CASES, PROBLEMS, AND MATERIALS

SECURITY INTERESTS IN PERSONAL PROPERTY

FOURTH EDITION

by

RANDAL C. PICKER
Paul and Theo Leffmann Professor of Commercial Law
The University of Chicago Law School
Senior Fellow, The Computation Institute of the University of Chicago and
Argonne National Laboratory

FOUNDATION PRESS
2009

THOMSON REUTERS

© 1984, 1987, 2002 FOUNDATION PRESS
© 2009 By THOMSON REUTERS/FOUNDATION PRESS

      195 Broadway, 9th Floor

      New York, NY 10007

      Phone Toll Free 1–877–888–1330

      Fax (212) 367–6799

      foundation-press.com

Printed in the United States of America

ISBN 978–1–59941–639–7

 TEXT IS PRINTED ON 10% POST CONSUMER RECYCLED PAPER

PREFACE

This book focuses on Article 9 of the Uniform Commercial Code on secured transactions in personal property. A revised Article 9 went effective in most states on July 1, 2001. The revised statute substantially re-works the prior statute and revises the numbering system completely but, at the same time, leaves most of the core concepts of Article 9 in place. With the third edition of the book—finished in September, 2002—we had just begun the transition. With the completion of this fourth edition in March, 2009, we are meaningfully on the road to seeing how Revised Article 9 operates.

The new edition reflects that. The third edition contained 48 main cases; 17 of those are gone and 29 new cases have been added. The organization of the book remains the same as does its central sense of how Article 9 is best taught. I think that there are three selling points for this book. First, the book is organized around 105 problems (see the Table of Problems for a quick list of these). These problems highlight what is at work in the statute in a simple set of facts and typically build up to the more complicated facts captured in a particular case. If you don't like the problems or don't think Article 9 should be taught using problems, you won't like the book. Second, I like my cases fat. I do not edit cases down to a six-word holding. I like a rich sense of the facts and I try to give the judges room to speak. If you did the math above, the new edition still has only 60 main cases. Third, I have a comprehensive set of PowerPoint slides that match with the problems. I find that a good way to lay out the problems in class. A teacher's manual is pretty dull and static, but the PowerPoint slides can be put to work directly.

This is the fourth edition of this casebook. The first two editions were done by my colleagues Tom Jackson and Douglas Baird. Douglas took secured transactions from Tom at Stanford, and I took the same course from Douglas at the University of Chicago. The nature of learning and teaching makes it hard for me to know exactly what I owe to Douglas and what to Tom through Douglas, but I am confident that my debts are substantial to both. Their names have dropped off of this fourth edition, but I hope that their influence is embedded in the book word by word.

Very little outside material is used in the casebook, but I do appreciate the opportunity to quote portions of the following works: Grant Gilmore, Security Interests in Personal Property (Little Brown & Co., 1965) and a model security agreement by Steve Weise.

I taught a version of the fourth edition in Fall, 2008 and appreciate the chance to inflict a working draft on my students at the University of Chicago Law School. They worked with the book with the diligence and eagerness that I expect of them but try not to take for granted. Jeff Luna provided able research assistance on this fourth edition, just as Alan Littmann and Basil Alsikafi did on the third edition.

I should also thank the John M. Olin Foundation and the Paul H. Leffmann Fund for general research support. I am also the Paul H. and Theo Leffmann Professor of Commercial Law. Good anything is rarely cheap and good teaching and research require real resources. As someone who teaches about debt, I am perpetually aware of whether I am paying properly my intellectual debts and I hope this book reduces my outstanding claims somewhat.

Additional materials may be found through my official University of Chicago website at http://www.law.uchicago.edu/faculty/picker/ where you will find a link to my personal home page. Questions or comments can be directed to me at r-picker@uchicago.edu.

RANDAL C. PICKER
Chicago
March, 2009

TABLE OF CONTENTS

TABLE OF CASES

Principal cases are in bold type. Non-principal cases are in roman type. References are to Pages.

TABLE OF STATUTES

TABLE OF PROBLEMS

CHAPTER ONE

INTRODUCTION

Secured transactions are at once obscure—tell people that you teach or are taking a course in secured transactions and you are sure to get a blank stare—and ubiquitous. Buy a house using borrowed money, and you almost certainly will enter into a secured transaction in real property. Buy a car and finance it through GMAC, General Motor's finance arm, and you will have entered into a second secured transaction, this time in personal property. Secured transactions range from a $10 loan at the local pawnshop secured by a pledge of a ring, to the lien on the car held by GMAC, to multibillion-dollar loans secured by all of a firm's assets. In each of these transactions, a borrower posts collateral to a lender to facilitate the loan. The idea of giving collateral in personal property—or, in language we will quickly adopt, of granting a security interest—and its consequences are the focus of this book.

This book then addresses the subject of secured transactions in personal property. Note the focus on "personal property," meaning, of course, property other than real estate. A corporation can own personal property, and indeed part of what makes secured lending interesting is the billion-dollar secured transaction involving corporate personal property. Notwithstanding the focus on personal property, you should not think for a minute that secured transactions in real property are unimportant. Quite the opposite. At any given time in the United States, several trillion dollars in outstanding loans are secured by mortgages on real property. And almost all of the recent attention on secured transactions has been on the so-called "subprime" mortgage meltdown in residential real-estate mortgages. Rather, the focus of this book reflects the scope of the law applicable to secured transactions. Different laws apply to lending against real and personal property. With some exceptions, most notably the federal Bankruptcy Code, most of the relevant law is state law. State laws on secured transactions in real property vary widely. Although common elements can be

1

identified across the states, no single scheme, or perhaps more important-ly, no single legal text, predominates.

Happily, the situation is far different for lending against personal prop-erty. Article 9 of the Uniform Commercial Code on Secured Transactions has formed the basis for the laws on the subject in each of the fifty states. It is therefore possible to offer a comprehensive introduction to the law of secured transactions in personal property in the United States in a book that weighs less than five pounds. After a quick look at the status of an unsecured creditor, this chapter lays out the basic infrastructure created by Article 9. The nature of such an undertaking is that it inevitably omits de-tails. In the law, details matter—some would say details are everything in the law—and, unfortunately, details may matter more in secured transac-tions than they do in most areas of the law. It will nonetheless be easier to absorb these details if the basics are well understood.

SECTION I. THE LIFE OF THE UNSECURED CREDITOR

It is difficult to comprehend what it means to be a secured creditor with-out understanding the life of the unsecured creditor. So start with a con-crete situation. Debtor is in the widget business and, as would be true of a business of any size, many assets are required to run it. Debtor uses a pa-tented process and special equipment to turn raw material into widgets. Debtor sells the widgets under its trademark, sometimes for cash, some-times on credit. The promises made by customers to pay constitute Deb-tor's accounts receivable.

On February 1st, Debtor approaches Bank for a loan of $10,000. If Bank lends on an unsecured basis, only two steps are required: money is lent by Bank to Debtor and Debtor promises to repay it. Oh sure, there will be lots of paper—promissory notes to evidence Debtor's obligation to repay and to set interests rates, other fees and a repayment schedule, and perhaps even a detailed loan agreement. Nonetheless, the basics of an un-secured loan are the lending of money and a promise to repay it, and noth-ing more.

Assume that Bank makes an unsecured loan of $10,000 and that the full amount of the loan, plus simple interest at 10%, is due in one year. The following February 1st, Bank seeks to collect its $11,000. If all goes well, Debtor cheerfully pays in full, and we can stop. Matters are more in-teresting if Debtor cannot pay. One question is obvious: What rights does

Bank have against Debtor? A second question is less obvious: What rights does Bank have relative to Debtor's other creditors?

Start with the first question. If Bank was careful, it checked before making its loan to confirm that Debtor had substantial assets. Debtor has refused to turn over any of those assets to Bank. Unless the debtor is just being spiteful, the debtor is almost surely in financial trouble. In most commercial dealings, in the absence of a dispute over performance of a contract, parties rarely simply refuse to pay, unless they are in financial trouble. Bank will seek to collect its debt under applicable state law.

Although state laws differ in their details, the basic pattern is fairly standard. Bank cannot simply descend on Debtor and grab a widget machine. In making an unsecured loan, Bank received no special rights in any of Debtor's assets. Putting to one side pre-judgment remedies, a creditor typically cannot invoke the powers of the state to collect her debt until a money judgment has been issued in favor of the creditor. Consequently, Bank first must go to court to prove that Debtor owes Bank the money. This process—usually called "proving up a judgment"—often is little more than a formality, as Debtor may not even contest the judgment. Nonetheless, this first step requires going to court, with the attendant out-of-pocket costs and delay.

Bank now has a judgment in hand—and has become a *judgment creditor*—but what Bank really wants is cash. The judgment is an essential step, but Bank must take two more steps. Bank must deliver the judgment or another paper describing the judgment to the sheriff of the jurisdiction where Debtor's property is located. The sheriff, in turn, will then seize the property from the debtor, or will *levy* on it. The sheriff will sell the property pursuant to established procedures and will pay the creditor the proceeds of the sale, after deducting the sheriff's expenses.

It is quite improbable that Bank is the only creditor with a bone to pick with Debtor. Debtor's refusal to pay Bank in the face of Bank's willingness to sue suggests that Debtor is in financial trouble. Debtor's other creditors will also seek to collect their debts. The just-described process of judgment, delivery, levy and sale describes the rights of one creditor against a debtor, but says nothing of the rights of one creditor against other creditors. If the debtor is insolvent, the *relative* rights of the creditors will determine how much each gets paid.

In some states, priority is determined by the date of the judgment. The first creditor to get a judgment is entitled to payment first, up to the full amount of the judgment. In other states, a judgment creditor is protected against the competing claims of unsecured creditors or transferees, but more is needed to be protected against the claims of other creditors seeking priority. The judgment creditor becomes an *execution creditor* by delivering an official notice of the entry of the judgment—the *execution*—to the local sheriff. Once the execution has been delivered to the sheriff, the creditor will have taken all of the steps necessary to create a priority to much of the debtor's property. Priority among competing execution creditors is then determined by the time of delivery of the execution to the sheriff. Note that in either case—when priority is dated from entry of the judgment or from delivery of the execution to the sheriff—unsecured creditors race to the assets by jumping through the appropriate state law hoops. Each unsecured creditor must undertake a slow and expensive process, and the till may be empty when the creditor finally reaches in for its share.

This has been a contextless hypothetical; as law students, you expect these, but we should make these ideas more concrete, and the next case, a 5-4 decision from the U.S. Supreme Court, does exactly that.

Grupo Mexicano de Desarrollo, S.A. v. Alliance Bond Fund, Inc.

United States Supreme Court, 1999.
527 U.S. 308.

■ JUSTICE SCALIA delivered the opinion of the Court.

This case presents the question whether, in an action for money damages, a United States District Court has the power to issue a preliminary injunction preventing the defendant from transferring assets in which no lien or equitable interest is claimed.

I

Petitioner Grupo Mexicano de Desarrollo, S.A. (GMD) is a Mexican holding company. In February 1994, GMD issued $250 million of 8.25% unsecured, guaranteed notes due in 2001 (Notes), which ranked *pari passu* in priority of payment with all of GMD's other unsecured and unsubordinated debt. Interest payments were due in February and August of every year. Four subsidiaries of GMD (which are the remaining petitioners) guaranteed the Notes. Respondents are investment funds which purchased approximately $75 million of the Notes.

Between 1990 and 1994, GMD was involved in a toll road construction program sponsored by the Government of Mexico. In order to elicit private financing, the Mexican Government granted concessions to companies who would build and operate the system of toll roads. GMD was both an investor in the concessionaries and among the construction companies hired by the concessionaries to build the toll roads. Problems in the Mexican economy resulted in severe losses for the concessionaries, who were therefore unable to pay contractors like GMD. In response to these problems, in 1997, the Mexican Government announced the Toll Road Rescue Program, under which it would issue guaranteed notes (Toll Road Notes) to the concessionaries, in exchange for their ceding to the Government ownership of the toll roads. The Toll Road Notes were to be used to pay the bank debt of the concessionaries, and also to pay outstanding receivables held by GMD and other contractors for services rendered to the concessionaries (Toll Road Receivables). In the fall of 1997, GMD announced that it expected to receive approximately $309 million of Toll Road Notes under the program.

Because of the downturn in the Mexican economy and the related difficulties in the toll road program, by mid-1997 GMD was in serious financial trouble. In addition to the Notes, GMD owed other debts of about $450 million. GMD's 1997 Form 20-F, which was filed with the Securities and Exchange Commission on June 30, 1997, stated that GMD's current liabilities exceeded its current assets and that there was "substantial doubt" whether it could continue as a going concern. As a result of these financial problems, neither GMD nor its subsidiaries (who had guaranteed payment) made the August 1997 interest payment on the Notes.

Between August and December 1997, GMD attempted to negotiate a restructuring of its debt with its creditors. On August 26, Reuters reported that GMD was negotiating with the Mexican banks to reduce its $256 million bank debt, and that it planned to deal with this liability before negotiating with the investors owning the Notes. On October 28, GMD publicly announced that it would place in trust its right to receive $17 million of Toll Road Notes, to cover employee compensation payments, and that it had transferred its right to receive $100 million of Toll Road Notes to the Mexican Government (apparently to pay back taxes). GMD also negotiated with the holders of the Notes (including respondents) to restructure that debt, but by December these negotiations had failed.

On December 11, respondents accelerated the principal amount of their Notes, and, on December 12, filed suit for the amount due in the United

States District Court for the Southern District of New York (petitioners had consented to personal jurisdiction in that forum). The complaint alleged that "GMD is at risk of insolvency, if not insolvent already"; that GMD was dissipating its most significant asset, the Toll Road Notes, and was preferring its Mexican creditors by its planned allocation of Toll Road Notes to the payment of their claims, and by its transfer to them of Toll Road Receivables; and that these actions would "frustrate any judgment" respondents could obtain. Respondents sought breach-of-contract damages of $80.9 million, and requested a preliminary injunction restraining petitioners from transferring the Toll Road Notes or Receivables. On that same day, the District Court entered a temporary restraining order preventing petitioners from transferring their right to receive the Toll Road Notes.

On December 23, the District Court entered an order in which it found that "GMD is at risk of insolvency if not already insolvent"; that the Toll Road Notes were GMD's "only substantial asset"; that GMD planned to use the Toll Road Notes "to satisfy its Mexican creditors to the exclusion of [respondents] and other holders of the Notes"; that "[i]n light of [petitioners'] financial condition and dissipation of assets, any judgment [respondents] obtain in this action will be frustrated"; that respondents had demonstrated irreparable injury; and that it was "almost certain" that respondents would succeed on the merits of their claim. It preliminarily enjoined petitioners "from dissipating, disbursing, transferring, conveying, encumbering or otherwise distributing or affecting any [petitioner's] right to, interest in, title to or right to receive or retain, any of the [Toll Road Notes]." The court ordered respondents to post a $50,000 bond.

The Second Circuit affirmed. 143 F.3d 688 (1998). * * *

III

We turn, then, to the merits question whether the District Court had authority to issue the preliminary injunction in this case pursuant to Federal Rule of Civil Procedure 65.[3] The Judiciary Act of 1789 conferred on the

---

[3] Although this is a diversity case, respondents' complaint sought the injunction pursuant to Rule 65, and the Second Circuit's decision was based on that rule and on federal equity principles. Petitioners argue for the first time before this Court that under Erie R. Co. v. Tompkins, 304 U.S. 64 (1938), the availability of this injunction under Rule 65 should be determined by the law of the forum State (in this case New York). Because this argument was neither raised nor considered below, we decline to consider it.

federal courts jurisdiction over "all suits ... in equity." 1 Stat. 78. We have long held that "[t]he 'jurisdiction' thus conferred ... is an authority to administer in equity suits the principles of the system of judicial remedies which had been devised and was being administered by the English Court of Chancery at the time of the separation of the two countries." Atlas Life Ins. Co. v. W.I. Southern, Inc., 306 U.S. 563 (1939). "Substantially, then, the equity jurisdiction of the federal courts is the jurisdiction in equity exercised by the High Court of Chancery in England at the time of the adoption of the Constitution and the enactment of the original Judiciary Act, 1789 (1 Stat. 73)." A. Dobie, Handbook of Federal Jurisdiction and Procedure 660 (1928). "[T]he substantive prerequisites for obtaining an equitable remedy as well as the general availability of injunctive relief are not altered by [Rule 65] and depend on traditional principles of equity jurisdiction." 11A Charles Alan Wright, Arthur R. Miller, & Mary Kay Kane, Federal Practice and Procedure § 2941, p. 31 (2d ed. 1995). We must ask, therefore, whether the relief respondents requested here was traditionally accorded by courts of equity.

A

Respondents do not even argue this point. The United States as *amicus curiae*, however, contends that the preliminary injunction issued in this case is analogous to the relief obtained in the equitable action known as a "creditor's bill." This remedy was used (among other purposes) to permit a judgment creditor to discover the debtor's assets, to reach equitable interests not subject to execution at law, and to set aside fraudulent conveyances. It was well established, however, that, as a general rule, a creditor's bill could be brought only by a creditor who had already obtained a judgment establishing the debt. See, e.g., Pusey & Jones Co. v. Hanssen, 261 U.S. 491, 497 (1923); Hollins v. Brierfield Coal & Iron Co., 150 U.S. 371, 378-379 (1893). The rule requiring a judgment was a product, not just of the procedural requirement that remedies at law had to be exhausted before equitable remedies could be pursued, but also of the substantive rule that a general creditor (one without a judgment) had no cognizable interest, either at law or in equity, in the property of his debtor, and therefore could not interfere with the debtor's use of that property. As stated by Chancellor Kent: "The reason of the rule seems to be, that until the creditor has established his title, he has no right to interfere, and it would lead to an unnecessary, and, perhaps, a fruitless and oppressive interruption of the exercise of the debtor's rights." Wiggins v. Armstrong, 2 Johns. Ch. 144, 145-146 (N.Y. 1816).

The United States asserts that there were exceptions to the general rule requiring a judgment. The existence and scope of these exceptions is by no means clear. Cf. G. Glenn, The Rights and Remedies of Creditors Respecting Their Debtor's Property §§ 21-24, pp. 18-21 (1915). Although the United States says that some of them "might have been relevant in a case like this one," it chooses not to resolve (or argue definitively) whether any particular one would have been. For their part, as noted above, respondents do not discuss creditor's bills at all. Particularly in the absence of any discussion of this point by the lower courts, we are not inclined to speculate upon the existence or applicability to this case of any exceptions, and follow the well-established general rule that a judgment establishing the debt was necessary before a court of equity would interfere with the debtor's use of his property.

The dissent concedes that federal equity courts have traditionally rejected the type of provisional relief granted in this case. It invokes, however, "the grand aims of equity," and asserts a general power to grant relief whenever legal remedies are not "practical and efficient," unless there is a statute to the contrary. This expansive view of equity must be rejected. Joseph Story's famous treatise reflects what we consider the proper rule, both with regard to the general role of equity in our "government of laws, not of men," and with regard to its application in the very case before us:

> Mr. Justice Blackstone has taken considerable pains to refute this doctrine. "It is said," he remarks, "that it is the business of a Court of Equity, in England, to abate the rigor of the common law. But no such power is contended for. Hard was the case of bond creditors, whose debtor devised away his real estate.... But a Court of Equity can give no relief...." And illustrations of the same character may be found in every state of the Union.... In many [States], if not in all, a debtor may prefer one creditor to another, in discharging his debts, whose assets are wholly insufficient to pay all the debts.

1 Commentaries on Equity Jurisprudence § 12, pp. 14-15 (1836).

We do not question the proposition that equity is flexible; but in the federal system, at least, that flexibility is confined within the broad boundaries of traditional equitable relief. To accord a type of relief that has never been available before—and especially (as here) a type of relief that has been specifically disclaimed by longstanding judicial precedent—is to invoke a "default rule," not of flexibility but of omnipotence. When there are indeed new conditions that might call for a wrenching departure from past practice, Congress is in a much better position than we both to perceive them and to design the appropriate remedy. Despite the dissent's allusion to the "increasing complexities of modern business relations," and to the bygone "age of slow-moving capital and comparatively immobile wealth," we suspect there is absolutely nothing new about debtors' trying to avoid paying their debts, or seeking to favor some creditors over others—or even about their seeking to achieve these ends through "sophisticated ... strategies." The law of fraudulent conveyances and bankruptcy was developed to prevent such conduct; an equitable power to restrict a debtor's use of his unencumbered property before judgment was not.

Respondents argue (supported by the United States) that the merger of law and equity changed the rule that a general creditor could not interfere with the debtor's use of his property. But the merger did not alter substantive rights. "Notwithstanding the fusion of law and equity by the Rules of Civil Procedure, the substantive principles of Courts of Chancery remain unaffected." Stainback v. Mo Hock Ke Lok Po, 336 U.S. 368, 382, n. 26 (1949). Even in the absence of historical support, we would not be inclined to believe that it is merely a question of procedure whether a person's unencumbered assets can be frozen by general-creditor claimants before their claims have been vindicated by judgment. It seems to us that question goes to the substantive rights of all property owners. In any event it appears, as we have observed, that the rule requiring a judgment was historically regarded as serving, not merely the procedural end of assuring exhaustion of legal remedies (which the merger of law and equity could render irrelevant), but also the substantive end of giving the creditor an interest in the property which equity could then act upon.

We note that none of the parties or *amici* specifically raised the applicability to this case of Federal Rule of Civil Procedure 18(b), which states:

> Whenever a claim is one heretofore cognizable only after another claim has been prosecuted to a conclusion, the two claims may be joined in a single action; but the court shall grant relief in that action only in accordance with the relative substantive rights of the parties. In particular, a plaintiff may state a claim for money and a claim to have set aside a conveyance fraudulent as to that plaintiff, without first having obtained a judgment establishing the claim for money.

Because the Rule was neither mentioned by the lower courts nor briefed by the parties, we decline to consider its application to the present case. We note, however, that it says nothing about preliminary relief, and specifically reserves substantive rights (as did the Rules Enabling Act, see 28 USC 2072(b)[7]. * * *

C

As further support for the proposition that the relief accorded here was unknown to traditional equity practice, it is instructive that the English Court of Chancery, from which the First Congress borrowed in conferring equitable powers on the federal courts, did not provide an injunctive remedy such as this until 1975. In that year, the Court of Appeal decided Mareva Compania Naviera S.A. v. International Bulkcarriers S.A., 2 Lloyd's Rep. 509. *Mareva*, although acknowledging that the prior case of Lister & Co. v. Stubbs, [1890] 45 Ch. D. 1 (C.A.), said that a court has no power to protect a creditor before he gets judgment, relied on a statute giving courts the authority to grant an interlocutory injunction "'in all cases in which it shall appear to the court to be just or convenient,'" 2 Lloyd's Rep., at 510 (quoting Judicature Act of 1925, Law Reports 1925(2), 15 & 16 Geo. V, ch. 49, § 45). It held (in the words of Lord Denning) that "[i]f it appears that the debt is due and owing—and there is a danger that the debtor may dispose of his assets so as to defeat it before judgment—the Court has jurisdiction in a proper case to grant an interlocutory judgment so as to prevent him *[sic]* disposing of those assets." 2 Lloyd's Rep., at 510. The *Mareva* injunction has now been confirmed by statute. See Supreme Court Act of 1981, § 37, 11 Halsbury's Statutes 966, 1001 (4th ed. 1985).

Commentators have emphasized that the adoption of *Mareva* injunctions was a dramatic departure from prior practice.

> Before 1975 the courts would not grant an injunction to restrain a defendant from disposing of his assets pendente lite merely because the plaintiff feared that by the time he obtained judgment the defendant would have no assets against which execu-

---

[7] Several States have adopted the Uniform Fraudulent Conveyance Act (or its successor the Uniform Fraudulent Transfers Act), which has been interpreted as conferring on a nonjudgment creditor the right to bring a fraudulent conveyance claim. Insofar as Rule 18(b) applies to such an action, the state statute eliminating the need for a judgment may have altered the common-law rule that a general contract creditor has no interest in his debtor's property. Because this case does not involve a claim of fraudulent conveyance, we express no opinion on the point.

> tion could be levied. Applications for such injunctions were consistently refused in the English Commercial Court as elsewhere. They were thought to be so clearly beyond the powers of the court as to be "wholly unarguable."

Hetherington, Introduction to the Mareva Injunction, in Mareva Injunctions 1, 3 (M. Hetherington, ed. 1983). * * *

The parties debate whether *Mareva* was based on statutory authority or on inherent equitable power. Regardless of the answer to this question, it is indisputable that the English courts of equity did not actually *exercise* this power until 1975, and that federal courts in this country have traditionally applied the principle that courts of equity will not, as a general matter, interfere with the debtor's disposition of his property at the instance of a nonjudgment creditor. We think it incompatible with our traditionally cautious approach to equitable powers, which leaves any substantial expansion of past practice to Congress, to decree the elimination of this significant protection for debtors.

IV

The parties and *amici* discuss various arguments for and against creating the preliminary injunctive remedy at issue in this case. The United States suggests that the factors supporting such a remedy include

> simplicity and uniformity of procedure; preservation of the court's ability to render a judgment that will prove enforceable; prevention of inequitable conduct on the part of defendants; avoiding disparities between defendants that have assets within the jurisdiction (which would be subject to pre-judgment attachment "at law") and those that do not; avoiding the necessity for plaintiffs to locate a forum in which the defendant has substantial assets; and, in an age of easy global mobility of capital, preserving the attractiveness of the United States as a center for financial transactions.

Brief for United States as *Amicus Curiae* 16.

But there are weighty considerations on the other side as well, the most significant of which is the historical principle that before judgment (or its equivalent) an unsecured creditor has no rights at law or in equity in the property of his debtor. As one treatise writer explained:

> A rule of procedure which allowed any prowling creditor, before his claim was definitely established by judgment, and without

reference to the character of his demand, to file a bill to discover assets, or to impeach transfers, or interfere with the business affairs of the alleged debtor, would manifestly be susceptible of the grossest abuse. A more powerful weapon of oppression could not be placed at the disposal of unscrupulous litigants.

Wait, Fraudulent Conveyances, § 73, at 110-111.

The requirement that the creditor obtain a prior judgment is a fundamental protection in debtor-creditor law—rendered all the more important in our federal system by the debtor's right to a jury trial on the legal claim. There are other factors which likewise give us pause: The remedy sought here could render Federal Rule of Civil Procedure 64, which authorizes use of state prejudgment remedies, a virtual irrelevance. Why go through the trouble of complying with local attachment and garnishment statutes when this all-purpose prejudgment injunction is available? More importantly, by adding, through judicial fiat, a new and powerful weapon to the creditor's arsenal, the new rule could radically alter the balance between debtor's and creditor's rights which has been developed over centuries through many laws—including those relating to bankruptcy, fraudulent conveyances, and preferences. Because any rational creditor would want to protect his investment, such a remedy might induce creditors to engage in a "race to the courthouse" in cases involving insolvent or near-insolvent debtors, which might prove financially fatal to the struggling debtor. (In this case, we might observe, the respondents did not represent all of the holders of the Notes; they were an active few who sought to benefit at the expense of the other noteholders as well as GMD's other creditors.) It is significant that, in England, use of the *Mareva* injunction has expanded rapidly. "Since 1975, the English courts have awarded *Mareva* injunctions to freeze assets in an ever-increasing set of circumstances both within and beyond the commercial setting to an ever-expanding number of plaintiffs." Wasserman, Equity Renewed: Preliminary Injunctions to Secure Potential Money Judgments, 67 Wash. L. Rev. 257, 339 (1992). As early as 1984, one observer stated that "[t]here are now a steady flow of such applications to our Courts which have been estimated to exceed one thousand per month." Shenton, Attachments and Other Interim Court Remedies in Support of Arbitration, 1984 Int'l Bus. Law. 101, 104.

We do not decide which side has the better of these arguments. We set them forth only to demonstrate that resolving them in this forum is incompatible with the democratic and self-deprecating judgment we have long since made: that the equitable powers conferred by the Judiciary Act of 1789 did not include the power to create remedies previously unknown to equity jurisprudence. Even when sitting as a court in equity, we have no authority to craft a "nuclear weapon" of the law like the one advocated here. Joseph Story made the point many years ago:

> If, indeed, a Court of Equity in England did possess the unbounded jurisdiction, which has been thus generally ascribed to it, of correcting, controlling, moderating, and even superceding the law, and of enforcing all the rights, as well as the charities, arising from natural law and justice, and of freeing itself from all regard to former rules and precedents, it would be the most gigantic in its sway, and the most formidable instrument of arbitrary power, that could well be devised. It would literally place the whole rights and property of the community under the arbitrary will of the Judge, acting, if you please, *arbitrio boni judicis*, and it may be, *ex aequo et bono*, according to his own notions and conscience; but still acting with a despotic and sovereign authority. A Court of Chancery might then well deserve the spirited rebuke of Seldon; "For law we have a measure, and know what to trust to—Equity is according to the conscience of him, that is Chancellor; and as that is larger, or narrower, so is Equity. Tis all one, as if they should make the standard for the measure the Chancellor's foot. What an uncertain measure would this be? One Chancellor has a long foot; another a short foot; a third an indifferent foot. It is the same thing with the Chancellor's conscience."

1 Commentaries on Equity Jurisprudence § 19, at 21.

The debate concerning this formidable power over debtors should be conducted and resolved where such issues belong in our democracy: in the Congress.

* * *

Because such a remedy was historically unavailable from a court of equity, we hold that the District Court had no authority to issue a preliminary injunction preventing petitioners from disposing of their assets pending adjudication of respondents' contract claim for money damages. We reverse the judgment of the Second Circuit and remand the case for further proceedings consistent with this opinion.

It is so ordered.

■ JUSTICE GINSBURG, with whom JUSTICE STEVENS, JUSTICE SOUTER, and JUSTICE BREYER join, dissenting.

I

Uncontested evidence presented to the District Court at the preliminary injunction hearing showed that petitioner Grupo Mexicano de Desarrollo, S.A. (GMD), had defaulted on its contractual obligations to respondents, a group of GMD noteholders (Alliance), that Alliance had satisfied all conditions precedent to its breach of contract claim, and that GMD had no plausible defense on the merits. Alliance also demonstrated that GMD had undertaken to treat Alliance's claims on the same footing as all other unsecured, unsubordinated debt, but that GMD was in fact satisfying Mexican creditors to the exclusion of Alliance. Furthermore, unchallenged evidence indicated that GMD was so rapidly disbursing its sole remaining asset that, absent provisional action by the District Court, Alliance would have been unable to collect on the money judgment for which it qualified.

Had it been possible for the District Judge to set up "a piepowder court ... on the instant and on the spot," Parks v. Boston, 32 Mass. 198, 208 (1834) (Shaw, C.J.), the judge could have moved without pause from evidence taking to entry of final judgment for Alliance, including an order prohibiting GMD from transferring assets necessary to satisfy the judgment. Lacking any such device for instant adjudication, the judge employed a preliminary injunction "to preserve the relative positions of the parties until a trial on the merits [could] be held." University of Texas v. Camenisch, 451 U.S. 390, 395 (1981). The order enjoined GMD from distributing assets likely to be necessary to satisfy the judgment in the instant case, but gave Alliance no security interest in GMD's assets, nor any preference relative to GMD's other creditors. Moreover, the injunction expressly reserved to GMD the option of commencing proceedings under the bankruptcy laws of Mexico or the United States. In addition, the District Judge recorded his readiness to modify the interim order if necessary to keep GMD in business. The preliminary injunction thus constrained GMD only to the extent essential to the subsequent entry of an effective judgment.

The Court nevertheless disapproves the provisional relief ordered by the District Court, holding that a preliminary injunction freezing assets is beyond the equitable authority of the federal courts. I would not so disarm the district courts. As I comprehend the courts' authority, injunctions of this kind, entered in the circumstances presented here, are within federal equity jurisdiction. Satisfied that the injunction issued in this case meets the exacting standards for preliminary equitable relief, I would affirm the judgment of the Second Circuit.

II

The Judiciary Act of 1789 gave the lower federal courts jurisdiction over "all suits ... in equity." § 11, 1 Stat. 78. We have consistently interpreted this jurisdictional grant to confer on the district courts "authority to administer ... the principles of the system of judicial remedies which had been devised and was being administered" by the English High Court of Chancery at the time of the founding. Atlas Life Ins. Co. v. W.I. Southern, Inc., 306 U.S. 563, 568 (1939).

As I see it, the preliminary injunction ordered by the District Court was consistent with these principles. We long ago recognized that district courts properly exercise their equitable jurisdiction where "the remedy in equity could alone furnish relief, and ... the ends of justice requir[e] the injunction to be issued." Watson v. Sutherland, 5 Wall. 74, 79, 18 L.Ed. 580 (1867). Particularly, district courts enjoy the "historic federal judicial discretion to preserve the situation [through provisional relief] pending the outcome of a case lodged in court." 11A Charles Alan Wright, Arthur R. Miller, & Mary Kay Kane, Federal Practice and Procedure § 2943, p. 79 (1995). The District Court acted in this case in careful accord with these prescriptions, issuing the preliminary injunction only upon well-supported findings that Alliance had "[no] adequate remedy at law," would be "frustrated" in its ability to recover a judgment absent interim injunctive relief, and was "almost certain" to prevail on the merits. The Court holds the District Court's preliminary freeze order impermissible principally because injunctions of this kind were not "traditionally accorded by courts of equity" at the time the Constitution was adopted. In my view, the Court relies on an unjustifiably static conception of equity jurisdiction. From the beginning, we have defined the scope of federal equity in relation to the *principles* of equity existing at the separation of this country from England, see, e.g., Payne v. Hook, 7 Wall. 425, 430 (1869), we have never limited federal equity jurisdiction to the specific practices and remedies of the pre-Revolutionary Chancellor.

Since our earliest cases, we have valued the adaptable character of federal equitable power. We have also recognized that equity must evolve over time, "in order to meet the requirements of every case, and to satisfy the needs of a progressive social condition in which new primary rights and duties are constantly arising and new kinds of wrongs are constantly committed." Union Pacific R. Co. v. Chicago, R.I. & P.R. Co., 163 U.S. 564, 601 (1896). A dynamic equity jurisprudence is of special importance in the commercial law context. As we observed more than a century ago: "It must not be forgotten that in the increasing complexities of modern business relations equitable remedies have necessarily and steadily been expanded, and no inflexible rule has been permitted to circumscribe them." Union Pacific R. Co., 163 U.S., at 600-601. On this understanding of equity's character, we have upheld diverse injunctions that would have been beyond the contemplation of the eighteenth century Chancellor.

Compared to many contemporary adaptations of equitable remedies, the preliminary injunction Alliance sought in this case was a modest measure. In operation, moreover, the preliminary injunction to freeze assets *pendente lite* may be a less heavy-handed remedy than prejudgment attachment, which deprives the defendant of possession and use of the seized property. Taking account of the office of equity, the facts of this case, and the moderate, status quo preserving provisional remedy, I am persuaded that the District Court acted appropriately.

I do not question that equity courts traditionally have not issued preliminary injunctions stopping a party sued for an unsecured debt from disposing of assets pending adjudication. (As the Court recognizes, however, the historical availability of prejudgment freeze injunctions in the context of creditors' bills remains cloudy.) But it is one thing to recognize that equity courts typically did not provide this relief, quite another to conclude that, therefore, the remedy was beyond equity's capacity. I would not draw such a conclusion.

Chancery may have refused to issue injunctions of this sort simply because they were not needed to secure a just result in an age of slow-moving capital and comparatively immobile wealth. By turning away cases that the law courts could deal with adequately, the Chancellor acted to reduce the tension inevitable when justice was divided between two discrete systems. But as the facts of this case so plainly show, for creditors situated as Alliance is, the remedy at law is worthless absent the provisional relief in equity's arsenal. Moreover, increasingly sophisticated foreign-haven judgment proofing strategies, coupled with technology that permits the nearly instantaneous transfer of assets abroad, suggests that defendants may succeed in avoiding meritorious claims in ways unimaginable before the merger of law and equity. I am not ready to say a responsible Chancellor today would deny Alliance relief on the ground that prior case law is unsupportive.

The development of *Mareva* injunctions in England after 1975 supports the view of the lower courts in this case, a view to which I adhere. As the Court observes, preliminary asset-freeze injunctions have been available in English courts since the 1975 Court of Appeal decision in Mareva Compania Naviera S.A. v. International Bulkcarriers S.A., 2 Lloyd's Rep. 509. Although the cases reveal some uncertainty regarding *Mareva's* jurisdictional basis, the better-reasoned and more recent decisions ground *Mareva* in equity's traditional power to remedy the "abuse" of legal process by defendants and the "injustice" that would result from defendants "making themselves judgment-proof" by disposing of their assets during the pendency of litigation. Iraqi Ministry of Defence v. Arcepey Shipping Co., 1 All E.R. 480, 484-487 (1979) (internal citations omitted). That grounding, in my judgment, is secure.

III

A

The Court worries that permitting preliminary injunctions to freeze assets would allow creditors, "'on a mere statement of belief that the defendant can easily make away with or transport his money or goods, [to] impose an injunction on him, indefinite in duration, disabling him to use so much of his funds or property as the court deems necessary for security or compliance with its possible decree.'" Ante (quoting De Beers Consol. Mines, Ltd. v. United States, 325 U.S. 212, 222 (1945)). Given the strong showings a creditor would be required to make to gain the provisional remedy, and the safeguards on which the debtor could insist, I agree with the Second Circuit "that this 'parade of horribles' [would] not come to pass." 143 F.3d 688, 696 (1998).

Under standards governing preliminary injunctive relief generally, a plaintiff must show a likelihood of success on the merits and irreparable injury in the absence of an injunction. Plaintiffs with questionable claims would not meet the likelihood of success criterion. The irreparable injury requirement would not be met by unsubstantiated allegations that a defendant may dissipate assets. As the Court of Appeals recognized, provisional freeze orders would be appropriate in damages actions only upon a finding that, without the freeze, "the movant would be unable to collect [a money] judgment." 143 F.3d, at 697. The preliminary asset-freeze order, in short, would rank and operate as an extraordinary remedy.

Federal Rule of Civil Procedure 65(c), moreover, requires a preliminary injunction applicant to post a bond "in such sum as the court deems proper, for the payment of such costs and damages as may be incurred or suffered by any party who is found to have been wrongfully enjoined." As an essential condition for a preliminary freeze order, a district court could demand sufficient security to ensure a remedy for wrongly enjoined defendants. Furthermore, it would be incumbent on a district court to "match the scope of its injunction to the most probable size of the likely judgment," thereby sparing the defendant from undue hardship. See Hoxworth v. Blinder, Robinson & Co., 903 F.2d 186, 199 (C.A.3 1990).

The protections in place guard against any routine or arbitrary imposition of a preliminary freeze order designed to stop the dissipation of assets that would render a court's judgment worthless. The case we face should be paradigmatic. There was no question that GMD's debt to Alliance was due and owing. And the short span—less than four months—between preliminary injunction and summary judgment shows that the temporary restraint on GMD did not linger beyond the time necessary for a fair and final adjudication in a busy but efficiently operated court. Absent immediate judicial action, Alliance would have been left with a multimillion dollar judgment on which it could collect not a penny.[6] In my view, the District Court properly invoked its equitable power to avoid that manifestly unjust result and to protect its ability to render an enforceable final judgment.

At the hearing on the preliminary injunction, the District Judge asked: "We have got a case where there is no defense presented, why shouldn't I be able to provide [Alliance] with [injunctive] relief?" Why, the District Judge asked, should GMD be allowed "to use the process of the court to

---

[6] Before the District Court, Alliance frankly acknowledged the existence of other, unrepresented creditors. While acting to protect its own interest, Alliance asked the District Court to fashion relief that "does not just directly benefit us, but benefits ... the whole class of creditors" by creating "an even playing field" among creditors. (Alliance suggests that District Court direct GMD to set up a trust in compliance with Mexican law in order to oversee distributions to creditors). The Court supplies no reason to think that Alliance should have abandoned its rock-solid claim just because other creditors, for whatever reason, failed to bring suit.

delay entry of a judgment as to which there is no defense? Why is that equitable?" The Court gives no satisfactory answer.

B

Contrary to the Court's suggestion, this case involves no judicial usurpation of Congress' authority. Congress, of course, can instruct the federal courts to issue preliminary injunctions freezing assets pending final judgment, or instruct them not to, and the courts must heed Congress' command. Indeed, Congress has restricted the equity jurisdiction of federal courts in a variety of contexts. See Yakus v. United States, 321 U.S. 414, 442, n. 8 (1944) (cataloging statutes regulating federal equity power).

The Legislature, however, has said nothing about preliminary freeze orders. The relevant question, therefore, is whether, absent congressional direction, the general equitable powers of the federal courts permit relief of the kind fashioned by the District Court. I would find the default rule in the grand aims of equity. Where, as here, legal remedies are not "practical and efficient," Payne, 7 Wall., at 431, the federal courts must rely on their "flexible jurisdiction in equity ... to protect all rights and do justice to all concerned," Rubber Co. v. Goodyear, 9 Wall., 805, 807 (1870). No countervailing precedent or principle holds the federal courts powerless to prevent a defendant from dissipating assets, to the destruction of a plaintiff's claim, during the course of judicial proceedings. Accordingly, I would affirm the judgment of the Court of Appeals and uphold the District Court's preliminary injunction.

COMMENTS AND QUESTIONS

1. Pari passu? Arbitrio boni judicis? Ex aequo et bono? Lawyers love the Latin, don't they? What *do* these phases mean?

2. As a matter of first principles, why should it matter whether an unsecured creditor has first obtained a judgment before exercising any control over the property of the debtor? To answer that question, should we know something about the relative ease of proof of the underlying alleged debt as against proof of the alleged actions that the debtor is taking in dissipating the assets? Also, can we answer this question in isolation, or should we consider the full set of choices available to a potential creditor?

3. What should we make of FRCP 18(b)? The parties didn't raise it and the Court notes that the FRCP is trumped by the provisions of the Rules Enabling Act. Should we think of the issue in *Grupo Mexicano* as being substantive or procedural?

4. Lawyers love the English, too, as you could not help but note the obsession with the English in this case. Is this ancestor worship, a historical accident, or something commanded by the relevant texts?

5. For a historical review of equity remedies and a critical appraisal of *Grupo Mexicano*, see Steven B. Burbank, The Bitter with the Sweet: Tradition, History, and Limitations on Federal Judicial Powers – A Case Study, 75 Notre Dame L. Rev. 1291 (2000).

Section II. Reading the UCC and Aids to Understanding

It is worth pausing to note what the Uniform Commercial Code is and is not. It is a model law promulgated by The National Conference of Commissioners on Uniform State Laws and the American Law Institute. Current responsibility for the Code rests in the main with the Permanent Editorial Board of the UCC, which in turn is comprised of representatives from the Conference and from the ALI. The UCC, which grew out of work commenced by Karl Llewellyn and Soia Mentschikoff in the 1940s, has evolved over time. Official versions are dated and the 1962 and 1972 official versions of Article 9 have been especially significant. Minor changes were made to the official version of Article 9 in 1987 to reflect the promulgation of Article 2A, covering leases of personal property. More substantial changes were made in 1994, when the revised version of Article 8 on securities was issued.

Most importantly, we are now in the midst of a transition period for Article 9. In 1998, a substantially revised version of Article 9 was issued by the ALI and NCCUSL. This is the first major revision of the statute since 1972, and probably will establish the basic framework for Article 9 transactions for the next two or three decades. The unfortunate reality is that transitions from one official UCC to a second are quite difficult, and that is especially true in secured transactions, where it is contemplated that the arrangements between the parties will last for many years.

We have already made it through one transition: all 52 states have enacted Revised Article 9 (What? They added two states and I didn't know? 50 states, plus the District of Columbia and the U.S. Virgin Islands). But Article 1 of the UCC provides some crucial general terms that apply throughout all of the UCC and, as of September, 2008, only roughly two-thirds of the states have enacted Revised Article 1. (You can find out the status in any state by going to NCCUSL's website at www.nccusl.org.) Beyond this, we are just building up a real caselaw under the new statute. We still are litigating old deals—deals implemented under the old statute—and it takes time for litigation to work its way up the court system. Litigants will inevitably look to cases under the old statute when they make their cases. All of that means that at least for awhile, we will all need to be adept at moving back and forth between the old statute and the new statute.

We can get quite concrete about how to do that. Pick up your copy of Article 9 and look at it. In addition to the table of contents, you will find two key tables. One is the table of dispositions. This shows where old sections have gone in the revised statute. So, if you decide tomorrow to read a case from 1994, you will see statutory references in that case, and you will need to map those references to the new statute. The table of dispositions helps you do this. The second table is the table indicating sources or derivations of new Article 9 sections and conforming amendments. Here is how this helps: you are looking at Article 9 and would like to do some research on a particular issue. You find no cases under the new section—and this will happen for some time—so you want to see if there are cases before the revision. You will use the table of derivations to map from the new statute to the old statute and from there to the cases.

In this book, as a matter of convention, most of the non-case references will be to the new statute. A reference to the old statute will say so, or will be indicated as F9-xxx. In cases, some old statutory references remain, but I have moved towards references to the current statute and those replacement references are set forth in square brackets. As you should now understand, all I have done is systematically used the table of disposition to save you the trouble of doing so.

If I haven't scared you off, the good news is twofold. First, with a handful of exceptions, most of the most basic concepts of Article 9 have not changed. Second, you have the chance to get in on the ground floor of a new statute. There are many new wrinkles in the statute, and you will get a chance to see them develop from the beginning.

A few more disclaimers and we can begin. Do not lose sight of the fact that Article 9 is just a model statute; it is not law. Laws, of course, are issued by the individual state legislatures. States can and do enact nonuniform amendments to the Code. A particular state may embrace 95% of the official version of Article 9, and a lawyer who relies on the official version in practicing in that state will, at best, be right only 95% of the time. As a result, the version of Article 9 as enacted in a particular state *must* be consulted before practicing in that state. With that disclaimer, this book will ignore, except in rare instances, particular changes made by the states. We will thus focus on the current official text of Article 9. As noted already, Article 1 is also relevant as it sets out general guidelines and definitions used throughout the rest of the UCC.

In addition to the text of the UCC, official comments are set out for the provisions. The comments will often help clear up ambiguities in the text, though they should not be understood to override clear textual provisions. The comments are often cited by the courts, as we will see, in their efforts to decipher the relevant statutory provisions. (For a general discussion of the role of the comments, see Note, The Jurisprudence and Judicial Treatment of the Comments to the Uniform Commercial Code, 75 Cornell L. Rev. 962 (1990).) In addition, cross-references and definitional cross-references are given at the end of the comments. Finally, in 1990, the Permanent Editorial Board started issuing new commentaries interpreting provisions of Article 9 in the light of the evolving caselaw. These should prove influential and therefore should be considered in examining the provisions.

SECTION III. CREATING AND PERFECTING SECURITY INTERESTS

The Basic Secured Transaction. Recall that unsecured lending consists of an exchange of money for a promise of repayment. Secured lending adds two steps. First, the debtor must create a security interest in favor of the secured creditor. Second, to enjoy the full benefits of a security interest, the secured creditor must give notice to the public of its interest. Figure 1.1 sets out the four steps:

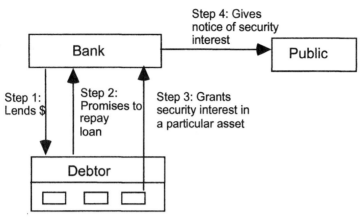

Figure 1.1: Attachment and Perfection of Security Interests

Steps 1 and 2 are the basic steps required to create an unsecured loan. In step 3, the debtor grants the creditor a security interest in some or all of its personal property. In step 4, the newly-secured creditor gives the public notice of its interest. You should not attach any special significance to the order in which the transaction in Figure 1.1 is set out. For the careful lender, step 4, giving notice to the public, will come first, followed by steps 2 and 3, and only then does the debtor get its hands on the cash in step 1. There may be a bit of a delay between giving the notice and the other steps, and we will see why that might be. Nonetheless, for current purposes, think of the transaction as set forth above.

In understanding steps 3 and 4 and what distinguishes a secured creditor from an unsecured creditor, two types of rights are important: property rights and priority rights. Property rights describe the special rights the secured creditor acquires against its debtor. The secured creditor receives property rights against the debtor to short-circuit the collection process faced by an unsecured creditor. The grant of the security interest creates these rights. The second key idea is priority rights. An unsecured creditor competes with other unsecured creditors for the debtor's limited assets and runs the risk that nothing will remain when the creditor goes to collect. In contrast, if the secured creditor gives notice to the public of its security interest, the secured creditor reserves a place in line for its collateral. It creates a priority to those assets.

Attachment and Perfection. To drop down one level of detail, under 9-609 and 9-610 of Article 9 of the UCC, if the debtor defaults, the secured creditor can repossess the property without going to court first (if it can do so without a breach of the peace) and can sell the property and keep the proceeds. These are the key property rights of the secured creditor and they exist as soon as the debtor grants a security interest to the creditor, even if the creditor never gives notice of that interest to the public. The security interest itself is granted pursuant to the provisions of 9-109, 9-201 and 9-203, and the process of granting a security interest is called *attachment*.

Notice matters, though, in an important way. If notice is given—if, in the language of Article 9, the security interest is *perfected*—the secured creditor receives priority rights. These are the rights of one creditor against other creditors. The secured creditor's interest is prior to that of an unsecured creditor, prior to that of a judgment creditor and prior to that of an execution creditor. The secured creditor gets to collect first. In effect, by taking a security interest in the beginning, the secured creditor opts out of the race to the assets that typifies the position of the unsecured creditor. (As we will explore later, though, secured creditors do need to worry about other secured creditors.)

Creating the Security Interest under Article 9. Article 1 of the Uniform Commercial Code contains general definitions and rules of construction applicable in the other articles. 1-201(b)(35) defines "security interest" as "an interest in personal property or fixtures which secures payment or performance of an obligation." (Look also at 1-203 which addresses separating security interests and leases.) Article 9 is limited to security interests in personal property, and the definition of security interest is the primary source of this limit. (See also 9-109.) The security interest is an "interest" in property. This definition tells us nothing about the nature of that interest; that will require careful review of Article 9, though as noted, 9-609 and 9-610 will loom large. It is an interest that "secures payment or performance of an obligation." Security interests are inextricably linked to their underlying obligations, though at times the link will be so tight as to make it difficult to separate the security interest and the obligation. (This will arise when a security interest secures a *nonrecourse* obligation.)

9-203 relies on two main methods for creating a security interest: through a written contract or through transfer of possession of the property. Throughout much of the history of secured transactions, the transfer of possession—the *pledge*—was the only effective way of creating a security interest. Security pursuant to a written contract is a relatively recent innovation and even today is not found in all countries. The requirement that the borrower give up possession of the collateral to the secured creditor severely limited the usefulness of the secured transaction. A business that handed over its equipment to a third party would be out of business quickly, as transferring possession of the assets would take them out of their most productive use. Pledging might work for small items held by consumers—as it still does in pawnbroking today—but, at least in its pure form, it was a weak and ineffective device for business.

The Ostensible Ownership Problem. The early law's focus on possession reflected its view that a contrary rule would lead to fraud and deception. For real property, a substantial paper trail of deeds and transfers of ownership existed. The owner of Blackacre would be determined not by reference to who possessed the property but rather by what the public records revealed. In contrast, few, if any, systematic records were kept of ownership of personal property. As a result, possession of personal property gave rise to a permitted inference of ownership of that property. Possession and ownership were treated as one.

Now insert security interests into this system. If the debtor transferred a security interest yet kept possession, possession and ownership were separated. If these "secret liens" were valid, it was no longer prudent to infer ownership from possession. An "ostensible ownership" problem would arise: the debtor would appear to own property, but, in truth, a third party would have an interest in it. The concern that the ostensible ownership problem would lead to widespread fraud led to a simple, bright-line rule: a valid security interest could be created only by transferring possession of the property. No separation of ownership and possession was allowed.

Not really. The purported "solution" to the ostensible ownership problem simply created such a problem and in fact *required* a separation of ownership and possession. When the common law debtor delivered a ring in pledge to the creditor, the debtor was still the owner of the ring. The creditor as the new possessor appeared to own the ring—if we followed out the common law inference of ownership from possession—when in fact the rights in the ring were limited to those specified in the contract between the debtor and the creditor. The pledge system therefore had substantial weaknesses. The requirement of delivery substantially undercut its usefulness, since it took property out of productive uses. Moreover, the rationale for the system—preventing fraud by linking ownership and possession—was internally incoherent.

9-203 still permits security interests to be created by transferring possession, but most are created via contract. In most cases, three requirements must be met. First, there must be a signed agreement between the creditor and the debtor, a security agreement for short. The term "security agreement" is defined in 9-102(a)(73), but it is essentially just a contract that creates a security agreement. Security agreements are often quite lengthy, but at the heart of any security agreement is something usually referred to as the "grant clause." That clause says something like "Debtor hereby grants a security interest in its inventory to Creditor." (The security agreement will often contain an elaborate definition of inventory.) Second, the debtor must have rights in the collateral. This is usually straightforward, as the debtor will grant a security interest in property it owns, but, as always, fringe cases complicate the analysis. Third and finally, the creditor must give "value" to the debtor. "Value" is a defined term, see 1-204, but usually just means lending money or entering into a commitment to lend money. Once these three conditions are met, the security interest attaches, unless the parties expressly delay the attachment. See 9-203.

When the security interest has attached, the secured creditor can enforce Article 9's property rights. In the main, these are rights applicable when the debtor defaults. 9-609 and 9-610 are of particular importance. 9-609 allows the secured creditor to repossess the collateral after a default without going to court, so long as the secured creditor can do so without a breach of the peace. Note that this latter limit makes it easy to overstate the difference between secured and unsecured creditors, at least on this dimension. If the debtor is willing to part with the property voluntarily, the unsecured creditor need not obtain a money judgment either, since nothing prevents the debtor from simply paying the unsecured creditor voluntarily, in cash or in other property. If the debtor will not pay voluntarily and wants to block a repossession under 9-609, at least for tangible property, the secured creditor must go to court as well. Once the property is in hand, 9-610 lets the secured creditor dispose of the property to pay off the debt. The disposition must be commercially reasonable, a requirement enforced by penalties under 9-625.

Perfecting the Security Interest. So far we have focused on how property rights are created against the debtor; these rights are the first of the two defining characteristics of secured credit. The second characteristic is the priority right that the secured creditor enjoys against other creditors. A separate process—*perfection*—is necessary to create rights against third parties. In Figure 1.1, this is step 4: the public is notified that a security interest was created in step 3. 9-308 to 9-316 set out Article 9's requirements for perfection.

The basic rule for perfection is set forth in 9-308(a): perfection occurs when the security interest has attached and the steps for perfection set out in 9-310 through 9-316 have been completed. There are many intricacies to these rules, but until recently, the process of perfection has been conceptually quite simple: a secured creditor perfected through filing a financing statement or through taking possession of the property. Revised Article 9 has added taking control of collateral, see 9-314, as a third important approach to perfection. Control represents a natural evolution of the idea of possession. As to filing, filing of what and where? The paper to be filed is called a financing statement, or sometimes a UCC-1. See 9-521.

9-502(a) sets out the contents required in the financing statement: the names of the debtor and the secured creditor, and the statement must indicate the collateral "covered" by the financing statement. The prior version of Article 9 required that the debtor sign the financing statement, but this has been dropped in the hopes of facilitating electronic filing. A signature was just one way—but certainly not the only way—of evidencing that the debtor had authorized the filing of the financing statement. Revised Article 9 continues to insist that the debtor must authorize the filing of the financing statement. See 9-509(a).

The requirement that the financing statement indicate the collateral covered by the financing statement is conceptually quite important. This makes Article 9 a *reified priority system*. Priority is defined with reference to particular property. The secured creditor has priority in inventory or equipment or something else. The secured creditor does not have a general priority over all of the debtor's assets. In fact, this country's laws make it rather difficult to create such a priority. 9-109 excludes many situations from Article 9, and this effectively makes residual state law applicable. As a result, a creditor wishing to take a security interest in all assets must proceed methodically from property type to property type and in so doing invoke Article 9, real estate law and other residual state law.

Filing Location. This tells us *what* the secured creditor must file if that is the method it uses to seek priority. The *where* of filing is given by 9-301 and 9-501 together. 9-301 creates a special choice-of-law rule for Article 9. Note that not only is the priority system reified—tied to particular types of property—it is tied to particular states. You file somewhere in Arkansas or Ohio or whatever state is the relevant state; we do not have a central filing system for the United States as a whole. Consequently, we must sort out which state is the relevant state for filing. 9-301 lays this out. Revised Article 9 departs from the prior statute in an important way. Under the old statute, both the location of the collateral and the location of the debtor were relevant. When collateral had a natural location, that location controlled; otherwise, the location of the debtor controlled. Most goods, such as equipment and inventory, have a natural location. Other goods are usually mobile—most vehicles qualify—and therefore have no natural location. This is true of intangible property as well, such as a receivable or a trademark. For property without a natural location, the location of the debtor controlled. If a debtor granted a security interest in, say, inventory and accounts receivable, the secured creditor would have had to file two financing statements, one for the inventory in its location, and a second for the accounts receivable in the location of the debtor. In contrast, Revised Article 9 focuses instead on the location of the debtor. See 9-301. This should considerably simplify filing financing statements and reduce the number of relevant jurisdictions in complicated transactions.

If the secured creditor has met all of Article 9's requirements, it holds a perfected security interest. That is, the secured creditor has taken all of the steps required by Article 9 to vest rights against third parties. That is *not* to say that the perfected secured creditor always triumphs in a contest with third parties; we can have contests between creditors holding perfected security interests in the same collateral, or between a perfected secured creditor and a levying lien creditor, or between a perfected secured creditor and a purchaser of the collateral. We turn to these issues next.

SECTION IV. PRIORITY OF SECURITY INTERESTS

What does the secured creditor get by being perfected? Before examining this, consider an "Irrelevance Proposition": Secured transactions are irrelevant if the debtor's business does well. It is when the debtor fails and there is a fight over its assets that the relative rights among creditors matter. Three sections, 9-201, 9-317 and 9-322, are of particular relevance. 9-201 establishes our baseline presumption: "[e]xcept as otherwise provided in [the Uniform Commercial Code] a security agreement is effective according to its terms between the parties, against purchasers of the collateral, and against creditors." 9-317 sets out the rights of secured creditors, unsecured creditors and lien creditors, while 9-322 controls basic disputes among secured creditors.

Start with disputes between secured creditors and non-secured creditors. 9-317(a)(2) states that an unperfected security interest is subordinate to the interest of a lien creditor. "Lien creditor" is defined in 9-102(a)(52); for now, think of a lien creditor as an unsecured creditor that has acquired a lien on the debtor's property through the state law collection process. 9-317 states that the unperfected secured creditor's interest is inferior to that of the lien creditor. This language has always been interpreted to mean—and the official UCC comments to 9-317 make this clear—that a perfected security interest is superior to the rights acquired by a lien creditor. Again, that should be straightforward given the baseline established by 9-201. (As always, there are qualifications to the rule that a perfected secured creditor is superior to a lien creditor, but we'll ignore details for now.)

To be concrete, suppose that on January 1st, Finco lends $10,000 to Corp, unsecured; on February 1st, Bank lends $10,000 to Corp, takes a security interest in collateral held by Corp and files an appropriate financing statement. On March 1st, Finco becomes a lien creditor. Who has priority? Under 9-317, Finco, as a lien creditor, loses to a perfected secured creditor, so Bank wins. This is a straightforward example of a first-in-time priority system: Bank wins because it acquired the first perfected property interest. Change the facts. Bank lends on February 1st as before but files its financing statement on March 2nd. Now, Finco became a lien creditor at the time that Bank was an unperfected secured creditor, and under 9-317(a)(2), Bank loses to Finco.

The Reified Priority System. Before looking at Article 9's priority rules, consider an example that should be clear once we recall that Article 9 implements a reified priority system. On January 1st, Finco lends $10,000 to Corp, takes a security interest in equipment and files an appropriate financing statement. On February 1st, Bank lends $10,000 to Corp, takes a security interest in inventory and files an appropriate financing statement. On March 1st, Creditco lends $10,000 on an unsecured basis. Two weeks later on March 15th the inventory is worth $5,000, the equipment, $15,000, and the debtor has no other assets. Who has priority? (Ignore for now the fact that the inventory on March 15th is almost surely different from the inventory on February 1st, the date Bank created its security interest in inventory. This raises many interesting questions that will be considered when we reach the topic of after-acquired property (see 9-204).)

Start with the basic priority principle for secured credit under Article 9: priority is defined in particular categories of property. Finco acquired special rights in equipment but not in inventory. Bank acquired special rights in inventory but not in equipment. Creditco has no special rights at all. Finco would collect its full $10,000 from the equipment worth $15,000. The balance of $5,000 would go first to junior secured creditors in the equipment, but there are none; next, to lien creditors, none again; and, finally, to unsecured creditors. This means Creditco, but it may mean Bank as well. It in fact does. As the only secured creditor in inventory, Bank gets first crack at it. Bank collects the $5,000 from the inventory and then is owed $5,000. Bank is an unsecured creditor for this amount. It has exhausted its special rights against the inventory and it has no special rights in the equipment. Creditco and Bank are on par as to the final $5,000. In bankruptcy, they would share this pro rata—see Bankruptcy Code ("BC") 726(b)—meaning here that with Bank owed $5,000 and Creditco owed $10,000 giving total debts of $15,000, Creditco would receive 10,000/15,000 or 2/3 of the $5,000 or $3,333 and Bank would receive 5,000/15,000 or 1/3 of the $5,000 or $1,666. Outside bankruptcy, the first unsecured creditor to the assets wins, so the unsecured creditors race to the assets. This will lead to wide variations in individual collections, limited by the fact that creditors can push the debtor into bankruptcy involuntarily and thereby opt into the pro-rata distribution rules.

To recap, Article 9's principle that priority is defined by particular assets resolves cases in which there are no overlapping security interests. When security interests do overlap, the first-in-time rule establishes priority. In the prior example, assume that Bank took a security interest in equipment in addition to the security interest in inventory. Nothing in Article 9 would prevent this, as Article 9 says nothing about how much security a secured creditor can take. Now we do have a conflict among secured creditors. Both Finco and Bank claim a perfected security interest in the equipment. Recall what was said before: having a perfected security interest means that the secured creditor has a prior position against unsecured creditors. But as between secured creditors holding a perfected security interest in the same asset, we need a different rule.

9-322 gives the basic rule. This section covers a number of situations, but 9-322(a) establishes the basic rule for two ordinary secured creditors claiming a security interest in the same collateral. On January 1st, Finco lends $10,000 to Corp, takes a security interest in equipment and files an appropriate financing statement. On February 1st, Bank lends $10,000 to Corp, takes a security interest in the same equipment and files an appropriate financing statement. 9-322(a)(1) provides that the earlier of first to file or perfect wins. Focusing on the earlier of first to file or perfect is necessary given that Article 9 often allows secured creditors to perfect through filing or through taking possession. In this example, both creditors perfected through filing and 9-322(a)(1)'s rule reduces to a very simple rule: the first to file wins. Finco therefore has priority.

Notwithstanding the apparent simplicity of this rule, it is easy to lose sight of what it means. Suppose that on January 1st, Finco lends $10,000 to Corp, takes a security interest in equipment but files no financing statement. On February 1st, Bank lends $10,000 to Corp, takes a security interest in the same equipment and files an appropriate financing statement. On February 2nd, Finco files an appropriate financing statement. Who has priority? First to file wins. Even though Finco lent money and took a security interest before Bank did, it did not make that interest public. By failing to file, Finco ran the risk—realized here—that an otherwise later secured creditor will file first. When Bank checked the public records before making its loan, it found nothing to put Bank on notice of Finco's interest.

Finco lent first and filed second and therefore was junior; so goes the first-to-file rule. This rule also means that a creditor that files first and lends second takes priority. On January 1st, Finco files a financing statement authorized by Corp for collateral described as equipment but lends no money. On February 1st, Bank lends $10,000 to Corp, takes a security interest in equipment and files an appropriate financing statement. On March 1st, Finco lends $10,000 to Corp and takes a security interest in equipment. Who has priority? The first to file wins. Finco filed first and this suffices to reserve priority for Finco for any later lending and grant of a security interest in equipment. Bank was put on notice of Finco's reserved place in line by the financing statement. Bank took a big risk by lending to Corp without reaching some sort of agreement with Finco about the pending financing statement.

The basic first-to-file rule also forms the basis for Article 9's rule regarding *future advances*. On January 1st, Finco lends $1,000 to Corp, takes a security interest in equipment and files an appropriate financing statement. On February 1st, Bank lends $10,000 to Corp, takes a security interest in the same equipment and files an appropriate financing statement. On March 1st, Finco takes a second security interest in the equipment and lends an additional $9,000. Who has priority? Again, the first secured creditor to file wins. Finco has priority for both loans. The second loan is in the nature of a future advance, a loan made after the initial loan. (If one wanted to be technical, the second loan might not be considered a future advance as it was made pursuant to a different contract.) The future (or subsequent) advance question created problems for early secured transactions law, but Article 9's rule is clear and follows directly from the basic first-in-time principle. See 9-204, 9-323. Article 9 refuses to embrace this rule in full, though, as a different rule applies between a secured creditor and a lien creditor or some third-party purchasers. See 9-323.

Perfection through Possession. Whether the first-to-file system is a good system is debatable, but, with some exceptions, it is Article 9's system. One important exception is perfection through possession; a second exception in Revised Article 9 is perfection through control, which bears a close relationship to possession. As noted, in early secured transactions law, possession was the only way to create a lien enforceable against third parties. For many kinds of property, possession remains an acceptable means for perfecting; for some, it is the exclusive means. This creates some complexities for determining priority. On January 1st, Finco lends Corp $10,000, takes a security interest in a laptop computer and perfects by taking possession. On February 1st, Bank lends $10,000 to Corp, takes a security interest in the computer and files an appropriate financing statement. On March 1st, Finco files a financing statement for the computer and gives up possession to Corp. Who has priority? If the simple first-to-file rule applied, Bank would hold priority. 9-322(a)(1) creates a richer rule: the earlier of first to file or perfect wins, so long as there was never a time at which the secured party had neither filed nor perfected. The date of the first filing is February 1st, the date Bank filed. The date of the first perfection is January 1st, the date Finco first satisfied all of the requirements for perfection. As Finco filed a financing statement before giving up possession of the laptop, the date it perfected through possession controls. Finco therefore has priority.

SECTION V. CHANGES AND STALE INFORMATION

Businesses are dynamic; they change locations, they change names. Most businesses are in the business of buying and selling something. When an asset is sold, something is given in return for it. It may be cash or a check or it may be a promise to pay at a later date. The same is true when an asset is purchased. The buyer gives up something of value to get the new asset. We must consider how we overlay our system of security interests and record public notice on fundamentally changing businesses. The nature of the limited notice required of the secured creditor gives rise to complications when a key condition that existed at the time of the original notice changes. To put the point differently, change makes the information on file stale.

Burdens of Monitoring and Inquiry. A record notice system takes a snapshot at a particular point in time. As part of a notice system, we have to allocate the consequences of this stale information. How we allocate these consequences in turn creates incentives either for a secured creditor to update the filing or for a prospective secured creditor to verify that the record information is current. In very general terms, burdens of monitoring or inquiry will be imposed. If the prior secured creditor runs the risk of losing that position through a change, it will have to monitor the debtor to detect possible changes and update the public records. If the prior security interest and the status it has survives the change, the public record deceives a subsequent secured creditor. It must make costly inquiries and this will necessarily raise the price of credit. The goal of Article 9 should be to minimize the sum of the costs of monitoring and the costs of inquiry resulting from how the consequences of change are allocated.

Consider an example. On January 1st, Bank lends $10,000 to Corp, takes a security interest in equipment and files an appropriate financing statement. The filing will have the debtor's name on it and will be indexed under that name. See 9-519(c)(1). That means that anyone wishing to determine whether there are financing statements pending against Corp will submit a request in the filing office under that name. On February 1st, Corp changes its name to Company. The next day, Finco approaches Company to make a loan and conducts a search of the public records to determine whether the firm has prior secured creditors.

Consider the range of possible rules. We might impose the risk of stale information on the secured creditor who has already filed. Under that rule, Finco can check the records under the debtor's current name and be confident of priority if no statements are found. Such a rule would force Bank to watch Corp closely to ensure that it did not change its name or to charge an interest rate commensurate with the risk that it might. Alternatively, we might impose the risk of stale information on the later secured creditor. Under that rule, Finco has a burden of inquiry: it must find out what prior names Company has had. Searching under the name Company alone will not protect Finco, if, as happened here, another creditor filed against a prior name.

Do not think for a moment that the debtor will be able to take advantage of the initial secured creditor. There are no new tricks here. Instead, the debtor's inability to commit to the first secured creditor that no name change will ensue reduces the scope of real freedom available to the debtor. The parties cannot put into place a contract that ensures that the debtor will take the step in their joint interest, but instead must assume that the debtor will change its name, to the detriment of the first secured creditor, if it is in the debtor's interest to do so.

Knowledge-Based Rules. We could impose a more tailored rule. We could say that if the original secured creditor learns of the name change, it has a duty to update the files, and in the absence of so doing, it bears the risk of stale information. And, you might think that this rule would track the context in which name changes would occur. Many name changes are driven by the needs of corporate image. US Steel's business changes and it becomes USX. I don't know what that means, but it doesn't suggest molten steel, and that's the point. The public's nickname for Allegheny Airlines is "Agony Airlines"—which is hardly a selling point—so it becomes USAir. There is good reason to think that the secured creditor may be told of this kind of name change—indeed, the whole world will learn of the change. Nonetheless, other name changes may occur precisely to confuse and deceive. The initial secured creditor will not be told of these changes, unless it is in cahoots with the debtor. The tailored rule just suggested would track what the initial secured creditor would likely know.

But it is far from obvious that this rule is an improvement over the prior rules. When Finco considers whether to make a loan, it knows that checking under the current name alone puts it at risk. Company may have changed its name recently, and if the first-filed secured creditor did not know of the change, it will retain priority. Also, the one thing we know about a knowledge-based rule is that it will lead to litigation. After the fact, much will turn on whether the later secured creditor can make a showing that the first-filed secured creditor knew of the name change. In this situation and in others like it, the legal rules have to allocate the risk of stale information. Doing so is unavoidable. In this particular case, Article 9 resolves this question by protecting the initial secured creditor for all collateral held by the debtor prior to the name change and for any additional collateral acquired within four months thereafter. See 9-507(c).

Selling and Buying Property. A second example should confirm the pervasive problem of changed conditions in a system of record notice. On January 1st, Bank lends $10,000 to Corp, takes a security interest in "computers, now and hereafter owned by Corp" and files a financing statement listing the collateral as "computers." On February 1st, Corp decides to get a new computer. It buys a new computer from Retailer for cash and swaps its old computer for a copier owned by Company. When all is said and done, Corp owns a new computer and the copying machine while Company owns Corp's old computer.

This is a relatively straightforward transaction; the only mildly unusual aspect to it is that the old computer was exchanged for other equipment rather than sold for cash. But this simple situation raises a number of important questions relating to the interaction between changed conditions and secured creditors. Focus on (1) the new computer in Corp's hands; (2) the old computer, now in Company's hands; and (3) the copier now held by Corp. Corp's new computer is *after-acquired property*. As the name suggests, it is property acquired by the debtor after the date of the initial grant of a security interest. 9-204 allows a security interest to cover after-acquired property. The language "now and hereafter" is expressly temporal and is a common way of granting a security interest in after-acquired property. Bank therefore has a security interest in Corp's new computer. Whether it is perfected depends on whether the language "computers" in the financing statement suffices for both property owned at the time the financing statement is filed and that acquired later. It does. The purpose of the financing statement is notice; once on notice, an interested party should inquire about the full extent of the prior interest. That reasoning, of course, isn't wholly consistent with Article 9, though, as it would suggest we could dispense with the description requirement in its entirety. We will pursue this issue later; for now, note the relationship between the range of inquiries that will be made and the information contained in the financing statement. Bank therefore holds a perfected security interest in the new computer.

Next consider the old computer now owned by Company. Bank took a security interest in it to make sure that value would be available to it should Corp get in financial trouble. We once again face an allocation problem, or two allocation problems actually. Consider first the inquiries Company should make as a prospective purchaser. If Bank's perfected security interest survives the sale, Company will risk loss of the computer if Corp defaults on its loan from Bank. Under that rule, Company will either have to search the public records or adjust the purchase price. Note that Company will almost surely ask Corp to represent and warrant that there are no outstanding liens against the computer, but if Corp breaches that promise, Company will hold an unsecured claim for damages. On the other hand, if the security interest is cut-off by the sale, Bank once again faces a monitoring burden. As we will see, Article 9 draws a fairly predictable line. It would be virtually intolerable in retail transactions to expect the purchaser to determine whether the seller had granted a security interest in its inventory. Imagine going into a store such as Sears to buy a washing machine and having to inquire about Sears' capital structure. In rough terms, sales from inventory are free of a security interest. See 9-320(a). The secured creditor clearly should understand that Sears is going to sell the washing machines. But for many other sales, the sale was not contemplated in advance, and the security interest does survive the sale. This would be true of Corp's sale of the computer, unless Bank consented to the sale. See 9-315(a)(1). Bank's financing statement will also remain effective. See 9-507(a).

The old computer leads to a second allocation problem. To see this, assume that on March 1st, Finco approaches Company to make a loan. Finco will search the records for financing statements filed against Company. Bank's statement against Corp will not turn up. If Bank's prior perfected security interest in the computer continues notwithstanding the sale, Finco will either have to inquire into Company's source of title for its equipment or adjust its charges accordingly. If the security interest does not continue, Bank will once again be forced to monitor for possible sales or charge higher prices. Again, we must allocate the burden of inquiry and the burden of monitoring. As noted above, as to the computer, which was equipment in Corp's hands, Bank's perfected security survives the sale. Finco must adjust its behavior accordingly.

We still have not discussed the copier. Recall that Corp swapped its old computer for the copier. What rights, if any, does Bank have to the copier? Bank's security interest and financing statements extended only to computers. This covered the computers originally owned by Corp and those acquired later. But neither the security interest nor the financing statement covered the copier. Notwithstanding this, Bank may hold a perfected security interest in the copier. Article 9 confers rights in property received in exchange for collateral. The property received in exchange is called *proceeds*, see 9-102(a)(64), and the secured creditor automatically receives a security interest in identifiable proceeds, unless it waives it. See 9-203(f) and 9-315(a)(2). Bank will therefore have a security interest in the copier.

Whether it is perfected turns on 9-315(d) and that need not detain us here, except to note that Bank may be perfected as to the copier, even though it is *not* listed as collateral in the financing statement. As should be clear, this once again places great stress on Article 9's system of public notice. Finco approaches Corp to make a loan. It finds Bank's financing statement listing its collateral as computers. Can Finco lend safely against the copier? Once again, it may need to inquire into how Corp acquired the copier.

SECTION VI. MISCELLANEOUS MATTERS

We have just seen the heart of secured transactions in personal property under Article 9. Much detail has been omitted, so this is really no more than a sketch of the major issues and a few of the ways that Article 9 addresses them. There are three other issues that are worth mentioning before moving on to our detailed inquiry into secured transactions.

Purchase Money Security Interests. Consider an example. On January 1st, Bank lends $10,000 to Corp, takes a security interest in "computers, now and hereafter owned by Corp" and files an appropriate financing statement. On February 1st, Corp decides to add another computer. Corp approaches Retailer to buy the new computer. Retailer is willing to finance the purchase price but only if it receives a first priority interest in the new computer. Given the earlier-filed financing statement in favor of Bank, in the absence of special provisions in Article 9, Retailer would have to negotiate a subordination agreement with Bank. A subordination agreement is a contract between two creditors pursuant to which one creditor agrees to accept a position junior to that of the other creditor. Unsurprisingly, nothing in Article 9 bars such agreements. See 9-339.

Negotiating such an agreement may be sufficiently costly so as to make financing by Retailer impossible. If one thought that such agreements would be given as a matter of course but would not be reached because of the cost, a better outcome could be reached if Article 9 simply allowed the financing seller to take a first position for the collateral it sells. Article 9 does just this through the notion of a *purchase money security interest*. A seller who finances its sale, or another creditor whose extension of credit can be traced directly to an acquisition, achieves a first priority for the collateral sold, if it complies with certain statutory requirements. See 9-103 and 9-324.

Priorities in Paper Collateral. As is true of all statutes, Article 9 does not exist in a vacuum. At various points, Article 9's priority system reflects concerns central to other areas of the law. This is true of the system of priorities in paper collateral—instruments, such as checks, are the best example of this—where the notion of negotiability matters a great deal. Without considering all of the details of this notion—currently embodied in Article 3 of the UCC, covering commercial paper—the key idea is that transfer of possession (often coupled with an endorsement) of a promise to pay money vests certain rights in the recipient. Possession of this promise to pay carries even greater weight than possession usually does for personal property. Article 9 embraces this idea by making perfection through filing an inferior means of perfecting for paper collateral. A secured creditor that perfects through filing can lose priority to another who perfects through taking possession. See 9-330, 9-331.

Interfacing Article 9 with Other Law. The line between Article 9 and issues of negotiability is only one instance in which we must sort out the relative roles of two otherwise distinct bodies of law. The same problem arises when the line blurs between personal property and real property. This is the law of *fixtures* and is covered by 9-334 and 9-102(a)(41). Another context is given by interests in property other than security interests. Security interests arise through consent. In contrast, state and federal law may establish nonconsensual statutory liens that arise out of some relationship between the debtor and a third party. For example, the Comprehensive Environmental Response, Compensation, and Liability Act of 1980, codified at 42 USC 9601-57, gives the federal government a lien on damaged real property cleaned up by the government. It matters a great deal whether that lien is junior to or superior to a competing security interest.

As to state law liens, Article 9 addresses these issues at various points—9-333—and the other law in question may do so as well. As to liens under federal law, Article 9 could just subordinate consensual security interests to those liens, but otherwise, as state law, it cannot address the question of the relative priority of federal liens and Article 9 security interests. The relevant federal statute must be consulted. The most important of these relating to personal property are federal tax liens and liens in favor of the Pension Benefit Guaranty Corporation. Finally, and probably most importantly, the rights of a secured creditor cannot be fully understood without a firm grasp of the Bankruptcy Code. Security matters most when the firm fails; many failing firms resolve the rights against them in bankruptcy court. That means that we need to understand the Bankruptcy Code too.

CHAPTER TWO

ATTACHMENT

9-109, the basic section defining the scope of Article 9, states that it applies to "a transaction, regardless of its form, that creates a security interest in personal property or fixtures by contract." Whether a security interest has been created, though, depends on whether the parties have met Article 9's formal requirements. If so, the security interest "attaches" and is enforceable between the parties, 9-203(a), (b), and is also effective (i.e., enforceable) against general creditors as well. See 9-201. If the security interest is attached (and no more), it is not effective against perfected secured creditors, lien creditors, or, most significantly perhaps, the trustee in bankruptcy. To protect the merely-attached security interest from these risks, an additional step is required: the secured party must have "perfected" its security interest—a status that usually requires more, but never requires less, than "attachment," 9-308(a). The additional steps necessary for perfection (such as the filing of a financing statement) are the ones that are designed to put third parties on notice of the agreement between the secured party and the debtor. These additional steps are, however, irrelevant until the agreement becomes enforceable as between the two parties (or, to use the language of Article 9, until the security interest "attaches"). Thus, attachment is a necessary step in the life of a security interest, for it both defines the moment when the interest first becomes enforceable at all and supplies a necessary ingredient to the desired status of a perfected security interest.

9-203(b) sets forth the basic rule for the creation of a security interest. Putting to one side special rules for certain property types, it sets out five requirements: (1) we must have a security interest; (2) either the secured party has possession of or control over the collateral under an agreement with the debtor or the debtor has authenticated a security agreement; (3) absent possession or control, the security agreement must contain an adequate description of the collateral; (4) the debtor must have rights in the collateral or the power to transfer rights in the collateral; and (5) value must be given. In this chapter, we look at each of these in turn.

SECTION I. THE IDEA OF A SECURITY INTEREST

Section 1-201(b)(35) sets forth the definition of a security interest. The first sentence provides that security interest "means an interest in personal property or fixtures which secures payment or performance of an obligation." Consider that sentence and the following fact patterns:

2-1: THE SIMPLE SECURITY INTEREST

- Debtor approaches Bank for a $10,000 loan. Bank is willing, so long as adequate security is given.
- Debtor executes a promissory note in Bank's favor and also signs a separate document stating that "Debtor hereby grants a security interest in its copier, serial no. 12345678, to Bank to secure the debt evidenced by that certain promissory note of even date herewith." Bank then lends Debtor $10,000.
- ¤ What are Bank's rights? See 1-201(b)(35), 9-203.

Description of collateral.

2-2: AFTER-ACQUIRED PROPERTY

- Debtor, a seller of rare books, expects to receive good title to a first edition of *Das Kapital* in six months, but it has no interest in the book today. Of course, Debtor wants to borrow money today.
- Banks lends Debtor $10,000 pursuant to a contract that provides *value* that "Debtor hereby grants a security interest in all of its inventory, equipment, and general intangibles of whatever kind or type, now or hereafter owned by Debtor, including, without limitation, that certain first edition of *Das Kapital* that Debtor expects to own in six months." *Debtor didn't own rights to this*
- Six months later, with the loan and the contract still outstanding, Debtor receives title to the book. *9-204*
- ¤ Does this create a security interest in the book at any time, and if so, when? See 9-204(a), 9-203(a), (b).

2-3: WAIVING THE RIGHT TO SEIZE COLLATERAL

- Bank lends Debtor $100,000 under a contract that provides that "Debtor hereby grants Bank a security interest in equipment, but

Bank hereby waives its rights under 9-609 to repossess the collateral after a default."

¤ Does Bank have a security interest under Article 9? See 9-609.

2-4: WAIVING PRIORITY RIGHTS

- Bank lends money as before, but the contract provides that "Debtor hereby grants Bank a security interest in equipment, but Bank must share the value of such equipment on a pro rata basis with Debtor's unsecured creditors if Bank repossesses and sells such equipment."

¤ Does Bank have a security interest under Article 9?

2-5: BUILDING THE SECURITY INTEREST BRICK-BY-BRICK

- Bank lends money as before, but the contract provides that "on default, Bank has the right to exercise those rights that a secured creditor would have under 9-609 of the Uniform Commercial Code." *Is this language enough for authentication?*

¤ Does Bank have a security interest under Article 9?

- Suppose that the contract instead said "on default, Bank shall have the rights that a secured creditor would have under Part VI of Article 9." *cannot monitor the collateral?*

¤ Does that change the outcome?

2-6: RESTRICTIONS ON ALIENATION *negative pledge clause ≠ security interest.*

- *(no grant.)* On February 1st, Debtor borrows $10,000 from Bank and posts as collateral a rare first edition of Adam Smith's *The Wealth of Nations*. Debtor further agrees that it will not sell the book. *Not security int. promise not to sell the book.*

- *(no int. in property)* On March 1st, Debtor purports to sell the book to Purchaser, notwithstanding its promise to Bank. Purchaser is unaware of that promise. *— This sale is not ineffective.*

¤ Is the sale effective? What are Bank's rights? If Purchaser knew of the covenant not to sell, would that change the outcome? See 9-401. *↓ breach of contract.*

If there was SI, then bank has right to it and can sue the purchaser.

With these examples in mind, focus on the key question presented in the following case: Does Chrysler have a security interest in the liquor license?

In re Clark

United States Bankruptcy Court, W.D. Pennsylvania, 1989.
96 Bankr. 605.

■ WARREN W. BENTZ, BANKRUPTCY JUDGE

* * * In July 1986, the debtor, Dick Clark (hereinafter "Clark") entered into a loan transaction with Chrysler First Consumer Discount Company ("Chrysler"), the proceeds of which were used to purchase the Wagon Wheel Restaurant, later renamed the "Laurel Valley Inn." To secure Clark's obligation to repay, Chrysler attempted to protect its position by having Clark execute two instruments. Among them was a first mortgage in favor of Chrysler covering the premises purchased. The second, which was titled "Acknowledgement" (hereinafter the "Acknowledgement"), referred exclusively to liquor license TR-1793 (hereinafter the "License"), the terms of which agreement provide:

ACKNOWLEDGEMENT

We, the undersigned, do hereby acknowledge, consent and agree that liquor license TR-1793 issued by the Pennsylvania Liquor Control Board for use at premises situate(d) at R.D. # 1, Box 19, Ligonier, Pennsylvania 15650, will not be removed from said premises, nor transferred without the prior written consent of Finance America Consumer Discount Company, until mortgage loan from Finance America Consumer Discount Company to Diane C. Clark and Dick J. Clark a/k/a Richard J. Clark is paid in full.

> LAUREL VALLEY INN
> By /s Diane C. Clark
> By /s Dick J. Clark
> By /s Richard J. Clark

Furthermore, Clark signed a UCC-1 financing statement listing the License as additional collateral to secure repayment of the loan. The financing statement was subsequently filed in Westmoreland County and with the Commonwealth of Pennsylvania prior to the close of the transaction.

Subsequent to Chrysler's having advanced the funds and the execution of the Acknowledgement, the Pennsylvania Legislature amended 4-468 of the Liquor Code on June 29, 1987, adding subsection (d) which provides:

[handwritten marginal note: Negative pledge clause 9-401]

4-468. Licenses not assignable; transfers.

... (d) The license shall constitute a privilege between the Board
and the licensee. As between the licensee and third parties, the
license shall constitute property.

Finally, Clark filed his Petition for Relief under the Bankruptcy Code on
or about April 26, 1988, thereby staying the enforcement of Chrysler's asserted security interest, whereupon it filed the Motion for Relief of the
Automatic Stay and Request for Adequate Protection now before this
court.

Chrysler also properly states the issues:

1. Whether or not the executed Acknowledgement is sufficient
to satisfy the formal requirements of an enforceable security
agreement?

2. Whether or not Chrysler's security interest attached at the
time the Pennsylvania Liquor Code was amended in 1987 to
state that a liquor license was to be treated as personal property
as between the licensee and third parties?

Section [9-203] of the Uniform Commercial Code sets forth the requirements for an enforceable security interest. * * * Chrysler argues that it
gave value when it advanced the sum of $85,000 to Clark enabling him to
finance and close the purchase transaction shortly after the advance was
made, and that determining whether Chrysler has an enforceable security
interest in the License merely requires a finding that a security agreement
was executed between the parties and that Clark ultimately acquired
"rights in the collateral" citing Kendrick v. Headwaters Production Credit
Assoc., 523 A.2d 395 (1987).

Section [1-201(b)(35)] defines "security interest" as follows: "A security
interest means an interest in personal property or fixtures which secures
payment or performance of an obligation." [9-201] provides that: "Except
as otherwise provided by this title, a security agreement is effective according to its terms between the parties, against purchasers of the collateral
and against creditors." [9-102(a)(73)] provides the following definition:
"'Security Agreement.' An agreement which creates or provides for a security interest."

Chrysler states correctly that the Code does not carefully define what
exactly constitutes a security agreement, so that we must look to case law,
citing In re Bollinger Corp., 614 F.2d 924 (3rd Cir. 1980). That court observed certain prior interpretations * * * under which a "creditor's assertion

of a secured claim must fall in the absence of language connoting a grant of a security interest." The court in *Bollinger* further noted that the requirement of "grant" language had been criticized and not followed by other courts which adopted a less strict rule, quoting with approval:

> A writing or writings, regardless of label, which adequately describes the collateral, carries the signature of the debtor, and establishes that in fact, a security interest was agreed upon, would satisfy both the formal requirements of the statute and the policies behind it. [In re Numeric Corp., 485 F.2d 1328, 1331 (1st Cir. 1973)]

The *Bollinger* court concluded: "The intention of the parties to create a security interest may be gleaned from the expression of future intent to create one in the promissory note and the intention of the parties as expressed in letters constituting their course of dealing."

Chrysler argues that the Acknowledgement (1) rendered the debtor unable to transfer the License thereafter to anyone else, including creditors and (2) precluded the debtor from transferring the License to a different premises, and is therefore sufficient as a security agreement. Chrysler concludes that it has a security interest in the License. However, while the Acknowledgement does constitute an agreement, and the parties are bound by its terms, and it identifies the License, its terms only provide limitations on the transfer of the License; the terms of the agreement do not indicate an intent to give to Chrysler a security interest in the License. Chrysler may prohibit a transfer of the License from the premises or prohibit the transfer of the License to an outside party, but it is given no right in the writing to foreclose on the License, to take possession of it, to have it canceled, to have it transferred to itself, to have any of the rights of a secured party under the Uniform Commercial Code, nor may Chrysler in any other manner derive a benefit from it except insofar as it may extract a ransom by being able to preclude a transfer by the debtor to another party or by the debtor to another premises.

We liken Chrysler's rights to the rights of a party to maintain a debtor's chicken within an enclosed, fenced-off area, under an agreement that the creditor might maintain the fence in place, preventing the chicken from being removed or used in any other place, or sold or transferred to any other person by the debtor, yet the secured creditor has no right in himself, on default or otherwise, to remove the chicken for his own benefit.

The outcome would be different if the writing had stated that Chrysler would have a security interest, for then Chrysler would have the right of possession under the Uniform Commercial Code upon default. And again, if the agreement had given, or evidenced an intent to give, Chrysler the right to possession upon default, then such a right could be enforced under the Uniform Commercial Code. But here, there is nothing to indicate an intent to give to Chrysler a security interest in the liquor license.

No doubt the debtors would have given Chrysler a security interest in the License if Chrysler had asked for it. It is apparent that Chrysler did not ask for a security interest. The obvious reason why Chrysler did not request a security agreement or security interest in the License was the fact that, under the state of the law at that time, the License was not property and no security interest could be obtained in it by a creditor.

Thus, the attempted security interest must fail.

The above conclusion makes unnecessary our consideration of the other issue, that is, whether Chrysler's security interest would have attached at the time the Pennsylvania Liquor Code was amended in 1987. This court's view, though now unimportant to disposition of this case, is that when the legislation was enacted in 1987 changing the law so that thereafter a liquor license does constitute property, all of the elements would have fallen into place to create a valid security interest under [9-203] if the Acknowledgement had contained language evidencing an intent to grant a security interest. In many transactions, the financing statements, security agreements and value have been advanced prior to the time the debtor has an interest in the collateral. When the debtor acquires an interest in the collateral (e.g., when the purchased item is delivered to the debtor), that being the last necessary element of a valid security interest, the security interest thereupon attaches. There is no reason why such rule should not apply to a liquor license. Here, however, the fundamental element of a valid underlying security interest is missing. * * *

COMMENTS AND QUESTIONS

The best discussion of the original definition of the security interest is Grant Gilmore's:

> This, like most definitions of basic terms, is essentially a declaration of faith. Who can meaningfully define the number "one"

or the verb "to be"? It is clear that there must be some sort of "obligation" which underlies or supports the interest; this will normally be a money debt but could conceivably be something else ("payment or performance"). The subject matter of the interest must be "personal property or fixtures"—that is, property within the coverage of Article 9 and the rest of the Code. No attempt is made to explain what constitutes an "interest" in property or *** when an interest "secures" an obligation. It is not suggested that anything useful could have been done to explain the phrase "an interest ... which secures ... an obligation": the draftsman's art does not go so far. What is important to remember is that, ultimately, the Article 9 security interest floats, unmoored, in a void. Whether any particular transaction creates "an interest ... which secures ... an obligation" is a question for judicial determination.

*** Article 9, for all its comprehensiveness, is a statute drafted to regulate certain well-known or institutionalized types of financing transactions. It is fair enough to say that a transaction which sets out to be one of those types should conform to the Article 9 rules or fall by the wayside. But beyond the area of institutionalized transaction, there stretches a no-man's land, in which strange creatures do strange things. For these strange things there are no rules; it makes no sense to measure them against the rules which professionals have developed for professional transactions. The best that can be done is to let the courts pick their way from case to case, working out their solutions ad hoc and ad hominem.

*** It should be noted that there are two quite different aspects to the question: Is this interest a Code security interest? One is attacking, negative and hostile. The claimant who wishes to defeat or set aside an interest says: This is a security interest, it does not comply with the Code's formal requirements or the perfection requirements; it is therefore invalid or unenforceable. The other is affirmative or constructive. The holder or beneficiary of some kind of interest says: This is a security interest; I am therefore entitled to the rights of a security party (including the right to file for protection against my debtor's other creditors). Conceivably, different considerations might apply to the resolution of the question, depending on whether the attempt was to defeat an interest or to claim rights under it, with more liberality being shown to the affirmative than to the negative claimant.

1 Grant Gilmore, Security Interests in Personal Property 334-337 (1965).

SECTION II. THE REQUIREMENT OF AN AUTHENTICATED AGREEMENT

The key formal requirement for a generic security interest is given in 9-203(b)(3)(A): "the debtor has authenticated a security agreement that provides a description of the collateral." What does it mean to say that a secured creditor has to have "authenticated" a security agreement before a security interest can attach or become enforceable? (For some help, see 9-102(a)(7).) In a transaction of any size, there will be a blizzard of documents evidencing the original transaction, plus a course of dealing after the fact. To what extent will we force subsequent secured parties to piece together the relationship from these documents and the dealings? Alternatively, should we enforce the authenticated agreement requirement rigorously and thereby force parties creating security interests to be especially careful?

In re Bollinger Corp.

United States Court of Appeals, Third Circuit, 1980.
614 F.2d 924.

■ ROSENN, CIRCUIT JUDGE

This appeal from a district court review of an order in bankruptcy presents a question that has troubled courts since the enactment of Article Nine of the Uniform Commercial Code (UCC) governing secured transactions. Can a creditor assert a secured claim against the debtor when no formal security agreement was ever signed, but where various documents executed in connection with a loan evince an intent to create a security interest? The district court answered this question in the affirmative and permitted the creditor, Zimmerman & Jansen, to assert a secured claim against the debtor, bankrupt Bollinger Corporation in the amount of $150,000. We affirm.

I

The facts of this case are not in dispute. Industrial Credit Company (ICC) made a loan to Bollinger Corporation (Bollinger) on January 13, 1972, in

[Handwritten margin notes:]
Attachment 9-203:
· value
· collateral
· agreement to create SA.
Actual agreement + formalities needed for SA.
· Agreement (grant)
Formalities (statute of frauds) require:
· authenticated writing
OR
· possession

In re Bollinger:

A creditor can assert a secured claim against the debtor when no formal agreement was signed, but where various documents ... executed in ... connection w/ a loan evince an intent to create an SI.

→ promissory note, financing statement, letters constituting course of dealing

the amount of $150,000. As evidence of the loan, Bollinger executed a promissory note in the sum of $150,000 and signed a security agreement with ICC giving it a security interest in certain machinery and equipment. ICC in due course perfected its security interest in the collateral by filing a financing statement in accordance with Pennsylvania's enactment of Article Nine of the UCC.

Bollinger faithfully met its obligations under the note and by December 4, 1974, had repaid $85,000 of the loan leaving $65,000 in unpaid principal. Bollinger, however, required additional capital and on December 5, 1974, entered into a loan agreement with Zimmerman & Jansen, Inc. (Z&J), by which Z&J agreed to lend Bollinger $150,000. Z&J undertook as part of this transaction to pay off the $65,000 still owed to ICC in return for an assignment by ICC to Z&J of the original note and security agreement between Bollinger and ICC. Bollinger executed a promissory note to Z&J, evidencing the agreement containing the following provision:

> *Security.* This Promissory Note is secured by security interests in a certain Security Agreement between Bollinger and Industrial Credit Company ... and in a Financing Statement filed by (ICC) ..., and is further secured by security interests in a certain security agreement to be delivered by Bollinger to Z and J with this Promissory Note covering the identical machinery and equipment as identified in the ICC Agreement and with identical schedule attached in the principal amount of Eighty-Five Thousand Dollars. ($85,000).

No formal security agreement was ever executed between Bollinger and Z&J. Z&J did, however, in connection with the promissory note, record a new financing statement signed by Bollinger containing a detailed list of the machinery and equipment originally taken as collateral by ICC for its loan to Bollinger.

Bollinger filed a petition for an arrangement under Chapter XI of the Bankruptcy Act in March, 1975 and was adjudicated bankrupt one year later. In administrating the bankrupt's estate, the receiver sold some of Bollinger's equipment but agreed that Z&J would receive a $10,000 credit on its secured claim.

Z&J asserted a secured claim against the bankrupt in the amount of $150,000, arguing that although it never signed a security agreement with Bollinger, the parties had intended that a security interest in the sum of

$150,000 be created to protect the loan. The trustee in bankruptcy conceded that the assignment to Z&J of ICC's original security agreement with Bollinger gave Z&J a secured claim in the amount of $65,000, the balance owed by Bollinger to ICC at the time of the assignment. The trustee, however, refused to recognize Z&J's asserted claim of an additional secured claim of $85,000 because of the absence of a security agreement between Bollinger and Z&J. The bankruptcy court agreed and entered judgment for Z&J in the amount of $55,000, representing a secured claim in the amount of $65,000 less $10,000 credit received by Z&J.

Z&J appealed to the United States District Court for the Western District of Pennsylvania, which reversed the bankruptcy court and entered judgment for Z&J in the full amount of the asserted $150,000 secured claim. The trustee in bankruptcy appeals.

II

Under Article Nine of the UCC, two documents are generally required to create a perfected security interest in a debtor's collateral. First, there must be a "security agreement" giving the creditor an interest in the collateral. [9-203(b)(3)(A)] contains minimal requirements for the creation of a security agreement. In order to create a security agreement, there must be: (1) a writing (2) signed by the debtor (3) containing a description of the collateral or the types of collateral. The requirements of [9-203(b)(3)(A)] further two basic policies. First, an evidentiary function is served by requiring a signed security agreement and second, a written agreement also obviates any Statute of Frauds problems with the debtor-creditor relationship. The second document generally required is a "financing statement," which is a document signed by both parties and filed for public record. The financing statement serves the purpose of giving public notice to other creditors that a security interest is claimed in the debtor's collateral.

Despite the minimal formal requirements set forth in [9-203] for the creation of a security agreement, the commercial world has frequently neglected to comply with this simple Code provision. Soon after Article Nine's enactment, creditors who had failed to obtain formal security agreements, but who nevertheless had obtained and filed financing statements, sought to enforce secured claims. Under F9-402, a security agreement may serve as a financing statement if it is signed by both parties. The question arises whether the converse is true: Can a signed financing statement operate as a security agreement? The earliest case to consider this question was American Card Co. v. H.M.H. Co., 196 A.2d 150, 152

(1963) which held that a financing statement could *not* operate as a security agreement because there was no language *granting* a security interest to a creditor. Although [9-203(b)(3)(A)] makes no mention of such a grant language requirement, the court in *American Card* thought that implicit in the definition of "security agreement" under [9-102(a)(73)] was such a requirement; some grant language was necessary to "create or provide security." This view also was adopted by the Tenth Circuit in Shelton v. Erwin, 472 F.2d 1118, 1120 (10th Cir. 1973). Thus, under the holdings of these cases, the creditor's assertion of a secured claim must fail in the absence of language connoting a grant of a security interest.

The Ninth Circuit in In re Amex-Protein Development Corp., 504 F.2d 1056 (9th Cir. 1974), echoed criticism by commentators of the *American Card* rule. The court wrote: "There is no support in legislative history or grammatical logic for the substitution of the word 'grant' for the phrase 'creates or provides for'." It concluded that as long as the financing statement contains a description of the collateral signed by the debtor, the financing statement may serve as the security agreement and the formal requirements of [9-203(b)(3)(A)] are met. * * *

Some courts have declined to follow the Ninth Circuit's liberal rule allowing the financing statement alone to stand as the security agreement, but have permitted the financing statement, when read in conjunction with other documents executed by the parties, to satisfy the requirements of [9-203(b)(3)(A)]. The court in In re Numeric Corp., 485 F.2d 1328 (1st Cir. 1973) held that a financing statement coupled with a board of directors' resolution revealing an intent to create a security interest were sufficient to act as a security agreement. The court concluded from its reading of the Code that there appears no need to insist upon a separate document entitled "security agreement" as a prerequisite for an otherwise valid security interest.

> A writing or writings, regardless of label, which adequately describes the collateral, carries the signature of the debtor, and establishes that in fact a security interest was agreed upon, would satisfy both the formal requirements of the statute and the policies behind it.

The court went on to hold that "although a standard form financing statement by itself cannot be considered a security agreement, an adequate agreement can be found when a financing statement is considered together with other documents." * * *

In the case before us, the district court went a step further and held that the promissory note executed by Bollinger in favor of Z&J, standing alone, was sufficient to act as the security agreement between the parties. In so doing, the court implicitly rejected the *American Card* rule requiring grant language before a security agreement arises under [9-203(b)(3)(A)]. The parties have not referred to any Pennsylvania state cases on the question and our independent research has failed to uncover any. But although we agree that no formal grant of a security interest need exist before a security agreement arises, we do not think that the promissory note standing alone would be sufficient under Pennsylvania law to act as the security agreement. We believe, however, that the promissory note, read in conjunction with the financing statement duly filed and supported, as it is here, by correspondence during the course of the transaction between the parties, would be sufficient under Pennsylvania law to establish a valid security agreement.[3]

III

We think Pennsylvania courts would accept the logic behind the First and Ninth Circuit rule and reject the *American Card* rule imposing the requirement of a formal grant of a security interest before a security agreement may exist. When the parties have neglected to sign a separate security agreement, it would appear that the better and more practical view is to look at the transaction as a whole in order to determine if there is a writing, or writings, signed by the debtor describing the collateral which demonstrates an intent to create a security interest in the collateral.[4] In con-

---

Assignment Theory.

[3] The district court held alternatively that the assignment of the 1972 security agreement between Bollinger and ICC to Z&J was sufficient to give Z&J a secured claim in the amount of $150,000. The 1972 security agreement contained a "future advances" clause, allowing ICC to use the collateral for its original loan to Bollinger as security for any future sums advanced by it to Bollinger, as permitted by [9-204(c)]. Z&J argued that its loan to Bollinger qualified as a future advance under the assigned security agreement, thereby giving it a security interest in the amount of $150,000. Although we have serious reservations whether the "future advances" clause was broad enough to encompass a loan made by a third party, we need not consider this alternative theory offered by the district court because we are convinced that the documents executed between Bollinger and Z&J were sufficient to secure Z&J.

[4] We do not intend in any way to encourage the commercial community to dispense with signing security agreements as a normal part of establishing a secured transaction. Lawsuits over the existence of a security agreement may be avoided by executing

nection with Z&J's loan of $150,000 to Bollinger, the relevant writings to be considered are: (1) the promissory note; (2) the financing statement; (3) a group of letters constituting the course of dealing between the parties. The district court focused solely on the promissory note finding it sufficient to constitute the security agreement. Reference, however, to the language in the note reveals that the note standing alone cannot serve as the security agreement. The note recites that along with the assigned 1972 security agreement between Bollinger and ICC, the Z&J loan is "further secured by security interests in a certain Security Agreement *to be delivered* by Bollinger to Z&J with this Promissory Note, ..." (Emphasis added.) The bankruptcy judge correctly reasoned that "[t]he intention to create a separate security agreement negates any inference that the debtor intended that the promissory note constitute the security agreement." At best, the note is some evidence that a security agreement was contemplated by the parties, but by its own terms, plainly indicates that it is not the security agreement.

Looking beyond the promissory note, Z&J did file a financing statement signed by Bollinger containing a detailed list of all the collateral intended to secure the $150,000 loan to Bollinger. The financing statement alone meets the basic [9-203(b)(3)(A)] requirements of a writing, signed by the debtor, describing the collateral. However, the financing statement provides only an inferential basis for concluding that the parties intended a security agreement. There would be little reason to file such a detailed financing statement unless the parties intended to create a security interest. The intention of the parties to create a security interest may be gleaned from the expression of future intent to create one in the promissory note and the intention of the parties as expressed in letters constituting their course of dealing.

The promissory note was executed by Bollinger in favor of Z&J in December 1974. Prior to the consummation of the loan, Z&J sent a letter to Bollinger on May 30, 1974, indicating that the loan would be made "provided" Bollinger secured the loan by a mortgage on its machinery and

---

a separate security agreement conforming to the minimal requirements of [9-203(b)(3)(A)]. Our discussion today only predicts, after our examination of the relevant case law, that Pennsylvania courts would adopt a pragmatic view of the issue raised here and recognize the intention of the parties expressed in the composite documents and not exalt form over substance.

equipment. Bollinger sent a letter to Z&J on September 19, 1974, indicating:

> With your [Z&J's] stated desire to obtain security for material and funds advanced, it would appear that the use of the note would answer both our problems. Since the draft forwarded to you offers full collateralization for the funds to be advanced under it and bears normal interest during its term, it should offer you maximum security.

Subsequent to the execution of the promissory note, Bollinger sent to Z&J a list of the equipment and machinery intended as collateral under the security agreement which was to be, but never was, delivered to Z&J. In November 1975, the parties exchanged letters clarifying whether Bollinger could substitute or replace equipment in the ordinary course of business without Z&J's consent. Such a clarification would not have been necessary had a security interest not been intended by the parties. Finally, a letter of November 18, 1975, from Bollinger to Z&J indicated that "any attempted impairment of the collateral would constitute an event of default."

From the course of dealing between Z&J and Bollinger, we conclude there is sufficient evidence that the parties intended a security agreement to be created separate from the assigned ICC agreement with Bollinger. All the evidence points towards the intended creation of such an agreement and since the financing statement contains a detailed list of the collateral, signed by Bollinger, we hold that a valid Article Nine security agreement existed under Pennsylvania law between the parties which secured Z&J in the full amount of the loan to Bollinger.

IV

The minimal formal requirements of [9-203(b)(3)(A)] were met by the financing statement and the promissory note, and the course of dealing between the parties indicated the intent to create a security interest. The judgment of the district court recognizing Z&J's secured claim in the amount of $150,000 will be affirmed.

Each side to bear its own costs.

COMMENTS AND QUESTIONS

1. Is there any doubt in Bollinger that Z&J has a security interest, given the assignment of the original loan to them? Isn't the real question whether it has more than one security interest? How should that influence how the letters and other evidence are viewed?

2. Footnote 3 presents an alternative theory to validate the new loans made by Z&J, namely, that they should be considered to be future advances under the original loan made by ICC. You should make a mental note of that possibility, as we will return to it—or at least a close cousin to it—when we consider the *Fretz* case (Republic National Bank v. Fitzgerald (In re E.A. Fretz Co.), 565 F.2d 366 (5th Cir. 1978)).

In re Weir-Penn, Inc.

United States Bankruptcy Court, N.D. West Virginia, 2006.
344 Bankr. 791.

■ PATRICK M. FLATLEY, BANKRUPTCY JUDGE

United Bank, Inc. ("United Bank"), filed a motion for relief from the automatic stay of the Bankruptcy Code to repossess convenience store property and enforce its security rights under State law. Thomas H. Fluharty, the Chapter 7 trustee (the "Trustee") for Weir-Penn, Inc. (the "Debtor"), opposes the motion on the basis that United Bank is not a secured creditor because it cannot produce an authenticated security agreement. The Debtor joins in the Trustee's objection. * * *

The Debtor operated Convenient Food Mart # 3818 in Weirton, West Virginia. On October 31, 1997, the Debtor borrowed $110,000 from United Bank, which allegedly took a security interest in the Debtor's assets, including: equipment, inventory, and accounts. United Bank filed a UCC-1 financing statement on November 6, 1997, but it cannot produce a copy of the security agreement purportedly executed by the Debtor. Anthony J. Gentile, Sr., the market president for United Bank, signed an affidavit on February 21, 2006, stating that the security agreement could not be located, and that it had likely been destroyed in a September 2004 or January 2005 flood.

The Debtor refinanced the October 31, 1997 loan twice: first, on July 8, 1999, for $40,135; then on September 10, 2002, for $110,000. United Bank filed a UCC-3 continuation statement on September 9, 2002. When the Debtor defaulted on the note on January 12, 2006, the payoff amount was $66,747.

On February 10, 2006, the Debtor filed its Chapter 7 bankruptcy petition. On March 21, 2006, the assets subject to United Bank's alleged security interest were sold by the Trustee for $21,000. Those funds are being held by the Trustee pending the determination of United Bank's lien rights, if any, in the proceeds.

United Bank asserts that the absence of a separate, written security agreement signed by the Debtor does not negate its security interest in the Debtor's convenience store assets. United Bank contends that the Debtor signed the financing statement listing the collateral subject to its interest—satisfying the writing requirement—and that the associated documentary evidence establishes the intent of the parties to give United Bank a security interest in the same categories of collateral listed on the financing statement.

The West Virginia Commercial Code (the "Commercial Code") sets forth the requirements to create an enforceable security interest [in] * * * 9-203(b). Here, there is no dispute that subsections (1) and (2) are satisfied. Without an authenticated security agreement that provides a description of the collateral, however, United Bank does not have an enforceable security interest.

The Commercial Code defines a "security agreement" as "an agreement that creates or provides for a security interest." 9-102(a)(76). No requirement exists that there be a separate written document labeled "security agreement" that has express language granting a security interest: once a debtor signs the financing statement the writing requirement is met, and the determination of whether the parties intended to create a security interest is an issue of fact that is garnered by reviewing "a collection of documents, no one of which contains granting language, but which in the aggregate disclose an intent to grant a security interest in specific collateral." Terry M. Anderson, Marianne B. Culhane, and Catherine Lee Wilson, Attachment and Perfection of Security Interests Under Revised Article 9: A "Nuts and Bolts" Primer, 9 Am. Bankr. Inst. L.Rev. 179, 188 (2001).

In this case, the Debtor has signed a financing statement indicating that the Debtor may have granted United Bank a security interest in the categories or types of property listed. A considerable number of cases have held that a financing statement alone—the purpose of which is only to provide notice that a creditor may, or may not, have a security interest in the listed property—cannot double as a security agreement. Because a signed financing statement is deemed to satisfy the Statute of Frauds, however, the only other purpose behind requiring an "authenticated security agreement" is evidentiary as it relates to the intent of the parties to grant the creditor identifiable security. 9-203 cmt. 3 ("Under subsection (b)(3), enforceability requires the debtor's security agreement and compliance with an evidentiary requirement in the nature of a statute of frauds.").

Sufficient evidence exists in this case to establish the intent of the parties to create a security interest in the categories or types of property listed on the Debtor's financing statement. The September 10, 2002 promissory note states:

9. SECURITY. This Loan is secured by separate security instruments prepared together with this Note as follows:

Document Name	Parties to Document
Deed of Trust-Leasehold ...	Weir-Penn, Inc.

and by the following previously executed, security instruments or agreements: UCC Financing Statement on all business assets bearing file # 048209 recorded 11/16/1997 with the WV Secretary of State and executed by Weir-Penn, Inc as debtor and United National Bank (nka United Bank, Inc.) as Secured Party.

(Doc. No. 16, Exhibit C).

Accordingly, the September 10, 2002 promissory note, which is also signed by the Debtor, contains a security clause that states that the loan is secured by "previously executed, security instruments or agreements." The only item listed under this clause is the UCC Financing Statement. Taken together, the note evidences the intent of the parties to create a security interest ("This Loan is secured by ...."), and the financing statement, incorporated by reference in the security clause of the promissory note, provides a description of the collateral.[3] E.g., In re Bollinger Corp., 614 F.2d

---

[3] Two additional documents exist that support the court's conclusion that the promissory note and the financing statement, taken together, satisfy the requirement of an authenticated security agreement. First, the Debtor apparently executed a corporate resolution granting Mr. Cottrill, the Debtor's president, the authority to execute a

924, 927-28 (3rd Cir. 1980) (holding that the financing statement alone met the requirement for a writing signed by the debtor and describing the collateral, and that the promissory note evidenced the intention of the parties to create a security interest in the listed collateral).

The financing statement signed by the Debtor meets the basic 9-203(b)(3)(A) requirements that there be a writing, signed by the Debtor, describing the collateral. The intent of the parties to create a security interest in the collateral listed on the financing statement is gleaned from the September 10, 2002 promissory note, which states that the note is secured by the financing statement. Accordingly, the Court will grant United Bank relief from the automatic stay to recover the proceeds of the sale of the collateral securing its September 10, 2002 loan to the Debtor. * * *

COMMENTS AND QUESTIONS

Is this the same case as *Bollinger*? Said differently, *Bollinger* is a case where notwithstanding a clear intent to execute a new security agreement, none was ever executed. That put the court to the choice of finding no security interest was created or somehow leaping from intent to completion. In *Weir-Penn*, doesn't the best evidence suggest that a security agreement was indeed executed? Does that matter? Should we treat the missing security agreement the same as the never-executed security agreement?

COMMENTS AND QUESTIONS: JUSTIFICATIONS FOR THE REQUIREMENT OF AN AUTHENTICATED SECURITY AGREEMENT

What are the reasons for the requirement that there be either possession by the secured party or a descriptive agreement authenticated by the debtor? What harm might flow from allowing parties to create non-possessory

---

security agreement with United Bank. The authorization is neither signed by the corporate secretary that purportedly conferred the authorization, nor is it dated. The second document is the waiver of lien rights of the Debtor's landlord in favor of United Bank. The Debtor was not a party to that agreement. The documents support the conclusion, however, that the Debtor intended to grant a security interest to United Bank and that United Bank believed that it had obtained one from the Debtor.

security interests orally? A key issue to keep in mind is that secured trans-actions are three-party transactions, at least in all cases that matter. What-ever the merits of the traditional Statute of Frauds, in most cases it applies in a two-party context. Secured transaction disputes are very different. The dispute will usually arise between a secured creditor and another creditor. The security agreement will be between the debtor and the secured party. The competing creditor will have no first-hand knowledge of the security agreement. The debtor may be insolvent and thus may have little stake in the outcome. Thus, absent a requirement of an authenticated agreement, the secured creditor could have a great deal of latitude in how it describes the agreement between the debtor and the secured party. The requirement of an authenticated agreement limits this possibility.

Does this suffice as a justification for the requirement? If authenticated agreements were not required, how would prospective creditors respond to the possibility that the debtor could have created any number of oral secu-rity agreements? Perhaps we need a more selective mechanism. The re-quirement of an authenticated security agreement bars *all* debtors from making oral agreements. Don't we just need a device by which the debtor can bind itself not to create oral security agreements?

SECTION III. DESCRIPTION OF THE COLLATERAL

When third parties are trying to sort out rights to a debtor's assets after it has become insolvent, a description in a security agreement may be of more use than a security agreement containing only words of grant. Does the need of third parties for such descriptions tell us what kind of language is sufficient to be "a description of the collateral" within the meaning of 9-203? A written description of the collateral in the security agreement is a proxy for possession of the collateral by the secured party, but it is at best an imperfect one. There seem to be at least three basic sorts of problems with descriptions. First, a description may be so broad as to tell us nothing about what property might be involved, but nevertheless be unambiguous precisely because it is so all-encompassing: "all debtor's property of what-ever kind, now existing or hereafter acquired." Second, a description may exist that, though perhaps more focused, may also be ambiguous: "debtor's car" (when the debtor has two cars). Third, a description may exist that, though focused, is erroneous: "debtor's 2006 Pontiac" (when the car in question is a 2005 Pontiac).

2-7: DEFINING KEY TERMS

- Debtor, a manufacturer, executes a security agreement that grants Bank "a security interest in all of Debtor's equipment, now and hereafter owned, to secure all debts to Bank hereunder."

¤ Debtor owns a special computerized lathe, office computers and copiers, plus an assortment of office furniture. Does Bank have a security interest in each of these? Does "equipment" reasonably identify the collateral under the standard of 9-108?

¤ Suppose that the grant clause reads instead "a security interest in all of Debtor's equipment (as defined in 9-102(a)(33)), now and hereafter owned, to secure all debts to Bank hereunder." Does this change the outcome? See 9-108(b)(3), (e).

Baldwin v. Castro County Feeders I, Ltd.

Supreme Court of North Dakota, 2004.
678 N.W.2d 796.

■ GILBERTSON, CHIEF JUSTICE

A South Dakota circuit court determined Castro County Feeders I, Ltd. (Castro County) had an enforceable security interest in the proceeds of a sale of seventy-eight cattle owned by Ryan Baldwin (Baldwin). Baldwin sold the cattle through Livestock Sales in Wagner, South Dakota. * * *

Both parties to this controversy reside in the State of Texas. Castro County runs a feedlot operation wherein it contracts to feed cattle placed in its lots as well as to provide the vitamins, minerals, and medicine necessary for the proper care of the cattle. Baldwin owns and operates a business specializing in the purchase and sale of cattle. As part of his business, Baldwin often placed his cattle with Castro County. Castro County would feed the livestock for a period of time and then release the cattle to Baldwin for transport and sale in Kansas. Generally, the sale proceeds were made payable to Baldwin and Castro County in order to reimburse it for the feed and related services provided to Baldwin's cattle. * * *

The circuit court determined Castro County had a valid security interest in Baldwin's cattle sold in Wagner. SDCL ch. 57A-9, South Dakota's codified version of Article 9 of the Uniform Commercial Code, governs secured transactions. * * *

The primary question Baldwin raises on appeal is whether the Agreement between himself and Castro County functions as a valid security agreement as required by 9-203(b)(3)(A). * * * Baldwin questions whether the Agreement provides a sufficient description of the collateral. * * * In particular, Baldwin argues the Agreement insufficiently described the collateral because it gave Castro County a security interest in all cattle "being specifically located in Lot(s) # _____ at Castro County Feeders, I, Ltd., Hart, Castro County, Texas."[4] In other words, Baldwin believes the Agreement failed to sufficiently identify the cattle at issue in this case because it did not specify the feedlots in which his cattle were located. We disagree * * *.

To determine whether the description was sufficient, we must look to 9-108. Pursuant to subsection (a), the "test" for sufficiency is whether the description (specific or not) "reasonably identifies what is described." In the instant case, the description was "livestock." This is an example of an identification of collateral by category, which is specifically permitted under 9-108(b)(2). ("Except as otherwise provided in subsection (d), a description of collateral reasonably identifies the collateral if it identifies the collateral by ... (2) category[.]") Comment 2 to UCC § 9-108 states:

> The purpose of requiring a description of collateral in a security agreement under 9-203 is evidentiary. The test of sufficiency of a description under this section, as under F9-110, is that the description do the job assigned to it: make possible the identifica-

---

[4] The complete Cattle Feeding Agreement definition of "collateral" included:

> [A]ll of Feeder's interest in farm products, limited to livestock, whether now owned or hereafter created, acquired or arising; all of Feeder's feed, vitamins, minerals, and medicine; all of Feeder's contracts for the future purchase or future sale or delivery of the livestock; all of Feeder's contract rights and accounts receivable, checks, drafts, notes, general intangibles and all the sale of any of the foregoing Collateral; all right, title, and the interest of Feeder as partner, joint venturer, co-owner or otherwise with respect to any properties of the foregoing description; all of the foregoing, whether now owned or hereafter acquired; and all such Collateral being located on the real property described in Exhibit "A" and including without limitation all additions, accessions, substitutions and replacements of, for, or to all or any of the foregoing together with all proceeds and products of all or any of the foregoing, such livestock being specifically located in Lot(s) # _____ at Castro County Feeders, I, Ltd., Hart, Castro County, Texas. It is expressly agreed that the Collateral is perishable in nature and is of a type requiring immediate sale to recognize the full value.

As noted above, the Lot # space was left blank in the original Agreement.

tion of the collateral described. This section rejects any requirement that a description is insufficient unless it is exact and detailed (the so-called "serial number" test).

Moreover, "livestock" is included in the definition of "farm products." Therefore, even if the agreement had only provided for an interest in Baldwin's "farm products," the description would have been sufficient to include "livestock." Specifically, 9-102(34) provides * * * . In Mushitz v. First Bank of South Dakota, 457 N.W.2d 849, 853 (S.D. 1990) we held the description of "all farm machinery ... and livestock owned by [debtor]" constituted a sufficient description of the collateral. We held that such descriptions reasonably identify what they describe.

Here, the Agreement did not attempt to give Castro County a security interest in all of Baldwin's property as prohibited by 9-108(c). Although the parties did not specify a particular lot or lots, the Agreement restricted the security interest to the cattle Baldwin delivered to Castro County's feedlot complex in the city of Hart, Texas. According to the Agreement, Baldwin also granted Castro County a security interest in the sale of these cattle. We believe this description was sufficient to make the collateral objectively determinable. A reasonable reading of the Agreement gave Castro County a security interest in only those cattle of Baldwin's to which it advanced feed and related services. It was not necessary for the agreement to list each individual head of livestock to which Castro County's security interest attached. Moreover, it was also reasonable for the Agreement to leave a specific lot number blank given the fact the cattle were not usually located in one of Castro County's lots when sold.

We believe the Agreement between Baldwin and Castro County constituted an authenticated security agreement that sufficiently described the collateral as those cattle to which Castro County provided feed and related services. Baldwin stipulated he owned the cattle placed at Castro County. Castro County provided value by advancing Baldwin's cattle feed and related services. Thus, the requirements for valid security interest as defined by 9-203 were met. * * *

COMMENTS AND QUESTIONS

1. Track the punctuation carefully in the definition of collateral in foot-note 4 of the Cattle Feeding Agreement. What role is the Lot number and the associated blank intended to play in the agreement?
2. The court ultimately limits the security agreement to those as to which Castro "advanced feed and related services." Where exactly does that come from?

2-8: FOOLISH RELIANCE?

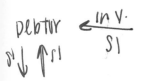

- Debtor buys inventory from Supplier. Supplier finances those pur-chases and Debtor signs a security agreement granting Supplier a security interest in "all inventory provided by Supplier." Debtor au-thorizes Supplier to file a financing statement covering "all inven-tory."
- Bank subsequently lends Debtor new funds and takes a security in-terest in "all Debtor's inventory" and files an authorized financing statement covering the same.
- Debtor subsequently buys new inventory from Supplier, financed by Supplier, and grants Supplier a security interest in "all Debtor's inventory."
- ¤ As between Bank and Supplier, who has priority over Debtor's in-ventory?

Shelby County State Bank v. Van Diest Supply Co.

United States Court of Appeals, Seventh Circuit, 2002.
303 F.3d 832.

■ DIANE P. WOOD, CIRCUIT JUDGE

Hennings Feed & Crop Care, Inc. (Hennings) filed a voluntary bankrupt-cy petition under Chapter 11 on August 23, 1999, after Van Diest Supply Co. (Van Diest), one of its creditors, filed a complaint against it in the Central District of Illinois. Shelby County State Bank (the Bank), another creditor of Hennings, brought this action in the bankruptcy proceeding against Van Diest and the Trustee for Hennings to assert the validity of the Bank's security interest in certain assets of Hennings. Van Diest was included as a defendant because the scope of Van Diest's security interest in Henning's assets affects the extent of the Bank's security interest. The Bank and Van Diest cross-moved for summary judgment, and the bankruptcy court granted the Bank's motion, finding that Van Diest's security interest was limited to the inventory it sold to Hennings (as opposed to the whole of Hennings's inventory). Van Diest appealed that order, and the district court reversed, finding that Van Diest's security interest extended to all of the inventory. * * *

I

Hennings, a corporation based in Iowa, was in the business of selling agricultural chemicals and products. As is customary, several of Hennings's suppliers extended credit to it from time to time to finance its business operations, and obtained liens or other security interests in Hennings's property and inventory to safeguard their advances.

The Bank is among Hennings's creditors. In December 1997, the Bank extended credit to Hennings for $500,000. In May 1998, the Bank increased this amount to a revolving line of credit of some $4,000,000. Hennings in return granted the Bank a security interest in certain of its assets, including inventory and general intangibles. Van Diest, also a creditor, entered into several security agreements with Hennings and its predecessor over the years to protect its financing of materials supplied to Hennings. These agreements were covered by the Uniform Commercial Code, which Iowa has adopted (including the revised Article 9).

A financing statement entered into by Hennings and Van Diest on November 2, 1981, provided for a blanket lien in "[a]ll inventory, notes and accounts receivable, machinery and equipment now owned or hereafter acquired, including all replacements, substitutions and additions thereto." On August 29, 1983, Hennings and Van Diest entered into a new security agreement (the Security Agreement), the language of which is at the core of this dispute. The Security Agreement was based on a preprinted standard "Business Security Agreement" form. In the field for the description of collateral, the parties entered the following language, drafted by Van Diest, describing the security interest as being in

> [a]ll inventory, including but not limited to agricultural chemicals, fertilizers, and fertilizer materials sold to Debtor by Van Diest Supply Co. whether now owned or hereafter acquired, in-

cluding all replacements, substitutions and additions thereto, and the accounts, notes, and any other proceeds therefrom.

The Security Agreement contained a further preprinted clause providing

as additional collateral all additions to and replacements of all such collateral and all accessories, accessions, parts and equipment now or hereafter affixed thereto or used in connection with and the proceeds from all such collateral (including negotiable or non-negotiable warehouse receipts now or hereafter issued for storage of collateral). * * *

II

As this case requires the interpretation of a contract, which is a question of law, we review the district court's decision de novo. The facts underlying the contract interpretation are not disputed in this case.

In accordance with the Security Agreement's undisputed choice of law provision, we apply Iowa law.

A. Ambiguity of the "After-Acquired" Clause

In the process of divining the meaning of a contractual clause, a court must first establish whether the language in dispute supports more than one interpretation. The existence of such an ambiguity is a question of law, and under Iowa law, "[t]he test for ambiguity is objective: whether the language is fairly susceptible to two interpretations." DeJong v. Sioux Ctr., Iowa, 168 F.3d 1115, 1119 (8th Cir. 1999).

The description of the security interest in this case is a textbook example of ambiguous language: a term (all inventory) is followed by a qualifier (including all ...) and then another (sold to Debtor by Van Diest). It is a basic rule of English syntax (of all syntax, in fact) that a modifier should be placed directly next to the element it aims to modify: placing two modifiers in a row leads to the question whether the latter one modifies only the first modifier, or modifies the entire term. In the first edition of his book on statutory interpretation, Sutherland described the "doctrine of the last antecedent" as providing that "[r]elative and qualifying phrases, grammatically and legally, where no contrary intention appears, refer solely to the last antecedent." J.G. Sutherland, Statutes and Statutory Construction § 267, at 349 (1st ed. 1891).

The Supreme Court recognized the existence of the "last antecedent" rule as early as 1799 in Sims' Lessee v. Irvine, 3 U.S. (3 Dall.) 425, 444

(1799) ("The rule is, that 'such' applies to the last antecedent, unless the sense of the passage requires a different construction."). The Supreme Court of Iowa has also often endorsed resort to the doctrine in an attempt to resolve problems caused by ambiguously placed modifiers. The rule is now thought to extend generally to the placement of all modifiers next to the term to be modified.

B. Canons of Interpretation and Extrinsic Evidence

As a linguistic matter, therefore, the sentence is ambiguous. As both the Supreme Court and Iowa courts have recognized (and, indeed, as Sutherland himself pointed out) the rule is helpful in determining the existence of the ambiguity, but not in solving the puzzle when both readings are plausible. Unless one always followed a rigid formalistic approach, the rule would not cast light on which of the two interpretations should prevail. Instead, courts (including those in Iowa) turn to other canons of interpretation. Under Iowa law, those other canons should be used to resolve an ambiguity before parol evidence may be introduced. The rules in Iowa are the familiar ones used in contract interpretation in United States courts: the contract must be construed as a whole; the court requires a fair and reasonable construction; avoid illegality; the interpretation must account for surrounding circumstances; and the parties' own practical construction is relevant. Iowa also applies the rule requiring the court to construe terms against the drafter of the instrument (still known to those fond of Latin phrases as the rule of *contra proferentem*); it favors specific terms over general terms; and it favors handwriting to typing and typing to printing.

Construing the contract before us as a whole leaves as many doubts as we had at the outset: nothing within it bears on the intended scope of the phrase "including but not limited to agricultural chemicals, fertilizers, and fertilizer materials sold to Debtor by Van Diest Supply Company." Van Diest could have acquired a security interest in everything that Hennings owned in inventory (as it had done, for instance, with the 1981 security agreement), or it could have limited its interest to the goods it supplied to Hennings. Without resort to other interpretive principles or to outside evidence, such as evidence of custom in the trade, it is impossible for a court to decide which reading the parties intended to adopt.

We do agree with the Bank's claim, however, that it would be bizarre as a commercial matter to claim a lien in everything, and then to describe in detail only a smaller part of that whole. This is not to say that there is no use for descriptive clauses of inclusion, so as to make clear the kind of entities that ought to be included. But if all goods of any kind are to be included, why mention only a few? A court required to give "reasonable and effective meaning to all terms," AmerUs Bank v. Pinnacle Bank, 51 F.Supp.2d 994, 999 (S.D. Iowa 1999), must shy away from finding that a significant phrase (like the lengthy description of chemicals and fertilizers we have here) is nothing but surplusage.

Iowa law permits courts to consider the parties' conduct, such as the prior security agreements that Van Diest entered into with Hennings, as one way of resolving the ambiguity. Those earlier agreements at times provided for a blanket security with collateral in all inventory. This, too, is not terribly helpful here. On the one hand, the prior use of a general claim for all inventory demonstrates the availability in the trade of such a term and the willingness of Hennings, on occasion at least, to enter into such broad lien grants. On the other hand, it tends to show that the parties knew how to achieve such a result if they wanted to. There must be a reason why the historically used "all inventory," was modified in this case.

More useful is the parties' own practical construction of this particular agreement—a source that Iowa courts agree may be consulted without opening the door entirely to parol evidence. After the Security Agreement was executed, Van Diest sent to other lenders notices of its interest thereunder. In all the notices, it claimed a "purchase money security interest" only in the inventory it sold to Hennings. In a July 1993 letter to the Bank, for instance, Van Diest described its security interest as being in "[a]ll of Debtor's property (including without limitation all inventory of agricultural chemicals and additives thereto) purchased or otherwise acquired from the Secured Party...." In the parenthetical, Van Diest then construed its own interest as being limited to the goods it sold to Hennings—not to the whole of Hennings's inventory, as it now claims.

It is true that this canon of construction treads remarkably close to the ground covered by extrinsic evidence. Furthermore, the course of dealing between principal parties A and B is not likely to shed light on the way that third party C should have understood an agreement. Where a third party disputes a reading of a contract, it is not in a good position to use course of dealing or other extrinsic evidence to support its position. It was not a part of the negotiations and does not have the access that we otherwise presume of both parties to outside materials relating to the contract.

The Bank also argues that contractual terms must be interpreted in a "commercially reasonable" fashion, even though the Bank has not supported this specific proposition with references to Iowa law. Nevertheless, the somewhat broader requirement of a generally fair and reasonable construction is amply recognized in Iowa. Of two plausible interpretations, we should assume the parties meant one that was fair and reasonable. The problem once again is that there is nothing inherently commercially unreasonable about either of the two possible readings. Under the circumstances, it would have been quite reasonable for Van Diest to get as much security from Hennings as it could, as the latter managed to ratchet up millions of dollars in debt before it went bust (it owes the Bank some $1,412,233.10; Van Diest had, at the time of the petition, some $2,890,288.75 in unpaid invoices; countless other creditors have lined up). On the other hand, it might have been unreasonable for Hennings to commit all of its potential collateral to Van Diest, if so doing might have made it more difficult for the company to obtain credit from others.

C. *Contra Proferentem*

As between the two parties to a contract, there is another doctrine that often resolves ambiguities: it is the rule requiring that ambiguous language must be construed against its drafter. Not only should the drafter be penalized by bearing the costs ex post of having cut corners ex ante, the penalty of interpretation against the drafter also aims to avoid overbearing behavior between contracting parties where the drafter, often the one in the better bargaining position, tries to pull a fast one over the party who can merely accept or reject the contract as a whole. Although this doctrine of *contra proferentem* is perhaps on the wane in some jurisdictions, it is alive and well in Iowa * * * .

Unlike many jurisdictions that relegate the contra proferentem rule to the status of "tie-breaker," Iowa takes a strong view of the rule, holding that ambiguous language is to be "strictly construed against the drafter." Iowa Fuel & Minerals, Inc. v. Iowa State Bd. of Regents, 471 N.W.2d 859, 863 (Iowa 1991).

Here, the drafting party was Van Diest. It was Van Diest that was trying to obtain a security interest in certain property of Hennings, in order to protect its advances to the latter. At least if this were a case against Hennings, the use of the *contra proferentem* rule would provide a way out of the ambiguity in the key contractual language: construing it against Van Diest, the security interest extends only to the products Van Diest sold to Hennings, not to "all inventory." It is not such a case, however, and so we turn to the final consideration that persuades us that the Bank must prevail.

D. Third-Party Interests

The most compelling reason to construe the language of this agreement against Van Diest is the fact that it was Van Diest that drafted the security agreement, and that the language of that agreement plays an important part for third-party creditors. Those creditors have no way of knowing what transpired between the parties; there is no parol evidence to which they may turn; and they have no way to resolve ambiguities internal to a contract. Here, we are not facing a garden-variety breach of contract action between the two contracting parties, both of whom were present during the negotiations. Instead, this case involves the effect of a contract between two parties (Hennings and Van Diest) on a third party (the Bank). The Bank, as we have already mentioned, is a stranger to the agreement, albeit one whose rights are affected by it. As the Bank could not have invested resources ex ante to avoid problems arising from ambiguous language, while Van Diest could have, it should be Van Diest who pays the price ex post.

A security agreement is a special kind of contract for which an important audience is third parties who need to know how much collateral has become encumbered. A potential creditor's decision whether to provide credit to Hennings (or anyone else), is contingent on the creditor's understanding of the extent of pre-existing security interests. An unclear statement of that extent should be avoided at all costs: if the creditor reads it reasonably, but too narrowly, when extending credit, it will be out of luck when the debtor defaults. If the potential creditor on the other hand takes a more conservative position and, fearful of the ambiguity, decides not to extend credit, the party seeking that credit is penalized in its access to capital by the shoddy work of its prior creditor—another result to be avoided.

By perfecting its security interest, Van Diest purported to give prospective creditors of Hennings notice of Van Diest's existing interest in Hennings's goods. A prospective creditor should have been able to look at Van Diest's filing and determine on that basis whether to extend credit to Hennings. Here, the Bank presumably did so, especially when it received Van Diest's letter in July 1993 telling it that the Van Diest security interest covered only goods bought from Van Diest. Whether this statement alone would have justified reliance on the Bank's part is debatable; but coupled with the language in the perfected Security Agreement that was susceptible to this interpretation, reliance was certainly reasonable.

The Supreme Court has also noted the special position that third parties occupy, given their limited ways of learning about the existence or the precise extent of a security interest. In United States v. McDermott, 507 U.S. 447 (1993), the Court expressed concern over the possibility that an after-acquired security interest clause might prevent the Government from asserting its interests. Like the Bank, the Government could not have protected itself by contracting with the parties or by analyzing the terms of the clause. The underlying rationale for the decision is equally applicable here: for the notice requirement to be a valid instrument of protection for potential creditors, that notice must be clearly expressed, and it must be such as is needed to inform the behavior of the potential creditor. "When two private lenders both exact from the same debtor security agreements with after-acquired-property clauses, the second lender knows, by reason of the earlier recording, that that category of property will be subject to another claim, and if the remaining security is inadequate he may avoid the difficulty by declining to extend credit." Id. at 454. When the earlier recording is ambiguous, the "second lender" does not know what collateral will be at its disposal.

In a broad sense, the problem of later creditors is similar to the problem of any third-party beneficiary. * * * [S]ecurity agreements should be construed if at all possible without resort to external evidence, and they should be construed in a way that recognizes the important role they play for third-party creditors. Doing so here leads to the same result we have already reached: Van Diest's security interest extends only to the inventory it furnished. The limiting clause modifies the term "all inventory," and it is not surplusage.

III

For these reasons, we REVERSE the judgment of the district court and REMAND the case to the bankruptcy court for the entry of judgment in favor of the Bank.

COMMENTS AND QUESTIONS

1. After you read a case like *Shelby County State Bank*, your immediate reaction should be to put pen to paper (or, more likely, fingers to key-

board). Given how the court read the key language in the security agreement, how would you re-write it to eliminate any possible ambiguity? In doing that, you must be careful to avoid just fighting the last war: in eliminating one possible ambiguity, what others do you risk introducing?

2. Go back and look carefully and the definitions of "inventory" (set out in 9-102(a)(48)) and "farm products (in 9-102(a)(34)). Is the fertilizer in *Shelby County* inventory or farm products? What determines that?

3. In James Talcott, Inc. v. Franklin National Bank, 194 N.W.2d 775, 782 (1972), the court stated that:

> The principal function of a description of the collateral in a security agreement is to enable the parties themselves or their successors in interest to identify it, particularly if the secured party has to repossess the collateral or reclaim it in a legal proceeding. If the debtor himself is willing to give a creditor a security interest in everything he owns, the code does not prevent it, whether his action is prudent or not. Upon default, the creditor takes everything to which the debtor previously agreed; hence, identification is no problem.

> The description of the collateral in the extension agreement did what it was meant to do—namely, it included all of the goods then owned, or to be owned in the future, by the debtor. The term "goods" was defined to be those goods as comprehended within the meaning of Article 9 of the code. The definition selected is embodied in the statute, a definition that is used and applied frequently. The parties sought to create a security interest in substantially all of the debtor's property. This is what was stated and that is what was meant. The parties did not particularize any further, and the statute does not require it.

> It would appear that the policy of Art. 9 is to uphold security agreements according to their terms. [9-201] states in part:

> "Except as otherwise provided by this chapter a security agreement is effective according to its terms between the parties, against purchasers of the collateral and against creditors."

> A security agreement should not be held unenforceable unless it is so ambiguous that its meaning cannot reasonably be construed from the language of the agreement itself.

4. For additional discussion of these issues, see David L. Kuosman, Sufficiency of the Description of Collateral in a U.C.C. Section 9-203 Security Agreement: A Critique of White & Summers' Approach, 65 U. Colorado L. Rev. 151 (1993).

5. Again, note the approach taken to supergenerics in 9-108(c).

SECTION IV. RIGHTS IN THE COLLATERAL

The concept that a security interest cannot attach until the debtor has rights in the collateral generates few problems in the context of a typical secured transaction. Nonetheless, it is important to understand some basic fact patterns:

2-9: RIGHTS IN THE COLLATERAL I
- Debtor approaches Bank for a loan. Debtor owns a printing press and offers to post it as collateral. A security agreement is executed stating that "Debtor hereby grants to Bank a security interest in Debtor's printing press to secure all debts of Debtor to Bank."
- ¤ What are Bank's rights?

2-10: RIGHTS IN THE COLLATERAL II
- Debtor approaches Bank for a loan. Debtor offers to post Da Vinci's "Mona Lisa" as collateral. A security agreement is executed stating that "Debtor hereby grants to Bank a security interest in the Mona Lisa to secure all debts of Debtor to Bank."
- ¤ What are Bank's rights?

2-11: CATEGORIZING THE COLLATERAL
- Debtor is a small business and has the usual range of office equipment. It owns its computers but it leases its copiers.
- On January 1st, Bank lends $10,000 to Debtor, takes a security interest in "equipment as defined in the UCC" and files an appropriate financing statement which lists the collateral as "equipment."
- ¤ What are Bank's rights in the computers? The copiers? See 9-102(a)(33), 9-102(a)(11).

2-12: THE LIMITS OF THE SECURED CREDITOR'S RIGHTS
- Debtor again owns computers and leases copiers.

- On January 1st, Bank lends $10,000 to Debtor, takes a security interest in "the debtor's leases in copiers" and files an appropriate financing statement.
- ¤ Does Debtor have sufficient "rights in the collateral" to use the copiers as security in a transaction with Bank? See, e.g., In re Holiday Airlines Corp., 647 F.2d 977 (9th Cir. 1981). If so, what does Bank effectively get as collateral? The leases? The copiers?

It is worth noting that Old Article 9 referred only to "rights in the collateral," F9-203(1)(c), while Revised Article 9 looks to whether "the debtor has rights in the collateral or the power to transfer rights in the collateral to a third party." 9-203(b)(2). As Official Comment 6 emphasizes, this clearly broadens the circumstances under which an effective security interest can be created.

In analyzing situations in which this issue arises, it may be helpful to break the inquiry into three separate parts. First, does the debtor have sufficient rights in the collateral to permit a security interest of a creditor to attach at all? This usually will be a simple inquiry. Yet we need not head for the secured transactions hills to find cases in which there will be much doubt over the debtor's interest in the collateral. For example, until a buyer acquires a "special property interest" under 2-501, it is difficult to see how the buyer could have any rights in the goods being sold and, hence, how the buyer could have "rights in the collateral" for purposes of the attaching or perfecting of a security interest of a creditor of the buyer. But once the buyer acquires a special property interest, 2-502 suggests that the buyer has *some,* albeit limited, rights in the goods. Are those sufficient for the debtor to have "rights in the collateral" within the meaning of 9-203(b)(2)? In determining when the security interest of a creditor of the buyer attaches or is perfected, should we look to the buyer's acquisition of a special property interest in goods, the buyer's acquisition of title to the goods, the buyer's obtaining possession of the goods, some combination of the above, or something else? Should we care, in other words, for purposes of determining the issue of "rights in the collateral," that the buyer's rights in the goods may increase over time?

Second, once we have surmounted the first inquiry—does the debtor have sufficient rights in the collateral for the security interest to attach—we can turn to a second question: what is the nature of the debtor's interest in the property? Article 9 sets forth an elaborate framework for classifying personal property. Parties often will embrace that scheme in their transactions. As a consequence, it is important to classify the debtor's interest appropriately, both under the relevant documents and under the Article 9 categories.

Third, we must focus on precisely what rights the secured creditor gets. This inquiry really involves an application of the derivation principle, that is, when would a creditor asserting a security interest in collateral be able to defeat a person, other than the debtor, who claims "ownership" of the collateral? This, in essence, is asking not so much whether the debtor has *any* rights in the collateral, but rather *when* the debtor can pass on to a secured party greater rights than the debtor itself has. The added language in 9-203(b)(2) clearly contemplates circumstances in which the debtor will be able to transfer more than it has. A debtor who leases a copier surely can grant a security interest in that lease. But, are Bank's rights limited to whatever rights Debtor had under the lease, or are there circumstances in which Bank's rights are greater than those held by Debtor? That is to say, might the secured creditor enjoy a right to the collateral that no longer is derivative of the debtor's rights: even though the debtor would lose to the "owner" in a two-party dispute, the debtor has been able to pass on to the secured party a right that the debtor itself does not enjoy—a right to take precedence over the asserted "owner" of the goods.

The rights-in-the-collateral question frequently arises in the small, closely-held business. In these situations, the lines between the personal and the corporate may be especially thin. Moreover, even if formalities are strictly observed, the corporate shareholder may be perfectly willing to create an exception to the broad protection offered by corporate limited liability. An important creditor may refuse to do business with the corporation, absent additional protection from the shareholder. This protection can take many forms. The shareholder can offer a guarantee, meaning that the corporate debt also becomes a personal debt of the shareholder. This guarantee could be unsecured, meaning that, absent voluntary payment, the creditor would have to sue in state court for seizure of the shareholder's personal assets. Alternatively, the corporate creditor may even insist that the personal obligation of the shareholder be secured by the shareholder's personal assets.

The fact pattern that follows offers another variation on this situation.

2-13: THIRD PARTIES AND COLLATERAL

- Corp approaches Bank for a loan. Bank concludes that Corp has too little property to collateralize the requested loan. Owner, the sole shareholder of Corp, offers to post a painting she owns personally as collateral for the loan to Corp.

  ¤ Does Article 9 permit this? How should this transaction be structured? See 9-102(a)(28).

Peoples Bank v. Bryan Bros. Cattle Co.

United States Court of Appeals, Fifth Circuit, 2007.
504 F.3d 549.

■ REAVLEY, CIRCUIT JUDGE

This case is to determine ownership of cattle and whether two contesting banks held a security interest in them. The district court granted summary judgment for the buyer of the cattle on the ground that the apparent seller was the owner and passed title to the buyer free of a lien. We hold that a fact issue exists on the ownership of the apparent seller, and we reverse the judgment.

Bryan Brothers Cattle Company and B&S Cattle Company ("Bryan") paid Glenbrook Cattle Company ("Glenbrook") for the cattle, but two banks—Peoples Bank and Cornerstone Bank—claim that Brooks L. "Louie" Dickerson was the owner and had previously granted them liens on the cattle. Each bank claims priority to the other. No other parties are before us now, and the decision depends, first, on whether Bryan has to pay one of these banks or did Bryan buy the cattle free of liens as the district court held, and second, if Bryan has to pay again, to which bank. We hold that Cornerstone has the superior lien on Dickerson's cattle and that the ownership of Glenbrook presents an issue precluding summary judgment.

I. Background

On October 5, 1999, Dickerson granted a security interest in the cattle he owned to Cornerstone in exchange for a loan. Cornerstone filed a financing statement with the Mississippi Secretary of State on October 14, 1999 and named "Louie Dickerson" as the debtor.

In 2001, Dickerson, Ellen Hardy, Bill Weeks and John David Weeks discussed forming an enterprise involving cattle, with Dickerson apparently as the catalyst for the idea. Between that time and February 2002, the parties began formulating the plan. Hardy and the Weeks brothers contributed cash (for example, Hardy put in $230,000), and it appears that Dickerson devised the business plan and began putting the operational and financial side of the business into place. The enterprise was to be called Glenbrook Cattle Company. There is a dispute about the intended role of the parties in the enterprise for example, whether Dickerson was to be the sole owner or if each of the parties had an ownership stake. This is at the heart of the present legal dispute, and the relationship among the parties is detailed below.

On February 13, 2002, Dickerson established a bank account at BancorpSouth Bank in Senatobia, Mississippi in the name of "Louie Dickerson, dba Glenbrook Cattle Company." The account was listed as existing for a sole proprietorship, and the taxpayer ID for the account was Dickerson's social security number. This is the only bank account that Glenbrook held or maintained in any capacity, although Dickerson had a number of other bank accounts at BancorpSouth and other banks (with those accounts listed under his personal name, as well as under the names of his other businesses).

On November 8, 2002, a Certificate of Formation for a Limited Liability Company ("LLC") was filed in the Office of the Mississippi Secretary of State under the name Glenbrook Cattle Company, with Dickerson as the registered agent. It appears that no official action was taken with regard to the LLC subsequent to the certificate filing.

At about the same time, in November 2002, Dickerson borrowed money from Peoples in exchange for a security interest in the cattle he owned or later acquired. Peoples filed one financing statement in November 2002 and two others in September 2003. The financing statements listed "Brooks L. Dickerson," Dickerson's legal name, as the debtor.

Starting in early 2002, Glenbrook began to operate as a cattle pre-conditioning business in Tate County, Mississippi. Dickerson handled the financial side of the business including the billing and receivables, apparently with little input from the other principals. Glenbrook hired Clayton Zweirschke as the farm manager, responsible for the day-to-day running of the pre-conditioning program.

Bryan has maintained a cattle operation in Happy, Texas for many years. Typically, Bryan takes physical possession of cattle in Texas following completion of a pre-conditioning period. Bryan first bought cattle pre-conditioned by Glenbrook in July 2002. Dennis Bryan, one of the principals in the company, and Zweirschke developed a business relationship, which resulted in Bryan's regularly buying cattle from Glenbrook. At that time, Glenbrook bought cattle from sale barns, pre-conditioned the cattle and then, at the end of the pre-conditioning period, placed the cattle on the market to sell to the highest bidder, which sometimes was Bryan.

Beginning in 2003, Glenbrook changed its cattle operations, which altered the arrangement with Bryan. Under the new arrangement, Bryan placed orders for certain cattle at the beginning of each week. Zweirschke forwarded these orders to commission buyers at the sale barns. During the week, these buyers purchased the cattle, forwarding the invoices to Glenbrook. Each day, the sale barns shipped the cattle to Glenbrook, where the cattle received a Bryan brand and a color-coded ear tag. Glenbrook then notified Bryan of the various purchases and sent Bryan a copy of the invoices and a bill of sale. After Bryan wired funds to Glenbrook during each week, Glenbrook mailed a check to the sale barn. At the end of the pre-conditioning period, Glenbrook shipped the cattle to Bryan in Texas, charging $.70 per pound of weight gained during the pre-conditioning period.

In May 2004, approximately 1,600 head of cattle, intended for Bryan, were in various stages of Glenbrook's pre-conditioning program. On May 19, 2004, Zweirschke contacted Bryan and told it to immediately arrange shipment of the cattle currently in Glenbrook's pre-conditioning program, because Glenbrook was out of money to purchase feed and vaccines.

As Bryan and Zweirschke were in the process of shipping the cattle, a local justice court issued a restraining order prohibiting the further shipment of the cattle. Bryan deposited money with the court, took possession of the majority of the remaining cattle, and removed the case to federal court. The federal district court clerk is now holding $342,500.00 on deposit. The court ultimately granted Bryan's motion for summary judgment, holding that Bryan purchased the cattle free and clear of liens. The court determined that the financing statements Peoples and Cornerstone filed were perhaps effective as to Dickerson individually, but that their security agreements were not perfected as to Glenbrook, which bought and sold the cattle at issue. The court also denied Peoples' claim that its security agreement was superior to Cornerstone's.

II. Discussion

Peoples and Cornerstone appeal the district court's summary judgment that Bryan purchased the cattle from Glenbrook free and clear of their security interests. Peoples also appeals the court's denial of its motion regarding the superiority of its security interest to Cornerstone's.

We hold that there is a fact issue precluding summary judgment for Bryan. We agree with the rejection of Peoples' claim of security interest superiority. * * *

B. Did Bryan Brothers Purchase the Cattle "Free and Clear"?

Peoples and Cornerstone argue that because liens were properly perfected on Dickerson and his property, the property sold by Glenbrook, which operated as Dickerson's sole proprietorship, was sold subject to their security interests. Bryan counters that the cattle were not subject to Peoples' or Cornerstone's liens on Dickerson's property because Bryan purchased the cattle from Glenbrook, which operated as either a partnership or a LLC (i.e., an entity separate from Dickerson's individual holdings), and thus Dickerson could not encumber Glenbrook's property. We hold that there is a fact issue as to whether Glenbrook operated as a sole proprietorship, partnership, or LLC. Thus, summary judgment as to this issue is improper.

1. The Security Interests Attach Only if Glenbrook Was a Sole Proprietorship of Dickerson

Under the Food Security Act ("FSA"), "a buyer who in the ordinary course of business buys a farm product from a seller engaged in farming operations shall take free of a security interest created by the seller, even though the security interest is perfected ... and the buyer knows of the existence of such interest." 7 USC 1631(d). The parties do not dispute that the purchase of cattle here is covered by the FSA. But under the FSA a buyer of farm products takes subject to a security interest created by the seller in particular circumstances, including when "in the case of a farm product produced in a State that has established a central filing system ... [1] the buyer has failed to register with the Secretary of State of such State prior to the purchase of farm products ... and [2] the secured party has filed an effective statement or notice that covers the farm products being sold ...." Id. 1631(e)(2). Mississippi has a central filing system but Bryan failed to register with the Mississippi Secretary of State prior to the purchase of the cattle. Therefore, the question is whether Peoples and Cornerstone filed statements that were effective and covered the cattle sold to Bryan.

If Glenbrook operated as a partnership or LLC, Peoples and Cornerstone's statements do not cover the cattle sold to Bryan because the banks did not have a valid security interest in Glenbrook's property. In Mississippi, a security interest is enforceable against the debtor and third parties with respect to collateral when, among other things, "the debtor has rights in the collateral." 9-203(b).

If Glenbrook operated as a partnership or LLC, Dickerson did not have sufficient "rights in the cattle" to encumber them. Mississippi recognizes a partnership as a separate entity that may sue or be sued in the partnership's name. Miss. Code Ann. 13-3-55. Partnership property includes all property brought into the partnership when formed or subsequently acquired by purchase on account of the partnership. Id. 79-12-15(1). Consequently, if Glenbrook existed as a partnership, the partnership owned the cattle and this partnership property is distinct from Dickerson's personal property. Id. 79-12-15(2) ("Unless the contrary intention appears, property acquired with partnership funds is partnership property.") A partner's right in specific partnership property is not assignable (except in connection with the assignment of rights of all partners), and it is not subject to attachment or execution, except on a claim against the partnership. Id. 79-12-49(2)(b), (c). Consistent with these principles, in a personal loan agreement Dickerson could not, without the consent of any of the other Glenbrook principals, encumber property Glenbrook owned. Dickerson could not encumber property that was not his own. See In re Whatley, 874 F.2d 997, 1004 (5th Cir. 1989) (stating the standard rule that "one cannot generally encumber another's property").

If Glenbrook operated as a LLC, the Peoples and Cornerstone security interests do not attach to the cattle. In Mississippi, a "member [of a LLC] has *no interest* in specific limited liability company property." Miss. Code Ann. 79-29-701 (emphasis added). The entity has independent power to, among other things, purchase and own personal property, sell or pledge personal property, and secure its obligations with a pledge of its personal property. Id. 79-29-108(2). It follows that an individual owner (Dickerson) of a LLC owned by multiple parties, cannot encumber specific LLC property in a personal loan agreement with a creditor. Thus, if Glenbrook existed as a LLC owned by the four parties, Bryan takes the cattle free and clear of the Peoples and Cornerstone loans.

Peoples argues that Dickerson could encumber the cattle Glenbrook sold, pointing to cases decided under Mississippi law where a security interest was held to attach to collateral because the debtor had sufficient "rights in collateral." However, these cases do not lead to the conclusion that Dickerson could encumber Glenbrook's property if Glenbrook existed as a partnership or LLC owned by multiple parties.

Peoples points to *In re Whatley*. In *Whatley*, this court held under Mississippi law that a corporation, owned by a husband and wife, had sufficient rights in collateral (farming equipment) to grant a security interest in the farming equipment to a lender, even though the husband, not the corporation, technically owned the farming equipment. The court reasoned that, while one generally cannot encumber another's property, the well-recognized exception of "consent by the property owner" allowed the security agreement the husband signed to be valid on behalf of the corporation. Here, the consent theory does not apply because, if Glenbrook was owned by three other parties, Dickerson could not, without the consent of these parties, encumber the cattle owned by the entity in which each had an ownership stake.

If Glenbrook existed as Dickerson's sole proprietorship, the security interest attaches to the cattle Bryan purchased. Bryan does not contest that an individual has sufficient "rights in collateral" under Mississippi law to grant a security interest in collateral his sole proprietorship owns. However, Bryan points out correctly that, under the FSA provision at issue here, a buyer of farm products who has failed to register with a state's central filing system takes subject to a security interest the seller creates only if the secured party has filed an *"effective financing statement"* covering the farm products being sold. 7 USC § 1631(e)(2). Bryan argues that the financing statements that listed Dickerson (not Glenbrook) as the debtor were not effective as to the cattle that Bryan bought from Glenbrook.

Under the FSA, an effective financing statement must contain, *inter alia*, the name of the person indebted to the secured party. Id. 1631(c)(4)(C)(ii). The FSA and its implementing regulations do not indicate whether a financing statement that lists an individual's name is effective against entities that purchase farm products from the individual's sole proprietorship doing business under a trade name. In the absence of further provision in the FSA or case law, we will look to Mississippi law that also requires a financing statement to provide the name of the debtor. 9-502(a)(1).

Peoples and Cornerstone properly obeyed the Mississippi Code by listing the debtor under Dickerson's individual name, rendering their financing statements effective if Glenbrook was Dickerson's sole proprietorship. "A financing statement that provides only the debtor's trade name does not sufficiently provide the name of the debtor." 9-503(c). However, the Mississippi Code states that a financing statement that provides the name of the debtor is not rendered ineffective by the absence of the debtor's trade name. 9-503(b)(1). The Official Comment to 9-503 states that "the actual individual or organizational name of the debtor on a financing statement is both necessary and sufficient, whether or not the financing statement provides trade or other names of the debtor ...." 9-503 cmt. 2. The banks' financing statements were not rendered ineffective by the absence of Dickerson's trade name *if* Glenbrook operated as Dickerson's sole proprietorship.

2. Was Glenbrook a Sole Proprietorship, Partnership, or LLC?

The district court erred in granting summary judgment to Bryan because a genuine issue of material fact exists as to Glenbrook's business form. Peoples presents sufficient evidence that Glenbrook existed as a sole proprietorship to overcome Bryan's summary judgment motion. The record shows that Dickerson opened the BancorpSouth bank account to which Bryan wired the funds for the cattle transaction at issue in the name of "Louie Dickerson, dba Glenbrook Cattle Company." Second, this bank account—Glenbrook's only one—was held as a sole proprietorship. Third, the taxpayer identification number for Glenbrook's account is Dickerson's social security number. Fourth, the bills of sale for the transaction with Bryan were signed by "Louie Dickerson/Glenbrook Cattle Company." Taken together, these facts raise a material issue as to whether Dickerson operated Glenbrook as a sole proprietorship, precluding summary judgment for Bryan.

There is substantial evidence that Glenbrook was a partnership, however. For example, a partnership appears to have been the intent of the initial principals-Dickerson, Hardy, and the Weeks brothers. While this evidence is sufficient to defeat Peoples' summary judgment motion, Bryan cannot establish as a matter of law that Glenbrook existed as a partnership. * * * Ultimately, while there are indications that Glenbrook existed as a partnership, this is not established as a matter of law. Taken as a whole, the evidence shows a material fact issue on the matter of partnership.

The district court rested its summary judgment for Bryan on the conclusion that Glenbrook existed as a LLC as a matter of law. But virtually all we have on this matter is the Certificate of Formation for a LLC filed on November 8, 2002 in the Office of the Mississippi Secretary of State under the name Glenbrook Cattle Company, with Dickerson as the regis-

tered agent. Without more, the LLC story is not developed enough to establish the operation of Glenbrook as a LLC at the relevant times in this
case. * * *

COMMENTS AND QUESTIONS

1. What do you make of the new language in 9-203(b)(2)—"the power to
    transfer rights in the collateral?" Where will that language apply?
2. For additional discussion of the rights in the collateral issue, see Mar-
    git Livingston, Certainty, Efficiency and Realism: Rights in Collateral
    under Article 9 of the Uniform Commercial Code, 73 N.C.L. Rev.
    115 (1994); Joseph W. Turner, Rights in Collateral under UCC
    § 9-203, 54 Mo. L. Rev. 677 (1989); and Ralph C. Anzivino, When
    Does a Debtor Have Rights in the Collateral Under Article 9 of the
    Uniform Commercial Code?, 61 Marq. L. Rev. 23 (1977).

Bank of America, N.A. v. Moglia

United States Court of Appeals, Seventh Circuit, 2003.
330 F.3d 942.

■ POSNER, CIRCUIT JUDGE

Outboard Marine Corporation is in Chapter 7 bankruptcy, and among its
holdings are the assets, currently worth some $14 million, in what is
known as a "rabbi trust." Bank of America, as the agent of Outboard's secured creditors, claims a security interest in these assets, while the trustee
in bankruptcy claims them for the unsecured creditors. The security
agreement on which Bank of America relies covers all Outboard's "general
intangibles," a term of great breadth in commercial law, see 9-102(a)(42)
and official comment 5(d), and broadly defined in the agreement as well to
include, besides a number of irrelevant enumerated items, "all other intangible personal property of every kind and nature." The term describes
the assets of the rabbi trust, but the bankruptcy court, seconded by the district court, held that they nevertheless were not subject to the security
agreement, and so ruled for the trustee. * * *

A rabbi trust, so called because its tax treatment was first addressed in an IRS letter ruling on a trust for the benefit of a rabbi, Private Letter Ruling 8113107 (Dec. 31, 1980), is a trust created by a corporation or other institution for the benefit of one or more of its executives (the rabbi, in the IRS's original ruling). The main reason (recited at the outset of the trust document in this case) for such a trust is that, should the control of the institution change, the new management might reduce the old executives' compensation, or even fire them; the trust, which consistent with this purpose is not funded until the change of control occurs, cushions the fall.

But as the IRS explained in the letter ruling, unless an executive's right to receive money from the trust is "subject to substantial limitations or restrictions," rather than being his to draw on at any time (making it income to him in a practical sense), the executive must include any contribution to the trust and any interest or other earnings of the trust in his gross income in the year in which the contribution was made or the interest obtained. The "substantial limitations or restrictions" condition was satisfied in the transaction on which the IRS ruled. The trust agreement provided that the rabbi would not receive the trust assets until he retired or otherwise ended his employment by the congregation. Until then the corpus of the trust and any interest on it would be owned by the congregation, so the rabbi would have neither legal nor equitable right to the money. And, what is key in this case, the trust instrument provided that "the assets of the trust estate shall be subject to the claims of [the congregation's] creditors as if the assets were the general assets of [the congregation]."

The word "creditors" is not defined either in the IRS's letter ruling or in the trust agreement in this case; but a "Model Rabbi Trust" agreement approved by the IRS states that the assets of the trust are subject to the claims of the settlor's "general creditors," Rev. Proc. 92-64, 1992-2 C.B. 422 (July 28, 1992), a term invariably used to refer to a debtor's *unsecured* creditors. The cases assume rather than hold that "general creditor" means "unsecured creditor," but what else could it mean? What work does "general" do unless to distinguish unsecured from secured creditors? Bank of America has no answer to that question.

Outboard is conceded to have established a bona fide rabbi trust, so that its contributions to the trust and the income that those contributions generated were not includible in the executives' gross income. Therefore, if the validity of a rabbi trust depends on its assets' being reserved for the employer's unsecured creditors, we can stop right here and affirm; the

Bank of America, as a secured creditor, would have no right to the assets—otherwise the trust's beneficiaries would not have received the favorable tax treatment accorded the beneficiaries of a rabbi trust, and they did receive it. But it is uncertain whether such a reservation actually is essential to the favorable tax treatment of a rabbi trust. All that the tax law requires is that there be substantial limitations on the beneficiaries' access to the trust assets, and a reservation of the assets in the event of bankruptcy to both the secured and the unsecured creditors of the settlor, rather than to the unsecured creditors, might well be thought substantial. For the reservation would keep those assets, most of them at any rate, out of the beneficiaries' hands—though this is provided that the limitation were coupled with a limitation on the beneficiaries' having free access to the assets of the trust before they leave their employment with the grantor. Without such a limitation, the reservation of creditors' rights would be illusory—the beneficiaries would pull the money out of the trust as soon as insolvency loomed on the horizon—and indeed the trust's assets might well be taxable as income to the beneficiaries. But we recall that, consistent with this concern, the assets of the rabbi trust were owned by the congregation until the rabbi's employment ended.

We say that a limitation to all, rather than just to the unsecured, creditors "might be" rather than "would be" substantial enough to satisfy the Internal Revenue Service because executives often are creditors of their firm; if they were secured creditors and their security interest embraced the assets of the trust, their claims to those assets would be superior to those of the firm's unsecured creditors, which would tend to make the limitation that is fundamental to the favorable tax treatment of the rabbi trust—that the creditors have a superior claim to the beneficiaries—illusory. But the trust instrument in this case took care of that concern by providing that Outboard's executives could not obtain a security interest in the trust's assets.

Even if the executives would not have sacrificed their favorable tax treatment had the trust instrument reserved the assets of the trust for all the company's creditors, secured and unsecured alike, in the event of bankruptcy, the instrument did not do this; it reserved those assets for the unsecured creditors. It states (we italicize the key terms) that the "Trust Corpus ... shall remain at all times subject to the claims of the *general creditors* of [Outboard]. Accordingly, [Outboard] shall not create a *security interest* in the Trust Corpus in favor of the Executives, the Participants [a term that apparently refers to retired executives] or *any creditor*." In the event of insolvency, the trustee "will deliver the entire amount of the Trust Corpus only as a court of competent jurisdiction, or duly appointed receiver or other person authorized to act by such court, may direct to make the Trust Corpus available to satisfy the claims of the Company's *general creditors.*"

This couldn't be clearer: secured creditors have no claim to the trust assets. And judges usually interpret written contracts (the instrument creating the rabbi trust in this case was an agreement nominally between Outboard and the trustee of the trust, Northern Trust Company, but realistically between Outboard and the executives who were the beneficiaries of the trust) according to the conventional meaning of their terms, that is, literally. This is especially appropriate in the case of a negotiated contract involving substantial stakes between commercially sophisticated parties, as in this case, who know how to say what they mean and have an incentive to draft their agreement carefully. Such a style of interpretation protects the parties against the vagaries of the litigation process—a major reason for committing contracts to writing—without too great a risk of misinterpretation.

But literal interpretation of written contracts, even when the parties are sophisticated and the stakes substantial, is merely presumptively the right approach to take. Even sophisticated lawyers and businessmen sometimes stumble in their use of language, or use language that is specialized to their trade and departs from normal usage, or fail to anticipate contingencies that may make the language of the contract yield absurd results if it is read literally, and if these circumstances are evident to the court the contract will not be interpreted literally. Bank of America argues in this vein that *of course* all that Outboard intended to do in the passages of the trust agreement that we quoted was to create a rabbi trust, that is, a grantor trust that would enjoy a favorable tax status, and so if a rabbi trust does not necessarily forfeit its favorable tax status by reserving the trust assets for secured as well as unsecured creditors, neither does the trust agreement. The security agreement, which we quoted at the beginning of this opinion, contains no language to suggest that the assets of the rabbi trust would be excluded from Bank of America's security interest just because they are pledged to any creditor and not just to unsecured creditors.

This argument is not negligible but neither is it sufficiently compelling to rebut the presumption in favor of literal interpretation to which we referred. Rather the contrary. The language of the Model Rabbi Trust would make it natural for Outboard to assume that to create a valid rabbi trust it would *have* to reserve the trust's assets for its general creditors, which undoubtedly it would understand to mean its unsecured creditors. The assumption may have been incorrect, more precisely may have been excessively cautious; but it provides the best guide to the meaning that Outboard and the executives ascribed to the agreement. The executives in particular would tend to favor the cautious approach rather than jeopardize their tax benefits for the sake of Outboard's secured creditors. And though they might benefit indirectly, and Outboard directly, from the company's being able to pledge more of its assets to secure a loan to the company, this benefit—since the assets in a rabbi trust are likely to be only a small fraction of the company's total assets—would probably be outweighed by the risk of forfeiting favorable tax treatment by departing from the template of the Model Rabbi Trust.

The trust agreement does not merely reserve the trust's assets for the general creditors, moreover; it forbids Outboard to create a security interest in favor not only of the executives (which might make the trust illusory and forfeit the beneficiaries' favorable tax treatment) but also of any creditor. So even if Outboard thought that the term "general creditors" includes secured creditors, the agreement explicitly forbids the creation of a security interest in the trust assets. The trust instrument took as it were the extra step to make clear that the parties *really* intended to reserve the trust assets for Outboard's unsecured creditors. The security agreement, as we said, does not exclude the assets in the rabbi trust; but to determine what assets it does include (because they are not listed in the agreement), one must look beyond the security agreement. And when one looks one finds the trust instrument, which excludes those assets. It is important to note in this connection that the rabbi trust was funded before the security agreement between Outboard and Bank of America was executed. Had it been funded after, Outboard's contribution of assets to the trust would have been subject to the security agreement regardless of the terms of the trust. For Outboard could not be permitted to impair the bank's security interest by putting some of the assets covered by the agreement into a trust that the bank could not reach.

Bank of America has a second string to its bow: it argues that Illinois law, which the parties agree governs the interpretation of the trust agreement, will enforce a contractual antiassignment provision, such as the provision in the trust instrument that forbids assigning a security interest in the assets of the rabbi trust to creditors, against an assignee only if the provision states that the assignor has no power, and not merely no right, to assign. So, the argument continues, because the trust instrument does not say in so many words that any attempt by Outboard to create a security interest in the trust assets would be void, ineffectual, etc., the creation of such an interest is not prohibited although a party (including any third-party beneficiaries, which Outboard's general creditors may or may not be—we needn't decide), could sue for damages in the event of a breach of the provision.

Clauses in conveyances, or in other instruments contractual or otherwise that create property rights, that forbid the recipient of the property to sell it free and clear—or in legal jargon that create a "restraint on alienation"—are traditionally disfavored. Gale v. York Center Community Co-op., Inc., 171 N.E.2d 30, 33 (1961). Sometimes they are disfavored because they are thought to create monopoly, concentrate wealth, or cater to "the capricious whims of the conveyor." Id. But more often and more realistically it is because they can increase transaction costs by preventing subsequent purchasers or assignees from knowing what they are getting. A legal requirement that the restraint be express, recorded, or otherwise readily ascertainable by potential purchasers and assignees minimizes, and often eliminates, those additional costs; if the recipient's purchaser knows exactly what he is (not) getting, a refusal to enforce the restriction merely confers a windfall on him.

The requirement of express and readily ascertainable notice is satisfied here. When Bank of America made its credit agreement with Outboard, it knew, if it bothered to read the trust agreement along with the other documents that defined Outboard's assets, as it should have done and no doubt did do, that the security interest it was acquiring would not cover the assets (currently some $14 million) in the rabbi trust. Nothing would have been added to the trust agreement but empty verbiage had it said "and not only is Outboard forbidden to create a security interest in these assets in favor of any creditor, but if it tries to do so its action shall be null, void, and of no effect." Of course, if Illinois required those magic words, as many states still do, to rebut the presumption of nonassignability, then Bank of America could argue persuasively that it had relied on their absence when it signed the security agreement. But Illinois does not require them * * *.

Illinois's approach implements the modern view, expressed in Restatement (Second) of Contracts § 322(2) (1981), that an antiassignment provision in a contract is unenforceable against an assignee "unless a different intention is manifested." Magic words are not required: "Where there is a promise not to assign but no provision that an assignment is ineffective, the question whether breach of the promise discharges the obligor's duty depends on all the circumstances." Id., comment c. The circumstances here weigh heavily in favor of enforcing the antiassignment provision when we consider the alternative remedy that is all that a "magic words" state would allow in the absence of the magic words—a suit for damages for breach of the provision. If the credit agreement between Outboard and Bank of America violated it by creating a security interest in the trust assets, then the contract breaker, and therefore the defendant in such a suit, would be Outboard, which is to say the trustee, while the plaintiffs would be the general creditors—the trustee also. Enough said. * * *

AFFIRMED.

COMMENTS AND QUESTIONS

Enough said? Some think not (ok, me). For more analysis of *Moglia*, see Randal C. Picker, Pulling a Rabbi Out of His Hat: The Bankruptcy Magic of Dick Posner, 74 U. Chi. L. Rev. 1845 (2007).

SECTION V. VALUE

Under 9-203(b)(1), a security interest is only enforceable if "value has been given." With the reworking of Article 1 of the UCC in 2001, "value" is now defined in its own separate section, 1-204. Its definition is broad enough so as to leave little room for dispute as to whether it exists. If an entity gives money to a debtor, it gives value. If an entity promises to give money to a debtor, it gives value. Value sufficient to support a security interest is given if that security interest is acquired for a pre-existing claim. Value is given if an entity agrees to act as an accommodation party or if it guarantees someone's debts—if, in other words, it *contingently* lends money. More generally, value is defined to include anything that would be sufficient consideration to support a simple contract—whether monetary in nature or not—as well as binding commitments to extend credit. See, e.g., In re Reliable Manufacturing Corp., 703 F.2d 996 (7th Cir. 1983) (transaction involved A Corp agreeing to buy stock in B Corp. from X and Y, B

Corp guaranteeing A Corp's obligation; B Corp's guarantee secured by B Corp's equipment; *held,* value requirement met because purpose is to require "an obligation which may properly be secured ... . A security interest given in consideration for the obligation of a third party clearly effectuates this purpose ... . It is enough, in fact, that there be detriment to the secured party even if there is no benefit to the owner of the assets subject to the security interest."). It is not, however, the same definition of "value" that is used in Article 3 for purposes of deciding whether someone has given value so as to be a "holder in due course," 3-302, 3-303, nor is it the same, necessarily, as the concept of "new value" or "debt" used in the Bankruptcy Code.

The value requirement has presented few problems and has generated little litigation, in part because there are few cases in which determining *if* value has been given is difficult. Because a security interest is defined in 1-201(b)(35) as an interest in property that secures payment or performance of an obligation, the value requirement is inherent in the concept of *enforcement;* unless there is a default in some obligation that gives rise to a right to realize on collateral, there is nothing to sue on.

To the extent that the "value" inquiry is likely to cause serious problems, it comes from the instances in which the *timing* of perfection becomes important. 9-308(a) states that a security interest is perfected "if it has attached and all of the applicable requirements for perfection ... have been satisfied." Although most priority disputes are resolved on a "first-to-file" rule, in which "attachment" is not relevant to the priority question, attachment will be relevant for priority purposes when perfection is accomplished by some means other than filing (e.g., possession). Parties may also postpone the moment of attachment by "explicit agreement," 9-203(a); see Allegaert v. Chemical Bank, 657 F.2d 495 (2d Cir. 1980). Determining *when* "value" has been given, then, does have some practical consequences and may pose some difficulties even though the answer to the question of *whether* value has been given is relatively easy.

2-14: TIMING OF VALUE
- On June 1st, Bank agrees to loan A Corp up to $1,000,000 to buy C Corp's accounts receivable, which A Corp is negotiating to buy from C Corp.
- Bank's loan will be secured by A Corp's inventory and equipment. It is a condition precedent to Bank's loan that A Corp and C Corp reach a written agreement respecting the sale of C Corp's recei-

vables. Even if A Corp and C Corp reach such an agreement, A Corp has no obligation to draw on Bank's loan.

- On July 1st, A Corp and C Corp sign their agreement and Bank, at A Corp's request, gives C Corp a check for $900,000, the purchase price.

¤ When is "value" given? 1-204.

SECTION VI. THE SECURITY AGREEMENT

You are now ready to read a real security agreement. As these things go, the contract set out below is a straightforward document, yet notwithstanding that, you will see many things that mean very little to you. Transaction lawyers routinely start with a document from a prior deal, and then "mark up" that document for a new deal. Only the first contract ever written in the history of humanity was actually written on a blank slate; every contract after the first has just been a mark-up.

This matters for a couple of reasons. First, contracts evolve over time, and provisions added at an earlier time may cease to be meaningful later but nonetheless stay in the contract as they do no positive harm. This makes contracts longer than they would otherwise be, but no individual attorney—especially a young law-firm associate—has any real incentive to delete these sections from the contract. Second, if you write a contract, you will start with a prior contract. You will undoubtedly be in a hurry to write the contract, but you must—really, must—stop and understand *every* term of the contract before you complete a draft. You can't learn anything otherwise, and you certainly cannot negotiate a document with opposing counsel without understanding what it means. The simple approach is to ask for each section of the contract: "Why is this here? What does it accomplish? In what situations that might arise will these be useful? Does it help the secured party, the debtor or both?"

Security Agreement

This Security Agreement ("Security Agreement") is made the 1st day of July, 2001, between Vending Machine Manufacturing Co., a Delaware Corporation ("Debtor") and Finco, an Illinois Corporation ("Secured Party").

This Security Agreement is entered into with respect to:

> (i)   a loan (the "Loan") to be made by Secured Party to Debtor pursuant to a Loan Agreement (the "Loan Agreement") dated the same date as this Security Agreement;
>
> (ii)   the sale by Debtor and the purchase by Secured Party of Accounts;
>
> (iii)   the sale by Debtor and the purchase by Secured Party of Chattel Paper;
>
> (iv)   the sale by Debtor and the purchase by Secured Party of Payment Intangibles; and
>
> (v)   the sale by Debtor and the purchase by Secured Party of Promissory Notes.

Secured Party and Debtor agree as follows:

1. Definitions.

1.1 *"Collateral."* The Collateral shall consist of all of the personal property of Debtor, wherever located, and now owned or hereafter acquired, including:

> (i)   Accounts;
>
> (ii)   Chattel Paper;
>
> (iii)   Inventory;
>
> (iv)   Equipment;
>
> (v)   Instruments[, including Promissory Notes];
>
> (vi)   Investment Property;
>
> (vii)   Documents;
>
> (viii)   Deposit accounts;
>
> (ix)   Debtor's claim for interference with contract against Big Soda Pop Company;
>
> (x)   Letter-of-credit rights;
>
> (xi)   General intangibles[, including payment intangibles];
>
> (xii)   [Supporting obligations];
>
> (xiii)   [to the extent not listed above as original collateral, proceeds and products of the foregoing].

1.2 *"Obligations."* This Security Agreement secures the following:

(i)   Debtor's obligations under the Loan, the Loan Agreement, and this Security Agreement;

(ii)   all of Debtor's other present and future obligations to Secured Party;

(iii)   the repayment of (a) any amounts that Secured Party may advance or spend for the maintenance or preservation of the Collateral and (b) any other expenditures that Secured Party may make under the provisions of this Security Agreement or for the benefit of Debtor;

(iv)   all amounts owed under any modifications, renewals or extensions of any of the foregoing obligations;

(v)   all other amounts now or in the future owed by Debtor to Secured Party; and

(vi)   any of the foregoing that arises after the filing of a petition by or against Debtor under the Bankruptcy Code, even if the obligations do not accrue because of the automatic stay under Bankruptcy Code § 362 or otherwise.

(vii)   This Security Agreement does not secure any obligation described above which is secured by a consensual lien on real property.

1.3 *UCC.* Any term used in the Uniform Commercial Code ("UCC") and not defined in this Security Agreement has the meaning given to the term in the UCC.

2. Grant of Security Interest.

Debtor grants a security interest in the Collateral to Secured Party to secure the payment or performance of the Obligations.

3. Perfection of Security Interests.

3.1 *Filing of financing statement.*

(i)   Debtor authorizes Secured Party to file a financing statement (the "Financing Statement") describing the Collateral.

(ii)   Debtor authorizes Secured Party to file a financing statement (the "Financing Statement") describing any agricultural liens or other statutory liens held by Secured Party.

(iii) Secured Party shall receive prior to the Closing an official report from the Secretary of State of each Collateral State, Chief Executive Office State, and the Debtor State (each as defined below) (the "SOS Reports") indicating that Secured Party's security interest is prior to all other security interests or other interests reflected in the report.

3.2 *Possession*.

(i) Debtor shall have possession of the Collateral, except where expressly otherwise provided in this Security Agreement or where Secured Party chooses to perfect its security interest by possession in addition to the filing of a financing statement.

(ii) Where Collateral is in the possession of a third party, Debtor will join with Secured Party in notifying the third party of Secured Party's security interest and obtaining an acknowledgment from the third party that it is holding the Collateral for the benefit of Secured Party.

3.3 *Control Agreements*. Debtor will cooperate with Secured Party in obtaining a control agreement in form and substance satisfactory to Secured Party with respect to Collateral consisting of:

(i) Deposit Accounts;

(ii) Investment Property;

(iii) Letter-of-credit rights; and

(iv) Electronic chattel paper.

3.4 *Marking of Chattel Paper*. Debtor will not create any Chattel Paper without placing a legend on the Chattel Paper acceptable to Secured Party indicating that Secured Party has a security interest in the Chattel Paper.

4. Post-Closing Covenants and Rights Concerning the Collateral.

4.1 *Inspection*. The parties to this Security Agreement may inspect any Collateral in the other party's possession, at any time upon reasonable notice.

4.2 *Personal Property*. The Collateral shall remain personal property at all times. Debtor shall not affix any of the Collateral to any real property in any manner which would change its nature from that of personal property to real property or to a fixture.

4.3 *Secured Party's Collection Rights.* Secured Party shall have the right at any time to enforce Debtor's rights against the account debtors and obligors.

4.4 *Limitations on Obligations Concerning Maintenance of Collateral.*

>   (i)   Risk of Loss. Debtor has the risk of loss of the Collateral.
>
>   (ii)   No Collection Obligation. Secured Party has no duty to collect any income accruing on the Collateral or to preserve any rights relating to the Collateral.

4.5 *No Disposition of Collateral.* Secured Party does not authorize, and Debtor agrees not to:

>   (i)   make any sales or leases of any of the Collateral;
>
>   (ii)   license any of the Collateral; or
>
>   (iii)   grant any other security interest in any of the Collateral.

4.6 *Purchase Money Security Interests.* To the extent Debtor uses the Loan to purchase Collateral, Debtor's repayment of the Loan shall apply on a "first-in-first-out" basis so that the portion of the Loan used to purchase a particular item of Collateral shall be paid in the chronological order the Debtor purchased the Collateral.

5. Debtor's Representations and Warranties.

Debtor warrants and represents that:

5.1 *Title to and Transfer of Collateral.* It has rights in or the power to transfer the Collateral and its title to the Collateral is free of all adverse claims, liens, security interests and restrictions on transfer or pledge except as created by this Security Agreement.

5.2 *Location of Collateral.* All collateral consisting of goods is located solely in the States (the "Collateral States") listed in Exhibit B.

5.3 *Location, State of Incorporation and Name of Debtor.*

>   (i)   Chief executive office is located in the State (the "Chief Executive Office State") identified in Exhibit B.
>
>   (ii)   State of incorporation is the State (the "Debtor State") identified in Exhibit B.

(iii)   Exact legal name is as set forth in the first paragraph of this Security Agreement.

6. Debtor's Covenants.

Until the Obligations are paid in full, Debtor agrees that it will:

(i)   preserve its corporate existence and not, in one transaction or a series of related transactions, merge into or consolidate with any other entity, or sell all or substantially all of its assets;

(ii)   not change the state of its incorporation; and

(iii)   not change its corporate name without providing Secured Party with 30 days' prior written notice.

7. Events of Default.

The occurrence of any of the following shall, at the option of Secured Party, be an Event of Default:

(i)   Any default, Event of Default (as defined) by Debtor under the Loan Agreement or any of the other Obligations;

(ii)   Debtor's failure to comply with any of the provisions of, or the incorrectness of any representation or warranty contained in, this Security Agreement, the Note, or in any of the other Obligations;

(iii)   Transfer or disposition of any of the Collateral, except as expressly permitted by this Security Agreement;

(iv)   Attachment, execution or levy on any of the Collateral;

(v)   Debtor voluntarily or involuntarily becoming subject to any proceeding under (a) the Bankruptcy Code or (b) any similar remedy under state statutory or common law;

(vi)   Debtor shall fail to comply with, or become subject to any administrative or judicial proceeding under any federal, state or local (a) hazardous waste or environmental law, (b) asset forfeiture or similar law which can result in the forfeiture of property, or (c) other law, where noncompliance may have any significant effect on the Collateral; or

(vii)   Secured Party shall receive at any time following the Closing an SOS Report indicating that Secured Party's security interest is not prior to all other security interests or other interests reflected in the report.

8. Default Costs.

Should an Event of Default occur, Debtor will pay to Secured Party all costs reasonably incurred by the Secured Party for the purpose of enforcing its rights hereunder, including:

(i)   costs of foreclosure;

(ii)   costs of obtaining money damages; and

(iii)   a reasonable fee for the services of attorneys employed by Secured Party for any purpose related to this Security Agreement or the Obligations, including consultation, drafting documents, sending notices or instituting, prosecuting or defending litigation or arbitration.

9. Remedies Upon Default.

9.1 *General.* Upon any Event of Default, Secured Party may pursue any remedy available at law (including those available under the provisions of the UCC), or in equity to collect, enforce or satisfy any Obligations then owing, whether by acceleration or otherwise.

9.2 *Concurrent Remedies.* Upon any Event of Default, Secured Party shall have the right to pursue any of the following remedies separately, successively or concurrently:

(i)   File suit and obtain judgment and, in conjunction with any action, Secured Party may seek any ancillary remedies provided by law, including levy of attachment and garnishment.

(ii)   Take possession of any Collateral if not already in its possession without demand and without legal process. Upon Secured Party's demand, Debtor will assemble and make the Collateral available to Secured Party as it directs. Debtor grants to Secured Party the right, for this purpose, to enter into or on any premises where Collateral may be located.

> (iii)   Without taking possession, sell, lease or otherwise dispose of the Collateral at public or private sale in accordance with the UCC.

10. Foreclosure Procedures.

10.1 *No Waiver.* No delay or omission by Secured Party to exercise any right or remedy accruing upon any Event of Default shall: (a) impair any right or remedy, (b) waive any default or operate as an acquiescence to the Event of Default, or (c) affect any subsequent default of the same or of a different nature.

10.2 *Notices.* Secured Party shall give Debtor such notice of any private or public sale as may be required by the UCC.

10.3 *Condition of Collateral.* Secured Party has no obligation to clean-up or otherwise prepare the Collateral for sale.

10.4 *No Obligation to Pursue Others.* Secured Party has no obligation to attempt to satisfy the Obligations by collecting them from any other person liable for them and Secured Party may release, modify or waive any collateral provided by any other person to secure any of the Obligations, all without affecting Secured Party's rights against Debtor. Debtor waives any right it may have to require Secured Party to pursue any third person for any of the Obligations.

10.5 *Compliance With Other Laws.* Secured Party may comply with any applicable state or federal law requirements in connection with a disposition of the Collateral and compliance will not be considered adversely to affect the commercial reasonableness of any sale of the Collateral.

10.6 *Warranties.* Secured Party may sell the Collateral without giving any warranties as to the Collateral. Secured Party may specifically disclaim any warranties of title or the like. This procedure will not be considered adversely to affect the commercial reasonableness of any sale of the Collateral.

10.7 *Sales on Credit.* If Secured Party sells any of the Collateral upon credit, Debtor will be credited only with payments actually made by the purchaser, received by Secured Party and applied to the indebtedness of the Purchaser. In the event the purchaser fails to pay for the Collateral, Secured Party may resell the Collateral and Debtor shall be credited with the proceeds of the sale.

10.8 *Purchases by Secured Party.* In the event Secured Party purchases any of the Collateral being sold, Secured Party may pay for the Collateral by crediting some or all of the Obligations of the Debtor.

10.9 *No Marshalling.* Secured Party has no obligation to marshal any assets in favor of Debtor, or against or in payment of:

(i)   the Note;

(ii)   any of the other Obligations; or

(iii)   any other obligation owed to Secured Party by Debtor or any other person.

11. Miscellaneous

11.1 *Assignment.*

(i)   *Binds Assignees.* This Security Agreement shall bind and shall inure to the benefit of the heirs, legatees, executors, administrators, successors and assigns of Secured Party and shall bind all persons who become bound as a debtor to this Security Agreement.

(ii)   *No Assignments by Debtor.* Secured Party does not consent to any assignment by Debtor except as expressly provided in this Security Agreement.

(iii)   *Secured Party Assignments.* Secured Party may assign its rights and interests under this Security Agreement. If an assignment is made, Debtor shall render performance under this Security Agreement to the assignee. Debtor waives and will not assert against any assignee any claims, defenses or set-offs which Debtor could assert against Secured Party except defenses which cannot be waived.

11.2 *Severability.* Should any provision of this Security Agreement be found to be void, invalid or unenforceable by a court or panel of arbitrators of competent jurisdiction, that finding shall only affect the provisions found to be void, invalid or unenforceable and shall not affect the remaining provisions of this Security Agreement.

11.3 *Notices.* Any notices required by this Security Agreement shall be deemed to be delivered when a record has been (a) deposited in any United States postal box if postage is prepaid, and the notice properly addressed to the intended recipient, (b) received by telecopy, (c) received through the Internet, and (d) when personally delivered.

11.4 *Headings.* Section headings used in this Security Agreement are for convenience only. They are not a part of this Security Agreement and shall not be used in construing it.

11.5 *Governing Law.* This Security Agreement is being executed and delivered and is intended to be performed in the State of Illinois and shall be construed and enforced in accordance with the laws of the State of Illinois, except to the extent that the UCC provides for the application of the law of the Debtor States.

11.6 *Rules of Construction.*

    (i)   No reference to "proceeds" in this Security Agreement authorizes any sale, transfer, or other disposition of the Collateral by the Debtor.

    (ii)   "Includes" and "including" are not limiting.

    (iii)   "Or" is not exclusive.

    (iv)   "All" includes "any" and "any" includes "all."

11.7 *Integration and Modifications.*

    (i)   This Security Agreement is the entire agreement of the Debtor and Secured Party concerning its subject matter.

    (ii)   Any modification to this Security Agreement must be made in writing and signed by the party adversely affected.

11.8 *Waiver.* Any party to this Security Agreement may waive the enforcement of any provision to the extent the provision is for its benefit.

11.9 *Further Assurances.* Debtor agrees to execute any further documents, and to take any further actions, reasonably requested by Secured Party to evidence or perfect the security interest granted herein or to effectuate the rights granted to Secured Party herein.

The parties have signed this Security Agreement as of the day and year first above written at Chicago, Illinois.

"DEBTOR"

Vending Machine Manufacturing Co.

a Delaware corporation

By: _____

Jane Drink-Soft

President

By: _____

Bob Soft-Drink

Secretary

CHAPTER THREE

PERFECTION

In this chapter, we discuss the mechanics of perfecting, and keeping perfected, security interests—the process that converts unperfected security interests into perfected ones. Before doing so, though, it is important to understand that just being perfected does not mean that the secured creditor wins when a dispute arises. Any number of secured creditors can hold perfected security interests in the same collateral at the same time. How much protection a creditor with a "perfected" security interest has is a question of priority, which we consider in the next chapter.

As to perfection itself, 9-308(a) provides:

> Except as otherwise provided in this section and Section 9-309, a security interest is perfected if it has attached and all of the applicable requirements for perfection in Sections 9-310 through 9-316 have been satisfied. A security interest is perfected when it attaches if the applicable requirements are satisfied before the security interest attaches.

As you will see when you look at 9-310 through 9-316, Article 9 has three basic approaches to perfection of a security interest: possession of the collateral, control over the collateral and filing of a financing statement. For some collateral types, more than one approach is acceptable, but for others, one way or the other is the exclusive means of perfecting. This legal pattern creates some risks for secured creditors. A secured creditor who takes possession of collateral may rudely learn later that filing was required.

We start with perfection through filing, see 9-310(a), and postpone until later in this chapter perfection by possession, perfection through control, and perfection by other means. The formal requisites of a financing statement are set out in 9-502, and are quite straightforward, in large part because Article 9 has a system of notice filing. 9-502(a) provides that:

> Subject to subsection (b), a financing statement is sufficient only if it: (1) provides the name of the debtor; (2) provides the name of the secured party or a representative of the secured party; and (3) indicates the collateral covered by the financing statement.

Each of these requirements raises issues; we will consider cases on each.

The financing statement exists for third parties. Indeed, whether a financing statement is filed does not affect the rights and obligations between the secured party and the debtor. The filing system also does not benefit general unsecured creditors before they obtain a property interest, either directly, as with a judicial lien, or indirectly, through the powers of the trustee in bankruptcy to assert the rights of a lien creditor. But having a filing system for the benefit of certain third parties and having one that in fact benefits them are not the same. A creditor may know about a security interest without any assistance from the filing system. And creditors may remain ignorant of a security interest, because they have not bothered to check the filing system at all.

In practice, however, the question of whether a filing is improper oftentimes does not turn on whether it actually affected anyone. If a secured creditor has not perfected its interest, it will lose to a lien creditor who obtains a lien on its collateral before the security interest is perfected. 9-317(a)(2). Because the rights of an unperfected secured creditor are typically set against the rights of a trustee in bankruptcy, who under BC 544(a) has the rights of a *hypothetical* lien creditor on the date of the filing for bankruptcy, the inquiry is necessarily abstract.

SECTION I. CATEGORIZING THE COLLATERAL

Consider the following fact pattern.

3-1: CATEGORIZING THE COLLATERAL

- Bank lends $10,000 to Corp, takes a security interest in a glomph and files a financing statement describing the collateral as a "glomph."
- ¤ Is Bank perfected?
- Bank lends $10,000 to Corp, takes a security interest in a glomph under an agreement with Debtor and takes possession of the glomph.

¤ Is Bank perfected?

• Bank lends $10,000 to Corp, takes a security interest in a glomph, takes possession of the glomph and files a financing statement describing the collateral as a "glomph."

¤ Is Bank perfected?

———————————————

Like many statutes that construct a framework for transactions, Article 9 sets out a series of definitions. Those are intended to be airtight, so that none of the property types embraced by Article 9 somehow slip through its grasp. That means, as the next case suggests, that we need to learn how to navigate the definitions.

Fordyce Bank & Trust Co. v. Bean Timberland, Inc.

Supreme Court of Arkansas, 2007.
251 S.W.3d 267.

■ TOM GLAZE, ASSOCIATE JUSTICE

This appeal requires our court to determine whether appellees Potlatch Corp. ("Potlatch") and Idaho Timber Corp. ("Idaho") are buyers in the ordinary course of business under the Uniform Commercial Code (UCC). See 9-320.

The appellant in this case, Fordyce Bank & Trust Co. ("Fordyce" or "the Bank"), issued several loans to appellee Bean Timberland ("Bean") so that Bean could purchase timber from various landowners. Bean gave the bank security interests in the purchased timber, and the proceeds from the sale of the timber were intended to repay the loans the Bank had made to Bean. The Bank, intending to perfect its security interests, filed its UCC Financing Statements with the Secretary of State's Office. However, when Bean sold the timber to the various lumber mills with which it did business, including Potlatch and Idaho, Bean failed to remit the sales proceeds to the Bank.

The Bank filed suit against Bean, Potlatch, and Idaho on February 19, 2004. * * * [T]he Bank contends in its third point on appeal that Potlatch and Idaho could not have been buyers in the ordinary course of business because the wood they purchased from Bean was not "inventory." The Bank urges that the trial court erroneously concluded that the cut timber was "the type of inventory" covered by the buyer-in-the-ordinary-course-of-business protection. The Bank states that the UCC provides such protection in this case only if the goods can be classified as inventory.

Under the UCC, "a security agreement is effective according to its terms between the parties, against purchases of the collateral, and against creditors." 9-201(a). In this case, the security agreement is between the Bank and Bean. That security agreement between the Bank and Bean, filed in the Secretary of State's office, was intended to secure the payment and performance of Bean's debts, liabilities, or obligations to the Bank, and it gave the Bank a security interest in cut timber.

The Bank concedes that the timber, once cut, becomes ordinary goods. *See* Comment to 9-501 ("Once cut, however ... [*t*]*he timber then becomes ordinary goods.*") (emphasis added). However, the Bank urges that the cut timber, which is "goods," is not "inventory." This distinction is important to the Bank because the Commentary to 9-320(a) states that the protection afforded to buyers in the ordinary course of business "applies primarily to inventory collateral." *See* Comment to 9-320.

All parties to this case agree that the cut timber is "goods." According to the Commentary to 9-102, there are "four mutually-exclusive 'types' of collateral that consist of goods: 'consumer goods,' 'equipment,' 'farm products,' and 'inventory.' " The Commentary continues as follows:

> The classes of goods are mutually exclusive. For example, the same property cannot simultaneously be both equipment and inventory.
>
> ....
>
> Goods are inventory if they are leased by a lessor or held by a person for sale or lease.... Goods to be furnished or furnished under a service contract, raw materials, and work in process also are inventory. Implicit in the definition is the criterion that the sales or leases are or will be in the ordinary course of business....

Comment to 9-102. If cut timber constitutes "goods," it must be inventory if it is not consumer goods, equipment, or farm products.

Consumer goods are goods "that are used or bought for use primarily for personal, family, or household purposes." 9-102(a)(23). Clearly, cut timber would not fall into this category. Equipment means "goods other than inventory, farm products, or consumer goods." 9-102(a)(33). The Commentary notes that, generally speaking, "goods used in a business are equipment if they are fixed assets or have, as identifiable units, a relatively long period of use." See 9-102. This obviously does not describe cut timber. Finally, farm products are defined in 9-102(a)(34), as follows:

> "Farm products" means goods, other than standing timber, with respect to which the debtor is engaged in a farming operation and which are:
>
> > (A) crops grown, growing, or to be grown, including:
> >
> > > (i) crops produced on trees, vines, and bushes; and
> > > (ii) aquatic goods produced in aquacultural operations;
> >
> > (B) livestock, born or unborn, including aquatic goods produced in aquacultural operations;
> > (C) supplies used or produced in a farming operation;
> > or
> > (D) products of crops or livestock in their unmanufactured states.

Again, cut timber does not fall within any of these descriptions. Because timber is "goods," but it is not consumer goods, equipment, or farm products, then logically it must be inventory. Inventory means "goods, other than farm products, which ... are held by a person for sale or lease or to be furnished under a contract of service; ... or ... consist of raw materials, work in process, or materials used or consumed in a business." 9-102(a)(48)(B) & (D). The cut timber at issue in this case was held by Bean for sale to Potlatch and Idaho; therefore, the timber certainly meets the definition of inventory.

The Bank nonetheless urges that cut timber is not inventory because, if it is not, then Potlatch and Idaho are not entitled to the protections afforded to buyers in the ordinary course of business. However, although the Bank cites several cases from other jurisdictions that describe inventory as usually consisting of merchandise, the Bank offers no authority to the effect that cut timber cannot constitute inventory. Accordingly, we hold that the trial court correctly concluded that the cut timber at issue in this case is "inventory," and Potlatch and Idaho are buyers in the ordinary course of business. * * *

COMMENTS AND QUESTIONS

Make sure to examine Article 9's definitional scheme carefully. The court in *Bean Timberland* is correct to note that Article 9 creates four mutually-exclusive sub-categories within "goods." Official comment 4.a. to 9-102 makes that clear and also emphasizes that there may be some difficult boundary cases. But *Bean Timberland* treats inventory as the residual—leftover—category. Is that right? Make sure to look at the definition of consumer goods in 9-102(a)(23); equipment in 9-102(a)(33); farm products in 9-102(a)(34); and inventory in 9-102(a)(48). Where do the leftover goods go?

Vienna Park Properties v. United Postal Savings Ass'n (In re Vienna Park Properties)

United States Court of Appeals, Second Circuit, 1992.
976 F.2d 106.

■ MESKILL, CHIEF JUDGE

* * * In 1984, the debtor in this bankruptcy case, Vienna Park Properties (Vienna Park), a limited partnership, purchased 300 condominium units (the Properties) located in Vienna, Virginia. Congressional Mortgage Corporation (Congressional) loaned Vienna Park the bulk of the money for the purchase. Congressional secured repayment of this loan by obtaining a Deed of Trust to each of the 300 condominium units. All 300 Deeds of Trust were recorded in the county in which the Properties are located. Each Deed of Trust contains a clause assigning to Congressional the rents of the Properties as additional security for the loan.

Vienna Park financed a portion of the remaining purchase price through the seller of the condominiums, Vienna Park Associates (VPA). To secure this second loan, Vienna Park granted VPA 300 second Deeds of Trust, each subordinate to Deeds of Trust granted Congressional for each unit.

Vienna Park and VPA also established an escrow fund (the Escrow Fund) that initially contained $2.5 million, $500,000 of which was contributed by Vienna Park. The remainder of the funds was drawn from the money that Congressional loaned to Vienna Park. The Escrow Account was held by a bank during the period of the VPA/Vienna Park loan and was to be used to manage the properties by a management agent designated by VPA. Thus, VPA effectively retained management control of the Properties during the period of the loan. The management agent was empowered to borrow money for the Escrow Fund if the fund were to become depleted. The management agent was also allowed to pledge the assets of the Escrow Account as collateral.

Upon satisfaction of Vienna Park's obligations to VPA, the escrow agreement was to terminate, and Vienna Park had the right to receive any funds that then remained in the Escrow Account. Vienna Park assigned to Congressional this right to the residual of the Escrow Account as further collateral to secure the loan from Congressional to Vienna Park.

In due course, Congressional assigned 162 of the 300 Deeds of Trust to United Postal Savings Association (United Postal) and the remaining 138 Deeds of Trust to Trustbank Federal Savings Bank (Trustbank) (United Postal and Trustbank are collectively referred to herein as "the Banks"). Trustbank has since been declared insolvent and is represented in this proceeding by the Resolution Trust Corporation. Congressional also assigned to each bank a portion of its security interest in Vienna Park's right to the residual of the Escrow Account, roughly in proportion to the assignments of the Deeds of Trust.

Vienna Park made no payments to either United Postal or Trustbank on the notes securing the loan after July 1989. As a result, both banks notified Vienna Park in August 1989 that it was in default and that the loan would be accelerated if the default was not cured within thirty days. United Postal accelerated its portion of the loan on September 19, 1989 and on October 30, 1989 demanded the rents of the Properties pursuant to the assignment of rents provisions in the Deeds of Trust. Trustbank similarly demanded the rents on October 30, 1989.

In late October 1989, the Banks commenced foreclosure proceedings on the Properties. On November 21, 1989, before the Banks had successfully foreclosed on the Properties, Vienna Park filed a petition for reorganization under Chapter 11 of the Bankruptcy Code. The foreclosure proceedings thus were automatically stayed. See BC 362(a).

* * * Vienna Park sought a determination in the bankruptcy court that the right to receive funds remaining in the Escrow Account was property of the estate not subject to the Banks' security interests. The bankruptcy court found that the collateral in that case was a "general intangible" under Virginia law and that because the Banks had failed to file a financing

statement, the security interests were unperfected. On appeal, the district court agreed with the bankruptcy court. Accordingly, the trustee had the power to void those interests under BC 544, which grants bankruptcy trustees the powers of hypothetical lien creditors under non-bankruptcy law.

* * * [T]his appeal involves the contending rights of the estate and the Banks in the funds contained in the Escrow Account. The district court held that the collateral was a "general intangible," a security interest which, under Virginia law, may only be perfected by filing a financing statement. The Banks argue that the collateral instead was money and that the security interest was perfectible by possession. Under the district court's holding, Vienna Park is able to void the Banks' security interest in the Escrow Account.

The Escrow Account was established by Vienna Park, VPA and certain principals of VPA as a form of security for the loan from VPA to Vienna Park. The escrow agreement directed that the funds contained in the Escrow Account be held by an escrow agent, invested at the direction of the management agent designated by VPA and used by that management agent to manage the Properties. The purpose of the Escrow Account was to pay certain operating expenses of the condominium project. On termination of the escrow agreement, the escrow agent was to disburse to Vienna Park the balance of the funds remaining in the Escrow Account.

Vienna Park and the management agent assigned to Congressional "their rights to receive funds now or hereafter deposited in the Escrow Account in accordance with the Escrow Agreement." This assignment was made "as collateral security for the full and prompt payment and performance by [Vienna Park] of its obligations under the Notes and Deeds of Trust." Congressional assigned to United Postal approximately 54 percent of "its interest in the Escrow Account ... including, but not limited to, its right to receive funds now or hereafter deposited [t]herein in accordance with the Escrow Agreement." The remaining portion of Congressional's interest in the Escrow Account was similarly assigned to Trustbank in January 1985. No financing statement was ever filed with respect to the Banks' security interest in Vienna Park's rights to the funds in the Escrow Account.

Under BC 544, the trustee is vested with the power to void certain transfers of property, including certain transfers of security interests. * * * Because the site of the transaction was Virginia, we examine Virginia law to determine the rights of such a hypothetical lien creditor under BC 544(a).

Because this issue involves a security interest, it is governed by Virginia's version of Article 9 of the Uniform Commercial Code (UCC). [9-317(a)(2)] states that "an unperfected security interest is subordinate to the rights of ... (b) a person who becomes a lien creditor before the security interest is perfected." Thus, if the trustee demonstrates that the Banks' security interest in Vienna Park's right to the escrow funds was not perfected, the trustee will be able to void that interest and Vienna Park's right to those funds will become an unencumbered part of the estate.

The steps required for perfection of a security interest under Virginia law vary depending on the nature of the collateral. [9-310(a)] provides that "[a] financing statement shall be filed to perfect all security interests except" for certain security interests specifically set forth. The district court held that the Banks' security interest was a security interest in a general intangible, see [9-102(a)(42)], which is not one of the interests specifically excepted from [9-310(a)'s] filing requirement.

The Banks argue that their security interest is excepted from the filing requirement of [9-310] because the collateral is "a security interest in collateral in possession of the secured party under F9-305." [9-310(b)(6)]. The Banks contend that the collateral in this case is not a general intangible but rather is money. A security interest in money can be perfected through possession by the secured party or an agent. See [9-313]. Possession of the funds by the escrow agent, in this case a bank, arguably satisfied the possession requirement of [9-313]. If the collateral is properly classified as money, the Banks arguably have perfected their security interest.

"Money" is defined by the Virginia UCC as "a medium of exchange authorized or adopted by a domestic or foreign government as a part of its currency." [1-201(b)(24)]. This general definition controls because Article 9 of the Virginia UCC does not specifically define "money."

There is no question that the funds held in the escrow account, United States dollars, are "money" within this definition. However, Vienna Park did not have an unencumbered present right to these funds at the time it granted the security interest. Rather, it merely possessed a contractual right to receive any funds remaining in the Escrow Account upon fulfillment of its obligations to VPA. The most Vienna Park could transfer at the time of the security agreement was a contingent right to receive an uncertain amount of money in the future.

A contractual right to obtain money at some future time is not the same thing as money itself. The UCC recognizes this in several of its provisions. See, e.g., [9-102(a)(2)] (defining "account" as "any right to payment for goods sold or leased or for services rendered which is not evidenced by an instrument or chattel paper"); [9-102(a)(11)] (defining "chattel paper" as "a writing or writings which evidence both a monetary obligation and a security interest in or a lease of specific goods"). * * *

The collateral in this case therefore was not "money" as that term is used in [9-313]. The Banks do not contend that the collateral could properly be classified as any of the other types of collateral in which a security interest can be perfected by possession under [9-313]. Nor do the Banks contend that the security interest is excepted from the filing requirement of [9-310(a)] in any manner except through operation of [9-313]. Although the district court was likely correct in classifying the collateral as a general intangible, it is enough that the collateral is not among the exceptions to [9-310(a)'s] general filing requirement.

Thus, under Virginia law, in order to perfect its security interest in Vienna Park's right to receive the residue of the Escrow Account the Banks were required to file a financing statement. As they concede that they did not do so, the security interest was unperfected. Thus, under Virginia law, that interest is subordinate to the rights of a person who becomes a lien creditor prior to perfection. [9-317(a)(2)]. As the Bankruptcy Code endows the trustee with the power of a hypothetical lien creditor at the beginning of the bankruptcy case, BC 544(a)(1), the district court properly held that the Banks' security interest in the proceeds of the Escrow Account was voidable. * * *

COMMENTS AND QUESTIONS

1. *Vienna Park Properties* considers two possible categories for the escrow account: money and general intangibles. Is there a third alternative? Consider the definition of "deposit account" given in 9-102(a)(29). Does the escrow account qualify? If not, why not? Suppose that it did: what consequences? In that regard, note 9-314(a).

2. The current structure of Article 9 makes it critical to classify collateral appropriately. Return to problem 3-1 and ask again, how should we classify a glomph? You should have reacted: "I have no idea what a glomph is, so how should I know how to classify it?" That, of course, turns out to be the point. Many potential items of collateral will be classified easily, but others, especially more recent creations in intellectual property and complex financial devices, may be hard to classify. You should keep the glomph fact pattern in mind, and should not assume that you just *know* what a particular item actually is.

SECTION II. REQUIREMENT OF THE DEBTOR'S NAME

Turn to 9-521 and examine the uniform form of financing statement. This looks fairly mechanical: names and addresses, taxpayer ID numbers, a collateral description requirement, etc. You should not be misled: if you have a good grant clause in your security agreement and an effective financing statement, you are usually in pretty good shape. Screw up the financing statement by delegating these "mechanical" forms to the insufficiently attentive, and you may risk your entire transaction. So be warned.

Beyond this, Article 9 creates a quite nuanced approach to financing statements. 9-502(a) states that a financing statement is sufficient if it provides the names of the debtor and the secured party and indicates the collateral covered by the financing statement. This seems hard to square with the form in 9-521, which seems to contemplate much more information. The mailing addresses of the debtor and the secured party appear on the 9-521 form, and the failure to include these addresses is a mandatory basis for a filing officer to refuse to accept a tendered financing statement. See 9-520(a), 9-516(b)(4), (5). Notwithstanding that, should the financing officer accept the statement—this acknowledges that filing officers will make their share of mistakes—the financing statement is effective, 9-520(c), so long as it is otherwise proper.

This is tricky to the outsider, but reasonably clear once it is considered. Statements without appropriate addresses should not be accepted for filing, but if accepted, the absence of the addresses will not render the financing statement ineffective. (It could conceivably, in unusual circumstances, have consequences for priority. See 9-338.) Note also that the financing statement need not be signed by the debtor—this should facilitate electronic filing—but the filing of the financing statement still must be authorized by the debtor. See 9-509.

Since the filing of financing statements is done by the debtor's name, 9-519(c)(1), perhaps the central requirement for a financing statement is that the debtor's name be sufficiently accurate so that subsequent creditors can find the financing statement when they search the files. Even separate from the question of name changes, which present their own problems, there can be genuine confusion or disagreement over the name of a debtor. 9-503 attempts to resolve much of the uncertainty that existed under prior law by specifying a sufficient name for a variety of entities. In addition, 9-503(b) and (c) address questions regarding the use of a debtor's trade name, that is, a name by which the debtor is commonly known but which is different from its legal name. 9-506 addresses the consequences of mistakes, particularly in the debtor's name, and also must be consulted.

There has been a flurry of cases under the new statute on the debtor's name. These cases should make your blood run cold. You will see small mistakes—mistakes that any one of us could make quite easily—with devastating consequences for the secured lender. You just have to get the debtor's name right in the financing statement—not just close, oh so close—but actually right, though some courts may let you off the hook.

Read 'em and weep.

In re Tyringham Holdings, Inc.
United States Bankruptcy Court, E.D. Virginia, 2006.
354 Bankr. 363.

■ DOUGLAS O. TICE JR., CHIEF JUDGE

Trial was held on November 13, 2006, on plaintiff's complaint to determine the validity, priority, or extent of a lien under a consignment held by defendant Suna Bros. Inc. The issue is whether Suna's financing statement was seriously misleading because it was not filed under the correct name of the debtor. For the reasons set forth below, the court finds that the financing statement is seriously misleading. Therefore, the defendant's lien is unperfected, and plaintiff may sell the collateral free and clear of any lien or interest of Suna.

* * * The financing statement was filed by Suna on June 10, 2005, and listed the debtor's name as "Tyringham Holdings." The debtor is a Virginia Corporation and is listed as "Tyringham Holdings, Inc." on the public records of the Virginia State Corporation Commission. An official UCC search certified by the State Corporation Commission revealed a search conducted under the name "Tyringham Holdings, Inc.," which did not reveal the Suna financing statement.

Where a filed financing statement is required to perfect a security interest, it must substantially satisfy the requirements of a financing statement. Generally, the name of a corporate debtor, as indicated on the public record of the debtor's jurisdiction of organization, must be listed on the financing statement for it to be valid. 9-503(a)(1). Where the requirements are substantially satisfied, a financing statement "is effective, even if it has minor errors or omissions, unless the errors or omissions make the financing statement seriously misleading." 9-506(a). By law, "[e]xcept as otherwise provided in subsection (c), a financing statement that fails sufficiently to provide the name of the debtor in accordance with §9-503(a) is seriously misleading." 9-506(b). There is no question in this case that the name of the debtor in the Suna financing statement, "Tyringham Holdings," was not the same corporate name as that on the public record for the state of Virginia, "Tyringham Holdings, Inc." Therefore, unless excepted by 9-506(c), the financing statement is seriously misleading and is ineffective to perfect Suna's security interest.

The exception in subsection (c) represents a shift between the previous version of Article 9 and Revised Article 9 in dealing with errors on financing statements. Prior to the revisions enacted in 2001, Virginia's version of Article 9 had no equivalent to subsections (b) and (c). Instead, the governing principle for financing statement sufficiency was a diligent searcher standard. Subsection (c) now provides a more concrete rule for determining if errors are seriously misleading, providing that:

> If a search of the *records of the filing office* under the *debtor's correct name,* using the *filing office's standard search logic,* if any, would disclose a financing statement that fails sufficiently to provide the name of the debtor in accordance with § 8.9A-503(a), the name provided does not make the financing statement seriously misleading.

9-506(c) (emphasis added).

According to the statute, the appropriate standard by which to judge a search is the filing office's standard search logic for a search under the debtor's correct name, in the filing office's database. Several cases in other jurisdictions, applying parallel provisions in their respective Uniform Commercial Codes, emphasize that the filing office's standard search logic is the governing factor in determining whether a financing statement is seriously misleading. Therefore, it is clear in these jurisdictions that the filing office's standard search logic governs.

In the time period between filing of the financing statement and the trial in this Adversary Proceeding, a number of UCC searches were performed by private search companies such as Corporation Service Company, Access Information Services, Inc., and UCC Retrievals, Inc. Each of these searches disclosed the existence of the Suna financing statement. No evidence was presented as to the underlying methodology behind the Corporation Service Company or Access Information Services, Inc., searches. At trial, a witness for Suna testified that she had conducted the search by UCC Retrievals, Inc., under the name "Tyringham Holdings." Her search disclosed the existence of the Suna financing statement. Her rationale for searching under the name "Tyringham Holdings" rather than the correct "Tyringham Holdings, Inc.," was that she considered the term "Inc." to be a "noise word." Noise words for these purposes are words that are removed or ignored in the process of performing an electronic database search for financing statements. The witness classified "Inc." as a noise word because it is one of such words on a list promulgated by the International Association of Corporation Administrators (IACA). Other abbreviations on the IACA "noise word" list include "Corporation," "Corp," "Company," "Co," "Limited," and "Ltd."

Suna repeatedly emphasizes that these private searches used "standard search logic" to disclose the Suna financing statement. Suna would have this court read out the portion of the statute that specifies whose "standard search logic" is employed in the analysis. The relevant standard is clearly no longer the diligent searcher's standard search logic nor a private search organization's standard search logic, but it is instead the filing office's standard search logic.

The Virginia State Corporation Commission has promulgated filing rules in 5 Va. Admin. Code 5-30-70(E) that describe the standard search logic employed by the commission when conducting a search. Search results are produced by the application of standardized search logic to the

name presented to the filing officer, along with several additional requirements, including the following subsection 4:

> "Noise words" include, but are not limited to, "an," "and," "for,"
> "of," and "the." The word "the" always will be disregarded and
> other noise words appearing anywhere except at the beginning
> of an organization name will be disregarded. Certain business
> words are modified to a standard abbreviation: company to "co,"
> corporation to "corp," limited to "ltd," incorporated to "inc."

5 Va. Admin. Code 5-30-70(E)(4). The State Corporation Commission
has not adopted the full list of noise words promulgated by the IACA.

Plaintiff called as a witness an employee of the Virginia State Corporation Commission, who described the coding of the UCC search program
utilized by the Corporation Commission in its official UCC searches. As
explained by the witness, the search logic modifies a given entry by removing certain items from the name entered by a searcher, including punctuation, spaces, and the five noise words listed in the State Corporation
Commission Rules. This creates a search key which is then matched to
names on filed financing statements, which have likewise been modified in
accordance with the same standards.

No evidence was presented to show that the private searches were conducted in accordance with the *Virginia State Corporation Commission's*
standard search logic on the *debtor's correct name.* The only private search
supported by additional evidence at trial was the one conducted by UCC
Retrievals, Inc. This search was conducted using the State Corporation
Commission's website, but only after the witness truncated the name, "Tyringham Holdings, Inc." to "Tyringham Holdings," based solely on her
own belief that "Inc." was a noise word in the state of Virginia. The
searcher entered "Tyringham Holdings" into the search field and retrieved
the Suna financing statement. No evidence was presented that the searcher ever entered "Tyringham Holdings, Inc.," into the search field and recovered the Suna financing statement.

Suna attempts to argue that the State Corporation Commission's
search logic is faulty because it does not filter out "Inc." as a noise word,
even though the IACA considers it as such. According to Plaintiff's witness, the State Corporation Commission is in the process of revising its
list of noise words and changing the search logic to include terms such as
"inc." However, the standard in place at all times relevant to this case did
not include "Inc." as a noise word; at present, the underlying search engine

code filters out only five articles as noise words. Suna makes much of the fact that noise words in the filing rules contained at 5 Va. Admin. Code 5-30-70(E)(4) "include, but are not limited to" the five articles filtered out by the search engine. Suna essentially argues that the search engine improperly employs the search methodology prescribed by the statute, because it in fact filters out *only* the five articles and thus is "limited to" those words only. Regardless of whether this argument makes logical sense, the court cannot conclude on the basis of the statutory language that "Inc." should be considered a noise word. The third sentence of subsection 4 says that "Certain business words are modified to a standard abbreviation...," the last of which is "incorporated" to "inc." 5 Va. Admin. Code 5-30-70(E)(4). If "inc" is a standard abbreviation, it cannot simultaneously be a disregarded noise word according to the State Corporation Commission's standard search logic as embodied by this statute and the search engine code utilizing it. As a result, it is clear that "Inc." is not a noise word for purposes of a Virginia UCC search, and the State Corporation Commission's search logic is functioning as it was presently intended to function in this respect.

None of the cases cited by Suna support its proposition that the language of 9-503(c) does not mean what it says regarding the use of the *filing office's* standard search logic. The closest Suna comes is in its discussion of Planned Furniture Promotions, Inc. v. Youngblood, Inc. 374 F.Supp.2d 1227 (M.D. Ga. 2005), where the United States District Court for the Middle District of Georgia ruled that a party's omission of "Inc" from the end of the debtor's name was not seriously misleading because a search "would almost assuredly turn up a financing statement...," and "a diligent creditor searching the filing records under the name Benjamin S. Youngblood, Inc. would be put on notice to inquire into the interests of a debtor listed as Benjamin Scott Youngblood." Id. at 1234. This case essentially ignores the provisions of the Georgia UCC referring to the filing office's standard search logic and appears to rest on pre-revised Article 9 law dealing with the diligent searcher standard. * * * This court finds the logic of *Planned Furniture Promotions* inapplicable to the present case and finds persuasive the number of cases that apply the plain language of the UCC, requiring a search using the filing office's standard search logic. Thus, a search using the correct debtor name under the filing office's standard search logic—as embodied by any relevant statute and search engine programming that implements the search logic—must reveal the financing statement filed under the incorrect name or it will be deemed seriously misleading.

While application of the filing office's standard search logic may lead to situations where it appears that a relatively minor error in a financing statement leads to a security interest becoming unperfected, it is not that difficult to ensure that a financing statement is filed with the correct name of the debtor. Little more is asked of a creditor than to accurately record the debtor's name, and according to the statute, failure to perform this action clearly dooms the perfected status of a security interest.

The official search certified by the State Corporation Commission, under the correct name, "Tyringham Holdings, Inc.," fails to disclose the Suna financing statement. Thus, the only search which used the correct name under the standard search logic actually employed by the State Corporation Commission did not disclose the Suna financing statement. As a result, the court must conclude that the financing statement is seriously misleading and is insufficient to perfect Suna's security interest in the collateral. Therefore, Suna's security interest in the collateral is unperfected and the collateral may be sold free and clear of any lien held by Suna. * * *

Pankratz Implement Co. v. Citizens Nat. Bank

Supreme Court of Kansas, 2006.
130 P.3d 57.

■ Davis, J.

* * * The facts in this case are uncontroverted. On March 18, 1998, Rodger House purchased a Steiger Bearcat tractor from Pankratz Implement Co. (Pankratz). House signed a note and security agreement in favor of Pankratz using his correct name, Rodger House. Pankratz listed the debtor's name in the agreement as "Roger House" instead of "Rodger House." Pankratz, in turn, assigned its interest in the note and the collateral to Deere and Company (Deere). Deere then filed a financing statement with the Kansas Secretary of State on March 23, 1998, using the same misspelled name, Roger House.

On April 8, 1999, House executed a note and security agreement in favor of Citizens National Bank (CNB), from which House obtained a loan. House pledged as collateral, among other things, all equipment "that I now own and that I may own in the future." On March 4, 1999, CNB filed a financing statement with the Kansas Secretary of State using the correct name of the debtor, Rodger House.

On June 10, 2002, House filed a petition for bankruptcy under Chapter 7 in the United States Bankruptcy Court for the District of Kansas. On July 1, 2002, Deere reassigned the House note and security interest to Pankratz. Pankratz obtained relief from the automatic stay pursuant to BC 362 and filed suit in the district court against CNB seeking a declaratory judgment concerning its purchase money security interest. * * *

The sole question presented for resolution on undisputed facts is one of law to be determined under recently enacted amendments to Article 9 of the UCC. * * * Although the general issue in this case has been litigated previously in Kansas courts, no Kansas court has addressed the issue since the Revised Article 9 became effective on July 1, 2001. Thus, the case presents an issue of first impression. * * *

Our construction of the above statutes provides the following analysis under the facts of this case. 9-503(a)(5)(A) provides that a financing statement sufficiently provides the debtor's name only if the financial statement provides the individual name of the debtor. In this case, Pankratz used an incorrect name by misspelling the debtor's name in the financing statement. Pankratz argues that the misspelled name was only a minor error under 9-506(a) and was not seriously misleading.

9-506(a) provides that a financing statement "is effective, even if it has minor errors or omissions, unless the errors or omissions make the financing statement seriously misleading." Except as otherwise provided in subsection (c) a financing statement that fails sufficiently to provide the name of the debtor in accordance with 9-503(a) is seriously misleading. Pankratz' use of the debtor's misspelled name failed to provide the individual name of the debtor in accord with 9-503(a); however, according to the safe harbor provisions of 9-503(c), the error may not be seriously misleading.

9-506(c) provides that

> "[i]f a search of the records of the filing office under the debtor's correct name, *using the filing office's standard search logic*, if any, would disclose a financing statement that fails sufficiently to provide the name of the debtor in accordance with 9-503(a) and amendments thereto, the name provided does not make the financing statement seriously misleading." (Emphasis added.)

Under such circumstances a search using the debtor's correct name would reveal the prior security interest of Pankratz with the misspelled debtor's name and its financing statement would not be seriously misleading.

However, the undisputed facts in this case establish that a search under the debtor's correct name using the filing office's standard search logic did not disclose Pankratz' financing statement with the debtor's misspelled name. The express provisions of 9-506(b) provide that "[e]xcept as otherwise provided in subsection (c), a financing statement that fails sufficiently to provide the name of the debtor in accordance with 9-503(a) and amendments thereto, is seriously misleading." Thus, Pankratz' financing statement using the misspelled name of the debtor, while prior in time, was seriously misleading * * *.

* * * Pankratz advances several arguments in support of its position that the misspelled name of the debtor is only a minor error not seriously misleading. Pankratz asserts that the name requirements are not sufficiently defined especially for individuals under the new amendments and that a careful reading of subsection (c) does not support the bright-line rule * * * that failing to meet the requirements of subsection (c) makes the financing statement seriously misleading. The object of Pankratz' arguments is to place upon the party claiming a superior lien the responsibility to conduct a diligent search of past records filed with the Secretary of State to determine whether a prior lien exists. If the name requirements of the debtor are not fixed and certain, the use of a nickname or a misspelled name on the financing statement filed with the Secretary of State may require just such a search on the part of the party claiming a superior lien.

On the other hand, if the legislature intended by its amended version of the UCC set forth above to fix and make certain the name of the debtor requirement, such a change shifts the responsibility of the one filing with the Secretary of State to follow the name requirement with the effect being that the party searching for prior liens on the same property may rely on the name used on the financing statement eliminating the need to conduct diligent searches. We believe that the language used by the legislature and the intent behind the adoption of the most recent amendments had the effect of shifting the responsibility of getting the name on the financing statement right to the filing party, thereby enabling the searching party to rely upon that name and eliminating the need for multiple searches using variations of the debtor's name. This would have the effect of providing more certainty in the commercial world and reducing litigation as was required prior to the amendments to determine whether an adequate search was made.

The facts in this case establish that two types of searches for prior liens were available to a creditor hoping to perfect his or her lien upon specific property. The first is the temporary internet search logic found at www.accesskansas.org. The facts establish that a search using the debtor's name in this case would have disclosed Pankratz' financing statement with the misspelled name of the debtor. However, the provisions of K.A.R. 7-17-24, as set forth below, make it clear that such a search shall not constitute an official search by the Secretary of State.

> "During the transition period of July 1, 2001 through June 30, 2006, public access to a database that produces search results beyond exact name matches may be provided by the secretary of state. The supplemental database [www.accesskansas.org.] shall not be considered part of the standard search logic and shall not constitute an official search by the secretary of state." K.A.R. 7-17-24.

The database provided a further disclaimer:

> "Searches conducted on the internet are not official searches under Revised Article Nine of the Uniform Commercial Code. This search engine is intended to provide a more flexible search logic so as to identify UCC filings under the old law, which employed different name requirements. Therefore searches conducted on this page will not determine whether a name is seriously misleading under 9-506. If you want an official search using the correct and current search logic given in KAR 7-17-22, contact the Kansas Secretary of State's Office at (785) 296-4564."

The "standard search logic" noted in 9-506(c) and provided by the Secretary of State is the official and only search that determines whether a name is seriously misleading under 9-506. See K.A.R. 7-17-21 and 7-17-22.

Pankratz, in support of its first argument, acknowledges that under 9-506(c), a search of the records of the Secretary of State, using the debtor's correct name and the filing office's standard search logic, would not disclose his financing statement using the misspelled name of the debtor, Roger House. However, Pankratz argues that the Court of Appeals erred in concluding under these circumstances that the financing statement is seriously misleading. Pankratz believes that the correct interpretation of

9-506(c) is that of Professors Barkley and Barbara Clark in volume one of their treatise, The Law of Secured Transactions Under the Uniform Commercial Code ¶ 2.09(1)(e), P.2-164 (2003):

> " '[R]ead carefully, ... § 9-506(c) provides only that a financing statement is not seriously misleading if, using standard search logic, a search under the debtor's correct name would reveal the statement containing the debtor's incorrect name. It does not provide that a financing statement is not seriously misleading *only* if a search using the debtor's correct name would reveal the statement containing the debtor's incorrect name in the circumstances .... [§ 9-506(c)] does not say that financing statements that do not satisfy subsection (c)'s "safe harbor" are seriously misleading and therefore ineffective. Thus ... § 9-506(c) leaves open the possibility that an error in the debtor's name does not render the financing statement seriously misleading, even if a search using the debtor's correct name and standard search logic would not turn up the statement.' " (Quoting Jordan, Warren, and Walt, Secured Transactions in Personal Property, p. 59 [2000]).

The above observation quoted by Professors Clarks is correct in that the provisions of subsection (c) are positive in recognizing that if a search under the debtor's correct name discloses the financing statement filed with a minor error, then the minor error does not make the filed statement seriously misleading. It does not say that such a filed statement that is not disclosed using standard logic search is seriously misleading. If all we were dealing with was subsection (c), then there would be the possibility that an error in the filed financing statement not meeting the safe harbor provisions of subsection (c) would not render the financing statement seriously misleading. However, as more fully discussed below, consideration of both amendments *in para materia* rather than focusing exclusively on subsection (c) supports the opposite conclusion.

Pankratz relies heavily upon Professors Clarks' interpretation as it relates to the crux of its argument. Pankratz argues that there is then no bright-line standard and the ultimate determination regarding the effectiveness a filed financing statement with an incorrect name that is not disclosed under the provisions of subsection (c) must be resolved on a case-by-case basis. Thus, depending again upon the diligence of the search by the creditor claiming a superior interest by reason of his or her later filed statement, the case must be resolved through a judicial determination of whether a particular financing statement is "seriously misleading."

The answer to this argument lies in the consideration of the two amendments together and interpreted as a whole scheme adopted by the Kansas Legislature rather than to focus exclusively upon one section alone. The answer also depends upon the express language used in both amendments, as well as the intent of the legislature in the adoption of the changes enacted.

A reading of the provisions of 9-503 with the provisions of 9-506 makes clear that the safe harbor provision of 9-506(c) applies to both 9-506 and 9-503. "A financing statement sufficiently provides the name of the debtor ... [i]f the debtor has a name, *only if it provides the individual or organizational name of the debtor.*" (Emphasis added.) 9-503(a)(5)(A). Referring to the case before us, the error in Pankratz' filed financing statement was the misspelling of the debtor's first name. Thus, Pankratz' financing statement failed to use the "name of the debtor" and therefore does not satisfy the provisions of 9-503(a). However, the provisions of 9-506(a) provide that "[a] financing statement substantially satisfying the requirements of this part is effective, even if it has minor errors or omissions, unless the errors or omissions make the financing statement seriously misleading." Pankratz' financial statement has a minor error; under 9-506(b), if the financing statement "*[e]xcept as otherwise provided in subsection (c)* [safe harbor provision], ... fails sufficiently to provide the name of the debtor in accordance with 9-503(a) and amendments thereto [only if the financing statement provides the name of the debtor], [it] is seriously misleading." The undisputed evidence establishes that Pankratz' financing statement did not satisfy the provisions of subsection (c), the safe harbor provisions, in that a search using debtor's correct name did not disclose Pankratz' statement.

Pankratz failed to satisfy the requirement of using the correct name of the debtor and thus did not satisfy the name requirements of 9-503(a)(5)(A). Nevertheless, minor errors will not destroy the effectiveness of that statement unless the errors make the statement seriously misleading. Pankratz' failing to meet the naming requirements is seriously misleading except in the case where a search using the debtor's correct name discloses the defective financing statement. In this case it did not and therefore remains seriously misleading. 9-506(b).

Pankratz' second argument focuses on the naming requirements set forth in 9-503. Pankratz asks what constitutes a sufficient name, a term not defined in the statute. Pankratz argues there is no requirement that a legal name must be used and bolsters this argument by pointing out the differences in the statute's loose requirements for an individual name and the exactness of the requirements for an organizational name. Pankratz' attack is aimed at the conclusion that if there is no exactness required for the name placed upon the financing statement, a nickname or even a slight variation in the name used would satisfy 9-503. If this is the case, then it follows that the law would therefore require a case-by-case determination regarding the sufficiency of the name with the result that the creditor claiming a superior lien on the property would be required to conduct a diligent search using variations of the debtor's name before it could be said that the prior filed statement is ineffective.

Pankratz is correct that 9-503 provides no specific rule or guidance concerning what constitutes a sufficient debtor "name." The term "name," name of debtor, debtor's name, or "correct name" is not defined in Article 9. At the same time, the statute sets forth exact requirements for the name of registered organizations. According to Pankratz, the difference in language indicates a legislative "loud silence," which means that there is no specific mandate to use the individual debtor's legal name in all circumstances. If there are no requirements as to the individual name, errors in the debtor's name in a financing statement must be judged on a case-by-case basis and the very minor error in this case, misspelling the debtor's first name by leaving out a "d" in Rodger, is only a minor error under 9-506(a).

Pankratz, as well as the district court, in this case relied upon the recent United States Bankruptcy Court decision In re Kinderknecht, 300 Bankr. 47 (Bankr. D.Kan. 2003), and cases cited therein. In that case, Terry J. Kinderknecht granted defendants a security interest in two farm implements, and they promptly filed financing statements on the collateral in the name "Terry J. Kinderknecht." Kinderknecht later filed a petition for Chapter 7 bankruptcy relief in his legal name "Terrance J. Kinderknecht," listing defendants as secured creditors. The trustee brought a strong-arm proceeding to set aside the security interests as not having been properly perfected in accordance with Kansas law. *** The court *** denied the claim of the trustee and held that use of the individual name "Terry J. Kinderknecht" in the financing statements did not make the financing statements insufficient or seriously misleading.

The trustee in the *Kinderknecht* case filed a timely appeal and the parties consented to jurisdiction of the United States 10th Circuit Bankruptcy Appellate Panel without a hearing before the United States District Court for the District of Kansas. In re Kinderknecht, 308 Bankr. 71 (B.A.P. 10th Cir. 2004) * * *. The 10th Circuit reasoned that 9-503

"was enacted to clarify the sufficiency of a debtor's name in financing statements. The intent to clarify when a debtor's name is sufficient shows a desire to foreclose fact-intensive tests, such as those that existed under the former Article 9 of the UCC, inquiring into whether a person conducting a search would discover a filing under any given name. Requiring a financing statement to provide a debtor's legal name is a clear cut test that is in accord with that intent.

"Furthermore, § 9-503, read as a whole, indicates that a legal name should be used for an individual debtor. In the case of debtor-entities, § 9-503(a) states that legal names must be used to render them sufficient under § 9-502(a). Trade names or other names may be listed, but it is insufficient to list a debtor by such names alone. A different standard should not apply to individual debtors. The more specific provisions applicable to entities, together with the importance of naming the debtor in the financing statement to facilitate the notice filing system and increase commercial certainty, indicates that an individual debtor must be listed on a financing statement by his or her legal name, not by a nickname.

"Our conclusion that a legal name is necessary to sufficiently provide the name of an individual debtor within the meaning of § 9-503(a) is also supported by four practical considerations. First, mandating the debtor's legal name sets a clear test so as [to] simplify the drafting of financing statements. Second, setting a clear test simplifies the parameters of UCC searches. Persons searching UCC filings will know that they need the debtor's legal name to conduct a search, they will not be penalized if they do not know that a debtor has a nickname, and they will not have to guess any number of nicknames that could exist to conduct a search. Third, requiring the debtor's legal name will avoid litigation as to the commonality or appropriateness of a debtor's nickname, and as to whether a reasonable searcher would have or should have known to use the name. Finally, obtaining a debtor's legal name is not difficult or burdensome for the creditor taking a secured interest in a debtor's property. Indeed, knowing the individual's legal name will assure the accuracy of any search that creditor conducts prior to taking its secured interest in property." 308 Bankr. at 75-76.

We believe the decision and reasoning of the 10th Circuit is sound and accurately reflects the legislative intent behind the adoption of new amendments to the UCC. Pankratz fails to harmonize what it calls a legislative silence in 9-503(a) with the specific provisions of 9-506. It is illogical to assert that the legislature would intend a rigorous requirement for business entity names and a vague, less rigorous standard for individual names, which would operate, by implication, as a kind of safe harbor, and then, in 9-506(c), expressly provide another safe harbor provision for the use of incorrect names on a filed financing statement.

The Kansas Secretary of State, in his amicus brief, supports the position taken in the *Kinderknecht* appeal by pointing out that the codified financial statement form, 9-521, requires the "debtor's exact full legal name." Moreover, the Official UCC Comment 2 to 9-503 stresses that "[t]he requirement that a financing statement provide the debtor's name is particularly important" and that "the actual individual or organizational name of the debtor on a financing statement is both necessary and sufficient." Because the primary purpose of a financing statement is to provide notice to third parties that the creditor has an interest in the debtor's property and the financing statements are indexed under the debtor's name, it is particularly important to require exactness in the name used, the debtor's legal name.

Finally, the Official UCC Comment 2 to 9-506 demonstrates the importance of the naming requirements as they relate to the concept of "seriously misleading":

> "Subsections (b) and (c), which are new, concern the effectiveness of financing statements in which the debtor's name is incorrect. Subsection (b) contains the general rule: a financing statement that fails sufficiently to provide the debtor's name in accordance with Section 9-503(a) is seriously misleading as a matter of law. Subsection (c) provides an exception: If the financing statement nevertheless would be discovered in a search under the debtor's correct name, using the filing office's stan-

> dard search logic ... then as a matter of law the incorrect name does not make the financing statement seriously misleading."

The purpose of the Revised Article 9 as a whole is the simplification of formal requirements, and the purpose of 9-506 in particular is to lessen the need for judicial hairsplitting (and, by implication, to move toward a bright-line rule). Harmonizing 9-506 with these purposes thus becomes the goal of any interpretation, despite the fact that other interpretations may be implied through omission in the statutory language. Pankratz argues that the legislature intended a case-by-case determination of "seriously misleading," based upon the absence of definitive language regarding the naming requirements for individuals in 9-503(a). Such an interpretation is contrary to the Comment's policy statement that the Revised Article 9 seeks to simplify filing requirements and to move away from judicial interpretation. Rather than judicial determinations, the Official UCC Comment 2 to 9-506 makes clear that

> "subsection (a) is in line with the policy of this Article to simplify formal requisites and filing requirements. It is designed to discourage the fanatical and impossibly refined reading of statutory requirements in which courts occasionally have indulged themselves.... Subsection (b) contains the general rule: a financing statement that fails sufficiently to provide the debtor's name in accordance with Section 9-503(a) is seriously misleading as a matter of law. Subsection (c) provides an exception...."

* * * The Kansas Court of Appeals in its decision, the express provisions of the revised amendments read *in para materia*, and the Official UCC Comments are all in accord that the primary purpose of the revision of the name requirement is to lessen the amount of fact-intensive, case-by-case determinations that plagued earlier versions of the UCC, and to simplify the filing system as a whole. The object of the revisions was to shift the responsibility to the filer by requiring the not too heavy burden of using the legal name of the debtor, thereby relieving the searcher from conducting numerous searches using every conceivable name variation of the debtor. The effect of the revision is to provide more certainty in the commercial world and reduce litigation to determine whether an adequate search was done. The cases cited by Pankratz in support of its position mostly were decided prior to the adoption of the revisions. The more recent cases decided after the revisions of UCC Article 9 are in accord with the Court of Appeals' decision in this case.

* * * We conclude that such authority, as well as the express provisions of 9-503 and 9-506 construed *in pari materia*, demonstrate that Pankratz' filed financing statement was "seriously misleading." * * *

In re Jim Ross Tires, Inc.

United States Bankruptcy Court, S.D. Texas, 2007.
379 Bankr. 670.

■ MARVIN ISGUR, BANKRUPTCY JUDGE

* * * Jim Ross Tires, Inc. ("Debtor") filed a chapter 7 bankruptcy petition on July 10, 2006. The Trustee has objected to the proofs of claim filed by Am-Pac Tire Dist., Inc ("Am-Pac") and Tradition Bank.

On July 27, 2006, Am-Pac filed a proof of claim of $130,130.13 asserting a secured claim and lien on all of the Debtor's assets including accounts receivable, equipment and inventory. The proof of claim is supported by three financing statements, dated December 2, 2002, November 15, 2005, and December 27, 2005. The Trustee objects arguing that the Financing Statements do not meet the requirements necessary to perfect AmPac's interest in Debtor's assets. Accordingly, the Trustee seeks to recharacterize AmPac's claim as unsecured.

The Trustee argues that the 2005 Financing Statements are inadequate because the Financing Statements do not reference an interest in collateral sufficient to create a security interest. Both Financing Statements state that the collateral covered is a "promissory note." The Trustee asserts that the term "promissory note" is an insufficient description of the collateral. AmPac does not dispute this argument. Accordingly, any dispute over the validity of the 2005 Financing Statements is moot. The 2005 Financing Statements are ineffective to perfect AmPac's interest.

The Trustee argues that the 2002 Financing Statement is inadequate because it does not properly list the Debtor's name as required by the Texas Business and Commerce Code. The Trustee, therefore, asserts that the 2002 Financing Statement is also ineffective to support AmPac's secured interest.

On July 20, 2006, Tradition Bank filed an unsecured claim in the amount of $94,948.57 and a secured proof of claim in the amount of $63,033.56. To support its proof of claim, Tradition Bank provided two

Financing Statements, dated July 30, 1998 and October 7, 2004. The Trustee asserted at the May 23, 2007 hearing that the 1998 Financing Statement had expired. Tradition Bank did not dispute this assertion. The Court, therefore, finds the 1998 Financing Statement is insufficient to support Tradition Bank's claim. As to the 2004 Financing Statement, the Trustee asserts that, like AmPac's 2002 Financing Statement, the Debtor's name is not properly stated as required by the Texas Business and Commerce Code.

* * * Among these other powers is ability of the trustee to avoid certain liens and transfers avoidable by creditors under state law. The first of these, as enumerated under the Bankruptcy Code, is found in BC 544. This section is frequently referred to as the "strong-arm clause." It is in this section that a trustee has the authority to avoid unperfected security interests. * * * Essentially, BC 544(a)(1) provides that a trustee may avoid any interest voidable by a hypothetical judicial lien creditor. The trustee, therefore, steps not only into the debtor's shoes, but certain creditors' shoes as well. The trustee's powers as a judicial lien creditor are governed by state law.

Under Texas law, the Texas Business and Commerce Code provides that a security interest is subordinate to the rights of a person that becomes a lien creditor before the security interest is perfected. 9-317(a). A "lien creditor" is defined in the Texas Business and Commerce Code to include "a trustee in bankruptcy from the date of the filing of the petition." Id. at 9-102(a)(52)(C). Therefore, under Texas law, the moment Debtor filed for bankruptcy, the Trustee became a lien creditor whose rights trump those holding unperfected security interests. * * *

The Texas Business and Commerce Code provides a list of what information must be included on the financing statement for the statement to perfect the creditor's security interest. The first of these requirements is that the financing statement "provides the name of the debtor". 9-502(a)(1). The proper statement of the debtor's name is governed by 9-503 which states that for a registered organization, the name on the financing statement must "provide[ ] the name of the debtor indicated on the public record of the debtor's jurisdiction of organization that shows the debtor to have been organized". 9-503(a).[4] * * *

---

[4] Effective June 15, 2007, 9-503 has been amended to read: (a) A financing statement sufficiently provides the name of the debtor: (1) if the debtor is a registered organization, only if the financing statement provides the name of the debtor indi-

Debtor's name on the 2002 Financing Statement filed by AmPac is stated as "JIM ROSS TIRES, INC. dba HTC TIRES & AUTOMOTIVE CENTERS". The name of Debtor as indicated by the Texas Secretary of State is "Jim Ross Tires Inc." As stipulated by the parties, Debtor's assumed name, "HTC Tires & Automotive Centers", expired on August 7, 2000, and was not renewed. AmPac argues that even though the statement of Debtor's name on the 2002 Financing Statement is not exactly as that "indicated on the public record of debtor's jurisdiction of organization," AmPac's inclusion of the dba at the end of the name is irrelevant to a determination of compliance with 9-503(a). AmPac argues that 9-503 sets only a "minimum limitation" for stating the debtor's name and if the correct name is otherwise included in the statement, any other information should be rendered "superfluous" and ignored for purposes of this analysis.

AmPac supports its argument by emphasizing subsections (b) and (c) of 9-503. 9-503(b) provides that a "financing statement that provides the name of the debtor in accordance with Subsection (a) is not rendered ineffective by the absence of: (1) a trade name or other name of the debtor ..." 9-503(b). 9-503(c) states that a "financing statement that provides only the debtor's trade name does not sufficiently provide the name of the debtor." Id. at 9-503(c). AmPac also references comment 2 to 9-503 which states:

> Together with subsections (b) and (c), subsection (a) reflects the view prevailing under former Article 9 that the actual individual or organizational name of the debtor on a financing statement is both necessary and sufficient, whether or not the financing statement provides trade or other names of the debtor ...

Id. at cmt. 2. Considering subsections (b) and (c) and the related comment together, AmPac asserts that the inclusion of dba's or other trade names was considered by the legislature, is entirely permissible, and should be of no consequence in this proceeding to an analysis of compliance with 9-503(a).

The Court disagrees. While it is clear that the legislature considered certain effects of dba usage in satisfying 9-503(a), the Court finds that the

---

cated on the debtor's formation documents that are filed of public record in [of] the debtor's jurisdiction of organization to create the registered organization and that show [shows] the debtor to have been organized, including any amendments to those documents for the express purpose of amended the debtor's name.

interpretation AmPac applies is overly broad and inoperable in application when considered with other sections of the Code. Specifically, AmPac's asserted interpretation, if applied, conflicts with the purposes of the indexing system when evaluated against the administrative procedures for indexing and searching UCC records filed with the Texas Secretary of State.

The Texas Administrative Code provides specific rules for the data entry of names in UCC filings. For organization names, the Code provides that:

> Organization names are entered into the UCC information management system exactly as set forth on the form, even if it appears that multiple names are set forth in the document or if it appears that the name of an individual has been included in the field designated for an organization name.

Tex. Admin. Code 95.407(1). The requirement that the indexing officer enter the name exactly as provided is absolutely necessary based on the procedures for searching the Secretary of State's database. Search requests are performed by "set[ting] forth the full correct name of a debtor ... consist [ing] of the name of the organization as stated on the articles of incorporation." Id. at 95.501. The following rule applies to the actual search:

> Search results are created by applying standardized search logic to the name presented to the filing officer by the person requesting the search. Human judgment does not play a role in determining the results of the search. The following, and only the following rules are applied to conduct searches.
>
> (1) There is no limit to the number of matches that may be returned in response to the search criteria.
>
> (2) No distinction is made between upper and lower case letters.
>
> (3) Punctuation marks and accents are disregarded.
>
> (4) Words and abbreviations at the end of a name that indicate the existence or nature of an organization as set forth in the "Ending Noise Words" list as promulgated and adopted by the International Association of Corporation Administrators[5] as from time to time, are disregarded ...

---

[5] Noise words include: Agency, Association, Assn, Associates, Assc, Assoc, Attorneys at Law, Bank, National Bank, Business Trust, Charter, Chartered, Company, Co, Corporation, Corp, Credit Union, CU, Federal Savings Bank, FSB, General

(5) The word "the" at the beginning of the search criteria is disregarded.

(6) All spaces are disregarded.

(7) For first and middle names of individuals, initials are treated as the logical equivalent of all names that begin with such initials, and no middle name or initial is equated with all middle names and initials ...

(8) After taking the preceding rules into account to modify the name of the debtor requested to be searched and to modify the names of debtors contained in active financing statements in the UCC information management system, the search will reveal only names of debtors that are contained in active financing statements and, as modified, exactly match the name requested, as modified.

Id. at 95.503. The applicant is to search by the "full correct name of a debtor." Id. at 95.501. There is no rule modifying the search terms based on a dba. Nor is there any rule that the indexing officer consider and separate a stated dba from the debtor's name. See Id. at 95.407(1). The Administrative Code clearly states that only exact matches and those modified by the rules are returned. Id. at 95.503(8). Therefore, in this proceeding, if a subsequent creditor searches under debtor's correct name, Jim Ross Tires, Inc., because a dba is not a grounds for modifying the name of the debtor and only exact matches are returned, any financing statement filed with a dba will inevitably fail to appear.

The same analysis applies to Tradition Bank's claim. Debtor's name on the 2004 Financing Statement filed by Tradition Bank is stated as "JIM ROSS TIRE INC". Tradition Bank argues that there is "nothing in the standard search logic which would prohibit the official search engine from finding the 2004 UCC merely because an 's' is missing at the end of the

---

Partnership, Gen part, GP, Incorporated, Inc, Limited, Ltd, Ltee, Limited Liability Company, LC, LLC, Limited Liability Partnership, LLP, Limited Partnership, LP, Medical Doctors Professional Association, MDPA, Medical Doctors Professional Corporation, MDPC, National Association, NA, Partners, Partnership, Professional Association, Prof Assn, PA, Professional Corporation, Prof Corp, PC, Professional Limited Liability Company, Professional Limited Liability Co, PLLC, Railroad, RR, Real Estate Investment Trust, REIT, Registered Limited Liability Partnership, RLLP, Savings Association, SA, Service Corporation, SC, Sole Proprietorship, SP, SPA, Trust, Trustee, As Trustee.

name." Tradition Bank, therefore, asserts the error lies with the Texas Secretary of State's application of 95.503. The Court disagrees. There is no rule stated in 95.503 that the letter "s" modifies the search for the debtor's name. As stated above, only exact matches are returned. Accordingly a search under Debtor's correct name will not return this Financing Statement.

As the comments to 9-503(a) emphasize, the requirement of the debtor's name is "particularly important" because "[f]inancing statements are indexed under the name of the debtor, and those who wish to find financing statements search for them under the debtor's name." 9-503 cmt. 2. The Court will not construe 9-503 in a manner which essentially overrides the intent and purposes of the filing system.[6] In this proceeding, as to AmPac, the dba expired approximately seventeen months prior to the filing of the financing statement—it is not included in Debtor's correct name. Likewise, Tradition Bank failed to include the required "s" in Debtor's name. It is undisputed that Jim Ross Tires Inc. was the name of public record. Accordingly, neither AmPac nor Tradition Bank have met the requirements of 9-503(a) necessary to perfect their Financing Statements.

The failure of Debtor's name to comply with 9-503, however, is not necessary fatal to the perfection of AmPac's and Tradition Bank's security interests. Recognizing the possibility of errors in the statement of the debtor's name, the legislature enacted 9-506(b) and (c) to address "the effectiveness of financing statement in which the debtor's name is incorrect." 9-506 cmt. 2. 9-506 provides the following:

> (a) A financing statement substantially satisfying the requirements of this subchapter is effective, even if it has minor errors or omissions, unless the errors or omissions make the financing statement seriously misleading.

---

[6] The Court also notes that practically under AmPac's interpretation, creditors could file financing statements with any extraneous words following the proper name and claim to be perfected. For example, a creditor could intend to file a financing statement for Smith, Inc. Based on the Administrative Code, the computer ignores the word "Inc." as a noise word, leaving the computer to process only the word "Smith". Tex. Admin. Code 95.503(4). Under AmPac's interpretation of 9-503(a), a creditor could file a financing statement under the name of Smith Fashion Store or Smith Auto Repair and the creditor could expect to be perfected for an organization whose actual name was Smith, Inc.

(b) Except as otherwise provided in Subsection (c), a financing statement that fails sufficiently to provide the name of the debtor in accordance with Section 9-503(a) is seriously misleading.

(c) If a search of the records of the filing office under the debtor's correct name, using the filing office's standard search logic, if any, would disclose a financing statement that fails sufficiently to provide the name of the debtor in accordance with Section 9-503(a), the name provided does not make the financing statement seriously misleading.

9-506. The comments to 9-506 describe subsection (b) and (c) as stating a "general rule" and an "exception". Id. at cmt. 2. Essentially, even if a debtor's name is misstated on the financing statement, as long as a search under the debtor's correct name would locate the financing statement, the misstatement should not be considered "seriously misleading" as a matter of law. If not "seriously misleading", the financing statement is effective, despite the error, to allow for perfection of the creditor's security interest. The policy of this section is considered "to simplify formal requisites and filing requirements."

AmPac and the Trustee have stipulated that a search under the name "Jim Ross Tires, Inc." does not reveal the existence of the 2002 Financing Statement.[7] Similarly, the Trustee asserts, and Tradition Bank does not dispute, that under a standard search, Tradition Bank's Financing Statement does not appear. The Business and Commerce Code is clear. Absent the exception of 9-506(c), if the debtor's name is not provided in accordance with 9-503, the financing statement is "seriously misleading" and therefore ineffective. 9-506(b). AmPac and the Trustee's stipulation is conclusive that AmPac's Financing Statement does not fit within the exception. Likewise, Tradition Bank has failed to show its statement is not "seriously misleading". The Court, therefore, finds pursuant to 9-506, the statement of Debtor's name on both AmPac's and Tradition Bank's financing statements is "seriously misleading" as a matter of law. * * *

Tradition Bank additionally argues that it should be perfected because its 2004 Financing Statement can be located by using a non-standard "wildcard" search. Since the 2004 Financing Statement can be found with

---

[7] To locate the December 2002 Financing Statement, a search must be conducted using the name, "Jim Ross Tires, Inc. dba HTC Tires & Automotive Centers" or "Jim Ross Tires, Inc. dba HTC Tires and Automotive Centers".

non-standard search logic, Tradition Bank asserts that the Trustee, as one government agency, is ignoring that it is possible to find this Financing Statement and is relying on another government agency to deprive Tradition Bank of its property interest without due process.

The Court finds this argument without merit. The Texas legislature has codified the requirements for determining the effectiveness of financing statements. Tradition Bank did not comply with 9-503 in properly stating Debtor's name. If the debtor's name does not exactly comply with that as required under 9-503, the legislature provided relief under 9-506. 9-506, however, specifically defines the requirement for relief. The statute is not ambiguous. It states that if a search using the "standard search logic" fails to disclose the financing statement, the statement is "seriously misleading" and ineffective. 9-506(c). The Court will not expand this relief to include a Court created non-standard search logic exception to the general rule.

Based on the foregoing, all other arguments are moot. AmPac and Tradition Bank failed to state Debtor's correct name on the Financing Statements as required by 9-503(a). The parties do not fit within the exception of 9-506. Accordingly, the Court finds that the Financing Statements are ineffective to grant security interests in Debtor's collateral. Although this result is harsh, the Court must examine the result in the context of claims between competing creditors. The moment Debtor filed bankruptcy, the Trustee had the authority of a hypothetical judicial lien creditors whose priority, by statute, is superior to that of unperfected creditors. 9-317(a). In that context, the Court must either (i) find for the creditor who did comply with the filing requirements and gave value (i.e., the hypothetical lien creditor); or (ii) find for the creditor who did NOT comply with the filing requirements and gave value. In consideration of the Trustee as a hypothetical judicial lien creditor, the result is apparent. The Trustee's objections are sustained. A separate order will issue.

Peoples Bank v. Bryan Bros. Cattle Co.

United States Court of Appeals, Fifth Circuit, 2007.
504 F.3d 549.

■ REAVLEY, CIRCUIT JUDGE

* * * Because we reverse the summary judgment awarding Bryan the cattle, we must review whether the court correctly denied the motion of Peoples on its claim that its security interest is superior to Cornerstone's. Peoples says its interests are superior, despite the fact that Cornerstone filed its financing statement in 1999, whereas Peoples filed in 2002 and 2003. We hold that the court correctly rejected the priority of Peoples.

Peoples argues that Cornerstone does not have a security interest in the cattle because its financing statement did not use Dickerson's legal name. Cornerstone's financing statement identified "Louie Dickerson" as the debtor instead of by his proper legal name, "Brooks L. Dickerson." Cornerstone argues that its financing statement was not seriously misleading and that Peoples had actual knowledge that Dickerson was known as "Louie Dickerson."

The Mississippi Code, which has enacted a version of the UCC filing statute, states that a financing statement must "[p]rovide[ ] the name of the debtor." 9-502(a)(1). If the debtor is an individual, the financing statement must contain the individual's name. 9-503(a)(4)(A). "A financing statement substantially satisfying the requirements of [the Code] is effective, even if it has minor errors or omissions, unless the errors or omissions make the financing statement *seriously misleading*." 9-506(a) (emphasis added). Failing to sufficiently name the debtor is seriously misleading and makes the financing statement ineffective. 9-506(b).

Cornerstone's financing statement was not seriously misleading. "The purpose of the filing system is to give notice to creditors and other interested parties that a security interest exists in property of the debtor .... Perfect accuracy, however, is not required as long as the financing statement contains sufficient information to put any searcher on inquiry." *In re Glasco, Inc.*, 642 F.2d 793, 795 (5th Cir. 1981) (internal citations and quotations omitted). Peoples was put on inquiry notice that a security interest in the property of "Brooks L. Dickerson" could be listed under the name "Louie Dickerson." Dickerson held himself out to the community as Louie Dickerson, and he used this name in bank accounts, bills of sale, and with others with whom he did business. This is important because evaluating whether a filing is seriously misleading requires a court to examine the facts in a particular case, and the focus should be "on whether potential creditors would have been misled as a result of the name the debtor was listed by" in the financing statement. Id. at 795-96.

Moreover, Peoples had actual notice that Dickerson was known as both "Louie Dickerson" and "Brooks L. Dickerson." In its own files, Dickerson is identified by both names in numerous places. Peoples was not seriously misled by Cornerstone's financing statement. * * *

COMMENTS AND QUESTIONS: THE DEBTOR'S NAME

As a group, these cases set forth many of the frequent mistakes for the debtor's name. *Tyringham Holdings* deals with plausible noise words, meaning words that it would be easy for an individual filling out the financing statement to ignore. And we could imagine that an intelligent search system—take Google as our best case—would filter out these terms in assessing matches. *Pankratz Implement* might just be a typo case—typing "Roger" when "Rodger" was required—or the natural tendency of individuals to code less familiar terms as more common usages. The *Kinderknecht* case, discussed in *Pankratz*, is the stuff of everyday life: everyone calls "Terrance J. Kinderknecht" "Terry" and so Terry it is on the financing statement. And *Jim Ross Tires* involves another typo—the missing "s" in "Tires" in one financing statement—and then the addition of a trade name in the second financing statement. How could more information be hurtful?

The answer to that turns on the design of the statute. Article 9 contemplates that financing statements will be filed in the debtor's legal name—and no more and no less, see 9-502(a) and 9-503—and that subsequent searcher's need do no more than search under that same name. See 9-506(c). 9-506(c), in turn, depends on the "filing office's standard search logic, if any."

As you might guess, to promote uniformity across the states, there has been a push to have a standard standard search logic. *Tyringham Holdings* mentions the International Association of Commercial Administrators, or IACA, for short, found at www.iaca.org. IACA has its own model rules—available at www.iaca.org/node/46—and also links to the administrative rules as adopted in particular states.

COMMENTS AND QUESTIONS: THE 9-506(a) SAFE HARBOR

We need to figure out what to do with mistakes in financing statements. One mistake, discussed below, is a fumble by the filing office itself. In other cases, the secured party may have blown the statement before even heading to the filing office. How should we deal with these mistakes? Strict liability, meaning any mistake, and the financing statement is ineffective? Perhaps some mistakes should matter, and others should not, but what standard would we use to separate the categories?

9-506(c) proceeds from the premise that the focus should be the ability of a subsequent party to find the financing statement:

> If a search of the records of the filing office under the debtor's correct name, using the filing office's standard search logic, if any, would disclose a financing statement that fails sufficiently to provide the name of the debtor in accordance with Section 9-503(a), the name provided does not make the financing statement seriously misleading.

This is a safe harbor for particular kinds of financing statement mistakes. Other mistakes are addressed by 9-506(a):

> A financing statement substantially satisfying the requirements of this part is effective, even if it has minor errors or omissions, unless the errors or omissions make the financing statement seriously misleading.

COMMENTS AND QUESTIONS: MISFILINGS BY THE FILING OFFICER

Will a security interest be perfected if the parties comply with all the provisions of Article 9, but the financing statement is indexed improperly (or lost) by the filing officer and is therefore inaccessible to any potential creditor who looks for it in the right place? 9-516(a) provides that "communication of a record to a filing office and tender of the filing fee or acceptance of the record by the filing office constitutes filing." 9-517, a new section in Revised Article 9, provides that "[t]he failure of the filing office to index a record correctly does not affect the effectiveness of the filed record." This makes explicit that potential creditors searching the files rather than the secured party who previously filed bears the risk that the filing officer will make a mistake.

Even if the mistake is wholly the fault of the filing officer, the secured party who presents the financing statement is not the only innocent party potentially involved; subsequent secured parties who engage in a proper (but fruitless) search also are "innocent." These subsequent searchers lack an effective way of discerning the filing officer's mistake. Is that true, however, of the original secured party? Should it matter whether the dispute is with (a) a subsequent *secured party* or (b) the trustee in bankruptcy (who represents the *unsecured* creditors)? What if the subsequent secured party actually searched the files? Should it make a difference? What if it is shown that the filing officer erroneously fails to file a financing statement but instead returns it to the secured party, who thereupon learns that its financing statement has not been filed? Two months later, another potential creditor searches the files, finds nothing, and then loans money to the debtor, taking a security interest. Who prevails?

SECTION III. THE SECURED CREDITOR'S NAME

9-502(a) requires two names in the financing statement—the debtor's name and the secured creditor's name—which doubles the number of mistakes that can be made. Nonetheless, because financing statements are indexed in the debtor's name, mistakes in the secured creditor's name may be less important. The key difference is that a mistake in the debtor's name may prevent the statement from ever being found; a mistake in the secured creditor's name will not reduce the chance of finding the statement itself. Consider this way to frame the inquiry: when confronted with the legal name and the name used on the financing statement, would a reasonable person be put on notice that the two entities might actually be the same entity? While that is the wrong approach when applied to the debtor's name—given the mistake, the financing statement might never be found and no one would ever be confronted with both names together—it may very well be sensible when applied to mistakes in the secured creditor's name. Consider that idea in connection with the fact patterns that follow.

3-2: MISTAKES IN THE LEGAL NAME

- The secured creditor's legal name is "Really Big Bank, Inc." and it does business under that name only.
- The financing statement shows the name as "Big Bank, Inc."
- The statement lists the correct address for the secured creditor.

¤ Has the secured creditor perfected?

3-3: LEGAL NAMES AND TRADE NAMES
- The secured creditor's legal name is "Really Big Bank, Inc."
- It does business as "BigBank."
- The financing statement shows the name as "BigBank, Inc."
- The statement lists the correct address for the secured creditor.
- ¤ Has the secured creditor perfected?

3-4: THE OMITTED SECURED CREDITOR'S NAME
- Debtor borrows money from two related secured creditors.
- The financing statement lists the debtor's name correctly but omits the name of the second secured creditor.
- ¤ Has the second secured creditor perfected?

Trust Corp. v. Patterson (In re Copper King Inn, Inc.)

United States Court of Appeals, Ninth Circuit, 1990.
918 F.2d 1404.

■ TROTT, CIRCUIT JUDGE

We are asked to decide whether Trust Corporation of Montana ("Trust Corporation") has a perfected security interest in furniture and equipment owned by Copper King Inn, Inc. ("Copper King"), a Montana corporation currently in Chapter 11 bankruptcy. We agree with the bankruptcy court that it does not.

Copper King owned and operated a hotel in Butte, Montana. In 1984 it began to have trouble paying its debts. John T. Noonan and Robert C. Patterson, who were officers, directors and shareholders of Copper King, came to the corporation's rescue, extending loans of $62,500 each in exchange for interest bearing promissory notes. No security was given at the time. Copper King was unable to pay when the notes became due on December 31, 1984, so repayment was deferred until July 31, 1985. When the deadline arrived, Copper King was still in financial straits, and therefore repayment was postponed indefinitely.

Northwest Capital Management & Trust Company ("Northwest") entered the picture at this point. Northwest was predecessor in interest to the Trust Corporation, appellant in this case. It also served as trustee for John T. Noonan Pension & Profit Sharing Plans. On February 1, 1986, Noonan directed Northwest to loan Copper King $100,000. Copper King gave Northwest a one-year interest bearing promissory note in return. In addition, Noonan and Patterson had Copper King sign a security agreement in which it pledged its furniture and equipment to secure both the recent $100,000 loan from Northwest and the earlier $62,500 loans. The agreement erroneously listed Noonan as the creditor of the $100,000 loan. However it also referred to the promissory note Copper King had executed in favor of Northwest, a copy of which was attached.

During the same period, a financing statement was filed with Montana's Secretary of State. The statement listed Patterson and Noonan as secured creditors of Copper King in the total amount of $225,000, and described the items secured. The statement made no mention of Northwest.

On January 15, 1987, Copper King filed a petition under Chapter 11 of the Bankruptcy Code. Copper King's second amended plan for reorganization listed Noonan, Patterson, and (by this time) Trust Corporation as secured creditors in the amount of $225,000. James McDermand, Donald Johnson and Arthur West, dissenting shareholders in Copper King and appellees in this case, filed an objection to the plan on February 12, 1988, challenging the secured status of the three creditors. The bankruptcy court set a hearing for March 9, 1988 to consider these and other objections.

At the hearing, counsel debated the validity of the secured claims. The bankruptcy court instructed them to submit briefs and on June 22, 1988 issued an order in favor of appellees. The order recognized the $100,000 loan from Northwest constituted a security agreement, but held it was not perfected because the financing statement filed with the Secretary of State had not listed Northwest as a creditor. As successor in interest to Northwest, Trust Corporation inherited nothing. * * *

We next address whether Trust Corporation has a perfected security interest in Copper King's furniture and equipment. State law controls the validity and effect of liens in the bankruptcy context. Our analysis therefore is governed by Montana law.

Montana law provides that a "financing statement must be filed to perfect all security interests" except in certain circumstances. [9-310(a)]. Furthermore,

> [a] financing statement is sufficient if it gives the names of the debtor and the secured party, is signed by the debtor, gives an address of the secured party from which information concerning the security interest may be obtained, gives a mailing address

and the county of residence of the debtor, and contains a statement indicating the types or describing the items of collateral. [9-503(a)]. The financing statement here satisfied all the above requirements save one: it did not list Northwest as a secured party. Robert C. Patterson and John T. Noonan were the only creditors so mentioned.

Trust Corporation concedes this omission, but claims it is not decisive. It correctly notes that * * * [9-506(a)] states: "[a] financing statement substantially complying with the requirements of this section is effective even though it contains minor errors which are not seriously misleading." [9-506]. We are not persuaded, however, that the omission of a creditor's name is a minor error.

The structure of the code section is highly suggestive of this result. The first subsection of [9-502] sets forth the information that should be contained in all financing statements. This includes the name and address of the debtor and creditors and a description of collateral. The remaining sub-sections cover specific filing procedures, format instructions and special exceptions. Failure to comply with one of these more technical rules might constitute a "minor error." A deviation in format, for instance, could be considered harmless if the essential terms of the security arrangement were disclosed, albeit in improper order. It is unlikely, however, that the Montana legislature intended to excuse the omission of basic data such as the names of the parties to the security agreement.[7]

As the bankruptcy court recognized, the omission of a creditor's name could be seriously misleading, especially in situations like the one presented here, where officers and shareholders in the debtor company are also its creditors. Potential lenders have a special interest in knowing the identity of such creditors because of the obvious possibility that the insider relationship may lead to collusive behavior that could disadvantage them. Though the financing statement in this case indicated the full amount of debt, it did not disclose the true source of the credit. Noonan's own name was listed, but his company, John T. Noonan Pension & Profit Sharing Plans, and its trustee, Northwest, were nowhere mentioned. The existence

---

[7] The Montana courts have not addressed this question, however the State Supreme Court, in dicta, has stated that "[t]here is no requirement that a party actually see the financing statement in order to have actual knowledge of its contents. However, the party must know the names of the parties, their addresses, and a description of the collateral." First Nat'l Bank of Glasgow v. First Sec. Bank of Montana, 721 P.2d 1270, 1274 (1986) (citations omitted). * * *

of these shadow entities would have been highly significant to anyone contemplating a loan to Copper King. In view of the commercial realities of this case, we find the financing statement was seriously misleading.

Trust Corporation responds that inquiries could have been made to Noonan, who would have clarified any ambiguity. This argument carries little weight. There is no guarantee an inquirer would have received a correct answer in these circumstances, where the incentive to provide misinformation may often be great. More fundamentally, an interested party generally would have little reason to doubt the accuracy of the financing statement in the first place, and therefore little reason to inquire further than the face of the document. Thus, the fact that a listed party stands ready to explain truthfully the nature of the security arrangement, or divulge the existence of other secured creditors, makes little difference. A potential creditor should not have to ask. Potential creditors are entitled to assume that facially adequate financing statements are complete in all material respects.

The fact that no one was deceived in this case also is irrelevant; general UCC principles require courts to measure the accuracy of financing statements from the standpoint of the hypothetical creditor. Faced with the financing statement in this case, a hypothetical creditor could easily have been led astray. * * *

Trust Corporation next cites In re Fried Furniture Corp., 293 F. Supp. 92 (E.D.N.Y. 1968), where a bank and a small business administration both served as secured creditors, though only the bank was listed on the financing statement. The court found the omission insignificant when examined in light of the federal law encouraging joint lending between local banks and small business administrations. No such statutory relationship exists in this case. *Fried Furniture* admittedly can be read for the broader proposition that so long as a financing statement discloses the total debt, potential creditors have no interest in learning the identity of all the secured parties. We reject this principle as unsound, at least in those cases involving insider relationships, where distinguishing between the various creditors becomes more important. * * *

We are mindful that in analyzing the sufficiency of financing statements courts should guard against "the fanatical and impossibly refined reading of such statutory requirements in which courts have occasionally indulged themselves." [9-506, Comment 2]. At the same time, we do not view omission of a creditor's name as a minor detail, especially in the special circumstances surrounding this case. The bankruptcy court's decision, and the district court's affirming order, are therefore affirmed.

COMMENTS AND QUESTIONS

1. How would the *Bollinger* court have addressed the inconsistency between the security agreement and the promissory note for the $100,000 loan from Northwest?
2. Could the secured creditors in *Copper King Inn* have squeezed their facts into the agency pigeonhole (see problem 3-5 below)?
3. The secured creditors argued that notice was created in the financing statement given that the total debt owed was set forth, and relied, as indicated in the case, on the *Fried Furniture* decision. We do not generally use the total debt owed in implementing the policies behind 9-502. Should we?

3-5: SECURED CREDITORS AND AGENTS

- Debtor borrows money from two secured creditors.
- Pursuant to an intercreditor agreement between the secured creditors, Trustco is appointed collateral agent for both secured creditors.
- The financing statement lists the debtor's name correctly and lists the secured creditor as "Trustco, as agent."
- ¤ Has either secured creditor perfected? See 9-502(a)(2), 9-503(d) and 9-102(a)(72)(E).

Cohen v. KB Mezzanine Fund II, LP (In re SubMicron Systems Corp.)

United States Court of Appeals, Third Circuit, 2006.
432 F.3d 448.

■ AMBRO, CIRCUIT JUDGE

Appellant Howard S. Cohen ("Cohen"), as Plan Administrator for the bankruptcy estates of SubMicron Systems Corporation, SubMicron Systems, Inc., SubMicron Wet Process Stations, Inc. and SubMicron Systems Holdings I, Inc. (jointly and severally, "SubMicron"), challenges the sale to an entity created by Sunrise Capital Partners, LP ("Sunrise") of SubMicron's assets under BC 363(b), which authorizes court-approved sales of assets "other than in the ordinary course of business." Sunrise negotiated directly with several—but not all—of SubMicron's creditors before presenting its bid to the District Court. These creditors—The KB Mezzanine Fund II, LP ("KB"), Equinox Investment Partners, LLC ("Equinox"), and Celerity Silicon, LLC ("Celerity") (collectively, the "Lenders")—agreed to contribute toward the purchase of SubMicron's assets new capital along with all of their claims in bankruptcy against Sub-Micron in exchange for equity in the entity formed by Sunrise to acquire the assets—Akrion LLC ("Akrion"). Akrion in turn "credit bid" the full value of the Lenders' secured claims contributed to it as part of its bid for SubMicron's assets pursuant to BC 363(k). * * *

Before its sale in bankruptcy, SubMicron designed, manufactured and marketed "wet benches" for use in the semiconductor industry. By 1997, it was experiencing significant financial and operational difficulties. To sustain its operations in the late 1990s, SubMicron secured financing from several financial and/or investment institutions. On November 25, 1997, it entered into a $15 million working capital facility with Greyrock Business Credit ("Greyrock"), granting Greyrock first priority liens on all of its inventory, equipment, receivables and general intangibles. The next day, SubMicron raised another $20 million through the issuance of senior subordinated 12% notes (the "1997 Notes") to KB/Equinox (for $16 million) and Celerity (for $4 million) secured by liens behind Greyrock on substantially all of SubMicron's assets. Submicron subsequently issued a third set of notes in 1997 (the "Junior 1997 Notes") for $13.7 million, comprising $8.7 million of 8% notes and a $5 million note to The BOC Group, Inc. The Junior 1997 Notes were secured but junior to the security for the 1997 Notes. Despite this capital influx, SubMicron incurred a net loss of $47.6 million for the 1997 fiscal year.

A steep downturn in the semiconductor industry made 1998 a similarly difficult year for SubMicron. By August of that year, it was paying substantially all of the interest due on the 1997 Notes as paid-in-kind senior subordinated notes. On December 2, 1998, SubMicron and Greyrock agreed to renew the Greyrock line of credit, reducing the maximum funds available from $15 to $10 million and including a $2 million overadvance conditioned on SubMicron's securing an additional $4 million in financing. To satisfy this condition, on December 3, SubMicron issued Series B 12% notes (the "1998 Notes") to KB/Equinox (for $3.2 million) and Celerity (for $800,000). The 1998 Notes ranked *pari passu* with the 1997 Notes and the interest was deferred until October 1, 1999. SubMicron incurred a net loss of $21.9 million for the 1998 fiscal year, and at year's end its liabilities exceeded its assets by $4.2 million.

SubMicron's financial health did not improve in 1999. By March of that year, its management determined that additional financing would be required to meet the company's immediate critical working capital needs. To this end, between March 10, 1999 and June 6, 1999, SubMicron issued a total of eighteen Series 1999 12% notes (the "1999 Tranche One Notes") for a total of $7,035,154 (comprising nine notes to KB/Equinox totaling $5,888,123 and nine notes to Celerity totaling $1,147,031). The 1999 Tranche One Notes proved insufficient to keep SubMicron afloat. As a result, between July 8, 1999 and August 31, 1999, KB/Equinox and Celerity made periodic payments to SubMicron (the "1999 Tranche Two Funding") totaling $3,982,031 and $147,969, respectively. No notes were issued in exchange for the 1999 Tranche Two Funding. Between the 1999 Tranche One Notes and the 1999 Tranche Two Funding (collectively, the "1999 Fundings"), KB/Equinox and Celerity advanced SubMicron a total of $9,870,154 and $1,295,000, respectively. (The 1999 Fundings were recorded as secured debt on SubMicron's 10-Q filing with the Securities and Exchange Commission.) Despite the cash infusions, during the first half of 1999 SubMicron incurred a net loss of $9.9 million. On June 30, 1999, SubMicron's liabilities exceeded its assets by $3.1 million.

By January 1999, KB/Equinox had appointed three members to Sub-Micron's Board of Directors. All appointees were either principals or employees of KB/Equinox. By June 1999, following resignations of various SubMicron Board members, KB/Equinox employees Bonaparte Liu and Robert Wickey, and Celerity employee Mark Benham, represented three-quarters of the Board, with SubMicron CEO David Ferran the lone Board member not employed by KB/Equinox or Celerity. * * *

Having established that the District Court properly concluded the 1999 Fundings were debt, we turn to Cohen's assertion that the Lenders did not present a valid *secured* claim. In determining whether claims asserted by creditors in bankruptcy are secured, state law applies. See In re Bollinger Corp., 614 F.2d 924, 925 n. 1 (3rd Cir. 1980). Cohen concedes that, whether one applies Delaware, Pennsylvania, California or New York law, the requirements to obtain a security interest are the same. Thus each state's codification of Uniform Commercial Code F9-203 and F9-302 existing in 1999 requires a written security agreement in favor of the lender describing the collateral and, for the collateral in question (inventory, equipment, receivables and general intangibles), the filing of a properly executed financing statement (unless the inventory and equipment are possessed by the lender or its representative, something normally, and here highly, impractical).

Cohen contends that the Lenders did not comply with state UCC law (and thus the requirements for assertion of a secured claim). The main source of contention is that financing statements filed by the Lenders only list "Equinox Investment Partners, LLC, as Collateral Agent," as the secured party. Cohen asserts that the listing of Equinox solely (and not also KB and Celerity) rendered the financing statement ineffective under the then-extant F9-402(1), which stated that a "financing statement is sufficient if it gives the names of the debtor and the secured party, is signed by the debtor, gives an address of the secured party from which information concerning the security interest may be obtained, gives a mailing address of the debtor and contains a statement indicating the types, or describing the items, of collateral." Official Comment 2 to then-F9-402 indicated that Article 9 employed a "notice filing" system whereby financing statements needed only to indicate that a secured party *"may* have a security interest in the collateral described. Further inquiry from the parties concerned ... [may] be necessary to disclose the complete state of affairs." (Emphasis added.) In this context, "[t]he Uniform Commercial Code does not require that the secured party as listed in [a financing] statement be a principal creditor and not an agent." Indus. Packaging Prods. Co. v. Fort Pitt Packaging Int'l, Inc., 161 A.2d 19, 21 (Pa. 1960). Because the financing statements name both SubMicron as debtor and Equinox as secured party, provide mailing addresses for both entities, and describe the collateral that is subject to the security agreement, we conclude that any interested party would be on notice to communicate with Equinox regarding the status of its (and its principals') interest in SubMicron's assets. This is sufficient for Article 9 perfection purposes.

We also conclude that, on the record before us, there can be no doubt that KB and Celerity were intended secured parties served by their agent, Equinox. Indeed, in the schedule of liabilities filed with the District Court, SubMicron lists KB and Celerity as secured noteholders. The District Court found on the basis of overwhelming evidence that KB and Celerity were intended secured parties with respect to the 1999 Fundings and we discern no basis to believe this determination was erroneous. In sum, we conclude that the Lenders presented valid secured claims for the 1999 Fundings. * * *

COMMENTS AND QUESTIONS

1. How does *SubMicron Systems* differ from *Copper King Inn?* Aren't we missing secured creditor names in both cases?

2. 9-502(a)(1) clearly contemplates that the financing statement can contain the name of "a representative of the secured party." When must that representative status be established? At the time that the financing statement is filed originally? Could a representative take on new secured parties after the fact? What consequences would that have for the filing system?

SECTION IV. IDENTIFICATION OF THE COLLATERAL

Since the financing statement is intended to give notice to third parties that someone has, or may have, a security interest in collateral, the financing statement must be findable. Litigation over whether or not a financing statement has been properly filed is widespread. Less litigation involves the collateral description requirement. If there was no collateral description requirement for the financing statement at all, what would be lost? How much information is necessary to put third parties on notice? The mere existence of a filing may put them on notice and tell them all that they need to know: check with the secured party. Does the debtor have an incentive to ensure that the financing statement contains enough information? 9-502(a)(3) requires the financing statement to "indicate[] the collateral covered by the financing statement." Is this intended to be a different test than the requirement for a security agreement in 9-203(b)(3)(A)— that it contain "a description of the collateral"? Are the reasons for requiring some sort of reference to the collateral in the financing statement the same as the reasons for requiring a description of the collateral in the security agreement? What is the relationship of 9-502(a)(3) and 9-108 addressing the sufficiency of a description? Revised Article 9 addresses this explicitly. 9-504 provides that:

> A financing statement sufficiently indicates the collateral that it
> covers if the financing statement provides: (1) a description of

the collateral pursuant to Section 9-108; or (2) an indication that the financing statement covers all assets or all personal property.

This is an important change. It ties the description requirement for the financing statement directly to 9-108, and it expressly approves the use of "supergenerics," namely, a description of "all assets" or "all personal property." Such a description is insufficient for a security agreement, see 9-108(c). Under the prior version of Article 9, supergeneric descriptions in financing statements were of uncertain status, but the better reasoned cases found them insufficient. See, e.g., In re Boogie Enterprises, Inc., 866 F.2d 1172 (9th Cir. 1989).

As the next case makes clear, we are still left with basic questions of interpretation.

Thorp Commercial Corp. v. Northgate Industries, Inc.

United States Court of Appeals, Eighth Circuit, 1981.
654 F.2d 1245.

■ McMILLIAN, CIRCUIT JUDGE

Franklin National Bank (the Bank) appeals from an order of the District Court for the District of Minnesota granting summary judgment to Thorp Commercial Corp. (Thorp) dismissing the Bank's counterclaim against Thorp for conversion. The conversion counterclaim arose out of Thorp's collection of proceeds from accounts receivable of a third party (the debtor, Northgate Industries, Inc.) who was indebted to both the Bank and Thorp. The Bank argues that the district court erred in holding that the Bank's claim to a security interest in certain of the debtor's accounts receivable failed as against Thorp because the Bank had not filed an adequate financing statement before Thorp perfected its own security interest in the accounts receivable. For the reasons discussed below, we reverse the district court's judgment and remand for further proceedings consistent with this opinion.

At issue in this appeal are security interests taken by both the Bank and Thorp in accounts receivable of a debtor, Northgate Industries, Inc., a firm engaged in repair of structures damaged by fires or other casualties. On May 13, 1971, the Bank lent the debtor $6,500 and under a security agreement took a security interest in collateral including all of the debtor's accounts receivable and proceeds. The security agreement indicated that ongoing financing arrangements were contemplated, because the security agreement purported to secure payment of all indebtedness existing or to be created afterward. The Bank duly filed with the Minnesota Secretary of State on May 21, 1971, a financing statement describing the collateral as "assignment accounts receivable" and "proceeds." * * *

Meanwhile, on April 2, 1972, Thorp set up its financing arrangement with the debtor by entering into a security agreement covering certain collateral, including the debtor's accounts receivable and specifying coverage of both existing accounts and accounts which would be subsequently acquired. Thorp filed a financing statement identical to its security agreement two days later.

Subsequently, both the Bank and Thorp made further loans to the debtor. Prior to the business failure of the debtor, Thorp collected about $685,000 in repayment of its advances and apparently was owed as much as $100,000 more by the debtor; the Bank seems to have advanced a smaller amount, but as much as $60,000 of the debtor's indebtedness to the Bank appears to remain unpaid. * * *

The present case is part of litigation that arose out of the failure of the debtor's business. * * * Thorp commenced a lawsuit against the Bank and others alleging common law fraud and violations of federal securities laws arising in part out of alleged improper relationships between officers of the Bank and the debtor. The Bank filed a counterclaim against Thorp for conversion. The counterclaim is based on a theory that Thorp had converted funds it received from the debtor, because the funds belonged to the Bank, which claimed a prior perfected security interest in the proceeds of the debtor's accounts receivable by virtue of its 1971 agreement and financing statement.

The district court dismissed the Bank's counterclaim because in its view the 1971 financing statement covered only accounts receivable in existence at the time and not accounts receivable subsequently created. The Bank has not disputed that Thorp also had a perfected security interest in the debtor's accounts receivable on the basis of Thorp's April, 1972, security agreement and financing statement securing collateral including the debtor's accounts. Under Article 9, where two creditors hold security interests in the same collateral of the kind involved in this case (a significant portion of the debtor's accounts receivable), the creditor which first perfects its security interest by filing a financing statement has the prior interest, regardless of the time of the creation of the security agreement. [9-322(a)(1)]. Thorp contended, and the district court agreed, that the

1971 financing statement filed by the Bank did not cover any accounts receivable coming into existence subsequent to the date the statement was filed. Thorp's April, 1972, financing statement would then be the earliest one covering the debtor's accounts receivable; therefore, Thorp would have the prior interest in the accounts and the Bank's conversion claim would fail. * * *

The UCC provisions governing secured transactions in the financing of accounts receivable set up a system designed to facilitate arrangements by which a debtor may obtain ongoing financing by using a significant portion of its accounts receivable as collateral. The creditor's security interest in the accounts receivable "attaches" when the debtor signs a valid security agreement covering the collateral, [9-203(b)(3)(A)]; the security interest is "perfected" when the creditor files a financing statement giving notice of the security interest, [9-310(a)]. Both the security agreement and financing statement may cover ongoing financing arrangements; once such an ongoing security arrangement attaches and is perfected, the creditor's interest in the accounts may be secured as collateral for future as well as past advances, despite the rollover process of closing of the debtor's existing accounts and opening of new accounts that were not in existence at the time the arrangement was set up.

The security agreement and financing statement have different functions under the UCC. The security agreement defines what the collateral is so that, if necessary, the creditor can identify and claim it, and the debtor or other interested parties can limit the creditor's rights in the collateral given as security. The security agreement must therefore describe the collateral. [9-203(b)(3)(A)]. The financing statement, on the other hand, serves the purpose of putting subsequent creditors on notice that the debtor's property is encumbered. The description of collateral in the financing statement does not function to identify the collateral and define property which the creditor may claim, but rather to warn other subsequent creditors of the prior interest. The financing statement, which limits the prior creditor's rights vis-à-vis subsequent creditors, must therefore contain a description only of the type of collateral. [9-502(a)(3)]. See James Talcott, Inc. v. Franklin National Bank, 194 N.W.2d 775, 782 & n.3 (1972). One corollary to this principle is that, as between two creditors with security interests in the accounts receivable of the same debtor, the first to provide notice by filing a financing statement has priority. * * *

Because the purpose of the financing statement is to warn subsequent creditors rather than to identify the collateral, the UCC makes clear that the collateral need not be specified in the financing statement but may be described by "type."[6] [9-504, 9-108]. The UCC commentary makes clear that it is ordinarily not expected that the financing statement itself will tell a subsequent creditor what collateral is already covered by a prior security interest. "The notice itself indicates merely that the secured party who has filed may have a security interest in the collateral described. Further inquiry will be necessary to disclose the complete state of affairs." F9-402, official comment 2.

The district court failed to focus upon whether the financing statement contained an adequate description of the type of collateral so that a subsequent creditor would reasonably make further inquiry; instead, the district court considered whether the financing statement adequately described the collateral itself. The district court found great significance in the word "assignment" and reasoned that "assignment accounts" could only refer to specific accounts listed in the security agreement or actually transferred in some other way prior to the filing of the financing statement. In the district court's view, the words "assignment accounts receivable" would not be adequate to cover future accounts receivable under [9-108], which provides, "[A]ny description of personal property ... is sufficient whether or not it is specific if it reasonably identifies what is described."

But, as noted above, the UCC requires a description of only the type of collateral, not the collateral itself, in the financing statement to perfect a security interest. Under [9-108], a description of the collateral in a financing statement "is sufficient whether or not it is specific if it reasonably identifies" the type of collateral. The drafters of the UCC contemplated that the financing statement would need to give only enough description of the collateral to induce a subsequent creditor to make further inquiries. F9-402, official comment 2. The description "reasonably identifies" the type of collateral, therefore, if it would reasonably induce further inquiry.[7]

---

[6] The creditor does have the option of describing the collateral by item in the financing statement, [9-504, 9-108], and therefore perfecting a security interest only in the specific items described. The apparent purpose would be to allow creditors the option to avoid filing a broad financing statement, covering collateral in which no security interest was actually claimed or contemplated as part of ongoing financing arrangements. See 1 G. Gilmore, Security Interests in Personal Property § 15.3, at 479-80 (1965). The financing statement in this case did not list specific accounts, however, but rather a type of collateral, "assignment accounts."

[7] One exception to this principle appears to arise in some cases where the financing statement fails to describe the collateral even by type, but instead simply designates

The district court's approach, however, has support under a line of cases in which courts have largely ignored the function of a financing statement to suggest further inquiry about the collateral. A split in authority exists in this area. For example, one court has held that a financing statement describing the collateral as "accounts receivable" did not cover accounts created after the financing statement was filed, reasoning that some subsequent creditors may have been misled by the failure to specify subsequently created accounts and that the prior creditor could easily have made the financing statement clearer. In re Middle Atlantic Stud Welding Co., 503 F.2d 1133 (3rd Cir. 1974). Other courts have, however, considered financing statements describing the collateral as "accounts receivable" or "accounts" as adequate to cover accounts created subsequent to the filing of the financing statement. Continental Oil Co. v. Citizens Trust & Savings Bank, 225 N.W.2d 209 (1974). Cf. In re Laminated Veneers Co., 471 F.2d 1124 (2d Cir. 1973) (court divided over whether description of collateral in financing statement as "equipment" is adequate to cover automobile).

A substantial theoretical difference seems to underlie these inconsistent results. Under one view a financing statement adequately covers collateral if it reasonably puts a subsequent creditor on notice of a need for further inquiry about the possibility that the collateral is subject to a prior security interest. The reasonableness of the notice would depend on balancing such factors as the difficulty of making further inquiry against factors such as the likelihood the type of collateral described in the financing statement might include the collateral which interests the subsequent creditor.

Under the second view of Article 9, a financing statement suffices to perfect a security interest in collateral if the financing statement itself contains a reasonable description of the collateral. The determination of reasonableness involves balancing such factors as the ease with which the

---

all of the debtor's property or uses some other vague or all-encompassing term. Some courts have held such a financing statement inadequate, because F9-402(1) specifically requires that the financing statement describe the collateral either by type or item. Other courts have, however, held such descriptions adequate to perfect a security interest in all of the debtor's property. Compare In re JCM Coop., Inc., 8 UCC Rep. 247 (W.D. Mich. Bankr. 1970) (Michigan law; financing statement covering "all ... personal property ..." sufficient to perfect security interest in inventory and proceeds), with In re Fuqua, 461 F.2d 1186 (10th Cir. 1972) (Kansas law; financing statement covering "all personal property" insufficient to perfect security interest in livestock and equipment).

prior creditor could make the description of the collateral more precise or clearer against factors like the danger that a subsequent creditor might fail to recognize that the collateral is covered. * * *

The [view that] requires that the financing statement by its own terms describe the collateral cannot be supported under Article 9. Article 9 simply does not require that the financing statement describe anything more than the type of collateral and leaves to interested parties the burden of seeking more information. Ultimately, such a requirement for a description of the collateral itself in a financing statement would eliminate the distinction between the financing statement and the security agreement, because the only way for a creditor to make sure that the financing statement describes the collateral would be to use the same description which identified the collateral in the security agreement setting up the security interest. Indeed, the district court suggested in the instant case that the "optimum practice" is for the creditor "to describe the collateral in the financing statement exactly as it appears in the security agreement." Such a requirement was rejected by the drafters of the UCC who specifically commented,

> the financing statement is effective to encompass transactions under a security agreement not in existence and not contemplated at the time the notice was filed, if the description of collateral in the financing statement is broad enough to encompass them. Similarly, the financing statement is valid to cover after-acquired property ... whether or not mentioned in the financing statement.

F9-402, official comment 2 (Official Draft 1972). One central purpose of allowing a broad financing statement is to allow a creditor that envisions an ongoing financing arrangement to protect the priority of its interest by filing at an early date a notice to third parties which will cover the existing arrangement and broad range of potential future modifications. By requiring a description of the collateral in the financing statement itself, courts would destroy this flexibility.[10]

---

[10] Another problem with requiring a description of the collateral in the financing statement is the possibility that a debtor might want to enter into a security agreement including information the debtor might not want to put on the public record for competitors to see. Cf. F9-208 [9-210] & official comment 2 (list of collateral available only to debtor so that casual inquirers and competitors cannot obtain it). A vague financing statement referring generally to the type of collateral can obviate this

The Minnesota courts have not addressed the precise question before us. In a case involving similar questions, however, the state supreme court explained,

> [o]nce a financing statement is on file describing property by type, the entire world is warned, not only that the secured party may already have a security interest in property of that type ..., but that it may later acquire a perfected security interest in property of the same type acquired by the debtor in the future.
>
> ....
>
> ... The code very simply and briefly provides for a notice-filing procedure with a minimum of information required to be publicized in a filed financing statement. All that is required is a minimal description, and it may be by type or kind. The statement need not necessarily contain detail as to collateral, nor any statement of quantity, size, description or specifications, or serial numbers. No preciseness is required with respect to whether the collateral exists at the time of filing or is to be acquired thereafter ....

James Talcott, Inc. v. Franklin National Bank, supra, 194 N.W.2d at 783, 786. Minnesota thus appears to be one of the jurisdictions which has adopted the first view discussed above, that a financing statement covers the collateral in question if it merely makes it reasonable for a subsequent creditor interested in the collateral to make further inquiries.

The Minnesota Supreme Court's reasoning seems fundamentally inconsistent with the Oklahoma court's decision in Georgia-Pacific Corp. v. Lumber Products Co., 590 P.2d 661 (Okla. 1979). If the financing statement covers not only existing security interests in the type of collateral described but also security interests which may arise in the future, then a financing statement covering "assignment accounts receivable" would cover any assignment of the debtor's accounts receivable that might exist or be made in the future. The word "assignment" might mean a specific assignment of named accounts receivable but is broad enough to refer to a general assignment of all the debtor's accounts receivable, including those acquired in the future. A subsequent creditor, faced with notice that a security interest may exist or be created in any or all of the debtor's accounts,

---

problem. The interest of a subsequent creditor can be protected in such a case from the danger that the prior financing statement will enable the prior creditor to obtain a superior security interest by a subordination agreement from the prior creditor.

would certainly have reasonable grounds for inquiring further before relying on any of the debtor's accounts for collateral. We conclude that under
Minnesota law applying the UCC the financing statement covering "assignment accounts receivable" was adequate to perfect the Bank's security
interest in accounts acquired subsequent to the filing of the financing
statement, whether or not there was a specific assignment of particular accounts.

In reaching this conclusion we do not overlook the district court's concern that a creditor should not benefit from use of a misleading or overreaching financing statement. The notice filing concept has a primary
purpose of facilitating ongoing financing arrangements not merely by the
first creditor on the scene but also subsequent creditors. The requirement
for filing a financing statement provides notice, at least theoretically, to
subsequent creditors of what assets may already be encumbered by prior
creditors. The financing statement would not provide notice where the
description of collateral is misleading, for example, if the description were
simply wrong or if the description seemingly would not cover the collateral
but contained coverage under some hidden ambiguity that could not be
considered reasonable notice. Cf. [9-506(a)] (financing statement is adequate despite minor errors which are not seriously misleading). Even assuming the words "assignment accounts receivable" could be interpreted
narrowly to refer to a single assignment of specific accounts receivable, the
words also have an obvious alternative broad meaning; in the present case
notice filing has served its purpose of alerting subsequent creditors to the
need for further inquiry. The UCC puts the burden on the subsequent
creditor to seek clarification.[11]

Accordingly, the judgment of the district court is reversed and the case
is remanded for further proceedings consistent with this opinion.

---

[11] There is no question in this case of "overreaching" by the subsequent creditor, a
problem which has been recognized by some commentators especially in the financing of purchases of consumer goods where the creditor may draw the financing
statement much broader than the actual collateral taken and thereby limit the debtor's access to further credit or give the first creditor unfair leverage over subsequent
creditors.

COMMENTS AND QUESTIONS

1. What role does the description requirement play? *Thorp* gives two visions. The first is that the financing statement itself must contain a reasonable description of the collateral. The second is that the financing statement suffices if it puts a subsequent creditor on notice of the need to inquire about the scope of the prior security interest. How should the role that financing statements play in assigning priority influence the choice between these two approaches?

2. For a discussion of the benefits and drawbacks of mere notice inquiry, see Linda J. Rusch, The Article 9 Filing System: Why a Race-Recording Model is Unworkable, 79 Minn. L. Rev. 565 (1995).

COMMENTS AND QUESTIONS: THE REQUIREMENT OF A DESCRIPTION IN THE FINANCING STATEMENT

If "notice" to inquire further is the sole purpose of a financing statement, why is there any requirement at all to "indicate[] the collateral covered by the financing statement"? Isn't the notice to inquire further accomplished simply by seeing the debtor's (and secured party's) name, without more? Is anything further gained by requiring a description of collateral? See Morris Shanker, A Proposal for a Simplified All-Embracing Security Interest, 14 U.C.C.L.J. 23 (1981) (questions why one requires a description if a security interest in all assets can be obtained "by simply copying from a boiler-plate list of words found in Article 9 ..."). Overbroad financing statements may make it more difficult for a debtor to get secured loans in the future. However, even in the case of filings that do not necessarily involve a series of transactions, the financing statement is effective to encompass transactions under a security agreement not in existence and not contemplated at the time the notice was filed, if the description of collateral in the financing statement is broad enough to encompass them. Similarly, the financing statement is valid to cover after-acquired property and future advances under security agreements whether or not mentioned in the financing statement.

Does the focus on notice miss something quite important about the role of the description requirement? Doesn't this overlook the important independent legal significance of the description in the financing statement? It is that description which defines the extent of the priority that a creditor may claim, regardless of whether that creditor currently holds a security interest to the full extent of the filed description. If the point of the financing statement is to allow a subsequent creditor to inquire regarding the debtor's preexisting security interests, no description need be required. Having the names of both the debtor and the secured creditor would allow any interested creditor to inquire regarding the underlying arrangements and to make whatever contractual agreement regarding priority as was desired. No description requirement is akin to creating a pure priority regime. If no description were required but one were allowed, a description would serve as the means by which the debtor limited the extent to which it had to negotiate contractual priority agreements with subsequent creditors. We would have to worry about the effect of this on nonconsensual creditors, but we are really talking about the default rule, as nothing prevents a creditor right now from achieving an all-encompassing priority through a comprehensive financing statement.

Article 9 rejects this. Instead, the breadth of the property description in the financing statement defines the extent of the protected priority. We could simply give the first-filing creditor a general priority over the assets of the debtor. We do not do that, and the way in which we limit the priority is through the description requirement. This makes Article 9 a *reified priority system*. Priority is defined with reference to particular property. The secured creditor has priority in inventory or equipment or something else. The secured creditor does not have a general priority over all of the debtor's assets. The purpose of the description in the financing statement is to define the extent of the creditor's potential priority. That means that there is a natural limiting device for overbroad descriptions. An overbroad description complicates the debtor's financing life going forward. If the financing statement is broader than the security agreement, other creditors will fear subsequent collateral grants to the first-filed creditor. They will insist on contractual subordination to achieve the codal subordination that would have otherwise been available through a more-tailored original financing statement.

3-6: THE SCOPE OF THE FINANCING STATEMENT
- On January 1st, Bank lends $10,000 to Corp, takes a security interest in equipment and files an appropriate financing statement.
- On February 1st, Bank lends an additional $10,000 to Corp, takes a security interest in equipment, but does not file an appropriate financing statement.

¤ To what extent is Bank perfected?

3-7: AMBIGUOUS DESCRIPTIONS

- Bank files an otherwise proper financing statement listing Debtor as debtor and Bank as secured party, and the collateral covered as "Debtor's car." (Assume no applicable certificate of title statute.) Debtor owns, however, at all relevant times, two cars.

¤ Is the financing statement effective? Does it matter whether Bank and Debtor have entered into a security agreement specifying one of the two cars as collateral? Does it matter whether Bank knows that Debtor has two cars? What if the security agreement between Bank and Debtor actually listed *both* of Debtor's cars as collateral?

- Simultaneously while loaning Debtor money, Bank files an otherwise proper financing statement listing Debtor as debtor and Bank as secured party, and the collateral covered as "Debtor's 1999 Pontiac." (Assume no applicable certificate of title statute.) Debtor, however, has owned at all relevant times a 1998 Pontiac, not a 1999 Pontiac.

¤ Is the financing statement effective? See 9-506(a). (Would a security agreement making the same mistake be effective?) What if Debtor owned a 1997 Buick at all relevant times, and never owned a Pontiac?

3-8: MISSING SCHEDULES

- Bank enters into an adequate written security agreement with Debtor, covering designated equipment. The financing statement describes the collateral as "various equipment, see Schedule 'A' attached hereto."

- Bank, when filing the financing statement, fails to include Schedule A.

¤ Does the financing statement, as filed, contain an adequate description for purposes of the requirements of 9-502(a)(3)?

¤ What if the typed language in the space provided below the printed legend "This financing statement covers the following types or items of property," simply stated "see Schedule A attached hereto" and no Schedule A was attached?

SECTION V. PERFECTION BY POSSESSION

While 9-310(a) suggests that Article 9 views filing as the principal method by which an *enforceable* security interest can be turned into a *perfected* security interest, filing is not necessarily the only way or even, sometimes, a permissible way, of perfecting a security interest in certain collateral. There are four other principal ways of perfecting Article 9 security interests in collateral not subject to federal rules under 9-109(c)(1) that you should be familiar with: (1) perfection by possession of the collateral under 9-313; (2) perfection through control; (3) automatic perfection under 9-309 (i.e., perfection upon attachment, without more); and (4) perfection by compliance with certificate of title (or similar) laws. In this section, we consider perfection through possession.

With respect to a great deal of collateral, the secured party has a choice: it may perfect either by possession of the collateral *or* by filing a financing statement. 9-313(a) provides that a security interest in negotiable documents, goods, instruments, money or tangible chattel paper may be perfected by taking possession. 9-312(a) provides that a security interest in chattel paper, negotiable documents, instruments or investment property may be perfected by filing. And 9-310 sets out the general rule, that unless otherwise called off, a financing statement must be filed to perfect a security interest. Taking all of this together, we see quickly that possession or filing works for instruments, goods, negotiable documents and tangible chattel paper. Money can only be perfected through possession (9-312(b)(3)).

The tricky questions regarding possession arise when the secured party does not have possession but wants to rely on possession by a third party. The statute addresses this at 9-312(c) and (d) and again at 9-313(c).

3-9: SIMPLE POSSESSION

- Debtor approaches Pawnbroker to borrow money. Debtor offers to post his gold watch as collateral for a $50 loan.
- Debtor receives a written receipt, which specifies an interest rate and a due date, and turns over possession of the watch.
- ¤ Has a perfected security interest been created?

3-10: POSSESSION AND BAILEES

- Suppose that the pawnbroker had run short on space and gave the watch to a third person to hold, as the pawnbroker's bailee.
- ¤ Does this change the outcome? See 9-313(c).
- Suppose the pawnbroker appointed the debtor as the pawnbroker's agent to hold the collateral.
- ¤ Does this change the outcome?

3-11: POSSESSION AND CLASSIFICATION

- Debtor wishes to borrow money from Bank and use as collateral her rare coin collection but, as an avid hobbyist, Debtor does not want to turn possession of the coin collection over to Bank.
- ¤ Can Bank perfect by filing a financing statement? Does it matter if Debtor's coin collection consists of: (a) Lincoln pennies; (b) $10 gold pieces; (c) Mexican pesos; (d) coins from ancient Greece and Rome? See 1-201(b)(24).

In a world in which assets are simple tangible assets—a plow or a hoe for example—there is no trouble identifying *what* must be possessed if the secured party chooses to rely on possession to perfect its security interest. As more and more value is represented by complex assets, which may have a mix of tangible and intangible components, possession becomes a more difficult undertaking. You should note that 9-313 makes an important change in the way in which possession by a third party operates. Former F9-305, set forth in full in the following case, simply required that a bailee in possession receive notice of the security interest of the secured party. In contrast, 9-313 requires that the "person in possession authenticate[] a record acknowledging that it holds possession of the collateral for the secured party's benefit."

Coral Petroleum, Inc. v. Banque Paribas (In re Coral Petroleum, Inc.)

United States Bankruptcy Court, S.D. Texas, 1985.
50 Bankr. 830.

■ MANUEL D. LEAL, BANKRUPTCY JUDGE

This matter, before the Court on plaintiff Coral Petroleum's complaint for a declaratory judgment, raises several complex issues. The major issues are

whether a 30 million dollar promissory note is to be classified as an instrument or a general intangible under the Uniform Commercial Code
and whether the defendants Banque Paribas and MBank, N.A. properly
perfected their security interests in the promissory note so as to prevent
the debtor from avoiding their respective interests under BC 544. Because
the Court concludes that the promissory note is an instrument, and because defendants Banque Paribas and MBank, N.A. did not take possession of the note or satisfy the requirements of establishing constructive
notice pursuant to [9-313(c)], the Court holds that their respective interests are unperfected and the debtor can recover the proceeds pursuant to
BC 544. Accordingly, the declaratory relief sought by the debtor is
granted and the motion to dismiss is denied. Intervenor MBank's motion
is also denied.

Debtor Coral Petroleum, Inc. commenced this adversary on July 8,
1983, by filing a complaint seeking a declaratory judgment that a lien on a
promissory note held by Banque Paribas, defendant herein, (hereinafter
"Paribas") is voidable under BC 544(a). By answer dated October 4, 1983,
Paribas moved for dismissal of the complaint in all respects, claiming that
its interest in the promissory note was superior to all other claimants.
MBank Houston, N.A. (hereinafter "MBank") intervened in the adversary
by court order entered on January 30, 1985, requesting that its interests be
recognized as superior to, or equal to, Paribas' interests. * * *

On or about September 17, 1982, Coral Petroleum Development, Inc.,
a Texas corporation and a wholly owned subsidiary of Coral, sold substantially all of its United States oil and gas producing properties to Tricentrol
Resources, Inc., a Delaware corporation. In return, Tricentrol Resources,
Inc., made and delivered to Coral Development, Inc., an interest-bearing
installment promissory note in the principal amount of 30 million dollars
(hereinafter "Tricentrol Note"). The obligation of Tricentrol Resources,
Inc., under the note was guaranteed by its parent corporation, Tricentrol,
PLC., pursuant to a written guarantee. On the same day, Coral Development, Inc., assigned the Tricentrol Note to Coral Petroleum, Inc., in consideration for intercompany advances.

On September 17, 1982, Coral entered into a credit agreement with the
First National Bank of Chicago (hereinafter "First Chicago") pursuant to
which First Chicago agreed to lend Coral up to 30 million dollars. Simultaneously, Coral made and delivered to First Chicago its interest-bearing
installment promissory note (hereinafter "Coral Note") in the principal
amount of 30 million dollars. As security for this loan, Coral pledged

among other things, the Tricentrol Note to First Chicago, delivered possession of the Tricentrol Note to First Chicago and executed a security agreement for the $30 million amount. Coral's borrowing under the credit agreement totaled 27 million dollars and on February 18, 1983, both the Coral Note and the credit agreement were amended to reflect Coral's having borrowed 27 million dollars. From October 27, 1982, to August 1, 1983, the note was in the exclusive physical possession of First Chicago in Chicago, Illinois. * * *

Banque Paribas and Coral entered into several loan agreements. On July 31, 1981, Coral borrowed 24.5 million dollars from Banque de Paris de Pays-bas (predecessor to Banque Paribas) coupled with a 10.5 million dollar loan from the Royal Bank of Canada. Paribas was granted an interest in certain collateral, including the following: "(iii) all other personal property now owned or hereafter acquired by the company, of every kind and description, tangible or intangible, including but not limited to, all money, goods, instruments, securities, documents, contract rights, patent and trademark rights, general intangibles, credits, claims demands and any other property, rights and interests of the company; (iv) any and all proceeds of the foregoing."

Paribas and Coral entered into a second loan agreement on August 30, 1982, in which Paribas lent Coral the principal amount of 40 million dollars, secured by a security agreement in certain collateral.

On January 27, 1983, a third loan was entered into between Coral and Paribas whereby Paribas loaned Coral 15 million dollars. In return, Coral granted Paribas a security interest in certain artwork that it owned and made two stock pledges, one of stock in Coral Petroleum Canada, Inc. and the other of stock in Coral Petro Development, Ltd., a Canadian Company. At the closing on January 27, 1983, of the 15 million dollar loan, Mr. Sudhaus, vice-president of Coral, signed a letter agreement which assigned all the payments received by Coral from the Tricentrol Note to Paribas. Mr. Sudhaus testified that Coral was willing to grant Paribas a security interest in the Tricentrol Note but never executed a document which specifically said that the excess funds of the Tricentrol Note would be "specific security" for the 15 million dollar loan. Following the closing of the 15 million dollar loan, Paribas filed a financing statement with the Texas Secretary of State relating specifically to Coral's artwork. Paribas also sent a letter to the gallery which held the artwork requesting that it sign an agency agreement designating Paribas as the secured party. However, no such filing or agreement was sent to First Chicago by

Paribas with respect to the Tricentrol Note. Mr. Forbes, a loan representative at First Chicago, testified that it was standard banking practice to obtain internal approval from senior management and a written agency agreement signed by all parties when a bank acts as agent or bailee for another secured party with respect to instruments in its possession.

Paribas perfected its security interest in Coral's general intangibles by filing statements with the Secretary of State of Texas on March 9, 1979, August 10, 1981, and October 27, 1981.

On January 18, 1977, Coral Petroleum, Inc., and Capital National Bank executed a security agreement in which Capital was granted a security interest in:

> [a]ll of the personal property and fixtures of the Debtor wherever located and whether now owned or in existence or hereafter acquired or created, of every kind and description, tangible or intangible, including, without limitation all inventory, equipment, farm products, documents, instruments, chattel paper, accounts, contract rights and general intangibles, such terms having the meaning ascribed by the Uniform Commercial Code.

MBank lent Coral 3 million dollars pursuant to a 1 million dollar promissory note executed on March 24, 1983, and a 2 million dollar promissory note executed on April 8, 1983. On February 11, 1977, MBank filed its financing statement covering Coral's general intangibles and instruments with the Secretary of State of Texas. On January 21, 1982, MBank filed a continuation statement with the Texas Secretary of State, as to its security interest

On August 29, 1980, several of the creditors of Coral, each of whom held perfected security interests in the same collateral, executed an inter-creditor agreement which provided, in essence, that a creditor with a "specific security interest" has "priority to the extent of all obligations, direct or contingent, of the debtor to such creditors secured thereby over any general collateral."[3] The inter-creditor agreement was signed by Banque de Paris et des Pay-Bas (now Banque Paribas), and Capital National Bank. First National Bank of Chicago was made a party to the inter-creditor agreement on or about February 18, 1983. (There was no testimony as to the events leading to First Chicago's joining this agreement.)

---

[3] The text of the Inter-Creditor Agreement is reprinted in the Appendix.

After filing its petition, Coral and First Chicago entered into an agreement whereby Coral was to sell the Tricentrol Note to First Chicago for 28.5 million dollars. The sale of the note would allegedly yield a surplus of 1.9 million dollars. First Chicago and Coral had negotiated the agreement prior to bankruptcy and were set to close the transaction on June 2, 1983, before the bankruptcy petition was filed. At that time, Mr. Sudhaus, vice-president of Coral, was located at Banque Paribas offices in New York. He asked Mr. Boyd and Mr. Forbes to meet him at Paribas' offices to close the transaction. There was conflicting evidence as to whether Paribas indicated its interest in the Tricentrol Note at that time. Both Boyd and Forbes testified that the subject of Paribas' interest did not come up in conversation on June 2, 1983, even though Paribas was well aware of the sales transaction involving the Note. Mr. Aiello, vice-president and general counsel of Paribas, testified that he mentioned to either Boyd or Forbes or both that Paribas had a "piece of the pie" on the surplus of the note. On the following day, June 3, 1983, Mr. Aiello sent a telex to First Chicago informing them that Paribas claimed an interest in the surplus of the Tricentrol Note.

Coral sought the approval of the bankruptcy court on the sale of the Tricentrol Note and Guarantee to First Chicago. Banque Paribas asserted that it was entitled to the proceeds of the Tricentrol Note by virtue of a junior security interest. The parties entered into a stipulation styled a partial compromise which was approved by the Honorable E.H. Patton, Jr., on August 1, 1983. Coral was allowed to sell the Tricentrol Note free and clear of all liens asserted on the Note to First Chicago with "any and all asserted liens, encumbrances, security and other interests in or to the Tricentrol Note attach (sic) to the surplus proceeds generated by the sale of the Tricentrol Note...." The surplus was remitted to Paribas pending the determination of the validity of Paribas' alleged interest. The order stated that if any court finds Coral to be entitled to the funds, Paribas will remit them with interest from the date of delivery to the date of disgorgement. The order provided the opposite result if Paribas prevailed. Nothing in the order was to prejudice the right of any party to come in and make a claim to the surplus funds.

Coral argues that the Tricentrol Note must be classified as an instrument under the Uniform Commercial Code. If this is the case, Paribas and MBank hold unperfected interests in the note due to their lack of possession of the Note. Paribas and MBank argue the note must be classified as a general intangible, and, as such, their respective filings operated to perfect their respective interests in the proceeds of the Tricentrol Note. Paribas further argues that it alone is entitled to the proceeds because the side letter of January 27, 1983, created a specific security interest which entitled Paribas to priority over Coral's other creditors pursuant to the terms of the inter-creditor agreement outlined above. MBank argues that this letter did not create a specific security interest and Paribas must share the proceeds of the Tricentrol Note pro-rata with all the other creditors who had an interest in the note. MBank further argues that a proportion of Paribas' interest is subordinate to MBank's by virtue of Paribas' actions in exempting certain loans made to Coral from the inter-creditor agreement. Finally, Paribas and MBank assert that if this Court finds the Tricentrol Note to be an instrument, as Coral alleges, they perfected their interest by notice to First Chicago.

* * * [T]his Court concludes the Tricentrol Note is an "instrument." * * *

Section F9-304(1) [9-312(a)] provides that "a security interest in money or instruments ... can be perfected only by the secured party's taking possession, except as provided in subsection (4) and (5) of this section...." Neither Paribas nor MBank had possession of the Note, so they cannot claim perfection pursuant to the above cited section.

Section F9-305 [9-313] provides that:

> A security interest in letters of credit and advices of credit Subsection (b)(1) of Section 5.116, goods, instruments (other than certificated securities), money, negotiable documents or chattel paper may be perfected by the secured party's taking possession of the collateral. *If such collateral other than goods covered by a negotiable document is held by a bailee, the secured party is deemed to have possession from the time the bailee receives notification of the secured party's interest.* A security interest is perfected by possession from the time possession is taken without relation back and continues only so long as possession is retained, unless otherwise specified in this chapter. The security interest may be otherwise perfected as provided in this chapter before or after the period of possession by the secured party. (Emphasis added)

Article 9 of the Uniform Commercial Code has no definition of a "bailee," therefore, pursuant to 1-103 this Court will look to common law principles for the definition. Since the Court has classified the Note as an instrument, Illinois law would apply. Under Illinois law, "a bailment is the delivery of goods for some purpose, upon a contract, express or implied, that after the purpose has been fulfilled they shall be redelivered to the bailor, or otherwise dealt with according to his directions, or kept till he reclaims them." Kirby v. Chicago City Bank and Trust Co., 403 N.E.2d 720, 723 (1980) quoting Knapp, Stout and Co. v. McCaffrey, 52 N.E. 98 (1899). A bailment is a consensual relationship that can be established by express contract or implication. An implied-in-fact bailment is determined by the surrounding facts such as benefits received by the parties, the parties intentions, the kind of property involved and the opportunity of each party to exercise control over the property. Texas law is similar to the law of Illinois.

Paribas asserts that its purported oral notification prior to bankruptcy and follow up telex after the bankruptcy was sufficient notification to First Chicago to make its interest perfected. Initially, there was no express agency agreement between First Chicago and Paribas. As to an implied bailment, Paribas has not produced enough evidence to support the establishment of this relationship. "A secured party depending for the perfection of its security interest upon the possession of a F9-305 bailee must establish the existence of a bailment consistent therewith." In re Kontaratos, 10 Bankr. 956, 968 (Bankr. D. Me. 1981). Paribas has failed to do so.

In the cases that held that a security interest was perfected in goods held by a bailee, the bailee was a third party who did not assert an interest in the bailed property. In our case, the bailee which Paribas alleges it notified of its interest is an interested stakeholder, namely the holder of a perfected security interest in the note. The reasoning for this distinction is clear although not expressly stated in the cases which address the point. By requiring the bailee to have no interest in the instrument in its possession, the danger of the bailee trying to pass the instrument off as his own is averted. The commercial world can rely upon an independent agent to represent accurately that the liens on the instrument do, in fact, exist. To require an interested party to inform the world of all other lien claimants, without an express agreement, would be a duty which the case law does not impose for the reason that the interested lienholder, who is also a bailee, would communicate conflicting signals to the commercial world for he would exercise unilateral control over the instrument while supposedly holding it for the benefit of another secured party. These are inconsistent positions that would cause chaos in commercial transactions.

Paribas has cited no cases which extend F9-305 to the fact situation of a senior perfected security interest holder acting as bailee for a junior perfected security holder. Paribas relies heavily on In re Chapman,

5 U.C.C.R.S. 649 (W.D. Mich. 1968), a case which held that "possession in one secured party should give notice of all secured interests known to the party having possession." However that case is easily distinguishable on its facts. The junior lien holder was in possession of the security and the court reasoned that anyone who inquired of the junior lien holder would not only obtain information of Thomas' secured interest but also of the senior lienholder. This is because when the borrower assigned the note as security for the junior interest, he did so subject to the senior lien in an assignment agreement. In our case, there was no such agreement. Coral did not give Paribas possession of the note subject to First Chicago's interest. * * *

Paribas' final argument on constructive possession is by analogy to F9-305 and by construction of the UCC to "permit the continued expansion of commercial transactions." This argument must be rejected for the following reasons. First Chicago testified at trial that it was standard banking procedure for the parties to an agency agreement to execute a formal written document. Paribas executed all of the necessary documents to perfect its security interest in the artwork and two stock pledges which were negotiated as the collateral for the 15 million dollar loan. Paribas did not execute an agency agreement or present any evidence that it had prepared a draft of an agency agreement to transmit to First Chicago. Paribas, as a major financial institution, must be charged with knowledge of the standard banking practice to establish a bailment relationship. Its inaction, coupled with its active role in perfecting its interest in other collateral, leads the court to the logical conclusion that Paribas did not believe that First Chicago was acting as its agent. * * * In our case, this Court cannot hold that First Chicago was Paribas' bailee without First Chicago having the opportunity to agree or to refuse to be Paribas' agent as to the Tricentrol Note. For this Court to so hold would be paramount to creating new law which this Court will properly leave to the legislative branch.

MBank raised the argument that since First Chicago was a party to the Inter Creditor-Agreement it had notice of all the other creditor's claim to the Tricentrol Note. This argument could be persuasive but insufficient evidence was produced to support this conclusion. The agreement, on its face, does not state explicitly or implicitly that any secured party who possesses an instrument acts as bailee or agent for all the other secured parties. The agreement deals with the priority between conflicting security interests which are *perfected* irrespective of the time and order of perfection, not the perfection of the security interest itself. In order to qualify as having a specific or general security interest under the Inter-Creditor Agreement, the creditor's security interest must be perfected. There was no evidence produced that First Chicago, by becoming a party to the Inter-Creditor Agreement intended to act as bailee for Paribas or MBank thereby perfecting their respective interests pursuant to F9-305. For the forementioned reasons, Paribas does not have a perfected security interest in the Tricentrol Note because it lacked possession. * * *

Having determined that the Tricentrol Note is an instrument and the Banks did not hold a perfected security interest, either by possession or notice under F9-305, this Court concludes that the debtor can avoid both Paribas' and MBank's interests pursuant to BC 544. * * * Accordingly, it is ordered that Paribas shall promptly remit to Coral the entire amount of the Tricentrol Note surplus, together with interest calculated at the highest rate which Paribas is currently charging to Coral, from the date Paribas received the funds to the date of disgorgement. * * *

APPENDIX

Inter-Creditor Agreement re: Coral Petroleum. Inc., Coral Petroleum (USA), Inc., Vulcan Refining Company, Coral Petroleum Syria, Inc., Kakwa Oil & Gas, Inc.

The subject (herein called the "Debtor") from time to time incurs obligations, direct and/or contingent, to each of the undersigned (herein called a "Creditor"), some or all of which obligations are secured, either wholly or partially, by Collateral. Each Creditor has filed or may file a financing statement under the Uniform Commercial Code and the Creditors desire to agree among themselves as to the relative priority of their respective security interests in Collateral. It is hereby agreed:

1. "Collateral" means all personal property and fixtures of the Debtor whether now or hereafter existing or now owned or hereafter acquired and wherever located, of every kind and description, tangible or intangible, including, but not limited to, all goods, documents, instruments, chattel paper, accounts, contract rights and general intangibles and including the products and proceeds thereof and accessions thereto, constituting security for obligations of the Debtor, direct or contingent.

2. "Specific Security Interest" means a perfected and enforceable security interest of a Creditor in any of the following Collateral, including the products and proceeds thereof and accessions thereto:

(a) Collateral in the possession of the Creditor (or an agent [or] bailee on its behalf); or

(b) Collateral made available to the Debtor by the Creditor (or its agent or bailee) pursuant to a trust receipt or other security agreement the effect of which is to continue the Creditor's security interest therein; or

(c) Collateral covered by a non-negotiable document issued in the name of the Creditor or as to which the Creditor (or an agent or bailee on its behalf) controls possession through a negotiable document; or

(d) Collateral which is an obligation owed by the Creditor to the Debtor; or

(e) Collateral which is specifically identified in a security agreement, or in another writing, delivered to the Creditor at or about the time the security interest attaches.

3. "General Security Interest" is any perfected and enforceable security interest of a Creditor in Collateral, however arising, other than a Specific Security Interest.

4. A Specific Security Interest of a Creditor in Collateral has priority to the extent of all obligations, direct or contingent, of the Debtor to such Creditor secured thereby over any General Security Interest of another Creditor in the same Collateral.

5. If Specific Security Interests of two or more Creditors attach to the same Collateral, the Specific Security Interest which is a purchase money security interest has priority over any other Specific Security, except that a Specific Security Interest of the type referred to in paragraph 2(c) hereof has, in the absence of notice of another security interest stamped on or affixed to the document (notwithstanding anything in paragraph 7 relating to notice), priority over any Specific Security Interest of the type referred to in paragraph 2(b), and Specific Security Interest of the type referred to in paragraph 2(b), and Specific Security Interests of two or more Creditors of the type referred to in paragraph 2(b) rank equally in priority.

6. The General Security Interest of each Creditor in Collateral ranks equally in priority with the General Security Interest of each other Creditor in the same Collateral.

7. The priorities specified herein are applicable irrespective of the time or order of attachment or perfection or security interests or the time or order of filing of financing statements or the giving or failure to give notice of the acquisition or expected acquisition of purchase money or other security interests.

8. Except as herein otherwise specifically provided, priority shall be determined in accordance with law. * * *

10. This Agreement shall be governed by the laws of the State of New York. Unless the context otherwise requires, all terms used herein which are defined in the Uniform Commercial Code shall have meanings therein stated. * * *

IN WITNESS WHEREOF, each Creditor has caused this Agreement to be duly executed as of the 29th day of August, 1980....

COMMENTS AND QUESTIONS

1. How would this case be decided under the Revised Article 9? Consider 9-313.

2. How would you re-write the Inter-Creditor Agreement, given how it played out in this situation?

3. For information on how Revised Article 9 treats the sale of promissory notes, see Julian B. McDonnell and John Franklin Hitchcock, Jr., The Sale of Promissory Notes Under Revised Article 9: Cooking Securitization Stew, 117 Banking L.J. 99 (2000).

COMMENTS AND QUESTIONS: THE MEANING AND CONSEQUENCES OF "POSSESSION"

Whether or not dealing with a bailee, one must decide, for purposes of 9-313, what "possession" means. What is the function of possession? Possession of chattels originally was the principal means of curing ostensible ownership associated with security interests. The rationale commonly put forth for 9-313 is that the lack of possession of collateral by the debtor and the actual possession of it by the creditor, the creditor's agent, or his bailee serves "to provide notice to prospective third party creditors that the debtor no longer has unfettered use of [its] collateral." In re Copeland, 391 F. Supp. 134, 151 (D. Del. 1975), modified on other grounds, 531 F.2d 1195 (3rd Cir. 1976). Does this provide the clue as to what should be the limits on what is considered to be "possession" by the secured party? Should it be lack of physical possession by the debtor? Lack of *control*? Both? Something else?

Why would a secured party *choose* possession instead of, or, as is commonly the case, in addition to, filing? In cases in which a secured party has a choice between perfecting by filing or by possession, a secured party may choose possession because, for example, it wants to prevent a debtor from losing, abusing, or otherwise injuring the collateral. Possession may also provide certain advantages to the secured party in bankruptcy, although the Bankruptcy Code has diminished most of them, see BC 542 and BC 543. Possession, furthermore, may allow the secured party to retain the collateral after default without first instituting a court hearing. See 9-609 and Flagg Bros., Inc. v. Brooks, 436 U.S. 149 (1978). Finally, possession may have certain cost advantages to the secured party, such as avoiding costs associated with filing a financing statement (e.g., a filing fee or the worries about ascertaining the debtor's exact name or location) or avoiding formalizing an agreement in a written security agreement. But the secured party also picks up certain duties with respect to collateral in its possession, 9-207. Moreover, possession also bears certain direct costs to the debtor: the debtor, at a minimum, now has to worry about the *secured party* losing, injuring, or perhaps selling or otherwise encumbering the asset. In certain cases, of course, the debtor is deprived of use of the collateral (a problem that is likely to be much more severe when the collateral is a drill press than when it is stocks and bonds). Do any of these reasons bear on how one should interpret "possession"?

SECTION VI. PERFECTION THROUGH CONTROL

Revised Article 9 makes few important changes to the fundamental principles of the statute. Perhaps the most important consistent change throughout Revised Article 9 relates to the expanded role for control as a means of establishing priority and perfection. This tracks generally the way that control has been used in Revised Article 8 relating to investment property. In Revised Article 9, control serves a number of important purposes in implementing key changes to the statute:

- *Deposit Accounts.* Original security interests in deposit accounts may now be taken and perfected under Article 9. Control operates as a way of policing the manner in which a security interest in a deposit account is perfected. Allowing filing to perfect the security interest in the deposit account would have made it quite easy—too easy in the eyes of many—to take a perfected security interest in a deposit account. Insisting on control over that account may mean that only genuine reliance creditors will take security interests in deposit accounts.

- *Filing Against Instruments.* A secured creditor can now perfect a security interest in an instrument through filing. Such a filing serves the purpose of providing notice of the security interest in the instrument, just as it always had for other categories of collateral. Still, there may be circumstances in which having the secured creditor take an additional step beyond filing adds value and having control serve as a superior method of perfection for instruments creates a carrot to get our secured creditor to take that additional step.

- *Supporting Obligations.* The explicit treatment of supporting obligations (9-102(a)(77)) and property securing such obligations necessitated a decision about the appropriate method of perfecting a security interest in these rights. Control is a natural way to implement a two-tier perfection system based on non-temporal priorities.

9-104 through 9-107 set forth the circumstances under which control has been established over deposit accounts (9-104), electronic chattel paper (9-105), investment property (9-106), and letter-of-credit rights (9-107). 9-314 legitimates control as a method of perfection for each of these property types and sets forth rules for the time when perfection by control takes place and how long that perfection continues. We also need to know whether any other perfection method works for these collateral types. For deposit accounts, other than as proceeds, control is the exclusive acceptable perfection method (9-312(b)). A security interest in investment property or chattel paper (including electronic chattel paper) may be perfected through filing (9-312(a)). A security interest in a letter-of-credit right may be perfected only through control, except that a security interest in any supporting obligation for collateral (including a letter-of-credit right (9-102(a)(77)) arises through perfection of a security interest in the collateral itself (see 9-308(d)) (9-312(b)(2)).

With the perfection rules in hand, we can then turn to priority. 9-327 through 9-330 set forth the priority rules relating to deposit accounts (9-327), investment property (9-328), letter-of-credit rights (9-329), and of a purchaser of chattel paper or an instrument (9-330). We also need to take account of rules outside of Article 9 that may affect priority, such as status as a holder in due course (9-331), as well as set-off rights against deposit accounts (9-340).

The issues raised by introducing control as a means of perfection are best raised in the following classic case:

Benedict v. Ratner

Supreme Court of the United States, 1925.
268 U.S. 353.

■ MR. JUSTICE BRANDEIS delivered the opinion of the Court.

The Hub Carpet Company was adjudicated bankrupt by the federal court for southern New York in involuntary proceedings commenced September 26, 1921. Benedict, who was appointed receiver and later trustee, collected the book accounts of the company. Ratner filed in that court a petition in equity praying that the amounts so collected be paid over to him. He claimed them under a writing given May 23, 1921—four months and three days before the commencement of the bankruptcy proceedings. By it the company purported to assign to him, as collateral for certain loans, all accounts present and future.

Those collected by the receiver were, so far as appears, all accounts which had arisen after the date of the assignment, and were enumerated in the monthly list of accounts outstanding which was delivered to Ratner September 23. Benedict resisted the petition on the ground that the original assignment was void under the law of New York as a fraudulent conveyance; that, for this reason, the delivery of the September list of accounts was inoperative to perfect a lien in Ratner; and that it was a preference under the Bankruptcy Act. He also filed a cross-petition in which he asked that Ratner be ordered to pay to the estate the proceeds of certain collections which had been made by the company after September 17 and turned over to Ratner pursuant to his request made on that day. The company was then insolvent and Ratner had reason to believe it to be so. These accounts also had apparently been acquired by the company after the date of the original assignment.

The District Judge decided both petitions in Ratner's favor. He ruled that the assignment executed in May was not fraudulent in law; that it created an equity in the future acquired accounts; that because of this equity, Ratner was entitled to retain, as against the bankrupt's estate, the proceeds of the accounts which had been collected by the company in September and turned over to him; that by delivery of the list of the accounts outstanding on September 23, this equity in them had ripened into a perfect title to the remaining accounts; and that the title so perfected was good as against the supervening bankruptcy. * * * On appeal, the Circuit Court of Appeals affirmed the order. * * * A writ of certiorari was granted by this Court. * * *

The rights of the parties depend primarily upon the law of New York. * * * It may be assumed that, unless the arrangement of May 23 was void because fraudulent in law, the original assignment of the future acquired accounts became operative under the state law, both as to those paid over to Ratner before the bankruptcy proceedings and as to those collected by the receiver; and that the assignment will be deemed to have taken effect as of May 23. * * * That being so, it is clear that, if the original assignment was a valid one under the law of New York, the Bankruptcy Act did not invalidate the subsequent dealings of the parties. * * * The sole question for decision is, therefore, whether on the following undisputed facts the assignment of May 23 was in law fraudulent.

The Hub Carpet Company was, on May 23, a mercantile concern doing business in New York City and proposing to continue to do so. The assignment was made there to secure an existing loan of $15,000, and further advances not exceeding $15,000 which were in fact made July 1, 1921. It included all accounts receivable then outstanding and all which should thereafter accrue in the ordinary course of business. A list of the existing accounts was delivered at the time. Similar lists were to be delivered to Ratner on or about the 23d day of each succeeding month containing the accounts outstanding at such future dates. Those enumerated in each of the lists delivered prior to September, aggregated between $100,000 and $120,000. The receivables were to be collected by the company. Ratner was given the right, at any time, to demand a full disclosure of the business and financial conditions; to require that all amounts collected be applied in payment of his loans; and to enforce the assignment although no loan had matured. But until he did so, the company was not required to apply any of the collections to the repayment of Ratner's loan. It was not required to replace accounts collected by other collateral of equal value. It was not required to account in any way to Ratner. It was at liberty to use the proceeds of all accounts collected as it might see fit. The existence of the assignment was to be kept secret. The business was to be conducted as theretofore. Indebtedness was to be incurred, as usual, for the purchase of merchandise and otherwise in the ordinary course of business. The amount of such indebtedness unpaid at the time of the commencement of the bankruptcy proceedings was large. Prior to September 17, the company collected from accounts so assigned about $150,000, all of which it applied to purposes other than the payment of Ratner's loan. The outstanding accounts enumerated in the list delivered September 23 aggregated $90,000.

Under the law of New York a transfer of property as security which reserves to the transferor the right to dispose of the same, or to apply the proceeds thereof, for his own uses is, as to creditors, fraudulent in law and void. This is true whether the right of disposition for the transferor's use be reserved in the instrument or by agreement *in pais,* oral or written; whether the right of disposition reserved be unlimited in time or be expressly terminable by the happening of an event; whether the transfer cover all the property of the debtor or only a part; whether the right of disposition extends to all the property transferred or only to a part thereof; and whether the instrument of transfer be recorded or not.[11]

If this rule applies to the assignment of book accounts, the arrangement of May 23 was clearly void; and the equity in the future acquired accounts, which it would otherwise have created, did not arise. Whether the rule applies to accounts does not appear to have been passed upon by the Court of Appeals of New York. But it would seem clear that whether the collateral consist of chattels or of accounts, reservation of dominion inconsistent with the effective disposition of title must render the transaction void. Ratner asserts that the rule stated above rests upon ostensible ownership, and argues that the doctrine of ostensible ownership is not applicable to book accounts. That doctrine raises a presumption of fraud where chattels are mortgaged (or sold) and possession of the property is not delivered to the mortgagee (or vendee). The presumption may be avoided by recording the mortgage (or sale). It may be assumed, as Ratner contends, that the doctrine does not apply to the assignment of accounts. In their transfer there is nothing which corresponds to the delivery of possession of chat-

---

[11] * * * N.Y. Personal Property Law, § 45; Laws, 1911, c. 626, authorizes the creation of a general lien or floating charge upon a stock of merchandise, including after-acquired chattels, and upon accounts receivable resulting from the sale of such merchandise. It provides that this lien or charge shall be valid against creditors provided certain formalities are observed and detailed filing provisions are complied with. It is possible that, if its conditions are performed, the section does away with the rule "that retention of possession by the mortgagor with power of sale for his own benefit is fraudulent as to creditors."

tels. The statutes which embody the doctrine and provide for recording as a substitute for delivery do not include accounts. A title to an account good against creditors may be transferred without notice to the debtor or record of any kind. But it is not true that the rule stated above and invoked by the receiver is either based upon or delimited by the doctrine of ostensible ownership. It rests not upon seeming ownership because of possession retained, but upon a lack of ownership because of dominion reserved. It does not raise a presumption of fraud. It imputes fraud conclusively because of the reservation of dominion inconsistent with the effective disposition of title and creation of a lien.

The nature of the rule is made clear by its limitations. Where the mortgagor of chattels agrees to apply the proceeds of their sale to the payment of the mortgage debt or to the purchase of other chattels which shall become subject to the lien, the mortgage is good as against creditors, if recorded. The mortgage is sustained in such cases "upon the ground that such sale and application of proceeds is the normal and proper purpose of a chattel mortgage, and within the precise boundaries of its lawful operation and effect. It does no more than to substitute the mortgagor as the agent of the mortgagee to do exactly what the latter had the right to do, and what it was his privilege and his duty to accomplish. It devotes, as it should, the mortgaged property to the payment of the mortgage debt." The permission to use the proceeds to furnish substitute collateral "provides only for a shifting of the lien from one piece of property to another taken in exchange." Brackett v. Harvey, 91 N.Y. 214, 221, 223. On the other hand, if the agreement is that the mortgagor may sell and use the proceeds for his own benefit, the mortgage is of no effect although recorded. Seeming ownership exists in both classes of cases because the mortgagor is permitted to remain in possession of the stock in trade and to sell it freely. But it is only where the unrestricted dominion over the proceeds is reserved to the mortgagor that the mortgage is void. This dominion is the differentiating and deciding element. * * *

The results which flow from reserving dominion inconsistent with the effective disposition of title must be the same whatever the nature of the property transferred. The doctrine which imputes fraud where full dominion is reserved must apply to assignments of accounts although the doctrine of ostensible ownership does not. There must also be the same distinction as to degrees of dominion. Thus, although an agreement that the assignor of accounts shall collect them and pay the proceeds to the assignee will not invalidate the assignment which it accompanies, the assignment must be deemed fraudulent in law if it is agreed that the assignor may use the proceeds as he sees fit.

In the case at bar, the arrangement for the unfettered use by the company of the proceeds of the accounts precluded the effective creation of a lien and rendered the original assignment fraudulent in law. Consequently the payments to Ratner and the delivery of the September list of accounts were inoperative to perfect a lien in him, and were unlawful preferences. On this ground, and also because the payment was fraudulent under the law of the State, the trustee was entitled to recover the amount. * * *

COMMENTS AND QUESTIONS: RETHINKING CONTROL

Step back and consider the decision on the merits. On one view, the Court tossed a major wrench into the basic gears of secured transactions. Receivables are the proverbial Heraclitan river, ever changing yet remaining the same. The floating stock of receivables changes, to be sure, day by day, but the individual items comprising the mass aren't the issue, the mass itself is. If a secured creditor cannot get an effective security interest on after-acquired receivables, we have removed an important source of collateral for supporting loans.

Of course, *Benedict* didn't say anything like this. Instead, the decision merely insists that the secured creditor police its debtor—control the debtor—if the security interest in receivables is to be effective. *Benedict* provides a road-map as to how to make these transactions effective. Indeed, lawyers were sufficiently successful that a robust industry in these arrangements arose. Nonetheless, the costs of these arrangements were ultimately seen to outweigh the benefits. In the drafting of Old Article 9, *Benedict* was overruled by statute; see F9-205 and its official comments. A fully-effective security interest could be granted in present and future receivables and the secured creditor need not police how the proceeds of these receivables are used.

It is interesting that the British system of fixed and floating charges is tied directly to these issues of control, and comes out squarely in favor of the regime defined by *Benedict* and abandoned by Article 9. In the British system, the freedom given to the debtor in the use of the charged property—the collateral—determines whether property may be subject to a fixed or a floating charge. Property that the debtor holds and uses but does not intend to transfer to third parties can be subject to a fixed charge. See R.M. Goode, Legal Problems of Credit and Security 9 (Sweet & Maxwell, 2nd ed. 1988). Equipment is a natural example: the debtor uses the equipment and in the ordinary course of business intends to hold it. After registration of the fixed charge—public recording—third parties take the property subject to the fixed charge. This is true both for purchasers and for execution creditors. Both of these results track the Article 9 rules for a security interest in equipment, as such a security interest would survive a sale, see 9-315(a)(1), 9-320(a), and would be prior to the interest of a lien creditor.

In contrast, assets that the debtor deals with freely as to third parties— inventory is the key example—cannot be subject to a fixed charge and may only be subject to a floating charge. The floating charge is in some sense inchoate: it is not effective against buyers and execution creditors prior to an event known as crystallization. As to these charges, Article 9 and the British system are in sync for buyers in the ordinary course. 9-320(a) cuts off a security interest in inventory, while the British buyer is not subject to the uncrystallized floating charge. The key difference is the treatment of a lien creditor. The Article 9 security interest in inventory is good against the lien creditor, both genuine lien creditors under 9-317(a) and hypothetical lien creditors under BC 544. The uncrystallized floating charge is not good against a lien creditor nor is it spared from the invasion of claims given a statutory preference in a liquidation. The structure of this system means that a group of assets—those that can be subject to no more than a floating charge—are always up for grabs. The holder of the floating charge can lose out to execution creditors prior to crystallization.

In this scheme, the control that the debtor exercises over inventory prevents the secured creditor from having a fully effective charge against those assets. This is similar in many ways to the scheme contemplated by *Benedict*, and all of this suggests that we should be cautious in embracing Article 9's choice in favor of perfected floating security interests on inventory and receivables without the secured creditor exercising some control over the collateral.

In fact, we might say more. Until very recently, Article 9 has had two primary ways of perfecting a security interest, filing and possession. Although filing may be an acceptable substitute for possession as to the notice provided to third parties, it is a very poor stand-in for possession when it comes to exercising control over the collateral. For the debtor to give up possession of the collateral also entailed giving up control over the collateral and assured all creditors of the debtor that the debtor could not mi-suse the asset. In contrast, filing has no direct consequence for control. The filed secured creditor can ignore the debtor and still enjoy priority based on its earlier financing statement.

Perfection through possession is in many ways a holdover from secured transactions' days in the primordial soup. It has been used only infrequent-ly as an instrument of policy for influencing outcomes, F9-308 being the prime example. That has left us with only one policy instrument, the fi-nancing statement, and we have done nothing with that, such as having different filing fees for different asset types or for situations where a credi-tor was taking a security interest in more than one asset type. (Fees could follow a step-ladder: take one asset type, pay once price, take two asset types, pay more, etc.) We also could introduce control much more gener-ally into Article 9 and use that as a policy instrument and, to some extent, Revised Article 9 has done so. Control might ensure that we avoid mis-matches between collateral and reliance and non-reliance creditors. To a large extent, reliance and control should travel together.

We can let our imaginations run as to the ways that control might be used. Consider two schemes briefly. We could expand the financing statement records to embrace control and non-control creditors (or active and passive secured creditors, if you prefer). The financing statement would permit a designation of the type of creditor. Passive creditors— either so designated or as the default designation—could be subordinated to later-filing active creditors, again by identification on the financing statement. Of course, all creditors would want to be active creditors, ab-sent a kicker, so the real question becomes what it should be. We could use filing fee differentials. This scheme is a before-the-fact designation scheme for control. An alternative is to allow a competitive market in ex-ercising control to evolve, with after-the-fact judicial evaluation of the contributions made by the creditors in exercising control over the debtor. We get some of that already now, since control is one of the indicia giving rising to liability in lender liability litigation. We would want to distin-guish bad control—typically relating to direct control over the decision-making of the debtor—from good control, which focuses on the treatment and use of the collateral.

We move from a secured transactions classic to new cases that start to work through control and deposit accounts under Revised Article 9. These cases probably have a short shelf-life, but we do need to work through some of the core mechanics of these issues.

3-12: TAKING A DEPOSIT ACCOUNT THE EASY WAY?
- Bank wants to take a perfected security interest in Debtor's deposit account. To do so, Debtor executes a security agreement granting Bank "a security interest in all deposit accounts of Debtor, whether now owned or hereafter acquired." Bank files a financing statement containing the same language.
- ¤ Does Bank have a perfected security interest? See 9-312(b)(1).

3-13: THE OLD DEPOSIT ACCOUNT SWITCHEROO
- Creditco wants to take a perfected security interest in Debtor's deposit account held with Bank. To do so, Debtor, Bank and Creditco enter into an appropriate control agreement under 9-104(a)(2).
- The next day, Debtor takes all of the money out of the deposit account with Bank and moves it to a new deposit account at Next-Bank.
- ¤ Does Creditco have control over the new deposit account at Next-Bank?

Counceller v. Ecenbarger, Inc.
Court of Appeals of Indiana, 2005
834 N.E.2d 1018.

■ BAILEY, JUDGE

Appellant-Intervenor John Counceller ("Counceller") appeals the small claims court's judgment in proceedings supplemental in favor of Appellee-Plaintiff Ecenbarger, Inc. d/b/a Applied Metal and Machine Works ("Applied Metal"). We affirm. Counceller raises three issues, which we consolidate and restate as whether the filing of the financing statement perfected his security interest in the deposit accounts at issue—i.e., accounts that belong to Defendant First Metals and Plastics Technologies, Inc. ("Defendant")—such that Counceller's interest enjoys priority over Applied Metal's judgment lien.

Counceller is the president and majority shareholder of Defendant and has individually loaned Defendant funds in excess of $200,000.00, which have not been repaid. On December 30, 2002, Counceller filed a financing statement with the Indiana Secretary of State, listing Defendant as the "Debtor." The financing statement gives Counceller an interest in "[a]ll Debtor's presently owned or hereafter acquired assets, including, without limitation, ... deposit accounts ... and all products and proceeds of the foregoing." At all times pertinent to this action, however, Defendant remained in control of the bank accounts at issue.

On June 15, 2004, Applied Metal received a default judgment against Defendant in the amount of $5,270.25, plus costs. Defendant has not moved for relief from this default judgment and its validity is not at issue in the present controversy. On July 26, 2004, Applied Metal filed a verified motion for proceedings supplemental to collect the unpaid portion of the judgment, i.e., $5,411.28, wherein it named National City Bank ("Bank") as a garnishee defendant. In its response to Applied Metal's request for interrogatories, Bank disclosed that Defendant maintains two checking accounts at its facility, with a combined balance, at that time, of $5,411.28.

On September 7, 2004, Counceller filed a Verified Petition to Intervene and Assert Claim, wherein he alleged that his filing of the financing statement gave him a security interest in the accounts at issue, which is superior to any subsequent creditors of Defendant, including Applied Metal. * * *

On September 28, 2004, Counceller filed his "Intervenor's Claim," alleging that his security interest in the bank accounts at issue was perfected upon the filing of the financing statement and, thus, is superior to Applied Metal's judgment lien. * * * On November 22, 2004, the small claims court denied Counceller's claim because he does not "control" the accounts at issue pursuant to 9-312(b)(1). * * *

On appeal, Counceller argues that the small claims court's judgment in favor of Applied Metal is clearly erroneous because his interest in the accounts at issue has priority over Applied Metal's judgment lien. In particular, Counceller contends that the financing statement served to perfect his security interest in the deposit accounts in dispute, regardless of his lack of control over such accounts. * * * [T]he parties agree that the only issue presently before this Court is whether Counceller has a perfected security interest in the deposit accounts in question, such that his interest is superior to Applied Metal's subsequently obtained judgment lien. Put another way, the sole issue presented is whether Counceller's interest was perfected upon the filing of the financing statement or whether, to perfect his interest in the bank accounts, he was required to maintain control over the accounts. To determine whether a valid security interest in the deposit accounts has been perfected, we look to the statutory provisions of the Uniform Commercial Code, which are controlling.

9-312(b) * * * governs the perfection of security interests in deposit accounts * * * . 9-315 provides, in relevant part * * *. Pursuant to these statutory provisions, the only way to perfect a security interest in a deposit account is by control under 9-312(b), unless the security interest is in proceeds and the original collateral—from which the proceeds derived—was perfected.

In the present case, the undisputed evidence reveals that Counceller did not control the deposit accounts at issue under 9-312(b). Nevertheless, Counceller maintains that the filing of the financing statement perfected his interest in the bank accounts, which contained proceeds from Defendant's inventory. The record is devoid of any evidence, however, demonstrating that the funds comprising the two accounts in dispute were the proceeds from Defendant's inventory. Rather, the evidence merely shows that such funds were used in the operation of Defendant's business, i.e., to pay the daily operating expenses of the business. Because Counceller has failed to prove that Defendant's deposit accounts were composed of inventory proceeds such that inventory was the original collateral, the exception to perfection by control provided in 9-315 does not apply.

Moreover, to the extent that the funds in question were proceeds from Defendant's original bank accounts, we note that the filing of the financing statement, alone, was still insufficient to perfect the security interest in proceeds because it was insufficient to perfect the original deposit accounts. As previously mentioned, pursuant to 9-315, a security interest in proceeds is a perfected security interest only if the security interest in the original collateral was perfected.

Here, because Counceller never controlled the bank accounts at issue pursuant to 9-312(b), his interest in such accounts was never perfected. Accordingly, Counceller's interest in Defendant's bank accounts is not entitled to priority over Applied Metal's judgment lien, because Counceller had never perfected his interest. Therefore, the trial court did not err by denying Counceller's claim.

For the foregoing reasons, we affirm the trial court's denial of Counceller's claim to Defendant's deposit accounts.

Affirmed.

3-14: ASSIGNING SECURITY INTERESTS I

- Debtor and Bank enter into a standard secured transaction in equipment with an appropriate security agreement and financing statement. Bank lends money to Debtor.
- Debtor subsequently enters into a similar secured transaction with Finco. Finco also files an appropriate financing statement.
- Bank subsequently sells its position to Creditco.
- ¤ Does Creditco have a perfected security interest? See 9-310(c). Who has priority between Creditco and Finco?

3-15: ASSIGNING SECURITY INTERESTS II

- Debtor and Bank enter into a standard secured transaction in equipment with an appropriate security agreement and Bank takes possession of the equipment. Bank lends money to Debtor.
- Debtor subsequently enters into a similar secured transaction with Finco, but Finco files an appropriate financing statement instead of taking possession.
- Bank subsequently sells its position to Creditco and delivers possession of the equipment to Creditco.
- ¤ Does Creditco have a perfected security interest? See Comment 4 to 9-310(c). Who has priority between Creditco and Finco?

3-16: ASSIGNING SECURITY INTERESTS III

- Debtor maintains a deposit account at Bank. Debtor signs an agreement granting Bank a security interest in the deposit account. Bank lends money to Debtor.
- ¤ Does Bank have a perfected security interest?
- Bank subsequently sells its position to Creditco, but the deposit account remains with Bank.
- ¤ Does Creditco have a perfected security interest? See Comment 4 to 9-310(c).

Beal Bank, S.S.B. v. Fewell (In re Fewell)

United States Bankruptcy Court, E.D. Arkansas, 2006.
352 Bankr. 98.

■ AUDREY R. EVANS, BANKRUPTCY JUDGE

Pending before the Court is the Motion for Relief from the Automatic Stay and for Abandonment of Collateral filed on behalf of Beal Bank, SSB on June 26, 2006. On July 6, 2006, the Debtor filed a Response to Motion for Relief and the Unsecured Creditors Committee filed an Objection to the Motion of Beal Bank for Relief from the Automatic Stay and for Abandonment of Collateral. * * *

The parties' stipulated facts are as follows:

1. Beal Bank, SSB ("Beal Bank") is the holder of a claim against the Estate that arises by virtue of various personal guarantees entered into by the Debtor Bobby Eugene Fewell ("Debtor") guaranteeing the prompt and punctual payment and performance of all sums owing by Pro Transportation, Inc. ("Pro Transportation") under a certain Note payable to Beal Bank, as assignee of U.S. Bank, N.A. ("U.S. Bank") (successor by merger to Mercantile Bank of Arkansas ("Mercantile Bank") and Firstar Bank, N.A. ("Firstar Bank")).

2. On July 26, 1999, Pro Transportation executed a Fixed Rate Commercial Promissory Note (the "Note") in favor of Mercantile Bank in the original principal sum of Nine Hundred Sixty-Two Thousand Seven Hundred Eighty-Three and 33/100 Dollars ($962,783.33). The Note was secured by a mortgage on certain property located in Pulaski County, Arkansas.

3. The Debtor personally guaranteed the prompt and punctual payment and performance of all sums owing by Pro Transportation to Mercantile Bank and its successors. The Debtor's personal guaranties of Pro Transportation's obligations are memorialized in the various agreements (referred to collectively as the "Guaranties") attached to the Joint Stipulation.

4. On or about October 26, 2000, the Debtor executed a Collateral Pledge Agreement (the "Pledge Agreement"), whereby the Debtor granted Firstar bank (successor by name change to Mercantile Bank) a security interest in a certificate of deposit in the principal amount of $200,000.00 (the "Certificate of Deposit") then held by Firstar Bank in the name of the Debtor. * * *

5. The Collateral Pledge Agreement granted Firstar Bank a security interest in the Certificate of Deposit to secure all obligations of the Debtor to Firstar Bank, including the obligations of the Debtor under the Guaranties.

6. U.S. Bank is the successor by merger to Firstar Bank and Mercantile Bank.

7. In June 2004, Beal Bank acquired the Note, and all related security interests, including the Guaranties and the Pledge Agreement, from U.S. Bank, pursuant to an Asset Sale Agreement dated June 10, 2004. * * *

8. On or about June 18, 2004, U.S. Bank assigned to Beal Bank all rights, title and interests to the Note and all security interests securing the Note, including the Guaranties and the Pledge Agreement. * * *

9. At the time that U.S. Bank assigned the Note, the Guaranties and the Pledge Agreement to Beal Bank, U.S. Bank held a perfected security interest in the Certificate of Deposit securing the Debtor's obligations under the Guaranties.

10. Pro Transportation defaulted under the Note.

11. On August 11, 2005, Beal Bank obtained a judgment against Pro Transportation in the Circuit Court of Pulaski County, Thirteenth Division, in the amount of $966,583.81.

12. The sum of $781,081.21 was credited against the judgment following the foreclosure of the mortgage and sale of the mortgaged property on September 8, 2005.

13. After crediting the foreclosure sale proceeds against the judgment, Pro Transportation is indebted to Beal Bank in the amount of $213,911.99 as of July 31, 2006, with interest accruing at a daily per diem of $44.59.

14. By virtue of the Guaranties, the Debtor is obligated to pay Beal Bank the sum remaining payable by Pro Transportation under the judgment.

15. The Debtor's payment of the sums owed to Beal Bank under the Guaranties is secured by the security interest in the Certificate of Deposit.

16. The Certificate of Deposit is a "deposit account" as defined in 9-102(29).

17. At all times prior to the assignment of the Note, the Guaranties and the Pledge Agreement to Beal Bank, U.S. Bank, or its predecessor in

interest, was the holder of the Note, the Guaranties and the Pledge Agreement.

18. At all times prior to the assignment of the Note, the Guaranties and the Pledge Agreement to Beal Bank, U.S. Bank has been the bank with which the Certificate of Deposit has been maintained and U.S. Bank has had continuous custody and control of the Certificate of Deposit.

19. U.S. Bank has been in continuous custody and control of the Certificate of Deposit from the date that the Note, the Guaranties and the Pledge Agreement were assigned to Beal Bank through present.

20. At no time did U.S. Bank authenticate a record acknowledging that it held the subject Certificate of Deposit for Beal Banks' benefit.

21. If the Court finds that Beal Bank has a perfected security interest in the Certificate of Deposit, the Debtor has little or no equity in the Certificate of Deposit.

22. If the Court finds that Beal Bank has a perfected security interest in the Certificate of Deposit, the Certificate of Deposit is not necessary to an effective reorganization.

ANALYSIS

* * * [T]he sole issue to be resolved by the Court is whether Beal Bank has a perfected security interest in the Certificate of Deposit. * * * It is Beal Bank's position that, when it took an assignment of the Note and collateral (including the Certificate of Deposit) from U.S. Bank, its security interest remained perfected as U.S. Bank's assignee. The Debtor and the Committee assert that Beal Bank failed to perfect an interest in the Certificate of Deposit because it did not obtain "control" as defined by 9-104. For the reasons set forth below, the Court agrees with Beal Bank that its security interest in the Certificate of Deposit was properly perfected * * *.

The parties have stipulated that the Certificate of Deposit is a "deposit account" as defined by 9-102(a)(29). Generally, a financing statement must be filed to perfect a security interest; however, a financing statement is not necessary to perfect a security interest in a deposit account. 9-310(a), (b)(8). In fact, pursuant to 9-312(b)(1), "a security interest in a deposit account may be perfected only by control...." Under 9-314, a party may perfect a security interest in a deposit account by satisfying the definition of "control" as defined in 9-104, and "remains perfected by control only while the secured party retains control." 9-314(a)-(b). * * *

The assignment of a perfected security interest is governed by 9-310(c), which provides that:

> If a secured party assigns a perfected security interest ..., a filing under this chapter is not required to continue the perfected status of the security interest against creditors of and transferees from the original debtor.

9-104(c). Although subsection (c) addresses when an additional filing will not be required for perfection, comment 4 states that "[s]ubsection (c) applies not only to an assignment of a security interest perfected by filing but also to an assignment of a security interest perfected by a method other than by filing, such as by *control* or by possession." 9-310, cmt. 4 (emphasis added). The security interest will remain perfected as against creditors and transferees of the original debtor, but additional action will be required for perfection against creditors and transferees of the assignor. In the present case, Beal Bank sought to enforce its security interest against the original debtor, and thus, Beal Bank argues it remained perfected pursuant to 9-310(c), cmt. 4.

The Debtor and the Committee argue that perfection under 9-104 and 9-313 require either actual possession of the account or, if the account is in possession of a party other than the debtor, perfection requires control. This argument is misplaced. 9-313(a) provides that "a secured party may perfect a security interest in negotiable documents, goods, instruments, money, or tangible chattel paper by taking possession of the collateral." However, comment 2 clarifies that possession will not be permitted to perfect a security interest in a deposit account. 9-313, cmt. 2. The parties stipulated that the Certificate of Deposit was a deposit account, thus, excluding the applicability of 9-313.

The Debtor and Committee also argue that Beal Bank's interpretation of 9-310(c), including comment 4, would create a statutory exception in direct conflict with 9-313 and the actual text of the Arkansas Code. As stated above, 9-313 is not applicable to deposit accounts, and, therefore, Beal Bank's interpretation of 9-310(c) and the comments would not create a statutory exception in direct conflict with 9-313. In addition, none of the statutes governing the perfection of a security interest in a deposit account, i.e., 9-312, 314, or 104, expressly address the impact of its assignment; and, therefore, 9-310 comment 4 does not directly conflict with the actual text of the Arkansas Code.

Neither party cited an Arkansas case governing the effect of an assignment on the perfection of security interest in deposit accounts, but at least one court has addressed the issue. See In re Verus Investment Mgmt., L.L.C., 344 Bankr. 536 (Bankr. N.D. OH 2006). In that case, under a similar statute, the court held that an assignee of a security interest in a deposit account will remain perfected so long as the assignor held the properly perfected security interest. Id. at 546 (citing UCC 9-310, comment 4).

For the foregoing reasons, the Court finds that Beal Bank has a perfected security interest in the Certificate of Deposit under 9-310(c). U.S. Bank properly perfected a security interest in the Certificate of Deposit, and Beal Bank holds its security interest in the Certificate of Deposit by assignment from U.S. Bank. U.S. Bank held its perfected security interest in the Certificate of Deposit prior to its assignment in June 2004, and it has maintained custody and control of the Certificate of Deposit from the date of the assignment to present. Pursuant to 9-310(c), a properly perfected security interest that is assigned to a third-party will remain perfected against the creditors and transferees of the original debtor. Subsection 310(c) applies to deposit accounts. See 9-310, cmt. 4. Accordingly, pursuant to 9-310(c), Beal Bank acquired a perfected security interest in the Certificate of Deposit through U.S. Bank's assignment of the perfected security interest. * * *

SECTION VII. MISCELLANEOUS PERFECTION APPROACHES

There are a handful of odds-and-ends on perfecting that we have not addressed:

SECURITY INTERESTS PERFECTED UPON ATTACHMENT

9-309 sets forth an extensive list of security interests that are perfected upon attachment. These include, among other things, a purchase money security interest in consumer goods; a sale of a payment intangible or a promissory note; certain assignments of health-care-insurance receivables; and certain security interests in favor of securities and commodities intermediaries. These are obviously very special rules, and the merits of each one can best be evaluated by consider the official comments to 9-309.

MOTOR VEHICLES AND CERTIFICATES OF TITLE SYSTEMS

Professor Gilmore observed that the automobile "has been one of the great sources of law in the twentieth century," and, in particular, "[a]s the most expensive chattel ever to come into general use, it generated novel methods of secured financing. Its unique mobility, combined with the high resale value of used cars, made theft both easy and profitable." 1 G. Gilmore, supra, at 550. One way in which the automobile has received distinct treatment is that it is one of the few items of personal property that is oftentimes subject to *title* recording laws. In this respect, it shares an attribute of real property, perhaps due to the automobile's relatively high value and reasonably specific identity (i.e., VIN number). Unlike real property, however, the automobile is certainly not fixed in location; it therefore creates the problem of changes in the relevant state's recording laws. (With respect to several other items of personal property of high value and great mobility—such as airplanes and ships—this problem has been solved in large part by a federal recording statute.)

Article 9's filing system could adequately deal with security interests in automobiles (and other vehicles). But Article 9 recognizes that a state may adopt a title recording system for such vehicles, which may preempt the general Article 9 rules. See 9-311(a)(2). That rule does not apply to cars held as inventory, as occurs at a dealer in new or used cars. See 9-311(d). A bank that lends to a car dealer perfects its security interest in the dealer's inventory—the cars on the lot—by filing in the ordinary UCC records.

So, to take the ordinary system, suppose that Bank finances the purchase of a new car by Consumer. How does Bank perfect its security interest? Unfortunately, the uniform law on this subject—the Uniform Motor Vehicle Certificate of Title and Anti-Theft Act—has been adopted in only a handful of states. That act requires, with the exception of a vehicle owned by a manufacturer or dealer held for sale or a vehicle owned by a non-resident of the state and not required by law to be registered in the state, § 2(a), "every owner of a vehicle which is in this state and for which no certificate of title has been issued by the Department [of Motor Vehicles ("DMV")]" shall apply for a certificate of title, § 4. Sufficient information must be provided to enable the DMV "to determine whether the owner is entitled to a certificate of title and the existence or non-existence of security interests in the vehicle," § 6. The certificate of title, when issued, provides not only "the name and address of the owner" but also "the names and addresses of any lienholders, in the order of priority as shown in the application," § 9. The certificate of title is mailed to the first lienholder named on the title, § 10.

Sections 20-23 of the uniform motor vehicle law regulate the perfecting of security interests in vehicles subject to it. The statute states that "a security interest in a vehicle of a type for which a certificate of title is required is not valid against creditors of the owner or subsequent transferees or lienholders of the vehicle unless perfected as provided in this act," § 20(a). Perfection is accomplished, § 20(b), by:

> the delivery to the [DMV] of the existing certificate of title, if any, an application for a certificate of title containing the name and address of the lienholder and the date of his security agreement and the required fee [and registration card]. It is perfected as of the time of its creation if the delivery is completed within ten (10) days thereafter, otherwise, as of the time of the delivery.

Although as noted before the Uniform Motor Vehicle Act has been enacted in only eleven states, virtually every jurisdiction now has a certificate of title statute requiring security interests to be noted on the title and has provided that this statute preempts the Article 9 filing system for automobiles and similar vehicles.

Certificate of title cases under Article 9 have largely involved one of two fact patterns. First is the case of a vehicle moving from a certificate of title state to a non-certificate of title state (or vice versa). Second is the problem of two certificates of title being issued in different states, but the second certificate fails to note (usually because of fraud or misbehavior by the debtor/owner) a security interest that was noted on the first state's certificate. Both cases, then, involve the question of whom the risk should be placed on in the case of interstate moves of the debtor's "location." The following problems explore both of these patterns, after starting with the question of which state should issue the original certificate in the first place.

In considering these fact patterns, focus on the following question: Is the confusion engendered in trying to mesh a variety of states' laws regulating motor vehicles with the "moving collateral" provisions of Article 9 worth this "semi-exclusion" from Article 9's filing requirements? That is to say, are the advantages of deference to certificate of title statutes (where they exist) worth the avoidance of duplication that would result if Article 9's filing system were not called off in cases where security interests must be recorded on the certificate of title? What, if any, residual problems would there be if Article 9 applied in full? Has Article 9 essentially achieved the same result as would be reached by way of full applicability of Article 9? What, if any, residual problems would there be if Article 9 were left as is, but all UCC jurisdictions could be persuaded to enact a uniform motor vehicles act?

3-17: WHICH STATE SHOULD ISSUE THE ORIGINAL CERTIFICATE?

- Debtor is a trucker. She resides in Michigan, but her work, naturally enough, takes her all over the country. The company she drives for has its main terminal in Indiana, a business office in Chicago, and its home office in Minnesota.

- Debtor purchases a truck which is financed on a secured basis by Bank. An application for a certificate of title is submitted to— somewhat surprisingly—the Alaska DMV. Nonetheless, the title is issued, listing Bank as lienholder and is delivered to Bank.

- Debtor files a Chapter 7 bankruptcy petition in a federal bankruptcy court in Michigan, and the trustee in bankruptcy claims that Bank's security interest is unperfected and therefore avoidable. The trustee acknowledges that Debtor's work does take her to Alaska, but that Michigan actually is the appropriate state for issuance of the certificate.

¤ Has a perfected security interest been created?

3-18: MOVING FROM STATE TO STATE

- Debtor buys a car, Bank finances the purchase. The certificate of title is issued in State A, with Bank listed as lienholder, and the certificate is delivered to Bank.

- On March 1st, Debtor moves to State B and takes her car with her. State B does not require notation on the certificate of title for perfection of a security interest.

- On April 1st, Debtor borrows from Finco on a secured basis and appropriate steps are taken under the law of State B for Finco's security interest to be perfected.

¤ How would a priority dispute between Bank and Finco be resolved if it arises on May 1st? July 15th?

¤ Suppose that State B did require notation on the certificate of title for perfection of the security interest. Would that have altered the likely course of events, assuming that Debtor would not have re-sorted to affirmative fraud?

3-19: FRAUDULENT CERTIFICATES

- Debtor buys a car, Bank finances the purchase. The certificate of title is issued in State A with Bank listed as lienholder, and the certificate is delivered to Bank.
- On March 1st, Debtor moves the car to State B, where Debtor fraudulently procures a "clean" certificate of title, even though Bank continues to possess the original certificate of title.
- On April 1st, Debtor borrows from Finco against the clean certificate, and appropriate steps are taken for Finco's security interest to be noted on the clean certificate. Finco takes possession of that certificate.

¤ Does the fact that the second certificate is fraudulent prevent Finco from acquiring a perfected security interest in the car? If not, who has priority? How should the dispute be resolved if it arises on May 1st? July 15th? Does it matter whether both states require notation on the certificate of title?

¤ Suppose that Debtor instead sold the car to Buyer, an ordinary consumer. What is the status of Bank's security interest?

3-20: THE MEANING OF "REGISTRATION"

- Debtor buys a car, Bank finances the purchase. The certificate of title is issued in New Hampshire, with Bank listed as lienholder, and the certificate is delivered to Bank.
- On March 1st, Debtor moves to New York, applies to the New York DMV, and receives New York registration papers and licenses. No new certificate of title is issued.
- On August 1st, Debtor files a Chapter 7 bankruptcy petition in New York. The bankruptcy trustee once again claims that Bank is unperfected. The trustee notes that more than four months have passed since Debtor's move and that a new New York registration was issued. Hence, says the trustee, Bank is unperfected.

¤ Has the car been "registered in another jurisdiction" when a new registration and license have been issued, but no new certificate of title was issued?

3-21: RELATION BACK AND THE DATE OF PERFECTION OF THE SECURITY INTEREST

- On March 1st, Debtor buys a car and Bank finances the purchase.
- On March 15th, Creditor acquires a judgment against Debtor and seizes the car, thereby becoming a lien creditor.
- On March 25th, the certificate of title is issued with Bank listed as lienholder, and the certificate is delivered to Bank.

¤ Who has priority as between Bank and Creditor? Suppose that a state statute provides that "a lien or encumbrance on a motor vehicle or trailer is perfected by the delivery to the director of revenue of the existing certificate of ownership, if any, an application for a certificate of ownership containing the name and address of the lienholder and the date of his security agreement, and the required certificate of ownership fee. It is perfected as of the time of its creation if the delivery of the aforesaid to the director of revenue is completed within thirty days thereafter, otherwise as of the time of the delivery."

¤ What result if Debtor filed a Chapter 7 bankruptcy petition on April 1st? Would the trustee in bankruptcy be able to avoid Bank's security interest as an impermissible preference under BC 547? See Fidelity Financial Services, Inc. v. Fink, 522 U.S. 211 (1998).

CHAPTER FOUR

PRIORITY

Once a security interest has attached, a creditor obtains an interest in property of the debtor. There is, however, a significant difference between merely having a property right and having one that is superior to someone else's property right in the same asset. For example, to have a property right in, say, a drill press that is superior to the rights of the trustee in a bankruptcy proceeding, a secured creditor must, in addition to all the steps necessary for attachment, perfect the security interest by taking possession of the collateral or by filing a financing statement.

Even the holder of a *perfected* security interest, however, may under certain circumstances be subject to the claims of many other parties, including buyers, sellers, tax collectors, holders of statutory liens, trustees in bankruptcy, and other secured parties. In this chapter, we look at the provisions that determine whose rights take precedence—loosely speaking, the "priority" provisions. 9-201 is the starting place for a study of priorities—the rights of the secured creditor against the rights of others who claim an interest in the property. It provides:

> Except as otherwise provided in [the Uniform Commercial Code], a security agreement is effective according to its terms between the parties, against purchasers of the collateral, and against creditors.

9-201 provides that, as a general matter, a secured creditor prevails against all other parties, once its interest attaches—that is, once it has given value, the debtor has rights in the collateral, and the debtor has signed a written security agreement or the secured creditor has taken possession of or control over the collateral. This provision, of course, states only the rule, and not its exceptions. Part 3 of Article 9 is riddled with exceptions to 9-201 and, despite 9-201's bold assertion that only other provisions in the Uniform Commercial Code override it, obviously other statutory law (such as the Internal Revenue Code and the Bankruptcy Code) must be considered. Nevertheless, 9-201 establishes a presumption. If there is a priority contest and neither Article 9 nor some other statute or common law rule states that the other party wins, then the secured creditor prevails.

The basic rules that concern us in this chapter are encompassed in 9-317 and 9-322. 9-317 allows some general creditors to prevail over secured creditors. General creditors who reduce their claim to judgment and acquire a lien on the debtor's property under state law prevail over a secured creditor whose interest is *unperfected* at the time the lien is acquired. Given 9-201, a secured creditor whose interest is *perfected* takes priority over all general creditors, even those who have reduced their claim to judgment and have acquired a lien, as long as the lien is not acquired *before* the interest is perfected. Moreover, an *unperfected* secured creditor prevails over all general creditors who do not reduce their claims to judgment. See, e.g., 9-201; 9-317(a).

Article 9, as a general matter, resolves the priority of two secured creditors who have rights to the same asset by a rule of first-in-time, first-in-right. 9-322(a)(1). More precisely, the party that is first in time is the party that filed first or perfected first, whichever is earlier. This subsection contains within it two important and distinguishable ideas. First, the secured party that is first in time ought to be first in right. Second, you should determine who was first in time by looking at the earlier of the date of filing or the date of perfection.

Article 9, however, carves out exceptions for secured parties who enable the debtor to acquire new property and there are special rules that apply when property is commingled with other property that is subject to another security interest. The basic rule of 9-322(a)(1), however, establishes a principle that, between competing property claimants asserting an Article 9 interest, the first to cure the ostensible ownership problem is entitled to priority. 9-317(a) establishes a similar rule for Article 9 interests vis-à-vis other creditors who acquire a property right: The rights of the Article 9 creditor turn on whether the competing property interest arises before it cures the ostensible ownership problem the security interest creates. In most states, you do not become a lien creditor (and thus do not acquire a competing property interest) until you cure the ostensible ownership problem that interest creates.

With these ideas in mind, consider the following simple (but important) fact patterns:

4-1: THE REIFIED PRIORITY SYSTEM

- On January 1st, Finco lends $10,000 to Corp, takes a security interest in equipment and files an appropriate financing statement.
- On February 1st, Bank lends $10,000 to Corp, takes a security interest in inventory and files an appropriate financing statement.
- ¤ As of March 15th, who has priority? (Ignore for now the fact that the inventory on that date is almost surely different from the inventory on February 1st, the date Bank created its security interest in inventory. This raises many interesting questions that will be considered when we reach the topic of *after-acquired property* (see 9-204).)

4-2: THE SIMPLE FIRST-TO-FILE RULE

- On January 1st, Finco lends $10,000 to Corp, takes a security interest in equipment and files an appropriate financing statement.
- On February 1st, Bank lends $10,000 to Corp, takes a security interest in the same equipment and files an appropriate financing statement.
- ¤ Who has priority?

4-3: FIRST-TO-FILE (AND WE MEAN IT)

- On January 1st, Finco lends $10,000 to Corp, takes a security interest in equipment but files no financing statement.
- On February 1st, Bank lends $10,000 to Corp, takes a security interest in the same equipment and files an appropriate financing statement.
- On February 2nd, Finco files an appropriate financing statement.
- ¤ Who has priority?

4-4: FIRST-TO-FILE (AND WE REALLY MEAN IT)

- On January 1st, Finco files a financing statement authorized by Corp for collateral described as equipment but lends no money.
- On February 1st, Bank lends $10,000 to Corp, takes a security interest in equipment and files an appropriate financing statement.
- On March 1st, Finco lends $10,000 to Corp and takes a security interest in equipment.
- ¤ Who has priority?

J.I. Case Credit Corp. v. Foos

Kansas Court of Appeals, 1986.
717 P.2d 1064.

■ DAVID S. KNUDSON, DISTRICT JUDGE

This action was brought to determine priority of security interests in farm equipment. The competing secured creditors are J.I. Case Credit Corporation (Case) and The Bazine State Bank (Bank). The debtor is Clarence Foos. The equipment consists of a Case tractor and a Noble undercutter.

Foos had been a regular customer of the Bank for years. As early as 1966, the Bank filed a UCC financing statement which provided for a security interest in after-acquired farm equipment. From time to time, appropriate UCC continuation statements were filed.

On May 30, 1980, Foos purchased the Case tractor and Noble undercutter from Rural Equipment, Inc., of LaCrosse, Kansas (Rural Equipment). This was a secured transaction. Rural Equipment filed a financing statement with the Ness County Register of Deeds on June 18, 1980. Rural Equipment subsequently assigned its rights in the transaction to Case.

In July 1981 Foos failed to make a full installment payment due Case. An extension was agreed upon with that payment to be included when the next annual installment was due. In July 1982 Foos was unable to meet his payment obligations under the purchase agreement or the extension. Case insisted that the account be brought current or that Foos surrender the collateral. Foos turned to the Bank for help. Its loan officer, Larry Stieben, conferred with a Case representative who explained the status of Foos' account, including the balance owed and the number of annual installments remaining to be paid. In September 1982 the Bank loaned Foos sufficient funds to bring the account current.

When Case received the delinquent payment from Foos, its computerized billing and account system erroneously reported the entire contract was paid in full. The contract was stamped "paid" and mailed to Foos. Case also filed a UCC termination statement on November 24, 1982, terminating its security interest in the tractor and undercutter.

In December 1982 Foos met with Stieben to request a loan. Foos advised Stieben that Case no longer had a security interest in the purchased equipment as the contract had been paid. Stieben requested documentation and Foos produced the canceled contract stamped "paid" with a letter from Case stating the promissory note had been paid in full and Case had terminated its security interest in the equipment. Stieben then verified with the Ness County Register of Deeds that Case had filed a termination statement. Thus informed, the Bank did enter into the loan transaction with Foos, taking a security interest in the tractor and undercutter. A UCC financing statement was filed.

In February 1983 Case discovered the incorrect entries to the Foos account and notified him the contract had not been paid in full. Case also filed a new financing statement with the register of deeds. The statement was not signed by Foos. Foos failed to make any further payments and Case repossessed the equipment. Foos then filed an action against Case alleging unlawful repossession and criminal trespass. The instigation of that action caused Case to file this lawsuit against Foos and the Bank for judicial determination of the validity and priority of the competing security interests in the equipment.

The district court, upon written findings of fact and conclusions of law, entered judgment in favor of Case and against the Bank. It is from this judgment the Bank now appeals. The Bank raises three issues in this appeal: (1) Whether Case has a perfected security interest in the farm equipment; (2) whether the Bank has a perfected security interest in the farm equipment; and (3) whether the trial court's finding that the Bank did not exercise good faith is supported by substantial competent evidence.

* * *

At the time Foos entered into the secured transaction with Rural Equipment, the seller failed to perfect its purchase money security interest under [9-324(a)] as a financing statement was not filed within the required ten days. Rural Equipment did file a financing statement and thus perfected its security interest by filing on June 18, 1980. Conversely, the record is clear that at the time of Foos' purchase and through June 18, 1980, the Bank had no underlying security interest supporting its previously filed financing statement. [9-308] contemplates the existence of a security agreement before a security interest is perfected. Based upon these circumstances, we conclude Case had a perfected security interest in the tractor and undercutter from June 18, 1980, until its termination statement was filed on November 24, 1982, superior to any interest or claim asserted by the Bank.

What was the effect of Case's improvident filing of a termination statement? In our opinion, under [9-513], Case's security interest was at that moment no longer perfected. Case could, of course, continue to enforce its security interest in the equipment as long as only its debtor Foos was involved. However, a secured creditor with a perfected security interest must be given priority under [9-322(a)(1)] *** . It would thus appear the Bank's security interest perfected in December 1982 would be entitled to priority but for the trial court's finding the Bank did not act in good faith. The trial court, with implicit agreement of the parties, reasoned that Foos held voidable title to the equipment when he gave the Bank a security interest in the equipment. The court further reasoned the Bank was a purchaser [and] that 2-403(1) applied *** .

First, we do not believe Foos held voidable title to the equipment. Rather, he held title subject to the unperfected security interest of Case. 2-401(2) states:

> Unless otherwise explicitly agreed title passes to the buyer at the time and place at which the seller completes his performance with reference to the physical delivery of the goods, despite any reservation of a security interest....

We submit that full title passed to Foos at the time of sale in 1980. ***

Secondly, the trial court's application of 2-403(1) ignores the fact this is a priority dispute between competing security interests and therefore is to be resolved under Article 9 of the Code, not Article 2. This conclusion is supported by specific provisions in the Code. [9-110] states in material part: "A security interest arising solely under the article on sales (Article 2) is subject to the provisions of this article." [9-202] provides Article 9 is applicable to secured transactions "whether title to collateral is in the secured party or in the debtor."

Therefore, we conclude [9-322] sets forth the statutory rules that must be considered in determining the priority of competing security interests in collateral. In short, this statute was intended to be and is a "pure race" type statute. This means the secured creditor who wins the "race" to the appropriate filing office has priority without regard to the prevailing creditor's state of mind and knowledge. The Bank, having perfected its security interest in the equipment, is entitled to priority irrespective of its knowledge of Case's unperfected security interest in the same equipment. Any other conclusion would cause confusion and uncertainty in commercial transactions, undoing the clarity and preciseness intended under Article 9 of the Code. * * *

We need not and do not decide the effect of Case's effort to again perfect its security interest with the 1983 filing of a financing statement to remedy its prior improvident termination. Based upon our previous analysis and conclusions, such filing could at best have had only prospective effect.

Accordingly, we find the trial court erred in the following particulars: (1) 2-403(1) should not have been applied; and (2) [9-322] is applicable but does not require good faith by the secured creditor as it is a "pure race" statute.

The judgment of the trial court is reversed and the case is remanded for entry of judgment consistent with this opinion.

COMMENTS AND QUESTIONS: COMPETING SECURED CREDITORS: THE FIRST-IN-TIME RULE

What is the justification for the first-in-time rule? We should note initially that it operates merely as a baseline. If a party is willing to subordinate its claim to later claims, it is perfectly free to do so, either before it enters the transaction or at some later time. See 9-339. The question, then, is why this baseline is better than any other. Because parties are free to negotiate their own priority systems through subordination agreements, isn't it appropriate to ask what system of priority they would be most apt to negotiate if they were given the opportunity?

Engage in the following thought experiment: Ask what negotiations would be like if a secured creditor and debtor had to negotiate the priority that the secured party's claim would receive every time they entered into a transaction. (Assume, for the moment, that Article 9 offered no presumption one way or another.) The debtor would perhaps initially insist that it be allowed to give subsequent creditors a superior interest in the same collateral—an interest that would override the creditor's claim.

What would be the secured party's response? Wouldn't it fear that the debtor's ability to give others a security interest in the same collateral would lessen its own ability to come in and take possession of the property to satisfy the debt? An agreement giving the debtor the right to give later parties priority effectively gives the debtor the power to turn what was a secured loan into an unsecured one. The secured creditor, accordingly, would treat the transaction as one that was only partially secured. This, however, is inconsistent with the parties' initial decision that a fully secured loan was in their mutual self-interest.

It would seem to follow that, if both parties agree that there is an advantage in making the loan on a secured basis, they would also be likely to include a provision in their contract barring the debtor from granting any subsequent creditor a superior interest in the collateral. If a provision of this sort is not or cannot be included, many of the putative savings made possible by a secured transaction would be lost. If the parties included this provision, would it bind third parties? Assuming that the debtor, a secured party, and other creditors would generally negotiate for such a provision, does Article 9's implementation of a basic first-in-time rule simply supply an "off-the-rack" rule that we would expect the parties to reach if they could all negotiate together? For an analysis of this question, see Thomas H. Jackson & Anthony T. Kronman, Secured Financing and Priorities Among Creditors, 88 Yale L.J. 1143, 1162-64 (1979).

Merely because a first-in-time rule establishes a baseline that may suit most transactions, it does not follow that it will suit all transactions. What are the cases in which the first-in-time rule should be modified by the Code itself, rather than by private agreement? Does the thought experiment we just engaged in lead to the same result when the secured party wants a security interest in after-acquired property?

COMMENTS AND QUESTIONS: NOTICE FILING

Even assuming that a first-in-time rule is a good idea, does it follow that the party that is the first to *file* (assuming all parties perfect by filing) should be the party that is judged to be the first in time? The party that is the first to file has an advantage over all other potential lenders when the debtor seeks further credit on the basis of property that is described in its financing statement. As a factual matter, the equivalent of second mortgages arise rarely in secured transactions involving personal property. When they do arise, in large part because of the first-to-file rule, the secured party that would become the second to file negotiates directly with the first. Subsequent lenders usually will lend only if they can obtain subordination agreements from the first lender, in which the first lender agrees to subordinate its claim to any further funds it lends the debtor to the claims of the second. Such agreements create extra paperwork, and are possible only when the first lender is cooperative. (The alternative is for the second lender to take-out the first lender, meaning provide enough funds to the debtor to pay the first lender in full, plus provide the new funds the debtor needs, as took place in *Bollinger*.)

Who benefits from notice filing? Does Article 9's filing system follow from its first-to-file-or-perfect rule? Unlike a potential general creditor, a potential secured creditor needs to know whether an asset is or might become encumbered and whether competing claims will take priority over his claim. Unclear priority rules increase the cost of making secured loans. Article 9's priority rules are on the whole clear: the secured party who is first in time wins, and the secured party who is first to file is the first in time.

No other rule for dating priority seems as easy to apply. For example, the date the security interest comes into being depends on a number of facts that are hard to discover. For most collateral, a security interest attaches only after the parties have agreed to create a security interest and three conditions are satisfied: (1) the creditor has given value; (2) the debtor has acquired rights in the collateral; and (3) the debtor has authenticated a security agreement or the creditor has taken possession of or control over the collateral pursuant to an agreement. A rule that fixed the priority by the date on which any of these three events took place would be ambiguous from the perspective of third parties precisely because it would require potential creditors to rely on the debtor's records.

Moreover, information about the date an agreement was made, value was given, or the rights were acquired is both in the control of the debtor and less certain than a filing date. For example, "value" does not cover only cash outlays, it also includes any commitment to extend credit in the future. But whether the lender has made a commitment or has reserved the option to cancel the line of credit is sometimes left unclear in revolving credit arrangements. Similarly, a debtor's acquisition of rights in the collateral may be unclear. For example, when does a debtor acquire rights in the collateral if it has a machine built to its order? When the manufacturing is completed? When it acquires an Article 2 "special property" interest? When the risk of loss passes to it? All of these dates are hard for potential creditors to determine. Not even the date of signing a written security agreement will be clear, because agreements can be drafted "as of" certain dates. These dates do not precisely coincide with the date of signing; moreover, agreements can be amended and loans can involve several written documents, all of which can qualify as security agreements.

By contrast, Article 9's notice-filing system meshes perfectly with its first-to-file-or-perfect rule. It clearly establishes the priority of each secured creditor with respect to described collateral and little else and it does so based on the event that cures the ostensible ownership problem. The notice-filing system is of little use to general creditors who need an overview of the financial condition of their debtors, but it provides secured creditors most of the information they need, once one assumes that secured creditors typically do not take multiple security interests in the same property. See Douglas G. Baird, Notice Filing and the Problem of Ostensible Ownership, 12 J. Legal Studies 53 (1983). A creditor cannot safely enter a secured transaction if another creditor already has superior rights (albeit potential) to the same asset, unless the senior creditor executes a subordination agreement or the debtor can remove the financing statement under 9-513. Because executing subordination agreements is costly, Article 9's rules rest in some measure on the assumption that most secured parties do not want such junior interests. Is this assumption plausible? Or is it simply a self-fulfilling prophesy? Why would creditors be willing to take second mortgages on real estate, but not on personal property? Is it relevant that personal property is harder to value or that it typically depreciates more rapidly?

If the legal rule in fact accommodates the needs of the parties rather than vice-versa—that is, if creditors avoid inferior interests in personal property because of the nature of the property, rather than the legal rules governing it—secured creditors would not need to learn anything from the filing system other than the name of the person who might have a security interest and the type of collateral that may be covered. The benefits of Article 9's rules may outweigh the costs they impose on junior secured creditors. Even for those that seek such interests, a notice-filing system provides the information they need (the name of the secured party and the type of collateral involved) to begin negotiating a subordination agreement.

Does the justification we have given for notice filing withstand close scrutiny? Does it convince you that we should have *notice* filing, rather than *transactional* filing? In a world of transactional filing, the first creditor's priority is limited to the amount of money it extends in the original transaction or expressly commits to extending in the future. Other future advances require an additional filing. Interests in after-acquired property may require additional filings as well. What virtues does the first-to-file-or-perfect rule have that outweigh this cost? More narrowly put, the question becomes: What virtues does the notice filing system have that justify maintaining a first-to-file-or-perfect rule, rather than some other rule that determines priority? See also Peter F. Coogan, Article 9 of the Uniform Commercial Code: Priorities Among Secured Creditors and the "Floating Lien," 72 Harv. L. Rev. 838, 879-80 (1959).

A. CONTINUITY OF PERFECTION AND PRIORITY

We have three principal methods for perfecting a security interest: filing, control and possession. 9-322(a)(1) recognizes this, and the earlier-of-first-to-file-or-perfect rule meshes the alternative perfection approaches into single priority rule. The next two fact patterns examine the rules when a secured creditor ties its perfection to two different events, and seeks to link them together in a single unbroken chain of perfection. This is the "continuity of perfection" problem.

4-5: MIXED PERFECTION METHODS AND PRIORITY

- On January 1st, Finco lends Corp $10,000, takes a security interest in a laptop computer and perfects by taking possession.
- On February 1st, Bank lends $10,000 to Corp, takes a security interest in the computer and files an appropriate financing statement.
- On March 1st, Finco files a financing statement for the computer and gives up possession to Corp.
- ¤ Who has priority? See 9-308(c); 9-322(a)(1).

4-6: MIXED FINANCING STATEMENTS AND PRIORITY

- On January 1, 1979, Bank lends $10,000 to Corp, takes a security interest in equipment and files an appropriate financing statement.
- On February 1, 1979, Finco lends $10,000 to Corp, takes a security interest in the same equipment and files an appropriate financing statement.
- On December 1, 1983, Bank files a new financing statement covering the same collateral.
- On January 1, 1984, Bank's original statement lapses.
- ¤ Who has priority? See 9-308(c); 9-322(a)(1); 9-515(a).

In re Hilyard Drilling Co.

United States Court of Appeals, Eighth Circuit, 1988.
840 F.2d 596.

■ WOLLMAN, CIRCUIT JUDGE

Hilyard Drilling Co., Inc. (Hilyard) filed a Chapter 11 bankruptcy petition on January 25, 1985. At that time, Hilyard had debts outstanding to
the National Bank of Commerce of El Dorado (NBC) and Worthen Bank
& Trust Co., N.A. (Worthen), both secured by perfected security interests
in Hilyard's accounts receivable. NBC appeals from the district court's af-
firmance of the bankruptcy court's judgment that Worthen had a first-
priority security interest in Hilyard's accounts receivable under Arkansas
law. We affirm.

On April 25, 1979, Hilyard granted NBC a security interest in all of its
existing and future accounts receivable, and the proceeds thereof. This security interest was perfected by the filing of appropriate financing statements on April 26, 1979.

On April 28, 1983, Paul C. Watson, Jr., Worthen's vice president,
wrote a letter to Hilyard, which stated in relevant part:

> Confirming our telephone conversation, our Loan Committee
> has approved a renewal of your $550,000 equipment line and
> your $500,000 short-term working capital line on the following
> conditions:
>
> 1. That Worthen take a second lien position on accounts receiv-
> able.
>
> * * * * *
>
> I do not think that any of these items present a problem to you
> since we have previously discussed these. I understand that you
> need to talk with [NBC] regarding the receivables. We ac-
> knowledge their first lien and would be happy to do so in writ-
> ing so that it is clear to everyone that our lien is junior to theirs.

NBC never requested a written acknowledgement. On June 14, 1983, Hilyard granted Worthen a security interest in the same accounts receivable.
Neither Worthen's loan documents nor the financing statements it filed
on June 14, 1983, stated that Worthen's security interest was subordinate
to NBC's security interest.

On July 8, 1983, in connection with the reworking of Hilyard's loans,
NBC filed a new financing statement giving notice of its security interest

in Hilyard's accounts receivable. NBC did not file a continuation statement within six months preceding April 25, 1984, the expiration date of its 1979 financing statement, as required by [9-515(c), (d)]. * * *

The schedule of assets filed in connection with Hilyard's Chapter 11 bankruptcy indicated that the debts to NBC and Worthen exceeded Hilyard's accounts receivable. Worthen filed a motion with the bankruptcy court for the determination of the priority of the security interests in Hilyard's accounts receivable. The bankruptcy court determined that Worthen's security interest was first in priority. On appeal, the district court affirmed the findings of the bankruptcy court. * * *

The effectiveness of a financing statement lapses five years from the date of filing, unless a continuation statement is filed prior to its lapse. [9-515(a)]. Thus, unless NBC filed a continuation statement, its April 26, 1979, financing statement lapsed on April 25, 1984, prior to the filing of Hilyard's bankruptcy petition. NBC argues that its July 8, 1983, financing statement should be treated as a continuation statement under [9-515(c), (d)]. We disagree.

Under [9-515(c), (d)], a continuation statement must be filed within six months prior to the expiration of the original filing and "must be signed by the secured party, identify the original statement by file number and state that the original statement is still effective."

NBC admits that its July 8, 1983, financing statement does not satisfy the specific statutory requirements for a continuation statement because it "was not filed within six months of the expiration of the original financing statement, it does not refer to the file number of that financing statement, and it does not state that the original financing statement is still effective." NBC nonetheless argues that its July 8, 1983, financing statement should be treated as a continuation statement because its failure to fulfill the requirements of [9-515(c), (d)] is "harmless error," comparable to that addressed in [9-506].

Without determining whether the harmless error concept applies to [9-515(c), (d)], the bankruptcy court found that NBC's July 8, 1983, financing statement did not substantially comply with the requirements for a continuation statement. This finding is not clearly erroneous.

Financing statements and continuation statements serve distinct and different purposes. A financing statement that does not refer to the original filing cannot suffice as a continuation statement. NBC's failure to file a continuation statement cannot be considered harmless error, because the second financing statement gave no indication that it was filed for the purpose of continuing any other financing statement.

In addition, the fact that Worthen was aware of NBC's once-perfected security interest does not render harmless NBC's failure to file a proper continuation statement. "[S]ince the purpose of statutory filing requirements is, in most instances, to resolve notice disputes consistently and predictably by reference to constructive or statutory notice alone * * * consideration of a junior creditor's actual notice of a now lapsed prior filing by a competing senior creditor" is precluded.

NBC argues that even if its July 8, 1983, financing statement is not considered a continuation statement, its security interest is first in priority because it was continuously perfected from April 26, 1979, pursuant to [9-308(c)] and [9-322(a)(1)].

* * * To interpret [9-308(c)] as providing that a security interest can be continuously perfected by consecutively filed financing statements contradicts the express language of [9-515(c)]. [9-308(c)] is applicable to security interests that are originally perfected in one way and then subsequently perfected in some other way, without an intermediate unperfected period. NBC, which initially perfected by filing, subsequently perfected in the same way, by filing, as opposed to "in some other way" as required by the statute. Accordingly, [9-308(c)] is inapplicable to NBC's security interest in Hilyard's accounts receivable. * * *

Worthen's security interest had first priority pursuant to [9-322(a)(1)]. NBC's April 26, 1979, financing statement lapsed due to its failure to file a continuation statement, leaving the underlying security interest unperfected. [9-515(c)] Following the lapse, the other perfected security interests in Hilyard's accounts receivable advanced in priority. Of the remaining perfected security interests, Worthen's interest had priority because it was first in time of filing or perfection. * * *

COMMENTS AND QUESTIONS

1. How does the result in *Hilyard Drilling* square with the language of 9-322(a)(1) ("[p]riority dates from the earlier of the time a filing covering the collateral is first made or the security interest or agricultural lien is first perfected, if there is no period thereafter when there is neither filing nor perfection")? After NBC filed its initial financing

statement, was there ever a point at which it was neither filed nor perfected? Of course, if we allowed a secured creditor to string together financing statements seriatim, what would this do to the integrity of the financing system?

2. Recall problem 4-5. Doesn't this create precisely the same problem for the financing system?

3. Isn't it true, though, that for 9-308(c) to be meaningful, we must reject a literal interpretation of 9-322(a)(1)? Or should we say instead that 9-308(c) speaks to one situation—different methods of perfection in sequence—without saying anything about a second situation—the same method of perfection in sequence?

4. Recall that 9-339 expressly provides that nothing in Article 9 undercuts subordination agreements. What should we make of the April 28, 1993 letter by Worthen to Hilyard? Can NBC claim it was a third-party beneficiary of that letter? As a matter of course, should NBC ask for subordination agreements in these situations, to guard against the possibility of a loss of priority? Is this overkill and precisely the sort of over-papering that gives lawyers a bad name, or is this prudent recognition of the fact that a client may find it difficult to file the continuation statement properly, as the lawyer may not be around to help?

B. THE NATURE OF PRIORITY

What does it really mean for one secured creditor to have priority over another secured creditor? The fact patterns that follow provide some simple background for the next cases.

4-7: PRIORITY IN DEFAULT SITUATIONS

- After a default by Debtor, Bank, a junior secured creditor, repossesses equipment from Debtor under 9-609. Bank gives notice that it intends to dispose of the collateral under 9-610, and takes steps to prepare the collateral for sale. Finco, the senior secured creditor, learns of the intended sale.

- ¤ What are Finco's rights? Would it matter whether Debtor was also in default to Finco? May Finco demand that Bank deliver the property to it? What rights does Bank have for the costs that it has incurred in repossessing the equipment and preparing it for sale? See 9-609 and 9-610.

- Finco does nothing and the equipment is sold.

¤ What are Finco's rights? May it demand that Bank deliver the proceeds of the sale to Finco? Again, what rights does Bank have as to the expenses it has incurred?

4-8: PRIORITY WITH MUTIPLE TYPES OF COLLATERAL: MARSHALING

- Finco holds a perfected security interest in equipment and inventory of Debtor. Bank has a perfected security interest only in inventory.
- Finco seeks to repossess inventory and sell it. Bank protests, arguing that Finco should be required to exhaust its interest in equipment first, prior to acting against the inventory.
- ¤ Who wins? Suppose Finco is the senior secured creditor on the inventory. Suppose Bank is. How should filing priority influence this situation?

Peoples Bank v. The Computer Room, Inc. (In re The Computer Room, Inc.)

United States Bankruptcy Court, N.D. Alabama, 1982.
24 Bankr. 732.

■ GEORGE S. WRIGHT, BANKRUPTCY JUDGE

The issue before the Court is whether the doctrine of marshaling of assets should be invoked.

I. FINDINGS OF FACT

1. The Computer Room, Inc. filed a Chapter 7 petition on November 25, 1981.

2. On July 1, 1981, the creditor, First Alabama Bank of Tuscaloosa, N.A. (FAB) perfected a general security interest in debtor's accounts receivable, inventory (including tangible personal property) and contract rights (Fund # 1), as security for a debt of $9,843.

3. On September 18, 1981, Peoples Bank of Tuscaloosa (Peoples Bank) perfected a security interest in a specific accounts receivable of the debtor (invoice from the State of Alabama Highway Department) (Fund # 2) as security for a loan of $6,808. This obligation was guaranteed individually by Jackson Mathews, who was President and a principal stockholder (Fund # 3). The debtor used the loan proceeds from Peoples Bank to purchase computer equipment necessary to complete contract work with the State of Alabama Highway Department.

4. On December 3, 1981, * * * the attorney for the debtor, Claude M. Burns, Jr., collected the specific accounts receivable from the State of Alabama Highway Department of $9,309, and also collected other accounts receivable and other funds of $4,044 making a grand total of $13,353, and has retained and invested such funds at interest by agreement of the parties.

5. On December 17, 1981, Peoples Bank filed an adversary proceeding to invoke the equitable doctrine of marshaling of assets.

6. Al Vreeland, as Trustee, has inventory in his possession of $29,100 cost value.

II. CONCLUSIONS OF LAW

The doctrine of marshaling of assets (or the "two funds" doctrine) is applied "when two or more creditors claim against one debtor and the first creditor can reach two properties held by the debtor whereas the second can reach only one." In re Beacon Distributors, Inc., 441 F.2d 547 (1st Cir. 1971).

The elements of marshaling of assets are:

1. That they are creditors of same debtor.

2. That there are two funds belonging to that debtor, and

3. That one of them alone has right to resort to both funds.

Diagrammatically, the marshaling of assets' doctrine is as set out below:

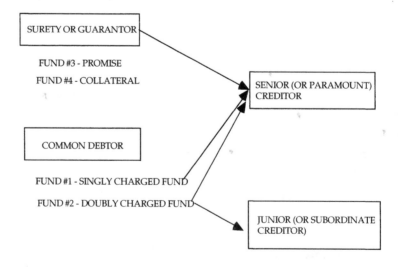

DOCTRINE[3,5]: Senior Creditor must exhaust Fund # 1 (Not Fund # 3 nor Fund # 4) before resorting to Fund # 2 so that Junior Creditor can collect Fund # 2.

A. History of Doctrine of Marshaling of Assets

In re Beacon Distributors, Inc., 441 F.2d 547 (1st Cir. 1971), outlines the history of the doctrine as follows:

> ... Derived from the case of Culpepper v. Aston, 2 Ch. Cas. 115, 117 (1682), the doctrine is almost the same today as it was then. Compare Lanoy v. Duke of Athol, 2 Atk. 444, 446 (Ch. 1742), with Meyer v. United States, supra. An early case on all fours with the instant one is Ex parte Kendall, 17 Ves. 514 (Ch. 1811). In that case a firm's senior partner died, and shortly thereafter the firm collapsed. The question before the Lord Chancellor was whether he should stay the creditors' dividend on the four surviving partners "until payment shall have been recovered out of [the decedent's] estate by those creditors, who are creditors upon both funds." Id. at 418. The Chancellor ruled that the doctrine did not apply. American courts have followed this ruling consistently, from the earliest days, e.g., Ayres v. Husted, 15 Conn. 504, 516 (1843); Dorr v. Shaw, 4 Johns. Ch. 17, 20 (N.Y. 1819), to the latest, In re Independent Truckers, Inc., 226 F. Supp. 440, Ohio App. 289, 194 N.E.2d 162 (1963).

* * * The security interest in the instant case is governed by the Uniform Commercial Code. [9-601] gives the senior secured party cumulative rights without requiring marshaling. The comment to [9-401] apparently

---

[3] There is a distinction between a surety (primarily liable) and a guarantor (secondarily liable). "A surety is usually bound with his principal by the same instrument, executed at the same time and on the same consideration.... On the other hand, the contract of guarantor is his separate undertaking, in which the principal does not join." Black's Law Dictionary (5th ed. 1979). However, there is no recognized surety-guaranty distinction in the application of the marshaling doctrine because these assets are not owned by a common debtor of both creditors (e.g. not contributed capital).

[5] In the 8th Circuit, In re Jack Green's Fashions for Men—Big and Tall, Inc., 597 F.2d 130 (8th Cir. 1979) general unsecured creditors (in lieu of a junior or subordinate secured creditor) as represented by a trustee in bankruptcy, have been allowed (erroneously in the opinion of this court) to invoke the marshaling doctrine. This is contra to the overwhelming majority rule which requires a secured creditor. * * *

recognizes marshaling as not being inconsistent with Article 9, so that 1-103 incorporates the marshaling of assets' doctrine.

The early case of Nelson v. Dunn, 15 Ala. 501, 517 (1849) adopted the doctrine of marshaling of assets in Alabama:

> It is furthermore, a well established rule in equity, that if a party has two funds, a person having an interest in one of them only, has a right in equity to compel the former to resort to the other, if it is necessary for the satisfaction of both. ***

Further, in 1923 Alabama codified the doctrine of marshaling of assets by a specific marshaling of liens statute, Ala. Code 35-11-4, as follows:

> 35-11-4. Order of resort to different things.
>
> Where one has a lien upon different things, and other persons have subordinate liens upon, or interests in, some but not all of the same things, the person having the prior lien, if he can do so without risk of loss to himself,[7] or of injustice to other persons, must resort to the property in the following order, on the written demand of any party interested:
>
> > (1) To the things upon which he has an exclusive lien;
> >
> > (2) To the things which are subject to the fewest subordinate liens;
> >
> > (3) In like manner inversely to the number of subordinate liens upon the same thing; and
> >
> > (4) When several things are within one of the following classes, and subject to the same number of liens, resort must be had
> >
> > > a. To the things which have not been transferred since the prior lien was created;
> > >
> > > b. To the things which have been so transferred without a valuable consideration; and
> > >
> > > c. To the things which have been so transferred for a valuable consideration in the inverse order of the transfer.

(Code 1923, 8938; Code 1940, T. 22, 4)

---

[7] The doctrine of marshaling of assets will not be invoked where the senior creditor will be prejudiced or has an increased risk of loss.

III. Application of Law to Facts

First Alabama Bank is the senior or paramount creditor with a security interest in inventory of $29,000 cost value and all accounts receivable ($13,352 so far collected), which are designated as Fund # 1—the singly-charged fund, which includes a specific accounts receivable from the State of Alabama Highway Department ($9,308 which has been collected).

Peoples Bank is the junior or subordinate creditor with a security interest in only one accounts receivable of the common debtor, The Computer Room, Inc., from the State of Alabama Highway Department of $9,308 (Fund #2—the doubly-charged fund) to secure a loan of $6,807. Inasmuch as all three elements of the doctrine of marshaling of assets have been satisfied, Peoples Bank can properly invoke the doctrine so as to require FAB to collect from the inventory and other accounts receivable (Fund # 1—the singly-charged fund) rather than from the specific account receivable from the State of Alabama Highway Department (Fund # 2—the doubly-charged fund).

The Court rejects the 8th Circuit anomaly, *In re Jack Green's Fashion for Men—Big and Tall, Inc.*, as being inconsistent with the historical background of the doctrine of marshaling of assets and further, as stated in the Matter of Samuels & Co., Inc., 526 F.2d 1238 (5th Cir. 1976)

> We do not sit as federal chancellors confecting ways to escape the state law of commercial transactions when that law produces a result not to our tastes. Doing what seems fair is heady stuff... Today's heady draught may give the majority a euphoric feeling, but it can produce tomorrow's hangover.

If the 8th Circuit rationale * * * were used in the instant case, the trustee in bankruptcy could force Peoples Bank to go against the personal guaranty of the principal stockholder, Jackson Mathews; but better reasoning supports the view that a separate guaranty of an officer, director, and principal stockholder is not a separate fund which the trustee in bankruptcy can force a senior creditor to exhaust. * * *

COMMENTS AND QUESTIONS: MARSHALING, EXTENDED PRIORITY AND THE INCOHERENCE OF NARROW ASSET PRIORITY

We have described Article 9 as creating a reified priority system, meaning one that ties priority to particular assets. That means that a security interest in, say, equipment creates no special rights in inventory. It turns out that isn't always true, at least not where the equitable doctrine of marshaling is introduced. Under 1-103, equitable doctrines still apply unless displaced by the UCC.

Consider the following facts. Bank lends Debtor $100 and takes a security interest in Debtor's equipment and inventory. Bank files appropriately. Subsequently, Finco lends Debtor $100 and takes a junior perfected security interest in the equipment, also with an appropriate filing. Debtor also owes Supplier $100 on an unsecured basis. Assume that Debtor fails and has equipment worth $100 and inventory worth $99. The priority as to the equipment is Bank, Finco, Supplier. As to the inventory, Bank has priority while both Finco and Supplier are unsecured.

The sequence in which we liquidate the collateral—inventory followed by equipment or equipment followed by inventory—matters a great deal. Start with inventory. Bank would take the full $99, and then would collect its remaining $1 from its first position against the equipment. That leaves $99 in equipment, and Finco takes all of that. Supplier gets shut out. Flip the collateral sequence. If Bank starts with equipment, it takes all of the value there. Finco collects nothing on its security interest in equipment. Both Finco and Supplier are unsecured against inventory, so they split the value evenly. Note the swing: in the first sequence, Bank collected $100, Finco $99 and Supplier $0, while on the second go-round, Bank received $100 and Finco and Supplier each took $49.50.

What controls the sequence in which we realize against the collateral? Very little actually and that should be a concern. So far, we have discussed priority by focusing on a particular asset and ranking the rights of creditors against that asset. We have done this asset by asset and have acted as if this creates a coherent priority scheme. As the last example should make clear, in a fundamental way it does not. We also need to order—to prioritize—the sequence in which we will proceed against different assets. We must prioritize the separate priority grants. Nothing in Article 9 makes it possible for the debtor to do so.

The problem is even more basic than the prior example suggests. It arises whenever we have a grant of a security interest. Take this in two steps. Modify the prior example by dropping the Bank's security interest in inventory. So, to reset, let Bank have the first security interest in the equipment, Finco the second. No creditor holds a security interest in the inventory. Again, the sequence in which these priorities are resolved may matter. Start with inventory, and then consider the equipment. Given the equal priority on the inventory, its value could be divided pro rata—$33 a piece—among the three creditors. Bank would then be owed $67, which, as the senior creditor on the equipment, it would collect in full. As the junior secured creditor, Finco would then be entitled to the remaining $33 from the equipment. Taken together, Bank would be paid in full, Finco would receive $66 and Supplier $33. Now flip the order: start with equipment and then consider inventory. Bank is first as to equipment, and therefore collects its full $100 from its value. As to inventory, Finco and Supplier have equal rights, so each collects $49.50. In both cases, Bank is paid in full, but again, the sequence in which we resolve the priorities against the property determines how the value is distributed between Finco, the junior secured creditor on equipment, and Supplier, the unsecured creditor.

Take one more step by dropping Finco's security interest in the equipment. Now the order of realization appears not to matter. If we proceed first against equipment, Bank collects $100, and Finco and Supplier split the $99 inventory evenly. If we proceed first against inventory, each creditor takes a $33 chunk. Bank is still owed $67, and collects that from the equipment for its full $100. The remaining $33 in equipment is split evenly between Finco and Supplier, so each collects a total of $49.50. In both cases, Bank gets $100 and Finco and Supplier each receive $49.50.

But the irrelevance of the sequence is an artifact of the numbers. Let the equipment be worth $80 and redo the calculations. Again, if we start with equipment, Bank collects $80. Bank is still owed $20 and collects that claim on a pro rata basis from the inventory. We now have unsecured debts of $220 against property worth $99. Bank's share is $9 (for a total of $89), while Finco and Supplier each take $45. Now start with inventory. Each creditor takes $33. Bank collects its balance from the equipment, giving it its full $100. $13 in equipment is left, and that is split evenly, giving Creditor and Supplier each a total of $39.50. Once again, the sequence in which we realize on the property matters. The size of the claim that Bank gets to use in the pro rata calculations used to distribute the inventory is determined by the order of realization.

This is a basic issue for Article 9's property-based priority rules. As soon as we allow for priority over particular property, to have an internally coherent system, we must address the order of realization against that property and the debtor's remaining property. As the examples emphasize, that order matters in a very powerful way. Our notion of priority should not be limited to the narrow asset priority that defines the reified priority system but must also grapple with the implicit priority issues by these sequencing examples.

How has the law fared? There is no overarching recognition of these issues; instead, we find pockets in the rules where these issues are considered. The equitable doctrine of marshaling is sometimes invoked if one creditor has two types of collateral while a second creditor has just one. In the first example, Bank had a security interest in equipment and inventory, while Finco was limited to equipment. Put generally, and subject to conditions, the doctrine of marshaling states that one secured creditor must satisfy its claim out of particular assets before looking to a second group of assets when another secured creditor has a security interest only on that second group of assets. Bank would be required to collect first from inventory before turning to the equipment. This is viewed as "fair" to the junior secured creditor who would otherwise collect nothing on its junior interest. The junior secured creditor did, after all, take some security interest, while unsecured creditors took none.

The equity of this is far from obvious. As the example emphasizes, what is at stake is the division of value between the junior secured creditor and the unsecured creditor. The doctrine of marshaling effectively extends the security interest held by the junior secured creditor to a second collateral type by resolving the realization-sequencing question to the benefit of the junior secured creditor. Of course, the junior secured creditor did not bargain for any explicit priority over the unsecured creditor as to the unencumbered assets. Both creditors were content to be on par as to those assets as unsecured creditors. Marshaling transmutes priority over one asset to unbargained-for priority over a second asset. Equity, it turns out, is quite tricky.

We might try other perspectives to speculate on the merits of this rule. The rule of marshaling maximizes the size of the assets subject to an effective security interest. In the example, marshaling means that both the inventory and the equipment are subject to effective security interests, as both Bank and Finco will vindicate their security interests. Absent marshaling, only the equipment would be subject to an effective interest. Is this a good or bad thing? On one view, unencumbered assets create common pool problems and we use security interests to structure competition among creditors. See Randal C. Picker, Security Interests, Misbehavior and Common Pools, 59 U. Chi. L. Rev. 645 (1992). Shrinking the encumbered assets reduces the risk of wasted competition over those assets.

In addition, marshaling enhances the likelihood that the junior secured creditor will get a return from monitoring. Indeed, the junior secured creditor could monitor either the inventory or the equipment and enhance its chance of collection.

For additional discussion, see J. Story, Commentaries on Equity Jurisprudence §§ 853-871, at 230-48 (14th ed. 1918) and Moses Lachman, Marshaling Assets in Bankruptcy: Recent Innovations in the Doctrine, 6 Cardozo L. Rev. 671 (1985).

Delaware Truck Sales, Inc. v. Wilson

New Jersey Supreme Court, 1993.
618 A.2d 303.

■ HANDLER, J.

On August 20, 1984, Delaware Repair Service, Inc. (Delaware Repair) entered into a financial agreement with Royal Bank of Pennsylvania (Royal Bank or bank). Royal Bank loaned $75,000 to Delaware Repair evidenced by a demand promissory note. Delaware Repair also secured the loan. It executed a financing statement covering all of its "inventory, equipment, fixtures, machinery, appliances, tools, furniture and furnishings, leasehold interests, accounts receivable, now and hereafter acquired." Royal Bank filed that financing statement with the Camden County Clerk on September 19, 1984, and with the Secretary of State on September 25, 1984. As further security for the loan to Delaware Repair, defendants, Edward Wilson, a principal of Delaware Repair, and his wife, Joan Wilson, personally guaranteed the loan, which in turn was secured by a mortgage on their residence.

Plaintiff, Delaware Truck Service, Inc. (Delaware Truck), a corporation engaged in the cargo-container-repair business, sold its assets to Delaware Repair. According to the sales contract, dated September 6, 1984, the assets transferred included: "the machinery and equipment of the Seller as set forth on Exhibit 'A' hereto the business and goodwill of the Seller and including all customer records and files presently in the hands of Seller." Delaware Repair agreed to pay Delaware Truck a total of $300,000, $30,000 in cash, plus a promissory note for $270,000 payable in sixty equal monthly installments. Defendant Edward Wilson and George Fandrick, both former employees of Delaware Truck, personally guaranteed payment on the note. The agreement provided that Delaware Repair would execute "financing statements" that would create a lien in favor of plaintiff covering all assets sold, plus a "secondary lien" on Delaware Repair's accounts receivable, "subject only to a prior lien in favor of Purchaser's institutional lender." Delaware Truck filed a financing statement covering Delaware Repair's "inventory, equipment, fixtures, machinery, appliances, tools, furniture and furnishings, now and hereafter acquired" with the Secretary of State on August 29, 1984 (which predated the signing of the sales agreement), and with the Camden County Clerk on September 13, 1984. It filed a separate financing statement on October 4, 1984, covering Delaware Repair's accounts receivable.

Delaware Repair eventually defaulted on its payments to Delaware Truck and Royal Bank. On May 27, 1988, Delaware Repair entered into an agreement with Delaware Truck whereby Delaware Repair acknowledged its inability to pay the $166,936 it owed plaintiff and surrendered to plaintiff all of the assets in which plaintiff held a security interest. According to the "Surrender Agreement," those assets included "inventory, equipment, fixtures, machinery, appliances, tools, furniture and furnishings, now and hereafter acquired," as well as its accounts receivable. The agreement also noted that the accounts receivable were "probably" subject to a "secondary lien * * * in favor of Royal Bank of Pennsylvania * * * ." In the months following the surrender of assets, plaintiff collected $98,600 from Delaware Repair's accounts receivable, and applied that money to Delaware Repair's debt.

In December 1988, Royal Bank sued Delaware Repair and the guarantors on the unpaid promissory note and obtained a default judgment against Delaware Repair and the guarantors in the full amount of $62,000. The record does not indicate that any of the defendants interposed any defenses. Thereafter, Royal Bank, apparently having learned that Delaware Truck had obtained and collected the debtor's accounts receivable, sought to recover from Delaware Truck the amounts thus realized. In April 1989, Royal Bank entered into a settlement agreement with Delaware Truck. Delaware Truck paid $59,500 in exchange for an assignment of Royal Bank's judgment against Delaware Repair and the guarantors, its security interests in Delaware Repair's assets, and the Wilsons' personal guaranty secured by the mortgage on the Wilson home. Royal Bank also entered into a subordination agreement with plaintiff whereby Royal Bank acknowledged that "every security interest held by Royal Bank in each and every asset of Delaware Repair Services, Inc. is subordinate to the security interest of Delaware Truck."

In April 1989, Delaware Truck filed suit against Delaware Repair, Edward and Joan Wilson, and George Fandrick seeking to collect on the note made by Delaware Repair in favor of plaintiff, as well as on Royal Bank's judgment. It sued to enforce both the note and personal guaranties. In July 1989, defendant Edward Wilson filed for personal bankruptcy. Plaintiff then filed a motion in bankruptcy court seeking to modify the automatic stay so that it could foreclose the mortgage on the Wilsons' residence, which constituted security for the Wilsons' personal guaranty. The bankruptcy court granted the motion, and plaintiff, as assignee of Royal Bank, filed the complaint in this action seeking to foreclose on the Wilsons' residence.

The Appellate Division * * * conclud[ed] that plaintiff could not foreclose on the mortgage. The Appellate Division found that Royal Bank was first to file a financing statement covering accounts receivable and therefore had priority over plaintiff's security interest in Delaware Repair's accounts receivable. The Appellate Division, however, further determined that because the moneys collected by plaintiff from Delaware Repair's accounts receivable should have been applied to Royal Bank's debt, the latter's debt had been satisfied and extinguished with the payment to Royal Bank.

Plaintiff first argues that it had priority with respect to Delaware Repair's accounts receivable, and therefore its realization of the proceeds from the accounts receivable prior to the assignment of Royal Bank's interests against Delaware Repair could not satisfy Delaware Repair's debt to Royal Bank.

Both creditors, Delaware Truck and Royal Bank, had perfected their respective security interests in Delaware Repair's assets through the execution of financing statements describing the collateral. * * * [W]e are thus satisfied that the Appellate Division correctly concluded that Royal Bank's priority interest in the accounts receivable of Delaware Repair was superior to the security interest of plaintiff.

After Delaware Repair's defaults, the creditors independently proceeded against the debtor to obtain satisfaction of their respective debts. Delaware Repair turned over all of its assets to Delaware Truck through a surrender agreement, which included its accounts receivable and inventory. Plaintiff realized $98,000 from the proceeds of the accounts receivable.

Royal Bank separately obtained a default judgment against Delaware Repair. Royal Bank then made a claim against Delaware Truck, presumably when it learned that Delaware Truck had obtained the accounts receivable and had proceeded to collect them. Royal Bank and Delaware Truck entered into an assignment and subordination agreement whereby Delaware Truck paid Royal Bank $59,500 and Royal Bank assigned to plaintiff its $62,000 default judgment against Delaware Repair, together with the personal guaranties and its secured collateral.

* * * According to the Appellate Division, Delaware Truck, as the junior creditor, when it came into possession of the accounts receivable by way of the surrender by Delaware Repair, held those receivables only as a trustee or agent on behalf of Royal Bank because the latter had a senior security interest in the receivables. Hence, plaintiff's collection of Delaware Repair's accounts receivable was deemed to be on behalf of Royal Bank, and its subsequent payment of the proceeds from the receivables to the bank satisfied and extinguished Delaware Repair's debt to Royal Bank. With the disappearance of the debt, the security for the debt likewise evanesced.

It is readily inferable that both Delaware Truck and Royal Bank, in the settlement between them, did not intend to satisfy and thereby discharge the underlying obligations of defendants to Royal Bank. Ordinarily, the intention of the parties determines whether a transfer of money by a third person to a creditor constitutes a discharge or purchase of an underlying debt or note. This rule may apply to transactions between junior and senior creditors.

Thus, from the face of the documents evidencing the transaction, it appears that Delaware Truck and Royal Bank mutually intended to transfer, not extinguish, Delaware Repair's underlying debt to Royal Bank. However, regardless of that intent, the Appellate Division may have been correct in concluding that the debt was extinguished as a matter of law. As stated earlier, Royal Bank had priority security interest in Delaware Repair's accounts receivable. That priority interest endured even after plaintiff liquidated the receivables and realized their proceeds. [9-315(a)] (stating that priority of a creditor holding a perfected security interest continues in proceeds from disposition of collateral). Consequently, in the absence of countervailing considerations, Royal Bank had a right to require plaintiff to disgorge the proceeds of the accounts receivable to the extent of its priority lien interest. Therefore, despite the contrary intentions of the parties, we cannot discount the force of the Appellate Division's conclusion that plaintiff was acting as a constructive trustee on Royal Bank's behalf.

The hesitancy that we have in affirming that determination is based on the absence in the record of evidence relating to the circumstances surrounding Royal Bank's claim against Delaware Truck and the settlement of that claim. The record does not sufficiently indicate whether Royal Bank knew, expected, or reasonably anticipated that the accounts receivable would be turned over to Delaware Truck and whether the collections of those receivables would be applied first to Delaware Repair's debt of Delaware Truck. Conversely, the record is silent with respect to Delaware Truck's knowledge or expectations in obtaining the accounts receivable and ignoring Royal Bank's priority when it collected the proceeds of those receivables. The record does not inform us whether Delaware Truck had any claim of right to the accounts receivable sufficient to justify its collection and application of some portion of their proceeds to its debt, or whether it had any valid defenses by way of bar or set-off to Royal Bank's later demand that the collected moneys be paid over. * * *

An additional circumstance that bears on the understanding and expectation of defendants with respect to whether the disposition of the accounts receivable served to extinguish Royal Bank's debt is the nature and purpose of the guaranty defendants gave Royal Bank and the understanding of defendants in providing that guaranty. The guaranty on its face gives broad rights to Royal Bank. It states that it is "a continuing, absolute and unconditional guaranty" and may be enforced "without first resorting to any security or other property or invoking other available rights or remedies." Thus, under the guaranty Royal Bank had virtually uncontrolled discretion to deal with the collateral, including the right to assign it. Arguably, those rights included the right to foreclose on the guarantors' mortgage and forego its other security interests. Thus, on Delaware Repair's default, Royal Bank was free to seek recourse directly against the guarantors and to enforce any of its security interests to satisfy its debt.

Moreover, under the doctrine of marshaling assets in an action against defendants, Royal Bank might have had an obligation under the personal guaranties to proceed against the real-estate mortgage in order to enable plaintiff to achieve a recovery out of the accounts receivable. Hence, in the context of this case, it would also be relevant to determine whether the guarantors, the Wilsons, when signing the guaranty and mortgage, knew or should have known that the bank could, in effect, forego its priority in the receivables, or, indeed, whether in the face of the Wilsons' imminent or actual bankruptcy, the bank would be required or expected to defer to Delaware Truck as the junior creditor with respect to the accounts receivable. Despite the broad range of remedial rights under the guaranty, the record is devoid of any evidence that would tend to show that Royal Bank reasonably would have pursued any particular remedy under the guaranty to the exclusion of another, or whether in its settlement with Delaware Truck it intended to select among the remedies provided by the guaranty.

Finally, it seems clear that defendants' claim that the personal guaranties were discharged because the collateral held by Royal Bank had been impaired through its liquidation is not sustainable. Guarantors may waive their rights to claim impairment of collateral as a defense in the guaranty agreement. Such a waiver, however, must be unequivocal before it will effectively preclude a guarantor from asserting the defense.

These several considerations appear material to whether plaintiff, Delaware Truck, improperly enhanced its position by paying itself $98,000 due Royal Bank and later by taking an assignment of the subject mortgage; and whether Royal Bank, though well within its rights to assign its default judgment and security interests, including defendants' personal guaranty secured by their residential mortgage, merely received a sum that was equivalent to the amount of the bank's judgment against defendants. Additional evidence should inform the determination of whether plaintiff and Royal Bank entered into a valid settlement permitting plaintiff to foreclose on defendants' residence.

We do not purport to resolve any of the factual issues that appear germane to proper determination of the claims in this case, or to intimate the weight, if any, to be ascribed to any facts that are found. While we cannot on this record indicate that any particular determination of these issues would dictate a resolution in favor of either party, the relevance of these issues forestalls a motion for summary judgment based on the current record.

In conclusion, we reverse the judgment of the Appellate Division, and remand this matter to the trial court for further proceedings consistent with this opinion.

■ POLLOCK, J., concurring.

* * * A fair reading of the record suggests that by applying the proceeds of the receivables to its own claim, Delaware Truck deprived Royal Bank of money to which it was entitled, forced the bank to threaten suit, and then resolved the dispute by paying the bank virtually all the money due on the

bank's loan. Thus, Delaware Truck enhanced its position, first by paying itself $98,600 due Royal Bank and later by taking an assignment of the subject mortgage. If Delaware Truck had paid the bank $62,000 from the proceeds of the receivables, the bank's loan would have been satisfied and Royal Bank would have canceled the mortgage. By misappropriating the proceeds of the receivables, Delaware Truck prevented the payment of Royal Bank's loan and facilitated the assignment of the subject mortgage, all to its benefit and the Wilsons' detriment. Having brought the bank to the bargaining table by not honoring the bank's senior security interest in the receivables, Delaware Truck improved its position to the prejudice of the Wilsons. Until it acquired Mrs. Wilson's guaranty and the subject mortgage, Delaware Truck had no claim against her or her family home. If it had paid Royal Bank from the proceeds of the receivables, Delaware Truck never would have acquired the mortgage from the bank. Only by misusing the proceeds was Delaware Truck able to acquire the mortgage that it now seeks to foreclose. * * *

The Appellate Division, however, concluded that because Delaware Repair should have applied the proceeds to Royal Bank's debt, that debt should be deemed satisfied. It relied on [9-322(a)(1)], which grants priority to the first creditor to perfect a security interest by filing. The court reasoned that Delaware Truck should have honored Royal Bank's senior security interest and paid the amount needed to satisfy the Wilsons' debt to the bank. Like the bank, the Wilsons had a right to expect that Delaware Truck would pay the bank before paying itself. Only by violating its duty under the Uniform Commercial Code was Delaware Truck able to bring the bank to the bargaining table and obtain the bank's consent to the agreement. From Royal Bank's perspective, once its loan was satisfied, it had no financial interest in the legal relationship between Delaware Truck and the Wilsons. Neither Delaware Truck nor Royal Bank inquired whether their agreement defeated the Wilsons' expectations.

* * * Like the bank, the Wilsons, as guarantors of Delaware Repair's debt to Royal Bank, had the right to expect that Delaware Truck would respect the seniority of the bank's security interest. Delaware Truck and Royal Bank could not deprive the Wilsons of that right without the Wilsons' consent. Hence, I disagree with the majority's suggestion that the Wilsons' expectations may be relevant because "the status of Delaware Truck in collecting the accounts receivable is determinative of its right as assignee to enforce Royal Bank's remedies against the debtors-guarantors * * *." The Wilsons' expectations are relevant not because Delaware

Truck's status is determinative, but because their expectations limit the extent to which Royal Bank and Delaware Truck may deal with the proceeds of Delaware Repair's receivables.

* * * I also believe that the majority misperceives the significance of the Wilsons' guaranty. By its terms, the guaranty was absolute, unconditional, and assignable. Under the circumstances of this case, however, Delaware Truck should not be allowed to avail itself of the guaranty or of its self-serving agreement with Royal Bank, an agreement that apparently was drafted by Delaware Truck's attorney without the knowledge or consent of the Wilsons. The reason is that the guaranty is subject to the Wilsons' expectation that Delaware Truck would pay Royal Bank from the proceeds of the receivables. Thus, the point is not that "Royal Bank might have had an obligation under the personal guaranties to proceed against the real-estate mortgage in order to enable plaintiff to achieve a recovery out of the accounts receivable." Rather, the point is that Delaware Truck and Royal Bank's agreement alone could not deprive the Wilsons of their rights, notwithstanding the terms of the guaranty. A contrary result could lead to a circuity of action: the Wilsons could recover from Royal Bank for its failure to apply the proceeds to the loan secured by their guaranty, and the bank could then recover from Delaware Truck for the misapplication of the proceeds.

Royal Bank recognized that its primary obligor was Delaware Truck. On discovering that Delaware Repair had misapplied the accounts receivable, the bank did not seek to foreclose on the Wilsons' home, but threatened to sue Delaware Truck. Had the Wilsons paid Royal Bank under their guaranty of Delaware Repair's loan, they would have been subrogated to the bank's rights against Delaware Truck for misappropriation of the proceeds of the receivables. In effect, the parties would have landed in their present position with the Wilsons entitled to credit against Delaware Truck for the misuse of the proceeds of Delaware Repair's receivables. * * *

The majority should not rely on the possibility that Royal Bank may have had an equitable obligation to marshal its assets in favor of Delaware Truck. As previously indicated, the critical relationship is not that between Royal Bank and Delaware Truck, except insofar as [9-322(a)(1)] obligates Delaware Truck to honor the bank's senior security interest. The focus should be on the relationship between Delaware Truck and the Wilsons.

Section [9-610] generally authorizes creditors to dispose of collateral to satisfy a defaulted loan. An earlier section, [9-315(a)], provides that a security interest continues in the proceeds from the disposition of collateral. No one disputes that the security interest of a creditor continues in the proceeds from the collection of accounts receivable. The priority of a creditor with a perfected security interest in the receivables continues in the proceeds. A creditor with a security interest in accounts receivable need not take possession of the receivables to perfect its lien. A secured creditor who disposes of proceeds in violation of Article 9 "is liable to the debtor and other secured parties for any loss caused by his failure to comply."

* * * By not turning over the proceeds to Royal Bank, Delaware Truck unjustly enriched itself and became a constructive trustee for the benefit of the Wilsons. * * *

On remand, I believe the trial court should focus on the Wilsons' right to expect Delaware Trust to turn over the proceeds to Royal Bank for application against Delaware Repair's $75,000 bank loan, which was secured by the subject mortgage.

COMMENTS AND QUESTIONS

1. What is the purported basis of the right that the concurring opinion sees the Wilsons as having regarding the settlement agreement between Royal Bank and Delaware Truck?

2. For a discussion of the relative rights and duties of junior and senior secured parties as applied to the foreclosure process under old Article 9, see C. Edward Dobbs, Foreword: Enforcement of Article 9 Security Interests—Why So Much Deference to the Junior Secured Party?, 28 Loy. L.A. L. Rev. 131 (1994).

SECTION II. RIGHTS BETWEEN SECURED AND UNSECURED CREDITORS

4-9: SECURED CREDITORS AND LIEN CREDITORS

- On January 1st, Bank lends and takes a security interest in collateral held by the debtor.

- On February 1st, Bank files an appropriate financing statement.

- On March 1st, a general unsecured creditor jumps through the state law hoops and becomes a lien creditor under 9-102(a)(52).

- ¤ Who has priority?

- On January 1st, Bank lends and takes a security interest in collateral held by the debtor.
- On February 1st, a general unsecured creditor jumps through the state law hoops and becomes a lien creditor under 9-102(a)(52).
- On March 1st, Bank files an appropriate financing statement.
- ¤ Who has priority?
- On January 1st, Bank files an appropriate financing statement.
- On February 1st, a general unsecured creditor jumps through the state law hoops and becomes a lien creditor under 9-102(a)(52).
- On March 1st, Bank lends and takes a security interest in collateral held by the debtor.
- ¤ Who has priority?

[handwritten margin note: Just filing — FS is not enough. Needs attachment.]

[handwritten margin note: elements: · value · authenticate · identity · collateral.]

[handwritten margin note: Perfect requires attachment. 9-203(b)]

4-10: NEGATIVE PLEDGES

- On January 1st, Creditco lends $10,000 to Debtor on an unsecured basis.
- On February 1st, Finco lends $20,000 to Debtor, and receives a negative pledge, meaning, of course, that the debtor promises that it will not grant a security interest in its assets.
- On March 1st, Debtor breaches that promise and borrows $30,000 from Bank who takes a security interest in all assets of the debtor.
- ¤ On April 1st, the debtor fails and has on hand $40,000 in assets, all of which is subject to the perfected security interest. How should these assets be divided?

Consider the role of 9-317(a) and the general relationship between secured and unsecured creditors in the following cases. Focus in particular on the limits that the priority scheme created in Article 9 should impose on the ability of a court to reach a desired outcome.

Aptix Corp. v. Quickturn Design Systems, Inc.

United States Court of Appeals, Federal Circuit, 2005.
148 Fed. Appx. 924.

■ GAJARSA, CIRCUIT JUDGE

Amr Mohsen ("Mohsen") appeals a decision by the United States District Court for the Northern District of California issued pursuant to Federal

Rules of Civil Procedure ("FRCP") 69(a) in which the court voided Mohsen's security interest in the assets of Aptix Corporation as a fraudulent transfer under California law. Quickturn Design Systems, Inc. ("Quickturn") filed the underlying motion to enforce the court's prior judgment awarding Quickturn $4.2 million in attorney fees stemming from a patent infringement suit filed by Aptix. Because the district court did not commit clear error in finding that Aptix granted the security interest to Mohsen with the actual intent to hinder Quickturn's satisfaction of the attorney fees award, we *affirm* the judgment.

I. BACKGROUND

Aptix is a developer of hardware-logic-emulation technology and the owner of U.S. Patent No. 5,544,069 ("the '069 patent"). Mohsen founded Aptix and at all relevant times was the majority shareholder, chief executive officer and chairman of the company. Mohsen is also the only inventor named on the '069 patent.

Quickturn is one of three primary competitors of Aptix in the hardware-logic-emulation technology field. Mentor Graphics Corporation ("Mentor") and its French subsidiary Meta Systems, Inc. ("Meta") also compete with Aptix. After Quickturn won a United States patent infringement suit against Mentor and Meta, Aptix entered into an agreement with Mentor and Meta whereby Aptix licensed the '069 patent and granted Meta the right to sue to enforce the patent. Mentor agreed to advance Aptix all costs of prosecuting a patent infringement suit against Quickturn. Aptix and Meta subsequently filed an infringement suit against Quickturn in the United States District Court for the Northern District of California.

On June 14, 2000, the court dismissed the Aptix/Meta complaint as a sanction for Aptix's having "engaged in a pattern of fraudulent behavior through Amr Mohsen, its founder, chairman, chief executive officer and lead inventor. Aptix tried to defraud defendant and the Court through the alteration and fabrication of evidence, perjury and the staged theft of evidence." The June 14, 2000 Order required Aptix and Quickturn to negotiate the amount of the attorney fees award by July 20, 2000. The parties agreed on a settlement amount of $4.2 million with Aptix retaining the right to object to certain categories of Quickturn's attorney fees and costs.

During the summer of 2000, Aptix was in financial trouble having unsuccessfully attempted to borrow money, raise equity financing and merge with another company. On July 25, 2000, Aptix and Mohsen entered into a security agreement whereby Aptix granted Mohsen a security interest in all of its assets in exchange for certain loan funds. Prior to July 2000, Mohsen had loaned at least $2 million to Aptix on an unsecured basis. Pursuant to the security agreement, Mohsen loaned Aptix at least $9.7 million between July 2000 and September 2003. In that same time frame, Mohsen received nineteen installments on the debt totaling approximately $1.5 million. Aptix used the money from Mohsen to maintain its operations by paying employees, vendors and other creditors.

On July 27, 2000, Aptix filed an objection to certain categories of Quickturn's attorney fees and costs. On August 10, 2000, Quickturn made its last filing on the issues surrounding the judgment by submitting a response to Aptix's objection. It was not until August 16, 2000, that Mohsen perfected his security interest by filing a UCC financing statement. On September 8, 2000, the court overruled Aptix's objections, awarded Quickturn the entire amount of attorney fees sought and entered final judgment in the case. * * *

On May 27, 2003 Quickturn levied on certain of Aptix's assets, creating an execution lien thereon, and the assets were delivered to the U.S. Marshal. Mohsen then made a third party claim to the assets based on his security interest executed in July 2000. Believing the security interest to be a fraudulent scheme to prevent Quickturn from recovering its award, Quickturn filed a motion to enforce judgment pursuant to FRCP 69(a). After an evidentiary hearing, the district court entered an order finding that Aptix had granted the security interest to Mohsen with "actual intent ... to hinder or delay satisfaction of the judgment due its creditor." Accordingly, the court voided Mohsen's security interest as a fraudulent transfer under California Civil Code 3439.04(a).

II. DISCUSSION

This court reviews "nonpatent issues according to the law of the regional circuit where appeals from the district court would normally lie." Univ. of Colo. Found., Inc. v. Am. Cyanamid Co., 342 F.3d 1298, 1305 (Fed. Cir. 2003). The district court's determination that Aptix granted the security interest to Mohsen with the intent to hinder or delay Quickturn's satisfaction of the judgment was a finding of fact that the Ninth Circuit reviews for clear error.

The district court applied California's fraudulent transfer statute in determining that the security interest granted to Mohsen should be voided. That statute reads:

(a) A transfer made or obligation incurred by a debtor is fraudulent as to a creditor, whether the creditor's claim arose before or after the transfer was made or the obligation was incurred, if the debtor made the transfer or incurred the obligation as follows:

(1) With actual intent to hinder, delay, or defraud any creditor of the debtor.

(2) Without receiving a reasonably equivalent value in exchange for the transfer or obligation, and the debtor either:

(A) Was engaged or was about to engage in a business or a transaction for which the remaining assets of the debtor were unreasonably small in relation to the business or transaction.

(B) Intended to incur, or believed or reasonably should have believed that he or she would incur, debts beyond his or her ability to pay as they became due.

Cal. Civ. Code 3439.04(a). Section 3439.04 has been construed to mean that a transfer is fraudulent if the provisions of either subdivision (a)(1) regarding actual intent *or* subdivision (a)(2) regarding the circumstances of the transfer have been satisfied.

The court relied on subdivision (a)(1) of § 3439.04 in finding that Aptix made the transfer to Mohsen with the actual intent to hinder or defraud Quickturn. In so finding, the district court identified three "badges of fraud" that supported an inference of fraudulent intent. At the time the court issued its order, the badges of fraud were not statutory, but appeared in the Legislative Committee commentary to 3439.04. In 2004, the California legislature added subsection (b) to 3439.04 which codified the following nonexclusive list of the badges of fraud:

(b) In determining actual intent under paragraph (1) of subdivision (a), consideration may be given, among other factors, to any or all of the following:

(1) Whether the transfer or obligation was to an insider.

(2) Whether the debtor retained possession or control of the property transferred after the transfer.

(3) Whether the transfer or obligation was disclosed or concealed.

(4) Whether before the transfer was made or obligation was incurred, the debtor had been sued or threatened with suit.

(5) Whether the transfer was of substantially all the debtor's assets.

(6) Whether the debtor absconded.

(7) Whether the debtor removed or concealed assets.

(8) Whether the value of the consideration received by the debtor was reasonably equivalent to the value of the asset transferred or the amount of the obligation incurred.

(9) Whether the debtor was insolvent or became insolvent shortly after the transfer was made or the obligation was incurred.

(10) Whether the transfer occurred shortly before or shortly after a substantial debt was incurred.

(11) Whether the debtor transferred the essential assets of the business to a lienholder who transferred the assets to an insider of the debtor.

Cal. Civ. Code 3439.04(b). The three badges of fraud relied on by the district court now appear as items (1), (4) and (9) on the codified list. The district court determined that while Aptix was insolvent it granted a security interest to an insider and that that transfer occurred just before a substantial judgment was to be entered against Aptix.

Before the district court, Mohsen argued that he should not be punished for simply lending money to Aptix so that it could continue as a going concern. The district court rejected this argument finding that Aptix and Mohsen had

> an arrangement by which Dr. Mohsen lends Aptix money, which Aptix uses to pay employee salaries and essential creditors in an effort to keep functioning.... Dr. Mohsen receives money back from Aptix on demand.... This setup allows ... Aptix to pay unsecured creditors as it sees fit, while effectively avoiding its obligations toward a judgment creditor that holds a judgment lien.

Id. Thus, the district court concluded that the arrangement was "not as innocent as Dr. Mohsen suggests." Id.

On appeal, Mohsen takes issue with both the district court's factual findings and the legal principles it applied. Mohsen's factual challenge is fundamentally a reassertion of the argument rejected by the trial judge, namely that the granting of the security interest to Mohsen was intended to benefit not defraud creditors by keeping Aptix operational. Borrowing a concept from bankruptcy cases, Mohsen argues that the on-going operation of Aptix was a "legitimate supervening purpose" such that the confluence of three badges of fraud was insufficient to establish actual intent to defraud.

Mohsen's reliance on the concept of a "legitimate supervening purpose" is misplaced. * * * Here, Mohsen attempts to rebut the presumption of fraudulent intent by focusing on the reason that Aptix needed to borrow money from Mohsen, i.e. it could not obtain funding elsewhere, and its ultimate use of the money, i.e. to pay employees and other creditors. Although Mohsen's argument may explain why Aptix entered into the loan arrangement with Mohsen, it does not explain why it was necessary for Aptix to grant Mohsen a security interest in substantially all of its assets when Mohsen had never required such an interest for his past loans. It also does not address the district court's express finding that the arrangement was not as innocuous or well-intentioned as Mohsen suggests. Mohsen failed to rebut the circumstantial inference arising from the badges of fraud and, therefore, it was not clear error for the district court to conclude that Aptix granted the security interest with the actual intent to defraud Quickturn.

Mohsen's legal arguments are also without merit. First, he argues that California law protects the right of debtors to "pay one creditor in preference to another, or ... give to one creditor security for the payment of his demand in preference to another." Cal. Civ. Code 3432. Mohsen fails to recognize, however, that the section of the California Civil Code on which he relies does not insulate debtors who make transfers with the intent to defraud creditors not party to the transaction. Kemp v. Lynch, 65 P.2d 1316 (1937) (a transfer that appears to be a lawful preference, but which is made with a fraudulent intent will be vitiated); Roberts v. Burr, 67 P. 46 (1901) (stating that a debtor may pay one creditor in preference to another in the absence of fraud).

Similarly, Mohsen argues that Aptix did not have the requisite fraudulent intent because it entered into the security agreement in order to benefit some of its creditors. This argument reads 3439.04(a)(1) as if it requires that the debtor intend to defraud *all* of its creditors, whereas the language actually used in the statute mandates only that the debtor act with the actual intent to "defraud *any* creditor" (emphasis added). * * *

■ NEWMAN, CIRCUIT JUDGE

I respectfully dissent. Dr. Mohsen loaned over nine million dollars to the company he had founded and operated, secured by the assets of the company. My colleagues hold that the purpose of making the secured loan was to defraud future creditors, based on two undisputed facts: that Dr. Mohsen expected an adverse attorney fee award in favor of Quickturn, and that his previous smaller loans to his company were unsecured. I cannot agree that the requirement of security for the larger loans establishes fraudulent intent.

The district court found that the facts established an intent by Aptix to prefer Dr. Mohsen as a creditor over Quickturn, and thus to "hinder or delay" the satisfaction of Quickturn's future judgment in terms of California Code 3439.04 (a transfer is fraudulent if made with "actual intent to hinder, delay, or defraud any creditor"). However, California law also establishes that "a preference, is not for that reason a transfer made to 'hinder, delay or defraud.'" Wyzard v. Goller, 28 Cal. Rptr. 2d 608 (1994). The *Wyzard* court explained that "it has been the rule for over 400 years, since the Statute of Elizabeth in 1571," that a transfer which establishes a preference is not thereby fraudulent. Id. (citing 13 Eliz., ch. 5 (1571)).

This rule is codified in California Code 3432, which states that "A debtor may pay one creditor in preference to another, or may give to one creditor security for the payment of his demand in preference to another." California precedent reaffirms that the preference itself does not establish wrongful fraudulent conduct. Id.

Although the panel majority is correct that an intent to prefer one creditor over another does not preclude the existence of a wrongful intent, it is clear from the district court's opinion that its inference was based solely on its belief that it was fraudulent for Aptix to prefer Dr. Mohsen by entering into a secured loan instead of an unsecured loan. The district court described as "not as innocent as Dr. Mohsen suggests" the "setup" whereby "Dr. Mohsen lends Aptix money, which Aptix uses to pay employee salaries and essential creditors in an effort to keep functioning." I point out that there is a large space between absence of innocence, and deliberate fraud. Undoubtedly all concerned knew that a secured creditor has priority over unsecured creditors. That does not establish an intent to defraud the unsecured creditors.

Precedent illustrates instances of fraudulent intent. In Kemp v. Lynch, 65 P.2d 1316 (1937) an ostensibly lawful preference made with "the understanding that it shall be a mere simulated transfer" was fraudulent. Unlike *Kemp*, here there was no simulated transfer, but regular monthly loans to meet payroll and other operating obligations. The facts of this case are more analogous to those of *Wyzard*, in which a secured loan was taken in order to pay an existing debt when it became known that an adverse judgment was imminent; the court held that there was no fraud in a transfer made "with recognition that the transfer will effectively prevent another creditor from collecting on his debt." Wyzard, 28 Cal. Rptr. 2d 608 (concluding that the facts did not raise a triable issue of fact as to fraud, notwithstanding the existence of three factors of fraud).

Aptix granted Dr. Mohsen a security interest; the money was needed and used for legitimate business purposes. The panel majority states that this "does not explain why it was necessary for Aptix to grant Mohsen a security interest" when "Mohsen had never required such an interest for his past loans." It is surely not fraudulent to obtain security for a loan of over nine million dollars, whatever the relationship between the lender and the recipient. Knowledge of a potential adverse judgment does not establish fraudulent intent when making a loan to meanwhile keep the company alive and operating.

The security interest here at issue was only to the amount of the loan. See 3439.04(b) (requiring that debtor not receive a "reasonably equivalent value in exchange for the transfer or obligation" in order to establish "constructive fraud"). The fact that the security was limited to the value of the loan is also relevant under subdivision (a), the subdivision under which the court found fraud, as in 3439.04(a)(8) (a "factor" in determining fraudulent intent is "[w]hether the value of the consideration received by the debtor was reasonably equivalent to the value of the asset transferred or the amount of the obligation incurred"). These provisions of the California Code hinge the determination of fraud on whether the exchange was for equivalent value, a fact here undisputed.

My colleagues have thus lapsed into error, in holding that the making of a secured loan instead of an unsecured loan in anticipation of an adverse judgment establishes deliberate wrongful conduct. The moneys obtained and the security interest granted for the loan were routine business practice. The secured nine million dollars here loaned provided essential funds to pay employees, vendors, and creditors. The facts of record do not establish fraud under California statute and precedent. I respectfully dissent from the panel majority's contrary holding.

COMMENTS AND QUESTIONS

1. What exactly has Dr. Mohsen done that is problematic? He puts in fresh money in a struggling business. He could have done that as an equity investment putting himself behind all creditors. Or he could have made an unsecured loan, as the majority seemingly thinks is required, putting the new debts on a level playing field with preexisting unsecured debts. But of course he didn't do that: he wanted priority for his new investments. Does Article 9 say anything about these questions?

2. I think that it is fair to say that the dissenting opinion is more faithful to the traditional lines separating fraudulent transfers from other transactions. But why are those lines drawn in the way that they are?

Be sure to read 9-401 and comment 5 to 9-401 before reading the next case. What role should 9-401 play in evaluating the negative pledge at stake in *Mudge*?

First Wyoming Bank, Casper v. Mudge

Wyoming Supreme Court, 1988.
748 P.2d 713.

■ URBIGKIT, JUSTICE

This is an appeal from an action instituted by Robert M. Mudge, Sybil A. Mudge, Edward W. Mudge, and Edna F. Mudge (Mudges), appellees, by a third-party complaint in response to a foreclosure action instituted by First Wyoming Bank, Casper (Bank), appellant, to foreclose a security interest in a corporate enterprise inventory. This third-party complaint was severed from the original foreclosure action when the earlier decision was appealed and the foreclosure decision affirmed in M & M Welding v. Pavlicek, Wyo., 713 P.2d 236 (1986). The third-party complaint alleging intentional interference with a contract by the Bank resulted in a jury verdict for the Mudges of $123,997.

We affirm this decision also, as essentially invoking a sufficiency-of-the-evidence inquiry. * * *

I. FACTS

* * * On July 31, 1981, the Mudges made an agreement to sell the family corporate welding business to Redding. This written agreement included

transfer of the Mudges' stock in M & M Welding, Inc., with inventory, equipment, and the business site real property. Additionally, the document contained a nonencumbrance covenant clause, Section 3(f), which later led to this litigation, and which provided:

> 3(f). It is agreed that the assets of M & M Welding, Inc., a Wyoming corporation, or its successor corporation shall not be mortgaged for more than the presently existing indebtedness without Sellers['] consent until the total purchase price herein agreed to be paid shall have been paid in full. Such consent shall not be unreasonably withheld.

To facilitate the security status of the transaction, the corporate stock was placed in escrow until the buyer completed payments under the contract while operating the business during the purchase payment period.

The sales transaction closed in September, 1981, and the buyer took over the operation of M & M Welding. Almost immediately, he applied to appellant for a loan of $100,000 to cover obligations from other investments. At some time, as evidenced by its inclusion in the Redding loan file, the Bank's lending officers had been given an unsigned copy of the purchase agreement that contained the nonencumbrance covenant. The date when the Bank actually received the agreement is disputed, as well as by whom it was seen. In any event, no encumbrance consent was ever obtained from the Mudges, and the Bank took a security interest in the inventory and equipment for the purpose of securing a first priority upon loan default.

Subsequently, Redding did go into default on his purchase payments, causing the Mudges to cancel the sales agreement and in August, 1982 reclaim the M & M stock from escrow. The Mudges first became aware of the security agreement given by Redding to the Bank when the Bank made foreclosure claim to the inventory and equipment as a result of the disputed security agreement, which action effectively shut down M & M Welding. To free up their collateral and be able to continue the business, the Mudges individually put up a letter of credit for $100,000, which was substituted for the property which was the subject of the pending bank foreclosure action. The Bank subsequently drew down the letter of credit. The Bank won the first go-around in *M & M Welding v. Pavlicek,* supra, but in the second round, now here on appeal, lost the jury verdict on a theory of intentional interference with a contractual relationship for the amount of the letter of credit, purchase cost, and interest. This court has

adopted the Restatement (Second) of Torts, § 766, p. 7 (1979) definition
of the tort of intentional interference with a contract:

> "One who intentionally and improperly interferes with the per-
> formance of a contract (except a contract to marry) between
> another and a third person by inducing or otherwise causing the
> third person not to perform the contract, is subject to liability to
> the other for the pecuniary loss resulting to the other from the
> failure of the third person to perform the contract." Davenport
> v. Epperly, Wyo., 744 P.2d 1110, 1111 (1987), quoting Toltec
> Watershed Improvement District v. Johnston, Wyo., 717 P.2d
> 808, 813-814 (1986). ***

Appellant next argues that it was erroneous not to grant appellant's motions for a directed verdict *** .

*** Evidentiary analysis establishes a justified basis for the jury to have
found as a predicate for liability that the Bank did not act in good faith in
inducing the borrower to violate his purchase agreement so that the lender
would obtain priority chattel security for its $100,000 loan. While the
Bank's motive to have a first priority in the collateral for loan is not in itself improper, the fact, as the jury concluded, that the Bank knew about
the restrictive covenant and then preempted the collateral in requiring the
Mudges to post a letter of credit to pay to get their property back, displayed a classic case of the tort of intentional interference with a contractual relation. In simplistic terms, it consisted of inducing the buyer to
break his purchase contract terms in order to offer a new loan security
priority to the Bank. ***

COMMENTS AND QUESTIONS: NEGATIVE PLEDGES AND PRIORITY

Return to the fact pattern before *Mudge*. Is this a situation where we have
a set of inconsistent priorities among our three creditors? The reasoning
would go something like this. The secured creditor has priority over the
unsecured creditor; that is what it means to be a secured creditor. The
negative pledge holder and the unsecured creditor are on par—the negative pledge holder did not seek priority over the unsecured creditor—and
the negative pledge holder and the secured creditor should be on par, as
that was the point of the negative pledge in the first place. That suggests

that all three creditors should be on par, but that is inconsistent with the idea that the secured creditor has priority over the unsecured creditor.

What should we do? Start with the unsecured creditor's rights under the negative pledge. The notion that this pure unsecured creditor should be on par with the secured creditor treats the pure unsecured creditor as a beneficiary of the negative pledge. A standard negative pledge bars security interests generally, and that would seem to benefit *all* unsecured creditors, not just the creditor who sought the restriction. That, though, is a bit odd. It is unlikely that the negative pledge holder cares about what happens to these stranger unsecured creditors. It might be more sensible to ignore that possibility and to treat the secured creditor as having priority over the unsecured creditor.

The next step is to separate property rights and private contractual rights, to treat property rights first and private contractual rights second. Here, that would mean that we should treat the negative pledge as a private contractual right between its holder and the secured creditor. The negative pledge morphs into a private contractual right of parity—of pro rata treatment—between the negative pledge holder and the secured creditor. This is how we implement the idea that general unsecured creditors should not benefit from the negative pledge.

First, distribute the $40,000 in accordance with the property rights against it. The secured creditor receives $30,000—respecting its property right through the security interest—while the negative pledge holder and the unsecured creditor—as unsecured creditors—split the remaining $10,000 pro rata ($6,667/$3,333). We are not done yet, as so far, the negative pledge hasn't accomplished much. Now make a second distribution, this time focusing on the negative pledge as this morphed private contractual right of parity between the secured creditor and the negative pledge holder. Together, in the first round of the distribution, these creditors received $36,667 on claims of $50,000. Pro rata treatment between them—parity between the negative pledge holder and the secured creditor under our interpretation of the negative pledge—means a 40%/60% split of the $36,667, or approximately $14,667 to the negative pledge holder and $22,000 to the secured creditor. The second step in the distribution gives nothing to the unsecured creditor, and this reflects the idea expressed above that the negative pledge holder does not intend the other unsecured creditors to benefit from the restriction. Note how the analysis hinges on the scope of the beneficiaries of the negative pledge. If instead the unsecured creditor is to benefit from the negative pledge, then there is no reason to distinguish the unsecured creditor and the negative pledge holder. Both should be treated on par with the "secured" creditor, and all $40,000 should be divided pro rata.

We might tap into doctrine and implement this idea through an action against the secured creditor for the breach of the negative covenant, such as the action for tortious interference with contract we see in *Mudge*. That would require that the secured creditor have knowledge of the restriction, and a secured creditor with knowledge who wished to avoid the consequences of the restriction would be forced to negotiate directly with the negative pledge holder. This also draws a natural line between property rights, good against the world, but as to which broad notice, though a public filing must be given, and private contractual rights, as to which no general notice must be given. On this view, the negative pledge is one example of this, a subordination agreement another. We might insist that the negative pledge/parity right be created affirmatively through a contract between the negative pledge holder and the secured creditor, but this is really just a question of default rules. That is, either we can insist on the contract just described, or allow the debtor and the negative pledge holder to enter into their contract, give notice of that contract to the secured creditor and insist that the secured creditor affirmatively contract with the negative pledge holder to override the negative pledge clause. The tortious interference with contract idea takes the latter approach.

Note that the negative pledge holder can limit the chance that a superior security interest will be granted. 9-203(a) provides that "a security interest attaches to collateral when it becomes enforceable against the debtor with respect to the collateral, unless an *agreement expressly postpones the time of attachment*." (emphasis added). The parties to a secured transaction can delay the time of attachment if they so choose. They may create conditional security interests that vest on the occurrence of a designated event, such as poor financial performance, entry of a judgment against the firm or a failure to satisfy financial ratios. A financing statement could be filed when the security agreement was executed and this would preserve the priority position of our springing secured creditor, should the spring be sprung. As to the negative pledge, take it, but file a financing statement and add a security interest that attaches on the grant of a security interest to second creditor. Under 9-322(a)(1), priority is keyed to the order of filing, not attachment, so the new secured creditor will be junior to the negative pledge holder/springing secured creditor. This result will make taking the security interest substantially less attractive, and should reduce the number of times the negative pledge is breached. Are there any risks in this approach? There may be a lurking preference issue under BC 547.

SECTION III. PURCHASE MONEY SECURITY INTERESTS

Article 9's treatment of the purchase money security interest (often a "PMSI") is embodied in 9-103 and 9-324. 9-103 tells us who is a purchase money lender and it incorporates a strict tracing requirement. 9-324 tells us what procedural requirements must be met for a purchase money lender to acquire priority over prior secured parties. If the purchase money lender does not meet these requirements, but still satisfies the requirements for becoming a perfected secured party, its rights are governed by 9-322(a)(1).

The predecessor to 9-103, F9-107, provided in full:

A security interest is a "purchase money security interest" to the extent that it is

(a) taken or retained by the seller of the collateral to secure all or part of its price; or

(b) taken by a person who by making advances or incurring an obligation gives value to enable the debtor to acquire rights in or the use of collateral if such value is in fact so used.

As should be clear, the drafters treated lenders who are not themselves sellers but who make enabling loans just as they treated sellers. Their ambition was to avoid distinguishing between classes of creditors on grounds that were entirely formal.

Note the strict tracing requirement of the rule of 9-103(a) and the steps that a purchase money lender should go through to ensure that its debtor not only buys the machine it promised to buy, but that it uses the lender's money to do it. Two safe ways to ensure that this requirement is met is for the lender to pay the seller directly or to write out the check that is handed to the debtor to the seller's order.

9-324(b) imposes special burdens on those who assert purchase money security interests in inventory, including timely advance notice to those holding competing security interests in the inventory. 9-324(a) allows those who assert purchase money interests in other kinds of property twenty days from the time the debtor receives possession of the collateral to file their interests. Moreover, the superpriority given to those with purchase money security interests in inventory does not extend to proceeds

that are not identifiable cash proceeds. Thus, when inventory is sold and
the proceeds of the sale are accounts, the priority contest between a purchase money financier of inventory and an accounts receivable financier as
to the accounts is decided by the first-to-file-or-perfect rule of
9-322(a)(1).

Now take a good look at 9-103. The new section is much longer than
F9-107. It adds a number of new ideas and addresses some key issues that
arose in the F9-107 caselaw. The section also represents a legislative compromise, as clarifications made in 9-103(e), (f) and (g) are not extended to
consumer-goods transactions, and courts instead are left on their own. To
understand the changes, examine 9-103 as you think through the following fact patterns:

4-11: THE SIMPLE PMSI

- Debtor, a small business, goes to Seller to buy a copying machine.
- Seller agrees to finance the purchase price, but requires that Debtor
  grant a security interest in the copier to secure payment.
- ¤ What kind of security interest does Seller receive? See 9-103,
  9-324.

4-12: PMSIS AND CURRENT ASSETS

- Bank lends Debtor $10,000, and takes a security interest in Deb-
  tor's equipment, inventory, proceeds and after-acquired property.
- Debtor sells the inventory for cash and does so in such a fashion
  that Bank's security interest in the inventory is cutoff after sale,
  such as would happen in a sale covered by 9-320.
- Debtor purchases new inventory from Supplier. Supplier finances
  the sale and takes back a security interest. Supplier files an appropriate financing statement before allowing Debtor to take possession of the inventory. Supplier also gives appropriate notice of all of
  this to Bank.
- ¤ What are the relative rights of Bank and Supplier?

4-13: PMSIS AND CATEGORIZATION OF THE COLLATERAL

- On February 1st, Bank enters into a security agreement with Debtor, a small accounting firm, and takes a security interest in inventory, equipment, accounts and general intangibles, then-owned and
  thereafter acquired. Bank files an appropriate financing statement.

- On March 1st, Seller sells a computer to Debtor on credit and takes back a security interest in the computer. Five days later, Seller files a financing statement for the computer.
- ¤ What are the respective rights of Bank and Seller?
- Change the facts. Seller manufacturers computers and sells them on credit to resellers. Seller keeps a purchase money security interest in the computers it sells. Debtor is one of those resellers. Five days after the sale to Debtor, Seller files an appropriate financing statement.
- ¤ What are the respective rights of Bank and Seller?

4-14: PMSIS AND MULTIPLE DEBTS

- Bank has a security interest in Debtor's equipment and is properly perfected.
- Seller sells a copying machine to Debtor taking back a security interest. Debtor's obligations under the contract include payment of the purchase price of $5,000, payment of interest of $500 and payment of attorney fees if the Debtor defaults.
- Seller files an appropriate financing statement within five days of closing.
- ¤ Assume the copier is equipment in Debtor's hands. What is Seller's status as to the purchase price? the interest obligation? the contingent debt for attorney's fees?

4-15: PMSIS AND THE DATE OF POSSESSION

- Debtor leases a computer from Seller for three months. It is a true lease, not a financing lease.
- At the end of the lease, Debtor purchases the computer from Seller. Seller finances the sale and takes back a purchase money security interest and files immediately after the sale.
- ¤ Does Seller have a PMSI?

4-16: PMSIS, DEFECTIVE NOTICE AND CIRCULAR PRIORITY

- On January 1st, Debtor grants Bank a security interest in current and after-acquired inventory. Bank files an appropriate financing statement.
- On February 1st, Debtor grants Finco a security interest in current and after-acquired inventory. Finco also files correctly.

- The next day, Supplier supplies new inventory and does so on a PMSI basis. Assume Supplier files before delivery. Supplier gives notice to Bank but fails to give notice to Finco.

¤ What are the relative priorities of Bank, Finco and Supplier?

COMMENTS AND QUESTIONS: THE JUSTIFICATIONS FOR A PURCHASE MONEY PRIORITY

Consider the following case: Bank acquires and perfects a security interest in all of Debtor's property now existing or hereafter-acquired. Seller retains a security interest in a machine it sells Debtor. Seller wants to argue that it does not need to satisfy any special requirements that Article 9 places on purchase money lenders. Debtor is incapable of conveying to Bank any greater rights than it had, and Bank acquired at most Debtor's equity in the machine. But Seller has not retained anything more than a security interest. See 1-201(b)(35). The Code treats purchase money lenders identically regardless of whether title was initially vested in them (as in the case of Seller) or in a third party (as in the case of a bank making a loan that enables a debtor to acquire goods from a manufacturer). See 9-103. However one determines property rights and priority rights under the Code, it may not be desirable to have the question turn on something like the rights a seller retains in the sales agreement that are invisible to third parties.

If Article 9's superpriority for purchase money lenders is not based on the 19th-century notion that the seller has never parted with a large number of the sticks in the bundle of rights associated with a particular piece of property, what is its justification? Perhaps we should remember our earlier observation that parties are free to rearrange priority rights among themselves. If parties had the time to think about it, would a lender that was first in time insist upon taking priority over most subsequent lenders, but nevertheless be willing to subordinate itself to a subsequent lender who enabled the debtor to acquire a new piece of property?

If a lender would be willing to subordinate itself to a subsequent lender who enabled the debtor to acquire a new piece of property, why wouldn't it be willing to subordinate itself to anyone who later provided additional funds to the debtor? What is the difference between a lender that enables a debtor to acquire new assets and a lender that gives a debtor funds to use in the ordinary course of its business? Isn't the debtor's financial health strengthened by the same amount in both cases?

In our earlier discussion, we tentatively concluded that a lender wants to insist on a first-in-time rule, because without it the lender has no assurance that its loan will in fact be fully secured. Although the lender can adjust for this in setting its interest rate, it will not capture all the benefits of secured credit. Why doesn't the purchase money lender undercut the benefits that the first party receives from its security interest in after-acquired property? Won't the secured party with an interest in after-acquired property charge a higher interest rate if it has to account for the possibility of purchase money lenders than if it does not?

A. The Scope of the Purchase Money Security Interest

9-103(a)(1) has eliminated some of the uncertainty that existed with regard to the scope of a permissible purchase money security interest. F9-107 provided, in relevant part, that "[a] security interest is a 'purchase money security interest' to the extent that it is (a) taken or retained by the seller of the collateral to secure all or part of its price ...." Consider that definition and the revised definition as you read the case that follows.

MBank Alamo N.A. v. Raytheon Co.

United States Court of Appeals, Fifth Circuit, 1989.
886 F.2d 1449.

■ Reavley, Circuit Judge

*** MBank Alamo National Association ("MBank") and E.I. DuPont de Nemours Company, Inc. ("DuPont") entered various security agreements with Howe X-ray ("Howe"). By January 10, 1983, in accordance with these agreements, both DuPont and MBank held perfected liens in Howe's present and future accounts receivable. MBank also held a perfected security interest in Howe's present and after acquired inventory.

Beginning in January 1983, Raytheon Company ("Raytheon"), an x-ray equipment manufacturer, entered a series of transactions with Howe who was one of its distributors. Raytheon agreed to ship x-ray equipment to Howe after Howe contracted with one of its customers for the sale, delivery, and installation of certain Raytheon equipment. In exchange, Howe agreed to assign the specific accounts receivable to Raytheon. Subsequent to the assignments, Raytheon filed financing statements in specific accounts receivable of Howe. Between July 1983 and December 1984, Raytheon collected over $850,000.

By November 1984, Howe had defaulted on its obligations to MBank and DuPont. MBank and DuPont, pursuant to their security interests, demanded payment from Raytheon from the accounts receivable that it had collected. Raytheon refused, claiming that it had a purchase money security interest ("PMSI") in the accounts receivable and that its interests were therefore superior to those of MBank and DuPont.

* * * The general rule provides that the first perfected security interest to be filed has priority and other perfected interests stand in line in the order in which they were filed. See [9-322(a)(1)]. PMSIs are excepted from the first-to-file rule and take priority over other perfected security interests regardless of the filing sequence. [9-324]. The district court found that Raytheon did not fall within the PMSI exception, that MBank had priority as the first to file, under [9-322(a)(1)], and that DuPont takes second priority since it filed next.[2]

Raytheon claims the district court erred by not recognizing its priority in the accounts receivable as a PMSI under [9-324(a)].[3] * * * As a threshold matter, Raytheon must establish that it meets the statutory definition of a PMSI. Raytheon contends that it fits the statutory requirements of a PMSI under [9-103(a)]. * * * To create a PMSI, the value must be given in a manner that enables the debtor to acquire [an] interest in the collateral. This is accomplished when a debtor uses an extension of credit or loan money to purchase a specific item.

The collateral at issue here is the accounts receivable. In an attempt to force its interest into the PMSI mold, Raytheon has characterized the transaction as follows: "Raytheon, by agreeing to extend credit on its equipment, enabled Howe X-Ray to enter into subsequent contracts of

[2] The district court also found that because MBank had a continuously perfected interest in the inventory since January 17, 1980, MBank has priority in the accounts as proceeds of inventory under [9-315]. Because we reach our decision under [9-322(a)(1)], we need not discuss this finding.

[3] Raytheon claims a PMSI in the accounts receivable and not in the inventory. Raytheon cannot claim a PMSI in this inventory because it did not comply with [9-324(b)], which requires a PMSI holder to notify in writing the holder of a conflicting security interest in the same inventory.

sale with its customers, thereby acquiring rights in the contract accounts which, upon the specific advance and delivery of equipment, blossomed into a right to the collateral accounts receivable." Raytheon, however, cannot force this transaction to fit. To accept this characterization, we would have to close our eyes to the true nature of the transaction.

Raytheon, in essence, is claiming that it advanced x-ray machines to Howe on credit, which then enabled Howe to purchase accounts receivable from its customers. This, however, does not comport with our view of commercial reality. While, as Raytheon suggests, it may be theoretically possible to create a PMSI in accounts receivable by advancing funds for their purchase, the same cannot be done by advancing x-ray machines. We view this as a two-step transaction in which Raytheon first advanced machines to Howe for retail sale and, once these machines were sold, Howe then assigned the accounts receivable to Raytheon. Through the credit advance, Howe acquired an interest in the machines, not the accounts receivable. Raytheon's credit advance, therefore, did not enable Howe to acquire an interest in the accounts receivable, as collateral within the meaning of the statute.

Additionally, in its characterization of the transaction, Raytheon is attempting to benefit from the PMSI's preferred status in a manner that was not contemplated by the UCC drafters. PMSIs provide an avenue for heavily burdened debtors to obtain credit for specific goods when creditors who have previously loaned money to the debtor may be unwilling to advance additional funds. By giving a PMSI holder a priority interest in the specific goods purchased, there is some incentive for a lender to advance funds or credit for the specific transaction. The scope of a PMSI holder's preferred interest, however, is specifically limited by the Code.

Under [9-324(b)], a PMSI in inventory is limited to that inventory or to "identifiable cash proceeds received on or before the delivery of the inventory to a buyer...." The drafters noted that general financing of an inventory business is based primarily on accounts resulting from inventory, chattel paper and other proceeds. F9-312, Official UCC Reasons for 1972 Change comment (4). Reasoning that "[a]ccounts financing is more important in the economy than the financing of the kinds of inventory that produce accounts, and [that] the desirable rule is one which makes accounts financing certain as to its legal position," they specifically excluded accounts resulting from the sale of inventory from the protections of a PMSI. Thus, financing statements that are filed on a debtor's accounts take precedence over any subsequent claim to accounts as proceeds of a

PMSI in inventory. Additionally, to protect lenders who make periodic advances against incoming inventory, the PMSI holder is required to notify other secured parties before it can take priority. [9-324(b)(2)]; 1972 Official UCC Comment comment 3.

The priority scheme, however, differs in the context of collateral other than inventory. Under [9-324(a)], a PMSI in collateral other than inventory entitles the holder to a superior interest in both the collateral and its proceeds regardless of any intervening accounts. The differing entitlement to proceeds is due to differences in the expectations of the parties with respect to the collateral involved.

Collateral other than inventory generally refers to equipment used in the course of business. Since, unlike inventory, "it is not ordinarily expected that the collateral will be sold and that proceeds will result, [the drafters found it] appropriate to give the party having a purchase money security interest in the original collateral an equivalent priority in its proceeds." F9-312, Official UCC Reasons for 1972 Change comment (3).

Howe's business primarily involved the sale of inventory, which included the Raytheon x-ray machines. The accounts receivable are proceeds resulting from the sale of the machines. MBank and DuPont took security interests in the accounts receivable, in accordance with their expectation that sale of the inventory would generate the accounts. If we were to accept Raytheon's argument that it holds a PMSI in Howe's accounts receivable, we would be giving Raytheon a priority interest in the proceeds of inventory, in direct contravention to the express intent of the drafters. Additionally, Raytheon would have successfully avoided the notice requirements of [9-324(b)(2)].

Raytheon argues, however, that the policies underlying PMSIs actually favor recognizing Raytheon's priority interest in Howe's accounts. It points out that Howe could find no other source of financing besides Raytheon and that "MBank and DuPont benefited by the financing arrangements because the extension of [credit] by Raytheon helped Howe X-ray stay in business thereby servicing its debts." Raytheon also contends that if the Code is interpreted to limit the security interests of creditors, such as Raytheon, to a mere promise of repayment and the grant of a PMSI in inventory, a "valuable source of credit" to similarly encumbered debtors would "dry up." This is because the risk of default is too great in the face of prior liens on the debtor's accounts.

The Code itself, however, answers this argument. The drafters were apparently well aware that the failure to extend a PMSI holder's priority status to the resulting accounts would provide less incentive for inventory financiers to provide credit. See F9-312, 1972 Official UCC Comment comment 8. Yet, they did not extend the protections of a PMSI and merely noted that "[m]any parties financing inventory are quite content to protect their first security interest in the inventory itself, realizing that when inventory is sold, someone else will be financing the accounts and the priority for inventory will not run forward to the accounts." The drafter's recognition of the problem and the statutory favoring of accounts financing demonstrate that the drafters were not overly concerned that this source of financing would "dry up."

Additionally, Raytheon had alternative means of securing its right to receive payment. Besides obtaining a PMSI in the inventory by complying with the [9-324(b)(2)] notice requirements, it could have entered subordination agreements with MBank and DuPont on the specific accounts resulting from the sale of Raytheon's x-ray machines. It also could have sold the machines to Howe's customers who would have paid Raytheon directly, with Howe receiving a commission on the sale. If Raytheon had followed either of these courses, it would not have subverted the notice and filing requirements of the Code. As this transaction goes beyond that contemplated by the PMSI provisions, we decline "to expand the scope of special protection afforded a purchase money security interest, lest in so doing we defeat the underlying purposes of the Code: to bring predictability to commercial transactions." Mark Prod. U.S., Inc. v. Interfirst Bank Houston, N.A., 737 S.W.2d 389, 393 (Tex. App.-Houston (14th Dist.) 1987).

Since Raytheon did not have a PMSI in Howe's accounts receivable, the first-to-file priority rules govern. As the last to file, Raytheon's interest is subordinate to those of MBank and DuPont. * * *

■ GOLDBERG, CIRCUIT JUDGE, dissenting.

* * * The nettle of this case is whether an account receivable should be considered "collateral" in the words of the purchase money security interest statute so that the purchase money interest has priority over a security interest previously perfected in an identical account. My belief is that accounts receivable are an appropriate form of collateral because they can be used to invigorate marginal businesses. I would thus hold that Raytheon

established a purchase money security interest in the specified accounts of Howe X-ray. * * *

The second element of a purchase money security interest is the requirement that Raytheon give value "to enable" Howe to acquire rights in the particular account receivable. This requirement means that the advance made by Raytheon must have made it possible for Howe X-ray to obtain the collateral. In the present case, the enabling requirement is satisfied because Raytheon's agreement with Howe, which preceded all of the particular transactions, was that Raytheon would advance an x-ray machine to Howe in exchange for an accounts receivable generated by Howe's sale of the machine to a customer. This preexisting agreement, together with the advance of the machine by Raytheon, enabled Howe to make the sale. At the same moment in time, in the twinkling of an eye, the sale created the particular account receivable payable to Howe which Howe then assigned to Raytheon pursuant to their preexisting agreement. "If the loan transaction appears closely allied to the purchase transaction, that should suffice. The evident intent of [9-103(a)] is to free the purchase-money concept from artificial limitations; rigid adherence to particular formalities and sequences should not be required." G. Gilmore, I Security Interests in Personal Property, 782 (1965). * * *

The most important policy justification for a purchase money security interest under [9-103(a)] is the protection that it gives to a debtor who is unable to raise additional funds to remain in business. Creditors who have previously loaned money to the debtor and taken a security interest in the debtor's goods may be unwilling to advance additional value or funds. These additional funds, however, could enable a debtor to purchase goods, make sales, and in turn, generate profits. Profits which could not only be used to create more business, but also, to allow the debtor to pay off the creditor's loans. The purchase money security provisions thus enable a leveraged debtor who is able to find a new lender to give that new lender a first claim on the new collateral purchased notwithstanding a prior filing by another creditor.

The arrangement between Raytheon and Howe exemplifies the use of accounts receivable to advance the policy rationale behind the purchase money security interest. It was the use of the accounts receivable by Raytheon as collateral for the x-ray machines that allowed Howe to continue to do business. The additional business that Howe was able to generate with the advance of the x-ray machines, at minimum, gave Howe an additional opportunity to stay in business. This opportunity was a benefit to creditors such as MBank and DuPont whose loans would not be repaid unless Howe had the ability to generate profits. It also demonstrated the importance of accounts receivable financing in another forum, the creation of purchase money security interests.

The use of accounts receivable as collateral in this case benefited MBank and DuPont as creditors because the consequences of an unpaid account were relatively greater to Raytheon. Raytheon, MBank and DuPont would each have been harmed if Howe's customers failed to pay their accounts. If an account receivable were to remain unpaid, Raytheon would lose the entire value of the x-ray machine advanced to Howe. In contrast, it is unlikely that the failure of one account would drive Howe into bankruptcy so that Howe would be unable to repay MBank and DuPont. Yet it is this additional risk taken by Raytheon which allowed Howe a profit that could be used to fund its business to the advantage of MBank and DuPont.

Finally, any obligation imposed on MBank and DuPont to determine whether Howe was using its accounts receivable to collateralize purchase money security transactions is diminished in two respects. First, as stated, it is these very purchase money transactions that allowed Howe an additional opportunity to service its debts to these creditors. Second, MBank and DuPont as creditors had already established relationships with Howe. In future transactions, it would not have been difficult for them to ascertain whether Howe was using any accounts to collateralize purchase money transactions with other creditors and draft the loan contracts accordingly. * * *

COMMENTS AND QUESTIONS

1. How does this case come out under the revised statute? F9-107 referred to "collateral" while current 9-103 refers to "goods." Why does the revised statute shrink the possible range for the PMSI device?

2. What is at stake in this case? As the majority notes, Raytheon had a choice as to how it structured this transaction. It could have just received subordinations from MBank and DuPont. Alternatively, it could have sold the machines directly to the customers, with Howe merely acting as agent. What complications would arise were the transaction structured this way? Does this change who is assessing the

credit risk of the ultimate customer? Could that be dealt with by having Howe guarantee customer payment?

3. Doesn't the subordination point made by the majority prove too
much? The same could be said of any purchase money creditor: if the
seller wants priority, negotiate for it with the person having the earlier
filing. The existence of some type of purchase money right means we
think it worthwhile to avoid these subordination negotiations, perhaps
because we believe that the result is most cases will be so clear that implementing this as a rule saves on transactions costs. How should that
influence how we articulate the precise lines drawn in 9-103 and
9-324?

4. An in-depth discussion of this case is provided by Sherri A. Saucer,
MBank Alamo N.A. v. Raytheon Co., A Strict Interpretation of Article
Nine's Purchase Money Security Interest, 36 Loy. L. Rev. 501 (1990).
And for more on purchase money security interests generally, see Hi-
deki Kanda and Saul Levmore, Explaining Creditor Priorities, 80 Virginia L. Rev. 2103 (1994); Alan Schwartz, A Theory of Loan Priorities, 18 J. Legal Studies 209 (1989).

COMMENTS AND QUESTIONS: CROSS-COLLATERALIZATION

Revised Article 9 introduced new text regarding so-called "cross-
collateralization" of purchase money security interests. Cross-
collateralization is a general notion and usually refers to circumstances under which one security interest secures a second debt. For example, in
bankruptcy, the filing of a bankruptcy petition divides the debtor's world
into prepetition and postpetition. Does a security interest that arises postpetition secure a prepetition debt? The "cross" here is that we are not asking about prepetition debts and prepetition security interests or postpetition debts and postpetition security interests but instead about a postpetition security interest and a prepetition debt. And we could of course ask
the same question about prepetition security interests and postpetition
debts. BC 552 will suggest why these questions arise.

Similar questions arise when we mix together PMSIs and ordinary security interests. Focus with care on 9-103(b)(2) as you consider the following fact pattern.

4-17: CROSS COLLATERALIZATION OF PMSIS

- On January 1st, Bank lends Debtor $10,000 to make possible the purchase of new equipment, a drill press. Debtor signs a security agreement in favor of Bank that provides that "Debtor hereby grants a security interest in equipment, now owned or hereafter acquired, to secure all obligations, now owed or to be owed, of Debtor to Bank." Bank files an appropriate financing statement.
- On February 1st, Bank lends Debtor a second $10,000 to enable Debtor to purchase a lathe.
- ¤ What security interests are held by Bank and are the security interests ordinary security interests or PSMIs? Does the lathe secure the January 1st loan? With what status? Does the drill press secure the February 1st loan? With what status? Does your answer change if we switch from purchases of equipment to purchases of inventory? See 9-103(b)(2). What turns on all of this?

B. Refinancings and the Transformation of the PMSI

A recurring issue under F9-107 was whether refinancing the original debt secured by the PMSI changes the character of the security interest. Read the case that follows, the "fix" in 9-103(f) and the exclusion for consumer-goods transactions in 9-103(h).

Billings v. Avco Colorado Industrial Bank

United States Court of Appeals, Tenth Circuit, 1988.
838 F.2d 405.

■ Logan, Circuit Judge

Russell Fred Billings and Julia Darlene Billings (debtors) appeal the order of the district court, affirming the bankruptcy court's denial of their motion pursuant to BC 522(f) to avoid a lien held by Avco Colorado Industrial Bank (creditor), and affirming the bankruptcy court's denial of confirmation of debtors' Chapter 13 plan. The sole issue on appeal is whether the refinancing of a purchase money loan, by which the old note and security agreement were canceled and replaced by a new note and security agreement, extinguished creditor's purchase money security interest in debtors' collateral, so that debtors may now avoid the lien and claim the collateral as exempt household goods.

Debtors purchased furniture on credit from Factory Outlet Store, giving Factory a purchase money security interest in the furniture. Factory then assigned the obligation to creditor. Thereafter, at the request of debtors, who apparently were having trouble making the payments, creditor refinanced the obligation, reducing debtors' monthly installment payments from $105.50 to $58.00. The parties canceled the old note and substituted therefor a new note and security agreement; this note extended the time for repayment and increased the interest rate. The back of the loan application stated that creditor would retain the purchase money security interest. Creditor took no additional collateral as security and loaned only an additional $9.67 to debtors.[2]

Debtors made one payment under the new schedule and then filed for bankruptcy. They then moved, pursuant to BC 522(f), to avoid creditor's lien on the furniture. Creditor objected to this avoidance, and to confirmation of the Chapter 13 plan, arguing that the goods were still secured by a purchase money security interest. After a hearing, the bankruptcy court found that debtors had not satisfied their burden of establishing that the parties intended the subsequent note to extinguish the original debt and purchase money security interest. The court rejected debtors' legal argument that refinancing automatically extinguishes a purchase money security interest. Accordingly, the court denied the motion to avoid the lien pursuant to BC 522(f) and denied confirmation of the debtors' plan. On appeal, the district court affirmed.

BC 522(f) provides in part: "Notwithstanding any waiver of exemptions, the debtor may avoid the fixing of a lien on an interest of the debtor in property to the extent that such lien impairs an exemption to which the debtor would have been entitled ... if such lien is ... a nonpossessory, non-purchase-money security interest in any ... household furnishings [or]

---

[2] Immediately before refinancing, debtors owed $1087.86 on the first note. After refinancing, debtors owed an additional $103.28: $89.61 for credit life and accident and health insurance, $4.00 for a filing fee, and $9.67 for cash advanced to debtors. Creditor does not claim a purchase money security interest in this addition to principal. The bankruptcy and district courts treated the $1087.86 owing at the time of refinancing as the total purchase money debt, and they applied the one $58 payment made on the new note as reducing the purchase money obligation to $1029.58. Neither party challenges this treatment.

household goods...." BC 522(f). Therefore, if the security interest held by creditor retains its status as a purchase money security interest despite the refinancing, then debtors may not avoid the security interest under BC 522(f).

The Bankruptcy Code does not define "purchase money security interest." For this definition, the courts have uniformly looked to the law of the state in which the security interest is created. See, e.g., Pristas v. Landaus of Plymouth, Inc., 742 F.2d 797, 800 (3rd Cir. 1984); In re Manuel (Roberts Furniture Co. v. Pierce), 507 F.2d 990, 992-93 (5th Cir. 1975). The Colorado Uniform Commercial Code defines "purchase money security interest" as [set forth in [9-103]]. This definition does not address the effect of refinancing on a purchase money security interest, and the Colorado state courts have not squarely faced the issue. In a different context, the Colorado Supreme Court has stated the general rule that: "the parties may, by giving a new note for an old one, thereby extinguish the original debt. Whether or not they do so depends upon various circumstances and their intent." Haley v. Austin, 223 P. 43, 45 (1924). From it we extrapolate the principle that under Colorado law the intent of the parties determines whether a refinanced debt will retain its purchase money character.

Other circuits, applying the same UCC provisions of other states, have considered directly the effect of refinancing on a purchase money security interest. These circuits have come to differing conclusions. Some hold that refinancing a purchase money loan by paying off the old loan and extending a new one automatically extinguishes the purchase money character of the original loan. See Dominion Bank of Cumberlands v. Nuckolls, 780 F.2d 408, 413 (4th Cir. 1985); In re Matthews (Matthews v. Transamerica Financial Services), 724 F.2d 798, 800 (9th Cir. 1984) (per curiam); In re Manuel, 507 F.2d at 993. Others hold that the purchase money status of a loan may survive refinancing. See Pristas, 742 F.2d at 801-02; First National Bank & Trust Co. v. Daniel, 701 F.2d 141, 142 (11th Cir. 1983) (per curiam). The Tenth Circuit has not ruled on this issue.

Courts holding that refinancing automatically extinguishes the purchase money character of an obligation create an easily applied, bright line rule. To reach this result, they have relied on one or both of two rationales. Some have reasoned that a purchase money security interest simply cannot exist when collateral secures more than its purchase price. See, e.g., In re Manuel, 507 F.2d at 993 ("the purchase money security interest cannot exceed the price of what is purchased in the transaction wherein the security interest is created, if the vendor is to be protected despite the absence of filing"). Other courts view the refinancing transaction as creating a new loan to pay off an "antecedent debt." The Official Commentary to the UCC states that security interests for antecedent debts cannot be purchase money security interests:

> When a purchase money interest is claimed by a secured party who is not a seller, he must of course have given present consideration. This Section therefore provides that the purchase money party must be one who gives value "by making advances or incurring an obligation:" the quoted language excludes from the purchase money category any security interest taken as security for or in satisfaction of a pre-existing claim or antecedent debt.

F9-107, Comment 2. ***

The problem with the first rationale—that the purchase money security interest cannot exist when collateral secures more than its purchase price—is that it ignores the precise wording of the UCC. [9-103] provides that a security interest is a purchase money security interest "to the extent that" the loan enables the debtor to purchase new property. This language would be meaningless if an obligation could never be considered only partly a purchase money debt. As the Third Circuit recently stated:

> By overlooking that phrase ["to the extent"], the "transformation" courts adopt an unduly narrow view of the purchase-money security device. Their reasoning is inconsistent with the Commercial Code, which gives favored treatment to those financing arrangements on the theory they are beneficial both to buyers and sellers.
>
> By contrast, acceptance of the "dual-status" rule, with its pro tanto preservation of purchase-money security interests, is more in harmony with the Code. Tolerance of "add-on" debt and collateral provisions, properly applied, carries out the approbation for purchase-money security arrangements and simplifies repeat transactions between the same buyer and seller.
>
> Moreover, this approach has the positive consequence of a larger number of sales, and the net effect is no more detrimental to the buyer than if a number of purchases had been made from different vendors.

Pristas, 742 F.2d at 801.

The problem with the second "transformation" rationale—that refinancing by canceling an old note and issuing a new note always constitutes payment of an "antecedent debt" as that term is used in Comment 2 to F9-107 of the UCC—is that it ignores the possibility that the refinancing merely renewed the debt, rather than creating a new debt. Certainly the prior debt could be satisfied and a new debt created by a novation extinguishing the old purchase money loan. But this should not occur automatically with every amended or renewed note.

In First National Bank & Trust Co. v. Daniel, 701 F.2d 141 (11th Cir. 1983) (per curiam), the Eleventh Circuit, applying Georgia law, held that a new note issued to refinance a debt did not constitute a novation. The issue in *Daniel* was whether refinancing extinguished a note and security interest executed before enactment of the Bankruptcy Code and created a separate and distinct obligation and security interest attaching after the Code's enactment date. This determination was necessary because, in United States v. Security Industrial Bank, 459 U.S. 70, (1982), the Supreme Court held that liens could be avoided under BC 522(f) only if they attached after the Code was enacted. The court in *Daniel* held that a new note which merely extended the payment period and which was collateralized by the same property did not constitute a novation under Georgia law; therefore, such a renewal note executed after the Code went into effect did not create a lien eligible for avoidance under BC 522(f).

District and bankruptcy courts in this circuit, applying their understanding of the laws of most states in our circuit, have rejected the "transformation" rationale, and have held that refinancing does not automatically transform a purchase money security interest. In In re Gibson, 16 Bankr. 257 (Bankr. D. Kan. 1981), the court addressed the same issue decided in *Daniel*, and followed Kansas precedent holding that refinancing a note does not automatically extinguish the original note and security interest. The *Gibson* court reasoned that because "the paying of the old note by execution of a renewal note is generally just a bookkeeping procedure," such a transaction would not extinguish the original note or security agreement unless the parties intended for the prior debt to be satisfied and a new debt created. Decisions in Wyoming, Colorado and Oklahoma have reached the same results.

We agree with and affirm the view stated in these opinions. The basic problem with the automatic "transformation" rule is that it discourages creditors who have purchase money security interests from helping their debtors work out of financial problems without bankruptcy and without surrendering the collateral securing the debt. The instant case is an excellent example. These debtors apparently needed lower monthly payments on their debt. In a "transformation" jurisdiction the creditor could not cooperate without giving up its right to protect its security if debtors filed bankruptcy. Perhaps it could allow debtors to be in partial default without a new note. But that informal arrangement has problems for both debtors and creditor: the defaulting debtors would be subject to foreclosure on their goods at any time; the creditor, if a bank carrying past due loans, would have problems with bank regulators and may be deemed to have agreed to a novation, even without a new note. In the unlikely event that debtors are aware of the "transformation" rule, they would have an incentive to renegotiate or renew in order to invalidate the purchase money lien. We note that debtors here made only one payment on the new note before filing for bankruptcy and seeking to set aside the lien. * * *

The transformation rule not only results in the automatic invalidation of liens under BC 522(f), but it also has broader ramifications as to Article 9 priorities:

> [I]n states where no filing is necessary to perfect a purchase money security interest in consumer goods, the creditor who did not file and later loses purchase money status becomes unperfected, see [9-309(1)], and loses in a priority dispute to other secured creditors who perfected, see [9-322(a)(1)], and to the trustee in bankruptcy. See BC 544. ... [I]n states such as Kansas where filing is required to perfect purchase money security interests in consumer goods, [9-309(1)], and in all other situations where filing is necessary to perfect, a creditor who obtained the "super priority" status offered under [9-324] will lose that priority. Therefore the second effect [of the transformation rule] is to jumble priorities among creditors....

Gibson, 16 Bankr. at 265. Thus, our conclusion that refinancing of a purchase money loan does not automatically extinguish the creditor's purchase money security interest in the debtor's collateral comports with the scheme of the UCC.

The bankruptcy court in the instant case found that the parties did not intend the new note to extinguish the original debt and security interest. That is also obvious from the renewal note itself and the security interest. The identical collateral remained, almost no new money was advanced, and the document stated specifically an intent to continue the purchase money security interest. Applying a clearly erroneous standard of review, as we must, we uphold the bankruptcy and district court's decision that the debtors could not avoid the creditor's interest under BC 522(f). The judgment of the United States District Court for the District of Colorado is affirmed.

COMMENTS AND QUESTIONS

For further analysis of this case in a broader review of consumer law, see Marion W. Benfield, Jr., Consumer Provisions in Revised Article 9, 74 Chi-Kent L. Rev. 1255, 1293 (1999).

C. UNDERSTANDING PRICE AND THE PURCHASE MONEY SECURITY INTEREST

The status in a bankruptcy of a security interest often turns on whether the security interest has purchase money status or whether the security interest is just a garden-variety security interest. Under BC 522(f)(1)(B), an individual debtor may avoid—kill off—certain "nonpossessory, nonpurchase-money" security interests. Some of the special rules in bankruptcy for aircraft equipment and leases and rolling stock—see, respectively, BC 1110 and BC 1168—again turn on whether the underlying security interest has purchase-money status. The next case looks at the "hanging paragraph" in BC 1325(a) and considers what counts as the price of the newly-acquired collateral under 9-103(a)(2).

4-18: LET'S BUY A NEW CAR
- Debtor buys a new car from OldDealer. OldDealer finances the sale as a secured transaction and its security interest is appropriately listed on the certificate of title. See 9-311(a)(2). Three years later, Debtor is ready for a new car. Debtor still owes OldDealer $15,000 and the used car has a fair-market value of $10,000 giving Debtor $5,000 in "negative equity."
- Debtor sells the used car to a third party for $10,000 and pays that to OldDealer. Debtor approaches NewDealer to buy a new car with a cash purchase price of $30,000. NewDealer agrees to lend $5,000 in cash to Debtor and to sell the new car for a price of

$28,000 for a total loan of $33,000. The deal is structured as a se-cured transaction and NewDealer's security interest is noted on the new car title. Debtor pays the $5,000 to OldDealer to pay that debt in full.

- ¤ Would you do this deal if you were the third party? How do we get rid of the lien noted on the original car title?
- ¤ What security interests are held by NewDealer and are the security interests ordinary security interests or PSMIs?
- ¤ Suppose that Debtor dealt only with Dealer for both transactions and that the used car was traded in to buy the new car with a credit for the used car of $10,000. Dealer would still be owed $5,000 for the old car and suppose that the loan was wrapped into the new loan as before for a total loan of $33,000. What security interests would be held by Dealer and would those be ordinary security interests or PSMIs? Make sure to consider the effect of 9-103(b)(2).

Graupner v. Nuvell Credit Corp. (In re Graupner)

United States Court of Appeals, Eleventh Circuit, 2008.
537 F.3d 1295.

■ VINSON, DISTRICT JUDGE

This case involves interpretation and application of the so-called "hanging paragraph" in Title 11, United States Code, BC 1325(a)(9), which was added to the Bankruptcy Code ("the Code") by the Bankruptcy Abuse Prevention and Consumer Protection Act of 2005. See Pub.L. No. 109-8, 119 Stat. 23 (2005) ("BAPCPA").[1] Specifically, we are called upon to decide if the anti-bifurcation provision in the hanging paragraph protects against "cramdown" of the negative equity in a trade-in vehicle. This issue has been confronted by a number of bankruptcy and district courts throughout the country (with widely divergent results), but it appears to be of first impression in this or any other circuit.

---

[1] The section in question has been called the hanging paragraph because, although it is set forth as a subparagraph following BC 1325(a)(9), it is not separately designated by letter or number. Rather, it just "hangs" without ordered designation and without surrounding context. It has been variously referred to by courts as section 1325(a)(9), section 1325(a)(*), and as the "hanging paragraph." For purposes of this opinion, we will use "hanging paragraph" in text and § 1325(a)(*) for citations.

I. BACKGROUND

The area of bankruptcy law involved in this case is somewhat complex and, as indicated above, rife with terms of art. For better understanding, we will set forth a brief discussion of the statutory background before turning to the facts and history of this particular case.

A. The Statutory Scheme

Bankruptcy rehabilitation under Chapter 13 of the Code commonly involves the adjustment of obligations owed to creditors holding liens on the bankruptcy debtor's property. Generally, lien creditors are deemed to hold a secured claim to the extent of the present value of the property that the lien encumbers, while the excess, if any, is treated as a separate and unsecured claim. BC 506(a)(1) of the Code provides in relevant part:

> (a)(1) An allowed claim of a creditor secured by a lien on property ... is a secured claim to the extent of the value of such creditor's interest in the estate's interest in such property ... and is an unsecured claim to the extent that the value of such creditor's interest ... is less than the amount of such allowed claim. Such value shall be determined in light of the purpose of the valuation and of the proposed disposition or use of such property[.]

BC 506(a)(1). In dealing with the allowed secured claims under BC 506(a), the Code provides for one of three possible treatments "with respect to each allowed secured claim:" (1) the creditor can accept the debtor's bankruptcy plan for repayment; (2) the debtor can surrender the property securing the claim to the creditor in lieu of repayment; or (3) the debtor can bifurcate the claim into a reduced secured portion equal to the present value of the collateral and an unsecured portion equal to the excess of the claim, and then receive a "cramdown" of the reduced secured claim upon the creditor. See generally BC 1325(a)(5). Under the "cramdown" option, as the Supreme Court has recognized, "the debtor is permitted to keep the property over the objection of the creditor; the creditor retains the lien securing the claim, and the debtor is required to provide the creditor with payments, over the life of the plan, that will total the present value of the allowed secured claim, *i.e.*, the present value of the collateral. The value of the allowed secured claim is governed by § 506(a) of the Code." Associates Commercial Corp. v. Rash, 520 U.S. 953, 957 (1997) (internal citations omitted). * * *

However, Congress viewed the pre-2005 use of "cramdown" as abusive, so it amended Section 1325(a) through BAPCPA and added the hanging paragraph, which provides:

> For purposes of paragraph (5), section 506 [cramdown] shall not apply to a claim described in that paragraph if the creditor has a purchase money security interest securing the debt that is the subject of the claim, the debt was incurred within the 910-day preceding the date of the filing of the petition, and the collateral for that debt consists of a motor vehicle (as defined in section 30102 of title 49) acquired for the personal use of the debtor, or if collateral for that debt consists of any other thing of value, if the debt was incurred during the 1-year period preceding that filing.

BC 1325(a)(*). ***

B. Facts and Procedural History

The facts of this case are simple, undisputed, and taken almost verbatim from the district court's order. On June 23, 2005, Stephen Michael Graupner ("Debtor") purchased a 2005 Chevrolet Silverado pick-up truck from a motor vehicle dealer in Georgia. The vehicle was for his personal use and had a "cash price" of $32,919.12. The dealer agreed to finance the sale pursuant to a retail installment contract, with the seller retaining a security interest in the vehicle to secure the unpaid balance of the total sales price.

As part of the transaction, the Debtor traded in a 2002 Chevrolet Silverado pick-up truck. That vehicle had a "negative equity," with the Debtor owing $6,347.50 more on the vehicle than its then-market value. There is nothing in the record of this case to indicate that the trade-in's negative equity was not bona fide and reasonable in amount. The total sales price of the new vehicle included the negative equity, which had the effect of increasing the purchase price. The total amount financed was $36,384.62. The dealer subsequently assigned the retail installment contract to Nuvell Credit Corporation ("Creditor"), which perfected its security interest by having its lien noted on the title to the new vehicle.

Three hundred and one days later, on April 19, 2006, the Debtor filed for Chapter 13 bankruptcy protection. The Creditor filed its secured proof of claim showing an amount due on the contract of $33,670.31. The Debtor retained the vehicle and listed it on his schedules as being valued at $23,375.00. The Debtor proposed a Chapter 13 plan that sought to modify the Creditor's secured claim of $33,670.31 by bifurcating it into secured and unsecured portions based on the retail value of the vehicle. The Creditor objected to the confirmation of the proposed plan, contending that its secured claim could not be modified through "cramdown" because it fell within the hanging paragraph. The parties agreed that the debt for the vehicle was acquired within 910 days of the filing for bankruptcy and that the vehicle was intended for the Debtor's personal use. Consequently, the only question to be decided in the bankruptcy court was whether the Creditor held a "purchase money security interest" in the vehicle. If it did, the debt could not be bifurcated.

Because the term "purchase money security interest" is not defined in the Code, the bankruptcy court began its analysis by stating that the question of "whether a creditor holds a purchase money security interest is a matter of state law." The bankruptcy court referred to Georgia's version of Article 9 of the Uniform Commercial Code * * *.

The bankruptcy court opined that while the definition of "purchase money obligation" in 9-103 appears clear at first glance, it becomes blurred and ambiguous when one attempts to define "price" in subsection (a)(2) because "the extent or reach of the term is uncertain." The bankruptcy court then went on to determine that "price" is more properly understood when viewed in conjunction with a separate, but related, section of the OCGA: the 1999 amendments to the Georgia Motor Vehicle Sales Finance Act ("MVSFA"), which specifically defines "cash sale price" to include "any amount paid to the buyer ... to satisfy ... a lien on or a security interest in a motor vehicle used as a trade-in on the motor vehicle which is the subject of a retail installment transaction under this article." See OCGA 10-1-31(a)(1). Reading these sections *in pari material*—which the bankruptcy court determined was proper in light of the ambiguity in 9-103(a)(2) and the relationship between the two statutes—the court held that "the Georgia General Assembly intended, with its 1999 amendment to the MVSFA, to permit negative equity in a trade-in vehicle to be added to the cash sales price of a new vehicle without precluding the financing creditor or its assignee from taking a purchase money security interest in the new vehicle." The Debtor was thus found to have a purchase money security interest in the vehicle pursuant to state law, which precluded bifurcation and "cramdown" under section 506. * * *

III. DISCUSSION

As we noted at the outset of this opinion, the issue presented in this case has been confronted by dozens of lower courts. These decisions generally fall into two broad camps. The first camp holds, as the bankruptcy court held here, that the creditor's purchase money security interest encompasses all components of the new vehicle purchase, including financing of negative equity. *** The second camp holds that certain components of the loan, most notably negative equity in a trade-in vehicle, do not constitute a purchase money security interest. ***

The latter group of cases lead to a further inquiry on how to treat "partial" purchase money securities, which has caused still more divergences in the law. Some courts have adopted the "dual-status rule" (which allows the court to treat the purchase-money portion as purchase-money, while the non-purchase-money portion remains non-purchase-money), whereas other courts have adopted the "transformational rule" (which holds that a security interest that is part purchase-money and part non-purchase-money completely loses its purchase-money character and is entirely "transformed" into a non-purchase-money security interest). ***

The ultimate issue we must decide is whether the Debtor's negative equity in his trade-in vehicle constitutes purchase money. Our Court has defined what is, and what is not, a purchase money security interest, and we apply that definition here:

> A security interest in collateral is "purchase money" to the extent that the item secures a debt for the money required to make the purchase. If an item of collateral secures some other type of debt, e.g., antecedent debt, it is not purchase money.

In re Freeman, 956 F.2d 252, 254-55 (11th Cir. 1992). So, the question is whether negative equity on a trade-in vehicle is "debt for the money required to make the purchase" of the new vehicle, or whether it is "antecedent debt." It is, as the split in the decided cases indicates, a close call.

Upon consideration, however, we agree with the bankruptcy court that, when looking to Georgia state law, negative equity is more properly regarded as the former and not the latter. When 9-103 and 10-1-31(a)(1) (MVSFA) are read *in pari materia* (which we believe is appropriate for all the reasons stated by the bankruptcy court), it is the only reasonable conclusion to reach. Because this issue was properly considered and analyzed at length by the bankruptcy court, and by certain of the courts in the "first camp" above, we see no reason to duplicate the analysis as the path is by now well-worn. We do add, however, that our decision finds support in the relevant UCC Official Comment and is consistent with legislative intent.

9-103 provides that "[a] security interest in goods is a purchase-money security interest ... to the extent that the goods are purchase-money collateral with respect to that security interest[.]" It then defines "purchase-money collateral" as "goods or software that secures a purchase-money obligation incurred with respect to that collateral." The term "purchase-money obligation" is defined, in turn, as "an obligation of an obligor incurred as all or part of the price of the collateral or for value given to enable the debtor to acquire rights in or the use of the collateral if the value is in fact so used." In sum, therefore, the focus of the definition of a purchase money security interest under the UCC is on the "purchase-money obligation" that is secured by the collateral, and this definition contains two prongs: (i) the price of the collateral; and (ii) value given to enable the debtor to buy the collateral. Official Comment 3 to the UCC explains:

> [T]he definition of "purchase-money obligation," the "price" of collateral or the "value given to enable" includes obligations for expenses incurred in connection with acquiring rights in the collateral, sales taxes, duties, finance charges, interest, freight charges, costs of storage in transit, demurrage, administrative charges, expenses of collection and enforcement, attorney's fees, *and other similar obligations.*

9-103, Official Comment 3 (emphasis added). Although the Debtor argues that negative equity is "not equivalent" to the various expenses listed in Comment 3, as the emphasized language indicates, the list is not exhaustive. The expenses identified in Comment 3 are merely examples of additional components of the "price" of the collateral or of "value given" to the debtor, and we see no persuasive reason why traditional transaction costs *and* the refinancing of reasonable, bona fide negative equity in connection with the purchase of the new vehicle should not qualify as "expenses" within the meaning of the comment. To be sure, as one court has rightly observed, the fact that "attorney's fees" are listed in Comment 3 "belies the notion that 'price' or 'value' is narrowly viewed as only those [traditional] expenses that *must* be paid to drive the car off the lot. Comment 3 expressly 'includes' the broad phrase 'obligations for expenses incurred in connection with acquiring rights in the collateral' " and, consequently, "the definitions of 'price' and 'value' should be interpreted broadly." In re Myers, 2008 WL 2445214, at *4 (Bankr. S.D. Ind. June 13, 2008) (emphasis in original).

Comment 3 further states that a purchase money security interest "requires a close nexus between the acquisition of collateral and the secured obligation." We believe there is such a "close nexus" between the negative equity in the Debtor's trade-in vehicle and the purchase of his new vehicle. The financing was part of the same transaction and may be properly regarded as a "package deal." Payment of the trade-in debt was tantamount to a prerequisite to consummating the sales transaction, and utilizing the negative equity financing was a necessary means to accomplish the purchase of the new vehicle. As the district court held in affirming the bankruptcy court, the negative equity was an "integral part of," and "inextricably intertwined with," the sales transaction. To hold otherwise would not be a fair reading of the UCC. * * *

COMMENTS AND QUESTIONS

1. You drive a new car off of the lot and what do you have? Negative equity. Not necessarily, but probably. A new car becomes used instantly and that reduces its value in the market, especially as soon as we factor in the lemons phenomenon. (People disproportionately want to get rid of bad used cars, not the good ones, and the current owner knows best whether her car is a lemon or a peach.) With a small down payment, voila, you get negative equity: the car is worth less than the amount of the debt secured by it.

2. What should we do about this, if anything? This means that the secured creditor is undersecured. Should we have a mechanism for reducing the amount of the debt to the value of the collateral? How do we think lenders and car dealers would respond to that?

CHAPTER FIVE

PROCEEDS AND TRANSFERS OF PROPERTY

It is a rare business that simply holds property unchanged until the end of time. Instead, businesses and individuals are continually selling or otherwise exchanging property they hold for cash or other property. There are many issues associated with these changes. First, when the debtor disposes of collateral and receives property back in return, what rights does the secured party have in the property that the debtor receives? This is the issue of *proceeds*, addressed in 9-315. Second, prior to the disposal of the collateral, the secured party had rights against it. How does the disposal affect those rights? Do they survive the transfer, meaning that the secured party can chase the property into the hands of the recipient? We will refer to this as the survival-on-transfer question; 9-315(a)(1) and 9-320 together establish the basic framework for it. If the security interest continues, must the secured party take steps to continue the perfection of its security interest? 9-507(a) addresses this.

How is the secured party's priority affected by the transfer? Prior to the transfer, priority was defined with reference to the financing statements filed against the secured party's debtor. If the secured party had filed first, it had priority. After the transfer, the secured party competes with creditors of the recipient of the transfer, some of whom may have filed financing statements long before the original secured creditor. Does the transfer change the secured creditor's priority? In this chapter, we start with the proceeds issue. We then turn to the survival-on-transfer question.

SECTION I. PROCEEDS

9-315(a)(2) provides that "[e]xcept as otherwise provided in this article and in Section 2-403(2) … a security interest attaches to any identifiable proceeds of collateral." 9-203(f) provides in turn that "[t]he attachment of a security interest in collateral gives the secured party the rights to proceeds provided by Section 9-315." Proceeds, in turn, are defined in 9-102(a)(64), and we will turn to that almost immediately, but for now think of proceeds as whatever stuff the debtor gets back when it gives up its rights to collateral. (Again, note that the fact that the debtor gives up its rights does not mean, necessarily, that the rights of the secured creditor to the collateral have come to an end. That is the survival-on-transfer question.)

To know what interest a secured creditor has in proceeds, we must consult the agreement and the rest of Article 9. Unless these sections are affirmatively misleading—and they are not—we should assume that they establish a strong presumption that the secured party gets a security interest in *identifiable* proceeds received by the debtor. Identifiability is an important limit, and we will return to it later. Assuming that one can "identify" the proceeds, 9-315(a)(2) states that a secured party's interest in those proceeds will attach. Attachment, of course, is only half the battle. A secured creditor will normally be concerned with the question of whether its security interest in proceeds is "perfected"—an issue to which 9-315(c), (d) and (e) speak.

9-315(d) creates a twenty-day grace period: If the original collateral was perfected, the secured party has an automatic twenty days of perfection for the proceeds after receipt of them by the debtor. This rule seems designed to lessen the necessity on the part of the secured party to monitor its debtor continuously: once every twenty days should be sufficient. Does the automatic perfection rule sensibly allocate risks between the perfected secured party and subsequent creditors of the debtor? If so, are the twenty days sufficient?

There are three ways in which a secured creditor can continue that perfected security interest beyond the twenty automatic days. 9-315(d)(3) provides, not surprisingly, that if affirmative action is taken within those twenty days to perfect the security interest in proceeds, perfection continues without interruption. 9-315(d)(2) provides that the security interest in proceeds remains automatically perfected if the proceeds are "identifiable cash proceeds." "Cash proceeds" are defined in 9-102(a)(9), and for cash proceeds, identifiability is covered by 9-315(b)(2): the secured party must "identif[y] the proceeds by a method of tracing, including application of equitable principles, that is permitted under law other than this article with respect to commingled property of the type involved." Finally, 9-315(d)(1) provides that the security interest in proceeds remains perfected if (i) the original collateral was covered by a filed financing statement; (ii) the proceeds are the type of collateral in which a security interest could have been perfected, as an original matter, by a filing in the same financing statement file or files; and (iii) the proceeds must not be acquired with cash proceeds.

The mechanics of these provisions are explored in the following materials. Start with the following fact pattern:

5-1: AN UNREMARKABLE PROCEEDS EXAMPLE

- On February 1st, Bank lends money to Debtor and takes a security interest in "all Debtor's paintings and other art work, proceeds thereof, and proceeds of proceeds of any sort." Bank files a proper financing statement containing the same description.

- On March 1st, Debtor trades one of the paintings for a new office computer.

- On April 1st, Debtor sells one of his paintings for $2,000 in cash and uses that $2,000 to buy another office computer.

- On June 1st, Debtor sells one of his paintings for $2,000 and deposits that money in his checking account, which has $1,000 in it at the time of the deposit. The next day, Debtor buys a $2,000 office computer and pays for it with a check drawn on his checking account.

- On July 1st, Debtor sells one of his paintings to Customer for $2,000 in a credit transaction, receiving Customer's promise to pay Debtor the $2,020 in one month (the extra $20 covers interest). One month after the sale, Customer pays Debtor the $2,020, via a check. The next day, Debtor deposits the check in its account with California Bank, and California Bank immediately credits Debtor's deposit account.

- ¤ What are Bank's rights as of February 1st? March 1st? April 1st? June 1st? June 2nd? July 1st? August 1st? August 2nd? Suppose that on June 1st the checking account had $10,000 in it. Would this change Bank's rights? See 9-315, 9-322.

A. THE DEFINITION OF PROCEEDS AND ATTACHMENT OF THE SECURITY INTEREST

Let's start with a plain-vanilla proceeds case and work our way up to harder cases.

Karle v. Visser

Supreme Court of Idaho, 2005.
118 P.3d 136.

■ SCHROEDER, CHIEF JUSTICE

This case involves an appeal from a district court decision that Arthur M. Bistline (Bistline) did not have a valid security interest in a pending action to collect on a promissory note.

On June 9, 1994, Doug and Vicki Visser (the Vissers) entered into an agreement to sell their dismantling and auto salvage business to Charles and Valerie Karle (the Karles) for the sum of $85,000.00. The overall transaction involved several different agreements, including both an Asset Transfer Agreement (ATA) and rental agreement to lease five acres of the Vissers' property associated with the salvage business. The lease provided that the Karles would pay a monthly rent of $1,200.00 in exchange for the Vissers making certain building and road improvements to the property and signing a covenant not to compete agreement. The Karles made a down payment of $20,000 and executed a promissory note for $65,000.00 plus interest at a rate of 9% per annum to be paid in monthly installments of $600.00.

The Karles made the monthly payments on both the lease and promissory note until December of 2000 at which time differences arose between the parties. The Karles filed suit against the Vissers for various claims, including breach of contract for failure to complete the road and building improvements under the lease. The Vissers answered and counterclaimed on the basis the Karles had breached the ATA and failed to pay rent under the lease for the months of January and February 2001.

A jury trial on these claims was held. The jury returned a verdict awarding damages in the amount of $53,932.50 to the Karles and ordering a reduction in their rent until the pledged road and building improvements were completed. The jury also awarded the Vissers $9,900.00 on their breach of contract claim under the ATA. Judgment was entered reflecting both these awards on April 15, 2002.

From April to July of 2002, the Karles continued to make monthly installment payments on the promissory note and paid the abated rent. A writ of execution reflecting the judgment was issued. At the time the amount of principal and interest owed by the Karles to the Vissers was approximately $51,520.55. On July 19, 2002, a Sheriff's sale was held. The Karles credit bid the sum of $10,500 for the judgment in favor of the Vissers and credit bid the sum of $22,500.00 on the Vissers' right title and interest in the ATA. The Sheriff refused to accept a credit bid by the Vissers on the ATA. The Vissers subsequently filed a motion to set aside the Sheriff's sale or, alternatively, to accept their credit bid. The district court denied this motion. After the credit bid was applied, the judgment in favor of the Karles for $53,932.50 was reduced to $20,923.50. When interest and fees were added, the amount left owing to the Karles was $26,371.00 as of September 18, 2003.

On January 8, 2003, Bistline entered into a Security Agreement (SA) with the Vissers in which he attempted to take a security interest in the promissory note as collateral for payment of the Vissers' outstanding and future attorneys' fees owed to Bistline. The SA identified the collateral as the promissory note and granted Bistline a security interest in:

> [R]ight title and interest in the collateral, and all proceeds from the sale or transfer of the collateral, and any judgments resulting from the collection of the Note that is the collateral, and any payments made pursuant to the terms and conditions of the collateral, no matter who hands those proceeds from the sale or transfer of the collateral, and judgments resulting from the collection of the Note that is the collateral, and payments made pursuant to the terms and conditions of the collateral, may go.

A UCC Financing Statement containing a description of the collateral and the security interest was filed with the Idaho Secretary of State on January 9, 2003.

On January 27, 2003, the Vissers filed a complaint against the Karles for alleged delinquency in payments on the promissory note. *Visser v. Karle*, Bonner County Case No. CV 03-00130. The Karles answered, arguing the note's obligations were canceled by virtue of the Sheriff's sale on July 19, 2002. On August 4, 2003, the district judge granted summary judgment in favor of the Vissers on Case No. CV 03-00130, finding the only issues to be determined were the remaining principal balance owed on the note and the amount of costs associated with collection on the note.

On December 18, 2003, the Karles filed another writ of execution with the Sheriff of Bonner County, this time against the Vissers' pending collection action, to collect on the remainder of their prior judgment. In response to the levy, Bistline filed a third party claim of exemption on behalf of the Vissers and himself. The Karles contested the claim of exemption. A hearing was held on the matter. The district court determined that Bistline did not have a valid security interest in the Vissers' pending action to collect on the note. Bistline appealed. At issue on appeal is whether a pending action to collect on a promissory note constitutes proceeds within the meaning of 9-102(a)(64) and whether the SA adequately took an interest in such proceeds. * * *

Bistline argues that the right to sue for collection on a note constitutes proceeds such that his interest in the promissory note automatically attached to the pending collection action. The Karles assert that Bistline failed to take a security interest in either a "chose in action" or "general intangibles" such that he did not take a valid and enforceable security interest in Visser v. Karle, Bonner County Case No. CV-03-00130.

The scope of Title 28, Chapter 9 of the Idaho Code governs secured transactions in promissory notes. * * * A valid and enforceable security agreement requires a sufficient description of the collateral to which the security interest will attach. Collateral is defined as "property subject to a security interest or agricultural lien" and includes any "proceeds" of the collateral. 9-102(a)(12)(A); 9-315(a)(2). Proceeds are defined as:

(A) whatever is acquired upon the sale, lease, license, exchange or other disposition of collateral;

(B) whatever is collected on, or distributed on account of, collateral;

(C) rights arising out of collateral;

(D) to the extent of the value of the collateral, claims arising out of the loss, nonconformity, or interference with the use of, defects or infringement of rights in, or damage to, the collateral; or

(E) to the extent of the value of collateral and to the extent payable to the debtor or secured party, insurance payable by reason of the loss or nonconformity of, defects or infringement of rights in, or damage to, the collateral.

9-102(a)(64) (emphasis added). This is an expanded definition of proceeds and "includes additional rights and property that arise out of collateral, such as distributions on account of collateral and claims arising out of the loss or nonconformity of, defects in, or damage to collateral. The term also includes collections on account of 'supporting obligations,' such as guarantees." Official Comment 9-101(4)(f).

A general intangible is a particular type of collateral and is defined as:

> [A]ny personal property, *including things in action*, other than accounts, chattel paper, commercial tort claims, deposit accounts, documents, goods, instruments, investment property, letter of credit rights, letters of credit, money, and oil and gas, or other minerals before extraction. The term includes payment intangibles and software.

9-102(a)(42) (emphasis added). Idaho's Official Comments note that "things in action' includes rights that arise under a license of intellectual property, including the right to exploit the intellectual property without liability for infringement." Official Comment 9-102(5)(d).

The Official Comments to Idaho's Revised U.C.C. and Idaho case law offer little guidance as to whether a pending action to collect on a promissory note is more akin to proceeds or a general intangible. *** Several states have found that a party may take a security interest in proceeds arising out of a chose in action or settlement of a pending lawsuit. *** The Supreme Court of Washington, however, has held that proceeds and general intangibles are not mutually exclusive. Rainier Nat'l Bank v. Bachmann, 757 P.2d 979, 984 (1988). In *Rainier*, a banks security interest in crops, dairy cattle and all proceeds was found to attach to government payments for cattle destroyed under a Dairy Termination Program (DTP). Relying on Osteroos v. Norwest Bank Minot, N.A., 604 F.Supp. 848, 849 (D.N.D. 1984), the Washington Supreme Court held that the government payments "constitute general intangibles as a category of collateral" and also "*constitute proceeds of crops so that failure to mention general intangibles in a security agreement or financing statement is not fatal.*" Rainier, 757 P.2d at 984 (emphasis added).

Bistline's security interest in the promissory note automatically attached to any proceeds of the note as defined by Idaho statute, including any rights arising out of the note. The right to collect on a note and to file a suit for collection is both a general intangible and proceeds of the collateral. Adopting the reasoning of *Rainier*, Bistline's failure to state a security interest in all general intangibles in his SA is not fatal to his claim. Bistline's interest in the note was sufficient to attach an interest to the pending collection action as proceeds of the note. The district court erred in finding Bistline's interest did not attach.

The Karles argue that the Vissers did not have any rights in the promissory note at the time they executed the SA and that Bistline had no interest in the note. While the record indicates the Sheriff executed on only the ATA, the party's pleadings indicate they understood the execution to incorporate the promissory note. However, the record also includes a summary judgment decision that the note was enforceable as against the Karles. Without further explanation or record to rely upon, it appears the Vissers retained rights in the promissory note following the Sheriff's sale. Bistline created a valid and enforceable security interest in the promissory note which automatically attached to the pending action to collect on the note.

The district court found that Bistline's SA limited the types of proceeds to which his security interest would attach. According to Bistline, proceeds are statutorily defined and if a party intends to limit the type of statutory proceeds to which its interest will attach, they must state an intent to do so in their security agreement. The Karles argue that the SA limited proceeds from the note to property acquired from the sale or transfer of the collateral or any judgments arising out of collection on the note.

The policy of the code with regard to sufficiency of description of collateral in a security agreement is liberal. 9-108. Form shall not prevail over substance. The Official Comment to 9-108 states:

> The purpose of requiring a description of collateral in a security agreement under Section 9-203 is evidentiary. *The test of sufficiency of a description under this section as under former Section 9-110, is that the description do the job assigned to it: make possible the identification of the collateral described.* This section rejects any requirement that a description is insufficient unless it is exact and detailed (the so-called 'serial number' test).

Official Comment, 9-108(2) (emphasis added).

Bistline took a valid and enforceable security interest in the promissory note which automatically attached to all statutorily defined proceeds of collateral. A party who seeks to limit the type of statutory proceeds to which its security interest will attach must state an intent to limit proceeds in the security agreement. Bistline did not state an intent to limit his security interest to specific statutory proceeds. Thus his interest attached to the pending lawsuit. This result is consistent with the letter and spirit of 9-108. Bistline identified specific proceeds in the SA, including any judgments arising out of a collection action. That Bistline could somehow retain a security interest in a collection judgment but not the pending collection itself is illogical and contrary to the policy of 9-108. Bistline's secured interest in the note automatically attached to the pending collection action. The district court's decision is reversed. * * *

COMMENTS AND QUESTIONS

1. Start with the default position of the secured creditor. 9-203(f) states that a secured creditor gets the rights to proceeds specified in 9-315. In turn, 9-315(a)(2) provides that "a security interest attaches to any identifiable proceeds of collateral." Is this automatic? Is it mandatory? That is, does a secured creditor need to specify that the collateral is "inventory and its proceeds" or would just "inventory" suffice? And why should a security interest in proceeds be mandatory? The scope of the collateral is generally a matter of negotiation between the debtor and the secured party. Why shouldn't that be true as well of an interest in proceeds?

2. In *Karle* itself, be sure to consider the actual language of the security agreement. Does that agreement specify a narrower class of proceeds than that set forth in 9-102(a)(64)?

Next consider the following hypothetical and then the case that follows.

5-2: TAKING THE SECURITY INTEREST IN PROCEEDS
- On February 1st, Bank lends money to Debtor, a TV station. Bank would like to take a security interest in all of Debtor's assets, including its operating license, but FCC policy forbids that. Bank takes a security interest in "the FCC license, to the extent permitted by law, and in all proceeds thereof."
- On March 1st, Debtor exchanges all of its assets, including the license, for the Hope Diamond. The FCC blesses the exchange.

¤ What does Bank have a security interest in as of February 1st? March 1st? If the Bank could not have a security interest in the license because of FCC policy, does that mean the Hope Diamond is not received in an exchange of "collateral," and hence prevents the diamond from being "proceeds"? See 9-102(a)(64).

¤ Why does this matter? Would it matter if Bank had an expansive after-acquired property clause in its original agreement with Debtor? Might the intervention of a bankruptcy proceeding impact that analysis? See BC 552.

Orix Credit Alliance, Inc. v. Mills (In re Beach Television Partners)

United States Court of Appeals, Eleventh Circuit, 1994.
38 F.3d 535.

■ HATCHETT, CIRCUIT JUDGE

In this appeal, we hold that a creditor may hold a valid security interest in the proceeds from the sale of a Federal Communications Commission (FCC) broadcasting license. * * *

Beach Television Partners (BTP) was a Florida general partnership that owned and operated two independent television stations. Orix Credit Alliance, Inc. (Orix) financed virtually all of BTP's broadcasting equipment, and to secure repayment, BTP granted Orix a security interest in all of its personal property including two FCC broadcasting licenses. On August 8, 1990, BTP filed a voluntary petition for reorganization under Chapter 11 of the Bankruptcy Code. After the bankruptcy court converted the bankruptcy filing to a liquidation under Chapter 7, the trustee for BTP requested and the FCC approved the sale of the two broadcast licenses to private parties for approximately $140,000.

On September 18, 1992, Orix moved that it be paid the proceeds from the sales. On January 26, 1993, the bankruptcy court denied Orix's motion, ruling that Orix did not have a valid security interest in the proceeds from the sale of the FCC broadcast licenses. On Orix's appeal, the district court affirmed the bankruptcy court's decision. This appeal ensued after the district court denied Orix's motion for a rehearing based on new case law.

This appeal presents only one issue for our review: whether a creditor may hold a valid security interest in the proceeds resulting from the sale of an FCC broadcasting license.

Prior to 1927, the private sector controlled the allocation of broadcast frequencies. Legislators soon realized, however, that "broadcast frequencies constituted a scarce resource" and thus the government should regulate allocations. The Federal Communications Act of 1934 (the Act) commissioned the FCC to fulfill this role. 47 USC 301 et seq. Section 307 of the Act vests in the FCC the exclusive authority to license the use of broadcasting frequencies for radio and television stations. 47 USC 307. In order to grant a license, the FCC must determine that the transfer will serve the public interest, convenience, and necessity. 47 USC 310(d). Thus, a licensee may not transfer or assign the license without the express permission of the FCC. 47 USC 310(d).

Based upon the FCC's exclusive authority under the Act to control the transfer of broadcast licenses, courts have traditionally held that licensees have no true ownership interest in their broadcast licenses. See FCC v. Sanders Bros. Radio Station, 309 U.S. 470 (1940) (noting that the Act prevents a person from holding a property interest in a broadcast license). Because [9-203(b)] requires an ownership interest in the underlying asset prior to the assignment of a security interest to a creditor, and courts typically have held that security interests in broadcast licenses are invalid, trustee contends that creditors holding such security interests possess no rights in the proceeds of the sale of the licenses. See In re Tak Communications, Inc., 985 F.2d 916 (7th Cir. 1993).

Nevertheless, recent FCC and court decisions have intimated that the courts' previous blanket invalidation of all security interests in broadcast licenses may be unwarranted. See In re Cheskey, 9 F.C.C.R. 986 (1994); In re Ridgely Communications, 139 Bankr. 374 (Bankr. D. Md. 1992). We agree with the developing case law that recognizing a security interest in the proceeds from the sale of an FCC broadcasting license does not contravene the FCC's authority to regulate broadcast frequencies.

The courts that adopted the former view primarily relied upon and deferred to the FCC's pronouncement in In re Radio KDAN, Inc., 111 F.C.C.2d 934 (1968) that a broadcast license "may not be hypothecated by way of mortgage, lien, pledge, lease, etc." Although such statements frequently arose in the context of dicta, they did evidence a clear FCC policy to prohibit the intrusion of commercial financing arrangements on the FCC's ability to regulate the transfer of broadcast licenses.

The FCC, however, has recently stated that a "security interest in the proceeds of the sale of a license does not violate Commission policy." In re

Cheskey, 9 F.C.C.R. 986 (1994). This clarification apparently vindicates the distinction between public and private rights adopted by the bankruptcy court in In re Ridgely Communications, Inc., 139 Bankr. 374 (1992). The *Ridgely* court reasoned that because "rights between licensees and the Commission are to be distinguished from rights between the licensee and a private third party," creditors can perfect a security interest in the private right of the *proceeds* from an FCC approved sale of a broadcast license. In re Ridgely, 139 Bankr. at 377-79. A security interest in the proceeds of an FCC-approved sale of a broadcast license in no manner interferes with the FCC's authority and mandate under the Act to regulate the use of broadcast frequencies.

Consequently, we hold that the district court erred in ruling that Orix did not have a valid security interest in the proceeds from the sale of the FCC broadcast licenses. * * *

COMMENTS AND QUESTIONS: MISSING ASSETS AND SECURITY INTERESTS

We should start with the state of the law and then consider the more conceptual issues posed by the case. In Federal Communications Commission v. Nextwave Personal Communications, Inc., 537 U.S. 293 (2003), the Supreme Court considered how BC 525 applied to efforts by the FCC to revoke communications licenses. BC 525 limits discriminatory actions that can be taken against debtors. In considering these issues, the Court turned to the question of security interests and licenses and noted that "[i]t is neither clear that a private party *can* take and enforce a security interest in an FCC license, see, e.g., In re Cheskey, 9 FCC Rcd. 986, ¶ 8 (1994), nor that the FCC *cannot*." Id. at 307 (emphasis in original). In Airadigm Communications, Inc. v. Federal Communications Commission (In re Airadigm Communications), 519 F.3d 640, 652 n. 2 (7th Cir. 2008), the court surveyed the uncertain status of the cases—citing *Orix Credit*—before concluding that it need not resolve the issue.

As to the underlying issues, the broadcast license cases illustrate rather nicely the line between property rights and priority rights and how that relates to whether a security interest exists. The FCC's policy that bars a security interest in the license itself as original collateral creates a missing asset, a hole as it were in the fabric of secured transactions. Notwithstanding this limit, creative lenders take a security interest in the proceeds of any sale of the license and sometimes also in the license-holder's right to petition the FCC for a sale of the license.

We need to draw lines carefully here. It is one thing to say that the FCC's limit on security interests prevents a secured creditor from repossessing the license pursuant to 9-609. See In re Ridgely Communications, Inc., 139 Bankr. 374 (Bankr. D. Md. 1992) and In re Tak Communications, 985 F.2d 916 (7th Cir. 1993). This is to say that the traditional property rights of the secured creditor against a debtor are cut-off by the FCC's policy. That is not to say, though, that a secured creditor should not be able to create priority rights to the value represented by the license. Suppose the station is sold as a going concern after the FCC approves the sale of the license. The former broadcaster has left the business and is now a shell corporation. The only thing that remains to be done is to divvy up the proceeds of the sale among the creditors and equityholders of the firm. Suppose that the debtor had signed an agreement with its main lender that provided the following: "debtor hereby grants a security interest in all of the assets of the firm, now or hereafter, owned excluding the broadcast license but including any proceeds of any FCC approved sale of the license." It is hard to see how this would raise any problems with control of the license while owned by the firm, and thus would seem acceptable given the FCC's views. Put differently, even if the property rights typically part of a security interest would run contrary to FCC policy, the priority rights clearly should not. Indeed, the FCC itself reached this conclusion in *Cheskey*, as described in *Orix Credit Alliance*.

These cases present an additional interesting question, namely, what is the appropriate way to take and perfect a security interest in the proceeds of property which itself cannot be Article 9 collateral (our "missing collateral")? Consider the grant above, which grants a security interest in "proceeds." Will this work? Perhaps not. The difficulty is that the definition of proceeds in 9-102(a)(64) is tied to "collateral." Thus, for something to be proceeds it must derive from property that was originally collateral. If you can't take a security interest in the FCC license, it can't be collateral, and it therefore cannot be Article 9 proceeds.

So what? After all, the lender took a security interest in all of the assets of the firm, and the new assets received in exchange for the license will be after-acquired property. The lender thus can obtain a security interest in the received assets, not as proceeds of collateral, but instead as new original Article 9 collateral. But we now encounter another roadblock and find a situation where the difference between whether the security interest arises through the proceeds interest or as after-acquired property actually matters. Suppose our distressed borrower files for bankruptcy. The licenses are to be sold under BC 363, and the lender wants its security interest to attach to the proceeds of the sale.

BC 552 may prevent this. BC 552(a) provides that a prepetition security agreement will not be effective to create a security interest in property acquired by the estate or the debtor after the commencement of the case. As a result, the property received in exchange for the license will not be encumbered under the after-acquired property clause of the prepetition security agreement. BC 552(b)(1) cuts back on the general rule of BC 552(a), as it provides that if the prepetition security agreement extended to "proceeds, product, offspring, or profits" of prepetition collateral, it also extends to them postpetition collateral, unless based on the equities of the case, the bankruptcy court orders otherwise.

But now we come to the rock and the hard place. As noted above, it is possible that a lender cannot take a direct proceeds interest under Article 9 if the property giving rise to the proceeds itself cannot be collateral. This means that the lender here should not fit within the protection of BC 552(b)(1), and should instead have to rely on its after-acquired property clause, which, in turn, is made ineffective by BC 552(a). Taken together, there seems to be no way for the security interest to attach to the postpetition proceeds of the license.

There is little to be said in favor of this result. The original FCC limitation on a security interest in the license may be understandable, but it has presumably unintended consequences for the proceeds, given the design of 9-315 and BC 552. Given that the FCC has no stake in the proceeds, we might consider whether the FCC would do a better job of vindicating its policies through another route. Allow a perfected security interest in the license but make it unenforceable as to the license itself. Bar the secured creditor from exercising any property rights against the license, such as repossession under 9-509 or sale under 9-510 or actions under BC 362. This would allow the rights to the proceeds to carry through as intended without putting at risk the original FCC policy regarding the license itself.

As to the mechanics, suppose the security agreement provides that debtor hereby grants a security interest in "the proceeds of the sale of broadcast licenses to lender to secure all debt owed by debtor to lender." Is that an adequate description under 9-203 and 9-108?

B. PROCEEDS AND PRIORITY

Consider how these transactions alter preexisting priority relationships:

5-3: PROCEEDS AND PRIORITY

- On February 1st, Bank lends money to Debtor and takes a security interest in Debtor's inventory and its proceeds. Bank files an appropriate financing statement.
- On March 1st, Finco lends money to Debtor and takes a security interest in Debtor's accounts and their proceeds.
- On April 1st, Debtor sells inventory and receives $10,000 in accounts in exchange.
- ¤ What are the relative priorities of Bank and Finco as of March 1st? April 1st?
- On February 1st, Bank lends money to Debtor and takes a security interest in Debtor's accounts and their proceeds. Bank files an appropriate financing statement.
- On March 1st, Finco lends money to Debtor and takes a security interest in Debtor's inventory and its proceeds.
- On April 1st, Debtor sells inventory and receives $10,000 in accounts in exchange.
- ¤ What are the relative priorities of Bank and Finco as of March 1st? April 1st?

Bank of Stockton v. Diamond Walnut Growers, Inc.

California Court of Appeals, 1988.
244 Cal. Rptr. 744.

[In 1981, the Bank of Stockton lent money on an unsecured basis to Bella-Farms Partnership, a walnut grower. Bella-Farms was a member of Diamond Walnut Growers, Inc., an agricultural marketing association. Diamond received walnuts from its members, sold them, and distributed the proceeds—called "member proceeds"—to the members. Diamond subsequently lent money to Bella-Farms and took a security interest in Bella-Farm's share of the member proceeds derived from the sale of the 1983 walnut crop. Diamond filed a financing statement for this loan with the California Secretary of State. Bella-Farms was unable to pay the bank on time. As part of a renegotiation of that loan, Bella-Farms gave the Bank of Stockton a security interest in Bella's 1983 crop and the proceeds thereof.

The bank filed appropriately with the Secretary of State and with the San Joaquin County recorder.]

■ BLEASE, ACTING PRESIDING JUSTICE

This is an appeal from a judgment declaring the priority between two creditors holding security interests, governed by the Commercial Code, arising from loans involving a walnut crop. Diamond Walnut Growers, Inc. (Diamond), an agricultural marketing association, made loans to one of its members, Bella-Farms Partnership (Bella-Farms), secured by Bella-Farm's share of the funds, called "member proceeds," to be received from the sale by Diamond of its 1983 walnut crop. The Bank of Stockton (Bank) also made a loan to Bella-Farms secured by the 1983 crop and by all "proceeds" from its sale. Prior to the harvest of the crop, Diamond and the Bank learned of the other's interest and agreed that the 1983 crop could be delivered to Diamond for marketing with the caveat that "[t]he parties do not intend by this agreement to change their respective rights and duties...." The crop was delivered to Diamond and sold by it, thus creating "member proceeds." This litigation ensued to ascertain the parties' competing claims to such funds in light of their agreement. The trial court ruled in favor of the Bank. * * *

The first complication arises because the Bank obtained a security interest in both the crop *and* proceeds and Diamond obtained a security interest only in the "member proceeds." However, this complication is easily resolved. As to the *crop*, the Bank is a secured creditor and Diamond is an unsecured creditor. Hence, as to the crop, the Bank's security agreement is effective "according to its terms" against Diamond. ([9-201].) But, as to the rights to receive "member proceeds," all other things being equal, both parties are perfected secured creditors and Diamond, which filed its UCC financing statement prior to the Bank's filing, would be accorded priority under the usual rule. Priority is assigned as to the particular collateral in issue. The party which has the highest priority or only security interest as to goods does not for that reason have priority as to the collateral, e.g., account or proceeds, derived from the sale of the goods.

Accordingly, the original rights of the Bank and Diamond under the Commercial Code are as follows. So long as the security interest in the crop exists, if Bella-Farms defaults under its security agreement with the Bank, the Bank has the right to employ the remedies provided in the Commercial Code, e.g. to take possession of the crop and thereafter to liquidate it. This action would prevent the advent of or extinguish the existence of proceeds, specifically the member proceeds account owing to Bella-Farms by Diamond. Upon the advent of proceeds of the crop, the Bank's security interest in the proceeds was perfected (by relation back to the original collateral) and upon default the Bank would have the right to possession of the proceeds, enforceable against anyone save a secured creditor with a higher priority. If the crop were lawfully marketed other than by delivery to Diamond, the Bank would be the sole secured creditor as to funds which were the proceeds of that transaction. However, as it turned out, the crop was delivered to Diamond. When the crop was sold by Diamond, there were created "member proceeds," the member's share of funds from the sale, pursuant to their agreement. The creation of "member proceeds" resulted in a fund from which Diamond's security interest could be satisfied. As we have shown, Diamond's interest in that account was perfected and Diamond had the right to the account against anyone save a secured creditor with higher priority. In this latter case, absent an agreement altering priority, Diamond would have a superior right to that of the Bank by virtue of its earlier filing of its UCC financing statement. That leads us to consider the agreement between Diamond and the Bank.

The rules provided by the Commercial Code may be varied by contract except as it otherwise provides. ([1-302].) Nothing in Article 9 prevents subordination of priority by agreement. ([9-339].) The Bank argues that the intention and effect of the agreement between it and Diamond was to change the priority of security interests as otherwise governed by the Commercial Code. It argues that the agreement fixes the time for resolution of the dispute at September 27, 1983, i.e., that the agreement amounts to a direction that the party that would have prevailed on that date should prevail thereafter. * * *

The agreement is cryptic with respect to its effect on the security interests of the parties. On the one hand it says that each party is reserving *all* rights and claims with respect to the 1983 crop and its proceeds. On the other hand it asserts that transfer of physical possession of the crop to Diamond shall not change the rights of the parties. * * * If the Bank thought the agreement was to have the effect of changing the rights and claims of the parties, i.e. of altering the Commercial Code rules for priority by importing priority in the crop as the rule for priority in the proceeds, it was incumbent upon it to so specify. Absent specification to the contrary, the rules provided by the Commercial Code are unaltered. The onus of showing that the agreement alters such rules is on the party which advocates that outcome. There is no such statement in the agreement. Rather, the tenor of the agreement is *preservation* of existing rights and claims. Accordingly, we read the agreement as meant to let the chips fall as they might with the proviso that no waiver of existing security interests could be implied from the transfer of physical possession of the crop to Diamond.

Thus read, the Bank's security interest in the walnuts continued despite transfer of their possession to Diamond. However, when the walnuts were sold by Diamond that security interest was extinguished. ([9-320].) Prior to that point the Bank could have foreclosed on the walnut crop. After the sale all that was left was the proceeds of the sale as to which Diamond had also perfected a security interest.

It is unfortunate that one of these creditors must lose out to the other. Other unsecured creditors may also have suffered in the demise of the Bella-Farms operation. At the outset the Bank had no security. Diamond was the only secured creditor and gave notice to all of its interest in the account of "member proceeds" that would arise after the delivery and sale of the crop as required under its membership contract with Bella Farms. Either through calculation or ignorance Diamond left itself at partial risk concerning the crop itself or its proceeds if the crop were lawfully marketed elsewhere. The Bank then filled this niche, leaving itself exposed to loss of its advantage if default did not occur soon enough or if it failed to take possession of the crop prior to extinction of its security interest in it. Neither the Bank nor Diamond has any compelling equitable claim vis-à-vis the other. They paid their money and took their chances.

The judgment is reversed. * * *

COMMENTS AND QUESTIONS

1. As *Diamond Walnut Grocers* must make painfully clear, how a priority dispute is resolved matters enormously. It is quite common to agree to sell the collateral and then litigate over the proceeds. The collateral may have a short shelf-life, storage charges may be accruing, and there is a continuing risk of loss. Notwithstanding the real advantages of converting the collateral into cash, no litigant would agree to do so if that would impair its position. This, of course, is precisely the fate of the Bank of Stockton in the above case. Put yourself into the shoes of the bank, and ask "what should we have done here to avoid this out-

come? What do we do next time to make sure this doesn't happen again?"

2. Given what was just said, doesn't the court offer much too narrow an interpretation of the contract that was signed in the case? Shouldn't the court have assumed that the bank would not permit a sale through Diamond if doing so would impair its position?

3. Why were the walnuts sold through Diamond? Would you advise the bank to sell elsewhere next time?

Perhaps the most important dispute that arises over proceeds involves proceeds that have made their way into a deposit account. Inventory is turned into an account, an account into a check, and the check is deposited at the bank. The debtor pays money from the account. Where does this leave the secured creditor who claims an interest in the deposit account as proceeds of collateral? The inclusion of deposit accounts into Article 9 means that Article 9 addresses both interests in the deposit account as original collateral and as proceeds of collateral. Read 9-322(c–f), 9-327 and 9-332, consider the following fact patterns.

5-4: CONTROL V. PROCEEDS INTEREST

- On February 1st, Bank lends money to Debtor and takes control under 9-104(a) of the Debtor's deposit account with the Bank.
- On March 1st, Finco lends money to Debtor and takes a security interest in Debtor's inventory, accounts and their proceeds.
- On April 1st, Debtor sells inventory to Customer and receives $10,000 in accounts in exchange. On May 1st, Customer pays Debtor via check, and Debtor deposits the check in its deposit account with Bank.
- ¤ What are the relative priorities of Bank and Finco as of April 1st? May 1st? See 9-315, 9-322(b) and 9-327.
- ¤ Suppose instead that Finco had completed its transaction on February 1st and Bank had finished its on March 1st. Would that change the outcome?

5-5: PROCEEDS V. PROCEEDS

- On February 1st, Bank lends money to Debtor and takes control under 9-104(a) of the Debtor's deposit account with the Bank.

- On March 1st, Finco lends money to Debtor and takes a security interest in Debtor's inventory, accounts and their proceeds.
- On April 1st, Debtor sells inventory to Customer and receives $10,000 in accounts in exchange. On May 1st, Customer pays Debtor via check, and Debtor deposits the check in its deposit account with Bank.
- On May 2nd, Debtor withdraws $10,000 in cash from the deposit account and buys new inventory.
- ¤ What are the relative priorities of Bank and Finco as of May 1st? May 2nd? See 9-315, 9-322 and 9-327

5-6: SENIORS AND JUNIORS

- On February 1st, Bank lends money to Debtor and takes a security interest in Debtor's inventory, accounts and their proceeds.
- On March 1st, Finco lends money to Debtor and takes a security interest in Debtor's inventory, accounts and their proceeds.
- On April 1st, Debtor sells inventory to Customer and receives $10,000 in accounts in exchange. On May 1st, Customer pays Debtor via check, and Debtor deposits the check in its deposit account with Bank. The next day, Debtor delivers a $10,000 check to Finco, which Finco collects in due course as of May 5th.
- ¤ What are the relative priorities of Bank and Finco as of April 1st? May 1st? May 5th? See 9-315, 9-322(b) and 9-332.

COMMENTS AND QUESTIONS: UNDERSTANDING DEPOSIT ACCOUNTS

The deposit account plays an unusually important role in secured transactions, as the day-to-day operations of the firm usually flow through that account. The standard path is a sale from inventory into cash or an account and then a check, but in both cases the value will often flow into the deposit account. Assuming that the tracing standards of 9-315(b) can be met, an inventory or accounts financier will end up with a security interest in the deposit account as proceeds of the original collateral.

Revised Article 9 also makes it possible for secured creditors to take a security interest in a deposit account as original collateral, but to do so, a secured creditor must take control over the deposit account. 9-312(b)(1), 9-314, 9-104. That means that we can have a number of different conflicts between secured creditors in a deposit account. We could have two control secured creditors in a dispute and 9-327(2), 9-327(3) and 9-327(4) set out the rules for that situation. We also can have a conflict between a control secured creditor and a secured creditor claiming a security interest in the deposit account as proceeds. 9-327(1) provides that the control secured creditor has priority over the proceeds-only secured creditor. Control beats non-control. This isn't about the time of perfection—remember the earlier-of-first-to-file-or-perfect rule in 9-322(a)(1) is precisely about *time*—but rather this is about one method of perfection—control—being superior to a second method of perfection. For more detail, see Randal C. Picker, Perfection Hierarchies and Non-Temporal Priority Rules, 74 Chi-Kent L. Rev. 1157 (1999).

So far, so good. Take the next step: ask what happens as value flows out of the deposit account to buy, say, new inventory. The secured creditor with control over the deposit account will seek to claim that inventory as a proceed of the deposit account. A creditor who had financed inventory originally would of course claim the inventory directly as original collateral and also might claim it indirectly as a proceed, though that would require tracing, so the original collateral claim would be far easier.

Where would we stand as to perfection and priority? Of course, for the ordinary inventory secured creditor, perfection flows from the financing statement filed to perfect it and that will establish the date for priority. For the control secured creditor claiming the inventory as proceeds, perfection will run for 20 days under 9-315(c) and 9-315(d), but absent an additional step in that window, perfection will cease. See Comment 8, Example 11, to 9-322.

SECTION II. TRANSFERS

9-315(a)(1) states that, except as provided elsewhere in Article 9 and in 2-403(2), "a security interest ... continues in collateral notwithstanding sale, lease, license, exchange, or other disposition thereof unless the secured party authorized the disposition free of the security interest ... ." 9-315(a)(2) then gives the security party rights in identifiable proceeds, so it appears that the secured party gets to double-dip: the secured party can chase the assets into the hands of the purchaser and also grab the proceeds from the debtor. And indeed comment 2 to 9-315 states baldy that "[t]he secured party may claim both any proceeds and the original collateral but, of course, may have only one satisfaction."

What should we make of this? Note two key points. First, 9-320 does call off the continuation rule, mainly for sales out of inventory. Second, the design point behind the continuation rule isn't really that collateral will grow and grow but rather to incentivize a buyer to protect the secured party. How so? The last thing a buyer wants to do is to hand over cash to a selling debtor and then take the property subject to the security interest. If that happened, an unpaid secured party could take the collateral from the buyer and the buyer would have nothing, no property and no cash. The buyer solves that problem by making sure that when the buyer pays the debtor/seller that the seller in turn pays that money to its original lender. The secured creditor will release its position once it is paid in full. This is the standard set of mechanics in buying a house and Article 9 imports this idea here through 9-315(a)(1). If the transaction is done correctly, the secured party won't end up with double collateral.

Turn to 9-320 and the circumstances in which a buyer takes free of a preexisting security interest in the property being sold. The core rule in 9-320(a) is that a buyer takes free of even a perfected security interest created by the buyer's seller even if the buyer knows of the existence of that security interest so long as the buyer qualifies as a "buyer in ordinary course of business." (9-320 carves out farm products from this framework as they are covered by a special federal statute.) Consider the following fact patterns:

5-7: SALES FROM INVENTORY

- Debtor, a retailer of home appliances, grants Bank a security interest in all of its personal property then owned and thereafter acquired. Bank files an appropriate financing statement.
- Consumer purchases a washing machine from Debtor.
- ¤ Does Bank's security interest in the washing machine survive the sale? Is it perfected, and, if so, for how long? See 9-320(a); 1-201(b)(9).

5-8: SALES BY CONSUMERS

- Consumer purchases a washing machine from Seller, who finances the sale and takes back a purchase money security interest.
- One year later, before Consumer has paid Seller in full, Consumer sells the washing machine to Neighbor.

¤ Does Seller's security interest in the washing machine survive the sale? See 9-320(b). Is it perfected, and, if so, for how long? See 9-309(1). How would the situation change if Seller had filed a financing statement? [What if Consumer had sold to Retailer rather than Neighbor?]

5-9: MULTIPLE TRANSFERS AND CONTINUATION OF THE SECURITY INTEREST

• Debtor has an outstanding security agreement with Bank covering all of Debtor's property. Bank is properly perfected. Bank's security agreement provides that payments for goods sold by Debtor are to be made to Debtor and Bank jointly.

• Debtor sells the goods to NewCorp, an entity owned by Debtor. NewCorp pays Debtor directly, knowingly violating the security agreement between Bank and Debtor.

• NewCorp in turn sells the goods to Customer. Customer is aware that NewCorp acquires some of its inventory from Debtor, and knows that Bank held a security interest in Debtor's property.

¤ Does Customer take free of Bank's security interest under 9-320(a)? See Official Comment 3 to 9-320. Is the language in 9-320(a) a trap for the unwary? Does whether a particular customer takes free of the security interest turn on whether its seller acquired the inventory in a transaction in which it qualified as a buyer in the ordinary course of business? Isn't the essential character of the goods as inventory unrelated to how the seller acquired them? Given that, what should the court do? For discussion, see First Bank of North Dakota (N.A.)-Jamestown v. Pillsbury Co., 801 F.2d 1036 (8th Cir. 1986).

Fordyce Bank & Trust Co. v. Bean Timberland, Inc.

Supreme Court of Arkansas, 2007.
251 S.W.3d 267.

■ TOM GLAZE, JUSTICE

This appeal requires our court to determine whether appellees Potlatch Corp. ("Potlatch") and Idaho Timber Corp. ("Idaho") are buyers in the ordinary course of business under the Uniform Commercial Code (UCC). See 9-320.

The appellant in this case, Fordyce Bank & Trust Co. ("Fordyce" or "the Bank"), issued several loans to appellee Bean Timberland ("Bean") so that Bean could purchase timber from various landowners. Bean gave the bank security interests in the purchased timber, and the proceeds from the sale of the timber were intended to repay the loans the Bank had made to Bean. The Bank, intending to perfect its security interests, filed its UCC Financing Statements with the Secretary of State's Office. However, when Bean sold the timber to the various lumber mills with which it did business, including Potlatch and Idaho, Bean failed to remit the sales proceeds to the Bank.

The Bank filed suit against Bean, Potlatch, and Idaho on February 19, 2004. In its complaint, the Bank alleged that Bean had known that the Bank had a valid first lien on the timber covered by the security interests. In addition, the Bank alleged that Potlatch and Idaho had both "negligently entered into contracts" with Bean for the purchase of timber and had "failed to exercise good faith" in those transactions. The Bank further contended that Potlatch and Idaho had been "negligent in failing to request a lien search of the UCC records [from] the Arkansas Secretary of State's Office." Had Potlatch and Idaho conducted a lien search, the Bank argued, they would have discovered the Bank's "properly recorded and perfected financing statement and security agreement granting [the Bank] a valid first lien[.]"

* * * Following the trial, the court later entered an order in which it found that Potlatch and Idaho were buyers in the ordinary course of business, and thus they were not required to perform a lien search on the timber purchased from Bean. * * *

We next turn to the Bank's second point on appeal, wherein it contends that the trial court erred in granting Potlatch's and Idaho's directed-verdict motions because there was sufficient evidence of negligence. Under Arkansas law, in order to prevail on a claim of negligence, the plaintiff must prove that the defendant owed a duty to the plaintiff, that the defendant breached the duty, and that the breach was the proximate cause of the plaintiff's injuries. In its complaint, the Bank asserted that Potlatch and Idaho were negligent in failing to request a lien search of the UCC records in the Arkansas Secretary of State's Office. In its second point on appeal, the Bank asserts that the trial court improperly granted Potlatch's and Idaho's motions for directed verdict despite testimony that Potlatch and Idaho should have known that their timber purchases from Bean were secured by financing, which would give rise to a duty to check for liens with the Secretary of State. Thus, to answer the question raised on appeal, this court must determine whether Potlatch and Idaho had a duty to perform a lien search; in turn, the answer to this question depends on whether Potlatch and Idaho were buyers in the ordinary course of business.

A buyer in the ordinary course of business is defined in [1-201(b)(9)], in pertinent part, as follows:

> "Buyer in ordinary course of business" means a person that buys goods in good faith, without knowledge that the sale violates the rights of another person in the goods, and in the ordinary course from a person, other than a pawnbroker, in the business of selling goods of that kind. *A person buys goods in the ordinary course if the sale to the person comports with the usual or customary practices in the kind of business in which the seller is engaged or with the seller's own usual or customary practices....*

(Emphasis added.)

Under 9-320(a), a buyer in the ordinary course of business "takes free of a security interest created by the buyer's seller, even if the security interest is perfected and the buyer knows of its existence." Thus, if Potlatch and Idaho were buyers in the ordinary course of business, they would be under no duty to perform a lien search, because even if they knew of a lien and had performed a lien search, they could nonetheless take free of the Bank's security interest.

To determine whether Potlatch and Idaho were buyers in the ordinary course of business, the court must look to see whether the sale to them "comport[ed] with the usual or customary practices in the kind of business in which the seller is engaged or with the seller's own usual or customary practices." See 9-320(a). Evidence presented at trial clearly showed that Potlatch and Idaho's practices were "usual or customary" in the timber business.

Bean sold timber to various mills as "gatewood." Gatewood is severed timber that is brought to a lumber mill's front gate by a logger; the wood is weighed and inventoried, and if the timber meets the mill's specifications, the mill will purchase it. If the wood does not meet specifications, the mill will not buy it. Numerous witnesses testified that purchases of gatewood are common in the Arkansas logging industry. For example, Robert Frey, the raw material procurement and marketing manager for Weyerhauser in Arkansas and Oklahoma, testified that the "basic way" the timber industry does business is for a mill to have written contracts with loggers or timber producers; those contracts would have specifications that set the mill's requirements for timber that it would accept.

Frey testified that lumber mills, such as Weyerhauser, would not typically go out and look at growing timber before it was cut, but would instead purchase it at the mill gates based on specifications. The gatewood system, according to Frey, was a "common way of doing business in the timber industry in Arkansas," and most companies that he knew about conduct business in this manner. Further, Frey testified that Weyerhauser does not perform title searches for liens and ownership on any gatewood timber. Frey also noted that, if Bean "delivers all of his product as gatewood, that is normal if that is how he does business. There is nothing wrong with that."

Frey testified that Weyerhauser does not conduct title searches at the county courthouse or at the Secretary of State's office on gatewood; however, it would do a title search and obtain a legal description of the tract for standing timber (as opposed to the cut timber of the type Bean sold) in order to make sure that the supplier was bringing the timber that the mill had contracted for. ***

In sum, the trial court had before it abundant evidence that purchasing gatewood without performing a lien search was the standard practice in the timber industry. Clearly, Bean's sales to Potlatch and Idaho, and Potlatch's and Idaho's practice of not conducting lien searches, "comport[ed] with the usual or customary practices in the kind of business in which the seller is engaged or with the seller's own usual or customary practices." See 9-320(a). As such, the trial court correctly determined that Potlatch and Idaho were buyers in the ordinary course of business. Further, because the mills were buyers in the ordinary course of business, they owed the Bank no duty to conduct a lien search. With no duty, there could be no breach of any duty. Therefore, the trial court properly granted a directed verdict on the Bank's negligence claims. ***

COMMENTS AND QUESTIONS: WHAT DID THE BUYER KNOW AND WHEN DID THE BUYER KNOW IT?

We have a little statutory work to do here. What exactly can the buyer know and still take free of the security interest? 9-320(a) itself suggests that the buyer take free even if the buyer knows of the existence of the security interest. But the buyer can only do so if the buyer qualifies as a buyer in ordinary course of business under 1-201(b)(9). So turn to that definition. As *Bean Timberland* makes clear, that depends on the practices of the industry, but before we get even to that point, we have to figure out what to make of the language that requires that the buyer do so "in good faith, without knowledge that the sale violates the rights of another person in the goods." And, for these purposes, good faith, defined in 1-201(b)(20), means "honesty in fact and the observance of reasonable commercial standards of fair dealing."

Of course, most buyers purchasing inventory won't know anything about whether their seller has created a security interest in it and those buyers should take free of the security interests. They will have been honest in fact and, while the fair dealing standard is loose, we don't typically expect a buyer to master its seller's capital structure. The secured creditor in *Bean Timberland* tried to suggest that buyers, at least in the timber industry, should do more, but made no headway with that argument. But suppose that the buyer does learn of a filed financing statement. Again that shouldn't create a problem for the buyer, given the approach taken to good faith in 1-201(b)(20) and the explicit statement in 9-320(a) that the buyer can know of a security interest and still take free of it.

So narrow further. What would it mean for the sale of the inventory to violate the rights of the secured party and how would the buyer know that? That is the set of circumstances that would have to arise for the buyer to take subject to the security interest (and read comment 3 to 9-320 to see this set out expressly). And this should be pretty narrow: the debtor can't run the business without selling inventory—selling stuff is the point of being in business after all—and an agreement that made a sale of inventory a violation of the security agreement should be seen as problematic. And even for less standard sales, it may be hard to show that the secured party has the requisite knowledge. See, for example, Key Corporate Capital, Inc. v. Tilley, 216 Fed. Appx. 193 (3rd Cir. 2007).

COMMENTS AND QUESTIONS: THE FOOD SECURITY ACT OF 1985

1. For those of you with a deep interest in farm products—and we know that you are out there—you should be aware of a federal override to 9-320(a). In the past, the financier of farmers fared better than the fin-

ancier of inventory. See, e.g., Thomas v. Prairie Home Cooperative Co., 237 N.W. 673 (1931). Courts rarely justified the distinction. Professor Gilmore suggested that the distinction had more to do with the likely players than with the nature of the goods involved. In the early part of this century, financiers of farmers were apt to be small local banks and buyers of goods were likely to be large food processors. By contrast, lenders with security interests in inventory were likely to be large finance companies and buyers were frequently consumers. 2 G. Gilmore, Security Interests in Personal Property 707 (1965).

2. The drafters of Article 9 continued the different treatment of buyers of inventory and farm products. Under 9-320(a), a buyer in ordinary course of business of farm products does not take free of security interests its seller has created. As a practical matter, however, courts frequently would find that the security interest did not survive the transfer to a buyer in ordinary course, especially where the secured party was not a local bank, but rather a branch of the United States government, such as the Farmers Home Administration. A common device was to find on the facts of the case that the secured party authorized the sale and waived the security interest. See, e.g., United States v. Central Livestock Association, Inc., 349 F. Supp. 1033 (D.N.D. 1972).

3. Effective in 1986, however, Congress preempted 9-320(a) as it applies to farm products. In the Food Security Act of 1985, Congress found that allowing secured creditors to enforce security interests against buyers in ordinary course subjected such buyers to the risk of double payment and this exposure "inhibits free competition in the market for farm products" and "constitutes a burden on and an obstruction to interstate commerce in farm products." 7 USC 1631(a). Instead of drafting a statute that allowed buyers in ordinary course of farm products to take free of security interests created by their sellers, however, Congress drafted a complicated statute that still allows secured creditors to prevail if they jump through the right hoops. A secured lender can trump the buyer in ordinary course of farm products if it makes a proper Article 9 filing and gives actual notice to the buyer.

CHAPTER SIX

CHANGES

In this chapter, we will have to confront the problem of realizing the goals of a system of notice filing when, after the date a financing statement is filed, the information on that financing statement becomes erroneous, even though it was correct on the date of the filing. When something like the debtor's name changes, *someone's* life is going to be made more difficult. The question, as always, is *who* should bear the risk of that change.

The absence of a prior claim to the debtor's property in the pertinent files does not eliminate the risk under Article 9 that someone will take priority over the secured creditor. A secured creditor may sometimes search the files but be unable to find the financing statement of an earlier creditor. For example, the previous secured party may have filed in another filing system, because at the time it lent to the debtor, the debtor lived in a different place. Moreover, the previous secured party may have filed in the same filing system, but the creditor may be unable to locate the filing because the debtor has changed its name.

The rules set forth in Article 9 are a compromise between placing the risk on the prior secured party (thereby encouraging it to monitor the debtor after extending credit and ensuring that creditors seeking security for their loans have readily available reliable information) and placing the risk on the subsequent secured party and requiring that party to adjust to the incompleteness of priority knowledge imparted by possession and the files. Though one could quarrel with the actual balance struck, some sort of compromise is inevitable. Secured parties must accept both a risk that the filing system is incomplete or inaccurate and a duty, after they extend credit, of imparting information about their interest. Reducing the risk parties face from prior creditors requires increasing the monitoring duties they must later bear. Similarly, reducing the monitoring duties on secured creditors to keep the files up to date requires increasing the risk placed on them of losing a property interest to a prior creditor. This tension exists any time one chooses between a negotiability-type rule (protecting subsequent parties by imposing a lighter search burden) and derivation-type rules (protecting prior parties with a lighter monitoring burden).

SECTION I. CHOICE OF LAW AND CHANGES OF LOCATION

Choice of law questions arise in every area of law and that includes Article 9. Choice of law matters most when laws differ across states. If each state had exactly the same law, the parties to a lawsuit wouldn't have anything at issue over which law applied to their dispute. But when differences in law arise, the parties have a strong stake in having the law applied that most favors their situation. Of course, Article 9 as such is a uniform law intended to be identical in all of the states. Differences creep in when a particular state changes the official text of Article 9 by making non-uniform amendments. Track the non-uniform amendments in a state to a particular enactment of Article 9 and you will quickly identify how choice of law may matter to a particular transaction.

But there is a second perhaps more fundamental way that choice of law matters for Article 9. The heart of Article 9 is notice through the financing statement system and a notice can't be effective unless someone can find it. As a state-based system, Article 9 will require that the financing statement be filed in a designated office in a particular state. Which state? A subsequent creditor can't find that statement unless the creditor can determine the state in which the financing statement should have been filed. So while standard choice of law disputes will arise when we have non-uniform enactments of Article 9, we still will need to go through a choice of law analysis in any case in which a financing statement is to be filed.

Revised Article 9 has made substantial changes in the rules controlling where a financing statement is to be filed. These changes should simplify matters considerably, and you will see that if you know a little about how things stood under the former statute. Under former Article 9, F9-401 was the Code's basic provision for answering the question of where a financing statement should be filed. But inherent in any use of F9-401 was another question: whether the proper state's enactment of Article 9 was being examined and applied. F9-401(4) stated that "[t]he rules stated in F9-103 determine whether filing is necessary in this state."

Maximizing the certainty of information in a filing system (and hence minimizing the costs of mistake by one party or another) demands *some* guidance as to where to file or look. Perfect guidance, however, may not be obtainable, at least at feasible cost levels, with respect to goods (and owners) that might, on occasion, move. For example, if a filing system is based on collateral location, any time the collateral is moved to a new filing jurisdiction, there is a risk that a party checking the new files will be misled. A rule that placed the risk on that party would lead, perhaps, to its checking files in other states or to its simply charging for the risk. Similarly, if the risk were placed on the original secured party, its response would be to check the location of the collateral more frequently or (if that got too expensive) to either take possession of the collateral or charge for the risk. F9-103 allocated the risk along a time plane. In situations where goods (or owners) had moved, several states were at least potential candidates for where one should or could file to perfect a security interest. F9-103 used two general filing-system principles: if collateral had a natural location, that location determined the state in which a financing statement should have been filed; if collateral did not have a natural location, the location of the debtor controlled.

Why should the "proper" state ever be in issue? Why shouldn't the parties be able to determine, pursuant to the general rule of 1-301, which state governs their transaction? The answer to both questions concerns the third-party notification function of financing statements: Article 9 needs to establish a determinate location (or set of locations) for filing so that subsequent parties can determine with precision *where* to look. This suggests why the general rule of 1-301 will not be satisfactory *insofar as rules governing third parties* are concerned. But it also suggests the advantages of having a conflicts-of-law rule for determining which state's law is applicable. In addition, the outcome of a lawsuit should not depend on where the suit is brought. That location will be a mere happenstance, which should be irrelevant; if it is not, location will become a strategic choice and the parties will fight over it.

F9-103(1)(b) set forth the general rule:

> [P]erfection, and the effect of perfection or non-perfection of a security interest in collateral are governed by the law of the jurisdiction where the collateral is when the last event occurs on which is based the assertion that the security interest is perfected or unperfected.

Note that the relevant language—"governed by the law of the jurisdiction"—is expressly choice-of-law language. Courts typically apply their own choice-of-law rules to select the substantive law that will apply in a particular case. Disputes that arise in a New Jersey state court, for example, will be subject to New Jersey's choice-of-law rules. Under the rule of Klaxon Co. v. Stentor Electric Mfg. Co., 313 U.S. 487 (1941), federal courts apply the choice-of-law rules of the state in which the court is located. At least in part, F9-103 was a choice-of-law statute for secured transactions.

The "last event" test set forth in F9-103(1)(b) was something of a misnomer. It was more usefully called an "all events" test. For a secured party, it meant essentially this: *Unless some other rule (such as the four-month rule in F9-103(1)(d)) provided otherwise, a security interest was perfected if there was ever a time when the goods were in a particular jurisdiction and the secured creditor had satisfied (at or before that time) the requirements for obtaining a perfected security interest under the laws of that jurisdiction.*

Revised Article 9 has altered this in important ways. All of subpart 1 of Part 3 of Article 9—9-301 to 9-307—is devoted to the law governing perfection and priority. 9-301 sets out the general rule, while special rules are given in 9-302 for agricultural liens; 9-303 for goods covered by a certificate of title; 9-304 for deposit accounts; 9-305 for investment property; and 9-306 for letter of credit rights. 9-307 gives the rule for determining the debtor's location. Even 9-301 can be carved down. 9-301(4) covers as-extracted collateral; 9-301(2) covers possessory security interests; and 9-301(3)(A) addresses fixture filings—you don't know what those are yet but you should recognize them as something out of the ordinary—while 9-301(3)(B) covers timber to be cut.

That leaves us with 9-301(1) and 9-301(3)(C):

> Except as otherwise provided in Sections 9-303 through 9-306, the following rules determine the law governing perfection, the effect of perfection or nonperfection, and the priority of a security interest in collateral:
>
> (1) Except as otherwise provided in this section, while a debtor is located in a jurisdiction, the local law of that jurisdiction governs perfection, the effect of perfection or nonperfection, and the priority of a security interest in collateral.
>
> ...

(3) Except as otherwise provided in paragraph (4), while negotiable documents, goods, instruments, money, or tangible chattel paper is located in a jurisdiction, the local law of that jurisdiction governs:

...

(C) the effect of perfection or nonperfection and the priority of a nonpossessory security interest in the collateral.

We must read carefully here, but if we do so, the statute serves as our guide. Both of these speak of the "local law of the jurisdiction" governing. That means the substantive law of that jurisdiction and not the choice-of-law rules. Absent that, we might get stuck in one of these choice-of-law loops, where State A refers us to State B, and then back to State A. So 9-301 speaks of local law, and that should be understood to mean the substantive law of the relevant jurisdiction. See 9-301, Official Comment 3.

But which local law? 9-301(1) looks to the debtor's location, while 9-301(3)(C) looks to the location of the collateral for particular types of collateral, including goods. This looks much like F9-103. But read more carefully. 9-301(1) addresses "perfection, the effect of perfection or nonperfection, and the priority of a security interest," while 9-301(3)(C) addresses only "the effect of perfection or nonperfection and the priority of a non-possessory security interest." The juxtaposition should highlight the key difference, even if that only means so much to you now: 9-301(1) "governs perfection," while 9-301(3)(C) does not. That means that *whether* a security interest is perfected is governed by the local law of the location of the debtor. The *consequences* of that status, depending on the type of property and other facts, may be governed by the local law of the location of either the debtor or the collateral.

We need two more steps, and then we can assess this. 9-307 gives the rules for the location of the debtor. That section is a little chunky, but look at three key subsections:

(a) ["Place of business."] In this section, "place of business" means a place where a debtor conducts its affairs.

(b) [Debtor's location: general rules.] Except as otherwise provided in this section, the following rules determine a debtor's location:

(1) A debtor who is an individual is located at the individual's principal residence.

(2) A debtor that is an organization and has only one place of business is located at its place of business.

(3) A debtor that is an organization and has more than one place of business is located at its chief executive office.

...

(e) **[Location of registered organization organized under State law.]** A registered organization that is organized under the law of a State is located in that State.

Here is where this matters. Under former Article 9, a secured creditor taking a security interest in all assets would need to file wherever the debtor was and wherever collateral was located. Collateral could be spread throughout the country and that necessitated many filings. The new approach avoids this. Under 9-307(e), a corporate debtor will be located where it is incorporated. Under 9-301(1), a secured creditor will file where the debtor is located. This means filing in one state for all of the collateral. For more on the benefits of this approach, see Lynn M. LoPucki, The Article 9 Filing System: Why the Debtor's State of Incorporation Should be the Proper Place for Article 9 Filing: A Systems Analysis, 79 Minn. L. Rev. 577 (1995).

Finally, 9-501 specifies exactly where to file in a particular state "if the local law of this State governs perfection of a security interest." Once we have figured out under 9-301 to 9-307 exactly which state's law governs perfection, we then turn to that state's version of 9-501 to determine where to file the financing statement.

We have one additional issue to address, but it will become clear that this issue is less significant under Revised Article 9. Tangible collateral moves around; you have a warehouse in Chicago, but need the goods at your Gary, Indiana store, so you ship them across state lines. The secured creditor is supposed to file in the location of the collateral. Illinois? Indiana? Both? Under former Article 9, the movement of the goods from one state to a second raised obvious questions. F9-103(1)(d) created a four-month rule which, in general terms, protected the original secured creditor for four months from the movement of the collateral into the new state, but which required filing in the new state during that period to continue perfection beyond the statutory window. (This slides over some details.) Dropping the location of the collateral as the basis for filing and switching to the location of the debtor means that collateral movement is much less important. Plus, the location of the debtor may change very infrequently:

corporations re-incorporate rarely, and individuals move out of state only so often. Still, we need to address what happens after a change of location, and 9-316(a) does this, as it continues the basic four-month rule of former Article 9.

Work through the next examples with some care. Look at 1-301 and F9-103(1), F9-103(3) and F9-401 to see how these fact patterns would have been treated under the former statute, and then turn to 9-301, 9-307 and 9-316 to analyze the facts under the new statute.

6-1: ROLLING DOWN THE HIGHWAY

- Debtor is located in Pennsylvania. Debtor enters into a secured lending arrangement with Bank. Debtor grants a security interest in inventory, accounts, contract rights and chattel paper and instruments relating to sales or services performed. Bank files appropriate financing statements in Pennsylvania.

- Debtor, of course, purchases additional inventory on an ongoing basis. The seller of the steel bars is based in Michigan.

- On February 1st, Debtor and Seller execute the sales papers transferring title to the debtor. On that date, the steel bars are at Seller's plant in Michigan.

- Five days later, Debtor picks up the bars and starts down the highway.

- ¤ Assume that a lien creditor of Debtor seizes the bars before they leave Michigan. A suit ensues in a Michigan state court over the respective priorities of lien creditor and Bank to the bars. Who has priority?

- Continue with the facts from above. Assume that the bars are not seized in Michigan and instead enter Ohio. A creditor levies in Ohio and brings suit in an Ohio state court.

- ¤ As between Bank and the lien creditor, who has priority?

- The bars are not seized in Ohio but instead cross over into Pennsylvania, where an unsecured creditor levies on them and brings suit in a Pennsylvania state court.

- ¤ As between Bank and the lien creditor, who has priority?

- Return to the facts of the second hypothetical. Assume that Seller seizes the bars while in Ohio. No dispute arises then. Seller applies the repossessed goods to reduce Debtor's obligation to it.

- Some time later, Debtor challenges the seizure as wrongful and brings suits in a Pennsylvania court.
- ¤ What are Bank's rights?
- ¤ This pattern is based on In re Slippery Rock Forging, Inc., 99 Bankr. 679 (Bankr. W.D. Pa., 1989), where the court concluded that Michigan law should apply, as it determined that the relevant "last event" for the purposes of F9-103(1)(b) was the manufacture of the bars. That should be a jarring result. Debtors acquire new material from the world over; the law of the location of manufacture or sale should have little role to play—one would think—in determining the status of a secured party with an interest in after-acquired property. Does the new approach solve this problem?

The new filing rules will make change-of-location cases much less frequent. This will result from the switch to a system tied to the debtor's location, coupled with making the state of incorporation the debtor's location for corporations (9-307(e)). Under 9-307(b)(3), there will still be a limited set of cases in which location turns on the location of the "chief executive office," mainly cases involving partnerships with more than one business location. Read the next fact pattern to make sure that you understand the basic rules regarding a change in the debtor's location.

6-2: REINCORPORATING

- On February 1st, Debtor, a New York corporation, enters into a security agreement with Bank covering inventory. Bank files an appropriate financing statement in New York.
- Two months later, Debtor reincorporates in New Jersey.
- ¤ Is Bank perfected on March 1st? On August 1st? Consider 9-301 and 9-316(a)(2); also consider comment 6 to 9-301.

The next case will give you a sense of the difficulties that arise when we tie legal outcomes to facts that are difficult to assess.

Mellon Bank, N.A. v. Metro Communications, Inc.

United States Court of Appeals, Third Circuit, 1991.
945 F.2d 635.

■ ROSENN, CIRCUIT JUDGE

This appeal, arising in the context of a failed leveraged buyout, had its roots in the congenial climate of mergers and acquisitions that beguiled corporate America during the decade of the nineteen-eighties. The appeal raises important questions regarding a bankruptcy trustee's avoidance powers under BC 547(b) and BC 548(a)(2). The debtor is Metro Communications (Metro), the corporation acquired in the leveraged buyout. Mellon Bank, N.A. (Mellon or Bank) financed the acquisition; Mellon lent the acquirer 1.85 million dollars to purchase all of the capital stock of the target corporation, Metro. Metro guaranteed and secured the acquisition loan with substantially all of its assets. Simultaneously with the leveraged buyout, Mellon extended a 2.3 million dollar credit line to Metro. At a later date, Mellon extended another 2.25 million dollars to Metro in the form of letters of credit. These loans were also collateralized by the security interest in substantially all of Metro's assets. Within a year of the leveraged buyout, Metro filed a bankruptcy petition under chapter 11.

The bankruptcy court held that Mellon's security interest in the three loans constituted a voidable preference under BC 547(b), finding that Mellon's security interest lapsed because it failed to re-file financing statements within four months of Metro's change in the location of its headquarters and that the refiling of the financing statements at the debtor's new location during the ninety day period preceding the filing of the bankruptcy petition constituted a voidable preference. * * * We reverse.

Metro Communications, also known as Metrosports, the debtor, had been in the business of television and radio sports syndication for about ten years prior to its bankruptcy. Metro, incorporated in Maryland in 1972, originally had its headquarters in Rockville, Maryland. Its business included acquiring the rights to broadcast sporting events, contracting with radio and television stations for such broadcasts, and selling rights to advertise during the broadcasts.

In April of 1984, Metro's stockholders sold all of their capital stock to Total Communications, Inc. (TCI), a wholly owned subsidiary of Total Communication Systems Co. (TCS). The principals of TCI created it solely for the purpose of acquiring the stock of Metro and becoming its sole shareholder. TCS, in turn, is the wholly owned subsidiary of Mass Communication and Management, Ltd. (MCM). * * *

To finance the purchase of the Metro stock, TCI borrowed $1,850,000 from Mellon on April 6, 1984. On the same day, Mellon loaned Metro $2,300,000 for use as working capital under a line of credit agreement. Pursuant to guaranty and suretyship agreements dated April 6, 1984, TCI guaranteed the repayment of the loan to Metro, Metro guaranteed the repayment of the loan to TCI, and TCS and MCM jointly guaranteed the repayment of both loans.

In addition to the guarantees, Metro entered into an agreement dated April 6, 1984, with Mellon Bank wherein Metro conveyed to the Bank a security interest in substantially all of Metro's property, including its general intangibles and accounts receivable. The security agreement provided that the collateral secured "all ... indebtedness, obligations and liabilities of [Metro] to the Bank, now or hereafter existing, including but not limited to those arising under the Guaranty, and those arising under the Metrosports Loan Agreement."

On September 7, 1984, Metro and Mellon entered into a Letter of Credit Agreement to finance Metro's purchase of broadcast rights for the PAC-10 Conference football season. * * *

The Bank perfected its security interests in the collateral pledged by Metro by filing UCC-1 financing statements in the Maryland State Department of Assessment and Taxation on April 9, 1984 and the Clerk's Office of the Circuit Court of Montgomery County, Maryland, on April 17, 1984. The Bank filed additional UCC-1 financing statements in the appropriate offices in Pennsylvania on February 1 to and including February 5, 1985. * * *

[Metro filed a voluntary petition under Chapter 11 of the Bankruptcy Code on March 15, 1985.]

The bankruptcy court concluded that Mellon Bank's security interest supporting the three loans—the acquisition loan, the working capital loan, and the letter of credit loan—constituted a voidable preference under BC 547(b). The court determined that the perfection of this security interest constituted a voidable preference because Mellon untimely refiled its financing statements in the debtor's new location. * * *

Whether the transfer occurred within the 90-day period turns on whether Mellon untimely refiled its security interest in Pennsylvania. Pa. F9-103(3) [9-301(1), 9-307, 9-316] governs the perfection of security interests in multi-state transactions. * * * The parties agree that at the time of the leveraged buyout, Metro had its chief executive office in Rockville, Maryland. Mellon filed in the appropriate offices in Maryland in April of 1984, thus perfecting its security interest. The issue is whether Mellon's refiling in Pennsylvania was within four months of the Metro's transfer of its chief executive office to Pittsburgh.

If the debtor moved its headquarters to Pennsylvania on or after October 5, 1984, Mellon's security interest in Metro's assets remained perfected. If the change of the chief executive office occurred prior to October 5, 1984, the lien of Mellon's statements would have lapsed, and the filing statements in Pennsylvania would constitute a reperfection rather than a continuation of the earlier perfected status. If the refilings constituted a reperfection, that new perfection occurred within the 90-day period of BC 547 and is thus vulnerable to attack.

The bankruptcy court determined that Metro moved its office "at least some time before October, and most apparently by late August." * * *

Turning to the bankruptcy court's factual findings as to when Metro moved its chief executive office, it appears that the court utilized the correct definition. The Official Comment to F9-103 explains that the "chief executive office does not mean the place of incorporation; it means the place from which in fact the debtor manages the main part of his business operations. This is the place where persons dealing with the debtor would normally look for credit information." Courts have used this language to develop a two-part test to determine the location of a debtor's chief executive office:

> (1) from which place does the debtor manage the main part of its business operations; and
> (2) where would creditors reasonably be expected to search for credit information?

The bankruptcy court's application of this definition, however, is questionable. The Banks rightly criticize the court's mechanistic application of factors deemed relevant in other cases. The Official Comment to F9-103 envisions a realistic test asking simply "where does the debtor manage the main part of its business" because that is where creditors are likely to search for information. To artificially break down that question into rigidly applied tests violates the practical nature of the inquiry as envisioned by the UCC.

The Banks correctly point out that when one corporation is acquired by another, the nature of the inquiry as to the location of the chief executive office must necessarily be tailored to that situation. Ascertaining the location of the headquarters of a wholly-owned subsidiary necessarily differs from determining the location of the chief executive office of a single corporation. Re-examining the evidence presented below with more illumination than that enjoyed by the bankruptcy court, it becomes apparent that the bankruptcy court basically concluded that Metro, over time, came under the control of its parent corporation, TCS, and thus Metro's headquarters became those of TCS. This conclusion is neither legally nor factually accurate.

The bankruptcy court's analysis is flawed in several respects. First, there is a presumption that a corporation, even when it is a wholly owned subsidiary of another, is a separate entity. The law recognizes the legal distinction of affiliated corporations as do business people. To require creditors to analyze and understand the internal power structure of related corporations to determine whether the wholly owned subsidiary was "truly independent" from its parent corporation is misplaced and would introduce great uncertainty into commercial transactions, especially with respect to the filing of financing statements.

The inappropriateness of the focus of the bankruptcy court's inquiry is underscored by the evidence it relied upon. The court found relevant internal memoranda allegedly revealing the "transfer of power [that] began gradually, and then proceeded rapidly." To require creditors to scrutinize internal documents to determine the "reality" of the power structure of affiliated corporations is impractical, imprudent, and unwarranted. If, as it must be, the focus of the inquiry is shifted from analyzing the relationship between the parent corporation and its subsidiary to where Metro, the debtor, in fact had its headquarters, overwhelming evidence supports the conclusion that Metro's chief executive office remained in Rockville, Maryland until it announced the transfer in the press in December of 1984.

As previously stated, Metro's business was the acquisition of syndication rights to sporting events as well as the sale of advertising. The bankruptcy court did not find that the activities of obtaining contracts and selling advertising were no longer centered in the Rockville office, but that these activities, over time, became subject to the final approval of Goldberg, the CEO and Chairman of the Board located in Pittsburgh.[1] The

---

[1] The evidence does show that accounting and financial services were consolidated in

court stated that "[b]y September the Rockville office had no more executive authority; it was merely a large sales arm of the Pittsburgh hub." Once again, however, to require the creditors of a corporation to speculate as to who is calling the final shots is impractical and irrelevant. The "main part" of Metro's activities was the acquisition of syndication rights and the sale of advertising; this activity remained centered in the Rockville office until it was closed in December of 1984.

Much evidence readily available to creditors and of a more objective nature demonstrated that Metro maintained its headquarters in Rockville until December of 1984. Most importantly, contracts for syndication rights list Rockville as the principal office as late as October 5, 1984. Tax forms filed in the beginning of 1985 list Rockville as the headquarters. Metro's own letterhead lists Rockville as headquarters until December 1, 1984. Representatives of athletic conferences and colleges continued to deal directly with the Rockville office at least through early October 1984. On October 5, 1984, the Big East Conference wrote to Gail Schelat, the chief financial officer of both TCS and Metro, confirming contract negotiations. That letter, however, was addressed to the Rockville office. All of this evidence strongly supports Rockville as the "place where persons dealing with the debtor would normally look for credit information." Official Comment to F9-103.

The only relevant piece of evidence in support of the court's conclusion that Metro's headquarters moved prior to October 5, 1984, was the July 12, 1984, newspaper announcement that stated that "TCS/Metrosports will be headquartered out of TCS's New Kensington, PA location." However, this announcement meant only that joint ventures embarked on by the newly related corporations would be coordinated out of the Pennsylvania location. Moreover, the effective date is not stated. The language used is telling—that the joint ventures will be "headquartered out of *TCS's New Kensington, PA location.*" Even this announcement did not imply that Metrosports, a separate corporate entity, had an office in New Kensington.

---

the Pittsburgh office shortly after the leveraged buyout. However, the location of these services is secondary to the main business of Metro corporation—obtaining syndication rights and selling advertising. Thus, the location of these services is not determinative. Moreover, it has become common practice for affiliated corporations to consolidate financial services for the corporate group in one location. The whereabouts of this streamlined accounting service does not give us much information about the location of the headquarters for each corporation.

Indeed, on the next page of the announcement, Metrosports' location is listed as Rockville, MD.

Finally, the most telling piece of evidence is not even mentioned by the bankruptcy court. On November 19, 1984, Metro announced that TCS/Metrosports was consolidating its operations and that accordingly, Metro's headquarters, "previously in Rockville, Maryland" were being moved to Pittsburgh "*effective on December 3, 1984*," and that "the firm expect[ed] to complete its consolidation of office and staff ... by December 31, 1984." (Emphasis supplied). Thus, the bankruptcy court's conclusion is directly contrary to the debtor's public announcement as to the location of its own headquarters.

In sum, the bankruptcy court's conclusion that Metro shifted its headquarters "at least some time before October" is fraught with error. First, the court impermissibly shifted the burden of proof. Second, the court engaged in an irrelevant inquiry as to the internal balance of power between corporate executives and whether the subsidiary corporation operations were controlled by the parent corporation. Third, the court ignored considerably critical evidence that Metro continued to handle negotiation of syndication contracts, Metro's central line of business primarily out of the Rockville office until at least October 5, 1984. Finally, the court disregarded the news release stating that Metro's headquarters would be moved on December 3, 1984. For these reasons, we conclude that the bankruptcy court erred in its mixed finding of fact and conclusion of law that Metro's headquarters moved "at least some time before October."

In any event, we need not decide the question whether the reperfection of a security interest in Pennsylvania during the 90-day preference period could be susceptible to attack under BC 547(b) in light of our holding that the bankruptcy court erred in its ultimate mixed finding of fact and conclusion of law that the debtor's headquarters moved prior to October 5, 1984. * * *

In sum, we conclude that the bankruptcy court erred in its conclusion that the debtor's chief executive office was relocated prior to October 5, 1984, and thus Mellon's refiling of its financing statements in the debtor's new location did not constitute a voidable preference under BC 547(b). * * *

COMMENTS AND QUESTIONS

As *Metro Communications* makes clear, the question of when the location of the debtor changes is largely a factual determination. Article 9 itself determines which facts are relevant and, in doing so, should focus on facts that are readily observable to third parties—potential secured creditors and judges—rather than making outcomes turn on difficult-to-determine facts such as where ultimate decisionmaking authority rests. The addition of new 9-307(e) will help substantially in this regard. Figuring out whether the debtor is a registered organization and in which state it is registered is much, much easier than sorting through messy factual situations of the sort presented in *Metro Communications*.

In the fact patterns that follow, assume that each relevant state has enacted the uniform version of Article 9.

6-3: UNANTICIPATED MOVEMENTS OF COLLATERAL

- On February 1st, Debtor, a New York corporation, enters into a security agreement with Bank covering inventory. Bank files an appropriate financing statement in New York.
- Two months later, Debtor moves property into New Jersey without Bank's knowledge.
- On May 1st, Debtor enters into a new security agreement with Finco, and Finco files an appropriate financing statement in New Jersey.
- ¤ On June 1st, who has priority? On August 1st?

6-4: SECURED CREDITOR V. BUYER AGAIN

- On February 1st, Debtor enters into a security agreement with Bank covering a glomph. Bank files a financing statement covering the glomph.
- ¤ A month later, Debtor sells the glomph to Buyer. Does Buyer take free of Bank's security interest in the glomph? See 9-315(a)(1); 9-320; 9-317(b). Was Bank perfected originally? If so and if Bank's security interest survives the sale, does it remain perfected? See 9-507(a), 9-316(a)(3); 9-102(a)(28).

6-5: SECURED CREDITOR V. BUYER AGAIN AND AGAIN

- On February 1st, Debtor, a New York corporation, enters into a security agreement with Bank covering equipment. Bank files a financing statement covering the equipment in the New York filing office.
- A month later, Debtor sells the equipment to Buyer, also a New York corporation. Assume that the sale does not qualify as a sale in the ordinary course of business under 1-201(b)(9).
- ¤ Is Bank perfected on April 1st? April 1st of the following year? Does Buyer take free of Bank's security interest? See 9-315(a)(1); 9-316(a)(3); 9-102(a)(28). Would the answer change if Buyer was instead a New Jersey corporation? See 9-316(b), 9-317(b).

With these three fact patterns in hand, we are ready to start down the Pearl River.

First Nat. Bank of Picayune v. Pearl River Fabricators, Inc.

Supreme Court of Louisiana, 2007.
971 So.2d 302.

■ KNOLL, JUSTICE

The difficult issue before us concerns our secured transaction laws pertaining to perfection of a security interest in collateral in one state and the failure to timely re-perfect the security interest in the collateral when the collateral is subsequently sold and moved to Louisiana. *** [W]e affirm the decision of the Court of Appeal, First Circuit, which found the secured creditor's security interest lapsed because of its failure to timely re-perfect its security interest in Louisiana.

FACTS

On December 11, 2000, Pearl River Fabricators, Inc. (Pearl River), a Mississippi business corporation with its principal office located in Picayune, Mississippi, borrowed $200,000 from the First National Bank of Picayune (FNB). To secure the loan, Pearl River executed a security agreement in favor of FNB, identifying certain collateral, including a "90 foot cutter head dredge" and a "sand and gravel shaker plant." On July 24, 2001, FNB filed and recorded a UCC-1 financing statement with the Chancery Clerk for Pearl River County, Mississippi, detailing its security interest in the above-described property.

The security agreement between Pearl River and FNB prohibited Pearl River from transferring "any of the collateral to any third party without the prior written consent of" FNB. Notwithstanding, on November 23, 2001, Pearl River, without notifying FNB, sold several pieces of equipment, including the cutter head dredge and the shaker plant it had at its Picayune, Mississippi plant, to Growth Fund Industries, Inc. (GFI), a for-profit domestic corporation created on October 5, 2001, in Indiana. Pearl River financed the equipment sale to GFI. In its agreement with Pearl River, GFI made a down payment of $45,000 and agreed to pay the remaining balance ($453,000) in sixty-one monthly installments. GFI never took physical possession of the equipment.

On December 11, 2001, GFI sold the cutter head and shaker plant to Phoenix Associates Land Syndicate, Inc. (Phoenix), a Nevada business corporation with its principal office in Madisonville, Louisiana. In the agreement among these parties, Phoenix agreed to pay GFI a $45,000 down payment and to pay the balance without interest as follows: 60 payments of $7,500, 1 payment of $3,000 and 1 balloon payment of $1,468,999.95.[1] On January 9, 2002, GFI filed a UCC-1 financing statement with the Louisiana Secretary of State and the Clerk of Court for St. Tammany Parish, identifying it as the secured party and Phoenix as the debtor. The financing statement identified the secured property, in part, as including a "90' X 22' X 5' Dredge Completely Powered" and "(1) 6' X 16'-Deck Shaker W/Standard Washbox." In May 2002, the equipment Phoenix acquired from GFI was transported by Pearl River from its principal office in Picayune, Mississippi to Phoenix's principal office in Madisonville, Louisiana.

On November 17, 2003, FNB filed a Louisiana UCC-1 financing statement with the St. Tammany Parish Clerk of Court. The financing statement identified FNB as the secured party and Pearl River as the debtor. The collateral was identified, in part, as "One (1) 90' x 22' x 5' Dredge completely powered, [and] One (1) 6' x 16' 3 deck shaker plant with stand and washbox."

---

[1] Despite the greatly differing sales prices, an examination of the sales agreements shows GFI sold nothing more to Phoenix than it received in the sale from Pearl River. The sole difference in the sale price is the final balloon payment Phoenix agreed to make to GFI.

On January 13, 2004, after Pearl River defaulted on its loan obligation, FNB filed its petition for executory process and sequestration against Pearl River in St. Tammany Parish. *** On May 3, 2004, the trial court *** found the property Pearl River collateralized for its loan from FNB and the equipment Phoenix purchased from GFI was one and the same. The trial court further rejected Phoenix's contention that it was necessary for FNB to refile its UCC-1 financing statement in Louisiana within one year, finding FNB/Pearl River's security agreement perfected in Mississippi was valid and enforceable in Louisiana. ***

On May 3, 2004, the trial court denied Phoenix's motion to dissolve the writ of sequestration and its request for damages. It found the property Pearl River collateralized for its loan from FNB and the equipment Phoenix purchased from GFI was one and the same. The trial court further rejected Phoenix's contention that it was necessary for FNB to refile its UCC-1 financing statement in Louisiana within one year, finding FNB/Pearl River's security agreement perfected in Mississippi was valid and enforceable in Louisiana. ***

DISCUSSION

FNB contends Phoenix should be charged with knowledge of the bank's security interest because it purchased equipment which, at the time of the sale, was located in Pearl River County, Mississippi, where the security interest was perfected and was a matter of public record. FNB further argues 9-316 and its re-perfection requirements are inapplicable because that statute and its re-perfection procedure only apply to a purchase or other transfer occurring in the destination state, after the collateral has been moved there.

Phoenix urges that FNB's position rests upon a knowledge requirement not found in 9-316 as reflected in the Legislature's recodification in 2001 and the deletion of the words, "after removal," from F9-103(1)(d)(i). It argues that utilizing well established Louisiana principles of statutory construction, this Court should interpret 9-316 as written, without a gloss that would either interject a knowledge requirement that does not exist or a limitation that the transfer must occur in the destination state *after* the collateral has been moved there. Phoenix contends that a plain reading of 9-316 compels the conclusion that FNB's security interest lapsed. Phoenix points out that although FNB admits it became aware of the transfer of the property on which it had a security interest in December 2002, it did not re-file its financing statement until November 17, 2003. Accordingly, Phoenix contends FNB's lack of due diligence should not be rewarded.

*** At the hearing on Phoenix's motion to dissolve the sequestration, Jerry T. Craft, Jr., the owner of Pearl River, testified his company built the equipment at issue in this case. He admitted the property was subject to a security interest in favor of FNB, that Pearl River transferred its interest in the equipment to GFI, that he never informed FNB of the sale of the equipment that secured its indebtedness as required by the contract it had with FNB, and that Pearl River delivered the equipment from Mississippi to Phoenix's Louisiana plant in the spring of 2002.

Counsel for FNB also referenced a stipulation among the parties that the equipment was located in Pearl River County, Mississippi at the time Pearl River granted FNB a security interest in the equipment. *** FNB contends Phoenix purchased its (FNB's) collateral in Mississippi and re-moved it to Louisiana several months later. FNB argues that if the pur-chase occurred in Mississippi, such purchase would have been subject to its recorded security interest in the equipment and no re-perfection was required.

The initial question thus presented is whether Phoenix purchased the equipment from GFI in Mississippi, where the equipment was located, or Indiana, where GFI was domiciled and where the purchase documents initiated. As defined in the UCC, "purchase includes taking by sale,...." [1-201(b)(29)]. Similarly, a purchaser "means a person who takes by pur-chase." Under 2-106, a "sale" consists in the passing of title from the seller to the buyer for a price. In the present case, it is clear that although the equipment GFI sold to Phoenix may have been located in Mississippi, the purchase documents were generated by GFI from its Indiana headquar-ters. As shown in the prior sale by Pearl River, title to the equipment passed to GFI on November 23, 2001. It was this title to the equipment GFI transferred to Phoenix on December 11, 2001. Thus, we find no me-rit to FNB's contention that Phoenix's purchase from GFI occurred in Mississippi.

The statute in question, 9-316, provides, in pertinent part:

   (a) General rule: effect on perfection of change in governing law. A security interest perfected pursuant to the law of the ju-risdiction designated in 9-301(1) or 9-305(c) remains perfected until the earliest of:

(1) the time perfection would have ceased under the law of that jurisdiction;

(2) the expiration of four months after a change of the debtor's location to another jurisdiction; or

(3) the expiration of one year after a transfer of collateral to a person that thereby becomes a debtor and is located in another jurisdiction.

(b) Security interest perfected or unperfected under law of new jurisdiction. If a security interest described in subsection (a) becomes perfected under the law of the other jurisdiction before the earliest time or event described in that subsection, it remains perfected thereafter. If the security interest does not become perfected under the law of the other jurisdiction before the earliest time or event, it becomes unperfected and is deemed never to have been perfected as against a purchaser of the collateral for value.

FNB first urges this Court to give 9-316(a)(3) its plain meaning. It contends the retroactive lapse rule did not come into play because there was no transfer of the property *after* it entered into Louisiana. In making this assertion, FNB argues that the re-perfection required in 9-316(a)(3) is only triggered where there is a "transfer" of property to a person "located in another jurisdiction." It points out that the word "transfer" does not simply refer to physical movement of property across state lines. Instead * * * FNB contends that because the property never changed ownership after it was moved to Louisiana, the one-year period was not triggered, and its security interest was never unperfected.

Phoenix points out that FNB's argument in this regard may have been viable under F9-103(1)(d)(i) which contained the words, "after removal." However, it contends the re-codification of F9-103(1)(d)(i) as 9-316(b) reflects a change of the law, and it further points out it is undisputed Pearl River's transfer to GFI and GFI's transfer to Phoenix occurred after the re-codification. It argues that the deletion of the words, "after removal," formerly contained in F9-103(1)(d)(i) strips FNB's assertion of any statutory basis. * * *

Prior to 2001, the principle of continued perfection of security interests in multi-state transactions was codified in F9-103(1)(d)(i). It provided, in pertinent part:

> [I]f the action is not taken before expiration of the period of perfection in the other jurisdiction or the end of four months after the collateral is brought into this state, whichever period first expires, the security interest becomes unperfected at the end of that period and is thereafter deemed to have been unperfected as against a person who became a purchaser *after removal*....

(Emphasis added).

After July 1, 2001, F9-103(1)(d)(i) was re-codified as 9-316(b) and re-worded as follows:

> (b) Security interest perfected or unperfected under law of new jurisdiction. If a security interest described in subsection (a) becomes perfected under the law of the other jurisdiction before the earliest time or event described in that subsection, it remains perfected thereafter. If the security interest does not become perfected under the law of the other jurisdiction before the earliest time or event, it becomes unperfected and is deemed never to have been perfected *as against a purchaser of the collateral for value.*

(Emphasis added).

Considering the wording of 9-316(b) and the failure of the Legislature to carry forward the words "after removal" formerly contained in F9-103(1)(d)(i), we find no merit to FNB's contention that the re-perfection rules do not apply, because Phoenix did not purchase the equipment after it had been moved to this jurisdiction.[12] To find otherwise would require us to ignore the wording of 9-316(b) and call for the interjection of language not contained in the statute. Clearly, Phoenix was a purchaser located in a jurisdiction other than Mississippi, i.e., Nevada, the state where it was organized, 9-307(e) ("A registered organization that is organized under the law of a State is located in that State."), and there was a transfer of title ownership to Phoenix through GFI's sale to it.

---

[12] In making this determination, we save for another day the question of whether the one-year period for re-perfection is triggered by the date of the transfer of ownership or by the date the collateral is moved to another jurisdiction. The facts of this case show FNB attempted to re-perfect its security interest in the equipment well past either triggering event.

The next issue before us involves the question of the proper interpretation to be given to the UCC provisions applicable to the retroactive lapse rule. FNB contends these provisions should be interpreted liberally and applied to the underlying purposes and policies. 1-103. In that light, FNB next urges us to adopt language included in comments on the retroactive lapse rule and common law jurisprudence that treats purchasers with notice of the underlying security interest differently from those without such notice. To the contrary, Phoenix contends that when presented with competing interpretation of the UCC, the laws must be applied as written, free of any gloss that common law jurisdictions may have added through the comments to the articles and their interpretive jurisprudence.

[1-103] provides that the provisions of Title 10, Commercial Laws, "shall be liberally construed and applied to promote its purposes and policies." The purposes and policies of Title 10 are:

> (a) to simplify, clarify and modernize the law governing commercial transactions;
>
> (b) to permit the continued expansion of commercial practices through custom, usage and agreement of the parties;
>
> (c) to promote uniformity of the law among the various jurisdictions.

[1-103]. ***

FNB references language in Example 6 of the Comments which states, "Buyer took subject to Lender's perfected security interest, *of which Buyer was unaware...* Having given value and received delivery of the equipment *without knowledge of the security interest* and before it was perfected [in the new jurisdiction], Buyer would take free of the security interest." (Emphasis added). Premised on that language, FNB urges that the official commentary to 9-316 recognizes a distinction between purchasers who already have notice of the underlying security interest perfected in another jurisdiction and those without such notice. Relying upon that language, FNB argues that creditors and purchasers who are already on notice of an underlying security interest do not require the protection of being re-notified vis-à-vis re-perfection of the security agreement in the new jurisdiction.

Phoenix counters with the assertion that nothing in the text of 9-316 supports FNB's position that 9-316(a) and (b) are only applicable when a third-party purchaser lacks knowledge of the pre-existing security interest. Thus, it concludes that when the express language of 9-316 does not contain the qualifying words "without knowledge," it is improper for the courts to supply such a qualification.

Moreover, we further observe that Example 6 of the Uniform Commercial Code Comments references 9-317(b) when it states that those without knowledge of a security interest will take free of the security interest if delivery is made before perfection of the security interest. La. Rev. Stat. Ann. 10:9-317(b) provides:

> (b) Buyers that receive delivery. Except as otherwise provided in subsection (e), a buyer, other than a secured party, of tangible chattel paper, documents, goods, instruments, or a security certificate takes free of a security interest or agricultural lien if the buyer gives value and receives delivery of the collateral before it is perfected.

In the 2001 Louisiana Official Revision Comments to La. Rev. Stat. Ann. 10:9-317, the following is stated:

> This section is uniform with revised U.C.C. Article 9, *except that in subsections (b), (c) and (d) the requirement of being "without knowledge" has been deleted.* This change is consistent with the Louisiana public records doctrine, which is predicated on filing and not knowledge. The Louisiana rule is that actual knowledge by third parties of an unrecorded interest is immaterial; proper filing is alone dispositive. This change also promotes judicial efficiency by facilitating proof in contested cases.

(Emphasis added).

Referencing the comments to La. Rev. Stat. Ann. 10:9-316 and the cross-reference therein to La. Rev. Stat. Ann. 10:9-317, we find further support for Phoenix's assertion that the plain language of La. Rev. Stat. Ann. 10:9-316 is dispositive of the issue presented. In conformity with the Louisiana rule which strongly adheres to the Louisiana public records doctrine, we find no support for FNB's reliance on the comments to La. Rev. Stat. Ann. 10:9-316. Moreover, at no time does FNB contend Phoenix had actual knowledge of FNB's recorded security agreement in Mississippi; it simply asserts Phoenix received shipment of the equipment from Mississippi. This fact alone does not meet the requirements of La. Rev. Stat. Ann. 10:1-201(25).

* * * In the present case, the Legislature did not qualify 9-316 to entities without knowledge of pre-existing security interests. Furthermore, as stated in [1-202], "[a] person 'knows' or has 'knowledge' of a fact when he has actual knowledge of it." FNB has not made a showing that Phoenix knew or had knowledge of the recorded Mississippi security agreement, only that the equipment was located in Mississippi at the time of its purchase from GFI. * * *

CONCLUSION

After conducting this statutory analysis of the rules relative to re-perfection, we realize the impact this holding has on lenders. Nonetheless, our ruling today effectuates the principles the Legislature adopted with regard to the rules relative to the re-perfection of security agreements. As the record shows in the case sub judice, FNB failed to re-perfect its security interest prior to the lapse of the one-year period delineated in 9-316. Pursuant to 9-316(b), FNB's failure to timely re-perfect its security interest in Louisiana prior to the lapse of its security interest resulted in its security interest becoming unperfected and deemed never to have been perfected against Phoenix. * * *

COMMENTS AND QUESTIONS

In a complicated set of facts, it is very important to get your bearings to figure out what is and is not relevant and then to sort through the relevant facts for a resolution. In *Pearl River Fabricators* itself, start with the movement of the collateral from Mississippi to Louisiana. Under former Article 9, collateral movement was quite important the location of the collateral determined the required location of filing for most goods. Former Article 9 anticipated these moves and put in place rules to manage them, most notably F9-103(1)(d)(i), which created a four-month rule requiring a new filing in the new jurisdiction if the original secured party was to maintain perfection.

Revised Article 9 has abandoned making the location of the collateral relevant for filing, so a collateral movement doesn't matter for the question of whether collateral perfected through filing is actually perfected. Read that sentence again, as it is easy to misunderstand, plus there is one fundamental way in which the statement is wrong. In 9-301, the location of the collateral matters for possessory security interests (9-301(2)); matters for as-extracted collateral (9-301(4)); and matters much more generally for goods and certain other types of collateral (9-301(3)(C)) but only for the effect of perfection or nonperfection and priority, but not, importantly, for perfection of the security interest in those types of collateral. That means, saying the first sentence again, that the location of the collateral doesn't matter for perfecting security interests perfected through filing.

But movement of the collateral across jurisdictions will change the local law applicable for, say, goods, as to the effect of perfection or nonperfection and priority (call this EPNP&P for short). This is exactly what 9-301(c) addresses. But so what, you say, where does that matter? It matters when the two states have different laws on EPNP&P. It matters when one state enacts the uniform version of Article 9 while a second enacts a non-uniform version and one that differs as to EPNP&P.

The fact that non-uniformities can make the movement of collateral matter is completely banal at one level but quite important at a second as *Pearl River* demonstrates. If Illinois adopted a priority rule that stated that the authors of Article 9 casebooks won all priority disputes, movement of the collateral into Illinois would matter. With non-uniform rules, all bets are off and collateral movements can be quite important. But that means that you need to be sensitive to possible non-uniformities. Louisiana has adopted a non-uniform version of 9-317(b) and that is a rule of priority picked up by 9-301(3)(C). That means that the movement of the collateral in *Pearl River Fabricators* from Mississippi to Louisiana might matter for the result in the case even though it would not had both jurisdictions enacted the uniform version of Article 9.

One other point of orientation in *Pearl River Fabricators*. Be sure to track how the original security interest survives the two sales in the case (or at least does so until we allow some version of 9-317(b) to operate). Is the first sale a sale by a buyer in ordinary course of business? Is the second? Even if the second would so qualify, does 9-320(a) cut-off that security interest? Note how the text is written: "takes free of a security interest created by the buyer's seller." What work does "buyer's seller" do?

For more on the case, see Ingrid Michelsen Hillinger, First National Bank of Picayune v. Pearl River Fabricators, Inc. and U.C.C. 9-316, Lexsee 2008 Emerging Issues 1598.

SECTION II. AFTER-ACQUIRED PROPERTY AND FUTURE ADVANCES

One of the most contentious issues historically in secured transactions relates to security interests in after-acquired property. The secured creditor seeks a security interest in the property the debtor has at a particular time, *plus*—and this is the critical point—property that the debtor will acquire going forward. How can a debtor grant an interest in property it does not yet have? It certainly can grant a security interest in the property once it has it and could do that by signing an additional security agreement each time the debtor received new property. That is obviously cumbersome, and there would seem to be much to be said for allowing the debtor to create in one transaction a mechanism that has the same effect as a continuing stream of additional security agreements. Article 9, of course, has embraced just this scheme. See 9-204. Put this way, there seems to be little to be said for the early twentieth-century cases that squarely rejected the result we now regard as commonplace. Yet the case set forth below, *Zartman*, has a surprising power and should be read carefully. After doing so, we turn to the problem of future advances, which, roughly, is a situation where a lender wishes, or may wish, to make a number of loans secured under a single security agreement. 9-204 validates this practice as well. The hypotheticals that follow set forth two paradigmatic fact patterns that you should have in mind as you read these materials.

There is no after acquired clause

6-6: INVENTORY TURNOVER

- On January 1st, Debtor borrows $10,000 from Bank pursuant to a security agreement granting Bank a security interest in "inventory." Bank files an appropriate financing statement.
- One month later, Debtor has sold all of its inventory and has replaced it with new inventory, identical to that it held before.
- ¤ What are Bank's rights?

6-7: MULTIPLE ADVANCES, SINGLE FINANCING STATEMENT

- On February 1st, Debtor borrows $10,000 from Bank pursuant to a security agreement granting Bank a security interest in equipment. Bank files an appropriate financing statement.
- One month later, Debtor seeks to borrow more money from Bank. Bank lends an additional $10,000 pursuant to an agreement that

provides that the new loan shall also be secured by equipment. No new financing statement is filed.

¤ What will be the Bank's status and when will its priority date from?

A. AFTER-ACQUIRED PROPERTY

Zartman v. First National Bank of Waterloo

Court of Appeals of New York, 1907.

189 N.Y. 267.

*** The object of this action was to determine the rights of the parties to a fund realized from a sale in bankruptcy of the property of the Waterloo Organ Company, a manufacturing corporation formerly carrying on the business of making and selling organs, pianos, and other musical instruments in the village of Waterloo. All the property of the company, both real and personal, was sold in one parcel, free from liens, by order of the United States District Court, and the value of such chattels included therein as were acquired by the company after it had given a corporate mortgage to secure its bonds issued and negotiated in the usual way was the sum of $15,480. The judgment directed in favor of the plaintiff consisted mainly of that sum, and there is no controversy over any other item. ***

■ VANN, J. (after stating the facts as above).

The question presented by this appeal is whether, in a mortgage given by a manufacturing corporation upon all its property, real and personal, to secure its negotiable bonds with the right of possession and enjoyment in the mortgagor for its own use and benefit until default, a clause, purporting in terms to cover after-acquired personal property, is good as to shifting stock and material on hand when possession was taken by the mortgagee pursuant to the provisions of the mortgage, one day after default in the payment of interest and three days before the commencement of bankruptcy proceedings against the mortgagor, as to the trustee in bankruptcy subsequently appointed therein.

*** To the extent that the mortgage covered personal property it was a chattel mortgage, but as it was executed by a corporation to secure the payment of its bonds and was duly recorded as a mortgage of real property, according to the provisions of the Lien Law, there was no necessity for filing or refiling it as a chattel mortgage. No question is raised as to the lien of the mortgage upon machinery, tools, and appliances belonging to the manufacturing plant, for the controversy is confined to musical instruments on hand, finished and unfinished, and materials from which other instruments might be made.

The learned counsel for the appellant, in an able argument, contends that while the mortgage did not create an absolute lien upon stock and materials acquired after its date, it operated as an executory contract to deliver possession upon default and to place the property as it then existed under the lien of the mortgage. He concedes that property of this nature is subject to seizure on execution by unsecured creditors during the period while it is subject to the disposal of the mortgagor, and until the trustee pursuant to the mortgage takes possession of it, but insists that the act of taking possession ripens the lien of the mortgage and makes it absolute as against general creditors or those with no prior lien.

The mortgage provided that, "until default shall be made in the payment of the interest or principal of the said bonds or some of them, * * * it shall be lawful for the said party of the first part and its successors peaceably and quietly to have, hold, use, possess and enjoy the said premises and property, with the appurtenances, and to receive the income and profits thereof to its own use and benefit without hindrance or interruption" from the mortgagee or its successors. This clause gave the mortgagor power to sell for its own benefit all materials and products until the trustee took possession after default in the payment of interest. No limitation is placed by the mortgage upon the use to be made of the proceeds derived from the sale of the stock and materials. * * * Conceding that the right of the mortgagor to receive the profits to its own use means a proper and legitimate corporate use, still the use permitted was independent of the mortgage or any lien supposed to be created thereby.

As was said in a case upon which both parties rely: "The right of the mortgagor in the meantime," that is, until default, "to the use of the earnings amounts, practically, to absolute ownership, and hence the mortgage cannot operate as a lien upon such earnings to the prejudice of the general creditors until actual entry and possession taken and then only upon what is earned after that time. The lien of the mortgage upon future earnings is consummated as against other creditors only by the fact of the possession of the property, and cannot have any retroactive operation, since it would then deprive the unsecured creditor of the fund, upon the faith of which he may have given credit to the mortgagor during the time when the latter was permitted to deal with and use it as its own. The lien upon the earnings, in favor of the bondholders, attaches only upon what is earned after the time when the lien is perfected by entry and possession." N.Y. Security & Trust Co. v. Saratoga Gas & El. L. Co., 159 N.Y. 137, 143.

If a lien was created by the mortgage upon property not in existence at its date, possession after it came into existence was of no importance. If no lien was created by the mortgage upon such property, the taking of possession pursuant to its terms did not create one as against general creditors, who are presumed to have dealt with the mortgagor in reliance upon its absolute ownership of the stock on hand. While the record of the mortgage was notice to all, it was notice of all its terms, which included the right of disposition for the use and benefit of the mortgagor, with no duty to apply the avails upon the mortgage indebtedness. If the question had arisen between the parties to the mortgage, equity might recognize a contract to give a lien and treat it as an actual lien; but it arises between the mortgagee and the general, unsecured creditors, who had little, if anything, to rely upon except the shifting stock, which, directly or indirectly, they themselves had furnished. The credit extended by them enabled the mortgagor to carry on business, and, if the product of that credit goes to the mortgagee, not only are they helpless, but, if the law is so declared, hereafter manufacturing corporations needing credit will be helpless also. If it is understood that a corporate mortgage given by a manufacturing corporation may take everything except accounts and debts, such corporations, with a mortgage outstanding, will have to do business on a cash basis or cease to do business altogether. Assuming that a court of equity may uphold and give effect to such a mortgage when the rights of the mortgagor and mortgagee only are involved, it will not aid the mortgagee at the expense of subsequent creditors when their rights are involved. It will not treat a contract to give a mortgage upon a subject to come into existence in the future as a mortgage actually then given, if the result would deprive the general creditors with superior equities so far as after-acquired property is concerned, of their only chance to collect debts. It is only when the rights of third parties will not be prejudiced that equity, treating as done that which was agreed to be done, will turn a contract to give a mortgage on property to be acquired into an equitable mortgage on such property as fast as it is acquired and enforce the same accordingly against the mortgagor, his representatives and assigns. In other words, the agreement and intention of the parties to a mortgage upon property not yet in existence will be given effect by a court of equity so far as practicable, provided no interest is affected except that of the mortgagor and mortgagee, who entered into the stipulation, but equity closes its doors and refuses relief if the interests of creditors are involved. The result thus announced is founded on principle and sanctioned by authority.

Was the alleged lien good at law? The authorities cited by both parties show that it was not for two reasons: First, because a man cannot grant what he does not own, actually or potentially. "Qui non habet, ille non dat." Second, because an agreement permitting the mortgagor to sell for his own benefit renders the mortgage fraudulent as matter of law as to the creditors represented by the plaintiff. * * *

As we have seen, equity takes hold of the subject with a strong hand in order to enable the mortgagee to get what the mortgagor intended to give, provided no other interest is involved, but when the creditors of the mortgagor enter the field equity goes no farther than the law and will simply enforce a lien if it exists without attempting to perfect it if something is lacking to make it complete. The taking of possession by the mortgagee is relied upon by the appellant to "ripen the lien," which, as is conceded, was inchoate before. If the contract between the mortgagor and mortgagee fell short of creating a lien, as was clearly the case, the act of taking possession did not enlarge, perfect, or complete it. A mortgagee cannot add to his title by his own act. The defendant did not have title to the after-acquired property when it took possession. All it had, as the courts hold, was the promise of the mortgagor to give title as the property came into existence. The mortgagor did not keep its promise by giving supplementary mortgages as pianos were made or materials were purchased, or in any other way. If it had, creditors would have been warned and could have avoided the danger. Time passed, and insolvency overwhelmed the mortgagor, when it was too late to give additional mortgages owing to the bankruptcy act. The plaintiff, as trustee in bankruptcy of the mortgagor, has the same rights as a creditor armed with an attachment or execution. When the general creditors intervened through the plaintiff, the mortgagee was simply in possession with title to the property that was in existence when the mortgage was given, but with no title to the shifting stock subsequently acquired. As to that property, it had only the promise of the mortgagor, which equity could help out by treating as done what was agreed to be done, but which it will not help out to the injury of unsecured creditors. The rights of the defendant, incomplete when it took possession, are incomplete still, for they can be perfected only by the aid of equity, and equity refuses to help under the circumstances of this case.

The judgment awarding the proceeds of the after-acquired property to the plaintiff was therefore properly rendered, and the action of the courts below should be sustained. * * *

COMMENTS AND QUESTIONS

1. Are the principles that a man cannot give what he does not have and that a mortgagor cannot retain dominion over that which it has already conveyed to its mortgagee a complete explanation for common law courts' resistance to "floating" liens (i.e., liens that automatically covered a shifting base of collateral) on inventory? The court in *Zartman* also thinks that a debtor should not have the unfettered ability to mortgage all of its property; that a "cushion," at least, of unsecured assets should be left for creditors who do not possess a security interest. If granting an overly-broad security interest is a problem, a filing requirement will not solve it. Is there, however, anything to this notion? How are general creditors hurt if, before they lend money, they know that there will be no "cushion" for them if the debtor's business collapses? Can't they simply refuse to extend credit or insist on taking a security interest themselves?

2. For a critical evaluation of this decision, see Steven L. Harris and Charles W. Mooney, Jr., The Politics of Article 9: A Property-Based Theory of Security Interests: Taking Debtors' Choices Seriously, 80 Va. L. Rev. 2021 (1994); for a more general discussion of the issues raised by *Zartman*, see Douglas G. Baird, The Importance of Priority, 82 Cornell L. Rev. 1420 (1997).

Peoples Bank v. Bryan Bros. Cattle Co.

United States Court of Appeals, Fifth Circuit, 2007.
504 F.3d 549.

■ REAVLEY, CIRCUIT JUDGE

* * * Peoples argues that Cornerstone's security agreement does not attach to the cattle because it does not explicitly include after-acquired property and Glenbrook acquired the cattle at issue nearly five years after Dickerson

executed the agreement. Cornerstone's security agreement states that Dickerson pledges "all livestock of every kind and description, including but not limited to beef and dairy cattle, branded or unbranded, plus any increase therefrom, and including steers and bulls now owned by debtor. All accession, additions, replacements, payments for participation in any state or federal farm programs and substitutions ... ."

We hold that Cornerstone's security agreement includes after-acquired property. The Mississippi Code does not require a financing statement to specifically contain an after-acquired property clause. 9-502 cmt. 2 and 9-204 cmt. 7. Interpreting the agreement to include after-acquired property is consistent with "[t]he vast majority of jurisdictions [which] hold that when a security interest is taken in the inventory of a business, after acquired inventory is automatically covered unless it is clearly set out that only certain items of inventory are to be covered." In re McBee, 714 F.2d 1316, 1330-31 (5th Cir. 1983). The rationale is that "it is obviously unreasonable to assume that anyone would have received or acquired or intended to acquire a security interest in an inventory with the rigid limitation that it should be limited to the same items which made up the inventory on the date the document was executed." Id.

The Tenth Circuit's decision in *In re Grey* is helpful. In *Grey*, the court held that a security agreement established the parties' intent to include after-acquired property where the agreement gave the bank a security interest in the debtor's livestock and farm equipment, which was updated monthly, and "any and all increases, additions, accessions, substitutions and proceeds thereto and therefor." *In re Grey*, 902 F.2d 1479, 1481 (10th Cir. 1990) (per curiam). The court held that the parties clearly intended to include after-acquired property because livestock and farm equipment "by its very nature rotated constantly and accordingly required a monthly update of the inventory."

Peoples posits that Cornerstone's security agreement did not include after-acquired property because Dickerson did not so intend. Notably, Dickerson gave another security interest to Cornerstone that included a specific after-acquired property clause. Peoples argues that the fact that Cornerstone's 1999 security agreement lacks similar language indicates that Dickerson did not intend to give Cornerstone a security interest in his after-acquired property.

The argument is unavailing. We follow *Grey* and *McBee* and hold that Cornerstone's security agreement includes after-acquired property. Like

Grey, Dickerson dealt in farm products, and it would be unreasonable to assume that Cornerstone would intend to acquire a security interest only in Dickerson's property as of 1999. The language in Cornerstone's security agreement is also very similar to that in *Grey*. * * *

B. Future Advances

A debtor and a secured creditor will often contemplate that a series of loans will be made. The lender may commit to these loans, but perhaps more often, will retain a substantial level of discretion over future loans. A critical question is what priority subsequent advances should enjoy. The basic first-to-file rule of 9-322(a)(1) should be understood to tie priority among secured creditors for future advances to the date of the financing statement. Courts have been reluctant to embrace that fully, see Coin-O-Matic Service Co. v. Rhode Island Hospital Trust Co., 3 UCC Rep. 1112 (R.I. Super. Ct. 1966), and that led, in 1972, to the addition of F9-312(7). Sometimes the cure is as bad as the disease, and it isn't obvious that F9-312(7) improved matters considerably. See State Bank of Sleepy Eye v. Krueger, 405 N.W.2d 491 (Minn. Ct. App. 1987). Revised Article 9 has gone back to the drawing board in 9-323, and we will see if it fares better with the courts.

6-8: ADVANCING AND RE-ADVANCING MONEY

- On February 1st, Debtor borrows $10,000 from Bank pursuant to a security agreement granting Bank a security interest in equipment. Bank files an appropriate financing statement. The security interest secures "all debts of Debtor to Bank, now and hereafter outstanding."
- One month later, Debtor pays Bank in full. The financing statement covering the original loan remains in place.
- On March 1st, Finco lends Debtor $10,000, takes a security interest in equipment, and files an appropriate financing statement.
- On April 1st, Bank lends another $10,000 to Debtor.
- ¤ What is the relative priority of Bank and Finco? Is the loan of April 1st, a "future advance" under 9-204 and 9-323? Was Bank perfected as of March 1st, even though it was not owed a dime on

that date? Should that matter for determining the relative priority of Finco and Bank?

6-9: FUTURE ADVANCES AND SECURED CREDITOR V. SECURED CREDITOR

- On February 1st, Debtor enters into a security agreement with Bank covering equipment securing "all debts now or hereafter owed by Debtor to Bank." Bank files an appropriate financing statement covering the equipment. Bank lends $10,000 to Debtor.
- One month later, Debtor enters into an identical deal with Finco, giving Finco a perfected security interest in the equipment. Finco also lends $10,000 to Debtor.
- One month later, Bank lends an additional $10,000 to Debtor.
- ¤ Some time after that, a priority dispute arises between Bank and Finco. The equipment is worth $20,000. How should that value be divided between Bank and Finco? See 9-322(a)(1); 9-323(b).

6-10: FUTURE ADVANCES AND SECURED CREDITOR V. LIEN CREDITOR

- On February 1st, Debtor enters into a security agreement with Bank covering equipment securing "all debts now or hereafter owed by Debtor to Bank." Bank files an appropriate financing statement covering the equipment. Bank lends $10,000 to Debtor.
- One month later, an unsecured creditor owed $10,000 becomes a lien creditor. The next day, the new lien creditor sends a fax to Bank to inform Bank of the lien creditor's new status.
- One month later, Bank lends an additional $10,000 to Debtor.
- ¤ Some time after that, a priority dispute arises between Bank and the lien creditor. The equipment is worth $20,000. How should that value be divided between Bank and the lien creditor? See 9-322(a)(1); 9-323(b). Suppose that the second loan by Bank had been made two months later rather than one month later. Would that change the result?

COMMENTS AND QUESTIONS: FUTURE ADVANCES, THE FIRST-IN-TIME RULE AND SITUATIONAL MONOPOLIES

One key question for a system of secured transactions is the extent of protection to be given to future advances. It is straightforward to imagine the possibilities here; indeed, Article 9 itself gives some sense of the possible variety. Rightly understood, 9-322(a)(1) and 9-323 protect the future advances of an initial secured creditor against loans by intervening secured creditors. See Comment 3 to 9-323. Note the risk that this poses for a junior secured creditor: any loan that it makes may be subordinated in an unlimited amount given the first-filed financing statement. In contrast, lien creditors and buyers not in the ordinary course of business do much better, as they enjoy some protection against future advances. 9-323(b) gives the rule for lien creditors: the secured creditor may lend for at least 45 days, plus the secured creditor can continue to lend on a prior basis so long as it does not learn of the position of the lien creditor. (Of course, the lien creditor can limit the window to just 45 days by giving notice of its interest to the secured creditor.) In similar fashion, buyers not in the ordinary course of business are protected under 9-323(d), though here a secured creditor can extend future advances and enjoy priority only for a period which is the lesser of 45 days and the point that the secured creditor learns of the purchase.

Does Article 9's future advance rule for secured creditors confer too much power—even monopoly power—on the first secured creditor? The argument would go something like this: no sensible lender would lend into a preexisting financing statement without obtaining a subordination agreement from the first lender. Thus, the first lender, by withholding the subordination, can prevent the debtor from obtaining funds elsewhere. This creates a monopoly, and thus the secured lender can extract higher interest rates in the subsequent borrowing arrangement. This problem could be solved by giving the debtor the power to cut-off priority for future advances by sending a notice to that effect to the first-filed lender. This system has been suggested for real estate transactions, see Grant S. Nelson & Dale A. Whitman, Rethinking Future Advance Mortgages: A Brief for the Restatement Approach, 44 Duke L.J. 657 (1995), and actually does apply in Great Britain. See R.M. Goode, Legal Problems of Credit and Security 21 (2nd ed., Sweet & Maxwell, 1988).

This is to move a little too quickly, though. Nothing just described should come as a major surprise to the debtor or to possible lenders. If having a monopoly is valuable for the initial lender—because it can extract excess value in later-stage lending—we should anticipate substantial competition originally among possible lenders to get that position. In a well-functioning market, lenders should compete away the financial benefits of the monopoly by offering lower initial rates to the debtor. So, the monopoly "problem" needs to be examined more carefully. Why might it be valuable—and here we should mean wealth enhancing for society generally—for a lender to have the right to block other lenders by refusing to subordinate possible future advances? Does this power protect the first lender against possible shifts in the debtor's assets—changes in investments, for example—that might be facilitated by new money but that might also impair the position of the first lender?

The next case is one of the better-known secured transactions decisions. Before reading it, examine the key provisions in Article 9 about secured creditors and their agents—9-102(a)(72)(E), 9-502(a)(2) and 9-503(d), (e)—and covering assignments of security interests, 9-310(c) and 9-514. Consider the following fact patterns. Then do not drown in the case's aquatic metaphor and thereby miss the important issues raised about assignments of security interests!

6-11: STARTING POINTS

[handwritten marginal note: read future advance clause]

- On February 1st, Debtor enters into a security agreement with Bank covering equipment securing "all debts now or hereafter owed by Debtor to Bank, whether arising from loans made directly by Bank to Debtor or from other obligations of Debtor that become owed to Bank." Bank files an appropriate financing statement covering the equipment. Bank lends $10,000 to Debtor.
- One month later, Debtor enters into an identical deal with Finco, giving Finco a perfected security interest in the equipment. Finco also lends $10,000 to Debtor.
- One month later, Creditco lends $10,000 to Debtor on an unsecured basis.
- ¤ Some time after that, a priority dispute arises and the equipment is worth $20,000. How should that value be divided between Bank, Finco and Creditco?

6-12: SWAPPING CREDITORS

- In the prior fact pattern, after the first three loans are made, Bank makes a fourth loan of $10,000 to Debtor. Debtor promptly pays that money to Creditco so that it is paid in full.
- ¤ Now a priority dispute arises and the equipment is again worth $20,000. How should that value be divided between Bank and Finco?

6-13: VULTURE CAPITALISM

- In the first fact pattern, after the first three loans are made, Bank pays Creditco $9,000 to buy its debt from Debtor.

- ¤ A priority dispute again arises and the equipment is worth $20,000. How should that value be divided between Bank and Finco?

Republic National Bank v. Fitzgerald (In re E.A. Fretz Co.)
United States Court of Appeals, Fifth Circuit, 1978.
565 F.2d 366.

■ JOHN R. BROWN, CHIEF JUDGE

This appeal presents a flood of interesting questions. The most intriguing issue is whether the Uniform Commercial Code * * * permits the use of "floating secured parties" in secured transactions. Under the bizarre facts of this case, we hold that it does not and reverse.

Diving Into The UCC Sea

On April 3, 1971, E.A. Fretz Co., Inc. (Fretz), a Texas Corporation, executed as "Debtor" three security agreements giving Revlon, Inc. as "Secured Party" a security interest in certain collateral, including all of Fretz's then or subsequently acquired equipment and inventory and the proceeds therefrom. The purpose of the agreements was to secure the payment of all debts owed by Fretz to Revlon and to present or future affiliates of Revlon and any debt owed by Fretz to others which Revlon may have obtained by assignment or otherwise.[2]

---

[2] The pertinent provisions of the agreements are as follows:

  1) *All debts*, liabilities, obligations, guarantees, covenants, and duties *owing by Debtor* and/or any of its present and future divisions and affiliates *to REVLON, INC. and/or all of its present and future divisions and affiliates*, of every kind and description (whether or not evidenced by any invoice or note or other instrument and whether or not for the payment of money), direct or indirect, absolute or contingent, *due or to become due, now existing or hereafter arising, including without limitation any debt, liability or obligation owing from Debtor and/or any of its present and future divisions and affiliates to others which REVLON, INC. and/or its present and future divisions and affiliates may have obtained by assignment or otherwise*, further including without limitation, expenses and attorneys' fees chargeable to Debtor's and/or any of its present and future divisions and affiliates account or incurred by REVLON,

A financing statement signed by Fretz and Revlon was filed with the Texas Secretary of State on April 5, 1971. The statement described the collateral and designated Fretz as the debtor and Revlon and only Revlon as the secured party. Revlon's New York address was also included.

On June 30, 1971, Fretz executed and delivered to Republic National Bank of Dallas (Republic) a security agreement giving the bank a secured interest in various collateral, including Fretz's inventory, then existing or subsequently acquired, and all proceeds therefrom. This agreement secured present and future indebtedness of Fretz owed to Republic. A financing statement, signed by Fretz and Republic, describing the collateral and respectively designating Fretz and Republic as debtor and secured party, was filed with the Secretary of State on August 11, 1971.

Prior to completing this transaction, Republic learned of "Revlon's" security interest in Fretz's inventory and the Revlon-Fretz financing statement. Indeed, Republic unsuccessfully attempted to persuade Revlon to subordinate its security interest to the one Fretz would grant to Republic.

On August 23, 1972, Fretz filed a voluntary petition in bankruptcy and adjudication followed. On September 19, Revlon-Realistic Professional Products, Inc. (RR) and Cosmetic Capital Corp. (CC), both wholly-owned subsidiaries of Revlon, assigned their claims against Fretz to Revlon.

Fretz's equipment and inventory were sold pursuant to court order. Valid liens and encumbrances were to attach to the proceeds of the sale which grossed $106,115. After applying all credits, and excluding interest, collection and attorneys' fees, Fretz was indebted to the following companies which claimed against the proceeds in the amounts shown:

INC. and/or its present and future divisions and affiliates, whether provided for herein or in any other agreement, and all filing, recording or searching fees paid by REVLON, INC. and/or any of its present or future divisions and affiliates. Any corporation which controls, is controlled by, or under common control with REVLON, INC. shall be deemed an affiliate of REVLON, INC. Any corporation which controls, is controlled by, or under common control with Debtor shall be deemed an affiliate of Debtor.

2) All existing and future indebtedness and liabilities of any and every kind or nature, now or hereafter owing by Debtor to Secured Party, howsoever such indebtedness shall arise or be incurred or evidenced.

Emphasis added.

(1) Texas Western Financial Corp.	$ 1,672
(2) Revlon, Inc.	29,488
(3) Revlon-Realistic	160,915
(4) Cosmetic Capital	32,487
(5) Republic National Bank	22,556

Revlon, RR, and CC applied for payment of their claims from the proceeds of the sale, asserting perfected security interests under the umbrella of Revlon's April 3, 1971, security agreements with Fretz. The Bankruptcy Judge entered findings of fact and conclusions of law allowing these claims in toto and leaving no proceeds available to pay Republic. Republic appealed to the District Court which affirmed the Bankruptcy Judge's order without opinion, and this appeal followed.

Floating Secured Parties Are All Wet

The Bankruptcy Judge concluded that the indebtedness owed by Fretz to RR and CC, which they had assigned to their parent, "was secured by the security interests of Revlon" and perfected by the filing of the Revlon-Fretz financing statement.

Republic recognizes that the UCC clearly contemplates and sanctions floating collateral (after-acquired property of the debtor) and floating debt (future advances). However, the UCC does not, according to Republic, contemplate "floating secured parties," that is, an open-ended class of creditors with unsecured and unperfected interests who, after the debtor's bankruptcy, can assign their claims to a more senior lienor and magically secure and perfect their interests under an omnibus security agreement and financing statement. We agree with Republic.

It is significant that the Bankruptcy Judge did not hold, either as a matter of fact or law, that the two Revlon subsidiaries were secured parties. Nor did he offer any legal explication of how they became entitled to perfected secured status by virtue of their post-bankruptcy claim assignments to Revlon. For reasons to be discussed below, we hold that since the Fretz-Revlon security agreements did not create security interests in favor of RR and CC, they were not secured parties whose interests could be validly perfected by the Fretz-Revlon financing statement. We further hold that the post-bankruptcy assignments of the subsidiaries' claims against Fretz to Revlon were ineffective to create perfected security interests in favor of Revlon-Realistic or Cosmetic Capital.

First, it is clear that Revlon-Realistic and Cosmetic Capital were not "secured parties" to the April 3, 1971 Fretz-Revlon security agreements. The pertinent portions of these contracts provide:

> E. A. FRETZ CO., INC. ... for the purpose of securing the indebtedness herein described and the further consideration of Ten Dollars ... to it in hand paid by REVLON, INC. ... whose mailing address is 767 Fifth Avenue, New York, New York, (hereinafter called, in accordance with the terms and provisions of the Uniform Commercial Code Secured Party).

Section [9-102(a)(72)] defines that term:

> "Secured party" means a lender, seller or other person *in whose favor* there is a security interest ....

(Emphasis added.) Fretz granted a security interest in favor of Revlon only.

Moreover, [9-203] states:

> ... [A] security interest is not enforceable against the debtor or third parties unless * * *
>
> (a) * * * the debtor has signed a security agreement which contains a description of the collateral ....

Comment 5 to F9-203 explains that the formal requisites are not only conditions to enforceability but are in the nature of a Statute of Frauds. Thus, the debtor must have signed the security agreement in favor of the secured party. Had Fretz, Revlon, or the Revlon affiliates desired to grant the security interest in favor of Revlon-Realistic and Cosmetic Capital and to have designated them secured parties in the agreements, such a desire would certainly have been simple to accomplish. They did not. No security interest was created in favor of RR or CC. Therefore, they had no interest which was perfected by the Revlon-Fretz financing statement.

But assuming for the sake of analysis that there was an interest which could have been perfected, could perfection be accomplished by virtue of the Fretz-Revlon financing statement or by post-bankruptcy assignment? We believe not.

RR and CC were not signatories to, nor were their addresses given on, the financing statement. Thus, the perfection requirements of [9-502] were not met.

Revlon argues that the Fretz-Revlon financing statement satisfied the purpose of the [9-502] requirements which is "simply to give notice that the secured party of record may have a security interest in the collateral described and to enable a prudent examiner to ascertain the exact state of affairs through further inquiry."

We believe that in the context of this case such an argument proves too much. We agree that the cases cited by Revlon and Comment 2 to F9-402 indicate that "simple notice" is all that is required. However,

> [t]he notice itself indicates merely that the *secured party who has filed* may have a security interest in the collateral described.

Comment 2, F9-402 (emphasis added). "Secured party" is a defined term. It means a party *in whose favor* a security interest is created. The quoted sentence cannot logically be read as though it stated, " ... secured party, and anyone in the world who subsequently assigned a claim to the secured party without ever filing a proper financing statement, may have a security interest in the collateral described." Just such a construction would necessarily follow were we to accept Revlon's contentions.

We believe that in a world of huge conglomerates a construction of the UCC's silence as to "floating secured parties" which would sanction such a weird device is clearly at odds with the "simple notice" requirements of [9-502]. Placing our imprimatur on floating secured parties would undercut "Article Nine's perfection requirement (which) reflects a Code policy against *secret* security." White & Summers, Uniform Commercial Code, § 24-3, p. 868 (1972) (emphasis added). Since the notice requirements are so simple to meet, the Revlon subsidiaries' failure to protect their interests in a timely fashion should not prejudice Republic.

The Bankruptcy Judge was apparently impressed with Revlon's argument that since Republic knew of "Revlon's"[16] security interest, the Code's notice requirements and their underlying purpose were satisfied. But knowledge cannot provide a substitute for creating valid security interests and perfecting them in accordance with Code provisions. Treating know-

---

[16] Finding of Fact No. 11 reads:

> Prior to obtaining its security interest on June 30, 1971, Republic knew that "Revlon" had a security interest in Fretz's inventory and that it had filed the financing statement described ... above ... . [Quotation marks those of the Bankruptcy Judge.]

It is significant that the Bankruptcy Judge was careful not to state that Republic knew of RR's and CC's security interests. As previously stated, the Fretz-Revlon agreements created a security interest only in Revlon, *not* in its subsidiaries.

ledge as controlling would turn Article 9 on its head. [9-317(a)] reads in relevant part:

> [A]n unperfected security interest is subordinate to the rights of
>
> (a) persons entitled to priority under Section [9-322].

Section [9-322] deals with priorities among conflicting security interests in the same collateral, [9-322(a)(1)] setting forth a first to file rule as to which knowledge is irrelevant.[17] See Comment 1 to F9-312. Adding knowledge into this formula would in effect rewrite [9-317] to provide:

> [A]n unperfected security interest is subordinate to the rights of persons entitled to priority under Section F9-312 unless those persons knew of the unperfected security interest.

Thus, this drastic result would totally undermine the "idea, deeply rooted at common law, of a race of diligence among creditors," Comment 1, F9-312, which is embodied in the Code.

Moreover, we question the significance and meaningfulness of "knowledge" under the facts of this case. Assume, for example, that a bank is contemplating making a loan and taking a security interest in inventory which will be subject to a senior lien in the same collateral. Assume further that the security agreement between the debtor and the senior secured party covers after-acquired property and future advances. At any point in time, the value of the bank's junior secured interest may vary, depending on the amount of future advances made by the senior lienor and the value of property subsequently acquired by the debtor which forms the collateral.

Surely floating debt and floating collateral provide all the uncertainty any creditor should be required to suffer. When floating secured parties are wading in the wings, clairvoyance, not mere knowledge, would be essential. We are unwilling to impose on any junior secured creditor, with knowledge or without, the additional risk that, at a date subsequent to his perfection, any affiliate of the senior creditor or any stranger to it unnamed as secured parties in a security agreement or a financing statement could be metamorphosed into senior secured parties by virtue of an assignment "or otherwise," pre- or post-bankruptcy. We also decline to impose upon a junior secured creditor the burden of a frequent check to determine

---

[17] It seems settled under [9-322(a)(1)] that knowledge of a prior unperfected security interest is irrelevant as far as general priorities are concerned, so that the security interest which is first perfected is superior to all subsequently perfected interests.

whether any unsecured parties have secretly assigned their claims to a senior secured party whose interest has been perfected. The risk and the burden would disrupt commercial transactions to an unwarranted and unnecessary degree. No reasonable bank would ever make a loan in the wake of so much floating. Fear of floundering on the rocks would be far too great. We believe that at the time a bank makes a loan, it should be secure in the knowledge of a precisely what, and how many, secured parties claim a prior interest in the same collateral. And it should be able to make that initial determination by resorting to financing statements which meet the "simple" [9-502] standards. * * *

Our view on this score is further reinforced by [9-310(c)], which reads:

> (2) If a *secured party* assigns a *perfected* security interest, no filing under this Chapter is required in order to continue the perfected status of the security interest against creditors of and transferees from the original debtor.

(Emphasis added.) Adoption of Revlon's contentions would be tantamount to holding that RR and CC could fit within [9-310(c)]. Such a result would render meaningless Article 9's definition of "secured party" and its perfection requirements. * * *

Waterloo

Nothing said herein should be construed to affect the valid claim of Revlon, Inc. for the debt owed to it and Texas Western. Revlon-Realistic does not have a lien on the proceeds. Cosmetic Capital does not have a lien on the proceeds superior to Republic's. We express no opinion on whether Cosmetic Capital's filing of a financing statement subsequent to the filing of the Fretz-Republic financing statement entitles it to any part of the proceeds once Republic's claim is paid. Republic's application for payment from the proceeds should be granted.

Reversed and Remanded.

COMMENTS AND QUESTIONS: FRETTING ABOUT *FRETZ*

Why can't Revlon-Realistic and Cosmetic Capital assert security interests in their own right? If one reads the security agreement as it is written, it sounds as though Fretz agreed to grant them a security interest. The court concludes otherwise, but is its argument convincing? Assume that it is not, so that you conclude that all the steps necessary for the attachment of the security interest have taken place. You then face an additional question: are the interests of Revlon-Realistic and Cosmetic Capital properly perfected? The court states that they did not sign the financing statement and their addresses do not appear on it, but are these errors seriously misleading? Can Realistic and Cosmetic fit under the substantial-compliance exception to the requirements of 9-502? See 9-506.

Assume that Realistic and Cosmetic are not subsidiaries of Revlon and that Republic is not in the picture. The transaction involved in *Fretz* amounted to the following. Realistic and Cosmetic each held claims against Fretz (for simplicity's sake, let us assume each held a claim for $10,000). These claims were unsecured claims and were worth, say, $5,000 each in Fretz's bankruptcy. Revlon, however, had more than adequate security for its claim against Fretz. Revlon buys Realistic's and Cosmetic's claims. If the transaction is allowed to stand, this will convert two claims worth $5,000 each into two claims worth $10,000 each. Presumably this is an advantageous transaction from both Revlon's perspective and from Realistic's and Cosmetic's perspective, for Revlon could pay something between $5,000 and $10,000 for each claim. But all their benefits come at the expense of Fretz's other unsecured creditors. The transaction makes them correspondingly worse off. This kind of after-the-fact reshuffling of priorities may be thought to be undesirable per se.

But before one jumps to that conclusion, can we restructure the transaction in *Fretz* to make it one that would pass muster under Article 9 (though perhaps not always under the Bankruptcy Code)? How is this case any different from one in which Revlon made new loans to Fretz and Fretz used the money to pay off Realistic and Cosmetic? In that case, Revlon pays $20,000 to Fretz, which pays $10,000 to each of Realistic and Cosmetic. The effect of this transaction is the same on other third-party creditors of Fretz. This transaction, moreover, fits squarely into Article 9's notice filing, first-to-file rule. Although this transaction is protected by Article 9, we may not need to worry about it as much. In the earlier case, Revlon simply negotiates with Realistic and Cosmetic to pay them something less than $10,000 each. Here, Revlon must pay Fretz the full $20,000. Even so, couldn't Revlon make a side deal with Realistic and Cosmetic to have them "kick back," say, $3,000 each, in exchange for Revlon agreeing to advance the money to Fretz for purposes of paying back Realistic and Cosmetic? But would this work without Fretz demanding some portion of the "surplus" as well?

Is this transaction significantly different from the one actually involved in *Fretz?* If Revlon does not pay 100 cents on the dollar for the claims it takes over, is its secured claim against Fretz the amount of the claim or the amount it lent Fretz? Why would parties engage in a transaction such as the one among Realistic, Cosmetic and Revlon? If it is done for no purpose other than to freeze out a rival creditor, why permit it? Is motive usually that clear? Couldn't Revlon argue that whatever the *effect* on third parties, its motive was simply profit? Whether a result of purpose or simply of effect, should this manipulation by creditors of their rights be a problem that Article 9 addresses or should one rely solely on federal bankruptcy law?

For more on *Fretz*, see Harry M. Fletchner, Inflatable Liens and Like Phenomena: Converting Unsecured Obligations into Secured Debt Under UCC Article 9 and the Bankruptcy Code, 72 Cornell L. Rev. 696 (1987).

SECTION III. NAME CHANGES, INCORPORATIONS AND MERGERS

Changes to the debtor's business structure or its name are common. Companies routinely engage in corporate makeovers in which they attempt to revamp the image they present to the public. Changing the corporation's name to reflect a new focus, or perhaps to convey almost no information, as when U.S. Steel becomes USX Corp., is often an important part of this. And we frequently go through waves of mergers and acquisitions. In all cases, we must confront the problems that these changes pose for secured transactions. Potentially the most serious of these problems arises when the change makes it more difficult for a subsequent secured party to *find* an earlier financing statement. We have seen this already when a change in the location of the debtor affects *where* a potential purchaser might look for a financing statement.

A. NAME CHANGES

Recall our discussion of mistakes made in the debtor's name. Do we want to treat risk allocation differently in the case of *change* than in the case of *mistake?* When a mistake is made *ab initio,* the resulting misfiling may make it effectively impossible for a subsequent secured party ever to find the financing statement. For example, if the debtor's name is "Jones" but the financing statement lists the debtor's name as "Kone," a subsequent party would have to have a fertile imagination indeed to reconstruct the error. But in the cases we are now dealing with, had the problem arisen initially as a "mistake," the "not seriously misleading" test would not have been met. The reason that we have a separate issue may, in part, rest on the fact that, in cases of *change,* a little detective work on the part of a subsequent party can oftentimes lead it back to the old financing statement. And the question posed is whether a prior secured party should be treated *more* leniently in the case of change than in the case of mistake because (a) it is comparatively more difficult for the prior secured party to keep abreast of changes than it is for that party to get it right in the first instance and/or (b) it is comparatively easier for subsequent parties to find the financing statement after a change than it is after a mistake.

Beyond this, we could take an additional step and require a secured party with knowledge of the debtor's change of name at any time to take steps to correct the financing statement. Do we want to bring a subjective, fact-specific test such as "knowledge" or "good faith" into the resolution of these disputes? If we do, do we also want to inquire into whether subsequent parties had knowledge of the *prior* name (so they could have searched under the prior name as well)? And what do we want to do with the secured party who does not know of its debtor's name change?

Note that in the case of a *corporation's* name change, neither party has an impossible task. A secured party who has filed a financing statement can check the Secretary of State's office periodically for corporate charter name changes. Subsequent parties can likewise trace corporate names backwards through the Secretary of State's corporate charter files. The recurrent question is: which of these parties should bear the risk of the name (or other) change? If the original secured party bears the risk of changes in the filing system, it will have to increase its monitoring of the debtor or, if that is not cost-effective, simply charge for the additional risk. If the original filing party is protected despite name changes by the debtor, then the subsequent party will have to increase its search or, if that is not cost-effective, charge for the additional risk. Here, as elsewhere, where the problem cannot be *avoided* at low cost, it seems sensible to ask: *who* can bear this risk most effectively? And in a computerized world, how sensible would it be to have the Secretary of State notify secured parties with financing statements on file of changes in their debtor's corporate name? It also may be important to place the burden on one party or the other, rather than place the burden some of the time on one and some of the time on the other, for both may then be guarding against the same thing.

In looking at this issue and others related to changes, we should keep in mind some basic questions. How sensibly does Article 9 allocate the risk of change? To what extent has Article 9 adopted different rules for all but identical issues? To what extent does Article 9 force each party to duplicate the others' efforts? Can you think of any reason why the drafters (assuming they thought about the issue at all) would have felt that a "name change" should be handled differently from these other changes?

6-14: NAME CHANGES

- On February 1st, Bank lends $10,000 to SmithCorp, takes a security interest in equipment and files an appropriate financing statement.
- On February 2nd, SmithCorp changes its name to JonesCorp.
- The next day, Finco approaches JonesCorp to make a loan. Finco lends $10,000 to JonesCorp, takes a security interest in equipment and files an appropriate financing statement.
- ¤ As of April 1st, what are the respective rights of Bank and Finco? See 9-507(c).
- Assume that Bank learns on January 31st that SmithCorp intends to change its name to JonesCorp. Nonetheless, Bank proceeds as before.
- ¤ Does this change the outcome?
- Assume that on January 30th, Debtor informs Bank that it will change its name from SmithCorp to JonesCorp soon after the loan is made.
- Unbeknownst to Bank, on January 31st—before the loan is made—SmithCorp changes its name to JonesCorp.
- On February 1st, documents are executed in the old name granting Bank a security interest in equipment and inventory and Bank files a financing statement in that name.
- Two months later, Finco lends on a secured basis taking a security interest in equipment and inventory. These statements are executed in the name of JonesCorp.
- ¤ What are the respective rights of Bank and Finco?

B. INCORPORATIONS

To get at the issues in this section, consider the following fact pattern:

6-15: INCORPORATION OF SOLE PROPRIETORSHIPS

- Individual operates a restaurant under the name "Joe's Place." The business is a sole proprietorship, meaning that the assets used in the business are owned by the individual personally.
- Individual enters into a secured loan with Bank covering all of his assets and after-acquired property. Bank files an appropriate financing statement under the name of Individual.
- A month later, on the advice of his tax attorney, Individual incorporates "Joe's Place, Inc." and transfers all of the assets associated with the restaurant—and all of its debts—to the new company.
- Joe's Place, Inc. immediately borrows on a secured basis from Finco. Finco files appropriately.
- ¤ Who has priority?

This fact pattern raises a number of issues. We have a transfer of collateral from one entity—the individual—to a second—the new corporation. As to the property transferred, we have to ask our usual questions arising with any change: Does the security interest survive the transfer? Does it remain perfected? What priority does it have? But, here, we must take an additional step. As the business starts to operate through the new corporation, it will acquire new property. The secured creditor signed a deal with the individual, not with the corporation. Does the security interest extend to property acquired by the corporation? These issues were thought to be sufficiently important that the revised statute puts in place a mechanism to address this problem. Read 9-102(a)(56), 9-102(a)(60), 9-203(d), 9-203(e), 9-326, 9-507 and 9-508.

COMMENTS AND QUESTIONS

1. Does Revised Article 9 solve the incorporation problem? When an individual running a business decides to incorporate that business, will the new corporation typically "acquire[] or succeed[] to all or substantially all of the assets of the other person"? Won't the individual have personal assets—a house, a car, a computer—that were not part of the business and that will not become corporate assets and won't that limit the application of the new debtor rules in the incorporation situation?

2. For more, see Gregory J. Morical, An Organization Approach to Resolving the Attachment and Perfection Problems of Identity Changes Under § 9-203(1)(A) & § 9-402(7) of the Uniform Commercial Code, 28 Ind. L. Rev. 43 (1994).

Play along with the court in the case that follows. Meaning, more directly, Florida's financing statements are available online at floridaucc.com. Go there and search under the names that you think Article 9 would require a subsequent secured party to search under. Pay attention to the fact that financing statements lapse under 9-515, so the actual financing statements in the case that follows may have moved from the current file to the lapsed file.

In re Summit Staffing Polk County, Inc.

United States Bankruptcy Court, M.D. Florida, 2003.
305 Bankr. 347.

■ PAUL M. GLENN, CHIEF JUDGE

* * * On October 16, 2002, a Chapter 7 petition was filed on behalf of Summit Staffing Polk County, Inc. (the Debtor). In the section of the petition requiring all other names used by the Debtor in the last 6 years, the name R & K Services was the only name entered. The street address of the Debtor was entered as 5903 Charloma Drive, Lakeland Fl 33813. In the list of equity security holders, the only entry was Randolf Vincent, with the same address as the Debtor.

From the affidavits, exhibits, and pleadings in support of the motions for summary judgment, the following facts appear to be uncontroverted:

1. On August 22, 2001, an agreement was entered between Associated Receivables Funding of Florida, Inc. (Associated Receivables) and Randy Vincent d/b/a Summit Staffing. Pursuant to the agreement, Vincent obtained operating funds from Associated Receivables, and sold and assigned certain accounts receivable to Associated Receivables. Vincent also granted Associated Receivables a security interest in all of his accounts receivable and in other collateral.

2. On September 4, 2001, a UCC Financing Statement was filed with the Secretary of State, Tallahassee, Florida, with Associated Receivables Funding, Inc. as the secured party, Randy A. Vincent as the debtor, and

"Summit Staffing" as an additional debtor. The addresses of the debtor and of the additional debtor were both shown as 5903 Charloma Drive, Lakeland, Florida 33813. The additional debtor was identified as a sole proprietorship.

3. On March 14, 2002, Summit Staffing of Polk County, Inc. was incorporated, and on March 15, 2002, the Articles of Incorporation were filed with the Florida Secretary of State.

4. Summit Staffing of Polk County, Inc. conducted the business formerly conducted by Randy A. Vincent d/b/a Summit Staffing. Summit Staffing of Polk County, Inc. obtained operating funds from Associated Receivables, and sold and assigned accounts receivable to Associated Receivables, in the same manner as had Randy Vincent doing business as Summit Staffing. No new written agreement was signed between Associated Receivables and Summit Staffing of Polk County, Inc., however, and no new financing statement was filed with the Secretary of State.

5. Summit Staffing of Polk County, Inc. filed its Chapter 7 petition in the bankruptcy court on October 16, 2002, showing its name as Summit Staffing Polk County, Inc.

6. As of the date the petition was filed, Cutrale Citrus owed the Debtor approximately $190,000 (the Cutrale accounts receivable). These accounts receivable had been sold and assigned by the Debtor to Associated Receivables. The entire balance owed to the Debtor accrued more than four months after the Debtor's incorporation. (Some of the accounts have been paid, and the proceeds are being held in trust pending the outcome of this motion.)

7. In her affidavit in support of her motion for summary judgment, the Trustee states that she conducted a UCC search through the official Florida Secured Transaction Registry Internet website using the actual corporate name of the Debtor, "Summit Staffing of Polk County, Inc." The trustee stated: "This UCC search did not result in the disclosure of Randy Vincent's financing statement and no secured interest in any of the Debtor's assets was found." * * *

Associated Receivables requests relief from the automatic stay to enforce its security interest in the Cutrale Citrus accounts receivable (the Cutrale accounts receivable). The Chapter 7 Trustee claims priority over the rights of Associated Receivables to the Cutrale accounts receivable. Both the Chapter 7 Trustee and Associated Receivables have filed motions for summary judgment. * * *

[Under BC 544(a)], the Trustee's powers are the same as those of a hypothetical creditor of a debtor who has completed the legal process for perfection of its lien upon all property available for the satisfaction of its claim against the debtor. The Trustee's lien takes priority over all unperfected liens or security interests. The extent of the Trustee's powers under section 544 is determined by the applicable non-bankruptcy law.

The applicable non-bankruptcy law in this case is Revised Article 9 of the Uniform Commercial Code as adopted in Florida, effective January 1, 2002. * * *

In this case, after entering the security agreement with Associated Receivables, the business changed its business structure from a sole proprietorship (Randy Vincent d/b/a Summit Staffing) to a corporation (Summit Staffing of Polk County, Inc.). The new corporation became generally obligated for the obligations of the sole proprietorship, including the obligation secured under the security agreement, and acquired or succeeded to all or substantially all of the assets of the sole proprietorship.

9-203(d) provides that, in certain circumstances, a new debtor may become bound by a security agreement entered into by another person. Accordingly, Summit Staffing of Polk County, Inc. became bound by the security agreement entered into by Randy Vincent d/b/a/ Summit Staffing.

9-508 governs the effectiveness of a financing statement if a new debtor becomes bound by a security agreement. This situation may arise when an original individual debtor incorporates his business, and the business continues to operate with the secured financing arrangements already in place. * * * Therefore, if a new debtor is bound by a security agreement entered into by another person, the financing statement naming the original debtor is effective to perfect a security interest in collateral in which the new debtor acquires rights for at least four months. Following that, the filed financing statement continues to be effective unless the difference between the name of the original debtor and that of the new debtor causes the financing statement to be seriously misleading.

All of the Cutrale accounts receivable accrued more than four months after Summit Staffing of Polk County, Inc. became bound under the security agreement entered into by Summit Staffing. Pursuant to 9-508(b), the financing statement disclosing Summit Staffing as the debtor continues to be effective to perfect the security interest in the Cutrale accounts receivable, unless the difference between the name Summit Staffing and the

name Summit Staffing of Polk County, Inc. causes the financing statement to be seriously misleading.

The standard for determining whether the financing statement is seriously misleading is set forth in 9-506. Pursuant to this section, if a search
of the records of the filing office under the debtor's correct name, using
the filing office's standard search logic, if any, would disclose a financing
statement that does not sufficiently provide the name of the debtor, the
name provided does not make the financing statement seriously misleading.

Accordingly, if a search of the records of the filing office under the
name Summit Staffing of Polk County, Inc., using the filing office's standard search language, would disclose the financing statement showing
Summit Staffing as the debtor, the financing statement is not seriously
misleading. In other words, the security interest of Associated Receivables
in the Cutrale accounts receivable was perfected by virtue of the filed financing statement if a search of the Florida Secured Transactions Registry
under the name Summit Staffing of Polk County, Inc. would disclose the
filed financing statement showing Summit Staffing as a debtor.

According to the affidavit filed by Associated Receivables in support of
its motion, a search of the Florida Secured Transaction Registry disclosed
the following debtors:

SUMMIT STAFFING	5903 CHARLOMA DRIV
SUMMIT STAFFING INC.	6905 WEST BROWARD
SUMMIT STAFFING SERVICES	8521 S ORANGE BLOSSOM TRAIL
	ORLANDO

The detailed record for SUMMIT STAFFING at 5903
CHARLOMA DRIV disclosed ASSOCIATED RECEIVABLES
FUNDING INC as the secured party, and the following as the debtor
parties:

SUMMIT STAFFING
5903 CHARLOMA DRIVE LAKELAND FL 33813

VINCENT RANDY A
5903 CHARLOMA DRIVE LAKELAND FL 33813

The corporate name of the Debtor in this case is Summit Staffing of Polk County, Inc., and the address of the corporation is 5903 Charloma Drive, Lakeland, Florida, 33813. A search of the records of the filing office under the debtor's correct name, using the filing office's standard search logic, disclosed the financing statement showing the debtor Summit Staffing with the address of 5903 Charloma Drive, Lakeland, Florida 33813, and the secured party as Associated Receivables.

Based on this, the Court determines that the earlier filed financing statement showing as a debtor Summit Staffing at 5903 Charloma Drive, Lakeland, Florida, is not seriously misleading, and is effective to perfect the security interest of Associated Receivables in the collateral of the Debtor, Summit Staffing of Polk County, Inc.

Accordingly, the Chapter 7 Trustee does not have priority over Associated Receivables to the Cutrale accounts receivable. The motion for summary judgment by Associated Receivables should be granted, and the motion for summary judgment by the Chapter 7 trustee should be denied. The automatic stay should be terminated and Associated Receivables should be entitled to pursue its in rem remedies against the collateral.

When a search is conducted in the Florida Secured Transaction Registry, a listing of debtors' names is produced. The listing is an alphabetical listing, and 20 names are displayed. If the debtor's actual name is produced, it is at the top of the list. If the debtor's name is not found, the next succeeding name on the alphabetical list is at the top of the list. To see the next preceding name on the alphabetical list, the searcher must use the "Previous" command on the screen. In fact, at the top of the list is the statement: "Use the Previous and Next buttons *to display additional search results*." (Emphasis supplied.) This statement directs the searcher to use the "Previous" command to see the immediately preceding names on the alphabetical list.

Certainly the searcher should do this. Since the name immediately following Summit Staffing of Polk County, Inc. is produced at the top of the alphabetical list, and since the filing office's directions state that the searcher should use the "Previous" command to display additional search results, clearly a searcher should check the preceding names on the alphabetical list.

Although it is clear that a searcher should check the immediately preceding names as well as the immediately succeeding names on an alphabetical list if there is not an exact match of the debtor's correct name, the issue of "reasonableness" develops at some point because the listing is an alphabetical listing. Although only three names begin with "Summit Staffing," there are several screens of debtors' names, with 20 names per screen, that begin with "Summit." Moreover, since the listing is an alphabetical listing, it is conceivable that one could use the "Previous" command to go back to the beginning of the alphabetical list.

The purpose of the UCC filing system is to provide public notice of UCC filings, and 9-506(c) is reflective of this purpose. If the erroneous financing statement is disclosed in a search using the debtor's correct name, then the financing statement is effective because notice of the filing has been accomplished. Revised Article 9 does not require that a searcher take actual notice of the filing, however. Whether the erroneous filing was actually found by the searcher or not, the fact that a financing statement would be disclosed in the results of a proper search is sufficient to exempt the financing statement from being seriously misleading.

Courts applying Former Article 9 imposed a duty on searchers to be reasonably diligent. In various cases and jurisdictions courts disagreed as to the actions that constituted a reasonably diligent search; however, courts generally agreed that a financing statement was not seriously misleading if it would be found by a reasonably diligent searcher.

Many courts held that a reasonably diligent searcher would conduct multiple searches using trade names, common misspellings of the debtor's name, and other reasonable search queries. However, even under Former Article 9, many courts rejected this burden and did not require searches under multiple names, but looked to the results of searches conducted using the debtor's correct name.

Revised Article 9 requires more accuracy in filings, and places less burden on the searcher to seek out erroneous filings. The revisions to Article 9 remove some of the burden placed on searchers under the former law, and do not require multiple searches using variations on the debtor's name. Revised Article 9 rejects the duty of a searcher to search using any names other than the name of the debtor indicated on the public record of the debtor's jurisdiction of organization. 9-506(c) exempts an erroneous filing from being seriously misleading only if it would be disclosed in a "search of the records of the filing office under the *debtor's correct name*." (Emphasis added.) * * *

Although Revised Article 9 does not require that a searcher exercise reasonable diligence in the selection of the names to be searched or the number of searches to conduct, the revisions to Article 9 do not entirely remove the duty imposed on a searcher to be reasonably diligent. One who searches the filings of a state must examine the results of a proper search with reasonable diligence. A searcher is not required to conduct multiple searches; however, a searcher must reasonably examine the results of the proper search using the debtor's correct name to determine if any financing statements relating to the debtor are disclosed by that search.

In Florida, where the results of a search produce an alphabetical listing of debtors, a searcher is still required to use reasonable diligence in examining the results of the search. If a reasonably diligent searcher would find the erroneous financing statement among the results of a proper search, then notice of the financing statement has been provided. Such a financing statement meets the requirements of 9-506(c) and is not seriously misleading.

The correct name of the Debtor in this case is Summit Staffing of Polk County, Inc., and the address of the corporation is 5903 Charloma Drive, Lakeland, Florida, 33813. A search of the records of the filing office under the debtor's correct name, using the filing office's standard search logic, discloses the financing statement showing the debtor Summit Staffing with the address of 5903 Charloma Drive, Lakeland, Florida 33813, and the secured party as Associated Receivables. The filed financing statement is not seriously misleading, and is effective to perfect the security interest of Associated Receivables in the Cutrale accounts receivable.

Accordingly, it is appropriate to deny the Trustee's Motion for Summary Judgment and to grant the Motion for Summary Judgment of Associated Receivables. * * *

COMMENTS AND QUESTIONS

1. Try our question again: does Revised Article 9 solve the incorporation problem? When an individual running a business decides to incorporate that business, will the new corporation typically "acquire[] or succeed[] to all or substantially all of the assets of the other person"? How does the court read 9-203(d)? What work is the text "by operation of law or by contract" doing?

2. Pay close attention to how the organization of the search database matters for the subsequent secured creditor. Even if such a creditor

need only search in the debtor's legal name, how many statements must a secured creditor consider when another twenty statements are always just a click away?

Georgia's statements are online as well at gsccca.org. Compare searching on that site with the Florida registry in the prior case.

Planned Furniture Promotions, Inc. v. Benjamin S. Youngblood, Inc.

United States District Court, M.D. Georgia, 2005.
374 F.Supp.2d 1227.

■ FITZPATRICK, DISTRICT JUDGE

Currently pending before the Court in this interpleader action is a Motion for Summary Judgment filed by Plaintiff Planned Furniture Promotion, Inc. ("PFP") and a Motion for Summary Judgment filed by Defendant United States of America, on behalf of the Internal Revenue Service ("IRS"). ***

On February 4, 1999, Defendants Benjamin and Laura Youngblood took out a loan with Defendant Citizens Bank of Fort Valley, Georgia ("the Bank"), in the amount of $550,000. The Youngbloods obtained the loan to help finance their furniture business. To secure their debt, the Youngbloods granted the Bank a security interest in "ALL INVENTORY, ACCOUNTS, FURNITURE, FIXTURES, EQUIPMENT, ALL ASSETS NOW OWNED OR HEREAFTER ACQUIRED OF OLD SALEM FURNITURE LOCATED AT 3565 HWY 205, CONYERS, GA & ANY OTHER LOCATION WHERE BUSINESS IS TRANSACTED." Because the Youngbloods used the loan proceeds to purchase the collateral specified in the security agreement, the Bank obtained a purchase money security interest which was perfected by the filing of a UCC-1 financing statement on February 22, 1999. Both the Loan Agreement and the financing statement list the debtors as Benjamin Scott Youngblood and Laura B. Youngblood. Not long after taking out this loan, on February 25, 1999, the Youngbloods' furniture business was incorporated as "Benjamin S. Youngblood, Inc." The Bank was not informed of this incorporation and the financing statement filed by the Bank in conjunction with the Youngbloods' loan was never updated to indicate the change.

On July 9, 2001, the Youngbloods entered into a Loan Modification Agreement with the Bank, changing the terms of the original loan to reflect a new loan amount of $474,872.93. With respect to the collateral, the Modification Agreement referenced the 1999 financing statement and recited the same collateral with a minor exception. The new agreement replaced the phrase "OLD SALEM FURNITURE" with "OLD SALEM FURNITURE AKA HONEY CREEK HOME FURNISHINGS." The collateral listed in the 1999 financing statement was not amended to identify the trade name Honey Creek Home Furnishings. The 2001 Modification Agreement again listed Benjamin Scott Youngblood and Laura B. Youngblood as debtors.

*** In the meantime, Defendant IRS had assessed tax deficiencies against Benjamin S. Youngblood, Inc. in the amount of $106,743.53. These deficiencies reflect unpaid federal employment taxes for the fourth quarter of 2000, all quarters of 2001, and the first quarter of 2002, and unpaid unemployment taxes for 2001. To protect the validity of its statutory lien interest as against Benjamin S. Youngblood, Inc.'s other creditors, the IRS filed five Notices of Federal Tax Liens against Benjamin S. Youngblood, Inc. ***.

*** The Court finds that, at the time the Bank loaned money to the Youngbloods in 1999, it acquired an enforceable security interest in all of the furniture store's inventory and other assets. *** To ensure the priority of its security interest as against third parties, the Bank perfected its interest by filing a UCC-1 financing statement on February 22, 1999. The financing statement listed the debtors as Benjamin Scott Youngblood and Laura B. Youngblood.

Having found that the IRS's federal tax lien and the Bank's security interest are valid, the Court now proceeds to determine which interest has senior priority status. ***

In order to perfect a security interest in a debtor's collateral, a financing statement must also provide the name of the debtor. See 9-502. As long as the name of the debtor is included in the financing statement, it is effective "even if it has minor errors or omissions, unless the errors or omissions make the financing statement seriously misleading." 9-506(a). A financing statement containing an error in the debtor's name is not seriously misleading "[i]f a search of the records of the filing office under the debtor's correct name, using the filing office's standard search logic, if any, would disclose [it]." 9-506(c). If a debtor's name change does make the financing statement seriously misleading, and the change is not corrected by amendment, the financing statement "is effective to perfect a security interest in collateral acquired by the debtor before, or within four months after, the change." 9-507(c)(2).

As noted above, the financing statement filed by the Bank on February 22, 1999, listed the debtors as Benjamin Scott Youngblood and Laura B. Youngblood. However, several weeks after the financing statement was filed, Mr. Youngblood incorporated his furniture store as Benjamin S. Youngblood, Inc. The Bank, which maintains it was not notified about the incorporation, never filed a new or amended financing statement to indicate the name change. The IRS argues that this change in the debtor's name rendered the financing statement seriously misleading and therefore ineffective to perfect a security interest with respect to any collateral acquired by the debtor more than four months after the change. See 9-508(b)(2) ("The financing statement is not effective to perfect a security interest in collateral acquired by the debtor more than four months after the [debtor's name] change, unless and amendment to the financing statement which renders the financing statement not seriously misleading is filed within four months after the change.").

To support its position, the IRS relies on two cases: First Agri Serv., Inc. v. Kahl, et al., 385 N.W.2d 191, 194 (1986) and Citizens Bank v. Ansley, 467 F.Supp. 51 (M.D. Ga. 1979), aff'd, 604 F.2d 669 (5th Cir. 1979). In *Kahl* the Wisconsin Supreme Court held that a financing statement listing Gary Kahl and Dale Kahl as debtors was seriously misleading and, therefore, ineffective to perfect a security interest in the collateral of the debtors' subsequently created partnership, "Kahl Farms." * * * The court found that a reasonably diligent third party searching solely under the name "Kahl Farms" would not have discovered the existence of financing statements filed under the names of the individual debtors. * * * In *Ansley* this Court held that a financing statement listing the debtor as "Ansley Farms" was not effective to perfect a security interest in collateral of an individual debtor named Emory Ansley. 467 F.Supp. at 55. * * *

In the present case, however, both *Kahl* and *Ansley* are readily distinguishable. The results in both *Kahl* and *Ansley* were compelled because of the dissimilarity between the true debtor and the debtor listed in the financing statement. Even though the debtors' names in those cases were not one hundred percent dissimilar—in each case the names shared at least one word in common—they were sufficiently distinct that filing under one name would not reasonably put a creditor on notice that he ought to conduct a separate search under another name to find competing security interests in the same collateral. Again, notice is the primary purpose of the UCC's filing requirements. If a filing is sufficient to put a creditor on notice of other potential security interests, it is not seriously misleading.

The corollary to the rule of complete dissimilarity is that a financing statement is not seriously misleading where, as here, the debtor's changed name is only nominally different than the debtor's name as originally listed. One of the debtors listed on the Bank's financing statement is "Benjamin Scott Youngblood." The debtor subsequently changed his business structure by incorporating under the name "Benjamin S. Youngblood, Inc." The IRS now claims that the Bank's security interest, perfected long before the federal tax lien arose, in the collateral of Benjamin Scott Youngblood (his furniture store's inventory and other assets) has lost its perfected priority status with regard to the collateral of Benjamin S. Youngblood, Inc. However, the Court is unable to conclude, as a matter of law, that this name change renders the original financing statement seriously misleading under 9-506. A search of the filing records under the name "Benjamin S. Youngblood, Inc." would almost assuredly turn up a financing statement filed under the name Benjamin Scott Youngblood. It is therefore reasonable to conclude that a diligent creditor searching the filing records under the name Benjamin S. Youngblood, Inc. would be put on notice to inquire into the interests of a debtor listed as Benjamin Scott Youngblood. As a result, the name change cannot be considered seriously misleading. Accordingly, the Bank's security interest remained perfected at all times and the IRS's motion for summary judgment must be denied. * * *

COMMENTS AND QUESTIONS

At the very end of the case, the court makes what is essentially a factual claim about the operation of the Georgia UCC records system. You can evaluate that claim directly by running your own searches. How well do you think that the court does?

C. MERGERS AND TRANSFERS

This fact pattern gives a stripped-down version of the case that follows:

6-16: NAME CHANGE? CORPORATE STRUCTURE CHANGE?

- Parent has two wholly-owned subsidiaries, FirstSub and Second-Sub.
- FirstSub enters into a secured financing arrangement with Bank covering, among other things, inventory. Bank files appropriately.
- Sometime later, SecondSub does the same with Finco, and Finco files an appropriate financing statement.
- SecondSub transfers assets to FirstSub, including SecondSub's inventory.
- FirstSub continues to operate and acquires more inventory.
- ¤ Three months later, a priority dispute arises between Bank and Finco. Who wins?

Bank of the West v. Commercial Credit Financial Services

United States Court of Appeals, Ninth Circuit, 1988.
852 F.2d 1162.

■ DAVID R. THOMPSON, CIRCUIT JUDGE

In these cross-appeals, Bank of the West, a California banking corporation ("Bank of the West" or "Bank"), and Commercial Credit Financial Services, Inc., a Delaware corporation ("CCFS"), appeal the district court's judgment for Bank of the West on its suit for conversion of collateral. * * *

On April 5, 1982, Bank of the West entered into a loan and security agreement with Allied Canners & Packers, Inc. ("Allied"), a wholly-owned subsidiary of Boles World Trade Corporation ("BWTC"). Bank of the West lent Allied $4,000,000 in exchange for a security interest in Allied's present and future-acquired inventory, accounts, and proceeds. The Bank perfected its security interest by filing a financing statement with the California Secretary of State on April 7, 1982.

In 1983, Allied's financial condition deteriorated and the Bank demanded repayment of the outstanding loan balance of $1,800,000. Allied persuaded the Bank to renegotiate the loan. This resulted in a restructuring agreement signed on January 13, 1984. Contemporaneously with the restructuring agreement, Allied signed a new security agreement granting Bank of the West a security interest in Allied's "present and hereafter acquired" accounts, inventory, and proceeds. As part of the loan renegotiations, there is evidence that BWTC suggested to Bank of the West that it would transfer a beverage wholesaling and importing business to Allied.

In January 1984, another wholly-owned BWTC subsidiary, Boles & Co., Inc. ("BCI"), entered into a factoring agreement with CCFS. The factoring agreement provided that BCI would assign its accounts to CCFS. CCFS would then collect amounts due from account debtors; three days after collection, CCFS would remit to BCI the amounts collected, less a 1% commission, and less any prior advances, plus interest. Advances were to be made on accounts which remained uncollected 33 days following assignment. In the factoring agreement, BCI granted CCFS a security interest in its present and after-acquired accounts. In a separate security agreement to secure advances made to BCI pending collection of accounts, BCI also granted CCFS a security interest in BCI's present and after-acquired inventory and proceeds. CCFS properly perfected its security interests by filing a financing statement with the California Secretary of State on January 5, 1984.

To understand the issues on appeal, it is necessary to consider the complicated corporate structure of the affiliated companies owned by BWTC. BWTC, formerly called Boles & Co., Inc., owned several subsidiary corporations, which engaged in several different businesses. Before August 1983, the former Boles & Co. (now called BWTC) conducted a beverage importing and wholesaling business. On August 15, 1983, the board of directors of the original Boles & Co. voted to change its name to BWTC and to contribute the beverage business to one of its wholly-owned subsidiaries, Minerals Trading Corporation. On the same day, the directors of Minerals voted to change its name to Boles & Co., Inc. (referred to as BCI), and to accept the contribution of the beverage business assets from BWTC. Between August 1983 and June 30, 1984, BWTC again reorganized its subsidiaries and transferred the beverage business from BCI to Allied. Allied changed its name to Boles International Beverage Co. ("Allied/BIBCO") by vote of its board of directors on December 6, 1983, but did not file a certificate of amendment with the California Secretary of State to reflect this name change until June 11, 1984.

*** [W]e accept the court's finding that between January 13 and June 30, 1984, BCI owned and operated the beverage business. In operating that business, BCI generated the accounts factored by CCFS. On July 1, 1984, the beverage business was transferred to Allied/BIBCO. Consequently, from and after that date, any accounts factored by CCFS were generated by sales of the beverage business inventory by Allied/BIBCO, or were accounts in existence at the time of the transfer.

ANALYSIS

The principal issue on appeal is the application of the California Commercial Code to determine which of two conflicting security interests in the beverage business's accounts has priority. * * *

The collateral claimed by both CCFS and Bank of the West consists of accounts generated from the sale of the beverage business's inventory *after the transfer of the beverage business from BCI to Allied/BIBCO*. The district court found that the "transfer" of the beverage business to Allied/BIBCO was effected by a process that ended by July 1, 1984. We already have said that this finding of fact is not erroneous. Consequently, the dispute is over those accounts factored between July 1, 1984 and October 15, 1984, the date on which the factoring agreement terminated. To understand the resolution of the priority dispute that we adopt in this opinion, it is necessary to consider the status of the parties' security interests before the transfer of the beverage business.

Until completion of the transfer on July 1, 1984, Bank of the West had no enforceable security interest in the beverage business's inventory or accounts. Bank of the West's debtor is Allied/BIBCO. A security interest cannot attach unless "the debtor has rights in the collateral." [9-203(b)(2)]. The district court specifically found that Allied/BIBCO did not acquire rights in the collateral until the transfer of the beverage business. Consequently, Bank of the West had no security interest in the accounts factored by CCFS under its agreement with BCI until the July 1, 1984 transfer.

From January 10, 1984 to July 1, 1984, CCFS had a perfected security interest in BCI's inventory, accounts, and proceeds. On January 10, 1984, BCI signed two agreements (the factoring agreement and the separate security agreement) granting CCFS security interests in BCI's present and future-acquired inventory, accounts, and proceeds. CCFS gave "value" to BCI by promising to advance it money on the strength of the accounts assigned under the factoring agreement. The district court specifically found that BCI had "rights in the collateral." Thus, CCFS's security interest attached to the pre-transfer collateral on January 10, 1984. CCFS filed a financing statement naming BCI as its debtor with the California Secretary of State on January 5, 1984. As a result, CCFS's security interest became perfected on January 10, 1984, the date on which its security interest in the collateral attached.

Bank of the West's security agreement with Allied granted the Bank a security interest in Allied's future-acquired inventory, accounts, and proceeds. As we have stated, Bank of the West's security interest attached to the transferred assets on July 1, 1984, when its debtor, Allied, acquired rights in the collateral. Bank of the West's security interest became perfected at the moment of attachment as a result of the Bank's financing statement naming Allied as its debtor, which was filed with the California Secretary of State on April 7, 1982. In addition to its perfected security interest in assets actually transferred from BCI to Allied, because of the after-acquired property clause in its security agreement, Bank of the West had a perfected security interest in all inventory, accounts, and proceeds thereafter acquired by Allied.

*** Two provisions of the commercial code are relevant to deciding whether CCFS's security interest continued after the transfer of the beverage business to Allied. We begin with [9-315(a)(1)] ***. Neither the factoring agreement nor the related security agreement expressly authorized BCI to transfer its assets to another corporation. There is no evidence to show that CCFS otherwise authorized this disposition of its collateral. California courts have made clear that implied authorizations of sales of the debtor's collateral will not be found absent clear evidence based on the prior conduct of the parties. Because there is no evidence that CCFS authorized BCI's disposition of the collateral, CCFS's security interest in the collateral actually transferred (inventory and accounts) and its proceeds continued after the transfer.

While [9-315(a)(1)] indicates that a security interest survives an unauthorized disposition of the collateral, we must look to [9-507] of the commercial code to determine whether CCFS's security interest in the collateral remained perfected after the transfer. *** We will not validate an attempt by BWTC to switch assets among its affiliated, wholly-owned subsidiaries so that the debt to Bank of the West is satisfied at the cost of CCFS's perfected secured claim against the beverage business's assets. ***

In summary, we hold that when BCI transferred its assets to Allied, this was not a bona fide third party transfer of collateral ***. Rather, BCI simply changed its corporate structure. When the transferor shifts assets to an affiliated company at the behest of their common parent company, and when the transaction has the same effect as a merger of the transferor into the transferee with the transferee as the surviving corporation, we cannot say that this is a simple transfer of collateral. * * * [W]e hold that CCFS's security interest continued perfected in those assets actually transferred to Allied as well as in those assets acquired by Allied during the four months following the July 1, 1984 transfer. Because the only collateral at issue in this case consists of those accounts factored in the 3.5-month period between July 1, 1984, and October 15, 1984, we need not consider whether the BCI-Allied transaction rendered CCFS's filed financing statement seriously misleading.

Having concluded that both Bank of the West and CCFS had perfected security interests in the inventory and accounts actually transferred from BCI to Allied/BIBCO, as well as the inventory and accounts acquired by Allied/BIBCO after the July 1, 1984 transfer, we must decide which of these security interests is entitled to priority. The district court resolved this question by looking to [9-322(a)(1)] * * * .

By applying [9-322(a)(1)] according to its literal language, the district court concluded that Bank of the West's security interest prevailed over that of CCFS. When BCI transferred the beverage business to Allied/BIBCO, Bank of the West's security interest attached under the after-acquired property clause in its security agreement. See [9-203, 9-204]. When Bank of the West's security interest attached, it automatically became perfected pursuant to the earlier filed financing statement naming Allied as its debtor. Bank of the West's financing statement was filed on April 7, 1982. CCFS's financing statement was filed January 5, 1984, and its security interest became perfected on January 10, 1984 when BCI executed the factoring and related security agreements. [9-322(a)(1)] sets forth a "first to file or first to perfect" rule of priority. Because Bank of the West's financing statement was filed first, the district court concluded that the Bank's security interest prevailed over that of CCFS.

The situation we have described above has until this case been regarded by the commentators as only a hypothetical scenario. It is a scenario offered by the commentators, however, to illustrate a failure of the commercial code to resolve a priority dispute properly. The difficulty noted by these commentators is this: Before the transfer from BCI to Allied, CCFS (the transferor's creditor) had a perfected security interest in the collateral. After the transfer, CCFS's perfected security interest suddenly is subordinated to the perfected security interest of Bank of the West (the transferee's creditor). CCFS, which had taken all steps required of it by the commercial code to announce its interest in the collateral *to potential credi-*

tors of the transferor (BCI), now finds its security interest subordinated to that of the *transferee's* (Allied's) *creditor*, (Bank of the West), whose security interest came into play only because BCI made an unauthorized disposition of the collateral to which the Bank's security interest attached solely by operation of an after-acquired collateral clause.

We agree with the commentators that applying [9-322(a)(1)] to resolve this priority dispute produces an unsatisfactory result. The principal reason that [9-322(a)(1)] fails to produce a proper result is that it does not appear the drafters contemplated *** the "dual debtor dilemma." *** Because [9-322(a)(1)] does not contemplate the dual debtor scenario, we must resolve this priority dispute by returning to first principles.

*** There are two reasons behind the rule of [9-322(a)(1)]. First, the "first to file or first to perfect" rule serves to modify the common law notion of "first in time, first in right." Harris, The Interaction of Articles 6 and 9 of the Uniform Commercial Code: A Study in Conveyancing, Priorities, and Code Interpretation, 39 Vand. L. Rev. 179, 222. [9-322(a)(1)] places a premium on prompt filing of financing statements as a means of protecting *future* creditors of the debtor. The financing statement alerts potential creditors that collateral against which they are contemplating making a loan already is encumbered. Thus, [9-322(a)(1)] penalizes a creditor who has a security interest but who does not promptly file a financing statement by awarding priority to a later creditor who acquires a security interest in the same collateral and who more promptly files a financing statement. The "first to file or first to perfect" rule of [9-322(a)(1)] thus addresses the problem of secret security interests that so concerned pre-Code courts. But in the present case, the notice giving function of [9-322(a)(1)] does not apply. Bank of the West is a creditor of another debtor entity, and the Bank's interest in the collateral arises solely out of an after-acquired property clause. Bank of the West cannot claim that it has relied to its detriment on the absence of a filed financing statement by CCFS.

A second purpose behind [9-322(a)(1)] is an implied commitment to a secured creditor who has filed a financing statement that, absent special considerations such as a purchase money security interest, see, e.g., [9-324], no subsequent creditor will be able to defeat the complying creditor's security interest. *** This has been described as the "claim staking" function of the financing statement. What this means is that by filing a proper financing statement in the proper place, a secured creditor has staked a claim to its collateral and knows that, absent special considerations, its claim will prevail against *subsequently arising* interests in the same property. By complying with the Code, the creditor is relieved of much of the responsibility of monitoring its debtor's collateral—the Code has allocated the burden of discovering prior filed financing statements to later lenders.

Applying [9-322(a)(1)] to the present case serves neither of the rationales behind the "first to file or first to perfect" rule. The notice giving function is irrelevant because the creditor of a different debtor whose sole interest in disputed collateral arises from an after-acquired property clause has no incentive to check for financing statements against the property of another debtor. Certainly the burden is on a transferee's creditor to search the title to property, but this duty arises only when the transferee's creditor first appears on the scene after the transfer. Likewise, it makes no sense to use [9-322(a)(1)] to defeat CCFS's perfected security interest when CCFS has taken all steps required of it by the Code to proclaim its interest in the collateral. CCFS is entitled to rely on the Code's promise that a creditor who fully complies usually may expect its security interest to be given priority in a dispute with another secured creditor. To apply [9-322(a)(1)] to this case would produce an undesirable result that does not follow from the principles that the section is meant to promote.

We think the correct result is reached in this case by applying the common sense notion that a creditor cannot convey to another more than it owns. Put another way, the transferee, Allied, cannot acquire any greater rights in the beverage business's assets than its transferor, BCI, had in them. Cf. 2-403(1). * * * And [9-315(a)(1)] provides that a security interest follows collateral into the hands of a transferee when there is an unauthorized disposition by the transferor. * * * If the transferee (Allied) takes the transferred collateral subject to the transferor's creditor's (CCFS's) security interest, certainly the transferee's creditor (Bank of the West) can have no greater rights in the collateral than does its debtor (Allied). Because [9-507] preserves CCFS's perfected security interest in the collateral actually transferred as well as in the property acquired in the four months after the transfer, CCFS's security interest continues to be superior to Bank of the West's interest during this period, even though Bank of the West's interest also is perfected. This result is consistent with the principles of the filing system that we have previously discussed. If the notice giving function does not apply because Bank of the West has no reason to check for filings against BCI, the claim-staking function that protects

CCFS should be enforced. CCFS has done all that the Code asks of it to protect its interest. Absent some countervailing consideration, CCFS should be entitled to rely on its perfected security interest.

CONCLUSION

BCI's transfer of the assets subject to CCFS's security interest was an un-authorized disposition of the collateral. Consequently, applying F9-306(2), CCFS's security interest followed the transferred assets into the hands of Allied. Because the transfer was in reality a change in corporate structure, CCFS's security interest remained perfected in all assets actually transferred as well as in those acquired by Allied in the four months after the transfer. Because Allied/BIBCO's interest in the assets transferred and those acquired in the four months thereafter is subject to CCFS's security interest, Bank of the West can have no greater rights in the collateral than its debtor. Therefore, CCFS's perfected security interest is superior to that of Bank of the West. Because Bank of the West's security interest is subordinate to that of CCFS, CCFS could not have converted Bank of the West's property when it factored the post-transfer account. As a result, we reverse the decision of the district court and remand the case for entry of judgment in favor of CCFS.

Reversed and Remanded.

COMMENTS AND QUESTIONS

1. This seems like a tricky case, but in a world of shuffling and reshuffling of corporations and their assets, this borders on plain vanilla. Given that, should Article 9 take this case head-on? Is this the case for 9-203(d)?

2. For more, see Margit Livingston, Certainty, Efficiency and Realism: Rights in Collateral Under Article 9 of the Uniform Commercial Code, 73 N.C. L. Rev. 115 (1994) and Dan T. Coenen, Priorities in Accounts: The Crazy Quilt of Current Law and a Proposal for Reform, 45 Vand. L. Rev. 1061 (1992).

CHAPTER SEVEN

Default

Recall where we started: we distinguished secured creditors from unsecured creditors by focusing on the special property and priority rights of the secured creditor. We have focused so far on the priority rights of the secured creditor—the ability of the secured creditor to acquire a superior position against a debtor's property. We have largely ignored the property rights of the secured creditor, and it is to that idea that we turn in this chapter. Property rights describe the special rights the secured creditor acquires against its debtor. The secured creditor receives property rights against the debtor to short-circuit the collection process faced by an unsecured creditor. The grant of the security interest creates these rights. You must understand that default rights are an integral part of the property rights that a secured party enjoys, and as such represent the other principal advantage that secured creditors have over unsecured creditors: the ability to use these default rights against a debtor without going through the unsecured creditor's collection process (which usually involves getting a judgment and an execution lien). But it is important not to overstate this advantage, for, should the debtor prove recalcitrant, a secured creditor will oftentimes have to enlist the assistance of a court to implement its default rights under Part 6 of Article 9.

The second principal feature of Part 6 of Article 9 arises out of the first. Because a secured party's default rights essentially involve implementation of its property rights, and not its priority rights, they concern primarily the rights of the secured party against the debtor, not the secured party's rights as against third parties (although these rights, as we will see, almost inevitably are implicated). Part 6 of Article 9, accordingly, is applicable whether or not the secured party has taken the steps to perfect its security interest.

SECTION I. OVERVIEW OF DEFAULT RIGHTS

In thinking about Part 6, recall our focus on the property rights of the secured creditor. These include the right to repossess collateral under 9-609, the right to sell the collateral to collect the debt under 9-610 and the right to retain the collateral in satisfaction of the debt under 9-620 to 9-622. The cases in this chapter focus on these issues in turn.

COMMENTS AND QUESTIONS: WHEN DOES A DEFAULT TAKE PLACE?

Part 6 of Article 9 is applicable "after default." 9-601(a). The key term "default," however, is nowhere defined. This omission was intentional and done on the ground that the parties should define the events constituting default. What happens, however, when the parties (or their attorneys) slip and default is not defined in the security agreement? Courts will then enter the picture, but the resulting scope of default may be quite limited. Even if a default is defined, a secured creditor, by agreement or course of conduct, may be estopped to assert an event of default.

The following represents a typical default clause for a large, negotiated deal; much briefer default clauses, of course, may do for simpler deals.

Section ___. Events of Default. The occurrence of any of the following shall constitute an "Event of Default" under this Security Agreement:

(1) Debtor shall default in the payment when due of any principal of or interest on the Loan;

(2) Debtor shall default in the payment when due of any other amount payable by Debtor to Secured Party or in the performance of any other obligation of Debtor to Secured Party including, without limitation, any obligation of Debtor under the Loan Agreement or under this Security Agreement;

(3) Any representation or warranty made in connection with the execution and delivery of the Loan Agreement or of this Security Agreement, or in any certificate or instrument furnished pursuant hereto or thereto, shall prove to be at any time incorrect;

(4) Debtor shall (i) default in the payment of principal of or interest on any obligation of Debtor (other than those covered by subsections (1) and (2) of this section), unless such obligation or such default is diligently being contested in good faith,

beyond any period of grace provided with respect thereto or (ii) default in the performance of any other term, condition or agreement contained in any such obligation or in any agreement relating thereto if the effect of such default is to cause or permit the holder or holders of such obligation (or trustee on behalf of such holder or holders) to cause such obligation to become due prior to its stated date of maturity and if the total amount of such indebtedness for borrowed money with respect to which such defaults or failures to pay are continuing exceeds One Hundred Thousand Dollars ($100,000);

(5)(i) Debtor shall become insolvent or admit in writing its inability to pay its debts as they mature; (ii) Debtor shall apply for, consent to, or acquiesce in the appointment of a trustee or receiver for Debtor or for a substantial part of the property of Debtor or, in the absence of such application, consent or acquiescence, a trustee or receiver shall be appointed for Debtor or for a substantial part of the property of Debtor and shall not be discharged within a period of 30 days; (iii) Debtor shall make or permit to be made an assignment of Debtor's assets for the benefit of its creditors; (iv) any bankruptcy, reorganization, debt arrangement, or other proceedings under any bankruptcy or insolvency law or a dissolution or liquidation proceeding instituted with respect to Debtor, (a) shall be implemented by, consented to, or acquiesced in by Debtor or (b) shall, if contested, not be dismissed within a period of 30 days; or (v) any judgment, writ of attachment or execution or any similar process shall be issued or levied against a substantial part of the property of Debtor and shall not be released, stayed, bonded, or vacated within a period of 30 days after its issue or levy;

(6) Reduction of the amount of voting stock of Debtor owned by Parent to less that 80 percent of the voting power of Debtor's issued and outstanding voting stock of all classes;

(7) Voluntary suspension by Debtor of its business or the sale by Debtor of a substantial part of its assets other than in the ordinary course of business;

(8) The Collateral becomes, in the judgment of Secured Party, unsatisfactory in character or value;

(9) Occurrence of a material adverse change in the financial condition of Debtor or entry of final judgment against Debtor that has a material adverse effect on the financial condition of Debtor, if such change or effect has not been remedied within 30 days after it occurs, or if such judgment has not been discharged or stayed within 30 days after entry thereof; or

(10) Secured Party shall believe that it has reasonable grounds for insecurity with respect to Debtor's performance of any of the obligations of Debtor specified in subsections (1), (2), or (4) of this section and Debtor, within 15 days after receipt of a demand by Secured Party for adequate assurance of due performance by Debtor, shall not have provided such adequate assurance of due performance.

Most security agreements provide that, upon an event of default, either the secured party may accelerate the unpaid balance or the unpaid balance accelerates automatically.

COMMENTS AND QUESTIONS: 9-601 AND THE USE OF AVAILABLE JUDICIAL PROCEDURES

Assuming that the secured party has discovered an event of default, the secured party may exercise rights arising from the security agreement, provided that they do not run afoul of 9-602, and also "may reduce a claim to judgment, foreclose, or otherwise enforce the claim, security interest, or agricultural lien by any available judicial procedure." 9-601(a)(1). If a secured party follows "any available judicial procedure," it is essentially suing on the debt, and pursuing the rights that any other creditor of the debtor would have. Everything is then carried out just as if the secured party never had a security interest, *except* that the secured party receives the benefit of the timing rules set forth in 9-601(e). So, using this remedy, the secured party may essentially proceed on the debt as if it did not have a security interest, except that it may refer to it for priority purposes, should that become relevant. Under the revised statute, the relevant date for this relation-back is that given by 9-322(a)(1).

It might seem strange to see a secured party pursuing this avenue, when one of the supposed virtues of a security interest is that it makes available the special procedures of Part 6 of Article 9. But there are several advantages. 9-601(f) provides that "[a] sale pursuant to an execution is a foreclosure of the security interest or agricultural lien by judicial procedure within the meaning of this section. A secured party may purchase at the sale and thereafter hold the collateral free of any other requirements of this article." Comment 8 to 9-601 states that such a sale is governed by other law and not by Article 9. Because the special procedures of Part 6 are avoided, the secured creditor need not worry about the failure to comply with those rules—a failure, we will see, that may have some costs. To consider another advantage of proceeding this way, say that a secured creditor has collateral worth $10,000 but is owed $100,000 by the debtor. Even if the secured creditor repossesses his collateral under Part 6, it may still have to file suit on the debt for the $90,000 deficiency; it may, in such cases, be easier simply to resort to available judicial remedies in the first instance.

Despite these advantages, the pursuit by a secured party of available remedies outside of Article 9 seems to be used only on rare occasions. One reason may be that secured creditors fear that courts may hold that pursuit of one remedy (non-Article 9 judicial procedures) constitutes an "election," and the creditor cannot later pursue another remedy.

McCullough v. Goodrich & Pennington Mortg. Fund, Inc.

Supreme Court of South Carolina, 2007.
644 S.E.2d 43.

■ TOAL, CHIEF JUSTICE

This certified question asks whether South Carolina recognizes a secured creditor's right to bring a claim against a third party for causing a reduction in the value of the secured party's collateral. After giving the question full consideration, we answer "no."

Beginning 1997, Goodrich & Pennington Mortgage Fund, Inc. ("G&P"), an originator of mortgage loans, entered into an agreement with Advanta Mortgage Corp., USA ("Advanta"), in which Advanta agreed to service G&P mortgages. (Under the agreement, "servicing" mortgage loans involved efforts to collect money due under the mortgages and taking appropriate action when the borrower on a mortgage loan defaulted on the obligation to pay.) Under a series of separate agreements, G&P was entitled to payments from Advanta related to the servicing of G&P's mortgage loans. In 2001, Advanta appointed Chase Home Finance, LLC ("Chase") as Advanta's attorney-in-fact for servicing the G&P mortgages.

In 1999, G&P entered into a series of loans with HomeGold Financial, Inc. ("HomeGold"). As collateral for the loans, G&P granted HomeGold a security interest in G&P's contractual right to receive payments under G&P's agreements with Advanta. G&P informed Advanta of this security interest and HomeGold ultimately loaned G&P one million dollars pursuant to the loan agreements.

G&P defaulted on the loan with HomeGold and in December 2005, HomeGold's bankruptcy trustee ("Trustee") filed a complaint in the United States District Court for the District of South Carolina. The complaint alleged breach of contract against G&P, and negligent/wrongful impairment of HomeGold's security interest in G&P's contractual right to receive payments against Advanta and Chase. Specifically, the Trustee alleged that G&P's default was a result of the negligent servicing of the mortgage loans by Advanta and Chase which failed to generate revenue for G&P so that G&P could fulfill its obligations to HomeGold.

The district court granted Advanta and Chase's motions to dismiss the Trustee's claim on the grounds that South Carolina did not recognize a cause of action for negligent/wrongful impairment of collateral. The Trustee moved the district court to reconsider the ruling and to certify the issue for review, and the district court granted the Trustee's motion for the limited purpose of certifying the question to this Court * * *.

This Court accepted the following certified question from United States District Judge G. Ross Anderson, Jr.:

> Does South Carolina law recognize a secured creditor's right to bring a claim for negligent/wrongful impairment of collateral where a third party's negligence or other actions caused the erosion, destruction, or reduction in value of the secured party's collateral?

This certified question asks whether South Carolina law recognizes a secured creditor's independent right to bring a claim against a third party for causing the reduction in value of the secured party's collateral. We answer "no."

In order for liability to attach based on a theory of negligence, the parties must have a relationship recognized by law as providing the foundation for a duty to prevent an injury. An affirmative legal duty may be created by statute, a contractual relationship, status, property interest, or some other special circumstance. However, this Court will not extend the concept of a legal duty of care in tort liability beyond reasonable limits.

With these principles in mind, we turn to the issue of whether South Carolina recognizes a legal duty between a secured creditor and a third party.

The Trustee contends that the contractual duties between G&P and Advanta provide the basis for the imposition of a duty of care running from Advanta to G&P's creditor, HomeGold. We disagree. *** The Trustee argues that HomeGold's security interest in G&P's rights to payment is a property interest which serves as the basis for the imposition of a duty in tort by Advanta to HomeGold. We disagree.

In South Carolina, legal title to mortgaged chattels vests in the mortgagee after default by the mortgagor. *Wilkes v. S. Ry. Co.*, 67 S.E. 292, 293 (1910). In recognition of this property interest, this Court has held that a mortgagee has the right to possession of the collateral and the right to recover damages from a third party for conversion, injury or destruction of the collateral. *Id.* at 67 S.E. at 293.

*** [T]his Court has previously expressed an unwillingness to recognize a duty of care based on a secured party's interest in rights to payment. In *Universal C.I.T. Credit Corp. v. Trapp*, 101 S.E.2d 829 (1958), the mortgagor of an automobile brought a claim for property damage against an at-fault driver (and his insurance company) for damage to the mortgagor's vehicle arising out of an automobile accident. Although the mortgagee notified the third party tortfeasor of its interest in the vehicle and requested joint payment of the settlement funds, the third party ignored the request and settled directly with the mortgagor. The mortgagee sued the third party for willfully and maliciously interfering with the mortgagee's right to recover damages.

Although this Court recognized that the property interests of the mortgagor and the mortgagee in the vehicle entitled them both to bring a claim against the third party for damage to the mortgaged chattel, this Court found no legal duty on the part of the third party to ensure that the mortgagee received its interest in the settlement funds.

Based on this Court's decision in *Universal,* and similar conclusions in other jurisdictions, we do not believe that a security interest in intangible collateral creates the same basis for a legal duty as a secured party's interest in tangible personal property. Accordingly, we answer that there is no property interest in intangible collateral giving rise to a claim by a secured creditor against a third party for negligent impairment of a security interest. ***

The Trustee argues that Article 9 of the Uniform Commercial Code (UCC) recognizes a duty upon which a secured creditor may bring an independent action against a third party for negligent impairment of collateral. We disagree.

Article 9 of the UCC is a comprehensive statutory scheme governing the rights and relationships between secured parties, debtors, and third parties. The Trustee argues that 9-607 permits a secured creditor to bring an action against a third party for impairment of collateral. Specifically, the Trustee points to subsection (a)(3) which provides that after default, a secured party may exercise the rights of the debtor with respect to third parties' obligations on the collateral. 9-607(a)(3). While this language appears to permit subrogation of the debtor's rights to the secured party—which could include a claim for damage or destruction to the collateral—it does not purport to permit a separate and independent tort claim by the secured party, and on behalf of the secured party, for impairment of collateral.

Other provisions within 9-607 also refute the Trustee's theory that a statutory duty exists between the secured creditor and a third party. Subsection (e) provides that "[t]his section does not determine whether an account debtor, bank, or other person obligated on collateral owes a duty to the secured party." 9-607(e). Furthermore, the Official Comment to 9-607 cautions that "the secured party's rights, as between it and the debtor, to collect from and enforce collateral against account debtors ... are subject to ... applicable law." 9-607 cmt. 6. As previously discussed, we do not find that "applicable law" in South Carolina recognizes a secured party's right to independently enforce the debtor's rights in intangible collateral.

Furthermore, a legal duty extending from a third party to a secured creditor is not necessary to protect a secured creditor. Under the UCC, a secured party such as HomeGold has a number of means available for protecting its interest in collateral. See 9-601 (providing that after default, a secured party may enforce a claim or security interest by any available judicial procedure); 9-609(a)(1) (providing that after default, a secured party may take possession of the collateral); 9-607(a)(1) (providing that after default, the secured party may notify a third party obligated on the collateral of the debtor's default and instruct the third party to make payment to the secured party); 9-607(a)(2) (providing that after default, the secured party may take proceeds of collateral to which it is entitled under 9-315) and 9-102(a)(64)(D) (defining "proceeds" to include any claims arising out of damage to collateral). This wide selection of remedies available to a secured creditor, in our view, counsels strongly against the recognition of a duty in tort between a third party and a secured creditor.

The UCC does not provide for an independent claim for impairment of collateral by the secured creditor against a third party. Instead, the UCC gives a secured creditor numerous options for protecting its security interest from a reduction in value due to third party actions. For these reasons, we do not find a statutory duty extending from a third party to a secured creditor. Accordingly, we answer that South Carolina law does not recognize a secured creditor's independent claim against a third party for negligent impairment of collateral. * * *

COMMENTS AND QUESTIONS

You shouldn't find the result in *McCullough* particularly surprising. Secured parties will almost surely need to protect their own interests and they should expect little extra help from the court system. Given that, what advice would you have given to the secured party about the steps it should have taken to protect its interests?

SECTION II. REPOSSESSION UNDER 9-609: THE BREACH OF THE PEACE LIMIT

9-609 provides, in relevant part, that:

> (a) **[Possession; rendering equipment unusable; disposition on debtor's premises.]** After default, a secured party:
>
> > (1) may take possession of the collateral; and
> >
> > (2) without removal, may render equipment unusable and dispose of collateral on a debtor's premises under Section 9-610.
>
> (b) **[Judicial and nonjudicial process.]** A secured party may proceed under subsection (a):
>
> > (1) pursuant to judicial process; or
> >
> > (2) without judicial process, if it proceeds without breach of the peace.

The breach of the peace limitation is critical to the scope of the rights available to the secured creditor. A severe limit means that secured credi-

tors must go to court routinely, and one of the purported benefits of secured credit is lost. A narrow limit may result in physical confrontations
between debtors and secured creditors, with a risk to third parties. In
thinking about the limit, you should focus on the different types of property that a debtor may have and how the breach of the peace standard may
interact with each. Consider the following fact pattern:

7-1: REPOSSESSION UNDER 9-609

- Debtor, a small retailer, grants Bank a security interest in all of its
  assets, including its inventory, equipment, accounts, and a truck
  used to make deliveries.

- The inventory and the equipment are stored inside Debtor's store,
  which, of course, is open to the public during normal business
  hours. The truck may be anywhere: it is often parked on the public
  parking lot next to Debtor's store, sometimes on a public street
  when making a delivery. The accounts exist on the books and
  records of Debtor.

- ¤ Debtor defaults, and Bank seeks to exercise its rights under 9-609.
  What are Bank's options? Break into the store at night and leave
  with the inventory and equipment? Walk in while the store is open
  and sneak off with inventory, piece by piece? Grab the truck from
  the parking lot or a public street? What should Bank do about the
  accounts? See 9-607.

As the prior fact pattern should suggest, repossessing property inside a
dwelling or a business will be quite difficult, if not impossible, absent the
consent of the debtor. And, of course, if the debtor would just consent to
hand over the property, the creditor wouldn't need to rely on 9-609 in the
first place. As a result, the cases under 9-609 focus on the most important
class of property kept outside—vehicles of all shapes and sizes.

Salisbury Livestock Co. v. Colorado Central Credit Union

Wyoming Supreme Court, 1990.
793 P.2d 470.

■ GOLDEN, JUSTICE

This is an appeal from a directed verdict granted to appellees Colorado
Central Credit Union, and Al Weltzheimer, Tom Clark, Gordon Srock,

and Darren Boling, (all appellees will be referred to as Colorado Central in the analysis) in a trespass action resulting from a vehicle repossession that occurred on appellant Salisbury Livestock Company's lands. The district court granted the directed verdict after finding that Colorado Central's entry to conduct the repossession was privileged and that reasonable men could not differ on the verdict. We do not agree. We reverse the directed verdict and remand for a new trial.

FACTS

Salisbury Livestock Company (Salisbury Livestock) initiated the trespass action in response to Colorado Central's repossession of vehicles owned by George Salisbury III (young Salisbury) from Wyoming property of Salisbury Livestock. Salisbury Livestock is a family corporation run by young Salisbury's father, George Salisbury, Jr.; it is registered in Wyoming and possesses land in Wyoming and in Colorado. The disputed repossession of the vehicles took place on Salisbury Livestock's Ladder Ranch, which is on the Wyoming side of the Wyoming-Colorado state border.

Young Salisbury had pledged the repossessed vehicles, along with three others, as collateral for a $13,000 loan from Colorado Central in October of 1984. This loan was made while he was living in the Denver area. He defaulted on the loan in March, 1986. He had defaulted on the loan once before, in October of 1985, and Colorado Central had repossessed one of his vehicles, which he subsequently redeemed. Colorado Central had then given young Salisbury an extension until February 15, 1986, meaning that he paid only interest from October, 1985, until February, 1986. He made the February, 1986 payment, but did not make any further payments.

At some time in early 1986 young Salisbury left Denver and returned to Slater, Colorado, where he resided near the Salisbury Livestock Wyoming property on which his mother and father lived. Colorado Central sent notice of default to his Slater, Colorado mailing address in May, 1986, but did not receive a response. In July, 1986, Colorado Central decided to repossess the vehicles pledged as security on the loan. Weltzheimer, Colorado Central's credit manager, hired C.A.R.S.-U.S.A., a car repossession company to retrieve the vehicles.

On the evening of July 27, 1986, C.A.R.S.-U.S.A. owner Clark and employees Srock and Boling (and one other C.A.R.S.-U.S.A. employee not made a party to the action) left Denver with two tow trucks to repossess young Salisbury's vehicles. Before leaving Denver, Clark had called young Salisbury's Slater, Colorado home and received directions for finding it from an unidentified woman. The repossession crew arrived at young Salisbury's home about 5:00 the next morning. They found one of the vehicles, a van, parked just off the highway in front of the house and with the key in the ignition. Clark looked inside a small shed or garage on the property and scouted the area around the house for the other vehicles, but did not find them.

Taking the van, they drove a short distance back up the road they had just traveled, Colorado Highway 129, to a large "Salisbury" sign that had been mentioned as a landmark by the unidentified woman Clark talked to on the telephone, and which they had noticed on their way to young Salisbury's home. The sign was adjacent to a private drive or roadway. Although they could not see any vehicles from the highway, the repossession crew turned down the drive. After traveling about fifty yards they spotted several vehicles in the ranch yard. When they reached the vehicles they identified two from their assignment form, a Corvette and a conversion van. They pushed the Corvette onto the drive so that they could reach it with one tow truck, backed up to the conversion van with the other tow truck, hooked both vehicles up, and towed them away.

At the time, it was light, and appellees reported that they heard people stirring in a nearby building. They did not attempt to obtain permission to enter the property or to take the vehicles. Clark testified that he did not plan on contacting anyone as it was his intention to avoid a confrontation. George Salisbury, Jr. testified that after the repossession he discovered that the repossessors had apparently broken a two-by-four that was lying on the ground near the repossessed vehicles.

After the repossession young Salisbury explained his financial problems to his father. The two agreed on a loan that permitted young Salisbury to redeem the vehicles on August 4, 1986, with a check drafted by his father. Salisbury Livestock, owner of the Wyoming property from which the Corvette and conversion van were towed, then initiated this trespass action. * * *

ANALYSIS

Salisbury Livestock contends that the directed verdict was improper, as entry was without privilege under [9-609] because an entry on lands of another without consent is a trespass, which is itself a breach of the peace. It argues that, if Restatement (Second) of Torts § 198 (1965) applies, the repossessors failed to make a demand for the vehicles, and that the time and manner of entry were otherwise unreasonable, so that the entry was not privileged. It disputes Colorado Central's assertion that it should be charged with knowledge of the loan to young Salisbury, and it claims that it is an innocent third party.

Colorado Central and the individual appellees respond that the trial court was correct that their entry was privileged by [9-609]. They point specifically to the statute's second sentence, which states, "[i]n taking possession a secured party may proceed without judicial process if this can be done without a breach of the peace." Appellees claim that their entry to repossess the pledged vehicles was therefore privileged because they did not breach the peace. They further rely on the district court's finding that [9-609] is underlain by Restatement (Second) of Torts § 198. Finally, responding to Salisbury Livestock's assertion that the corporation is a third party not involved in the loan transaction between Colorado Central and young Salisbury, they point to young Salisbury's statement on his loan application that he was a part owner of Salisbury Livestock, which, they argue, means the corporation had constructive knowledge of the loan. The argument proceeds that, if Salisbury Livestock is charged with knowledge of the loan, then consent in the loan agreement provides another good defense to the trespass claim.

Our review convinces us that Salisbury Livestock is entitled to have a jury decide the merits of its argument. There is no real disagreement as to whether a trespass occurred. The crux of this dispute is whether the entry to repossess was privileged either by the self-help statute or by consent. From our review of the evidence in a light favorable to Salisbury Livestock, we conclude that a reasonable jury could find that it was not.

* * * Section [9-609], in turn, incorporates the preexisting right of extrajudicial repossession. The drafters of the UCC did not intend that [9-609] create new rights or obligations concerning the self-help remedy. In the same vein, this court has said before that we will not presume that a statute changes the common law unless it does so explicitly. State v. Stovall, 648 P.2d 543, 548 (Wyo. 1982). The underlying common law governing this entry to repossess is expressed, as was recognized by the trial court, in Restatement (Second) Torts § 198.

Second, because the Wyoming statute is the enactment of a uniform law, our interpretation is governed by W.S. 8-1-103(a)(vii): "Any uniform act shall be interpreted and construed to effectuate its general purpose to make uniform the laws of those states which enact it." Consequently, to make a consistent application in this case, we must consider what self-help acts our sister jurisdictions have found protected by the same, or similar, statutory language.

Finally, we agree with the statement that "courts disfavor self-help repossession because, if abused, it invades the legitimate conflict resolution function of the courts." Note, Is Repossession Accompanied by Use of Stealth, Trickery or Fraud a Breach of the Peace Under Uniform Commercial Code Section 9-503?, 40 Ohio St. L.J. 501, 504 (1979). While recognizing that [9-609] extends a conditional self-help privilege to secured parties, we will read the statute narrowly to reduce the risk to the public of extrajudicial conflict resolution. Although it is apparent that the self-help remedy is efficient for creditors and results in reduced costs of credit for debtors, we must seek a reasonable balancing of that interest against private property interests and society's interest in tranquility.

We then look to the language of [9-609] to establish the parameters of the protection it offers to secured parties who seek to repossess collateral without judicial process. The statute provides in pertinent part that "[i]n taking possession a secured party may proceed without judicial process if this can be done without breach of the peace * * * ." Obviously, the key to whether a self-help repossession is privileged by the statute is whether the peace has been breached. Colorado Central agrees, but argues that the facts demonstrate that there was no breach of the peace. Salisbury Livestock would have us define breach of the peace as including simple trespass.

Section [9-609] does not define breach of the peace, and there is no definition offered elsewhere in the Wyoming statutes that address rights of secured parties.[3] In our review of decisions from other jurisdictions we find no consistently applied definition, but agree with the analysis of the Utah Supreme Court in Cottam v. Heppner, 777 P.2d 468, 472 (Utah 1989), that, "[c]ourts have struggled in determining when a creditor's trespass onto a debtor's property rises to the level of a breach of the peace. The two

---

[3] Wyoming's criminal breach of the peace statute, W.S. 6-6-102(a), reads, "[a] person commits breach of the peace if he disturbs the peace of a community or its inhabitants by using threatening, abusive or obscene language or violent actions with knowledge or probable cause to believe he will disturb the peace." Restatement (Second) of Torts § 116 is more useful in arriving at what constitutes a civil breach of the peace: "A breach of the peace is a public offense done by violence, or one causing or likely to cause an immediate disturbance of public order." We note that, although actual violence is not required to find a breach of the peace, a disturbance or violence must be reasonably likely, and not merely a remote possibility.

primary factors considered in making this determination are the potential for immediate violence and the nature of the premises intruded upon." These factors are interrelated in that the potential for violence increases as the creditor's trespass comes closer to a dwelling,[4] and we will focus our analysis on them. It is necessary to evaluate the facts of each case to determine whether a breach of the peace has occurred.

We agree with the trial court that the Restatement (Second) of Torts § 198 reasonableness requirement provides appropriate criteria for evaluating whether a creditor's entry has breached the peace. If, as here, there was no confrontation and the timing and manner, including notice or lack of notice, are found reasonable, the entry is privileged. If the jury should find that the manner or timing of this entry was unreasonable because it may have triggered a breach of the peace, it in effect finds the entry a breach of the peace and unprivileged. We foresee the possibility that a rational jury could reach the conclusion that this entry was unreasonable.

As asserted by Salisbury Livestock, one specific inquiry is whether, as discussed in Comment d, § 198, a demand for the property is required. The comment waives the requirement if such demand would be futile, but there must be a determination whether demand would have been futile in these circumstances. Young Salisbury had not responded to Colorado Central's demands for payment, but Salisbury Livestock, on whose property the vehicles were found, was not given an opportunity to deliver the pledged vehicles to Colorado Central or its representatives. Notice is not an express requirement of the statute, but is a common law element which helps to determine the reasonableness of the repossessors' actions. Because we recognize that there was no intent to alter the common law of repossession with [9-609], we believe the Utah Supreme Court's discussion of the § 198 notice requirement in Mortensen v. LeFevre, 674 P.2d 134 (1983) is applicable. Although that case did not involve a repossession, it did involve the § 198 "Privileges Arising Irrespective of Any Transaction Between the Parties," which is the situation with repossession from third party property.

Neither of the *Cottam* factors, nor the Restatement reasonableness analysis, requires or suggests that a trespass is necessarily a breach of the peace. Property owners may be entirely unaware of a trespass, so that there

---

[4] Decisions elsewhere have established a general rule that a creditor's entry into a residence without permission is a breach of the peace. J. White & R. Summers, Handbook of the Law Under the Uniform Commercial Code 26-6 (2d ed. 1980).

is no potential for immediate violence. Likewise, a peaceful, inadvertent trespass on lands remote from any home or improvements is unlikely to provoke violence. Therefore, we do not agree with Salisbury Livestock's contention that a trespass without more is a breach of the peace. A trespass breaches the peace only if certain types of premises are invaded, or immediate violence is likely.

However, we cannot agree with Colorado Central's assertion that there can be no finding of a breach of the peace because there was no confrontation. Confrontation or violence is not necessary to finding a breach of the peace. The possibility of immediate violence is sufficient. Two elements of this case create questions which we believe might lead reasonable jurors to a conclusion at odds with the trial court's directed verdict. First, this was an entry onto the premises of a third party not privy to the loan agreement. Particularly if there was no knowledge of young Salisbury's consent to repossession, this could trigger a breach of the peace. The few reported cases involving repossession from third party properties suggest that such entry is acceptable. See, e.g., Ford Motor Credit Company v. Ditton, 295 So.2d 408 (1974). However, these cases do not address third party residential property. When entry onto third party property is coupled with the second unusual element, the location and the setting of this repossession, the possibility of a different verdict becomes more apparent.

We have not located any cases addressing a creditor's entry into the secluded ranchyard of an isolated ranch where the vehicles sought are not even visible from a public place. The few cases involve urban or suburban driveways, urban parking lots, or business premises. See, e.g., Oaklawn Bank v. Baldwin, 709 S.W.2d 91 (1986); Ragde v. Peoples Bank, 767 P.2d 949 (1989). We believe that the location and setting of this entry to repossess is sufficiently distinct, and the privacy expectations of rural residents sufficiently different, that a jury should weigh the reasonableness of this entry, or whether the peace may have been breached by a real possibility of imminent violence, or even by mere entry into these premises: the area next to the residence in a secluded ranchyard.

Because these are factual questions on which reasonable minds may differ, it was error to grant the motion for a directed verdict. The jury must determine whether the peace was breached by this creditor's entry because of the premises entered or the real possibility of immediate violence given the setting and location of the repossession. The reasonableness of the time and manner of the entry must be considered in the context of the third party property status and the rural setting. Whether notice is necessary is also an appropriate consideration when evaluating the manner of repossession. If either time or manner, or both, are found unreasonable then the entry is not privileged. * * *

We are sensitive to the usefulness of self-help remedies for secured parties, and recognize that [9-609] authorizes secured parties to proceed by action if self-help will not result in a breach of the peace. However, we must balance this concern with our recognition of society's interest in tranquility, and the right of those not involved with the security agreement to be free from unwanted invasions of their land, which trespass law generally protects against. To achieve an equitable balance where there is conflict, the finder of fact must weigh the particular facts and determine whether the repossession was conducted reasonably.

We need not, and so do not, reach the question of exemplary damages. Any question of damages awaits a prerequisite finding that the repossessors committed an unprivileged trespass.

Reversed and remanded for a new trial.

■ CARDINE, CHIEF JUSTICE, dissenting.

I would affirm. The court in this opinion notes that the few reported cases in point would find this entry of directed verdict "acceptable." So would I.

Appellant seeks to recover damage because appellees' agent, while driving on appellant's gravel road, broke a 2 x 4 board. Thereafter, without a breach of the peace, appellees took possession of cars that they were entitled to possess. This they were privileged to do pursuant to [9-609], which provides:

> In taking possession a secured party may proceed without judicial process if this can be done without breach of the peace * * *

Undertaking to repossess these cars under the circumstances here existing may have been risky, but that is often the case with repossession by exercise of self help. It is not uncommon for the secured creditor to take possession of property from the debtor or from his presence without judicial process. If taking possession can be accomplished without a breach of the peace, it is entirely lawful.

The secured party in this case, Colorado Central Credit Union, took possession without a breach of the peace. This was lawful, and the judgment should be affirmed.

Williams v. Ford Motor Credit Co.

United States Court of Appeals, Eighth Circuit, 1982.
674 F.2d 717.

■ BENSON, CHIEF JUDGE

In this diversity action brought by Cathy A. Williams to recover damages for conversion arising out of an alleged wrongful repossession of an automobile, Williams appeals from a judgment notwithstanding the verdict entered on motion of defendant Ford Motor Credit Company (FMCC). * * * We affirm the judgment n.o.v. * * *

In July, 1975, David Williams, husband of plaintiff Cathy Williams, purchased a Ford Mustang from an Oklahoma Ford dealer. Although David Williams executed the sales contract, security agreement, and loan papers, title to the car was in the name of both David and Cathy Williams. The car was financed through the Ford dealer, who in turn assigned the paper to FMCC. Cathy and David Williams were divorced in 1977. The divorce court granted Cathy title to the automobile and required David to continue to make payments to FMCC for eighteen months. David defaulted on the payments and signed a voluntary repossession authorization for FMCC. Cathy Williams was informed of the delinquency and responded that she was trying to get her former husband David to make the payments. There is no evidence of any agreement between her and FMCC. Pursuant to an agreement with FMCC, S&S Recovery, Inc. (S&S) was directed to repossess the automobile.

On December 1, 1977, at approximately 4:30 a.m., Cathy Williams was awakened by a noise outside her house trailer in Van Buren, Arkansas. She saw that a wrecker truck with two men in it had hooked up to the Ford Mustang and started to tow it away. She went outside and hollered at them. The truck stopped. She then told them that the car was hers and asked them what they were doing. One of the men, later identified as Don Sappington, president of S&S Recovery, Inc., informed her that he was repossessing the vehicle on behalf of FMCC. Williams explained that she had been attempting to bring the past due payments up to date and informed Sappington that the car contained personal items which did not even belong to her. Sappington got out of the truck, retrieved the items from the car, and handed them to her. Without further complaint from Williams, Sappington returned to the truck and drove off, car in tow. At trial, Williams testified that Sappington was polite throughout their encounter and did not make any threats toward her or do anything which caused her to fear any physical harm. The automobile had been parked in an unenclosed driveway which plaintiff shared with a neighbor. The neighbor was awakened by the wrecker backing into the driveway, but did not come out. After the wrecker drove off, Williams returned to her house trailer and called the police, reporting her car as stolen. Later, Williams commenced this action.

The case was tried to a jury which awarded her $5,000 in damages. FMCC moved for judgment notwithstanding the verdict, but the district court, on Williams' motion, ordered a nonsuit without prejudice to refile in state court. On FMCC's appeal, this court reversed and remanded with directions to the district court to rule on the motion for judgment notwithstanding the verdict. The district court entered judgment notwithstanding the verdict for FMCC, and this appeal followed.

Article 9, which Arkansas has adopted and codified as [9-609], provides in pertinent part:

> Unless otherwise agreed, a secured party has on default the right to take possession of the collateral. In taking possession, a secured party may proceed without judicial process if this can be done without breach of the peace....

In Ford Motor Credit Co. v. Herring, 589 S.W.2d 584, 586 (1979), which involved an alleged conversion arising out of a repossession, the Supreme Court of Arkansas cited [9-609] and referred to its previous holdings as follows:

> In pre-code cases, we have sustained a finding of conversion only where force, or threats of force, or risk of invoking violence, accompanied the repossession. Manhattan Credit Co., Inc. v. Brewer, 341 S.W.2d 765 (1961); Kensinger Acceptance Corp. v. Davis, 269 S.W.2d 792 (1954).

The thrust of Williams' argument on appeal is that the repossession was accomplished by the risk of invoking violence. The district judge who presided at the trial commented on her theory in his memorandum opinion:

> Mrs. Williams herself admitted that the men who repossessed her automobile were very polite and complied with her requests. The evidence does not reveal that they performed any act which was oppressive, threatening or tended to cause physical violence. Unlike the situation presented in *Manhattan Credit Co. v. Brewer*, it was not shown that Mrs. Williams would have been forced

to resort to physical violence to stop the men from leaving with her automobile.

In the pre-Code case Manhattan Credit Co. v. Brewer, 341 S.W.2d 765 (1961), the court held that a breach of peace occurred when the debtor and her husband confronted the creditor's agent during the act of repossession and clearly objected to the repossession. In *Manhattan*, the court examined holdings of earlier cases in which repossessions were deemed to have been accomplished without any breach of the peace. In particular, the Supreme Court of Arkansas discussed the case of Rutledge v. Universal C.I.T. Credit Corp., 237 S.W.2d 469 (1951). In *Rutledge*, the court found no breach of the peace when the repossessor acquired keys to the automobile, confronted the debtor and his wife, informed them he was going to take the car, and immediately proceeded to do so. As the *Rutledge* court explained and the *Manhattan* court reiterated, a breach of the peace did not occur when the "Appellant (debtor-possessor) did not give his permission but he did not object."

We have read the transcript of the trial. There is no material dispute in the evidence, and the district court has correctly summarized it. Cathy Williams did not raise an objection to the taking, and the repossession was accomplished without any incident which might tend to provoke violence.

Appellees deserve something less than commendation for the taking during the night time sleeping hours, but it is clear that viewing the facts in the light most favorable to Williams, the taking was a legal repossession under the laws of the State of Arkansas. The evidence does not support the verdict of the jury. FMCC is entitled to judgment notwithstanding the verdict.

The judgment notwithstanding the verdict is affirmed.

■ HEANEY, CIRCUIT JUDGE, dissenting.

The only issue is whether the repossession of appellant's automobile constituted a breach of the peace by creating a "risk of invoking violence." The trial jury found that it did and awarded $5,000 for conversion. Because that determination was in my view a reasonable one, I dissent from the Court's decision to overturn it.

Cathy Williams was a single parent living with her two small children in a trailer home in Van Buren, Arkansas. On December 1, 1977, at approximately 4:30 a.m., she was awakened by noises in her driveway. She went into the night to investigate and discovered a wrecker and its crew in the process of towing away her car. According to the trial court, "she ran outside to stop them but she made no *strenuous* protests to their actions." (Emphasis added.) In fact, the wrecker crew stepped between her and the car when she sought to retrieve personal items from inside it, although the men retrieved some of the items for her. The commotion created by the incident awakened neighbors in the vicinity.

Facing the wrecker crew in the dead of night, Cathy Williams did everything she could to stop them, short of introducing physical force to meet the presence of the crew. The confrontation did not result in violence only because Ms. Williams did not take such steps and was otherwise powerless to stop the crew.

The controlling law is the UCC, which authorizes self-help repossession only when such is done "without breach of the peace * * * ." [9-609]. The majority recognizes that one important policy consideration underlying this restriction is to discourage "extrajudicial acts by citizens when those acts are fraught with the likelihood of resulting violence." Despite this, the majority holds that no reasonable jury could find that the confrontation in Cathy Williams' driveway at 4:30 a.m. created a risk of violence. I cannot agree. At a minimum, the largely undisputed facts created a jury question. The jury found a breach of the peace and this Court has no sound, much less compelling, reason to overturn that determination.

Indeed, I would think that sound application of the self-help limitation might require a directed verdict in favor of Ms. Williams, but certainly not against her. If a "night raid" is conducted without detection and confrontation, then, of course, there could be no breach of the peace. But where the invasion is detected and a confrontation ensues, the repossessor should be under a duty to retreat and turn to judicial process. The alternative which the majority embraces is to allow a repossessor to proceed following confrontation unless and until violence results in fact. Such a rule invites tragic consequences which the law should seek to prevent, not to encourage. I would reverse the trial court and reinstate the jury's verdict.

Stone Machinery Co. v. Kessler

Washington Court of Appeals, 1970.
463 P.2d 651.

■ EVANS, CHIEF JUDGE

Plaintiff Stone Machinery brought this action in Asotin County to repossess a D-9 Caterpillar Tractor which plaintiff had sold to defendant Frank Kessler under conditional sales contract. Service of process was not made on the defendant but plaintiff located the tractor in Oregon and repossessed it. The defendant then filed an answer and cross-complaint in the Asotin County replevin action, alleging that the plaintiff wrongfully and maliciously repossessed the tractor, and sought compensatory and punitive damages under Oregon law. Trial was to the court without a jury and the court awarded defendant compensatory damages in the sum of $18,586.20, and punitive damages in the sum of $12,000 on defendant's cross-complaint.

The operative facts are not in serious dispute. Defendant Kessler purchased, by conditional sales contract, a used D-9 Caterpillar Tractor from the plaintiff Stone Machinery, for the sum of $23,500. The unpaid balance of $17,500 was to be paid in monthly installments, with skip payments. The defendant's payment record was erratic and several payments were made late. However, payments of $3600 on March 29, 1966, and $1800 on July 18, 1966, put the contract payments on a current basis. The payment due on August 10, 1966 was not made and, on September 7, 1966, plaintiff's credit manager, Richard Kazanis, went to the defendant's ranch in Garfield, Washington, and demanded payment of the balance due on the contract or immediate possession of the tractor. At this time defendant had made payments on the purchase price totaling $17,200, including the trade-in. The defendant was unable to make full payment, or any payment at that time, and informed Mr. Kazanis that he would not relinquish possession of the tractor to him at that time, or at any time in the future, in the absence of proper judicial proceedings showing his right to repossess, and that "someone would get hurt" if an attempt was made to repossess without "proper papers." At that time the defendant informed Mr. Kazanis that he, the defendant, expected to be awarded a contract by the U.S. Bureau of Fisheries to do some work with the D-9 at their installation on the Grande Ronde River near Troy, Oregon, and that he would then be able to pay on the tractor.

On September 13, 1966, the plaintiff instituted this action in Asotin County, Washington, but the sheriff was unable to locate the tractor in that county. Thereafter, the plaintiff instituted another action in Garfield County, but the sheriff was unable to locate the tractor in that county. The evidence indicates that on September 24 Kessler took the tractor to Oregon to work the bureau of fisheries job.

On September 27, 1966, Mr. Kazanis, by use of an airplane, located the tractor on the Grande Ronde River, west of Troy, Wallowa County, Oregon. He then contacted the sheriff of Wallowa County and requested him to accompany them in the repossession of the tractor to prevent any violence by the defendant. The sheriff agreed to meet with Mr. Kazanis at Troy, Oregon, and on September 27, 1966, Mr. Kazanis in his private car, plaintiff's mechanic in a company pickup, and the plaintiff's truck driver in the company lo-boy truck, left Walla Walla, and the following morning met the Wallowa County Sheriff at Troy, where the sheriff was shown a copy of the conditional sales contract. The sheriff confirmed previous legal advice plaintiff had received that the plaintiff had the right to repossess the tractor (although not by the use of force) and thereupon the sheriff, in his official sheriff's car, followed by Mr. Kazanis in his private car, the mechanic in the pickup, and the truck driver in the lo-boy, proceeded to the scene where the defendant was operating the D-9 tractor in the Grande Ronde River approximately 7 miles west of Troy, pursuant to contract with the U.S. Bureau of Fisheries.

Upon arriving at the scene the sheriff, accompanied by Mr. Kazanis, walked to the edge of the river and motioned the defendant, who was working with the tractor in the river, to bring the tractor to shore. The sheriff was in uniform and wearing his badge and sidearms. The sheriff informed the defendant that the plaintiff Stone Machinery had a right to repossess the tractor, and stated, "We come to pick up the tractor." The defendant asked the sheriff if he had proper papers to take the tractor and the sheriff replied, "No." The defendant Kessler protested and objected to the taking of the tractor but offered no physical resistance because, as he testified, "he didn't think he had to disregard an order of the sheriff." The plaintiff's employee then loaded the tractor on the lo-boy and left for Walla Walla, Washington.

Within a few days the tractor was sold to a road contractor at Milton-Freewater, Oregon, for the sum of $7448 cash, on an "as is" basis. The sale price represented the balance due on the contract, plus the plaintiff's charges for repossession. * * *

Defendant Kessler's cross-claim is predicated on the theory that Stone Machinery Company committed a tort in Oregon. To resolve this question we must look to Oregon law. * * *

Retaking possession of a chattel by a conditional seller, upon the default of the buyer, is governed by [9-609]:

> Secured party's right to take possession after default. Unless otherwise agreed a secured party has on default the right to take possession of the collateral. In taking possession a secured party may proceed without judicial process *if this can be done without breach of the peace* or may proceed by action. * * *

(Italics ours.)

Defendant Kessler was admittedly in default for nonpayment of the August and September contract installments. By the terms of the above statute Stone Machinery had the right to take possession of the tractor without judicial process, but only if this could be done without a breach of the peace. The question is whether the method by which they proceeded constituted a breach of the peace.

No Oregon cases have been cited which define the term "breach of peace" so we must look to other authority. In 1 Restatement of Torts 2d, § 116 (1965), the term is defined as follows:

> A breach of the peace is a public offense done by violence, or one causing or likely to cause an immediate disturbance of public order.

In the case of McKee v. State, 132 P.2d 173, breach of peace is defined, as follows:

> To constitute a "breach of the peace" it is not necessary that the peace be actually broken, and if what is done is unjustifiable and unlawful, tending with sufficient directness to break the peace, no more is required, nor is actual personal violence an essential element of the offense. * * *

In the instant case it was the sheriff who said that he had no legal papers but that "we come over to pick up this tractor." Whereupon, the defendant Kessler stated, "I told him I was resisting this; there was an action started and I wanted to have a few days to get money together to pay them off." At this point defendant Kessler had a right to obstruct, by all lawful and reasonable means, any attempt by plaintiff to forceably repossess the tractor. Had the defendant offered any physical resistance, there existed upon both the sheriff and plaintiff's agents a duty to retreat. However, confronted by the sheriff, who announced his intention to participate in the repossession, it was not necessary for Kessler to either threaten violence or offer physical resistance. As stated by the court in Roberts v. Speck, 14 P.2d 33 at 34 (1932), citing from Jones on Chattel Mortgages (4th ed.), § 705:

> The mortgagee becomes a trespasser by going upon the premises of the mortgagor, accompanied by a deputy sheriff who has no legal process, but claims to act *colore officii*, and taking possession without the active resistance of the mortgagor. To obtain possession under such a show and pretense of authority is to trifle with the obedience of citizens to the law and its officers.

Acts done by an officer which are of such a nature that the office gives him no authority to do them are "*colore officii*."

In Burgin v. Universal Credit Co., [98 P.2d 291 (1940)] the conditional seller retook possession from the buyer, after default in payments, and in order to do so secured the presence of a police officer, without legal papers. The only act of the officer was to order the buyer to release the brakes and drive the car to the curb. The court said:

> Because a party to a contract violates his contract, and refuses to do what he agreed to do, is no reason why the other party to the contract should compel the performance of the contract by force. The adoption of such a rule would lead to a breach of the peace, and it is never the policy of the law to encourage a breach of the peace. The right to an enforcement of this part of the contract must, in the absence of a consent on the part of the mortgagor, be enforced by due process of law, the same as any other contract.

As stated in *Roberts v. Speck*, supra, and quoted with approval in *Burgin v. Universal Credit Co.*, supra,

> The reason for the rule requiring a person to resort to process of law in undertaking to acquire possession of property to which he is entitled by virtue of a contract which the person in possession, when such party refuses to peaceably surrender it, is the same whether the possession be acquired by virtue of the terms of a chattel mortgage or a conditional bill of sale. The law does not encourage people to resort to a breach of the peace. * * *.
> * * *

In the instant case, when the sheriff of Wallowa County, having no authority to do so, told the defendant Kessler, "We come over to pick up this tractor," he was acting *colore officii* and became a participant in the repossession, regardless of the fact that he did not physically take part in the retaking. Plaintiff contends that its sole purpose in having the sheriff present was to prevent anticipated violence. The effect, however, was to prevent the defendant Kessler from exercising his right to resist by all lawful and reasonable means a nonjudicial take-over. To put the stamp of approval upon this method of repossession would be to completely circumvent the purpose and intent of the statute.

We hold there is substantial evidence to support the trial court's finding that the unauthorized actions of the sheriff in aid of the plaintiff amounted to constructive force, intimidation and oppression constituting a breach of the peace and conversion of the defendant's tractor. * * *

COMMENTS AND QUESTIONS

1. Is it possible to square the results in *Salisbury Livestock* and *Williams*? Note that both involve repossession of vehicles, early in the morning, from property not solely in the control of the debtor.

2. To what extent should we take into account the individual characteristics of the debtor in evaluating the breach of the peace standard? For example, in making a forecast about the likelihood of violence should a midnight repossession be discovered in progress, should we take the gender of the debtor into account, if men are disproportionately prone to violence? Would that disadvantage women as a group? Should the gender of the debtor be relevant to evaluating the extent of the protest of the repossession? Would that help women as a group?

3. Exactly what is the problem in *Stone Machinery*? Should we understand 9-609 as giving the debtor the unilateral right to force the secured creditor to go to court to get the collateral? If not, didn't the secured creditor act with great care so as to avoid the possibility of a breach of the peace? Put differently, is 9-609 about controlling the risk of violence in repossession, or about giving debtors the ready ability to delay repossession?

4. What should be the role of judges and juries in evaluating the breach of the peace standard? Is there reason to believe that juries will systematically favor debtors in these cases?

5. What should be the role of pre-Code cases as precedent under 9-609? Does the open-textured language import pre-Code and non-Code standards into this area?

6. For more, see Jay M. Zitter, Secured Transactions: Right of Secured Party to Take Possession of Collateral on Default Under UCC § 9-503, 25 A.L.R.5th 696 (2001); Jean Braucher, The Repo Code: A Study of Adjustment to Uncertainty in Commercial Law, 75 Wash. U. L.Q. 549 (1997); Julie E. Cohen, Copyright and the Jurisprudence of Self-Help, 13 Berkeley Tech. L.J. 1089 (1998).

SECTION III. 9-610 AND THE COMMERCIALLY REASONABLE SALE

9-609 just establishes a right to repossess the property. Our secured creditor cares most about getting paid on its debt. 9-610 and 9-620 address that together, and it is critical to understand the strategic opportunities that those sections present together. You must understand before you consider the fact pattern that follows the key difference between the two sections. Under 9-610, the secured creditor sells the collateral and, under 9-615, applies the proceeds to its debt and the costs of sale. 9-615(d) entitles the secured creditor to sue the debtor for a deficiency if the proceeds generated from the sale do not cover the costs of the sale, plus the expenses of the sale. So, for example, if the secured creditor is owed $10,000, sells the collateral for $4,000, incurs $1,000 in expenses in conducting a commercially reasonable sale and otherwise complies with the statute, the secured creditor will still be owed $7,000. That amount represents the deficiency, and the secured creditor may assert that amount as an unsecured claim against the debtor. The value of that is, of course, uncertain, but could be substantial. If instead the sale generated $17,000 in proceeds, the secured creditor would collect its $11,000 in full, and would have to deliver the surplus, the $6,000, to the debtor. In contrast, under 9-620, the secured creditor simply keeps the collateral in partial or full satisfaction of the debt. There is no duty to deliver any surplus. The possibility of accepting collateral in partial satisfaction of the debt is a change in Revised Article 9, as the old statute, F9-505, allowed acceptance only in full satisfaction. Partial satisfaction is not permitted in consumer transactions. 9-620(g).

7-2: THE SECURED CREDITOR'S CHOICE
- Bank, owed $10,000, has repossessed equipment from Debtor.
- Bank believes that any deficiency claim it asserts against Debtor will ultimately be collected at 25¢ on the dollar, meaning, of course, that it will receive $250 on a $1000 unsecured claim.
- Bank would incur $1,000 to comply with 9-610.
- ¤ What should Bank do? Suppose Bank believes the property will generate $5,000 in a proper sale under 9-610? Suppose $15,000? If Bank proposes to retain the collateral in the second case, how will Debtor respond to the offer? Does it matter whether Debtor is solvent or insolvent?

The next case explores basic questions regarding the consequences if a secured creditor fails to comply with its duties. In reading the case, you should know that 9-626 resolves uncertainty in the cases by providing that in non-consumer transactions the so-called "rebuttable presumption" rule applies if the question of whether the secured party has complied with the statute is put in issue. Judge Easterbrook makes a strong case for a different rule. Does he persuade you that the drafters of Revised Article 9 made a mistake in 9-626?

In re Excello Press, Inc.

United States Court of Appeals, Seventh Circuit, 1989.
890 F.2d 896.

■ EASTERBROOK, CIRCUIT JUDGE

Secured creditors are usually the lucky ones in a bankruptcy proceeding, for they can turn to specific assets to satisfy their claims rather than joining the queue of claimants. Many times, however, the creditor is under-secured and must join the unsecured creditors to get back a portion of what is still owed. This case is about what such a creditor must do to share in the remaining assets.

I

Excello Press was a commercial printer in Elk Grove, Illinois; now it is a bankrupt. It filed under Chapter 11 in October 1985. Having tried, and failed, to sell the business, it is in the process of liquidation.

In late 1980 Metlife Capital Credit Corp. sold Excello two web presses (web presses print on continuous rolls of paper), an M110 and an M1000, for a little more than $3 million to be paid over ten years. Metlife retained a security interest. By the time of the bankruptcy Excello still owed Metlife about $2.7 million. Metlife attempted to collect from Excello under Article Nine, which governs a debtor's default under a security agreement.[1] The parties agree that New York's interpretation of the UCC governs, as the contract provides.

To liquidate its collateral, Metlife required a modification of the automatic stay imposed by BC 362(a). On April 4, 1986, the bankruptcy court entered an agreed order, which permitted Metlife to sell the two presses. Metlife promised to remove them from Excello's plant by April 30. The agreement also capped Metlife's deficiency claim at $900,000 should the presses fetch less than the $2.7 million debt—as they did. Metlife sold each press privately for $550,000, the M1000 on April 23 and the M110 in June. This left Excello's debt at more than $1.6 million, and Metlife filed the maximum claim of $900,000, to which Excello and its unsecured creditors' committee objected. The bankruptcy court held a hearing in November to resolve the dispute.

Over three days of testimony, Metlife argued that it had sold the presses in a commercially reasonable fashion, had received the fair market value, and was entitled to its deficiency judgment. Four witnesses testified that Metlife began to look for buyers in December 1985. Harris, the manufacturer, was enlisted to help in the marketing effort. More than 30 of the 150 largest printers were solicited, as were 13 other prospects and nine brokers in 15 states. Metlife introduced an appraisal dated March 1985, filed as part of the bankruptcy petition, estimating that the two presses together were worth $1.2 million. Excello owned one each of the same models clear of liens; it valued these at $1.55 million, the difference likely reflecting that each of Excello's presses could print five colors. (Metlife's could print only four.) Excello sold these presses at a public auction and received a total of $950,000. The difference might have tracked a change in the market, but the only testimony on the state of the market for presses of this kind was excluded as hearsay. Finally, Metlife observed that the cap

---

[1] Metlife argued to the bankruptcy judge that the financing agreements covering the presses are leases, as titled. Relying on In re Marhoefer Packing Co., 674 F.2d 1139, 1144-45 (7th Cir. 1982), the judge found that in substance they are security agreements. The parties do not question this determination on appeal, so neither shall we.

on its deficiency judgment gave it every incentive to maximize the return on the presses. Its deficiency judgment was going to be $900,000 unless it managed to get more than $1.8 million for the two presses, which was unlikely. So every extra cent received on the sale would go straight to its treasury, while the estate would pay out less than 100 cents on the dollar for any judgment, already limited by the cap, it obtained. (Metlife's $900,000 claim is worth only about $200,000.)

At the close of Metlife's case, Judge James granted judgment in Excello's favor. Excello argued that Metlife had not proved that it had given notice and conducted a commercially reasonable sale as required by the UCC. Metlife had mailed a written notice on April 23, the day before the first sale was finalized, simply stating that it was selling the presses, without indicating when. Relying on Executive Financial Services, Inc. v. Garrison, 722 F.2d 417 (8th Cir. 1983) (Missouri law), Judge James predicted that New York would establish that only written notice would satisfy the command that "reasonable notification of the time after which any private sale or other intended disposition is to be made shall be sent by the secured party to the debtor." [9-611 to 9-614]. The April 23 notice was not "reasonable notification," he found. When notice is not given, New York law creates a presumption that the collateral's fair market value at the time of the sale is equal to the amount of the debt. Judge James concluded that Metlife had not overcome this presumption. He would not consider the price Metlife had received at its sale because he rejected Metlife's employees' testimony about the sale as coming from biased parties. The other evidence was not enough to convince him that the presses were worth less than $2.7 million (the amount of the debt): the appraisal was almost two years old, the testimony about the market from Metlife employees was inadmissible hearsay, the prices paid at the auction of the Excello presses were "immaterial." What was missing? "[T]estimony of persons familiar with the business to apprise the Court of what is a fair market price of available goods—or available market for these goods."

Judge James reiterated these determinations when he denied Metlife's motion for reconsideration, and added a new ground for disregarding the price obtained from the sale: because Metlife hadn't given notice, it could not use the price achieved at the sale as evidence of market value. On this view, whether the sale had been conducted in a commercially reasonable fashion is irrelevant.

The district court affirmed. The judge found it unnecessary to determine whether New York would require written notice, because Metlife had not shown that it gave adequate oral notice. Agreeing that New York would require Metlife to rebut a presumption that the presses had a market value of $2.7 million, he deferred to the bankruptcy court's determination that the presumption had not been overcome and did not decide whether New York would prohibit recovery in the absence of notice. ***

II

The outcome turns on [9-611(b), 9-612] ***. The UCC doesn't define either "commercially reasonable" or "reasonable notification"; it also does not explain how these obligations relate to an action for deficiency. In order to sort this dispute out, we must look at how this subsection fits into the rest of Article Nine.

A

Both of the courts below started by asking whether Metlife had given "reasonable notification," assuming the answer would affect recovery of the deficiency. The significance of notice is not so obvious, however. The Code and its official comments are silent about the effect of non-compliance with [9-611(b), 9-612] on a deficiency action; the drafters of Article Nine did not consider the question. The only provision speaking to the debtor's entitlements is [9-625]: "If the disposition has occurred the debtor ... has a right to recover from the secured party any loss caused by a failure to comply with the provisions of this Part." Perhaps this remedy for non-compliance is exclusive—if the secured party has not fulfilled its obligations, the debtor can counter-claim for or obtain a set-off of any damages suffered in consequence of a commercially unreasonable sale or inadequate notice. ***

This approach is a logical outgrowth of the common law's allocation of responsibilities. An action for deficiency is one form of action for payment of a debt: the sale of the collateral is partial satisfaction. In the traditional debt action, the plaintiff need only establish that a debt is owed and its amount. Payment is an affirmative defense. A debtor's challenge to the disposition of collateral is a complaint that the payment, in the form of the repossessed collateral, is worth more than the credit given by the lender: there is no question that the debtor owes the lender, only how much of the debt has been repaid.

Attractive as this might be, it is a minority position among the states, and New York has evinced little interest in it. New York courts, in line with the majority of the other states' courts, say that compliance with

[9-611(b), 9-612] is part of the creditor's proof in a deficiency action. And even though there is nothing in the Code about who shall have the burden of persuasion with respect to compliance, these courts are nearly unanimous in assuming without discussion that it belongs to the secured party. Pursuing the analogy to the debt action, this is akin to placing on the creditor the burden of proving non-payment.

If secured parties are not likely to maximize the price obtained for repossessed collateral then it might be sound to place on them the burdens of production and persuasion, supplying an incentive to do so. A belief that secured parties consistently do not maximize has been deployed in support of a conclusion that all deficiency judgments should be barred. Philip Shuchman, Profit on Default: An Archival Study of Automobile Repossession and Resale, 22 Stan. L. Rev. 20 (1969) (study of 89 car repossessions in Connecticut). But why shouldn't they maximize? Even if the secured party could be assured of a judgment for the full deficiency, why would it forgo a dollar today for the chance to enforce a deficiency judgment tomorrow? The UCC provides that the proceeds from the sale of the collateral are applied first to the expenses incurred in its disposition; the remainder goes to satisfy the debt. [9-615]. So even if the return after expenses is small, the secured party will expend every cost-justified effort because it prefers money now to judgment later. See Alan Schwartz, The Enforceability of Security Interests in Consumer Goods, 26 J.L. & Econ. 117, 126-27 (1983) (demonstrating that rational creditors will maximize sale prices of repossessed collateral). Add the uncertainty of recovery in litigation and this preference for cash grows stronger. That the debtor has defaulted is an indication that it is unlikely to be good for all of any judgment the creditor is able to get. This case illustrates the point. Every dollar extra that Metlife got for the presses went straight into its pockets. Even if its possible judgment had not been capped at $900,000—$700,000 less than it was owed after selling the presses—it still would not have recovered more than 22 cents on the dollar. What reason could Metlife have had to do anything but maximize the resale price? True, it would have had little incentive to maximize any surplus (which must be paid to the debtor under [9-608(a)]), but all agree that the majority of cases, like this one, involve creditors who are under-secured.

One treatise argues that secured parties should bear the burden because they are in control of the procedures called into question. White & Summers, 2 Uniform Commercial Code § 27-16 at 617-18. This, however, is at best a reason to impose on them the burden of production, not the burden of persuasion. * * * Another justification for laying the burden on the creditor might be that the creditor as plaintiff must prove every element of its case, including compliance with [9-611(b), 9-612]. But this begs the question: *why* is compliance with [9-611(b), 9-612] an "element" of the claim? One only need think about the situation where the lender is over-secured and the debtor is owed the surplus to see the problem. If enough money is realized from the sale of the collateral to cover the debt, the debtor may have to sue the lender under [9-625] if it thought the surplus was not as great as it could have been. Many courts say that the debtor, as plaintiff, must prove that the creditor has not complied with [9-611(b), 9-612]. Yet there is no reason to make the burden of persuasion turn on the amount realized at the sale or the sequence of pleadings.

Despite our doubt that the courts of New York have fully considered the subject, we have no doubt about how New York's courts would approach the question if this case were pending there. Although no New York court has given reasons, and although the cases seem to reflect assumptions about a subject that has not been argued by the parties, a pervasive assumption is good evidence about how the courts will decide. New York regularly, albeit without explanation, lays the burden on the secured creditor. What happens when this burden is not met, however, is less clear.

B

Excello argues that Metlife did not comply with the notice requirement of [9-611(b), 9-612] because written notice is required and Metlife didn't give it. The UCC does not provide any definition of "reasonable notification," and, as with most of the issues raised in this appeal, the Court of Appeals of New York has not addressed the subject. Metlife points to several trial court decisions applying New York law holding that oral notification achieving actual notice is sufficient under [9-611(b), 9-612]. The bankruptcy judge disregarded these cases and agreed with Excello, relying on a case from the Eighth Circuit construing Missouri law. The Eighth Circuit focused on the phrase "shall be sent":

> It is difficult to believe that, in choosing this language, the draftsmen contemplated oral notice as being sufficient .... [9-611(b), 9-612] requires that the secured party "send" notice and [1-201(b)(36)] tells us that "'Send' in connection with any writing or notice means to deposit in the mail or deliver for transmission by any other usual means of communication with

postage provided for and properly addressed ...." It is most diffi-cult to fit an oral message into the quoted language. Rather the subsection seems to contemplate mail or telegraphic notice.

Executive Financial Services, Inc. v. Garrison, 722 F.2d 417, 418-19 (8th Cir. 1983), quoting from White & Summers, Uniform Commercial Code § 26-10 at 1112 (2d ed. 1980). Yet the UCC also provides that a person has "notice" of a fact "when (a) he has actual knowledge of it; or (b) he has received a notice or notification of it; or (c) from all the facts and circumstances known to him at the time in question he has reason to know that it exists." [1-202]. The very next section of Article Nine implies that the drafters did not use "send" to imply "written." [9-620] ("[w]ritten no-tice ... shall be sent ..."). "Send" can mean "give," which may be done oral-ly. There is little reason to rely on the definition of "send" over that of "notice" in order to impose the additional requirement of a writing. The purposes of the notice requirement are to allow the debtor to ensure that the sale is commercially reasonable, find another buyer, or redeem the debt. If the debtor knew enough to monitor the sale, that is sufficient. Did Excello receive notice in time to come up with another buyer or to request information on Metlife's plans so as to challenge them? If so, then Metlife fulfilled its obligation to provide "reasonable notification."

Unfortunately, this question remains unanswered. The district court's determination that Excello did not have actual notice flowed not from the facts but from its assumption that New York would follow Spillers v. First National Bank, 400 N.E.2d 1057, 1060 (4th Dist. 1980) ("It therefore be-came the duty of [the secured party] to notify petitioner of all and every proposed private sale, or sales. Simply being aware of an impending sale is insufficient.") (citation omitted). Spillers read the phrase "any private sale" in "reasonable notification of the time after which any private sale or other intended disposition is to be made" to mean "all and every proposed pri-vate sale." But this ignores the "after which" language. Notice of a private sale need only let the debtor know how much time he has before the colla-teral will be sold, not to whom or even if a definite buyer is lined up. To be reasonable, notice must assure that the debtor has sufficient time to take appropriate action to protect its interests. Notice provides time for the debtor to protect itself: to bid on the collateral, to find other buyers, to get involved in the process of selling it. There is nothing in [9-613(1)] which requires the creditor to tell the debtor anything more than the "time after which" the disposition will occur, so any notice after the first one in-dicating "the time after which" would be redundant. "Reasonable notification" does not relieve the debtor of all responsibility to act to defend its self-interest; the secured party need not put forth a steady stream of notices, while the debtor sits back and does nothing. Similarly, Excello's contention that they had to be notified of the time and place of the sale is silly. Knowing time and place is helpful for a public sale where monitoring the actual bidding and presentation of the collateral is feasible—indeed it is required by [9-611(b), 9-612]. When a sale is private, by contrast, the debtor needs to know how much time it has to scare up buyers, which is why the statute requires the creditor to tell the debtor the "time after which" the sale may occur, and why only one notice is required.

Metlife believes that its notice of April 23 was "reasonable notification" of the sale of the second press, which did not occur until June. But the notice boldly stated that the presses were going to be sold, without giving a "time after which" the sale was to occur. So Excello did not know how long it had to procure buyers, at least from the written notice. Metlife also urges us to rule that it gave "reasonable notification" because Excello had actual notice. By February 28, Excello knew that Metlife intended to sell the presses through a private sale rather than Excello's public auction. Excello helped Metlife identify potential buyers, and on several occasions assisted Metlife in demonstrating the presses to interested prospects, both proving, according to Metlife, that Excello had plenty of time to act. Since removing the presses from the debtor's plant was a very expensive proposition and likely to decrease the presses' value, Excello must have known that Metlife had a strong incentive to close a sale before April 30. All of this, Metlife argues, is enough to find that Excello had actual notice. That's a strong logical case, but whether a party actually knows something is a question of fact. And Excello has not had an opportunity to put in any evidence. Since this case must be remanded in light of the standards set out in Part II(C), we leave this question to be considered in the first instance by the bankruptcy court.

C

Excello presses on us an argument that the bankruptcy court rejected and the district court did not reach: that New York would bar a deficiency judgment if notice were inadequate. Several states have taken this position. We agree with the bankruptcy court, however, that New York would apply what has been termed the middle-of-the-road position (between barring a deficiency and leaving the debtor only a counterclaim under [9-625]:

> [D]espite failure of the secured party to give notice of sale of the security to the debtor as provided by the statute, and even despite the creditor's failure to conduct the sale in a commercially reasonable manner, the creditor may still recover a deficiency judgment ... except that in such cases the secured creditor must prove the amount of his deficiency and that the fair value of the security was less than the amount of the debt. This is sometimes expressed by stating that in such cases there is a presumption that the security was equal to the debt and that the secured party has the burden of proof to overcome such presumption.

Security Trust Co. v. Thomas, 399 N.Y.S.2d 511, 513 (4th Dept. 1977) (citations omitted) * * * .

Yet given that the secured party bears the burden of proving compliance with [9-611(b), 9-612], does this "rebuttable presumption" change anything? Not unless one takes the extra step, as bankruptcy and district courts did, of refusing to consider the price obtained after a sale without notice. This was, we believe, a step unauthorized by state law, for there is a substantial difference between discounting the weight of evidence and refusing to consider evidence. There may be good reason to discount the evidentiary value of the price, and to require other evidence of the fair market value, when the sale was not commercially reasonable: the price from a commercially unreasonable sale doesn't reveal much about the collateral's market value. And there may be good reason for believing that the failure to give notice decreases the likelihood that the sale was commercially reasonable, because lack of notice may remove from the process the party (the debtor) with the best ability to find buyers (and a good incentive to do so).

Even after discount, though, the sale conveys information. If despite the lack of notice the sale was commercially reasonable, the price is more than merely informative. The product of a commercially reasonable sale *is* the fair market value. If the secured party can prove that the sale was commercially reasonable, it has proved the market value of the collateral. * * * The price obtained in a commercially reasonable sale is not *evidence* of the market value, which can be discounted or thrown out. It *is* the market value. Whether the sale was commercially reasonable thus is the central inquiry. The third-party evidence (such as an appraiser's estimate), which the bankruptcy judge thought essential to establish the market value and which the district court called superior "direct evidence," is at best second-best. What someone pays in a commercially reasonable sale is the market price; an appraisal (that is, what an expert thinks someone would pay in a commercially reasonable sale) is useful only when the price of such a sale cannot be got at directly. If a creditor is able to meet the burden of proving that the sale was commercially reasonable, it has "rebutted the presumption," notice or not.

Lack of notice may make a difference, but only because it is suggestive on the question whether the sale was conducted in a commercially reasonable fashion. The UCC gives it no talismanic significance and allows the omission of notice when other devices protect the debtor. See [9-611(b), 9-612], excusing notice when the sale takes place on a "recognized market" or notice is too expensive. In the end, the "principal limitation on the secured party's right to dispose of the collateral is the requirement that he proceed in good faith (1-203) and in a commercially reasonable manner." F9-507 Official Comment 1. Whether a sale was commercially unreasonable is, like other questions about "reasonableness," a fact-intensive inquiry; no magic set of procedures will immunize a sale from scrutiny. Failure to give notice is evidence of commercially unreasonable behavior. It might indicate that the secured creditor was trying to avoid the debtor's monitoring and call for closer scrutiny; yet the omission might have been innocent, a result of a speedy sale needed to maximize the return, or irrelevant (if the debtor had knowledge anyway). The choice of public versus private sale also depends on the circumstances. Judge James seemed to think that a public auction (such as that conducted by Excello) is always commercially reasonable, so that Metlife could be censured for proceeding otherwise. The right inquiry is whether a particular method of sale was the commercially reasonable way to proceed under *these* circumstances with *this* equipment. And a party's good faith may be taken into account in evaluating whether the sale was on the up-and-up.

Some courts have talked about the possibility of a separate "proceeds test" to hold that the shortfall of the proceeds (compared with the debt) makes a sale commercially unreasonable without regard to the creditor's efforts to obtain a price as high as possible. A low price may signal the need for close scrutiny. A large deficiency might indicate the search for buyers had been inadequate; or it might simply reflect a greatly depreciated piece of collateral. So the "proceeds test" is simply another part of looking at the circumstances of the sale. Once the sale is shown to have been commercially reasonable, though, the size of the deficiency is irrelevant.

In the end, the court must decide what a reasonable business would have done to maximize the return on the collateral. It must consult "[c]ustoms and usages that actually govern the members of a business calling day-in and day-out [that] not only provide a creditor with standards that are well recognized, but tend to reflect a practical wisdom born of accumulated experience." Bankers Trust Co. v. J.V. Dowler & Co., 390 N.E.2d 766, 769 (N.Y. 1979). That inquiry, abjured in the first instance by the bankruptcy court, must be the center of attention on remand.

D

In addition to deciding that commercial reasonableness is irrelevant, Judge James also looked at Metlife's evidence and suggested that it is insufficient. It is unclear to us that the judge gave this independent weight, but to the extent the judge meant this to be a finding of fact, we hold it clearly erroneous. Judge James said that the sale was commercially unreasonable because Metlife had not presented the testimony of disinterested third parties on the question of valuation; he disregarded the testimony of two Metlife employees who described what Metlife had done to procure the best possible price. There is no general rule in deficiency actions, or any others, that interested parties cannot provide competent testimony. A judge may not say: "In my court, the testimony of the parties counts for naught." Triers of fact must evaluate the testimony with greater specificity; some interested witnesses will be credible and others not so, and the court must try to determine which is which rather than reject everything out of hand.

The bankruptcy judge paid scant attention to aspects of this record that seem to us important to any evaluation of the commercial reasonableness of a sale, such as Metlife's exhaustive search for buyers and the need to move the presses by the end of April. The bankruptcy judge rejected Excello's own 1985 appraisal of these two presses at $1.2 million as too old, an unsupported decision: there is no evidence that the market had changed since the time it was made, and presses one year older are worth less unless the market rose in the interim (which no evidence supports). Although Judge James said that the price Excello received for its five-color presses is immaterial, he gave no reasons and it is hard to see what they might be. Other things equal, five-color presses are worth more than four-color presses; no evidence suggests that the five-color presses were in worse shape. Excello had placed a greater value on its presses than on Metlife's in its bankruptcy schedules. The bankruptcy judge did not discuss why Excello's presses might have fetched less at what he presumed was a commercially reasonable auction than Metlife obtained from its private sale. Metlife knew in advance that its recovery was capped, which gave it every reason to conduct a commercially reasonable sale. Judge James did not mention this. There was also no explanation how Metlife could have been expected to receive $700,000 more than it did for the presses; all it had to do was show that the market value was less than $1.8 million to be entitled to a $900,000 deficiency judgment, and there is no evidence that the presses were worth anything near that.

III

To summarize, the main question in a deficiency action is the commercial reasonableness of the disposition of the collateral, with the secured party bearing the burden of persuasion. Oral notification producing actual knowledge is "notice." If the debtor did not receive notice, the court may use the omission (along with other factors) to inform its assessment of commercial reasonableness. Only if the secured party cannot establish the commercial reasonableness of its sale need it try to prove market value using secondary evidence, such as appraisals and sales of similar equipment. Because the bankruptcy and district judges cut short these inquiries, the judgment is reversed, and the case is remanded to the bankruptcy court for proceedings consistent with this opinion.

■ RIPPLE, CIRCUIT JUDGE, dissenting.

* * * With respect to the adequacy of notice of the sale of the collateral, there is, as my brothers note, a conflict of authority as to whether [9-611(b), 9-612] requires written notification to the debtor or whether oral notification is sufficient. However, this issue need not be decided in this case. Even assuming that New York does not require written notification under [9-611(b), 9-612], the district court determined that Metlife did not provide adequate oral notification. * * * The purpose of the notice requirement is not in serious dispute; it is designed "to give the debtor an opportunity to protect his interest in the collateral by exercising any right of redemption or by bidding at the sale, to challenge any aspect of the disposition before it is made, or to interest potential purchasers in the sale, all to the end that the merchandise not be sacrificed by sale at less than its true value" (citations omitted). First Bank & Trust Co. of Ithaca v. Mitchell, 473 N.Y.S.2d 697, 702 (Sup. Ct. 1984). The district court's assessment of the record in light of that purpose certainly is not clearly errone-

ous. Metlife acquired legal authority to sell the presses on April 4, 1986. Between that date and April 23rd, the date the first press was sold, Excello knew little more than that Metlife planned to sell the presses in a private sale and that the presses "should" be sold by April 30, 1986. Excello had to vacate its premises on that date, and there were tremendous costs involved with moving the presses if they had not yet been sold. According to Met-life, deinstallation of the presses "would cause a decline in value of at least $100,000 per unit." However, the April 30, 1986 deadline, while impor-tant, was apparently not essential. One of the presses was sold on April 23 for $550,000; the other was not sold until June and was also purchased for $550,000.

Having determined that Metlife did not give Excello adequate notice of the sale of the presses, our focus must shift to the effect of that failure.[2] There is some authority in New York for the proposition that inadequate notice bars any deficiency judgment. However, most courts, including many in New York, have taken the view that inadequate notice simply creates "a presumption that the security was equal to the debt and that the secured party has the burden of proof to overcome such presumption ...." Security Trust Co. v. Thomas, 399 N.Y.S.2d 511, 513 (1977). While I agree with the majority that it appears that New York would follow the latter line of cases if its Court of Appeals were confronted directly with the

---

[2] Contrary to the majority's position, whether the sale was commercially reasonable is not always "the main question in a deficiency action." * * * [T]he issue of commercial reasonableness is moot once the creditor fails to establish due notice. To succeed in a deficiency claim, a secured creditor must prove due notice of sale *and* commercial reasonableness. Having failed to prove one, the other becomes irrelevant and the creditor moves on to the next step—proof of the amount of the debt, the fair value of the collateral, and the resulting deficiency. In this second part of the analysis, I can-not agree with the majority's position that "[t]he price obtained in a commercially reasonable sale is not *evidence* of the market value ... [i]t *is* the market value." (em-phasis in original). The majority offers no authority to support this position, and Metlife's own witnesses testified that the manner in which collateral is sold affects the price it will bring. For example, the price obtained at auction is usually dimi-nished or liquidated. The sales price does not necessarily reflect the market value, therefore, even though the sale is conducted in a commercially reasonable manner. Indeed, the majority's view is a clear invitation to a creditor to ignore the notice re-quirements of [9-611(b), 9-612]. Under the majority's view, a secured creditor could hold a sale without appropriate notice, dispose of secured collateral, and still be able to recover a deficiency judgment so long as the creditor could prove the fair market value of the equipment sold.

issue, I do not believe that we need to resolve definitively the issue in this litigation. If inadequate notice is deemed an absolute bar to a default judgment, Metlife's deficiency claim must fail. If New York rejects the absolute bar rule, on the other hand, Metlife must overcome the presumption that the value of the presses equaled the amount of Excello's debt ($2.7 million). Assuming the rebuttable presumption rule is the rule in the State of New York, I agree with the bankruptcy and district courts that the presumption was not overcome. * * *

In sum, I believe it is unnecessary to resolve the issues of New York law. We need not determine whether New York requires written, instead of oral, notice under [9-611(b), 9-612] because neither was given. Similarly, we need not determine whether inadequate notice absolutely bars a deficiency judgment or, alternatively, gives rise to a rebuttable presumption that the value of the collateral equals the amount of the debt. Our only necessary task is to assess the determinations that Metlife failed to produce sufficient evidence of either adequate oral notification or of the collateral's market value in April and June, 1986. In my view, the structural relationship between trial and appellate courts—and the consequent deferential standard of review of the issues necessarily before us—requires that the judgment of the district court be affirmed.

Accordingly, I respectfully dissent.

COMMENTS AND QUESTIONS

We have a certain amount of ground to navigate when considering a case such as *Excello Press*. It arises under the prior version of the statute, but Revised Article 9 continues to embrace a standard of commercial reasonableness for disposition of collateral under 9-610. (And be sure to look at 9-627 too.) There is little reason to think that prior discussions of commercial reasonableness won't be influential as courts consider cases arising under Revised Article 9. And for more on that standard generally, see L.B. Wilkinson, Jr., Procedures v. Proceeds: Evaluation of the Commercial Reasonableness of Dispositions of Collateral Under Article 9 of the Uniform Commercial Code, 63 Tenn. L. Rev. 987 (1996).

And, while Revised Article 9 settles on the rebuttable presumption rule in new 9-626, it does so only for non-consumer transactions. 9-626(b) instructs the courts in consumer transactions to carry on as before without regard to the rules embraced in 9-626(a). Again, the old caselaw on how to think through the consequences of a secured creditor mistake will continue to matter for consumer transactions.

Finally, there is the question of the status of mistaken notices under the new statute. 9-611, 9-612, 9-613 and 9-614 now offer much greater detail on how notice is be given and in precisely what form. The statute also creates safe harbors that the secured party can satisfy and then rely on. See 9-612(b). But what if the secured party makes a mistake in providing notice? The new rebuttable presumption rule in 9-626(a) is intended to be invoked in situations where the secured party has failed to prove that "the collection, enforcement, disposition, or acceptance was conducted in accordance with the provisions of this part" relating to those acts. As the comments to that section make clear, other mistakes are to be covered by the more general actual damages rule of 9-625(b). Exactly where does a mistake in notice fit?

SECTION IV. RETENTION OF COLLATERAL UNDER 9-620

As noted before, a secured creditor has two alternative paths that it can pursue to obtain value from its collateral. We have just looked at sale under 9-610 and 9-615, and we now turn to retention of the collateral under 9-620. In fact pattern 7-2, we highlighted the incentives of the secured creditor in making this choice. Consider in fact pattern 7-3 how unsecured creditors might behave in this situation:

7-3: GETTING VALUE TO UNSECURED CREDITORS

- Bank, owed $7,500, has repossessed equipment from Debtor, and proposes to retain it under 9-620 in full satisfaction of its debt. Bank sends a notice to that effect to Debtor. The collateral is believed to be worth $10,000.

- Debtor has ten unsecured creditors, each owed $1,000, for a total of $10,000

- ¤ How should the $10,000 in value from the equipment be divided? How likely is it that notice to Debtor of the intent to retain will achieve this? Should Bank be required to give notice of the proposed retention to unsecured creditors? Would any unsecured creditor have reason to act, even if doing so was in the benefit of the group of unsecured creditors? Put differently, are there substantial free-rider problems here for the unsecured creditors?

Reeves v. Foutz and Tanner, Inc.

New Mexico Supreme Court, 1980.
617 P.2d 149.

■ SOSA, CHIEF JUSTICE

*** Plaintiffs Reeves and Begay are uneducated Navajo Indians whose ability to understand English and commercial matters are limited. Each of them pawned jewelry with the defendant whereby they received a money loan in return for a promise to repay the loan in thirty days with interest. The Indian jewelry left with defendant as collateral was worth several times the amount borrowed. The plaintiffs defaulted and defendant sent each of them a notice of intent to retain the collateral, though Reeves claimed she never received notice. The retention was not objected to by either plaintiff. Defendant then sold the jewelry in the regular course of its business.

The question we are presented with is whether a secured party who sends a notice of intent to retain collateral, in conformance with [9-620], may sell the collateral in its regular course of business without complying with [9-610]? We decide that the secured party in this case could not sell the collateral without complying with [9-610].

The Uniform Commercial Code provides a secured party in possession with two courses of action upon the default of the debtor. [9-610] provides generally that the secured party may sell the collateral, but if the security interest secures an indebtedness, he must account to the debtor for any surplus (and the debtor must account for any deficiency). [9-620] provides the secured party with the alternative of retaining the collateral in satisfaction of the obligation. Under this section, the secured party must give written notice to the debtor that he intends to keep the collateral in satisfaction of the debt. The debtor is then given thirty days to object to the proposed retention and require the sale of the property according to [9-610].

In the present case we will assume that defendant gave proper notice to both Reeves and Begay of its intention to retain the collateral and that neither objected within thirty days. The trial court found that the defendant, in accordance with its normal business practice, then moved the jewelry into its sale inventory where it was sold to Joe Tanner, president of defendant corporation, or to Joe Tanner, Inc., a corporation owned by Joe Tanner and engaged in the sale of Indian jewelry. There was no accounting to plaintiffs of any surplus. The trial court also found that the defendant did not act in good faith in disposing of the jewelry, taking into consideration the relative bargaining power of the parties.

The defendant argues that the trial court should be reversed because it applied [9-610]. It essentially argues that once it complied with [9-620] and sent the notice of intent to retain, it could do as it pleased with the property once the thirty days had elapsed without objection. The debtor-creditor relationship terminates, they claim, and the creditor becomes owner of the collateral.

The plaintiffs argue that the trial court was correct in applying [9-610] to require that any surplus from the sale of collateral be returned to the debtor. They urge that the intention of the secured party should control and where he intended to sell the collateral and did sell the collateral in the normal course of business, he must comply with [9-610] which governs sales of such collateral.

Neither party to this action has cited a case which has dealt directly with the issue here, but *amicus* has referred us to a Federal Trade Commission case on the subject where it was stated:

> In the Draftsmen's Statement of Reasons for 1972 Changes in Official Text, the Draftsmen summarized the purpose of [9-620] as follows:
>
> > "Under subsection (2) of this section the secured party may in lieu of sale give notice to the debtor and certain other persons that he proposes to retain the collateral in lieu of sale."
>
> The foregoing language strongly suggests that waiver of surplus and deficiency rights under [9-620] is appropriate only when prompt resale of repossessed collateral in the ordinary course of business is not contemplated by the creditor .... That being so, use of [9-620] by an automobile dealer, particularly one not disposed to pursue deficiency judgments, would appear calculated solely to extinguish surplus rights of consumers, which we do not believe was the intended purpose of [9-620].

In the Matter of Ford Motor Company, Ford Motor Credit Company, and Francis Ford Inc., 3 CCH Trade Reg. Rep. 21756, 21767 (FTC Docket No. 9073, Sept. 21, 1979). The Commission went on to say that a creditor of this type is not foreclosed from using [9-620] so long as he intends to retain the collateral for his own use for the immediately foreseeable future, rather than to resell the collateral in the ordinary course of business. We agree with the approach used by the Federal Trade Commission.

The Court of Appeals reasoned that once the creditor elected to retain the collateral, and followed the mechanics of [9-620], the property became his to keep or to sell. We do not find fault with this reasoning, but it misses the point. Defendant can do as he pleases with the property, but where he intends to sell the property in the regular course of his business, which is in substance selling the property as contemplated by [9-610], he must account for a surplus in conformity with [9-610].

The defendant also argues that plaintiffs could have objected to the retention, thus forcing a sale in compliance with [9-610]. But because there was never any actual intent to retain under [9-620], the failure of plaintiffs to timely object does not foreclose their claim. Moreover, the fact that plaintiffs could have objected means nothing in this context; their objection would only have served to cause a sale of the goods, which sale was already intended by defendant.

The defendant also argues that the trial court erred in finding that it acted in bad faith. We need not reach this question because bad faith was not material to the trial court's conclusions of law and judgment, which we find to be proper. * * *

COMMENTS AND QUESTIONS

1. Is this a case of bad facts making for bad law or does this case get these issues right? Under the court's rule, don't we end up with a messy, after-the-fact inquiry into the secured creditor's intent? As the cases will appear, the secured creditor will seek to claim that it had the requisite intent at the time of retention, but that changed circumstances led to a change in plan. How long must the secured creditor retain the property to be safe from these attacks?

2. Note the importance of 9-620 in allocating the risk of a change in the value of the collateral. Suppose that the secured creditor wants to delay the sale to speculate on a possible increase in value of the collateral. If the creditor has retained under 9-620, the creditor bears the full costs and benefits of the speculation. If the creditor has merely delayed proceeding under 9-610, the creditor bears neither the full costs of the speculation nor receives the full benefits. If the collateral rises in value,

the secured creditor receives each dollar of benefit, at least until the value of the collateral reaches the amount of the debt plus the costs. At that point, the debtor should exercise the option to redeem under 9-623 (though may not because of the debtor's indifference). How should we police this type of speculation?

3. For more, see Wendell H. Holmes, "Involuntary Strict Foreclosure" Under Section 9-505(2) of the Uniform Commercial Code: Tarpit for the Tardy Creditor, 26 Wake Forest L. Rev. 289 (1991).

CHAPTER EIGHT

THE LIMITS OF ARTICLE 9

Article 9 exists in a much larger legal context and therefore we must devote some effort to navigating the boundaries. 9-109 does this explicitly in that it excludes a number of important areas from its ambit. These include most real estate transactions, such as a mortgage on a house, security interests in areas covered by federal statutes plus many other more specialized areas. The first section of this chapter looks at three of these exclusions, first for security interests in copyrights and patents, then at certain other rights that arise under federal law and finally at how Article 9 interfaces with the doctrine of set-off. The next section of the chapter considers near-secured transactions—transactions such as bailments and leases—that is, transactions that may be seen to be close cousins of a secured transaction. In these cases, the characterization of the basic transaction—bailment or secured transaction, lease or secured transaction—is critical. As filing is required to perfect a security interest but is not required to maintain the interest of a bailor or lessor, how the deal is characterized determines the winners and the losers. Finally, in the third section, we look at 9-109(a)(3)'s inclusion of sales of accounts, chattel paper, payment intangibles and promissory notes in Article 9.

SECTION I. 9-109 AND EXCLUDED AREAS

A. INTELLECTUAL PROPERTY

The next two cases are interesting in their own right, as each provides a window into the world of intellectual property, that is, copyrights, patents, trademarks and the like. These cases also give us a chance to play comparativist. Pay close attention to the rules for security interests for intellectual property set forth in the United States Code and compare those provisions to their counterparts in Article 9. We will start with patents and then switch to copyrighted works.

8-1: HYPO HYPO

- On May 1st, Debtor executes a document in favor of Bank providing that "[d]ebtor hereby grants a security interest in patent no. 12345, to secure a $10,000 loan by Bank to Debtor of even date herewith." Bank files a standard financing statement in the appropriate state office.
- On June 1st, Debtor files for bankruptcy. Under BC 544, Debtor asserts bankruptcy's hypothetical lien creditor power and can avoid the security interest if it is unperfected.
- ¤ How should this case come out given the relevant section from the Patent Act, 35 USC 261?

> Subject to the provisions of this title, patents shall have the attributes of personal property. Applications for patent, patents, or any interest therein, shall be assignable in law by an instrument in writing .... An assignment, grant or conveyance shall be void as against any subsequent purchaser or mortgagee for a valuable consideration, without notice, unless it is recorded in the Patent and Trademark Office within three months from its date or prior to the date of such subsequent purchase or mortgage.

8-2: PATENTLY ABSURD?

- On May 1st, Debtor executes a document in favor of Bank providing that "[d]ebtor hereby grants a security interest under Article 9 in patent no. 12345, to secure a $10,000 loan by Bank to Debtor of even date herewith." Bank files a standard financing statement in the appropriate state office.
- On June 1st, Debtor grants a security interest under Article 9 in the same patent to Finco. Finco records with the U.S. Patent and Trademark Office.
- ¤ Who wins?

In reading the next case, be sure to focus on footnote 1 and the court's use of the term "lien creditor." Does its use square with that in 9-102(a)(52) and 9-317? If not, why not and with what consequences?

In re Cybernetic Services, Inc.

United States Court of Appeals, Ninth Circuit, 2001.
252 F.3d 1039.

■ GRABER, CIRCUIT JUDGE

As is often true in the field of intellectual property, we must apply an antiquated statute in a modern context. The question that we decide today is whether 35 USC 261 of the Patent Act, or Article 9 of the Uniform Commercial Code (UCC), as adopted in California, requires the holder of a security interest in a patent to record that interest with the federal Patent and Trademark Office (PTO) in order to perfect the interest as against a subsequent lien creditor.[1] We answer "no." * * *

The parties stipulated to the relevant facts: Matsco, Inc., and Matsco Financial Corporation (Petitioners) have a security interest in a patent developed by Cybernetic Services, Inc. (Debtor). The patent is for a data recorder that is designed to capture data from a video signal regardless of the horizontal line in which the data is located. Petitioners' security interest in the patent was "properly prepared, executed by the Debtor and timely filed with the Secretary of State of the State of California," in accordance with the California Commercial Code. Petitioners did not record their interest with the PTO. * * *

The parties do not dispute that Petitioners complied with Article 9's general filing requirements and, in the case of most types of property, would have priority over a subsequent lien creditor. The narrower question in this case is whether Petitioners' actions were sufficient to perfect their interest when the "general intangible" to which the lien attached is a patent. The parties also do not dispute that, *if* Petitioners were required to file notice of their security interest in the patent with the PTO, then the Trustee, as a hypothetical lien creditor under BC 544(a)(1), has a superior right to the patent.

---

[1] A "security interest" is an interest in personal property that secures a payment or the performance of an obligation. [1-201(b)(35)]. We refer to a person who holds a security interest in property but who does not hold title to that property as a "lien creditor." * * *

The Trustee makes two arguments. First, the Trustee contends that the Patent Act preempts Article 9's filing requirements. Second, the Trustee argues that Article 9 itself provides that a security interest in a patent can be perfected only by filing it with the PTO. We discuss each argument in turn.

* * * The Trustee argues that the recording provision found in 35 USC 261 requires that the holder of a security interest in a patent record that interest with the PTO in order to perfect as to a subsequent lien creditor. Section 261 provides:

> Ownership; assignment
>
> Subject to the provisions of this title, patents shall have the attributes of personal property.
>
> Applications for patent, patents, or any interest therein, shall be assignable in law by an instrument in writing. The applicant, patentee, or his assigns or legal representatives may in like manner grant and convey an exclusive right under his application for patent, or patents, to the whole or any specified part of the United States.
>
> A certificate of acknowledgment under the hand and official seal of a person authorized to administer oaths within the United States, or, in a foreign country, of a diplomatic or consular officer of the United States or an officer authorized to administer oaths whose authority is proved by a certificate of a diplomatic or consular officer of the United States, or apostille of an official designated by a foreign country which, by treaty or convention, accords like effect to apostilles of designated officials in the United States, shall be prima facie evidence of the execution of an assignment, grant or conveyance of a patent or application for patent.
>
> *An assignment, grant or conveyance shall be void as against any subsequent purchaser or mortgagee for a valuable consideration, without notice, unless it is recorded in the Patent and Trademark Office* within three months from its date or prior to the date of such subsequent purchase or mortgage.
>
> (Emphasis added.)

If the Trustee's reading of the relevant portion of 35 USC 261 is correct, then to the extent that Article 9 allows a different method of perfection, it would be preempted under either a "field" or "conflict" preemption theory. That is because recording systems increase a patent's marketability and thus play an integral role in the incentive scheme created by Congress. Recording systems provide notice and certainty to present and future parties to a transaction; they work "by virtue of the fact that interested parties have a specific place to look in order to discover with certainty whether a particular interest has been transferred." Nat'l Peregrine, Inc. v. Capitol Fed. Savs. & Loan Ass'n (In re Peregrine Entm't, Ltd.), 116 Bankr. 194, 200 (C.D. Cal. 1990). If, as the Trustee argues, the Patent Act expressly delineates the place where a party must go to acquire notice and certainty about liens on patents, then a state law that requires the public to look elsewhere unquestionably would undercut the value of the Patent Act's recording scheme. If, on the other hand, 35 USC 261 does not cover liens on patents, then Article 9's filing requirements do not conflict with any policies inherent in the Patent Act's recording scheme.

Article 9 itself recognizes the existence of preemption principles. [9-109(c)] expressly subordinates Article 9's requirements to those of federal law. That section provides that Article 9 does not apply to any "security interest subject to any statute of the United States to the extent that such statute governs the rights of parties to and third parties affected by transactions in particular types of property." [9-109(c)] may be broader than federal preemption doctrine under the Patent Act. The text of [9-109(c)] implies that Article 9's requirements are inapplicable to the extent that a federal law *governs* the rights of a party to a secured transaction, with or without a *conflict* between the state law and the scheme created by Congress in the Patent Act.

This possible difference in scope does not affect the result in the present case, however. As noted, the Trustee argues that 35 USC 261 *required* Petitioners to record their interest with the PTO. If that is true, then the Trustee has priority to the patent's proceeds, either because there is a clear conflict between the state and federal schemes and the state scheme is preempted, or because the Patent Act "governs the rights of parties" to the transaction and [9-109(c)] operates to nullify Article 9's filing requirements. We turn to that issue now.

2. The Patent Act Requires Parties to Record with the PTO Only Ownership Interest in Patents.

As noted, the Patent Act's recording provision provides that an "assignment, grant or conveyance shall be void as against any subsequent purchaser or mortgagee for a valuable consideration, without notice, unless it is recorded in the [PTO]." 35 USC 261. In order to determine whether Congress intended for parties to record with the PTO the type of interest that is at issue in this case, we must give the words of the statute the meaning that they had in 1870, the year in which the current version of 35 USC 261 was enacted.

* * * The first phrase in section 261's recording provision—"assignment, grant or conveyance"—refers to different types of transactions. The neighboring clause—"shall be void as against any subsequent purchaser or mortgagee"—refers to the status of the party that receives an interest in the patent. Therefore, for the Trustee to prevail in this case, (1) Petitioners' transaction with Debtor must have been the type of "assignment, grant or conveyance" referred to in section 261, and (2) the Trustee, who has the status of a hypothetical lien creditor, must be a "subsequent purchaser or mortgagee." We hold that neither condition is met.

As we will discuss next, our conclusion finds support in the text of 35 USC 261, keeping in view the historical definitions of the terms used in the recording provision; the context, structure, and policy behind section 261; Supreme Court precedent; and PTO regulations. We will begin by analyzing the statute's text and context, as interpreted by the Supreme Court. For the sake of clarity, we will discuss the two relevant phrases in the recording provision of section 261 separately.

a. The Phrase "Assignment, Grant or Conveyance" Concerns Transfers of Ownership Interests Only.

The historical meanings of the terms "assignment, grant or conveyance" all involved the transfer of an ownership interest. A patent "assignment" referred to a transaction that transferred specific rights in the patent, all involving the patent's title. A "grant," historically, also referred to a transfer of an ownership interest in a patent, but only as to a specific geographic area. Although older cases defining the term "conveyance" in the context of intangible property are sparse, and its historic meaning tended to vary, the common contemporaneous definition was "to transfer the legal title ... from the present owner to another." Abendroth v. Town of Greenwich, 29 Conn. 356 (1860). * * *

In summary, the statute's text, context, and structure, when read in the light of Supreme Court precedent, compel the conclusion that a security interest in a patent that does not involve a transfer of the rights of ownership is a "mere license" and is not an "assignment, grant or conveyance" within the meaning of 35 USC 261. And because section 261 provides that only an "assignment, grant or conveyance shall be void" as against subsequent purchasers and mortgagees, only transfers of ownership interests need to be recorded with the PTO.

In the present case, the parties do not dispute that the transaction that gave Petitioners their interest in the patent did not involve a transfer of an ownership interest in the patent. Petitioners held a "mere license," which did not have to be recorded with the PTO.

b. The Phrase "Subsequent Purchaser or Mortgagee" does not Include Subsequent Lien Creditors.

The Trustee's argument fails not only because a security interest that does not transfer ownership is not an "assignment, grant or conveyance," but also because he is not a subsequent "purchaser or mortgagee." Congress intended for parties to record their ownership interests in a patent so as to provide constructive notice only to subsequent holders of an ownership interest. Again, we derive our conclusion from the historical definitions of the words, from the context and structure of 35 USC 261, and from Supreme Court precedent.

The historical meaning of "purchaser or mortgagee" proves that Congress intended for the recording provision to give constructive notice only to subsequent holders of an ownership interest. For the sake of convenience, we begin with the definition of "mortgagee."

Historically, a "mortgagee" was someone who obtained title to property used to secure a debt. A "mortgage" must be differentiated from a "pledge," a term that is absent from the Patent Act. Professor Gilmore, in his treatise, Security Interests in Personal Property § 1.1, at 8, notes that the historical distinction between a pledge and a mortgage was that "the mortgagee got title or an estate whereas the pledgee got merely possession with a right to foreclose on default." * * * That the Patent Act refers to securing a patent through a "mortgage" but not through a "pledge" is significant, for both were common methods of using a patent as collateral. * * * It seems then, that by using the term "mortgagee," but not "lien" or "pledge," Congress intended in 1870 for the Patent Act's recording provision to protect only those who obtained title to a patent.

The term "purchaser" does not detract from this conclusion. 35 USC 261 instructs that an unrecorded "assignment, grant or conveyance" shall be void as against a subsequent "purchaser ... for a valuable consideration, without notice." The historical definition of a "purchaser for value and without notice" was a *bona fide* purchaser. A purchaser ...

who takes a conveyance purporting to pass the entire title, legal and equitable," who pays value and does not have notice of the rights of others to the property. Bouvier's Law Dictionary 1005 (Baldwin's Century ed. 1926). * * *

Congress, by stating that certain transactions shall be void as against a subsequent "purchaser or mortgagee" intended for the words to be read together: A "purchaser" is one who buys an ownership interest in the patent, while a "mortgagee" is one who obtains an ownership interest in a patent as collateral for a debt.

Our previous comments about the context and structure of 35 USC 261 support our conclusion that Congress intended to protect only subsequent holders of an ownership interest. As noted, the title of section 261 is "Ownership; assignment," which suggests that the recording provision is concerned only with ownership interests.

Similarly, the second paragraph delineates the types of transactions that section 261 covers—(1) the assignment of a patent, and (2) the grant or conveyance of an exclusive right in the patent to the whole or any specified part of the United States—each involving the transfer of an ownership interest in a patent. It follows that, when Congress referred to a "subsequent purchaser or mortgagee," it was simply describing the future recipients of those transactions. In one case the recipient bought the interest (purchaser), while in the other the recipient loaned money and received the interest as collateral (mortgagee). In either case, an ownership interest was transferred. * * *

In summary, the historical definitions of the terms "purchaser or mortgagee," taken in context and read in the light of Supreme Court precedent, establish that Congress was concerned only with providing constructive notice to subsequent parties who take an ownership interest in the patent in question.

The Trustee is not a subsequent "mortgagee," as that term is used in 35 USC 261, because the holder of a patent mortgage holds title to the patent itself. Instead, the Trustee is a hypothetical lien creditor. The Patent Act does not require parties to record documents in order to provide constructive notice to subsequent lien creditors who do not hold title to the patent.

3. Public Policies that Underlie Recording Provisions Cannot Override the Text of the Patent Act.

The Trustee argues that requiring lien creditors to record their interests with the PTO is in line with the general policy behind recording statutes. It may be, as the Trustee argues, that a national system of filing security interests is more efficient and effective than a state-by-state system. However, there is no statutory hook upon which to hang the Trustee's policy arguments. Moreover, we are not concerned with the policy behind recording statutes generally but, rather, with the policy behind 35 USC 261 specifically.

35 USC 261, as we have demonstrated and as its label suggests, is concerned with patent ownership. In that provision Congress gave patent holders the right to transfer their ownership interests, but only in specific ways. The congressional policy behind that decision was to protect the patent holder and the public for, as the Supreme Court put it,

> it was obviously not the intention of the legislature to permit several monopolies to be made out of one, and divided among different persons within the same limits. Such a division would inevitably lead to fraudulent impositions upon persons who desired to purchase the use of the improvement, and would subject a party who, under a mistake as to his rights, used the invention without authority, to be harassed by a multiplicity of suits instead of one, and to successive recoveries of damages by different persons holding different portions of the patent right in the same place.

Gayler v. Wilder, 51 U.S. (10 How.) 501, 519-20 (1850). The recording provision, if read to include ownership interests only, is perfectly aligned with that policy. By contrast, a security interest in a patent does not make "several monopolies ... out of one, ... divided among different persons within the same limits." Gayler, 51 U.S. at 519.

We must interpret 35 USC 261 in the light of the purposes that Congress was seeking to serve. Congress simply was not concerned with non-ownership interests in patents, and this limitation was well understood at the time. As explained in a venerable treatise on the law of patents:

> A license is not such a conveyance of an interest in the patented invention as to affect its ownership, and hence is not required to be recorded .... The value of the patented invention to the vendee may be impaired by such outstanding licenses, but of this he

> must inform himself at his own risk as best he may. The record
> of a license, not being legally required, is not constructive notice
> to any person for any purpose.

2 Robinson § 817, at 602-03 (footnotes omitted).

The Patent Act was written long before the advent of the "unitary" Article 9 security interest. But we must interpret 35 USC 261 as Congress wrote it. The Constitution entrusts to Congress, not to the courts, the role of ensuring that statutes keep up with changes in financing practices. It is notable that Congress has revised the Patent Act numerous times since its enactment, most recently in 1999, see Pub. L. 106-113, but it has not updated the Act's recording provision. We decline the Trustee's invitation to do so in Congress' place.

4. Cases Interpreting the Copyright Act do not Control.

The Trustee's final argument is that this court should follow *Peregrine*, in which a bankruptcy court held that the Copyright Act preempts state methods of perfecting security interests in copyrights. The court in *Peregrine* observed that the "federal copyright laws ensure predictability and certainty of copyright ownership, promote national uniformity and avoid the practical difficulties of determining and enforcing an author's rights under the differing laws and in the separate courts of the various States." 116 Bankr. at 199 (internal quotation marks omitted). The court reasoned that allowing state methods to stand would conflict with those goals.

Of course, *Peregrine* is not binding on this court although, in the present case, we have no occasion to pass on its correctness as an interpretation of the Copyright Act. We note, however, that the Copyright Act, by its terms, governs security interests. The Copyright Act governs any "transfer" of ownership, which is defined by statute to include any "hypothecation." 17 USC 101, 201(d)(1). A "hypothecation" is the "pledging of something as security without delivery of title or possession." Black's Law Dictionary 747 (7th ed. 1999).

By contrast, the Patent Act does not refer to a "hypothecation" and, as we have demonstrated, does not refer to security interests at all. The fact that one federal intellectual property statute with a recording provision expressly refers to security interests (the Copyright Act), while another does not (the Patent Act), is more evidence that security interests are *outside* the scope of 35 USC 261. * * *

6. There is no Conflict Between the Patent Act and Article 9 in this Case.

Because the Patent Act does not cover security interests or lien creditors at all, there is no conflict between 35 USC 261 and Article 9. Petitioners did not have to file with the PTO to perfect their security interest as to a subsequent lien creditor.

B. Article 9's Step-Back Provision

The Trustee's second major argument is that Article 9 itself requires that a creditor file notice of a secured transaction with the PTO in order to perfect a security interest. [9-311(a)] states that the filing of a financing statement pursuant to Article 9 "is not necessary or effective to perfect a security interest in property subject to ... [a] statute ... which provides for a national or international registration ... or which specifies a place of filing different from that specified in" Article 9. If [9-311(a)] applies, then a party *must* utilize the federal registration system in order to perfect its security interest.

The question, then, is whether the Patent Act is "[a] statute ... which provides for a national or international registration ... or which specifies a place of filing different from that specified in" Article 9. [9-311(a)]. The Patent Act is clearly a statute that provides for a national registration. But that begs the more focused question: a national registration *of what?* Courts have tended to use the context of the statute to amplify the bare text and to answer the focused question: a national registration *of security interests.* For example, in Aerocon Engineering, Inc. v. Silicon Valley Bank (In re World Auxiliary Power Co.), 244 Bankr. 149, 155 (N.D. Cal. 1999), the bankruptcy court observed that [9-311(a)], if read literally,

> would be absurd. It would provide that, whenever a particular type of collateral may be registered nationally, regardless of whether the federal statute specifies a place for filing a security interest different than that provided by the UCC, filing a UCC-1 financing statement would be neither necessary nor effective to perfect a security interest in the collateral.

Courts have thus read [9-311(a)] as providing that federal filing is necessary only when there is a statute that "provides for" a national registration *of security interests.* We agree with that interpretation.

Under that more restrictive definition, it is clear that the Patent Act is outside the scope of [9-311(a)]. As we have explained, a transaction that grants a party a security interest in a patent but does *not* effect a transfer of title is *not* the type of "assignment, grant or conveyance" that is referred to in 35 USC 261. The transaction in this case did not transfer an ownership interest. Therefore, [9-311(a)] did not require that Petitioners record their security interest with the PTO.

The Comments to Article 9 of the UCC support this view. Comment 8 states that F9-302(3)

> exempts from the filing provisions of this Article transactions as to which an adequate system of filing, state or federal, has been set up outside this Article and subsection (4) makes clear that when such a system exists perfection of a relevant security interest can be had only through compliance with that system.

The Comments instruct that "17 USC § § 28, 30 (copyrights), 49 USC § 1403 (aircraft), [and] 49 USC § 20(c) (railroads)" are examples of the "type of federal statutes" referred to in [9-311(a)]. Each of the statutes listed in the Comments refers expressly to security interests. See 17 USC 101; 49 USC 44107; 49 USC 11301. The Patent Act is not among them.

C. Conclusion

Because 35 USC 261 concerns only transactions that effect a transfer of an ownership interest in a patent, the Patent Act does not preempt Article 9, and neither [9-109(c)] nor [9-311(a)] applies. Consequently, Petitioners perfected their security interest in Debtor's patent by recording it with the California Secretary of State. They have priority over the Trustee's claim because they recorded their interest before the filing of the bankruptcy petition.

AFFIRMED.

COMMENTS AND QUESTIONS: SECURITY INTERESTS IN INTELLECTUAL PROPERTY

We all know the buzzwords: it's a high-tech world, a "knowledge-based" economy, where the traditional hard assets central to Article 9 are quickly being pushed to the periphery. The companies of this age are Microsoft and Disney, McDonald's and Nike. Intellectual property—patents, copyrights and trademarks—are the defining assets of these companies. The trademark Nike Swoosh is more visible at international sporting events than national flags, while the Golden Arches span the globe from Moscow, Idaho to Moscow, Russia. Disney's copyrighted characters are ubiquitous and ever-growing as its animators turn out yet another Summer blockbuster. Microsoft claims a mix of copyrights and patents on Windows and other programs.

Intellectual property issues will be at stake in a business secured transaction of any size. It would be nice if it were straightforward to take a security interest in intellectual property, but it isn't. Security interests in intellectual property occur at the crossroads of Article 9 and federal intellectual property law. The links between these areas are, at best, tangled. As a result, there is a substantial risk of error in this area—of becoming secured-transactions roadkill—and the careful lawyer elides that risk by filing everywhere that might be relevant.

Start within Article 9 itself. "General intangibles"—our residual category set out in 9-102(a)(42)—is the place to go, and a security interest in general intangibles is perfected through filing. 9-109(c)(1) provides that "[t]his Article does not apply to the extent that a statute, regulation or treaty of the United States preempts this article." This is standard: federal law displaces state law. The tricky question is understanding the scope of that preemption. Federal law might establish this scope directly, but somewhat surprisingly, state law may play a role as well. In that regard, consider the relevant chunks of 9-311:

> (a) **[Security interest subject to other law.]** Except as otherwise provided in subsection (d), the filing of a financing statement is not necessary or effective to perfect a security interest in property subject to:
>
>> (1) a statute, regulation, or treaty of the United States whose requirements for a security interest's obtaining priority over the rights of a lien creditor with respect to the property preempt Section 9-310(a);
>>
>> * * *
>
> (b) **[Compliance with other law.]** Compliance with the requirements of a statute, regulation, or treaty described in subsection (a) for obtaining priority over the rights of a lien creditor is equivalent to the filing of a financing statement under this article. Except as otherwise provided in subsection (d) and Sections 9-313 and 9-316(d) and (e) for goods covered by a certificate of title, a security interest in property subject to a statute, regulation, or treaty described in subsection (a) may be perfected only by compliance with those requirements, and a security in-

terest so perfected remains perfected notwithstanding a change
in the use or transfer of possession of the collateral.

State law can embrace federal law, even if federal law does not insist
that it do so. To be more concrete, federal law may create a recordation
system, and a security interest might be recorded in that system, as occurs
with the federal recording system for airplanes and engines. Federal law
might otherwise say very little about the security interest. 9-109(c)(1) suggests that federal law governs only to the extent that it affirmatively displaces state law. 9-311(b) requires filings in a federal filing scheme, even if
that scheme itself does not insist on complete federal control over filings.
That is, 9-311(b) looks only to the question of whether federal law
preempts 9-310(a) in evaluating a priority dispute between a secured
creditor and a lien creditor. Put differently, 9-311(b) incorporates a federal
filing scheme into Article 9 and displaces its normal internal filing rules.

Why? To see this, again consider the relevant section from the patent
law, 35 USC 261:

> Subject to the provisions of this title, patents shall have the
> attributes of personal property. Applications for patent, patents,
> or any interest therein, shall be assignable in law by an instru-
> ment in writing .... An assignment, grant or conveyance shall
> be void as against any subsequent purchaser or mortgagee for a
> valuable consideration, without notice, unless it is recorded in
> the Patent and Trademark Office within three months from its
> date or prior to the date of such subsequent purchase or mort-
> gage.

In reading this provision, *Cybernetic Services* focuses on the scope of two
different aspects, first "assignment, grant or conveyance" and second "subsequent purchaser or mortgagee."

Start with the second provision. Note what it says about lien creditors:
nothing. The voidness provision benefits only a purchaser or a mortgagee.
It should not benefit an unsecured creditor who levies on a patent, and,
most importantly, therefore should not benefit the trustee in bankruptcy as
a hypothetical lien creditor under BC 544(a). It is precisely such an interest that was being asserted in *Cybernetic Services*. Where does this put us?
Should we understand that a secured creditor who fails to record with the
PTO runs no risk against unsecured creditors?

Probably not. Section 261's preemption of Article 9 is seemingly quite
limited. A natural reading is that section 261 simply doesn't cover unse-

cured creditors and that the underlying state law—Article 9—applies. That would mean that a secured creditor with an interest in a patent must file in the state UCC system to be perfected against a lien creditor and need not—and cannot—file with the PTO to do so. See In re Transportation Design and Technology, Inc., 48 Bankr. 635 (Bankr. S.D. Calif. 1985), which held exactly this. *Cybernetic Services* reaches the same result in its examination of "subsequent purchaser or mortgagee" but does so less directly.

Turn from lien creditors to secured creditors and consider again problem 8-2 (Bank files in the UCC records while Finco records with the PTO). *Cybernetic Services* seems to tell us that Bank wins. The Ninth Circuit reads both key clauses in section 261 to apply only to transactions affecting the title to the patent. Although 9-202 makes clear that the location of title is irrelevant for most secured transactions, in a garden-variety secured transaction title will remain with the debtor. Such a secured transaction, on the analysis of *Cybernetic Services*, would not trigger the application of section 261. *Cybernetic Services* applies directly in only the Ninth Circuit, so secured lenders will need to be careful about assuming that its analysis will apply everywhere. This suggests continued filing with the PTO and in the UCC records would be wise.

Now that we have mastered (?) patents, switch to copyright. The core provision of U.S. copyright law is set out in a single sentence in 17 USC 102(a): "Copyright protection subsists, in accordance with this title, in original works of authorship fixed in any tangible medium of expression, now known or later developed, from which they can be perceived, reproduced, or otherwise communicated, either directly or with the aid of a machine or device." This turns out to be stunningly broad and comprehensive.

Write a poem on a piece of paper right now. Poetry worthy of Browning? It doesn't matter. While the patent system places hurdles in front of inventors—standards that must be met if a patent is to be granted—copyright law just insists on a work that the author made up and fixed. To hold a copyright in that work, you need not do *anything* more. You don't need to attach a notice—"Copyright © 2009. Randal C. Picker"—though doing so will create statutory benefits. (And before 1976, you did need to adhere to formalities to maintain copyright, but in 1976, U.S. copyright law changed by dropping some of its formal requirements to harmonize with the copyright law of other countries.)

You need not file the work with the U.S. government—we call that registering the work—though you need to do so if you want to file suit for infringements of the work. 17 USC 411(a). That means—and this turns out to matter for secured transactions in copyrighted works—that we can split copyrighted works into two groups: unregistered works and registered works.

8-3: FIRST-TO-FILE (OR NOT)?

- On May 1st, Debtor executes a document in favor of Bank providing that "[d]ebtor hereby grants a security interest in the copyright to the song 'New York, New York,' registration number 12345, to secure a $10,000 loan by Bank to Debtor of even date herewith."

- Two weeks later, on May 15th, Debtor enters into a second transaction, this time with Finco, and executes a similar document for a new loan from Finco. Finco consults every record imaginable before lending money, and finds nothing. Finco immediately records the transfer in the federal Copyright Office.

- ¤ One week later, on May 22nd, Bank records its transfer in the Copyright Office. How does this case come out if we treat the Copyright Office as the appropriate place for filing but otherwise ordinary UCC rules control? How does this case come out if applicable law is the relevant section from the Copyright Act, 17 USC 205:

> Sec. 205. Recordation of transfers and other documents
>
> (a) Conditions for Recordation. Any transfer of copyright ownership or other document pertaining to a copyright may be recorded in the Copyright Office if the document filed for recordation bears the actual signature of the person who executed it, or if it is accompanied by a sworn or official certification that it is a true copy of the original, signed document.
>
> * * *
>
> (c) Recordation as Constructive Notice. Recordation of a document in the Copyright Office gives all persons constructive notice of the facts stated in the recorded document, if—

(1) the document, or material attached to it, specifically identifies the work to which it pertains so that, after the document is indexed by the Register of Copyrights, it would be revealed by a reasonable search under the title or registration number of the work; and

(2) registration has been made for the work.

(d) Priority Between Conflicting Transfers. As between two conflicting transfers, the one executed first prevails if it is recorded, in the manner required to give constructive notice under subsection (c), within one month after its execution in the United States or within two months after its execution outside the United States, or at any time before recordation in such manner of the later transfer. Otherwise the later transfer prevails if recorded first in such manner, and if taken in good faith, for valuable consideration or on the basis of a binding promise to pay royalties, and without notice of the earlier transfer.

¤ Suppose that Finco learns of the transfer to Bank before completing its transaction and before Bank has recorded in the Copyright Office. Would this alter the outcome under the UCC? the Copyright Act?

• Suppose that Finco registers—files—with the Copyright Office notwithstanding the knowledge it has acquired of Bank's interest. Debtor now enters into a third transaction, granting a security interest in the copyright to Creditco. Creditco files immediately. Finally, Bank records its interest with the Copyright Office.

¤ What are the priorities under the UCC? the Copyright Act?

8-4: A MICKEY MOUSE PROBLEM?

• Disney enters into a contract with Proctor & Gamble to license Mickey Mouse for diaper decorations. The contract provides for monthly royalty payments paid by P&G to Disney.

• Disney in turn borrows money on a secured basis, posting the contract as collateral.

¤ How should this security interest be created and perfected? Should we treat the contract as an account receivable under 9-102(a)(2) and file in the UCC filing system? Is this an interest in intellectual property requiring a filing in the federal Copyright Office?

8-5: YESTERDAY ALL MY TROUBLES SEEMED SO FAR AWAY

- Paul, a songwriter, wakes up one morning, inspired. He quickly dashes off a song on a piece of paper. Paul then goes to Bank and seeks to borrow $10,000 based on the song. Surprisingly, Bank lends Paul the money. Paul executes a standard security agreement covering the song and Bank files a financing statement in the UCC records.

- The next day, Paul registers the song with U.S. copyright office. He then approaches Finco for a loan. Finco lends the money on a secured basis and files a record of that loan with the U.S. Copyright office.

- ¤ Who has priority between Bank and Finco? Is this a change of use situation contemplated by 9-311(b)?

Aerocon Engineering, Inc. v. Silicon Valley Bank (In re World Auxiliary Power Company)

United States Court of Appeals, Ninth Circuit, 2002.
303 F.3d 1120.

■ KLEINFELD, CIRCUIT JUDGE

In this case we decide whether federal or state law governs priority of security interests in unregistered copyrights.

Facts

Basically, this is a bankruptcy contest over unregistered copyrights between a bank that got a security interest in the copyrights from the owners and perfected it under state law, and a company that bought the copyrights from the bankruptcy trustees after the copyright owners went bankrupt. These simple facts are all that matters to the outcome of this case, although the details are complex.

Three affiliated California corporations—World Auxiliary Power, World Aerotechnology, and Air Refrigeration Systems—designed and sold products for modifying airplanes. The FAA must approve modifications of civilian aircraft by issuing "Supplemental Type Certificates." The three companies owned copyrights in the drawings, technical manuals, blue-prints, and computer software used to make the modifications. Some of these copyrighted materials were attached to the Supplemental Type Certificates. The companies did not register their copyrights with the United States Copyright Office.

The companies got financing from Silicon Valley Bank, one of the appellees in this case. Two of the companies borrowed the money directly, the third guaranteed the loan. The security agreement, as is common, granted the bank a security interest in a broad array of presently owned and after-acquired collateral. The security agreement covered "all goods and equipment now owned or hereafter acquired," as well as inventory, contract rights, general intangibles, blueprints, drawings, computer programs, accounts receivable, patents, cash, bank deposits, and pretty much anything else the debtor owned or might be "hereafter acquired." The security agreement and financing statement also covered "[a]ll copyright rights, copyright applications, copyright registrations, and like protections in each work of authorship and derivative work thereof, whether published or unpublished, now owned or hereafter acquired."

The bank perfected its security interest in the collateral, including the copyrights, pursuant to California's version of Article 9 of the Uniform Commercial Code,[3] by filing UCC-1 financing statements with the California Secretary of State. The bank also took possession of the Supplemental Type Certificates and the attached copyrighted materials. But the copyrights still weren't registered with the United States Copyright Office, and the bank did not record any document showing the transfer of a security interest with the Copyright Office. See 17 USC 205.

Subsequently, the three debtor companies filed simultaneous but separate bankruptcy proceedings. Their copyrights were among their major assets. Aerocon Engineering, one of their creditors (and the appellant in this case), wanted the copyrights. Aerocon was working on a venture with another company, Advanced Aerospace, and its President, Michael Gilsen, and an officer and director, Merritt Widen (all appellees in this case), to engineer and sell aircraft modifications using the debtors' designs. Their prospective venture faced a problem: Silicon Valley Bank claimed a securi-

---

[3] Although California adopted the revised Article 9 of the Uniform Commercial Code, effective July 1, 2001, the revised statute "does not affect an action, case, or proceeding commenced before July 1, 2001," 9-702(c). As this litigation was pending on that date, we apply the former Article 9.

ty interest in the copyrights. To solve this problem, Aerocon worked out a deal with Gilsen, Widen, and a company named Erose Capital (not a party in this case) to buy the debtors' assets, including their copyrights, from the bankruptcy trustees along with the trustees' right to sue to avoid Silicon Valley Bank's security interest. Once Aerocon owned the copyrights, it planned to exercise the trustees' power to avoid Silicon Valley Bank's security interest so that the venture would own the copyrights free and clear.

The transaction to purchase the copyrights and the trustees' avoidance action worked as follows. First, Aerocon paid the bankruptcy trustees $90,000, $30,000 for each of the three bankruptcy estates. Then, the trustees, with the bankruptcy court's approval, sold the estates' assets and avoidance action to Erose Capital, Gilsen, and Widen. Gilsen and Widen then sold their two-thirds interest to their company, Advanced Aerospace.

After this transaction was completed, for reasons not relevant to this appeal, Aerocon's planned joint venture with Advanced Aerospace and Gilsen and Widen fell through. In the aftermath, Erose Capital sold its one-third interest to Aerocon and Advanced Aerospace sold its two-thirds interest to Airweld. These transactions meant that Aerocon and Airweld owned the debtors' copyrights and the trustees' avoidance action as tenants in common.

Meanwhile, Silicon Valley Bank won relief from the bankruptcy court's automatic stay and, based on its security interest, foreclosed on the copyrights. Then the bank sold the copyrights to Advanced Aerospace (Gilsen's and Widen's company) which then sold the copyrights to Airweld. Had Aerocon's joint venture with Gilsen and Widen gone through, buying off the trustees' and the bank's interests in the copyrights would have been a sensible, if expensive, way to ensure that the venture owned the copyrights free and clear. But, of course, the venture did not go through, and Gilsen and Widen's affiliations had changed. Thus Gilsen and Widen's purchase from the bank and sale to Airweld meant that Aerocon, which had paid $90,000 for the copyrights and had owned them as a tenant in common with Airweld, now had a claim adverse to Airweld's, which purportedly owned the copyrights in fee simple.

Aerocon brought an adversary proceeding in each of the three bankruptcy proceedings against Silicon Valley Bank, Advanced Aerospace, Gilsen, Widen, and Airweld. (These adversary proceedings were later consolidated.) Aerocon sued to avoid Silicon Valley Bank's security interest and to recover the copyrights or their value from subsequent transferees Advanced Aerospace, Gilsen, Widen, and Airweld. *** The bankruptcy court then granted summary judgment to Silicon Valley Bank on all of Aerocon's claims on the ground that the bank had perfected its security interest in the copyrights under California's version of Article 9 of the Uniform Commercial Code. ***

Analysis

We have jurisdiction to review the judgment of the district court and we review de novo.

Copyright and bankruptcy law set the context for this litigation, but the legal issue is priority of security interests. The bankruptcy trustees sold Aerocon their power to avoid any security interest "that is voidable by a creditor that extends credit to the debtor at the time of the commencement of the case, and that obtains, at such time and with respect to such credit, a judicial lien ... ." See BC 544(a). Under this "strong-arm" provision, Aerocon has the status of an "ideal creditor" who perfected his lien at the last possible moment before the bankruptcy commenced, and if this hypothetical creditor would take priority over Silicon Valley Bank's lien, then Aerocon may avoid the bank's security interest.

Whether Aerocon's hypothetical lien creditor would take priority turns on whether federal or state law governs the perfection of security interests in unregistered copyrights. The bank did everything necessary to perfect its security interest under state law, so if state law governs, the bank has priority and wins. The bank did nothing, however, to perfect its interest under federal law, so if federal law governs, Aerocon's hypothetical lien creditor arguably has priority, although the parties dispute whether Aerocon might face additional legal hurdles.

We are assisted in deciding this case by two opinions, neither of which controls, but both of which are thoughtful and scholarly. The first is the bankruptcy court's published opinion in this case, Aerocon Engineering Inc. v. Silicon Valley Bank (In re World Auxiliary Power Co.), 244 Bankr. 149 (Bankr. N.D. Cal. 1999), which we affirm largely for the reasons the bankruptcy judge gave. The second is a published district court opinion, National Peregrine, Inc. v. Capitol Federal Savings & Loan Association (In re Peregrine Entertainment, Ltd.), 116 Bankr. 194 (C.D. Cal. 1990), the holdings of which we adopt but, like the bankruptcy court, distinguish and limit.

Our analysis begins with the Copyright Act of 1976. Under the Act, "copyright protection subsists ... in original works of authorship fixed in any tangible medium of expression...." While an owner must register his copyright as a condition of seeking certain infringement remedies, registration is permissive, not mandatory, and is not a condition for copyright protection. Likewise, the Copyright Act's provision for recording "transfers of copyright ownership" (the Act's term that includes security interests) is permissive, not mandatory: "Any transfer of copyright ownership or other document pertaining to copyright *may* be recorded in the Copyright Office ... ." 17 USC 205(a) (emphasis added). The Copyright Act's use of the word "mortgage" as one definition of a "transfer"[26] is properly read to include security interests under Article 9 of the Uniform Commercial Code.

Under the Copyright Act,

> [a]s between two conflicting transfers, the one executed first prevails if it is recorded, *in the manner required to give constructive notice* ... within one month after its execution ... or at any time before recordation ... of the later transfer. Otherwise the later transfer prevails if recorded first in such manner, and if taken in good faith, for valuable consideration ... and without notice of the earlier transfer.

17 USC 205(d) (emphasis added).

The phrase "constructive notice" refers to another subsection providing that recording gives constructive notice

> but only if—
>
> (1) the document, or material attached to it, specifically identifies the work to which it pertains so that, after the document is indexed by the Register of Copyrights, it would be revealed by a reasonable search under *the title or registration number* of the work; and
>
> (2) registration has been made for the work.

Id. 205(c) (emphasis added).

A copyrighted work only gets a "title or registration number" that would be revealed by a search if it's registered. Since an unregistered work

---

[26] 17 USC 101 ("A 'transfer of copyright ownership' is an assignment, mortgage, exclusive license, or any other conveyance, alienation, or hypothecation of a copyright....").

doesn't have a title or registration number that would be "revealed by a reasonable search," recording a security interest in an unregistered copyright in the Copyright Office wouldn't give "constructive notice" under the Copyright Act, and, because it wouldn't, it couldn't preserve a creditor's priority. There just isn't any way for a secured creditor to preserve a priority in an unregistered copyright by recording anything in the Copyright Office. And the secured party can't get around this problem by registering the copyright, because the secured party isn't the owner of the copyright, and the Copyright Act states that only "the owner of copyright ... may obtain registration of the copyright claim ... ." Id. 408(a).

Aerocon argues that the Copyright Act's recordation and priority scheme exclusively controls perfection and priority of security interests in copyrights. First, Aerocon argues that state law, here the California UCC, by its own terms "steps back" and defers to the federal scheme. Second, whether or not the UCC steps back, Aerocon argues that Congress has preempted the UCC as it applies to copyrights. We address each argument in turn.

A. UCC Step Back Provisions

Article 9 of the Uniform Commercial Code, as adopted in California, provides that unperfected creditors are subordinate to perfected, and as between perfected security interests, the first perfected interest prevails. The bank perfected first under state law by filing a financing statement with the California Secretary of State on existing and after-acquired copyrights. The UCC treats copyrights as "general intangibles." [9-102(a)(42)]. Security interests in general intangibles are properly perfected under the UCC by state filings such as the one made by the bank in this case.

To avoid conflict with the federal law, the UCC has two "step-back provisions," by which state law steps back and out of the way of conflicting federal law. The first, more general "step-back" provision says that Article 9 "does not apply ... [t]o a security interest subject to any statute of the United States to the extent that such statute governs the rights of parties to and third parties affected by transactions in particular types of property ... ." [9-109(c)(1)]. As applied to copyrights, the relevant UCC Official Comment makes it clear that this step-back clause does not exclude all security interests in copyrights from UCC coverage, just those for which the federal Copyright Act "governs the rights" of relevant parties:

> Although the Federal Copyright Act contains provisions permitting the mortgage of a copyright and for the recording of an

assignment of a copyright such a statute would not seem to contain sufficient provisions regulating the rights of the parties and third parties to exclude security interests in copyrights from the provisions of this Article.

The second step-back provision speaks directly to perfection of security interests. It exempts from UCC filing requirements security interests in property "subject to ... [a] statute ... of the United States which provides for a national ... registration ... or which specifies a place of filing different from that specified in this division for filing of the security interest." [9-311(a)(1)]. Compliance with such a statute "is equivalent to the filing of a financing statement ... and a security interest in property subject to the statute ... can be perfected only by compliance therewith ... ." [9-311(b)].

Under the UCC's two step-back provisions, there can be no question that, when a copyright has been registered, a security interest can be perfected only by recording the transfer in the Copyright Office. As the district court held in *Peregrine*, the Copyright Act satisfies the broad UCC step-back provision by creating a priority scheme that "governs the rights of parties to and third parties affected by transactions," [9-109(c)(1)], in registered copyrights and satisfies the narrow step-back provision by creating a single "national registration" for security interests in registered copyrights. Thus, under these step-back provisions, if a borrower's collateral is a registered copyright, the secured party cannot perfect by filing a financing statement under the UCC in the appropriate state office, or alternatively by recording a transfer in the Copyright Office. For registered copyrights, the only proper place to file is the Copyright Office. We adopt *Peregrine's* holding to this effect.

However, the question posed by this case is whether the UCC steps back as to unregistered copyrights. We, like the bankruptcy court in this case, conclude that it does not. As we've explained, there's no way for a secured creditor to perfect a security interest in unregistered copyrights by recording in the Copyright Office. The UCC's broader step-back provision says that the UCC doesn't apply to a security interest "to the extent" that a federal statute governs the rights of the parties. The UCC doesn't defer to the Copyright Act under this broad step-back provision because the Copyright Act doesn't provide for the rights of secured parties to unregistered copyrights; it only covers the rights of secured parties in registered copyrights. The UCC's narrow step-back provision says the UCC doesn't apply if a federal statute "provides for a national ... registration ... or which specifies a place of filing different from that specified in this division for filing of the security interest." [9-311(a)(1)]. The UCC doesn't defer to the Copyright Act under this narrow step-back provision because the Copyright Act doesn't provide a "national registration": unregistered copyrights don't have to be registered, and because unregistered copyrights don't have a registered name and number, under the Copyright Act there isn't any place to file anything regarding unregistered copyrights that makes any legal difference. So, as a matter of state law, the UCC doesn't step back in deference to federal law, but governs perfection and priority of security interests in unregistered copyrights itself.

B. Federal Preemption

It wouldn't matter that state law doesn't step back, however, if Congress chose to knock state law out of the way by preemption. Federal law preempts state law under three circumstances. The first is "express preemption," where Congress explicitly preempts state law. Keams v. Tempe Technical Institute, Inc., 39 F.3d 222, 225 (9th Cir. 1994) (internal quotation marks and citation omitted). The second is "field preemption," where Congress implicitly preempts state law by "occupy[ing] the entire field, leaving no room for the operation of state law." Id. at 225. The third is "conflict preemption," where we infer preemption because "compliance with both state and federal law would be impossible, or state law stands as an obstacle to the accomplishment and execution of the full purposes and objectives of Congress." Id. We presume that federal law does not preempt "state law in areas traditionally regulated by the States." Id. (internal quotation marks and citation omitted).

Aerocon argues, relying on *Peregrine*, that Congress intended to occupy the field of security interests in copyrights. Aerocon also argues that the UCC actually conflicts with the Copyright Act's text and purpose.

Because Aerocon relies so heavily on *Peregrine* and its progeny, we will briefly review the facts and holding of that case. In *Peregrine*, a bank had secured a loan with the debtor's copyrights in a library of films licensed out for exhibition and related accounts receivable and attempted to perfect its security interest by filing a UCC financing statement. The debtor later filed for bankruptcy and, as debtor-in-possession, sued in the bankruptcy court to avoid the bank's lien on the ground that the bank had failed to perfect its lien by failing to record it with the Copyright Office. The bankruptcy court held for the bank, and the debtor-in-possession appealed to the district court. The district court reversed, holding that "the comprehensive scope of the Copyright Act's recording provisions, along with the unique federal interests they implicate, support the view that federal law preempts state methods of perfecting security interests in copyrights ... ." 116 Bankr. at 199. The district court reasoned that federal law preempts state law because "the Copyright Act establishes a uniform method for recording security interests in copyrights" and creates a different priority scheme than state law, and because "competing recordation schemes ... lessen [ ] the utility of each."

Although *Peregrine* did not specify whether the copyrights at issue were registered, it is probably safe to assume that they were, and that the *Peregrine* court did not have a case involving unregistered copyrights, because the collateral at issue was a movie library that got licensed out to exhibitors and, in the ordinary course, copyrights in such films would be registered. Also, as the bankruptcy judge in the case at bar pointed out, *Peregrine's* "analysis only works if the copyright was registered." The district court in *Peregrine* held that Congress had preempted state law because of "the comprehensive scope of the Copyright Act's recording provisions." As applied to registered copyrights, the Act's recording scheme is comprehensive; it doesn't exclude any registered copyright from its coverage. But as applied to unregistered copyrights, the Act doesn't have comprehensive recording provisions. Likewise, *Peregrine* notes that "[t]o the extent there are competing recordation schemes, this lessens the utility of each." This holds true for registered copyrights. But there aren't two competing filing systems for unregistered copyrights. The Copyright Act doesn't create one. Only the UCC creates a filing system applicable to unregistered copyrights. *Peregrine* reasoned that creditors could get conflicting results under the UCC and the Copyright Act, because each provides a different priority scheme. That's true only for registered copyrights. The Copyright Act wouldn't provide a conflicting answer as to unregistered copyrights because it wouldn't provide any answer at all. *Peregrine's* holding applies to registered copyrights, and we adopt it, but as the bankruptcy court reasoned in the case at bar, it does not apply to unregistered copyrights.

* * * Moreover, * * * extension[] of *Peregrine* to unregistered copyrights would make registration of copyright a necessary prerequisite of perfecting a security interest in a copyright. The implication of requiring registration as a condition of perfection is that Congress intended to make unregistered copyrights practically useless as collateral, an inference the text and purpose of the Copyright Act do not warrant.

In the one instance where the Copyright Act conditions some action concerning a copyright on its registration—the right to sue for infringement— the Act makes that condition explicit. See 17 USC 411(a). Nowhere does the Copyright Act explicitly condition the use of copyrights as collateral on their registration. Second, the Copyright Act contemplates that most copyrights will not be registered. Since copyright is created every time people set pen to paper, or fingers to keyboard, and affix their thoughts in a tangible medium, writers, artists, computer programmers, and web designers would have to have their hands tied down to keep them from creating unregistered copyrights all day every day. Moreover, the Copyright Act says that copyrights "may" be registered, implying that they don't have to be, and since a fee is charged and time and effort is required, the statute sets up a regime in which most copyrights won't ever be registered.

Though Congress must have contemplated that most copyrights would be unregistered, it only provided for protection of security interests in registered copyrights. There is no reason to infer from Congress's silence as to unregistered copyrights an intent to make such copyrights useless as collateral by preempting state law but not providing any federal priority scheme for unregistered copyrights. That would amount to a presumption in favor of federal preemption, but we are required to presume just the opposite. The only reasonable inference to draw is that Congress chose not to create a federal scheme for security interests in unregistered copyrights, but left the matter to States, which have traditionally governed security interests.

For similar reasons, we reject Aerocon's argument that congressional intent to preempt can be inferred from conflict between the Copyright Act and the UCC There is no conflict between the statutory provisions: the Copyright Act doesn't speak to security interests in unregistered copyrights, the UCC does.

Nor does the application of state law frustrate the objectives of federal copyright law. The basic objective of federal copyright law is to "promote the Progress of Science and useful Arts," U.S. Constitution, article 1, section 8, by "establishing a marketable right to the use of one's expression" and supplying "the economic incentive to create and disseminate ideas." Harper & Row, Publishers v. Nation Enterprises, 471 U.S. 539, 558 (1985). Aerocon argues that allowing perfection under state law would frustrate this objective by injecting uncertainty in secured transactions involving copyrights. Aerocon conjures up the image of a double-crossing debtor who, having gotten financing based on unregistered copyrights, registers them, thus triggering federal law, and gets financing from a second creditor, who then records its interest with the Copyright Office and takes priority. We decline to prevent this fraud by drawing the unreasonable inference that Congress intended to render copyrights useless as collateral unless registered.

Prudent creditors will always demand that debtors disclose any copyright registrations and perfect under federal law and will protect themselves against subsequent creditors gaining priority by means of covenants and policing mechanisms. The several amici banks and banking association in this case argue that most lenders would lend against unregistered copyrights subject to the remote risk of being "primed" by subsequent creditors; but no lender would lend against unregistered copyrights if they couldn't perfect their security interest. As we read the law, unregistered copyrights have value as collateral, discounted by the remote potential for priming. As Aerocon reads the law, they would have no value at all.

Aerocon's argument also ignores the special problem of copyrights as after-acquired collateral. To use just one example of the multi-industry need to use after-acquired (really after-created) intangible intellectual property as collateral, now that the high-tech boom of the 1990s has passed, and software companies don't attract equity financing like tulips in seventeenth century Holland, these companies will have to borrow more capital. After-acquired software is likely to serve as much of their collateral. Like liens in any other after-acquired collateral, liens in after-acquired software must attach immediately upon the creation of the software to satisfy creditors. Creditors would not tolerate a gap between the software's creation and the registration of the copyright. If software developers had to register copyrights in their software before using it as collateral, the last half hour of the day for a software company would be spent preparing and mailing utterly pointless forms to the Copyright Office to register and record security interests. Our reading of the law "promote[s] the Progress of Science and useful Arts" by preserving the collateral value of unregistered copyrights, which is to say, the vast majority of copyrights. Aerocon's reading of the law—which would force producers engaged in the ongoing creation of copyrightable material to constantly register and update the registrations of their works before obtaining credit—does not.

Conclusion

Regarding perfection and priority of security interests in unregistered copyrights, the California UCC has not stepped back in deference to federal law, and federal law has not preempted the UCC. Silicon Valley Bank has a perfected security interest in the debtors' unregistered copyrights, and Aerocon, standing in the bankruptcy trustees' shoes, cannot prevail against it.

AFFIRMED.

COMMENTS AND QUESTIONS

Aerocon Engineering draws a clear line between unregistered and registered works. A secured creditor should file for unregistered works in the Article 9 filing system and for registered works with the U.S. Copyright Office. That is pretty clumsy and it poses a very old-fashioned collateral management problem for secured creditors. Think back to the regimes contemplated in cases like *Benedict v. Ratner* and *Zartman*. Secured creditors were to engage with their debtors actively receiving periodic lists updating the collateral. Won't secured creditors need to take exactly those steps for copyrighted works?

B. MORE FEDERAL RIGHTS

We return to the question of how licenses issued by the Federal Communications Commission fit in Article 9. The FCC has moved to holding periodic auctions of available spectrum. In running these auctions, the FCC has at least two goals in mind: (1) raise revenues for the government and (2) allocate the spectrum in a fashion that implements an intelligent communications policy. These policies may conflict and arguably did so when the FCC conducted the "C" and "F" block auctions. Consistent with a congressional directive and in an effort to make sure that the spectrum was distributed widely—with the hope that this would increase competition in the use of the spectrum—the FCC decided to finance the license fees and accept installment payments from winning bidders.

Students of auctions could have predicted what happened next. High bidders should fear the "winner's curse," meaning that auction winners probably over-pay on average. Why? The spectrum auctions are common-value auctions, meaning that each bidder will use the spectrum in roughly the same way. Each bidder is trying to assess the uncertain future value of the new spectrum. Think of this as each bidder drawing a ball from an urn of values. The auction winner will be the bidder who draws the highest value from the urn, but the best guess of the value of the spectrum is the average draw, not the high draw. Hence the winner's curse. Finance those winners and we should expect winners who can't pay their bills and now we are at the domain of secured transactions and bankruptcy.

In FCC v. NextWave Personal Communications, Inc., 537 U.S. 293 (2003), the Supreme Court addressed whether the FCC could automatically cancel the licenses of the purchasers that filed for bankruptcy. The Court concluded that it could not do so, at least not while it was acting in its regulatory capacity. BC 525 limits the power of the government to discriminate against bankrupt firms and the Court found that the FCC's automatic cancellation regime failed. But the Court separated the FCC's regulatory role from its rights as a secured creditor: "As we described in our statement of facts, the FCC purported to take such a security interest in the present cases. What is at issue, however, is not the enforcement of that interest in the bankruptcy process, but rather elimination of the licenses through the regulatory step of 'revoking' them—action that the statute specifically forbids." Id. at 307-08.

Given that, the next step forward is to consider the rules that control security interests taken by the FCC. Before doing that, consider the following fact patterns.

8-6: CODE BLUE

- Debtor runs its business based on a piece of software that it created. Bank is willing to lend money to Debtor but wants the software as collateral.
- Debtor makes a copy of the software and turns over possession of that copy to Bank. Debtor also installs a front-end to its copy of the software. That front-end requires a new monthly numeric code issued by Bank to operate the software. Absent the new code, Debtor can't access its copy of the software.
- Debtor fails to make a payment to Bank. In turn, Bank doesn't issue the next code to Debtor and Debtor can no longer access the software in its possession.
- ¤ What issues does this raise under Article 9? Is this the sort of disabling of collateral contemplated by 9-609(a)(2)?

8-7: FCC IN THE UCC?

- The FCC auctions spectrum licenses and finances the license fee. The FCC seeks to protect its financial interests in the payments, so it has the auction winners sign standard Article 9 security agreements covering the licenses. The FCC tries to perfect by filing ordinary financing statements in the applicable state UCC records.

¤ Is the FCC perfected? Is this transaction within or without the UCC under 9-109(c)(1) and 9-311?

8-8: CAN THEY TURN OFF THE SPECTRUM?

- As before, the FCC auctions, lends and takes a security interest in the license and files in the UCC records. But the FCC wants more. When it issues the licenses in the first place, it provides in the license that "the license is conditioned upon the full and timely payment of all monies due to the FCC under the license" and that "failure to comply with this condition will result in the automatic cancellation" of the license.

¤ Is the FCC perfected? When a debtor fails to pay and the license cancels, is the FCC disabling the collateral ala 9-609(a)(2) or is it doing something else?

Airadigm Communications, Inc. v. Federal Communications Commission (In re Airadigm Communications, Inc.)

United States Court of Appeals, Seventh Circuit, 2008.
519 F.3d 640.

■ FLAUM, CIRCUIT JUDGE

Debtor-appellant, Airadigm Communications, Inc. is a cellular-service provider. In 1996, it successfully bid for fifteen personal communications services ("PCS") licenses as part of an FCC auction and opted to pay off the licenses under an installment plan set up by the FCC. For Airadigm, however, the airwaves were too turbulent, and by 1999 it had filed for chapter-11 bankruptcy. Almost immediately, the FCC cancelled Airadigm's PCS licenses and filed a proof of claim in bankruptcy court for the remaining amounts owed under the installment plan. The ensuing reorganization proceeded under the assumption that the licenses were gone, having been validly cancelled. And although the ultimate reorganization plan set out several contingencies in the event the FCC reinstated the licenses—which it never did—it provided little else regarding the licenses' status after the reorganization. In 2003, the Supreme Court decided FCC v. NextWave Personal Communications, Inc., 537 U.S. 293 (2003), and held that the FCC could not cancel a debtor's PCS licenses just because it had filed for bankruptcy. The FCC conceded a few months later that it had been wrong to terminate Airadigm's licenses and reinstated them as though they had never been cancelled.

Airadigm filed a second chapter-11 petition in May 2006 to tie up the loose ends from the fairly significant legal developments that had come about since its first reorganization. As part of its second filing, Airadigm commenced this adversary proceeding against the FCC, seeking to eliminate the FCC's continuing interest in the licenses based on the 2000 reorganization plan. The bankruptcy court held that the 2000 plan had not affected the FCC's interests in the licenses and subsequently ratified a second plan with the FCC as a partially secured creditor. * * *

Section 309(j) of the Communications Act of 1934, as amended in 1993, authorizes the FCC to award licenses to use the electromagnetic spectrum "through a system of competitive bidding," that is, an auction. c. Congress recognized that an auction had several advantages over the available alternatives, such as the "development and rapid deployment of new technologies," 47 USC 309(j)(3)(A), and the "recovery for the public ... a portion of the value of the public spectrum resource," 47 USC 309(j)(3)(C). Despite these benefits, a market-based design could concentrate ownership of licenses in the hands of those relatively few businesses that could afford the up-front cost. As a result, the Communications Act directs the FCC to structure the auction to "avoid the excessive concentration of licenses," 47 USC 309(j)(3)(B), specifically by "consider[ing] alternative payment schedules ..., including ... guaranteed installment payments." 47 USC 309(j)(4).

Against this legislative backdrop, the FCC adopted rules to auction off portions of the spectrum used for personal communications services ("PCS"), that segment used for a number of forms of wireless communication. In re Implementation of Section 309(j) of the Communications Act, 9 F.C.C.R. 5532 (1994). The FCC specified two of the six frequency blocks being auctioned—Blocks C and F—for smaller businesses who, being unable to afford the lump sum, could pay for their licenses in installments. 47 CFR 24.709 (2007). To ensure payment, the FCC made payment-in-full a condition precedent to obtaining a license,

47 CFR 1.2110(g)(4)(iv), and executed a promissory note and security agreement to secure its interest in each license, id. 1.2110(g)(3). If the successful bidder fell into default, "its license [would] automatically cancel, and it [would] be subject to debt collection procedures." Id.

In 1996, the FCC conducted the auction. Airadigm was the highest bidder for fifteen licenses—thirteen of which were "C-block" and two of which "F-block" segments covering Michigan, Iowa, and Wisconsin—and agreed to pay off what it had bid in quarterly installments, plus interest, over a ten-year period. Airadigm paid 10% of the purchase price, signed fifteen promissory notes recognizing its debt to the FCC, and executed fifteen security agreements. The licenses themselves stated that they were conditioned on the "full and timely payment of all monies due pursuant to [FCC regulations] and the terms of the Commission's installment plan." The FCC then sought to perfect its interests in the licenses by, among other things, filing UCC financing statements with the office of the Wisconsin Secretary of State.

Airadigm soon met financial problems and could not meet its obligations to the FCC. In 1999, it filed a petition for reorganization in the Western District of Wisconsin. The FCC allowed Airadigm to continue using its portion of the spectrum but cancelled Airadigm's licenses and filed a proof of claim in the bankruptcy court for $64.2 million, Airadigm's remaining balance. In its proof of claim, the FCC stated that, because it had cancelled the licenses, it was an unsecured creditor. Hedging a bit, the FCC also said that if it did not actually have the authority to cancel the licenses, its debt was instead secured by the licenses themselves, attaching proof of its security interests to its claim. The FCC otherwise participated in Airadigm's bankruptcy, filing a notice of appearance and ultimately objecting to its treatment as an unsecured creditor under the plan.

The 2000 reorganization proceeded under the assumption that the FCC had properly cancelled the licenses. The plan provided that the FCC had an allowed claim of $64.2 million and laid out several contingencies should the FCC reinstate the licenses. The reorganization hinged on financing by a third party, Telephone and Data Systems ("TDS"). Should the FCC reinstate the licenses by February 2001, TDS would pay the FCC's claim in full. If the FCC did not reinstate the licenses by February 2001, but did so by June 2002, TDS had the option of paying off the claim, but was not obligated to do so. But if the FCC never reinstated the licenses or "fail[ed] to act ... in a timely manner," the plan provided that TDS would obtain all of Airadigm's assets except the licenses. The plan was otherwise silent as to the FCC's exact interests in the licenses and what would happen if the FCC reinstated them after June 2002. And the plan didn't expressly preserve the FCC's security interest in the licenses, instead stating that the plan "shall not enjoin or in any way purport to limit, restrict, affect or interfere with action initiated by the FCC in the full exercise of its regulatory rights, powers and duties with respect to the Licenses."

The FCC never reinstated the licenses and maintained its position that it had validly cancelled them after Airadigm's 1999 bankruptcy. In 2003, the Supreme Court held otherwise in FCC v. NextWave Personal Communications, Inc., 537 U.S. 293 (2003). In nearly identical circumstances, the FCC had cancelled NextWave's C-and F-block licenses after it had filed for bankruptcy. The Court held that this action violated the bankruptcy code and set aside the FCC's decision. After its own bankruptcy in 1999, Airadigm had filed a petition before the FCC seeking to reinstate its cancelled licenses. On August 8, 2003, the FCC denied this petition as moot, reasoning that, in light of *NextWave*, its cancellation of the licenses had been "ineffective." In re Airadigm Communications, Inc., 18 F.C.C.R. 16296 (Aug. 8, 2003). Airadigm thus had its licenses back as though they had never been cancelled.

In light of this development, Airadigm filed a second petition for reorganization on May 8, 2006. As part of that reorganization, Airadigm filed the present adversary proceeding against the FCC, seeking to divest it of any continuing interests in the licenses. The bankruptcy court granted the FCC's motion for summary judgment and rejected Airadigm's claims.

Ultimately, on October 31, 2006, the bankruptcy court approved a second plan of reorganization, to which the FCC raised two general objections. The first went to the payment options under the plan. Even though Airadigm owed the FCC $64.2 million, the plan treated the FCC as a secured creditor for only $33 million—the then-current market value for the licenses. As a result, the FCC would have two options with respect to Airadigm's debt: It could take an immediate payout of $33 million and lose its liens in the licenses; or it could treat its entire $64.2 million claim as secured and receive deferred payments totaling this greater amount over a number of years. Under the latter option (called a BC 1111(b) election), the FCC would retain liens for the full $64.2 million and Airadigm would purchase and hold $33 million of government-backed securities or low-risk annuities. Airadigm would use the interest or payments from these instruments to make deferred payments to the FCC over (at most) a thirty-year period. When the payments totaled $64.2 million, the liens would expire. If Airadigm sold the licenses before making full payment, the FCC would receive the proceeds of the sale and, if the sale amount was less than $64.2 million, retain its liens in the licenses.

The FCC argued in the bankruptcy court that this last provision did not square with the code. Specifically, the FCC argued that a "due on sale" provision set out in its regulations—stating that the full auction bill is due if Airadigm transfers the licenses to a third party that would not otherwise qualify for installment payments—was part of the lien it held in a license. The FCC wanted the full $64.2 million at the time of a sale to a non-qualifying third party, not the proceeds of the sale plus a continuing lien in the licenses. Thus, in the FCC's estimate, the plan's failure to preserve this provision meant that the FCC had not "retain[ed] its liens" as required by the bankruptcy code. The bankruptcy court disagreed, reasoning that due-on-sale provision was not part of the lien itself and was instead contractual and subject to modification in bankruptcy. * * * Both parties appealed to the district court, who affirmed the bankruptcy court's decisions in relevant respects.

* * * The 2000 reorganization proceeded under the assumption that the FCC had validly cancelled Airadigm's licenses after it declared bankruptcy in 1999, and thus the plan made no mention of the status of the FCC's security interests following the reorganization. But the *NextWave* decision proved this assumption wrong. The anti-discrimination provision of the bankruptcy code, BC 525(a), prohibits the FCC from cancelling PCS licenses just because a license-holder has entered bankruptcy. Now the parties dispute the effect of the 2000 reorganization plan's silence in light of *NextWave*. Both the bankruptcy court and the district court held that the silence did not extinguish the FCC's continuing interests * * * . For the reasons set out below, we affirm. * * *

Airadigm also appeals the lower courts' conclusions that the FCC's liens could not be avoided under BC 544(a) * * * . Airadigm, as the debtor-in-possession, has the "rights and powers of ... a creditor that extends credit to the debtor at the time of the commencement of the case, and that obtains, at such time and with respect to such credit, a judicial lien" on the property in question. BC 544(a)(1). This "strong arm" power functions much like a foreclosure. If at the time of Airadigm's filing some hypothetical unsecured creditor could have obtained a judicial lien superior to the interest of the party bringing a secured claim in the bankruptcy proceeding, the estate can avoid the interest. But unlike a regular foreclosure, the property simply becomes the estate's free of the secured lien. Here, if some hypothetical creditor could have obtained an interest superior to the FCC's at the time of Airadigm's filing, the FCC will become an unsecured creditor with respect to the licenses.

To resolve the question, we must look to the rules governing the FCC's interests in the licenses. For although the "strong arm" power comes from federal bankruptcy law, the rules governing the perfection of security interests do not. In the mine-run case—for example one concerning a private creditor's interest in a tractor or some type of inventory—state law governs. But when the property in question falls outside of state commercial codes by virtue of the federal interest or the nature of the property, federal law provides the rule of decision. Grogan v. Garner, 498 U.S. 279, 283-84 & n. 9 (1991). In such instances, if a federal statute speaks to the issue directly, the court will look no further. See United States v. Kimbell Foods, Inc., 440 U.S. 715, 726 (1979). Barring that, courts can either adopt state law as the rule of decision, see, e.g., Kimbell Foods, Inc., 440 U.S. at 729, or craft a federal rule of common law. See, e.g., Clearfield Trust Co. v. United States, 318 U.S. 363, 366 (1943). The issues before us are whether state or federal law governs the perfection of the FCC's interests in the licenses and, if the latter, what federal law demands.

Airadigm argues on appeal that Wisconsin law should govern the perfection of the FCC's interests in the licenses. After the 1996 auction, the FCC executed fifteen security agreements, and Airadigm signed fifteen promissory notes for the amounts owed. Initially, the FCC filed financing statements in Wisconsin to perfect its interests in the licenses. But financing statements lapse after five years, and the FCC didn't renew them when the time came in June and July 2002, waiting until June 2006 to file a continuation statement. See 9-515(a), (c). Due to this lapse, if Wisconsin law (or more generally the UCC) governs, the FCC's interests would be unperfected—and thus avoidable—due to this failure to renew.

But neither the UCC nor Wisconsin law decides the issue, as federal statutory and regulatory law prevent a hypothetical lien creditor from obtaining a superior interest in an FCC license for purposes of the bankruptcy code. The liens held by the FCC are unlike liens held by the federal government as part of other federal lending programs, where the lien secures the loan by attaching to property that is otherwise defined by state law. See, e.g., United States v. Kimbell Foods, Inc., 440 U.S. 715, 737 (1979). Instead, the property itself—the license—is a creature of federal law. Accordingly, federal law also defines the FCC's retained interest in

that license. And as defined by federal law, the FCC does not have to perfect its interest in a spectrum license because federal law prevents another
creditor from holding a superior interest.

The licenses created by the Communications Act, as amended in 1993,
"maintain the control of the United States over all the" invisible spectrum.
47 USC 301. The licenses give permission "for the use of such channels,
but not the ownership thereof," and "no such license shall be construed to
create any right, beyond the terms, conditions, and periods of the license."
Id. Although these licenses provide license-holders the right to exclude,
they are not freely transferable as no license "or any rights thereunder,
shall be transferred, assigned, or disposed of in any manner, voluntarily or
involuntarily, directly or indirectly, ... except upon application to the
Commission." 47 USC 310(d). Even then, the Commission will only approve the transfer "upon finding ... that the public interest, convenience,
and necessity will be served thereby." Id.

The rules governing the auctions themselves also preserve the FCC's
interests in the licenses. In 1993, Congress gave the FCC the authority to
"grant [a] license or permit to a qualified applicant through a system of
competitive bidding" that would "recover[ ] for the public ... a portion of
the value of the public spectrum resource made available for commercial
use." 47 USC 309(j)(1), (j)(3)(C). In so doing, the Commission was required to "consider alternative payment schedules and methods of calculation, including ... guaranteed installment payments." Id. at 309(j)(4)(a).
Pursuant to this authority, and after a notice-and-comment period, see In
re Implementation of Section 309(j) of the Communications Act,
9 F.C.C.R. 5532 (1994), the FCC crafted regulations governing the auction and the installment plan. These regulations conditioned a successful
bidder's use of the licenses "upon the full and timely performance of the
licensee's   payment   obligations   under   the   installment   plan."
47 CFR 1.2110(g)(4). And finally, the very "terms of the ... license[s]"—
which 47 USC 301 provided would define any "right" in them—stated
that they were "conditioned upon the full and timely payment of all monies due pursuant to" the regulations and the security agreements.

These statutory and regulatory provisions indicate that federal law prec-
ludes a private party from obtaining a superior interest to the FCC. Generally, when a lien-creditor forecloses on a lien, the affected property is
sold, and the lien-creditor recovers its debt from the proceeds of the sale.
In terms of priority, a lien-creditor receives payment prior to any secured
creditor whose interest is unperfected. See, e.g., 9-317(a)(2). In other

words, the unperfected secured creditor—in this case, the FCC—will not get paid anything unless there is money left over after superior creditors recover from the proceeds of the sale.

But if the forced sale of the PCS licenses were to occur with the FCC as merely an unperfected secured creditor, the sale would conflict with the statutes and regulations covering the FCC's licensing scheme. This conflict gives rise to a negative inference—controlling in this case—that federal law does not allow private creditors to obtain an interest in PCS licenses superior to the FCC's. In the first place, a judicially enforced sale would mean that a "transfer" of the licenses occurred without an "application to the Commission and upon finding by the Commission that the public interest, convenience, and necessity will be served thereby." 47 USC 310(d).

In addition, if the lien-holder were to be paid before the FCC, this would conflict with 47 USC 301 and 47 CFR 1.2110(g)(4). Section 301 provides for the "use" of licenses subject to the "terms, conditions, and periods of the license." And the "terms ... of the license[s]" require that the licensee make "full and timely payment of all monies due." The FCC's regulations, crafted after Congressional authorization and a notice-and-comment period, similarly predicate the auction-winner's use of the licenses on "the full and timely performance of the licensee's payment obligations under the installment plan." 47 CFR 1.2110(g)(4). Pursuant to Congress's command to "recover ... a portion of the value of the public spectrum resource," the FCC made full payment a regulatory condition on the use of the invisible spectrum when implementing the installment plan. Subordinating its interests to that of a private lien-creditor would conflict with the FCC's statutory and regulatory authority.

As a result, under federal non-bankruptcy law the rights afforded to a hypothetical lien creditor at the time of Airadigm's filing could not have been superior to the FCC's interests in the licenses. Accordingly, the lower courts were correct to conclude that Airadigm cannot avoid the FCC's interests in the licenses under BC 544(a). We conclude by noting that we do not decide whether a private party can in fact take an interest in the proceeds of PCS licenses.[2] This decision is unnecessary because, regardless

---

[2] A previous decision of this Court, In re Tak Communications, 985 F.2d 916 (7th Cir. 1993), held that a "creditor may [not] hold a security interest in [a] license." This decision reflected the FCC's stated policy at the time, see In re Tak, 985 F.2d at 918-19; In re Twelve Seventy, Inc., 1 F.C.C.2d 965, 967 (1965), and ended with

what interest a license-holder can give a creditor in these licenses, it could not be superior to the FCC's for purposes of BC 544(a). * * *

COMMENTS AND QUESTIONS

1. The court makes a great deal turn on the legal fact that the FCC, in its regulatory capacity, has to approve transfers of spectrum licenses. That quickly becomes a rule that prevents third parties from acting against the license, which in turn operates to prevent unsecured creditors from improving their position against the license by becoming lien creditors, and that finally takes us to a rule that means that the FCC seemingly doesn't need to file in the UCC system to perfect its security interest in the license.

2. Does that make too much of the regulatory powers held by the FCC? Shouldn't we separate their regulatory powers from rules regarding

---

the proviso that any change in this policy was "a matter for the FCC rather than the courts to decide." In re Tak, 985 F.2d at 919. A subsequent decision coming from within the FCC then expressly disagreed with *In re Tak*. The Chief of the Mobile Services Division held that, despite the FCC's general "policy against a licensee giving a security interest in a license," a "security interest in the proceeds of the sale of a license does not violate Commission policy." In re Cheskey, 9 F.C.C.R. 986, 987 & n. 8 (Mobile Serv. Div. 1994). Other circuits have found this statement persuasive. See, e.g., MLQ Investors, L.P. v. Pacific Quadracasting, Inc., 146 F.3d 746, 748-49 (9th Cir. 1998); In re Beach Television Partners, 38 F.3d 535, 537 (11th Cir. 1994). But the FCC has not argued before this Court that this decision is entitled to *Chevron* deference, which would have meant that the FCC effectively overruled *In re Tak*. See Nat'l Cable & Telecommunications Inc. v. Brand X Internet Svces., 545 U.S. 967, 982-84 (2005) ("A court's prior judicial construction of a statute trumps an agency construction otherwise entitled to *Chevron* deference only if the prior court decision holds that its construction follows from the unambiguous terms of the statute and thus leaves no room for agency discretion."). Nor is *Chevron* deference likely given that the Commission subsequently declined to adopt this policy in affirming the Chief's order in *Cheskey*. See In re Cheskey, 13 F.C.C.R. 10656, 10659-60 (1998) (expressly declining to reach issue); 47 USC 154(i) (powers of Commission), 155(c)(1)-(6) (powers, unused in *Cheskey*, to delegate authority to an employee of the FCC). Accordingly, because the answer to this question is not necessary for our decision and because "it is [not] clear that a private party *can* take and enforce a security interest in an FCC license," NextWave, 537 U.S. at 307, it is for a future case (or the FCC) to readdress the matter if necessary.

priority to the license? And try another angle on this. We have emphasized all along that for secured creditors we need to separate the property rights of the secured creditor from the priority rights. The regulatory block held by the FCC weakens the property rights of the secured
creditor, but those are limited already in many cases (by the breach-of-
the-peace limit and by the fact that debtors can easily file for bankruptcy and kick in bankruptcy's automatic stay (BC 362)). A secured
creditor—or an unsecured creditor looking to become a lien creditor—
will care more about the priority rights of the superior position. Does
the court do a good job of distinguishing property and priority rights?

3. Is this case importantly different from *In re Clark* (remember that one:
the liquor license and the acknowledgment barring transfer of it)?

4. What does this mean for taking a security interest in a spectrum license? The court leaves open the question of whether a security interest can be taken at all, but assume that one can. The FCC doesn't
seem to have to file in the UCC records. What does a private secured
creditor need to do?

C. SET-OFF RIGHTS

9-109(d)(10) provides that "[t]his article does not apply to a right of recoupment or set-off." Grant Gilmore had strong views on this exclusion:

> This exclusion is an apt example of the absurdities which result
> when draftsmen attempt to appease critics by putting into a sta-
> tute something that is not in any sense wicked but is hopelessly
> irrelevant. Of course a right of set-off is not a security interest
> and has never been confused with one: the statute might as ap-
> propriately exclude fan dancing. A bank's right of set-off against
> a depositor's account is often loosely referred to as a "banker's
> lien," but the "lien" usage has never led anyone to think that the
> bank held a security interest in the bank account. Banking
> groups were, however, concerned lest someone, someday, might
> think that a bank's right of set-off, because it was called a lien,
> was a security interest. Hence, the exclusion, which does no
> harm except to the dignity and self-respect of the draftsmen.

1 Grant Gilmore, Security Interests in Personal Property 315-316 (1965).
With the inclusion of deposit accounts in Article 9, it was thought necessary to address set-off again, and 9-340 does this. Consider the next fact

patterns and then case that follows. Focus on the key question: what exactly is the right of set-off, and how does it differ from a security interest, keeping in mind of course that these two interests have "never" been confused.

8-9: MUTUAL DEBTS AND SET-OFF

- Bank lends $10,000 to Debtor.
- Debtor deposits $5,000 in its checking account with Bank to bring the balance to $10,000.
- ¤ Does Bank have a security interest? Does Debtor? See 1-201(b)(35). If not, how should we characterize the relationships that exist between Bank and Debtor?

8-10: SET-OFF AND SECURITY INTERESTS

- Finco takes a security interest in Debtor's accounts and files an appropriate financing statement. Debtor receives a check in payment of a $5,000 account and deposits that into its checking account with Bank.
- Bank, delighted to see the deposit, sets off that deposit against a debt owed by Debtor to Bank of $10,000.
- ¤ Can Bank do that? Does Finco have priority over Bank's attempt at set-off? See 9-340.

Kentucky Highlands Inv. Corporation v. Bank of Corbin, Inc.

Court of Appeals of Kentucky, 2006.
217 S.W.3d 851.

■ COMBS, CHIEF JUDGE

Kentucky Highlands Investment Corporation ("Kentucky Highlands") appeals from a summary judgment granted by the Whitley Circuit Court in favor of the Bank of Corbin, Inc., ("the Bank"). The appeal involves a priority dispute between Kentucky Highlands and the Bank of Corbin. The Bank claimed a right of set-off against funds in a commercial deposit account. Kentucky Highlands asserted a perfected security interest in the same funds. After considering the relevant provisions of Kentucky's commercial code together with the arguments of counsel, we affirm the summary judgment of the trial court.

Kentucky Highlands was the primary lender to Tri-County Manufacturing and Assembly Incorporated ("Tri-County Manufacturing") and its affiliates, including Tritech Electronics, LLC ("Tritech"). Various loans extended to these debtors by Kentucky Highlands totaled more than five million dollars. Kentucky Highlands contended that the loans were secured by a properly perfected security interest in all of the debtors' personal property and an assignment of the debtors' customer accounts receivable.

Tritech maintained a commercial deposit account with the Bank of Corbin. The Bank obtained a security interest in the deposits held at the Bank pursuant to a loan agreement dated April 6, 2001, between Tritech and the Bank, and it held a well-established right of set-off against the account.

Customer payments generally were *not* deposited into Tritech's account. Instead, provisions of its loan agreements with Kentucky Highlands required Tritech to direct customers to remit their payments directly to Kentucky Highlands. The Tritech deposit account was funded primarily by transfers from an account held by Tri-County Manufacturing. Tri-County Manufacturing funded those advances on a line of credit provided by Kentucky Highlands. Kentucky Highlands was aware of Tritech's account with the Bank of Corbin. Pursuant to the provisions of 9-104(1), it could have taken steps to protect itself by taking control of the account. But it made no attempts to do so. ***

In March or April of 2002, the relationship between Kentucky Highlands and its debtors began to deteriorate. An audit conducted by Kentucky Highlands in mid-July 2002 indicated that its debtors had overstated available accounts receivable and inventory by nearly 1.5 million dollars. In a meeting held on July 24, 2002, the debtors were instructed by Kentucky Highlands not to collect any accounts receivable. By July 26, 2002, at the latest, Kentucky Highlands believed that its debtor's president was engaged in illegal activity. Nevertheless, Kentucky Highlands did not invoke or initiate any judicial process to assert control over Tritech's accounts receivable.

Kentucky Highlands alleged that from approximately July 2, 2002, and continuing through approximately August 2, 2002, Tritech began depositing customer payments totaling nearly $400,000.00 into its own account at the Bank. Kentucky Highlands claimed that the Bank was paying overdrafts on the account during this period of time. Kentucky Highlands alleged that the Bank applied the funds deposited by Tritech to its overdrafts and to its other credit accounts held by the Bank—despite the

Bank's knowledge that Kentucky Highlands held a properly perfected security interest in all of the debtors' accounts receivable.

On February 19, 2004, Kentucky Highlands filed a complaint against the Bank, alleging that Tritech had breached several of its agreements with Kentucky Highlands. Kentucky Highlands claimed that by depositing customer payments directly into its account with the Bank, Tritech converted funds belonging to Kentucky Highlands. Kentucky Highlands also alleged that the Bank knew—or should have known—that Tritech's deposits amounted to a conversion of its funds. Kentucky Highlands claimed that the Bank had colluded with its debtors to divert the proceeds of the collateral assigned to Kentucky Highlands. Kentucky Highlands charged that the Bank had "aided and abetted Tritech in this conversion of funds belonging to Kentucky Highlands." Kentucky Highlands sought recovery of the customer payments deposited into the subject account.

In its answer, the Bank denied the allegations. The Bank claimed that it had a superior right of set-off against the disputed funds under the provisions of Kentucky's commercial code (as amended) and that it had no duty to monitor deposits being made into the subject account or to scrutinize the status of the collateral claimed by Kentucky Highlands. Invoking the provisions of Kentucky's commercial code, the Bank filed a comprehensive motion for summary judgment.

In its response to the Bank's motion for summary judgment, Kentucky Highlands argued strenuously and persuasively that the decision of the Kentucky Supreme Court in General Motors Acceptance Corporation v. Lincoln National Bank, 18 S.W.3d 337 (Ky. 2000), ("GMAC"), controlled the dispute and that *GMAC* had not been superseded by subsequent amendments to the commercial code. * * *

The parties agree that the issues before us are governed by the provisions of Revised Article 9 of the Uniform Commercial Code (the UCC) as adopted by Kentucky and which became effective on July 1, 2001. Kentucky Highlands contends that the decision of the Supreme Court of Kentucky in *GMAC*, a case factually similar to the one before us, remained intact and unaffected precedentially—even after the General Assembly adopted revisions to Kentucky's commercial code in the wake of *GMAC*. Conversely, the Bank argues that the revisions to Article 9 rendered the decision in *GMAC* meaningless with respect to this case.

In *GMAC*, the Supreme Court of Kentucky was asked to decide whether a deposit bank could apply the cash proceeds of a creditor's collateral to cover its depositor's overdrafts. Relying on a decision rendered by the Supreme Court of Iowa in 1989, our Court concluded that the secured creditor had priority over the interest of the deposit bank in the account by virtue of its security agreement with the depositor, metaphorically holding that the bank could not bypass or "leapfrog" the secured creditor by reimbursing itself for overdrafts taken from deposits which were derived from identifiable cash proceeds of the secured creditor's collateral.

Kentucky Highlands argues that the decision "could hardly be more clear, or more clearly applicable to the case presented ... against the Bank." Applying the reasoning of *GMAC* to the facts of the case before us, Kentucky Highlands essentially contends that the Bank of Corbin could not reimburse itself for Tritech's overdrafts from an account into which customer payments had been deposited—payments (or collateral) that belonged to (and should have been paid directly to) Kentucky Highlands under its loan agreements with Tritech.

The Bank contends that the drafters of the UCC (and Kentucky legislators adopting and incorporating its provisions in our statutes) clearly intended to reverse the prevailing trend in existing law. That is, their adoption of the revisions to Article 9 was directly aimed at undoing the effects of the Supreme Court's decision in *GMAC*. According to the Bank,

> [t]he drafters of Revised Article 9 and the legislature determined that the interests of depository banks, the free flow of commerce and the checking system are superior to the interest of secured creditors in funds deposited into accounts at depository banks.

Consequently, the Bank argues that a new presumption of priority has been conferred upon depository banks and that secured creditors are required to take specific steps to preserve their interest in funds held by a bank.

We agree with the Bank's argument. By enacting the revisions, the drafters of Revised Article 9 and the legislature of Kentucky have clearly and deliberately shielded depository banks from claims and priority disputes with secured creditors.

Addressing the priority of conflicting security interests in a deposit account, 9-327 provides as follows:

> (1) A security interest held by a secured party having control of the deposit account under 9-104 has priority over a conflict-

ing security interest held by a secured party that does not have control.

(2) Except as otherwise provided in subsections (3) and (4) of this section, security interests perfected by control under 9-314 rank according to priority in time of obtaining control.

(3) Except as otherwise provided in subsection (4) of this subsection, *a security interest held by the bank with which the deposit account is maintained has priority over a conflicting security interest held by another secured party.*

(4) A security interest perfected by control under 9-104(1) has priority over a security interest held by the bank with which the deposit account is maintained. (Emphasis added.)

The official commentary to the UCC explains the bank's super-priority status as follows:

Under paragraph (3), the security interest of the bank with which the deposit account is maintained normally takes priority over all other conflicting security interests in the deposit account, *regardless of whether the deposit account constitutes the competing party's original collateral or its proceeds.* A rule of this kind enables banks to extend credit to their depositors without the need to examine either the public record or their own records to determine whether another party might have a security interest in the deposit account.

* * * *

A secured party who claims the deposit account as proceeds of other collateral can reduce the risk of becoming junior by obtaining the debtor's agreement to deposit proceeds into a specific cash-collateral account and obtaining the agreement of that bank to subordinate all its claims to those of the secured party. But if the debtor violates its agreement and deposits funds into a deposit account other than the cash-collateral account, the secured party risks being subordinated.

(Emphasis added). [1-110 permits the use of the official comments in the construction and application of Kentucky's enactment of Article 9.]

9-340 establishes similar priority rules with respect to the depository bank's right of set-off against funds in a customer account that might be subject to a claim by a secured creditor. 9-340 provides as follows:

(1) Except as otherwise provided in subsection (3) of this section, a bank with which a deposit account is maintained may exercise any right of recoupment or set-off against a secured party that holds a security interest in the deposit account.

(2) Except as otherwise provided in subsection (3) of this section, the application of this article to a security interest in a deposit account does not affect a right of recoupment or set-off of the secured party as to a deposit account maintained with the secured party.

(3) The exercise by a bank of a set-off against a deposit account is ineffective against a secured party that holds a security interest in the deposit account which is perfected by control under 9-104(c), if the set-off is based on a claim against the debtor.

9-340 places a bank's right of set-off ahead of the security interest of a secured party in the deposit account. Under this provision, a secured party's interest in the account will be subordinate *until and unless* the security interest in the deposit account is perfected "by control under 9-104(c)."

Kentucky Highlands contends that the priority rules established by 9-340 do not apply where a secured party claims a security interest in the *cash proceeds* deposited into the commercial account rather than a security interest in the deposit account itself. We disagree. That construction would fail to distinguish between a creditor who neglected to protect its interests and a conscientious secured party that took the necessary steps to establish its priority. The revisions to Article 9 recognize that very distinction. The result urged by Kentucky Highlands conflicts with the clear intention of revised Article 9: to provide a comprehensive and predictable framework by which parties may avoid priority disputes and to protect the interests of depository banks.

Under the revised portions of the UCC, depository banks receive an automatic perfected interest in the accounts of their customers. Kentucky Highlands was aware of its debtors' deposit account with the Bank of Corbin and yet acquiesced in its use without taking any action to assert priority as to proceeds to which it claimed entitlement. Kentucky Highlands was on notice that the Bank could assert a claim against the deposit accounts at any time. Although Kentucky Highlands was in a position to protect its priority through a variety of means, it nonetheless risked becoming subordinate by doing nothing. It is true that the Bank might have protected itself by simply refusing to honor its customer's overdrafts. However, the revised statute required Kentucky Highlands as a secured creditor to monitor its debtor's business and to police its own collateral-not to shift such duties onto the Bank. A depository bank no longer bears the burden to ascertain the source of funds deposited into its customers' accounts and to determine whether there is a creditor who may have a lien on those funds before a bank can assert its rights as a secured creditor—namely, its rights to set-off against the account.

We conclude that the provisions of 9-340 directly govern this priority dispute. A depository bank may properly exercise its right of set-off against a secured party who seeks to assert an interest in a commercial deposit account—regardless of whether the secured party claims a security interest in the deposit account as original collateral or as its proceeds. The trial court did not err by granting summary judgment to the Bank on this issue.

Next, Kentucky Highlands contends that the trial court erred by granting summary judgment to the Bank because it had offered sufficient evidence of collusion between the Bank and Tritech to deprive Kentucky Highlands of the value of its collateral. In support of its argument, Kentucky Highlands relies on the following provisions of 9-332:

> (1) A transferee of money takes the money free of a security interest unless the transferee acts in collusion with the debtor in violating the rights of the secured party.
>
> (2) A transferee of funds from a deposit account takes the funds free of a security interest in the deposit account unless the transferee acts in collusion with the debtor in violating the rights of the secured party.

The Official Comment explains as follows:

> [T]his section does not cover the case ... in which a bank debits an encumbered account and credits another account it maintains for the debtor.
>
> A transfer of funds from a deposit account, to which subsection (b) applies, normally will be made by check, by funds transfer, or by debiting the debtor's deposit account and crediting another depositor's account....

We are not persuaded that 9-332 is applicable to this case. By its terms, the statute is intended to provide broad protection for transferees of funds from a deposit account representing the proceeds of a secured creditor's collateral. More significantly, we are not persuaded that these provisions pertain to priority conflicts between a depository bank and a secured creditor concerning funds in the deposit account. A depository bank is not a transferee as described by the language of the statute.

Finally, we note that the provisions of 9-341 set forth the rights and duties of a bank with respect to deposit accounts as follows:

> Except as otherwise provided in 9-340(3) [where the secured party has become the bank's customer under 9-104(1)(c)], and unless the bank otherwise agrees in an authenticated record, a bank's rights and duties with respect to a deposit account maintained with the bank are not terminated, suspended, or modified by
>
> (1) The creation, attachment, or perfection of a security interest in the deposit account;
>
> (2) The bank's knowledge of the security interest; or
>
> (3) The bank's receipt of instructions from the secured party.

Again, the Official Comment provides a helpful explanation:

> This section is designed to prevent security interests in deposit accounts from impeding the free flow of funds through the payment system. Subject to two exceptions it leaves the bank's rights and duties with respect to the deposit account and the funds on deposit unaffected by the creation or perfection of a security interest or by the bank's knowledge of the security interest. In addition, the section permits the bank to ignore the instruction of the secured party unless it had agreed to honor them or unless other law provides to the contrary. *A secured party who wishes to deprive the debtor of access to funds on deposit or to appropriate those funds for itself needs to obtain the agreement of the bank, utilize the judicial process, or comply with procedures set forth in other law....*

(Emphasis added).

The Bank was statutorily authorized to ignore even direct "instructions" from Kentucky Highlands with respect to its conduct toward the deposit account. Kentucky Highlands failed to avail itself of direct agreement with the Bank or to become the Bank's customer as provided by statute in order to protect its interests. The Bank was entitled to judgment as a matter of law with respect to this issue, and the trial court did not err by granting the summary judgment.

The judgment of the Whitley Circuit Court is affirmed.

Comments and Questions

9-332 creates broad protections for transferees of money and of value from a deposit account. That is consistent with the notion that we want to protect the free flow of funds through the payments system. Be sure to read the comments to 9-332. As the court suggests, those comments suggest that the exceptions to the free-flow idea are to be read quite narrowly.

Section II. Characterization Problems and Excluded Transactions

Article 9 has special line-drawing rules in cases of certain types of transactions (leases and consignments, for example) involving tangible goods. Before examining those statutory rules, however, we begin by inquiring how to distinguish between a transaction governed by Article 9 and a transaction outside of Article 9 when no specific statutory attention has been paid to the problem. You should keep in mind at least two distinct questions. First, focusing on the language of Article 9, one might ask whether a supplier of goods can claim exemption from Article 9 merely by calling itself a bailor, or whether a supplier has to show that the transaction was not one "that creates a security interest," 9-109(a)(1)—whether, that is to say, the supplier has to show that its interest in the goods (as bailor or whatever) was not one that "secures payment or performance of an obligation," 1-201(b)(35). Second, and more broadly, what are the purposes being served by this line-drawing? However clear it may be that a transaction is a bailment on the one hand or a secured transaction on the other hand, why should the form of the transaction between the supplier and the processor determine the resolution of a dispute between the supplier and a different party (such as a secured creditor of the processor)? Is the ostensible ownership problem different in the two cases? Are there other reasons for differentiating between kinds of two-party transactions when sorting out third-party rights?

8-11: CHARACTERIZATION I: TRUE SALE OR ... ?

- On February 1st, Bank enters into a standard secured transaction with Debtor. The security agreement covers all personal property— not in those terms, of course, but building carefully collateral type by collateral type—and Bank files an appropriate financing statement. Bank lends money to Debtor.

- Debtor turns raw materials into finished goods. Wholesaler contracts with Debtor for those services. On March 1st, Supplier sells new raw materials to Wholesaler, who pays for those with cash. The next day, Wholesaler sells the raw materials to Debtor and does so on an unsecured basis.

- During good times, Debtor performs as usual and then sells the finished product to Wholesaler. Wholesaler then pays Debtor the difference between the price for the finished goods and the amount owed by Debtor to Wholesaler for the raw materials.

- ¤ Debtor fails. Debtor holds raw materials from Wholesaler and owes Wholesaler for past purchases. As between Wholesaler and Bank, who has priority in the raw materials held by Debtor?

8-12: CHARACTERIZATION II: BAILMENT OR ... ?

- A variation on the prior fact pattern. Debtor deals with Bank as before but Wholesaler buys raw materials from Supplier and just has those delivered to Debtor. Debtor doesn't buy the raw materials from Wholesaler but instead just agrees to hold them on behalf of Wholesaler.

- During good times, Debtor processes the raw materials into finished product and delivers those to Wholesaler (or to whomever Wholesaler designates). Wholesaler then pays Debtor a processing fee, set equal to exactly the same amount Wholesaler paid to Debtor in the prior fact pattern.

- ¤ Debtor fails and holds raw materials from Wholesaler. As between Wholesaler and Bank, who has priority in the raw materials held by Debtor?

8-13: CHARACTERIZATION III: SECURED TRANSACTION OR ... ?

- A variation on the two prior fact patterns. Debtor deals with Bank as before but now Wholesaler agrees to finance Debtor's purchases of raw materials from Supplier. Debtor and Wholesaler enter into a secured transaction covering inventory and accounts receivable. Wholesaler then lends money to Debtor and those funds are then traced into raw materials purchased by Debtor from Supplier.

- ¤ Debtor fails. As between Wholesaler and Bank, who has priority in the raw materials held by Debtor? Answer based on whether or not

Wholesaler filed an appropriate financing statement. Are there other steps that might be relevant for Wholesaler?

COMMENTS AND QUESTIONS: *MEDOMAK*, BAILMENTS, AND THE FINANCING BUYER

The three prior fact patterns are based on a well-known if now somewhat dated case, Medomak Canning Co. v. William Underwood Co., 25 UCC Rep. 437 (D. Me., 1977). As you consider the three fact patterns, focus on how title to the raw materials influences the outcome. Wholesaler wants to argue essentially that it is in fact the true owner of the goods in question. Wholesaler did not convey title to the goods to Debtor. Rather it gave the goods to Debtor so they could be processed and returned. Under this argument, Debtor was no more the owner of the goods than a dry cleaner becomes the owner of a suit it is given to clean. The derivation principle tells us that a dry cleaner cannot grant a creditor a security interest in a suit it is given to clean that will take precedence to the rights of the owner. The dry cleaner can convey only what it has and its rights are quite limited vis-à-vis the owner. Similarly, Wholesaler's argument concludes, the secured creditor in our hypos, Bank, cannot enjoy a security interest in the goods that takes precedence over the rights of Wholesaler. Debtor can convey to Bank a security interest only in what it has, and when it is merely processing goods for someone else, it has little of value to convey.

To prevail, Bank must argue that this characterization of the transaction is wrong. If Wholesaler is a "true" bailor then the transaction is just like that involving the dry cleaner, and Wholesaler prevails. To decide whether Wholesaler is a true bailor, we must look at the substance of the transaction and ask if it in fact has the attributes of a "true" bailment. Bank must argue that, under the better characterization, Wholesaler is nothing more than a secured creditor that is trying to escape its obligation to cure the ostensible ownership problem by calling itself something other than a secured creditor. Bank must argue that substance should take precedence over form and that, as a matter of *substance*, Wholesaler should be considered a secured creditor. In substance, Bank's argument would have to run: Wholesaler is simply a buyer who is financing its seller and who is taking a security interest in its seller's raw materials and finished product to protect itself in the event that its seller defaults.

We do not take the ostensible ownership problem secured credit causes seriously if we allow a secured creditor to escape from its obligation to give public notice of nonpossessory property interests simply by using magic words in the loan agreement with its debtor. The loan agreement is a private matter between the parties. Words in a loan agreement cannot affect the ostensible ownership problem. If we allowed labels to govern, ordinary secured parties could transform themselves into bailors without changing the substance of the transaction.

But as a general matter, we do not allow labels to govern: the major thrust of Article 9 is to allow substance to control. Article 9 is intended to control all consensual security interests in personal property, regardless of what the parties called them. A financing buyer should no more be able to label its transaction a sale and a bailment (and thereby escape the requirements of Article 9), than the equipment financier should be able to label its transaction a lease or the purchase money lender should be able to label its transaction a consignment, and thereby escape Article 9.

To say this, however, does not fully address the problem of Article 9's limited scope, for *some* leases and *some* bailments are outside its reach. We are left, therefore, with the problem of distinguishing the true bailor who leaves a suit with the dry cleaner to be pressed—a transaction excluded from Article 9—from the financing buyer who persuades its seller to transfer title to it but to retain the goods until the seller finishes making them—a transaction covered by Article 9.

Both a true bailment and a secured transaction create an ostensible ownership problem. Indeed, one can imagine a true bailment and a secured transaction creating the same ostensible ownership problem. We would face a true bailment if you were to take cloth that you owned to a tailor to get a suit made. A secured transaction would exist, however, if you prepaid a tailor to make a suit for you and persuaded the tailor to give you an interest in the fabric it bought so that you could take possession of it in the event that the tailor defaulted on its obligation to make the suit for you. In the early days of commercial law, courts accepted the need to have leases and bailments of personal property, but they did not accept the need for secured transactions. This perception (rather than a perception that secured transactions should be recorded, but leases and bailments should not be) first gave rise to differing treatment for leases and bailments on the one hand and secured transactions on the other. The distinction continued even after filing systems became widespread. True bailors, like true lessors, have no obligation to cure the ostensible ownership problem when they separate ownership from possession.

If you are a true bailor when you give your tailor the fabric, but are merely a financing buyer with a security interest when the tailor buys the fabric, what follows? The principal difference between the financing buyer and the true bailor seems to lie over who owns the goods at the start of the transaction. Can we settle on a rule that provides that a true bailor must, vis-à-vis its bailee, bear all the incidents of ownership at the start of the transaction? You are a true bailor when you give your cloth to the tailor, but not when the tailor buys the cloth and conveys an interest in it to you. In the first case, you bear all the risks of ownership with respect to the cloth. You can sue the tailor if its workmanship is shoddy, but you cannot reject the suit on the ground that you do not like the quality of the cloth. In the second case, you do not begin as the owner of the cloth, and you can reject the cloth if it is not up to the standard set forth in your contract with the tailor. In this case, you bear none of the incidents of ownership with respect to the cloth at the time the transaction with the tailor commences.

One way of trying to resolve problems like those *Medomak* presents (or indeed problems in commercial law generally) is to ask how the transaction might have been restructured, with as little substantive change as possible, so as to leave you feeling reasonably comfortable that almost any judge would find the Debtor-Wholesaler transaction, first, to be *excluded* from Article 9 and, second, to be *included* in Article 9. To do this, start with the definition of a security interest in 1-201(b)(35) and consider, as well, 9-109. And for more generally, see Douglas G. Baird and Thomas H. Jackson, Possession and Ownership: An Examination of the Scope of Article 9, 35 Stan. L. Rev. 175 (1983).

Revised Article 9 subsumes a narrow class of bailments into its overall approach to security interests. Consider a standard consignment transaction. A gallery sells art to the general public. The gallery could buy works from its artists in a standard sale transaction, but doing that forces the gallery to guess whether the public will actually be interested in a particular artist's work. *Nobody knows* is often described as the core problem of the arts and entertainment world, and if that is right, the gallery may want to avoid assuming the risk of non-sale to the public. How to do that? The consignment is the answer. The artist transfers physical possession of the art to the gallery but retains title. The gallery acts as agent for the artist and has the power to transfer title to purchasers.

Where does this leave creditors of the gallery? This is where Article 9 steps in, though it does so in a limited way. Consider again the definition of a security interest in 1-201(b)(35). The second sentence of that definition provides that " '[s]ecurity interest' includes any interest of a consignor * * * ." In corresponding fashion, 9-109(a)(4) provides that Article 9 applies to "consignment" transactions and that term is defined, in turn, in 9-102(a)(20). Next go back and look at the foundational definitions of Article 9—for debtor (9-102(a)(28)); secured party (9-102(a)(72)); and collateral (9-102(a)(12))—and see how each of those makes a slight tweak to cover consignments. The actual definition of consignment is narrow; indeed, it may not cover the gallery example above (why?).

What is the consequence of bringing these consignments into Article 9? 9-319 is the key provision, and on first reading at least, it is a little tricky. The key notion in 9-319(a) is "deemed title." In the actual transaction between the consignor and the consignee—the artist and the gallery assuming that the transaction makes it into Article 9 under 9-102(a)(20)—title stays with the consignor and the consignee takes nothing. If we just applied the derivation principle, creditors of the consignee would get nothing. The consignee would lack sufficient rights in the collateral for, say, the consignee to grant a security interest to a secured creditor.

9-319(a) changes that by deeming the consignee to have title to the consigned goods equivalent to that held by the consignor, unless, see 9-319(b), the consignor takes steps to achieve priority under Article 9 in the consigned goods. That will often require filing a financing statement, and be sure to look carefully again at the standard financing statement set out in 9-521(a) and note that filing by consignors—and others—is contemplated. If the consignor achieves priority under Article 9, then law other than Article 9 controls a contest between a consignor and creditors of the consignee. That law, in most cases though not necessarily universally, will be some version of the derivation principle and that will block creditors of the consignee from accessing the consigned goods.

To make sure you get that, work through the next fact pattern and then turn to the case that follows. Does that case involve a consignment or something else? What turns on that?

8-14: TO FILE OR NOT TO FILE

- Artist delivers paintings to Gallery for sale. Artist retains title and assume that on the underlying facts the transaction otherwise qualifies as a consignment under 9-102(a)(20).

- Bank enters into an ordinary secured transaction with Gallery taking a security interest in all of the Gallery's assets, including after-acquired property. Bank perfects appropriately.

- ¤ If Gallery fails, who wins as between Artist and Bank? Does it matter whether Artist filed a financing statement when she delivered her art to Gallery? See 9-319.

Pioneer Commercial Funding Corp. v. American Financial Mortg. Corp.

Supreme Court of Pennsylvania, 2004.
855 A.2d 818.

■ JUSTICE SAYLOR

This appeal is centered on a commercial priority dispute between a banking institution exercising setoff against a general deposit account and a company asserting a third-party interest in the account proceeds, in the nature of absolute ownership and/or a perfected security interest.

Appellee, Pioneer Commercial Funding Corp. ("Pioneer") is a publicly-traded company that operated as a real estate warehouse lender in California. As such, Pioneer provided funding to small-to medium-sized companies originating loans to home buyers. Pioneer obtained its own primary funding via a line of credit extended by a consortium of lenders operating through a Texas financial institution known as Bank One Texas, N.A. ("Bank One").

In the usual course of affairs, loan originators receiving funding from Pioneer repaid their obligations using the proceeds from bulk sales of the loans to one or more third-party investors comprising a secondary market, thus enabling Pioneer to meet its own obligations to Bank One. Pending such sales, under the terms of loan and security agreements, Pioneer maintained a security interest in, *inter alia*, the original promissory notes signed by home buyers, as well as proceeds from their sale. Perfection was accomplished by means of possession of the negotiable instruments in bearer form—as home purchase transactions closed, the loan originators endorsed the notes in blank and delivered them to Pioneer, together with blank assignments and other security documentation. 9-313. Pursuant to a three-party agreement between Pioneer, the loan originator, and Bank One, Pioneer delivered these collateral packages to Bank One, to secure Pioneer's own credit line pending the resale. (Under the three-party agreement, Bank One held the collateral as agent for its consortium of lenders, Pioneer, and the loan originator.) Upon the resale, the notes were endorsed and transmitted to the purchaser with a shipping request (including wiring instructions for the sale proceeds) and bailee letter, a document employed as a general convention in the warehousing lending industry to permit a secured creditor to release possession of negotiable instruments to prospective purchasers without surrendering perfection. 9-313(h). The purchaser, in turn, wired funds to a restricted Pioneer account at Bank One, and Bank One was repaid from that account, thus completing the transaction.

At the center of this litigation is a business arrangement that was markedly different from Pioneer's usual course dealings, involving a California loan originator known as RNG Mortgage Services, Inc. ("RNG") and American Financial Mortgage Corporation ("AFMC"), a Pennsylvania company in the same business. As background, in the spring of 1997, Pioneer committed to serving as RNG's warehouse lender, and the companies executed loan and security and three-party agreements establishing the usual governing terms and conditions. This relationship, however, was compromised after August of 1997, when RNG sought protection under Chapter 11 of the federal Bankruptcy Code. RNG's financial condition impaired its ability to attract investors from the secondary market, given its inability to assure them recourse, thus threatening its ability to survive as a going concern. About the same time as RNG was seeking avenues to allow it to continue its operations, AFMC was exploring expansion opportunities. Learning of RNG's circumstances, AFMC began investigating a possible acquisition of the California company's assets, the most valuable of which was its portfolio of unfunded mortgage commitments, referred to in the industry as a loan "pipeline."

Both AFMC and RNG thus had an interest in maintaining RNG as a going concern while AFMC considered the acquisition. To accomplish this, they devised an arrangement whereby AFMC would receive an effective assignment of the loans, assume recourse responsibility relative to them, and sell them in the secondary market. Pioneer was also made a party to the discussions, as AFMC and RNG desired to obtain continued funding from Pioneer for loans in the pipeline. Pioneer elected to participate for its own reasons, apparently related to its desire to obtain the existing business and the prospect of a future warehouse lending relationship with AFMC.

The dispositive issue in this appeal concerns the nature of the interest conferred upon AFMC in this arrangement, and, relatedly, the character of the interest reserved to Pioneer. Mechanically, Pioneer and AFMC executed a loan and security agreement and a three-party agreement (with Bank One), thus facially establishing the framework of a debtor/creditor relationship. Pioneer agreed to arrange for the notes to be endorsed and shipped to AFMC, along with a bailee letter indicating that Pioneer held a security interest in the notes and their proceeds, and also, retained title pending full payment. AFMC, in turn, was to consummate the sale to an institutional investor, and Pioneer was to be paid from the proceeds. Additionally, RNG committed to obtaining approval of this arrangement from the federal bankruptcy court supervising its operations.

RNG assembled the first loan portfolio to be administered in this manner, worth approximately $2.3 million, in mid-October of 1997. AFMC proceeded to obtain a purchase commitment from Norwest Funding, Inc. ("Norwest"), an institutional investor that had categorically refused to purchase loans directly from RNG. In connection with the purchase, Norwest required a series of seller representations and warranties, including AFMC's attestation to its absolute and unencumbered ownership of the notes, which facially contradicted the bailee letter transmitted from Pioneer to AFMC. The notes were released to AFMC, endorsed by it, and shipped by AFMC to Norwest. After reviewing the notes, Norwest subsequently transferred payment for those that it accepted via the Federal Reserve Wire Transfer Network ("FedWire") to an AFMC account maintained with Appellant, CoreStates Bank, N.A. ("CoreStates"), which had been denominated by AFMC as a "settlement account." Upon AFMC's request, CoreStates forwarded the funds to Bank One, to the credit of Pioneer's designated account.

After the first transaction, Pioneer expressed concern about AFMC's possession of the proceeds from the loan sales and requested that AFMC instruct Norwest to transmit proceeds from future sales directly to Pioneer's account at Bank One. Representatives of Pioneer, RNG, and AFMC all contacted Norwest to convey Pioneer's request.

As it turns out, Pioneer's concern was well founded, since, unbeknownst to it or AFMC, CoreStates was beginning an investigation of account activity of corporations in which AFMC's principal, Thomas Flatley, had an interest. The bank had discovered a substantial overdraft in an AFMC account, in the amount of approximately $4.5 million, and, as a result of its investigation, concluded the overdraft was a consequence of a sustained practice of check kiting, i.e., improper manipulation of accounts to allow the account holder to draw on funds that it did not in fact possess.[10] In response, on November 7, 1997, CoreStates imposed debit restraints on Flatley company accounts, including the AFMC settlement account.

Without knowledge of this debit restraint, RNG, Pioneer, AFMC, and Norwest proceeded with the sale of a second portfolio of loans to Norwest, this time valued at approximately $1.78 million, which occurred during the second week of November, 1997. The second transaction initially proceeded much as the first one had. Contrary to Pioneer's expressed wishes, and despite the request that AFMC had previously conveyed on Pioneer's behalf, AFMC again furnished instructions to Norwest to wire the proceeds of the sale to AFMC's self-described settlement account at CoreStates. Norwest complied with those instructions and transmitted the approximately $1.78 million to this account via FedWire in three installments. These funds became frozen as a result of CoreStates' debit restraint, and CoreStates refused requests from the various parties to either return the monies to Norwest or to forward them to Pioneer's account at Bank One.

Later that month, CoreStates consulted a specialist in banking law in connection with the AFMC overdrafts. The attorney advised the bank that it had the right to set off monies credited to AFMC deposit accounts against the overdraft indebtedness.[11] CoreStates subsequently swept and closed AFMC's accounts, including the settlement account, making corresponding entries in its books to afford AFMC credit against its indebtedness. In the ensuing months, CoreStates negotiated repayment terms

---

[10] Pursuant to a cash management agreement with CoreStates, funds accumulated in any of AFMC's accounts could be used to cover checks drawn on other accounts. However, the series of overdrafts resulting in AFMC's ongoing indebtedness of $4.5 million was well beyond the scope of such agreement.

[11] A bank's right of setoff arises under common law, subject to requirements of mutuality of obligation, maturity, deposit in a general account, and depositor ownership. It is undisputed that the first three of these four elements were met; the depositor ownership element, however, is a central subject of the remaining controversy.

with Mr. Flatley for the remainder of the indebtedness, which culminated in a workout agreement executed in March of 1998.

Pioneer, for its part, would no longer fund RNG, and RNG ceased doing business. Although Pioneer never received payment in relation to the second loan portfolio, it satisfied its own indebtedness to Bank One. Apparently as a result of a downward spiral triggered by its substantial losses in this regard, however, Pioneer itself ceased doing business in the summer of 1999.

Pioneer commenced the present civil action against CoreStates, AFMC, Flatley, and Norwest, in 1998. * * * CoreStates invoked decisional law holding that a bank's common law right of setoff has priority over a perfected security interest in collateral.[13] See Pennsylvania Nat'l Bank & Trust Co. v. CCNB Bank N.A., 667 A.2d 1151, 1154-55 (1995). Pioneer, on the other hand, relied substantially on a line of cases vindicating the interests of third-party owners over a bank's right of setoff, where the account holder possesses the third-party funds strictly as a fiduciary or agent. See, e.g., Sherts v. Fulton Nat'l Bank, 21 A.2d 18, 20 (1941).

* * * [T]he trial court refused CoreStates' request for a directed verdict grounded in these principles and its proposed jury instructions embodying them. Instead, the trial court issued a relatively short set of instructions that did not differentiate between (and indeed conflated) possession by a fiduciary or agent subject to another's absolute reservation of title (a true trust or bailment arrangement and the *Sherts* paradigm) and a perfected security interest in account proceeds (the *Pennsylvania National Bank & Trust* scenario). The court then described Pioneer's essential claim as an assertion of a security interest in the AFMC account proceeds, and relegated CoreStates' defenses to the claim that Pioneer simply had no security interest. Having reduced the issue to be decided by the jury to the single question of whether or not Pioneer possessed a security interest, the trial court advised the jurors that, if they answered this question in the affirmative, CoreStates had no right to set off and could be found liable for con-

---

[13] Under the Uniform Commercial Code, as reflected in the Pennsylvania Commercial Code, perfection of a security interest is maintained in identifiable proceeds upon the sale of collateral. 9-315(a)(2). Whether proceeds are capable of identification is determined according to common law tracing rules. Here, the proceeds from the sale of the second loan portfolio to Norwest remained clearly identifiable, by virtue of CoreStates' debit restraint.

version. Additionally, the Court issued a generalized punitive damages charge.

In the context of the court's charge, the jury returned a special verdict finding that Pioneer possessed an ownership interest in the funds deposited in the AFMC settlement account. The jurors thus found CoreStates and AFMC liable in conversion, and awarded Pioneer the $1.78 million sum that CoreStates had set off. The jury also found CoreStates (but not AFMC) liable for punitive damages, and, after a damages phase of trial, awarded Pioneer an additional $13.5 million in consequential damages (the amount by which its market capitalization had declined between the date of setoff and the date of trial), and set the punitive damages award at $337.5 million.

In response to post-trial motions by CoreStates, the trial court sustained the liability findings and the compensatory damages award, but remitted the punitive damages to $40.5 million, resulting in a judgment in favor of Pioneer in the amount of approximately $56 million. *** We allowed CoreStates' subsequent appeal, in which it has maintained, *inter alia*, that the jury's verdict was tainted by the common pleas court's decision to depart from prevailing principles of commercial law on the basis that such precepts lack relevance to a tort action grounded in conversion theory.

*** [T]he case was submitted to a jury lacking essential direction. Because of the trial court's approach, the jury never learned of the relevant distinction under Pennsylvania law between the *Sherts* scenario, involving pure fiduciary or agency relationships entailing absolute retention of title, and a sale-on-credit transaction. Indeed, the trial court misled the jury by affirmatively indicating, contrary to the holding of *Pennsylvania National Bank & Trust*, that a security interest created a sufficient ownership interest to defeat a bank's right of setoff.

*** In its brief, Pioneer contends that *Pennsylvania National Bank & Trust* is not persuasive, and therefore, this Court should take this opportunity to overrule it. *** Pioneer takes the position that the case should be limited to its facts, as it involved bank setoff in relation to a certificate of deposit as opposed to a deposit account. The certificate of deposit at issue, however, was of the non-negotiable variety, which has been held to constitute a general deposit account under the prior version of the Uniform Commercial Code, and notably, this treatment has been made express under the revised Uniform Commercial Code. See 9-102, cmt. 12 (stating that "[t]he revised definition [of deposit account] clarifies the proper treatment of nonnegotiable or uncertificated certificates of deposit," and observing that, unless of a type subject to transfer by delivery only without endorsement or assignment, a non-negotiable certificate of deposit is a deposit account). Moreover, the *Pennsylvania National Bank & Trust* court obviously viewed non-negotiable certificates of deposit and deposit accounts as being of the same order, since it predicated its decision on a series of decisions involving bank setoff of deposit accounts.

We appreciate the complexity of the priority issue resolved in *Pennsylvania National Bank & Trust,* and acknowledge the strong equities attaching to each of the competing interests as between banking institutions and companies funding purchase transactions in general commerce. We are also aware that the *Pennsylvania National Bank & Trust* panel afforded little in the way of concrete explanation concerning the balance that it struck in devising a common law priority rule.[25] To some degree, the inability to fully rationalize a particular priority structure is inherent in the nature of the undertaking—it is perhaps best conceptualized as an attempt to establish a framework pursuant to which parties can organize their financial dealings on a prospective basis with a fair degree of predictability. As such, and given the range and scale of interests involved, the exercise is far more amenable to legislative determination than to common law decision making. Indeed, as Pioneer acknowledges, legislative intervention did in fact occur—in 1998, the Uniform Commercial Code was revised to embrace the *Pennsylvania National Bank & Trust* holding, see 9-340(a) (establishing the general rule that "a bank with which a deposit account is maintained may exercise any right of recoupment or set-off against a secured party that holds a security interest in the deposit account"), which has since been adopted in fifty states.

---

[25] Prior to 1998 amendments to the Uniform Commercial Code, there was in fact a fairly strong current in a number of other jurisdictions favoring the interests of secured creditors over depository institutions, based on the general priority provision of Article 9. See 9-201(a) ("Except as otherwise provided by this Act, a security interest is effective according to its terms between the parties, against purchasers of the collateral and against creditors."). The contrary line of cases generally relied on the exclusion of prior UCC Section 9-104(i) (excluding from the coverage of Article 9 a transfer of any "deposit, savings, passbook, or like account with a bank, savings and loan association, credit union, or like organization"), to exempt setoff from consideration under Article 9 entirely and to interpose a common law priority rule.

Thus, the Pioneer/AFMC arrangement for sale of the second loan portfolio to Norwest was orchestrated at a time when Pennsylvania's common law matched the Uniform Commercial Code's present, statutory priority scheme, and, as reflected in that scheme, and taking due consideration of the respective interests involved, the common law priority scheme was at least a reasonable one. In these circumstances, we do not believe that the interests of justice require further evaluation of the potential for retrospectively modifying the now-supplanted common law to consider the wisdom of a closed-ended departure from current practice.

In summary, under prevailing Pennsylvania law as it existed at the time of trial, the controlling question in this case should have been whether Pioneer effectuated an absolute reservation of title in the second loan portfolio and its proceeds (i.e., a true bailment), versus whether it possessed a perfected security interest (or something of lesser priority). Since the common pleas court failed to make this distinction, at a minimum, the verdict must be vacated and the case returned for a new trial.

CoreStates also seeks review of the trial court's decision to deny it judgment notwithstanding the verdict on the ground that, as a matter of law, Pioneer's interest should be relegated, at most, to the security-interest category. In this undertaking, we review the record in the light most favorable to Pioneer to assess whether its evidence was sufficient to sustain the bailment theory.

As a threshold matter, we recognize that Article 9 of the Uniform Commercial Code was conceived with the goal of minimizing the role of actual, technical title in the governance of commercial transactions. See generally 9-202 (stating the general rule that the provisions of Article 9 "apply whether title to collateral is in the secured party or the debtor"). Significantly, parties are not constrained, however, in all instances to conduct their affairs under the Uniform Commercial Code's regime; for example, a true bailment relationship (a directed-purpose transfer to an agent of possession only, subject to absolute retention of title), is not covered by Article 9. In distinguishing between transactions governed by the Uniform Commercial Code versus those controlled by other law (here, a sale on credit versus a true bailment), the intention of the parties is obviously the preeminent consideration. To assess intent, courts will look not to any particular document or the form of the transaction, but rather, to the overall transaction and its substance. See generally 9-102, cmt. 3b.

In the present case, Pioneer, RNG, and AFMC participated in an unusual transaction designed to invest in AFMC the accouterments of ownership vis-à-vis the second loan portfolio. The undisputed objective was to satisfy Norwest's condition that it have a right of recourse against the seller. Although the transaction was unique, it was nevertheless organized around a loan and security agreement, the cornerstone of a UCC-based security relationship, see 9-201, the notes were endorsed to AFMC, AFMC in turn endorsed the notes as the sole party entitled to their enforcement, and the transaction was held out to third parties as a sale with the knowledge of all concerned. The situation is in no way akin to that which was present in *Sherts,* namely, setoff of an attorney's deposit account containing proceeds from receivables belonging to third-parties. The overall structure of the transaction, therefore, militates strongly in favor of treating the transaction as a sale on credit, subject to a security interest.

The strongest evidence of an intention on the part of Pioneer to retain absolute title is reflected in the bailee letter. As noted, the bailee letter is a standard, commercial device designed to assure continued perfection of a security interest; it is not designed to create a true or pure bailment relationship. Moreover, in the circumstances presented, the assertion in the bailee letter of an absolute retention of title is inconsistent with the overall structure of the transaction—indeed, if it were to have been enforced, the proviso would have wholly undermined the sale of the second loan portfolio on the designated terms. We therefore agree with CoreStates that to permit a factfinder to regard the trust proviso of the bailee letter as dispositive would afford too little recognition to the other documents and the overall character of the transaction. We also view the similar characterizations of the transaction by Pioneer's lay witnesses at trial as insufficient to overcome the understanding arising from the undisputed structure and purpose of the transaction.

Accordingly, based on the evidence viewed in the light most favorable to Pioneer, we hold as a matter of law, that the transfer of the second loan portfolio to AFMC was in the nature of a sale-on-credit transaction, subject to a security interest, as opposed to a true bailment. As such, the case need not be returned for fact finding on this subject. * * *

Finally, we observe that CoreStates has raised a number of other important legal issues in this appeal. Most significantly, the framing of the case in terms of Article 4A of the Uniform Commercial Code and the incorporating provisions of Federal Reserve Board Regulation J, 12 CFR 10.25(a), (b), governing fund transfers, has attracted the attention of multiple *amici,* including the Federal Reserve Banks. In this regard, CoreStates has maintained throughout the litigation that Article 4A's express authorization of bank setoff, see 4A-502(c) (providing, *inter alia,* that "the amount credited [via wire transfer] may be set off against an obligation owed by the beneficiary to the bank"), as incorporated into Regulation J, preempts common law distinctions based on ownership or secured status external to Article 4A as they might otherwise pertain to the lawfulness of bank setoff. In this regard, CoreStates' position appears to encompass the assertion that the *Sherts* holding has been preempted (or at least substantially displaced) by statute. This, in turn, has given rise to concerns on the part of another *amicus,* whose interests are representative of a substantial body of persons and organizations that are beneficiaries of statutory trusts arising by operation of federal law, for example, in proceeds from the sale of perishable agricultural commodities. See 7 USC 499e(c). This *amicus* presents the counter argument that Article 4A's setoff provision was intended to incorporate existing setoff and priority rules into the funds transfer arena, not to supplant them. Given our determination, above, however, there is simply is no conflict between Article 4A (or Regulation J) and Pennsylvania common law concerning any material point of the present dispute. Therefore, although we acknowledge the importance of this issue and the respective merits of the competing positions, according to the general principles by which we address controversies, resolution will be reserved for a case in which the question would be of controlling significance.

The order of the Superior Court is reversed and the matter is remanded for entry of judgment notwithstanding the verdict in favor of CoreStates.
* * *

COMMENTS AND QUESTIONS

For commentary on *Pioneer,* see Stephen C. Veltri, Marina I. Adams & Paul S. Turner, Payments: 2004 Developments, Survey: Uniform Commercial Code, 60 Bus. Law. 1669 (2005); Steven O. Weise, UCC Article 9: Personal Property Secured Transactions, Survey: Uniform Commercial Code, 60 Bus. Law. 1725 (2005).

Before reading the next case, take a good look at 1-201(b)(35) and 1-203. We have struggled to figure out the right way in the text to separate secured transactions from leases. At the time that *Marhoefer* was decided, the relevant text provided that:

> Whether a lease is intended as security is to be determined by the facts of each case; however, (a) the inclusion of an option to purchase does not of itself make the lease one intended for security, and (b) an agreement that upon compliance with the terms of the lease the lessee shall become or has the option to become the owner of the property for no additional consideration or for a nominal consideration does make the lease one intended for security.

1-203 follows the old structure in that it states that whether or not a particular transaction is intended to be one for security depends on all of the facts of the transaction, and then goes on to identify certain factors that are *not* to be dispositive of the question and then certain factors that *are* to be dispositive. Did the old statute cleanly resolve *Marhoefer*? Does the new one?

In re Marhoefer Packing Co.

United States Court of Appeals, Seventh Circuit, 1982.
674 F.2d 1139.

■ PELL, CIRCUIT JUDGE

This appeal involves a dispute between the trustee of the bankrupt Marhoefer Packing Company, Inc., ("Marhoefer") and Robert Reiser & Company, Inc., ("Reiser") over certain equipment held by Marhoefer at the time of bankruptcy. The issue presented is whether the written agreement between Marhoefer and Reiser covering the equipment is a true lease under which Reiser is entitled to reclaim its property from the bankrupt estate, or whether it is actually a lease intended as security in which case Reiser's failure to file a financing statement to perfect its interest renders it subordinate to the trustee.

I

In December of 1976, Marhoefer Packing Co., Inc., of Muncie, Indiana, entered into negotiations with Reiser, a Massachusetts based corporation engaged in the business of selling and leasing food processing equipment, for the acquisition of one or possibly two Vemag Model 3007-1 Continuous Sausage Stuffers. Reiser informed Marhoefer that the units could be acquired by outright purchase, conditional sale contract or lease. Marhoefer ultimately acquired two sausage stuffers from Reiser. It purchased one under a conditional sale contract. Pursuant to the contract, Reiser retained a security interest in the machine, which it subsequently perfected by filing a financing statement with the Indiana Secretary of State. Title to that stuffer is not here in dispute. The other stuffer was delivered to Marhoefer under a written "Lease Agreement."

The Lease Agreement provided for monthly payments of $665 over a term of 48 months. The last nine months payments, totaling $5,985, were payable upon execution of the lease. If at the end of the lease term the machine was to be returned, it was to be shipped prepaid to Boston or similar destination "in the same condition as when received, reasonable wear and tear resulting from proper use alone excepted, and fully crated." The remaining terms and conditions of the agreement were as follows:

1. Any State or local taxes and/or excises are for the account of the Buyer.

2. The equipment shall at all times be located at

> Marhoefer Packing Co., Inc.
> 1500 North Elm & 13th Street
> Muncie, Indiana

and shall not be removed from said location without the written consent of Robert Reiser & Co. The equipment can only be used in conjunction with the manufacture of meat or similar products unless written consent is given by Robert Reiser & Co.

3. The equipment will carry a ninety-day guarantee for workmanship and materials and shall be maintained and operated safely and carefully in conformity with the instructions issued by our operators and the maintenance manual. Service and repairs of the equipment after the ninety-day period will be subject to a reasonable and fair charge.

4. If, after due warning, our maintenance instructions should be violated repeatedly, Robert Reiser & Co. will have the right to cancel the lease contract on seven days notice and remove the said equipment. In that case, lease fees would be refunded pro rata.

5. It is mutually agreed that in case of lessee, Marhoefer Packing Co., Inc., violating any of the above conditions, or shall

default in the payment of any lease charge hereunder, or shall become bankrupt, make or execute any assignment or become party to any instrument or proceedings for the benefit of its creditors, Robert Reiser & Co. shall have the right at any time without trespass, to enter upon the premises and remove the aforesaid equipment, and if removed, lessee agrees to pay Robert Reiser & Co. the total lease fees, including all installments due or to become due for the full unexpired term of this lease agreement and including the cost for removal of the equipment and counsel fees incurred in collecting sums due hereunder.

6. It is agreed that the equipment shall remain personal property of Robert Reiser & Co. and retain its character as such no matter in what manner affixed or attached to the premises.

In a letter accompanying the lease, Reiser added two option provisions to the agreement. The first provided that at the end of the four-year term, Marhoefer could purchase the stuffer for $9,968. In the alternative, it could elect to renew the lease for an additional four years at an annual rate of $2,990, payable in advance. At the conclusion of the second four-year term, Marhoefer would be allowed to purchase the stuffer for one dollar.

Marhoefer never exercised either option. Approximately one year after the Vemag stuffer was delivered to its plant, it ceased all payments under the lease and shortly thereafter filed a voluntary petition in bankruptcy. On July 12, 1978, the trustee of the bankrupt corporation applied to the bankruptcy court for leave to sell the stuffer free and clear of all liens on the ground that the "Lease Agreement" was in fact a lease intended as security within the meaning of the Uniform Commercial Code ("Code") and that Reiser's failure to perfect its interest as required by Article 9 of the Code rendered it subordinate to that of the trustee. Reiser responded with an answer and counterclaim in which it alleged that the agreement was in fact a true lease, Marhoefer was in default under the lease, and its equipment should therefore be returned.

Following a trial on this issue, the bankruptcy court concluded that the agreement between Marhoefer and Reiser was in fact a true lease and ordered the trustee to return the Vemag stuffer to Reiser. The trustee appealed to the district court, which reversed on the ground that the bankruptcy court had erred as a matter of law in finding the agreement to be a true lease. We now reverse the judgment of the district court.

II

* * * The primary issue to be decided in determining whether a lease is "intended as security" is whether it is in effect a conditional sale in which the "lessor" retains an interest in the "leased" goods as security for the purchase price. By defining the term "security interest" to include a lease intended as security, the drafters of the Code intended such disguised security interests to be governed by the same rules that apply to other security interests. In this respect, [1-201(b)(35)] represents the drafter's refusal to recognize form over substance.

Clearly, where a lease is structured so that the lessee is contractually bound to pay rent over a set period of time at the conclusion of which he automatically or for only nominal consideration becomes the owner of the leased goods, the transaction is in substance a conditional sale and should be treated as such. It is to this type of lease that clause [1-203](b) properly applies. Here, however, Marhoefer was under no contractual obligation to pay rent until such time as the option to purchase the Vemag stuffer for one dollar was to arise. In fact, in order to acquire that option, Marhoefer would have had to exercise its earlier option to renew the lease for a second four-year term and pay Reiser an additional $11,960 in "rent." In effect, Marhoefer was given a right to terminate the agreement after the first four years and cease making payments without that option ever becoming operative.

Despite this fact, the district court concluded as a matter of law that the lease was intended as security. It held that, under clause (b) of [1-203], a lease containing an option for the lessee to purchase the leased goods for nominal consideration is conclusively presumed to be one intended as security. This presumption applies, the court concluded, regardless of any other options the lease may contain.

We think the district court's reading of clause (b) is in error. In our view, the conclusive presumption provided under clause (b) applies only where the option to purchase for nominal consideration necessarily arises upon compliance with the lease. It does not apply where the lessee has the right to terminate the lease before that option arises with no further obligation to continue paying rent. For where the lessee has the right to terminate the transaction, it is not a conditional sale.

Moreover, to hold that a lease containing such an option is intended as security, even though the lessee has no contractual obligation to pay the full amount contemplated by the agreement, would lead to clearly erroneous results under other provisions of the Code. Under [9-623] of the Code, for example, a debtor in default on his obligation to a secured party has a right to redeem the collateral by tendering full payment of that obligation. The same right is also enjoyed by a lessee under a lease intended as security. A lessee who defaults on a lease intended as security is entitled to purchase the leased goods by paying the full amount of his obligation under the lease. But if the lessee has the right to terminate the lease at any time during the lease term, his obligation under the lease may be only a small part of the total purchase price of the goods leased. To afford the lessee a right of redemption under such circumstances would clearly be wrong. There is no evidence that the drafters of the Code intended such a result.

We therefore hold that while [1-203(b)] does provide a conclusive test of when a lease is intended as security, that test does not apply in every case in which the disputed lease contains an option to purchase for nominal or no consideration. An option of this type makes a lease one intended as security only when it necessarily arises upon compliance with the terms of the lease.

Applying [1-201(b)(35) and 1-203], so construed, to the facts of this case, it is clear that the district court erred in concluding that the possibility of Marhoefer's purchasing the stuffer for one dollar at the conclusion of a second four-year term was determinative. Because Marhoefer could have fully complied with the lease without that option ever arising, the district court was mistaken in thinking that the existence of that option alone made the lease a conditional sale. Certainly, if Marhoefer had elected to renew the lease for another term, in which case the nominal purchase option would necessarily have arisen, then the clause (b) test would apply.[6] But that is not the case we are faced with here. Marhoefer was not required to make any payments beyond the first four years. The fact that, at the conclusion of that term, it could have elected to renew the lease and obtain an option to purchase the stuffer for one dollar at the end of the second term does not transform the original transaction into a conditional sale.

---

[6] Reiser concedes that had Marhoefer elected to renew the lease after the first term, the transaction would have been transformed into a sale. George Vetie, Reiser's treasurer, testified that the renewal option was actually intended as a financing mechanism to allow Marhoefer to purchase the stuffer at the end of the lease if it desired to do so but was either unable or unwilling to pay the initial purchase price of $9,968.

This fact does not end our inquiry under clause (b), however, for the trustee also argues that, even if the district court erred in considering the one dollar purchase option as determinative, the lease should nevertheless be considered a conditional sale because the initial option price of $9,968 is also nominal when all of the operative facts are properly considered. We agree that if the clause (b) test is to apply at all in this case, this is the option that must be considered. For this is the option that was to arise automatically upon Marhoefer's compliance with the lease. We do not agree, however, that under the circumstances presented here the $9,968 option price can properly be considered nominal.

It is true that an option price may be more than a few dollars and still be considered nominal within the meaning of [1-203]. Because clause (b) speaks of nominal "consideration" and not a nominal "sum" or "amount," it has been held to apply not only where the option price is very small in absolute terms, but also where the price is insubstantial in relation to the fair market value of the leased goods at the time the option arises.

Here, however, the evidence revealed that the initial option price of $9,968 was not nominal even under this standard. George Vetie, Reiser's treasurer and the person chiefly responsible for the terms of the lease, testified at trial that the purchase price for the Vemag stuffer at the time the parties entered into the transaction was $33,225. He testified that the initial option price of $9,968 was arrived at by taking thirty percent of the purchase price, which was what he felt a four-year-old Vemag stuffer would be worth based on Reiser's past experience.

The trustee, relying on the testimony of its expert appraiser, argues that in fact the stuffer would have been worth between eighteen and twenty thousand dollars at the end of the first four-year term. Because the initial option price is substantially less than this amount, he claims that it is nominal within the meaning of clause (b) and the lease is therefore one intended as security.

Even assuming this appraisal to be accurate, an issue on which the bankruptcy court made no finding, we would not find the initial option price of $9,968 so small by comparison that the clause (b) presumption would apply. While it is difficult to state any bright line percentage test for determining when an option price could properly be considered nominal as compared to the fair market value of the leased goods, an option price of almost ten thousand dollars, which amounts to fifty percent of the fair market value, is not nominal by any standard.

Furthermore, in determining whether an option price is nominal, the proper figure to compare it with is not the actual fair market value of the leased goods at the time the option arises, but their fair market value at that time as anticipated by the parties when the lease is signed. Here, for example, Vetie testified that his estimate of the fair market value of a four-year-old Vemag stuffer was based on records from a period of time in which the economy was relatively stable. Since that time, a high rate of inflation has caused the machines to lose their value more slowly. As a result, the actual fair market value of a machine may turn out to be significantly more than the parties anticipated it would be several years earlier. When this occurs, the lessee's option to purchase the leased goods may be much more favorable than either party intended, but it does not change the true character of the transaction.

We conclude, therefore, that neither option to purchase contained in the lease between Marhoefer and Reiser gives rise to a conclusive presumption under [1-201(b)(35) and 1-203] that the lease is one intended as security. This being so, we now turn to the other facts surrounding the transaction.

III

Although [1-203(a)] states that "[w]hether a lease is intended as security is to be determined by the facts of each case," it is completely silent as to what facts, other than the option to purchase, are to be considered in making that determination. Facts that the courts have found relevant include the total amount of rent the lessee is required to pay under the lease; whether the lessee acquires any equity in the leased property; the useful life of the leased goods; the nature of the lessor's business; and the payment of taxes, insurance and other charges normally imposed on ownership. Consideration of the facts of this case in light of these factors leads us to conclude that the lease in question was not intended as security.

First, Marhoefer was under no obligation to pay the full purchase price for the stuffer. Over the first four-year term, its payments under the lease were to have amounted to $31,920. Although this amount may not be substantially less than the original purchase price of $33,225 in absolute terms, it becomes so when one factors in the interest rate over four years that would have been charged had Marhoefer elected to purchase the machine under a conditional sale contract.[8] The fact that the total amount of

---

[8] The bankruptcy court found that Reiser was originally willing to sell Marhoefer the

rent Marhoefer was to pay under the lease was substantially less than that amount shows that a sale was not intended.

It is also significant that the useful life of the Vemag stuffer exceeded the term of the lease. An essential characteristic of a true lease is that there be something of value to return to the lessor after the term. Where the term of the lease is substantially equal to the life of the leased property such that there will be nothing of value to return at the end of the lease, the transaction is in essence a sale. Here, the evidence revealed that the useful life of a Vemag stuffer was eight to ten years.

Finally, the bankruptcy court specifically found that "there was no express or implied provision in the lease agreement dated February 28, 1977, which gave Marhoefer any equity interest in the leased Vemag stuffer." This fact clearly reveals the agreement between Marhoefer and Reiser to be a true lease. Had Marhoefer remained solvent and elected not to exercise its option to renew its lease with Reiser, it would have received nothing for its previous lease payments. And in order to exercise that option, Marhoefer would have had to pay what Reiser anticipated would then be the machine's fair market value. An option of this kind is not the mark of a lease intended as security.

Although Marhoefer was required to pay state and local taxes and the cost of repairs, this fact does not require a contrary result. Costs such as taxes, insurance and repairs are necessarily borne by one party or the other. They reflect less the true character of the transaction than the strength of the parties' respective bargaining positions.

IV

We conclude from the foregoing that the district court erred in its application of [1-201(b)(35) and 1-203] to the facts of this case. Neither the option to purchase the Vemag stuffer for one dollar at the conclusion of a second four-year term, nor the initial option to purchase it for $9,968 after the first four years, gives rise to a conclusive presumption under clause (b) of [1-203] that the lease is intended as security. From all of the facts sur-

---

stuffer under a conditional sale contract the terms of which would have been $7,225 down and monthly installments of $1,224 over a twenty-four month period. The total payments under such an agreement would have amounted to $36,601, substantially more than the amount Marhoefer was required to pay over four years under the lease.

rounding the transaction, we conclude that the agreement between Marhoefer and Reiser is a true lease.

COMMENTS AND QUESTIONS: DOING THE NUMBERS IN *MARHOEFER*

If you look across the wreckage of the secured transactions caselaw, you will find no shortage of sloppy transactions, transactions in which the parties gave almost no thought before the fact to what it was they were seeking to do, but where after the fact they have substantial incentives as to how the court sees the transaction. Part of what is unusual about the transactions in *Marhoefer* is that we seem to have concrete evidence that the parties sought to enter into two different transactions. It is surely possible that they intended the same substance in each transaction and they just dressed them up differently, but the more likely inference is that the substance of the two transactions was to differ.

Consider the terms of the lease. The original term was for 48 months, with the final nine payments payable in advance (for a total of $5,985), followed by 39 monthly payments at $665. The lease imposed restrictions on use and location and Reiser was given the right to take the stuffer back for failure to maintain, regardless of payments on lease. The lease had an option provision as well. At the end of the four years, Marhoefer could do one of three things: it could return the stuffer to Reiser; it could purchase it for $9,968; or it could renew the lease for four years at $2,990 per year, payable annually in advance, coupled with a $1 purchase option at end of the second four-year term. We might also note that the stuffer had an original purchase price of $33,225, and Reiser would have sold it to Marhoefer for $7,225 down and 24 monthly payments of $1,224.

Suppose that a sale agreement had been entered into between Marhoefer and Reiser providing for the following terms: a down payment of $5,986, 39 monthly payments of $665, and a balloon payment after the 48th month of $9,968. The first column of figures in the next table has the actual sale terms offered by Reiser, which, after some work with the numbers, suggests that the implicit annual interest rate was 12%. The second column uses that interest rate, the actual amount payable on transfer of the stuffer, and the planned number of payments to compute a fixed monthly payment on the assumption that the stuffer was sold up-front.

	Offered Sale	Sale w/o Balloon	Sale with Balloon
Purchase Price	$33,225	$33,225	$33,225
Down Payment Amount	$7,225	$5,985	$5,985
Final Balloon	$0	$0	$9,968
Secured Debt	$26,000	$27,240	$21,057
Annual Interest Rate	12%	12%	12%
Monthly Interest Rate	1%	1%	1%
Number of Periods	24	39	39
Fixed Monthly Payment	$1,224	$847	$655
Total Dollars Paid	$36,599	$39,015	$41,486

The third column calculates the monthly payment due, using the given interest rate, the up-front payment, and balloon payment to purchase at the end of the first four-year term. Note that the amount due, $655, is in the ballpark of the actual amount paid in the case, $665.

Had the transaction taken place under the terms of column 2—the sale without the balloon payment—shouldn't we treat this as a financed sale, with the interest of the seller being seen as a security interest? How does this differ from column 3, which we take to approximate the economic deal between Reiser and Marhoefer? Is the balloon payment optional or mandatory? Should this matter? Suppose that we knew with a certainty that the value of the sausage stuffer after four years was going to be $14,000. Should that affect the way in which we think about this transaction?

SECTION III. INCLUDED TRANSACTIONS: SALES OF ACCOUNTS AND THE LIKE AND SECURITIZATION

You might not notice it on your first pass through Article 9, but Article 9 covers more than just secured transactions: it also covers sales of accounts, chattel paper, payment intangibles and promissory notes. Go back and re-read 9-109(a)(3) (" ... this Article applies to ... (3) a sale of accounts, chattel paper, payment intangibles, or promissory notes") and the definition of "security interest" in 1-201(b)(35) ("[t]he term also includes any interest of a consignor and a buyer of accounts, chattel paper, a payment intangible, or a promissory note in a transaction that is subject to Article 9"). You might also consider the definitions of "collateral," "debtor," and "secured party" in 9-102. This should startle you: Article 9 does not cover sales of, say, green beans—we leave that to Article 2—and yet here it throws in sales of accounts, chattel paper, payment intangibles and promissory notes. Why?

The answer is that it has proven difficult over time to separate secured transactions involving accounts from sales of those accounts. If as a lawmaker or drafter you cannot do a good job of articulating a bright line separating two related transactions, you might be wise to treat them identically. The decision to bring these sales into Article 9 reflects exactly these concerns. See also 9-101, Official Comment 4.a. That said, you should also be careful that when you lump together two transactions, you may inadvertently invoke a legal result that you did not intend. These issues are important in their own right, but have taken on greater significance with the right of the practice of securitization.

We need to understand what it means to "include" specified sales within Article 9 and where, if ever, it matters whether we can distinguish sales of, say, accounts, from a secured transaction covering accounts. Start backwards. Separating true sales from secured transactions matters most as to two issues: (1) surplus and deficiency rights and (2) exclusion of assets from bankruptcy. 9-608(b) and 9-615(e) set forth the rule that if there is a true sale of accounts, chattel paper, payment intangibles or promissory notes, the debtor is not entitled to a surplus nor is the debtor liable for a deficiency. Said differently, if the debtor sells accounts to a purchaser, the purchaser has no right to go to the debtor to ask for more money if the accounts do not collect in full. The purchaser has, after all, purchased the account and has accepted ownership risk. At the same time, if the amounts collected on the accounts exceed the purchase price, the debtor/seller has no right to go to the purchaser and demand that the excess amounts—the surplus—be turned over to the seller.

Turn to the first issue. What does it mean to include a true sale of accounts and certain others within Article 9? The rules for accounts and chattel paper, on the one hand, and payment intangibles and promissory notes, on the other hand, differ, reflecting the difficulties of bringing new subject areas in an old statute. A true sale must be perfected. If it is not perfected, other creditors—and subsequent purchasers—can jump ahead of the purchaser under 9-318(b). 9-318(b) does this through a "deemed title" approach akin to what we saw for consignments under 9-319(a).

How do you perfect a true sale? For payment intangibles and promissory notes, the purchaser need do nothing; perfection is automatic. 9-309(3),

9-309(4). As Comment 4 to 9-309 makes clear, this continues prior practice, where no filing was required for a true sale of a payment intangible, as it was wholly outside of Article 9. In contrast, again continuing prior practice, filing is usually required for a true sale of accounts, see 9-310(a) and 9-309 Comment 3, though there are situations where the sale of accounts will be perfected automatically. 9-309(2). A true sale of chattel paper can be perfected by filing, 9-312(a), or by possession, if the chattel paper is tangible, 9-313(a), and recall that the new statute contemplates electronic chattel paper as a possibility. Possession will frequently have advantages. 9-330(a).

You now understand how to perfect a true sale. What happens if you do not do so? Consider the following fact patterns:

8-15: UNPERFECTED SALES?

- Debtor sells chattel paper to Buyer for $10,000. Buyer does not file a financing statement in connection with the purchase.

- ¤ Subsequently, an unsecured creditor works its way through the state law process to become a lien creditor. What rights does the new lien creditor have as to the sold chattel paper?

- ¤ Suppose instead that after the sale, Debtor tried to sell the same chattel paper to Purchaser. What rights can Purchaser obtain? Does it matter whether Purchaser files a financing statement?

8-16: TRUE SALES I

- Debtor again sells accounts with a face value of $25,000 to Factor who pays $24,000. Debtor warrants that the accounts are all fully collectable. Debtor agrees to pay to Factor the face amount of any account that cannot be collected.

- ¤ Has Debtor sold all of these accounts? If these aren't sales, what are they? What turns on this?

8-17: TRUE SALES II

- Debtor again sells accounts with a face value of $25,000 to Factor who pays $24,000. Debtor sells Factor a put, meaning that Factor has the right to sell back to Debtor accounts that cannot be collected.

- ¤ Again, has Debtor sold all of these accounts? If these aren't sales, what are they?

Before considering the case that follows, we should see if we can articulate the difference between a loan and a sale. That is what *Major's Furniture Mart* demands of us, but drawing that line can turn out to be surprisingly difficult. Article 9 itself punts, though the comments are a little fuzzy. Look at comment 4 to 9-109, comment 2 to 9-318 and comment 9 to 9-607 and consider the fact patterns that follow.

8-18: PLAIN VANILLA

- Bank lends Debtor $10,000, due in one year, with simple interest of 10%. (This means Debtor will owe Bank $11,000 at the end of the year.) Debtor grants Bank a security interest in a painting owned by Debtor and Bank files appropriately.
- ¤ Describe Bank's position.

8-19: FRENCH VANILLA PUTS?

- Debtor has a painting worth $10,000. Debtor sells painting to Bank for that amount and Bank pays in cash. Debtor and Bank further agree that Bank has the right to sell the painting back to Debtor for $11,000 in one year.
- ¤ Describe Bank's position.

8-20: DOUBLE-DUTCH CHOCOLATE PUTS AND CALLS OR PLAIN VANILLA?

- Debtor has a painting worth $10,000. Debtor sells painting to Bank for that amount and Bank pays in cash. Debtor and Bank further agree that Bank has the right to sell the painting back to Debtor for $11,000 in one year. Debtor and Bank further agree that Debtor has the right to buy the painting back from Bank in one year for $11,000.
- ¤ Describe Bank's position. Would the analysis change if we switched from a painting to accounts receivable?

Major's Furniture Mart, Inc. v. Castle Credit Corp.

United States Court of Appeals, Third Circuit, 1979.
602 F.2d 538.

■ GARTH, CIRCUIT JUDGE

This appeal requires us to answer the question: "When is a sale—not a sale, but rather a secured loan?" The district court held that despite the form of their Agreement, which purported to be, and hence was characterized as, a sale of accounts receivable, the parties' transactions did not constitute sales. * * *

I

Major's is engaged in the retail sale of furniture. Castle is in the business of financing furniture dealers such as Major's. Count I of Major's amended complaint alleged that Major's and Castle had entered into an Agreement dated June 18, 1973 for the financing of Major's accounts receivable; that a large number of transactions pursuant to the Agreement took place between June 1973 and May 1975; that in March and October 1975 Castle declared Major's in default under the Agreement; and that from and after June 1973 Castle was in possession of monies which constituted a surplus over the accounts receivable transferred under the Agreement. Among other relief sought, Major's asked for an accounting of the surplus and all sums received by Castle since June 1, 1976 which had been collected from the Major's accounts receivable transferred under the Agreement. * * *

The provisions of the June 18, 1973 Agreement which are relevant to our discussion provide: that Major's shall from time to time "sell" accounts receivable to Castle, and that all accounts so "sold" shall be with full recourse against Major's. Major's was required to warrant that each account receivable was based upon a written order or contract fully performed by Major's. ([9-102(a)(11)], classifies the accounts receivable which are the subject of the agreement as "chattel paper.") Castle in its sole discretion could refuse to "purchase" any account. The amount paid by Castle to Major's on any particular account was the unpaid face amount of the account exclusive of interest less a fifteen percent "discount"[5] and less another ten percent of the unpaid face amount as a reserve against bad debts.[6]

---

[5] The 15% "discount" was subsequently increased unilaterally by Castle to 18% and thereafter was adjusted monthly to reflect changes in the prime rate * * * .

[6] It becomes apparent from a review of the record that the amount which Castle actually paid to Major's on each account transferred was the unpaid face amount exclusive of interest *and* exclusive of insurance premiums less 28% (18% "discount" and 10% reserve).

In its brief on appeal, Castle sets out the following summary of the transactions that took place over the relevant period. It appears that the face amount of the accounts which were "sold" by Major's to Castle was $439,832, to which finance charges totaling $116,350 and insurance charges totaling $42,304 were added, bringing the total amount "purchased" by Castle to $598,486. For these "purchases" Castle

Under the Agreement the reserve was to be held by Castle without interest and was to indemnify Castle against a customer's failure to pay the full amount of the account (which included interest and insurance premiums), as well as any other charges or losses sustained by Castle for any reason.

In addition, Major's was required to "repurchase" any account "sold" to Castle which was in default for more than 60 days. In such case Major's was obligated to pay to Castle

> an amount equal to the balance due by the customer on said Account plus any other expenses incurred by CASTLE as a result of such default or breach of warranty, less a rebate of interest on the account under the "Rule of the 78's". * * *

Thus essentially, Major's was obligated to repurchase a defaulted account not for the discounted amount paid to it by Castle, but for a "repurchase" price based on the balance due by the customer, plus any costs incurred by Castle upon default.

As an example, applying the Agreement to a typical case, Major's in its brief on appeal summarized an account transaction of one of its customers (William Jones) as follows:

> A customer [Jones] of Major's (later designated Account No. 15,915) purchased furniture from Major's worth $1700 (or more). [H]e executed an installment payment agreement with Major's in the total face amount of $2550, including interest and insurance costs. * * * Using this piece of chattel paper, * * * Major's engaged in a financing transaction with Castle under the Agreement. * * * Major's delivered the Jones' chattel paper with a $2550 face amount of Castle together with an assignment of rights. Shortly thereafter, Castle delivered to Major's cash in the amount of $1224. The difference between this cash amount and the full face of the chattel paper in the amount of $2550, consisted of the following costs and deductions by Castle:

---

paid Major's $316,107. Exclusive of any surplus as determined by the district court Castle has retained $528,176 which it has received as a result of customer collections and repurchases by Major's. Collection costs were found by the district court to be $1,627.

1. $180 discount credited to a "reserve" account of Major's.
2. $300 "discount" (actually a prepaid interest charge).
3. $31 for life insurance premium.
4. $78 for accident and health insurance premium.
5. $153 for property insurance premium.
6. $588 interest charged to Jones on the $1700 face of the note.

Thus, as to the Jones' account, Castle received and proceeded to collect a piece of chattel paper with a collectible face value of $2550. Major's received $1224 in cash.

As we understand the Agreement, if Jones in the above example defaulted without having made any payments on account, the very least Major's would have been obliged to pay on repurchase would be $1,700 even though Major's had received only $1,224 in cash on transfer of the account and had been credited with a reserve of $180. The repurchase price was either charged fully to reserve or, as provided in the Agreement, 50% to reserve and 50% by cash payment from Major's. In the event of bankruptcy, default under the agreement or discontinuation of business, Major's was required to repurchase all outstanding accounts immediately. * * *

Under the Agreement, over 600 accounts were transferred to Castle by Major's of which 73 became delinquent and subject to repurchase by Major's. On March 21, 1975, Castle notified Major's that Major's was in default in failing to repurchase delinquent accounts * * *. Apparently to remedy the default, Major's deposited an additional $10,000 into the reserve. After June 30, 1975, Major's discontinued transferring accounts to Castle * * *. On October 7, 1975 Castle again declared Major's in default * * *.

Major's' action against Castle alleged that the transaction by which Major's transferred its accounts to Castle constituted a financing of accounts receivable and that Castle had collected a surplus of monies to which Major's was entitled. We are thus faced with the question which we posed at the outset of this opinion: did the June 18, 1973 Agreement create a *secured interest* in the accounts, or did the transaction constitute a *true sale* of the accounts? The district court, contrary to Castle's contention, refused to construe the Agreement as one giving rise to the sales of accounts receivable. Rather, it interpreted the Agreement as creating a security interest in the accounts which accordingly was subject to all the provisions of Article 9. * * *

Castle on appeal argues (1) that the express language of the Agreement indicates that it was an agreement for the sale of accounts and (2) that the parties' course of performance and course of dealing compel an interpretation of the Agreement as one for the sale of accounts. Castle also asserts that the district court erred in "reforming" the Agreement and in concluding that the transaction was a loan. In substance these contentions do no more than reflect Castle's overall position that the Agreement was for an absolute sale of accounts.

II

Our analysis starts with Article 9 which encompasses both *sales* of accounts and *secured interests* in accounts. Thus, the Code "applies * * * (a) to any transaction (regardless of its form) which is intended to create a security interest in * * * accounts * * *; and also (b) to any sale of accounts * * *" [9-109(a)(3)]. The official comments to that section make it evident that Article 9 is to govern *all* transactions in accounts. Comment 2 indicates that, because "[c]ommercial financing on the basis of accounts * * * is often so conducted that the distinction between a security transfer and a sale is blurred," that "sales" as well as transactions "intended to create a security interest" are subject to the provisions of Article 9. Moreover, a "security interest" is defined under the Act as "any interest of a buyer of accounts." [1-201(b)(35)]. Thus even an outright buyer of accounts, such as Castle claims to be, by definition has a "security interest" in the accounts which it purchases. * * *

The default section relevant here, which distinguishes between the consequences that follow on default when the transaction *secures an indebtedness* rather than a *sale*, provides:

> A secured party who by agreement is entitled to charge back uncollected collateral or otherwise to full or limited recourse against the debtor and who undertakes to collect from the account debtors or obligors must proceed in a commercially reasonable manner and may deduct his reasonable expenses of realization from the collections. *If the security agreement secures an indebtedness, the secured party must account to the debtor for any surplus,* and unless otherwise agreed, the debtor is liable for any deficiency. But, *if the underlying transaction was a sale of accounts,* contract rights, or chattel paper, *the debtor is entitled to any surplus* or is liable for any deficiency *only if the security agreement so provides.*

[9-608] (emphasis added).

Thus, if the accounts were transferred to Castle *to secure Major's' indebtedness,* Castle was obligated to account for and pay over the surplus proceeds to Major's under [9-608], as a debtor's (Major's') right to surplus in such a case cannot be waived even by an express agreement. [9-602(5)]. On the other hand, if a *sale of accounts* had been effected, then Castle was entitled to all proceeds received from all accounts because the June 18, 1973 Agreement does not provide otherwise.

However, while the Code instructs us as to the consequences that ensue as a result of the determination of "secured indebtedness" as contrasted with "sale," the Code does not provide assistance in distinguishing between the character of such transactions. This determination, as to whether a particular assignment constitutes a sale or a transfer for security, is left to the courts for decision. It is to that task that we now turn. * * *

IV

The comments to [9-608] (and in particular Comment 4) make clear to us that the presence of recourse in a sale agreement without more will not automatically convert a sale into a security interest. Hence, one of Major's arguments which is predicated on such a *per se* principle attracts us no more than it attracted the district court. The Code comments however are consistent with and reflect the views expressed by courts and commentators that "[t]he determination of whether a particular assignment constitutes a [true] sale or a transfer for security is left to the courts." F9-502, Comment 4. The question for the court then is whether the *nature* of the recourse, and the true nature of the transaction, are such that the legal rights and economic consequences of the agreement bear a greater similarity to a financing transaction or to a sale. * * *

In referring to the extremely relevant factor of "recourse" and to the risks allocated, the district court found:

> In the instant case the allocation of risks heavily favors Major's claim to be considered as an assignor with an interest in the collectibility of its accounts. It appears that Castle required Major's to retain all conceivable risks of uncollectibility of these accounts. It required warranties that retail account debtors—e.g., Major's customers—meet the criteria set forth by Castle, that Major's perform the credit check to verify that these criteria were satisfied, and that Major's warrant that the accounts were fully enforceable legally and were "fully and timely collectible."

It also imposed an obligation to indemnify Castle out of a reserve account for losses resulting from a customer's failure to pay, or for any breach of warranty, and an obligation to repurchase any account after the customer was in default for more than 60 days. Castle only assumed the risk that the assignor itself would be unable to fulfill its obligations. Guaranties of quality alone, or even guarantees of collectibility alone, might be consistent with a true sale, but Castle attempted to shift all risks to Major's, and incur none of the risks or obligations of ownership. It strains credulity to believe that this is the type of situation, referred to in Comment 4, in which "there may be a true sale of accounts * * * although recourse exists." When we turn to the conduct of the parties to seek support for this contention, we find instead that Castle, in fact, treated these transactions as a transfer of a security interest.

449 F. Supp. at 543.

Moreover, in looking to the conduct of the parties, the district court found one of the more significant documents to be an August 31, 1973 letter written by Irving Canter, President of Castle Credit, to Major's. As the district court characterized it, and as we agree:

> This letter, in effect, announces the imposition of a floating interest rate on loans under a line of credit of $80,000 per month, based upon the fluctuating prime interest rate. The key portion of the letter states:
>
> > Accordingly, your volume for the month of September cannot exceed $80,000. Any business above that amount will have to be paid for in October. I think you'll agree that your quota is quite liberal. The surcharge for the month of September will be 3% of the principal amount financed which is based upon a 9.5% prime rate. On October 1, and for each month thereafter, the surcharge will be adjusted, based upon the prime rate in effect at that time as it relates to a 6.5% base rate. * * *
>
> This unilateral change in the terms of the Agreement makes it obvious that Castle treated the transaction as a line of credit to Major's—i.e., a loan situation. Were this a true sale, as Castle now argues, it would not have been able to impose these new

conditions by fiat. Such changes in a sales contract would have modified the price term of the agreement, which could only be done by a writing signed by all the parties.

449 F. Supp. at 543.

It is apparent to us that on this record none of the risks present in a true sale is present here. Nor has the custom of the parties or their relationship, as found by the district court, given rise to more than a debtor/creditor relationship in which Major's' debt was secured by a transfer of Major's' customer accounts to Castle, thereby bringing the transaction within the ambit of [9-608]. To the extent that the district court determined that a surplus existed, Castle was obligated to account to Major's for that surplus and Major's' right to the surplus could not be waived, [9-602(5)]. Accordingly, we hold that on this record the district court did not err in determining that the true nature of the transaction between Major's and Castle was a secured loan, not a sale. * * *

Suppose that we have an unperfected true sale of accounts. What does that mean? Does the debtor retain an interest in the accounts? Can other creditors obtain a superior interest in the accounts? If the debtor retains an interest and the debtor files for bankruptcy, does that interest or the accounts themselves become part of the debtor's bankruptcy estate?

These are worthy issues generally but especially important for securitization transactions. These are transactions in which the debtor sells assets to a newly-created entity in exchange for cash raised by creating a capital structure for the new entity, such as selling securities in the public markets. If done right, the sale isolates the sold assets from the operating assets of the debtor. If the debtor gets into financial trouble and files for bankruptcy, the assets held by the special-purposed vehicle should be outside the debtor's bankruptcy.

In re LTV Steel Co.

United States Bankruptcy Court, N.D. Ohio, 2001.
274 Bankr. 278.

■ BODOH, BANKRUPTCY JUDGE

This cause is before the Court on the emergency motion of Abbey National Treasury Services PLC ("Abbey National") for modification of an interim order entered by the Court on December 29, 2000. That order permitted LTV Steel Company, Inc., Debtor and Debtor-in-Possession in these jointly administered proceedings ("Debtor"), to use cash assets that are claimed to be cash collateral in which Abbey National has an interest. A hearing was held on this matter on January 18, 2001. Richard M. Cieri, Esq. and Bruce Bennett, Esq. appeared on behalf of Debtor. Thomas D. Lambros, Esq., David Spears, Esq. and Lindsee P. Granfield, Esq. appeared on behalf of Abbey National. This is a core proceeding over which the Court has jurisdiction pursuant to 28 U.S.C. § 157(b)(2)(M) and (O). The following constitutes the Court's findings of fact and conclusions of law pursuant to Fed. R. Bankr. P. 7052.

Debtor is one of the largest manufacturers of wholly-integrated steel products in the United States. Debtor mainly produces flat rolled steel products, hot and cold rolled sheet metal, mechanical and structural tubular products, and bimetallic wire. Debtor currently employs approximately 17,500 people in various capacities, and Debtor is also responsible for providing medical coverage and other benefits to approximately 100,000 retirees and their dependents. Debtor and 48 of its subsidiaries filed voluntary petitions for relief under Chapter 11 of Title 11, United States Code, on December 29, 2000. These cases are jointly administered.

This is not the first occasion on which Debtor has filed for relief under the Bankruptcy Code. Debtor previously filed a voluntary Chapter 11 petition in the Bankruptcy Court for the Southern District of New York on July 17, 1986. Debtor successfully emerged from Chapter 11 on June 28, 1993. Indeed, the current controversy stems from a series of financial transactions that Debtor executed after its previous reorganization. The transactions in question are known as asset-backed securitization or structured financing ("ABS"), and are generally designed to permit a debtor to borrow funds at a reduced cost in exchange for a lender securing the loan with assets that are transferred from the borrower to another entity. By structuring the transactions in this manner, the lender hopes to ensure that its collateral will be excluded from the borrower's bankruptcy estate in the event that the borrower files a bankruptcy petition.

Abbey National is a large financial institution located in the United Kingdom. Debtor and Abbey National entered into an ABS transaction in October 1994. To effectuate this agreement, Debtor created a wholly-owned subsidiary known as LTV Sales Finance Co. ("Sales Finance"). Debtor then entered into an agreement with Sales Finance which purports to sell all of Debtor's right and interest in its accounts receivables ("receivables") to Sales Finance on a continuing basis. Abbey National then agreed to loan Two Hundred Seventy Million Dollars ($270,000,000.00) to Sales Finance in exchange for Sales Finance granting Abbey National a security interest in the receivables. On the date Debtor's petition was filed, Chase Manhattan Bank ("Chase Manhattan") was Abbey National's agent for this credit facility.

In 1998, Debtor entered into another ABS financing arrangement. To that end, Debtor created LTV Steel Products, LLC ("Steel Products"), another wholly-owned subsidiary. Debtor entered into an agreement with Steel Products which purports to sell all of Debtor's right, title and interest in its inventory to Steel Products on a continuing basis. Chase Manhattan and several other banking institutions then agreed to loan Thirty Million Dollars ($30,000,000.00) to Steel Products in exchange for a security interest in Steel Products' inventory. Abbey National is not involved in this ABS facility, and it had no interest in pre-petition inventory allegedly owned by Steel Products.

Neither Sales Finance nor Steel Products is a debtor in this proceeding. Nevertheless, Debtor filed a motion with the Court on December 29, 2000 seeking an interim order permitting it to use cash collateral. This cash collateral consisted of the receivables and inventory that are ostensibly owned by Sales Finance and Steel Products. Debtors stated to the Court that it would be forced to shut its doors and cease operations if it did not receive authorization to use this cash collateral. A hearing was held on Debtor's cash collateral motion on December 29, 2000 as part of the first day hearings.

Abbey National was not present at the cash collateral hearing. However, the Court notes that Abbey National had actual notice of the hearing, first, in the form of an e-mail sent by a Chase Manhattan employee to Abbey National on December 28, 2000, and second, in the form of a telephone call made from a Chase Manhattan employee to Abbey National on December 29, 2000. Furthermore, it is clear that Debtor had given advance notice of its intention to file for bankruptcy protection to Chase Manhattan, Abbey National's agent, in the week prior to December 29, 2000. Chase Manhattan was present at the December 29, 2000 hearing.

On December 29, 2000, Debtor and Chase Manhattan reached an agreement regarding an interim order permitting Debtor to use the cash collateral. Chase Manhattan did not formally consent to the entry of this order, as it could not secure Abbey National's consent to the form of the order, but Chase Manhattan did negotiate some of the terms of the order and did not raise an objection to its entry by the Court. The Court determined that entry of the interim order was necessary to permit Debtor to continue business operations, that the interests of Abbey National and all other creditors who had an interest in the cash collateral were adequately protected by the order, and that entry of the order was in the best interests of the estate and creditors of the estate. Accordingly, the Court entered the order tendered by Debtor, the relevant provisions of which are summarized below:

1. Recognition that there is a dispute between Debtor and the secured lenders of Sales Finance and Steel Products as to whether the transactions between Debtor and those entities were true sales or disguised financing vehicles;

2. An order requiring the secured lenders to turn over to Debtor the cash proceeds of the inventory and receivables which are to be used to provide working capital for Debtor;

3. Recognition that in the event the Court determines these transactions to be true sales, the secured lenders whose cash collateral was used will be entitled to administrative expense claims against the estate;

4. Adequate protection was provided to the secured lenders in the form of senior liens on the inventory and receivables and weekly interest payments to the lenders at pre-petition non-default rates.

It is this order that Abbey National seeks to modify. Specifically, Abbey National asks the Court to modify the interim cash collateral order *nunc pro tunc* to include the following provisions:

a. The Debtors shall transfer to Sales Finance all receivables created on or after December 29, 2000 and not previously sold to Sales Finance and that would have been sold to Sales Finance were it not for the occurrence of a Liquidation Event;

b. Steel Products would continue to purchase Inventory from the Inventory Sellers and Sales Finance would continue to purchase Receivables from the Receivables Sellers, each on the same basis and on the same terms as existed prior to the Petition Date;

c. The respective Collection Accounts would be administered by the Collateral Agent in the same manner as was administered prior to the Petition Date. Therefore, notwithstanding the occurrence of any Termination Date, collection on account of the Receivables would not be required to be applied to principal payments or amortization payments (other than any payments required in connection with the maintenance by the borrowers of their respective borrowing bases);

d. Steel Products and the Collateral Agent under the Inventory Facility would continue to automatically release all liens against the Receivables purchased by Sales Finance from Steel Products;

e. All minimum borrowing base and collateral value requirements set forth in the Receivables Facility and the Inventory Facility will continue in full force and effect;

f. In all other respects, the Receivables Facility and the Inventory Facility will continue to operate as required after the occurrence of a Liquidation Event including without limitation, the reimbursement of all expenses of each Receivables Lender and Inventory Lender.

(Abbey National's Emergency Motion to Modify Interim Order at 14-16).

Abbey National argues that the interim cash collateral order should be modified because * * * there is no basis for the Court to determine that the receivables which are Abbey National's collateral are property of Debtor's estate * * *.

* * * Abbey National's next argument is that the receivables which constitute its collateral are not property of Debtor's estate, and thus this Court lacked jurisdiction to enter the interim order. We shall construe this as an argument that the interim order is void pursuant to Rule 60(b)(4).

Section 541(a) of the Bankruptcy Code provides that upon the filing of a bankruptcy petition an estate is created consisting of "all legal or equitable interests of the debtor in property as of the commencement of the case." BC 541(a)(1). The estate created by the filing of a Chapter 11 petition is very broad, and property may be included in Debtor's estate even if Debtor does not have a possessory interest in that property. United States v. Whiting Pools, Inc., 462 U.S. 198, 204, 205-06 (1983).

Abbey National contends that the interim order is flawed because, on its face, the transaction between Debtor and Sales Finance is characterized as a true sale. Therefore, Abbey National argues, since Debtor sold its interests in the receivables to Sales Finance, Debtor no longer has an interest in the receivables and they are not property of the estate. However, Abbey National has admitted to the Court, both in its pleadings and in oral argument, that the ultimate issue of whether Debtor actually sold the receivables to Sales Finance is a fact-intensive issue that cannot be resolved without extensive discovery and an evidentiary hearing.

We find Abbey National's argument for "emergency" relief to be not well taken for several reasons. First, Abbey National's position in this regard is circular: we cannot permit Debtor to use cash collateral because it is not property of the estate, but we cannot determine if it is property of the estate until we hold an evidentiary hearing. We fail to see how we can conclude that the receivables are not property of Debtor's estate until an evidentiary hearing on that issue has been held. Because the determination of this issue must await further discovery, we decline to grant Abbey National relief from the interim order.

Furthermore, there seems to be an element of sophistry to suggest that Debtor does not retain at least an *equitable* interest in the property that is subject to the interim order. Debtor's business requires it to purchase, melt, mold and cast various metal products. To suggest that Debtor lacks some ownership interest in products that it creates with its own labor, as well as the proceeds to be derived from that labor, is difficult to accept. Accordingly, the Court concludes that Debtor has at least some equitable interest in the inventory and receivables, and that this interest is property of the Debtor's estate. This equitable interest is sufficient to support the entry of the interim cash collateral order.

Finally, it is readily apparent that granting Abbey National relief from the interim cash collateral order would be highly inequitable. The Court is satisfied that the entry of the interim order was necessary to enable Debtor to keep its doors open and continue to meet its obligations to its employees, retirees, customers and creditors. Allowing Abbey National to modify the order would allow Abbey National to enforce its state law rights as a secured lender to look to the collateral in satisfaction of this debt. This circumstance would put an immediate end to Debtor's business, would put thousands of people out of work, would deprive 100,000 retirees of needed medical benefits, and would have more far reaching economic effects on the geographic areas where Debtor does business. However, maintaining the current status quo permits Debtor to remain in business while it searches for substitute financing, and adequately protects and preserves Abbey National's rights. The equities of this situation highly favor Debtor. As a result, the Court declines to exercise its discretion to modify the interim order pursuant to Rule 60(b)(4). * * *

For the reasons stated above, the Court concludes that Abbey National's motion seeking to modify the Court's interim order permitting the use of cash collateral on December 29, 2000 is properly characterized as a motion seeking relief from judgment pursuant to Fed. R. Civ. P. 60(b). Furthermore, the Court finds that Abbey National has failed to establish that modification of the interim order is warranted. Accordingly, Abbey National's emergency motion is overruled.

An appropriate order shall enter.

COMMENTS AND QUESTIONS
1. What exactly are Sales Finance and Steel Products? Why were new, separate corporations created? Why did LTV sell its inventory to Steel Products? Does this mean LTV, a steel company, had no inventory? How do you run this kind of business without inventory?
2. Judge Bodoh emphasizes that LTV had 100,000 retirees who needed medical benefits. How should that fact influence the judge's decision? If it does influence his decision, if you were Abbey National or Chase Manhattan, how would you try to take that into account? Does that help or hurt LTV and the 100,000 retirees?

COMMENTS AND QUESTIONS: THE PRACTICE OF SECURITIZATION
We should be clear on the purpose of securitization: "Structured financings are based on one central, core principle—a defined group of assets can be structurally isolated, and thus serve as the basis of a financing that is independent as a legal matter, from the bankruptcy risks of the former owner of the assets." The Committee on Bankruptcy and Corporate Reorganization of The Association of the Bar of the City of New York, Structured Financing Techniques, The Business Lawyer (February, 1995). Assets that would otherwise be part of the bankruptcy estate had the original transaction been structured as a secured financing are outside of bankruptcy if the transaction structure is respected.

In a standard securitization, a new entity is created, a "special purpose vehicle" (SPV). (In *LTV Steel*, Sales Finance and Steel Products were SPVs.) Assets such as accounts receivable of an operating entity will be sold to the SPV in exchange for cash. The SPV will raise that cash by selling its own securities in public markets. The SPV will not be an operating entity, and will operate only as a conduit for translating its assets—the receivables—into cash to pay off the securities that it has issued. The SPV is designed to be "bankruptcy-remote" meaning, at a minimum, that it will not go into bankruptcy if the operating company that sold the receivables itself files a bankruptcy petition. Bankruptcy-remoteness can be created by making the SPV an entity of the sort that is not eligible for bankruptcy, see BC 109, or by controlling the decision-making ability of the entity, such as by requiring unanimous consent of the board of directors for a filing and by having an independent director.

You should be asking two questions: first, why do market participants value bankruptcy-remoteness?; and second, even if they find it privately useful, is it socially beneficial? As to the former, contrast the position of a standard secured creditor with that of the SPV. To be clear on what that means, assume that we got cash to the operating entity—this is the point of the securitization after all—by having the SPV lend money to the operating entity, secured by a first position on the receivables that would otherwise have been sold. The SPV again raises that cash by issuing securities. If the operating company filed under Chapter 11 of the Bankruptcy Code, the receivables would be property of the estate under BC 541, and would be "cash collateral" under BC 363. The debtor-in-possession—that is, the debtor after it files for Chapter 11 and retains control over its business under court supervision—will be able to use that collateral to operate its business if it can persuade the bankruptcy court that it can adequately protect the interests of the secured creditor. See BC 361, BC 363. There is no assurance that the secured creditor will receive interest in the bankruptcy proceeding, see BC 506, and it may get paid many years later under terms quite different from those originally negotiated. BC 1129.

In contrast, if the receivables are sold—and here we mean *really* sold, whatever that turns out to mean—in a transaction that does not have the taint of a fraudulent conveyance, we will respect this sale and the sold assets will not be involved in the bankruptcy of the operating company. That means that the debtor cannot use the receivables in the bankruptcy, and the SPV will not be subject to the treatment just-described for a secured creditor. This should make it clear why many potential investors want the protection of a bankruptcy-remote SPV.

How should society evaluate this transaction? Look first at the time of bankruptcy and then at the time of the transaction itself. Suppose, for example, that Debtor sold, for cash, a single share of Microsoft stock at the prevailing market price, and then filed for bankruptcy. This is the quintessential arms-length transaction, and there is no reason to think that we should overturn it after Debtor files for bankruptcy. Debtor has the cash in hand, and the estate has just swapped one asset for another. We should worry if a debtor sells property for less than it is worth, but we have fraudulent conveyance doctrines under state law and BC 548 to deal with these cases. Proper sales shouldn't trouble us then. Suppose that Debtor blows the cash from the stock sale on losing lottery tickets right before filing for bankruptcy. Should we now question the sale itself? We shouldn't. It is true that Debtor could not have used the Microsoft share to buy the tickets directly, and that the conversion of that share to cash helped Debtor undertake its desperate scheme to restore solvency. But we usually do not impose on purchasers the burden of seeing how the proceeds of the sale will be used; creditors should play that role.

Is a securitization transaction any different from any other pre-bankruptcy fair-market sale? All of these transactions will have the consequence of removing assets from the bankruptcy estate. Debtors flush with cash rarely file for bankruptcy, so we can be confident that the debtor will have dissipated the cash received for the receivables, just as occurred in the lottery example. This will make it more difficult for the debtor to reorganize, as it will have fewer liquid assets, such as receivables to work with. It is possible that the debtor will not fully internalize the costs to creditors of exacerbating the liquidity crisis that the debtor will face, but these are marginal effects to be sure.

Try a different angle on this. There is an academic literature that emphasizes that securitization may have the consequence of creating judgment-proof entities. See Lynn M. LoPucki, The Death of Liability, 106 Yale L.J. 1, 28-29 (1996); Lois R. Lupica, Asset Securitization: The Unsecured Creditor's Perspective, 76 Tex. L. Rev 595 (1998). This debate is ongoing and is far from unanimous. See James J. White, Corporate Judgment Proofing: A Response to Lynn LoPucki's The Death of Liability, 107 Yale L.J. 1363 (1998), and the further response by Lynn M. LoPucki, Virtual Judgment Proofing: A Rejoinder, 107 Yale L.J. 1413 (1998).

What are the benefits of securitization? Many believe that securitization is socially useful in that it may reduce the cost of obtaining cash by making it easier for certain borrowers to access public markets. See, e.g., Steven L. Schwarcz, Structured Finance: A Guide to the Principles of Asset Securitization (PLI, 2nd ed., 1993). Lowering transaction costs is generally something we want, and securitization may enable borrowers to exit thin markets and substitute into thicker, public markets.

CHAPTER NINE

SECURITY INTERESTS AND INTERESTS ARISING OUTSIDE ARTICLE 9

Consensual interests in personal property under Article 9 are just one of the many species of interests in property. The fate of the Article 9 secured creditor cannot be fully assessed if we look only at competing secured and unsecured creditors. These other interests must be dealt with when the debtor fails and should be assessed by a potential secured creditor when it lends money in the first place. Liens can arise under both state and federal law, and interests in personal property can arise through interests in real estate under the law of fixtures. We deal with each of these in turn, starting with a brief overview of the interaction of state law liens and Article 9. We then turn to a more extended treatment of federal tax liens, where we once again have the opportunity to examine how an alternative statutory structure deals with many important secured transactions issues (after-acquired property and future advances, for example). We close the chapter with a look at fixtures, property with a personal property past and future.

SECTION I. STATE LIENS

Security interests are created consensually: the debtor agrees to give the secured creditor an interest in property. Liens, in contrast, typically arise without the consent of the debtor, either pursuant to common law rules or specific statutes creating the liens. These liens therefore provide an additional source of conflict over a debtor's property. What priority does a state law lien or, for example, a federal tax lien have compared to an Article 9 security interest in the same property?

9-109(d)(2) provides that Article 9 does not apply to "a lien, other than an agricultural lien, given by statute or other rule of law for services or materials, but Section 9-333 applies with respect to priority of the lien." Note that, for the first time, Article 9 does apply to agricultural liens. This results in a number of particular provisions, see, e.g., 9-302 and 9-322(g), but we will say nothing more about this here. (For much more detail, see Donald W. Baker, Some Thoughts on Agricultural Liens under the New U.C.C. Article 9, 51 Ala. L. Rev. 1417 (2000); John Mark Stephens, Boon Or Boondoggle? Proposed Article 9 Revisions Incorporate Statutory Agricultural Liens For Better, Not Worse, 30 Tex. Tech L. Rev. 1199 (1999).) 9-109(d)(2) looks to 9-333, which states that:

(a) ["**Possessory lien.**"] In this section, "possessory lien" means an interest, other than a security interest or an agricultural lien:

(1) which secures payment or performance of an obligation for services or materials furnished with respect to goods by a person in the ordinary course of the person's business;

(2) which is created by statute or rule of law in favor of the person; and

(3) whose effectiveness depends on the person's possession of the goods.

(b) [**Priority of possessory lien.**] A possessory lien on goods has priority over a security interest in the goods unless the lien is created by a statute that expressly provides otherwise.

9-333 addresses a particular class of liens: those arising out of the provision of services or materials and that are tied to the possession of the collateral in question.

9-1: THE BASICS

- A business takes in a sensitive piece of equipment for repairs. New parts plus labor results in a bill of $1000.
- Before retrieving the equipment, the business collapses, and the bank holding a security interest in the collateral asks the repair shop to turn over the equipment.
- Relevant state law provides that the repair shop holds a lien on the equipment for the full amount of the bill, so long as the equipment remains in its possession.

¤ A dispute over priority arises: who wins? See 9-333; compare this with our approach to purchase money security interests in 9-103 and 9-324.

SECTION II. FEDERAL TAX LIENS

The federal government wants to collect its taxes, just as any other creditor wants to be paid what it is owed. The federal government frequently is one of the big creditors of failing enterprises. One might think that an enterprise that was doing poorly wouldn't owe any federal taxes. (If it had lots of taxable income, it wouldn't be a failing enterprise.) But tax liabilities may be assessed years after the taxable event. Businesses, moreover, may have federal tax obligations extending beyond the corporate income tax. Sometimes a business stops paying the government such things as withholding taxes when its fortunes take a turn for the worse.

Put yourself into the shoes of the government and try to figure out how you might maximize the chance of collecting these taxes. A creditor would take a security interest, but these obligations arise by operation of law, so the government could only take a lien. It does exactly that. Section 6321 of the Internal Revenue Code ("IRC"), 26 USC 6321, provides that:

> If any person liable to pay any tax neglects or refuses to pay the same after demand, the amount (including any interest, additional amount, addition to tax, or assessable penalty, together with any costs that may accrue in addition thereto) shall be a lien in favor of the United States upon all property and rights to property, whether real or personal, belonging to such person.

The general idea is clear, but a few of the details are murky. When *exactly* does the lien arise or, as we might put it, when does the lien attach? IRC 6321 is triggered by neglect in paying taxes or a refusal to pay after a demand. That suggests that the lien does not attach until that point as well. IRC 6322 tells us otherwise:

> Unless another date is specifically fixed by law, the lien imposed by section 6321 shall arise at the time the assessment is made and shall continue until the liability for the amount so assessed (or a judgment against the taxpayer arising out of such liability) is satisfied or becomes unenforceable by reason of lapse of time.

The "assessment" provided for by IRC 6322 consists of a "nonpublic administrative act," Peter F. Coogan, The Effect of the Federal Tax Lien

Act of 1966 Upon Security Interests Created Under the Uniform Commercial Code, 81 Harv. L. Rev. 1369, 1373 (1968). The federal government, accordingly, acquires a lien on all the taxpayer's property by means of an event that may be known neither to the taxpayer nor to third parties.

This is a problem obviously, and one that IRC 6323(a) attempts to address:

> The lien imposed by section 6321 shall not be valid as against any purchaser, holder of a security interest, mechanic's lienor, or judgment lien creditor until notice thereof which meets the requirements of subsection (f) has been filed by the Secretary.

Put differently, the government's property interest (its lien) is good against parties that acquire their interests after it has cured the ostensible ownership problem by making a public filing.

Where? Unfortunately, Congress did not simply adopt Article 9's filing system, a decision that simplifies things for the federal tax collector, but that undermines, at least in part, the concept of "integrating" federal tax lien policy with Article 9. IRC 6323(f)(1)(A)(ii) provides that, in the case of personal property, the filing should be made "in one office within the state (or the county, or other governmental subdivision), as designated by the laws of such State, in which the property subject to the lien is situated." If state law has not designated one such office, then the tax lien is to be filed "[i]n the office of the clerk of the United States district court for the judicial district in which the property subject to the lien is situated ... ," IRC 6323(f)(1)(B). 26 CFR 301.6323(f)-1(a)(2) provides that a state has not designated one such filing office "if more than one office is designated in the State, county, or other governmental subdivision for filing notices with respect to all of the personal property of a particular taxpayer."

Personal property, whether tangible or intangible, is situated "at the residence of the taxpayer at the time the notice of lien is filed." IRC 6323(f)(2)(B). Corporations and partnerships are deemed to reside at the place where the principal executive office of the business is located; taxpayers whose residence is "without the United States shall be deemed to be in the District of Columbia." IRC 6323(f)(2).

The tax lien filing is effective for ten years from the date of the *assessment* of the tax, while refilings are effective for ten years running from the close of the preceding filing or refiling period, IRC 6323(g)(3). If the government wants to continue the effectiveness of its tax lien filing "against any person without regard to when the interest of the person in the property subject to the lien was acquired," 26 CFR 301.6323(g)-1(a)(3), a refiling must be made within one year before the expiration of the prior period. The refiling must be made in the prior file and, in addition, if the Internal Revenue Service has received written information concerning a change in the taxpayer's residence, in the proper file in the taxpayer's new residence. IRC 6323(g)(2)(B).

Step back and examine the system created so far. The government takes a lien on all of its debtor's property to increase the chance of collecting the debts. That lien arises when the debt is assessed but is not valid against a competing secured creditor until an appropriate public filing is made. This also defines a priority rule, even though it is not couched as such. Security interests that arise prior to the tax lien filing enjoy priority, while those that arise thereafter are subordinated.

So far, so good. But, as we know now, there are an infinite variety of issues that arise and that that system should need to address. Take two of particular importance: after-acquired property and future advances. To get a handle on this, start with the definition of "security interest" used in IRC 6323:

> (h)(1) Security interest. The term "security interest" means any interest in property acquired by contract for the purpose of securing payment or performance of an obligation or indemnifying against loss or liability. A security interest exists at any time (A) if, at such time, the property is in existence and the interest has become protected under local law against a subsequent judgment lien arising out of an unsecured obligation, and (B) to the extent that, at such time, the holder has parted with money or money's worth.

9-2: STARTING POINTS

- On February 1st, the IRS assesses a tax against Debtor for $10,000.
- On March 1st, Bank lends Debtor $10,000, takes a security interest in equipment and files an appropriate financing statement.
- On April 1st, the IRS files under IRC 6323(f).
- ¤ A dispute over priority arises: who wins?

9-3: AFTER-ACQUIRED PROPERTY

- On February 1st, the IRS assesses a tax against Debtor for $10,000.
- On March 1st, Bank lends Debtor $10,000, takes a security interest in inventory, then-existing and thereafter arising, and files an appropriate financing statement.
- On April 1st, the IRS files under IRC 6323(f).
- On May 1st, a dispute over priority arises. The inventory on hand was all acquired by Debtor after April 1st.
- ¤ Who wins? When did Bank become the "holder of a security interest" as that phrase is used in IRC 6323(a)? At the time the security interest was created in the original inventory? At the time it was created in the new inventory? How should we interpret the "in existence" language in IRC 6323(h)(1)? Focus on the IRS: Under IRC 6321, does the IRS lien attach at all to after-acquired property?

This is as basic as it gets: we know that the inventory will turn over— repeatedly. We can be just as basic for future advances. IRC 6323(d) sets the stage for the fact pattern that follows:

> 45-day period for making disbursements. Even though notice of a lien imposed by section 6321 has been filed, such lien shall not be valid with respect to a security interest which came into existence after tax lien filing by reason of disbursements made before the 46th day after the date of tax lien filing, or (if earlier) before the person making such disbursements had actual notice or knowledge of tax lien filing, but only if such security interest
>
> > (1) is in property (A) subject, at the time of tax lien filing, to the lien imposed by section 6321, and (B) covered by the terms of a written agreement entered into before tax lien filing, and
> >
> > (2) is protected under local law against a judgment lien arising, as of the time of tax lien filing, out of an unsecured obligation.

9-4: FUTURE ADVANCES

- On February 1st, the IRS assesses a tax against Debtor for $10,000.

- On March 1st, Bank lends Debtor $10,000, takes a security interest in equipment to secure debts "now and hereafter owed by Debtor to Bank" and files an appropriate financing statement.
- On April 1st, the IRS files under IRC 6323(f).
- On May 1st, Bank lends an additional $10,000 to Debtor.
- ¤ On June 1st, a dispute over priority arises. Who wins? Again, when did Bank become the "holder of a security interest" as that phrase is used in IRC 6323(a)? Suppose that the property had been inventory instead of equipment and that the inventory had turned over after the IRS filed: would that alter the result?

If you have navigated this maze successfully, you should understand the key features of the IRC, as set out so far. First, the basic structure does not preserve the priority of the Article 9 secured creditor over property that turns over in the debtor's hands. The "in existence" restriction in the definition of security interest in IRC 6323(h)(1) means that an Article 9 secured creditor does not hold a security interest in property until the debtor has rights in the collateral. Once this is coupled with the basic priority rule of IRC 6323(c)—that the IRS lien is valid and superior against subsequent security interests once filed—we see that change-over in a debtor's property can flip the priority positions of the Article 9 secured creditor and the government. Second, the tax lien statute provides a protected window for future advances—the smaller of 45-days and knowledge (and compare 9-323 on this)—and one that applies only to the property held by the debtor at the time that the tax lien was filed.

This is pretty severe stuff, and it is therefore not surprising that there are additional rules that cut-back on what we have said so far. These are quite specific, and we will pursue only one here, the protections for "commercial transactions financing agreements." Read IRC 6323(c) and then consider the following case:

Rice Investment Co. v. United States

United States Court of Appeals, Fifth Circuit, 1980.
625 F.2d 565.

■ RANDALL, CIRCUIT JUDGE

In October, 1973, Rice Investment Company ("Rice") loaned Handy Stop, Inc. (the "Debtor") $67,583. In connection with the loan, the Debtor executed and delivered to Rice a security agreement pursuant to which the Debtor granted to Rice a security interest in all of the Debtor's inventory then owned or thereafter acquired. A financing statement was filed in the office of the Secretary of State of the State of Texas on October 29, 1973. The Debtor made payments on its indebtedness to Rice from time to time. In March, 1975, $46,317 remained owing from the Debtor to Rice.

The Debtor incurred liabilities for withholding and FICA taxes for the third and fourth quarters of 1973 and the first quarter of 1974 in the total amount of $11,853. Assessments of the taxes were made during March, 1974. Thereafter, a notice of a federal tax lien in the amount of $8,521 was filed on April 26, 1974, for the third and fourth quarters of 1973, and a further notice of a federal tax lien in the amount of $4,588 was filed on August 5, 1974, for the first quarter of 1974. The Internal Revenue Service levied upon the Debtor's inventory on August 18, 1974. The outstanding tax liability of the Debtor, including interest, at that time was $13,514. The perishable inventory was sold by the United States on August 28, 1974 for $750, and the nonperishable items were sold on November 14, 1974 for $3,500.

In September, 1974, Rice brought suit against the United States under 26 USC 7426 seeking recovery from the United States of the proceeds ($4,250) received by the United States from the sale of the Debtor's inventory. Rice's second amended complaint asserts that the lien of the United States under 26 USC 6321 in the inventory of the Debtor was junior to the lien of Rice under 26 USC 6323 and that the levy of the United States was therefore unlawful. During the proceedings, in response to interrogatories propounded by the United States, Rice acknowledged that it did not have any information in its possession by which it could determine the exact date on which the Debtor acquired the inventory which was seized by the Internal Revenue Service. Further, Rice admitted, in its motion for summary judgment, that none of the actual inventory on hand in October, 1973, when the security agreement was entered into, was part of the inventory seized and sold on August 28, 1974, and November 14, 1974.

On motions for summary judgment by both parties, the district court, without opinion, issued an order granting Rice's motion and denying the motion of the United States.

The question presented by this appeal is whether the federal tax lien filed by the United States on April 26, 1974,[2] pursuant to 26 USC 6321, primes the security interest held by Rice in the inventory which was seized by the United States on August 18, 1974. We hold that the lien of the United States does prime the security interest of Rice in such inventory, and accordingly, we reverse the summary judgment granted by the district court and remand with instructions to enter summary judgment for the United States.

Some History on the Problem

The opinion of this court in Texas Oil & Gas Corp. v. United States, 466 F.2d 1040 (5th Cir. 1972), contains a description of the history of the competition between federal tax liens and private liens. We will repeat here only so much of that history as is necessary for an understanding of the problem before the court.

Under 26 USC 6321, every federal tax which is not paid on demand becomes a lien "upon all property and rights to property, whether real or personal, belonging to" the taxpayer. After-acquired property, such as the Debtor's property in this case, is reached by the lien. The lien is effective from the date of assessment of the tax, IRC 6322, and has aptly been described as a secret lien. When the lien was first created in 1866, it prevailed, even though secret, against a bona fide purchaser for value. In 1913, however, Congress extended protection to purchasers, mortgagees and judgment creditors, and in 1939, to pledgees, against federal tax liens of which notice had not been filed in a designated office. Further, recognizing the impracticability of searching for tax liens in some cases, Congress in 1939 provided priority over filed tax liens under certain conditions for purchasers of, and lenders secured by "securities" and in 1964, for purchasers of motor vehicles. However, as against the rest of the world, including the taxpayer himself, the federal tax lien was effective upon assessment without any need for public notice.

The most basic principle employed in the adjudication of the priority of competing liens is "the first in time is the first in right." When a federal tax lien is one of the liens involved, however, the Supreme Court added a gloss on that principle by requiring that in order to be "first in time," the

---

[2] Since the amount of gross proceeds from the sale of the inventory ($4,250) is less than the amount of the lien ($8,521) as to which notice was filed on April 26, 1974, we concern ourselves here only with the lien filed on that date.

nonfederal lien must first have become "choate," i.e., the identity of the lienor, the property subject to the lien and the amount of the lien must be established beyond any possibility of change or dispute. Further, the determination of whether "a lien has acquired sufficient substance and has become so perfected as to defeat a later-arising or later-filed federal tax lien" is a matter of federal law.

As the federal law on "choateness" developed, few liens prevailed in the battle against federal tax liens. Even mortgages and other contractual security interests, despite their specially favored position under the federal statute, were vulnerable before 1966 to subsequently filed federal tax liens to the extent that the security embraced after-acquired property or involved disbursements (whether optional or obligatory) yet to be made, including foreclosure expenses and other outlays for which a mortgagee normally is entitled to a lien with the same priority as the principal debt. Plumb, Federal Liens and Priorities Agenda for the Next Decade, 77 Yale L.J. 228, 231 (1967) (footnotes omitted).

FEDERAL TAX LIEN ACT OF 1966

Congress enacted the Federal Tax Lien Act of 1966 in an effort to conform the lien provisions of the Internal Revenue Code to the concepts developed in the UCC. Another primary objective was to provide some limited but specific relief from the harshness of the choateness rule for, among others, commercial lenders whose loans and collateral may change daily.[17]

---

[17] S. Rep. No. 1708, 89th Cong., 2d Sess., reprinted in (1966) U.S. Code Cong. & Admin. News, pp. 3722, 3729. According to the Senate Report, protection for a security interest arising out of a commercial transactions financing agreement "is afforded only where the loan or purchase is made not later than 45 days after the tax lien filing (unless actual notice or knowledge of the filing is obtained sooner) and only where the inventory, accounts receivable, etc., are acquired before the 45 days have elapsed." The Senate Report states further as follows:

> In the case of inventory and accounts receivable financing, it is customary for a business, after establishing a line of credit, to receive advances from time to time as its needs arise. The security in such a case customarily is the inventory, accounts receivable, etc., which the business receives from time to time in the ordinary course of its business. The loan may be secured by these assets (including replacements of the initial assets) or these assets themselves (except inventory) may be sold to the financier. Under present law, a filed tax lien has priority over the rights of the lender or purchaser if the funds are not ad-

Section 6323 of the Internal Revenue Code, as amended by the Federal Tax Lien Act of 1966, sets forth certain limitations on the validity and priority of federal tax liens imposed by IRC 6321 as against certain persons, including the holder of a security interest in property which is the subject of such a lien. IRC 6323(c) is the provision designed to provide a safe haven for the holders of security interests arising in certain commercial financing arrangements. Subsection (c) provides, in relevant part, that

> even though notice of a lien imposed by section 6321 has been filed, such lien shall not be valid with respect to a security interest which came into existence after tax lien filing but which
>
> > (a) is in qualified property covered by the terms of a written agreement entered into before tax lien filing and constituting
> >
> > > (i) a commercial transactions financing agreement, ... and
> >
> > (b) is protected under local law against a judgment lien arising, as of the time of tax lien filing, out of an unsecured obligation.

The balance of subsection (c) and subsection (h) define the terms used in subsection (c). Four of those definitions are relevant for our purposes the definitions of "commercial transactions financing agreement," "qualified

---

vanced, or the security purchased, until after the tax lien filing. In addition, it has priority under present law if the initial assets are replaced with assets acquired after the tax lien filing. As a result, under present law for a lender or purchaser to be sure that no tax lien has recently been filed, he must search the records each time before making an additional advance or purchase. The provision added by the bill is designed to keep this obligation within practical bounds by giving the interests arising under the agreements providing for these loans or purchases priority over a filed tax lien if the loans or purchases are made not later than 45 days after the tax lien filing and before the lender or purchaser has actual notice of the filing. In this regard it should be noted that the standard of perfection (i.e., validity against judgment liens) in this regard is the same for a purchaser (including a bona fide purchaser) as it is for the holder of a security interest. This provision thus generally gives an inventory or accounts receivable, etc., financier assurance that his loans or purchases are not inferior to some recently filed tax lien as long as he searches the records at least once every 45 days.

See also H.R. Rep. No. 1884, 89th Cong., 2d Sess. (1966).

property," "commercial financing security" and "security interest." The term "commercial transactions financing agreement" is defined

> as an agreement (entered into by a person in the course of his trade or business)—
>
> (i) to make loans to the taxpayer to be secured by commercial financial security acquired by the taxpayer in the ordinary course of his trade or business,
>
> ...
>
> but such an agreement shall be treated as coming within the term only to the extent that such loan or purchase is made before the 46th day after the date of tax lien filing or (if earlier) before the lender or purchaser had actual notice or knowledge of such tax lien filing.

The term "qualified property," when used with respect to a commercial transactions financing agreement, is defined to include "only commercial financing security acquired by the taxpayer before the 46th day after the date of tax lien filing." See 26 CFR 301.6323(c)-1(d) ***. The term "commercial financing security" is defined to mean "(i) paper of a kind ordinarily arising in commercial transactions, (ii) accounts receivable, (iii) mortgages on real property, and (iv) inventory." Finally, subsection (h)(1) of IRC 6323 defines the term "security interest" as follows:

> The term "security interest" means any interest in property acquired by contract for the purpose of securing payment or performance of an obligation or indemnifying against loss or liability. A security interest exists at any time (a) if, at such time, the property is in existence and the interest has become protected under local law against a subsequent judgment lien arising out of an unsecured obligation, and (b) to the extent that, at such time, the holder has parted with money or money's worth.

Under subsection (c) of IRC 6323, the holder of a security interest competing for priority with a federal tax lien who is able to demonstrate that such security interest meets the requirements of subsection (c) and the related definition in subsection (h) achieves priority for such security interest over the federal tax lien by virtue of the introductory language of subsection (c) which renders the competing tax lien invalid as against such security interest. It is apparent, simply from reading subsections (c) and (h), that the holder of a security interest seeking to establish priority thereunder over a competing tax lien must clear several complex hurdles under such subsections, and the failure to clear any one of them leaves the holder outside the safe haven of subsection (c). In the case before the court, the United States argues that in view of Rice's admission that it did not have any information in its possession by which it could determine the date on which the Debtor acquired the inventory seized by the United States on August 18, 1974, Rice would be unable to carry its burden under IRC 6323 of proving that the inventory was "qualified property," i.e., property acquired by the Debtor before June 11, 1974 (the 46th day after the filing of the tax lien on April 26, 1974). We agree, and we hold that the security interest of the United States in the seized inventory is, accordingly, not invalid under IRC 6323 with respect to the security interest of Rice in such inventory. Our holding is based on the clear language of the statute, and is strongly supported by the equally clear legislative history. At least when the inquiry is solely whether an item of inventory is "qualified property," it is not necessary to resort to notions of "choateness" as a tool for statutory interpretation. In view of our holding, it is also unnecessary to analyze the status of Rice's security interest insofar as the other requirements of IRC 6323 are concerned, and we express no views with respect thereto. * * *

Rice urges that we construe the "in existence" language contained in the definition of "security interest" in subsection (h) of IRC 6323 to cover not only the inventory of the Debtor in existence on the date of the filing of the tax lien, but also any inventory which thereafter replaced such inventory. Rice argues that such a construction is particularly appropriate where, as was the case here, there has been only a single advance by the lender. To accept Rice's argument, however, would be to ignore the clear language of subsection (c) which requires that, wholly apart from the date on which the loan is made (which is itself the subject of certain independent requirements under IRC 6323 concededly met here), see 26 USC 6323(c)(2)(a), (d), the collateral must be "qualified property." It would also be to ignore the legislative history of the Federal Tax Lien Act of 1966 which evidences a clear intent not to give commercial lenders an infinite priority over the United States, but instead to limit such lenders to property acquired by the taxpayer debtor before the 46th day after the filing of the tax lien. Rice says that a decision in favor of the United States in this case will have the effect of requiring a secured lender to check each day to determine whether a federal tax lien has been filed with respect to each of its borrowers. While this may be something of an exaggeration, it is clear that subsection (c) of IRC 6323 requires a secured lender regularly to monitor the federal tax lien status of its borrowers because only the prompt ascertainment of the existence of a federal tax lien will put the secured lender in a position to protect its interest in the collateral. As this court noted in *Texas Oil & Gas*, "we realize that this disposition does not afford the protection that commercial lenders who deal with after-acquired property might prefer." 466 F.2d at 1053. But efforts to improve that protection should be directed to Congress and not to the courts.

Back to History

Since the security interest of Rice in the seized inventory is not entitled to priority over the federal tax lien under IRC 6323, Rice must demonstrate that it is entitled to priority under the federal law developed prior to the enactment of the Federal Tax Lien Act of 1966. However, it is clear that under the federal law on "choateness" described above, the federal tax lien filed by the United States on April 26, 1974, would be entitled to priority over the security interest of Rice in the inventory seized by the United States on August 18, 1974, because Rice, by its own admission, could not prove that the seized property was in existence and owned by the Debtor on the date the tax lien was filed, which would lead to the conclusion that the security interest of Rice in the seized inventory was not sufficiently choate on the date of the tax lien filing to prevail over the tax lien.

Our conclusion that Rice, having failed to secure a safe haven under IRC 6323, is left with the law on "choateness" and fails under that law is buttressed by this court's similar conclusion in *Texas Oil & Gas*. Having demonstrated, among other things, that the account receivable in that case did not constitute "qualified property" under IRC 6323, the court turned to a consideration of the status of the account under the federal law on "choateness":

> In the instant case, it is true that the bank had done all it could do under the UCC to secure its interest in taxpayer-debtor's accounts receivable. However, that conclusion simply does not answer the case law as it has developed in the area of tax liens. However "complete" a lender's perfection may be under state recording laws and however "specific" state law might deem that interest to be, it is federal law that determines the extent to which that state determination will protect a private lien from a federal tax lien. It appears clear from the case law that an account receivable not yet "acquired" at the time of the filing of a tax lien because the final transaction creating the account re-

ceivable was not yet in existence cannot be considered choate, save for those accounts receivable now protected by section 6323(c).

Texas Oil & Gas, 466 F.2d at 1051.

In our case, while Rice may well have done all that it could do under the UCC to perfect its security interest in the Debtor's after-acquired inventory, the security interest of Rice in inventory not yet acquired at the time of the filing of the tax lien cannot be considered choate for federal law purposes, and the federal tax lien prevails over such security interest.

Reversed and remanded with instructions to enter summary judgment for the United States.

Comments and Questions

We get a chance to do comparative law on the cheap when we look at the federal government's approach to federal tax liens. As you read and re-read IRC 6323, you should know enough by now to ask the basic questions that we should expect a system of secured transactions to confront. How does it deal with the possibility of unperfected interests? What third parties enjoy protection against the federal tax lien? What, for example, are the rights of buyers in the ordinary course of business? What about changes? We focused above on after-acquired property and future advances. We said nothing about proceeds, or about a change in the location of the debtor or the collateral. What about name changes, incorporations or mergers? To what extent does IRC 6323 address these issues? Does it approach these issues in a fashion that differs importantly from that taken by Article 9? What should the drafters of Article 9 learn from the tax lien statute, and vice versa?

The next case considers how Article 9's naming systems meshes with how the IRS approaches names.

United States v. Crestmark Bank (In re Spearing Tool and Mfg. Co.)

United States Court of Appeals for the Sixth Circuit, 2005.
412 F.3d 653.

■ Cook, Circuit Judge

In this case arising out of bankruptcy proceedings, the government appeals the district court's reversal of the bankruptcy court's grant of summary judgment for the government. For the following reasons, we reverse the district court, and affirm the bankruptcy court.

I. Background and Procedural History

In April 1998, Spearing Tool and Manufacturing Co. and appellee Crestmark entered into a lending agreement, which granted Crestmark a security interest in all of Spearing's assets. The bank perfected its security interest by filing a financing statement under the Uniform Commercial Code, identifying Spearing as "Spearing Tool and Manufacturing Co.," its precise name registered with the Michigan Secretary of State.

In April 2001, Spearing entered into a secured financing arrangement with Crestmark, under which Crestmark agreed to purchase accounts receivable from Spearing, and Spearing granted Crestmark a security interest in all its assets. Crestmark perfected its security interest by filing a UCC financing statement, again using Spearing's precise name registered with the Michigan Secretary of State.

Meanwhile, Spearing fell behind in its federal employment-tax payments. On October 15, 2001, the IRS filed two notices of federal tax lien against Spearing with the Michigan Secretary of State. Each lien identified Spearing as "SPEARING TOOL & MFG. COMPANY INC.," which varied from Spearing's precise Michigan-registered name, because it used an ampersand in place of "and," abbreviated "Manufacturing" as "Mfg.," and spelled out "Company" rather than use the abbreviation "Co." But the name on the IRS lien notices was the precise name Spearing gave on its quarterly federal tax return for the third quarter of 2001, as well as its return for fourth-quarter 1994, the first quarter for which it was delinquent. For most of the relevant tax periods, however, Spearing filed returns as "Spearing Tool & Manufacturing"—neither its precise Michigan-registered name, nor the name on the IRS tax liens.

Crestmark periodically submitted lien search requests to the Michigan Secretary of State, using Spearing's exact registered name. Because Michigan has limited electronic-search technology, searches disclose only liens matching the precise name searched—not liens such as the IRS's, filed under slightly different or abbreviated names.[2] Crestmark's February 2002 search results came back from the Secretary of State's office with a handwritten note stating: "You may wish to search using Spearing Tool & Mfg. Company Inc." But Crestmark did not search for that name at the time, and its exact—registered—name searches thus did not reveal the IRS liens. So Crestmark, unaware of the tax liens, advanced more funds to Spearing between October 2001 and April 2002.

On April 16, 2002, Spearing filed a Chapter-11 bankruptcy petition. Only afterward did Crestmark finally search for "Spearing Tool & Mfg. Company Inc." and discover the tax-lien notices. Crestmark then filed the complaint in this case to determine lien priority. The bankruptcy court determined the government had priority; the district court reversed. The questions now before us are whether state or federal law determines the sufficiency of the IRS's tax-lien notices, and whether the IRS notices sufficed to give the IRS liens priority.

II. Federal law controls whether the IRS's lien notice sufficed.

Crestmark argues Michigan law should control the form and content of the IRS's tax lien with respect to taxpayer identification. The district court, though it decided in favor of Crestmark on other grounds, rightly disagreed.

When the IRS files a lien against a taxpayer's property, it must do so "in one office within the State ... as designated by the laws of such State, in which the property subject to the lien is situated." IRC 6323(f)(1)(A). The Internal Revenue Code provides that the form and content "shall be prescribed by the [U.S. Treasury] Secretary" and "be valid *notwithstanding any other provision of law regarding the form or content of a notice of lien.*" IRC 6323(f)(3) (emphasis added). Regulations provide that the IRS must file tax-lien notices using IRS Form 668, which must "identify the taxpayer, the tax liability giving rise to the lien, and the date the assessment arose." 26 CFR 301.6323(f)-1(d)(2). Form-668 notice "is valid notwithstanding any other provision of law regarding the form or content of a notice of lien. For example, omission from the notice of lien of a description of the property subject to the lien does not affect the validity thereof even

---

though State law may require that the notice contain a description of property subject to the lien." 301.6323(f)-1(d)(1); see also United States v. Union Cent. Life Ins. Co., 368 U.S. 291, 296 (1961) (Michigan's requirement that tax liens describe relevant property "placed obstacles to the enforcement of federal tax liens that Congress had not permitted.").

The plain text of the statute and regulations indicates Form-668 notice suffices, regardless of state law. We therefore need only consider how much specificity federal law requires for taxpayer identification on tax liens.

III. The notice here sufficed.

An IRS tax lien need not perfectly identify the taxpayer. See, e.g., Hudgins v. IRS (In re Hudgins), 967 F.2d 973, 976 (4th Cir. 1992); Tony Thornton Auction Serv., Inc. v. United States, 791 F.2d 635, 639 (8th Cir. 1986). The question before us is whether the IRS's identification of Spearing was sufficient. We conclude it was.

The critical issue in determining whether an abbreviated or erroneous name sufficiently identifies a taxpayer is whether a "reasonable and diligent search would have revealed the existence of the notices of the federal tax liens under these names." Tony Thornton, 791 F.2d at 639. In *Tony Thornton*, for example, liens identifying the taxpayer as "Davis's Restaurant" and "Daviss (sic) Restaurant" sufficed to identify a business correctly known as "Davis Family Restaurant." Id. In *Hudgins*, the IRS lien identified the taxpayer as "Hudgins Masonry, Inc." instead of by the taxpayer's personal name, Michael Steven Hudgins. This notice nonetheless sufficed, given that both names would be listed on the same page of the state's lien index. 967 F.2d at 977.

Crestmark argues, and we agree, that those cases mean little here because in each, creditors could search a physical index and were likely to notice similar entries listed next to or near one another—an option which no longer exists under Michigan's electronic—search system. So the question for this case becomes whether Crestmark conducted a reasonable and diligent electronic search. It did not.

Crestmark should have searched here for "Spearing Tool & Mfg." as well as "Spearing Tool and Manufacturing." "Mfg." and the ampersand are, of course, most common abbreviations—so common that, for example, we use them as a rule in our case citations. Crestmark had notice that Spearing sometimes used these abbreviations, and the Michigan Secretary of State's office *recommended* a search using the abbreviations. Combined, these factors indicate that a reasonable, diligent search by Crestmark of the Michigan lien filings for this business would have disclosed Spearing's IRS tax liens.

Crestmark argues for the unreasonableness of requiring multiple searches by offering the extreme example of a name it claims could be abbreviated 288 different ways ("ABCD Christian Brothers Construction and Development Company of Michigan, Inc."). Here, however, only two relevant words could be, and commonly are, abbreviated: "Manufacturing" and "and"—and the Secretary of State specifically recommended searching for those abbreviations. We express no opinion about whether creditors have a general obligation to search name variations. Our holding is limited to these facts.

Finally, we note that policy considerations also support the IRS's position. A requirement that tax liens identify a taxpayer with absolute precision would be unduly burdensome to the government's tax-collection efforts. Indeed, such a requirement might burden the government at least as much as Crestmark claims it would be burdened by having to perform multiple lien searches. "The overriding purpose of the tax lien statute obviously is to ensure prompt revenue collection." United States v. Kimbell Foods, Inc., 440 U.S. 715, 734-35 (1979). "[T]o attribute to Congress a purpose so to weaken the tax liens it has created would require very clear language," which we lack here. Union Central, 368 U.S. at 294. Further, to subject the federal government to different identification requirements—varying with each state's electronic-search technology—"would run counter to the principle of uniformity which has long been the accepted practice in the field of federal taxation." Id.

Crestmark urges us to require IRS liens to meet the same precise-identification requirement other lien notices now must meet under Uniform Commercial Code Article 9. See 9-503(1) ("A financing statement sufficiently provides the name of [a] debtor [that is] a registered organization, only if the financing statement provides the name of the debtor indicated on the public record of the debtor's jurisdiction of organization which shows the debtor to have been organized."). We decline to do so. The UCC applies to transactions "that create[ ] a security interest in personal property or fixtures *by contract*." 9-109(1)(a) (emphasis added). Thus, the IRS would be exempt from UCC requirements even without the strong federal policy favoring unfettered tax collection.

More importantly, the Supreme Court has noted that the United States, as an involuntary creditor of delinquent taxpayers, is entitled to special priority over voluntary creditors. See, e.g., Kimbell Foods, 440 U.S. at 734-35, 737-38. Thus, while we understand that a requirement that the IRS comply with UCC Article 9 would spare banks considerable inconvenience, we conclude from Supreme-Court precedent that the federal government's interest in prompt, effective tax collection trumps the banks' convenience in loan collection. * * *

COMMENTS AND QUESTIONS

Parents go to school conferences to find out how their kids are doing. In the early years, you find out whether your child "plays well with others." Grade the IRS. In *Spearing Tool*, the IRS filed in the name most readily available to it and made no effort to file in a way that protected the integrity of the UCC financing system. We have discussed before the way in which validating name variants imposes costs on subsequent searchers. The number of possible variants rises quite quickly and will indeed give rise to "considerable inconvenience" for private creditors. The costs imposed on those parties must far exceed the burden that would be imposed on the IRS to identify the debtor's legal name. We should fix this, shouldn't we? For commentary, see Lynn M. LoPucki, The *Spearing Tool* Filing System Disaster, 68 Ohio St. L.J. 281 (2007); Steven O. Weise, 2006 Survey UCC Article 9, 61 Bus. Law. 1617 (2006).

SECTION III. FIXTURES

As noted before, Article 9 is not completely comprehensive. Its most basic limit is that it defines rights in personal property. An important class of secured transactions, mortgages of real estate, are completely outside of its ambit. See 9-109(d)(11). But, of course, once we set out these two separate categories, we inevitably spend time policing the boundary between them. This can arise many ways, one of particular interest relates to the law of fixtures.

9-5: STARTING POINTS
- Debtor owns land and a building subject to a real estate mortgage in favor of Mortgagco.

- Debtor also has signed a general security agreement with Bank covering equipment, inventory and other personal property, then-owned or acquired thereafter, and has filed a financing statement with the Secretary of State.
- Debtor intends to install a wrought-iron fence. Debtor buys the fence from Seller on credit, and Seller takes back a purchase money security interest. The fence is delivered to the property and installed.
- ¤ What are the relative rights to the fence of Mortgagco, Bank and Seller? How should Seller proceed to bolster its position? What should we make of the fact that, absent special rules, Bank will have filed in the Article 9 filing system and Mortgagco will have filed in the real estate records?

The basic first-to-file rule needs to be extended in some way to treat separate filing systems, or we need a way of unifying our treatment of objects like the fence. A unified system would require a filing in one location by all parties seeking a perfected security interest in the fence. Bank would either be forced to make an additional filing in the real estate records, or Mortgagco would be required to file in the Article 9 system. Seller then would file in the applicable system, but would file in only one system.

Alternatively, we could have two systems run in parallel. Disputes between creditors claiming through the real estate would be decided on the real estate records, those between personal property lenders in the Article 9 records. We would need to allocate disputes between real estate lenders and personal property lenders to one system or the other. Suppose we allocated the "interspecies" disputes to the real records. Bank would then need to file in both the Article 9 records and the real estate records to ensure its priority against all comers, and Seller would have to do the same. Mortgagco, in contrast, could file only in the real estate records and would thereby be protected. Bank very well might choose not to file in the real estate records—the only thing at stake is after-acquired property of a particular character—and would accept that it would lose against real estate creditors. Seller, of course, would need to file in both locations.

A dual system runs the potential of introducing circular priorities. Suppose that Bank files only in the UCC records, Mortgagco and Seller in the real estate records. Seller would be prior to Mortgagco, assuming we recognize the purchase money security interest here. Mortgagco would be prior to Bank, as this is a dispute between an Article 9 creditor and a real estate creditor, and the dual system gives priority to filing in the real estate records. Bank, in turn, would be prior to Seller, as this dispute involves Article 9 creditors, and Seller is unperfected there. Seller beats Mortgagco, Mortgagco beats Bank, and Bank beats Seller.

Enough about possibilities. Article 9's scheme is set forth in the main in 9-102(a)(40), 9-102(a)(41), 9-501(a)(1), 9-502(b) and 9-334. Consider first the definitions of "fixture" and "fixture filing." Article 9 defines fixtures as goods that have "become so related to particular real estate that an interest in them arises under real estate law." That is, we start with a well-defined item of personal property and somehow it is transformed into a fixture. The transformation itself is not controlled by Article 9 but rather by the applicable real estate law. A fixture filing is defined as a "filing of a financing statement covering goods that are or are to become fixtures and satisfying 9-502(a) and (b)."

With definitions out of the way, turn to 9-334 and its focus: establishing priority rules for disputes between Article 9 secured creditors and entities claiming an interest in the fixtures through the real estate. Note what 9-334 does not do: it does not set forth rules for a dispute between two Article 9 secured creditors. An Article 9 security interest in fixtures can be perfected either though a normal financing statement filing or by making a special fixture filing in the real estate records. See 9-501 Official Comment 4. For disputes within Article 9, such as that between Bank and Seller in the fact pattern above, the usual priority rules apply, meaning 9-322 and the purchase money priority in 9-324.

In contrast, 9-334 applies to a dispute between an Article 9 claimant and a real estate claimant, such as Mortgagco in the prior fact pattern. Consider then a priority dispute between an Article 9 secured creditor and the holder of a real property mortgage. Although it is easy to lose sight of this in reading 9-334, the principal rule of priority is simply a race in the real estate records. That is, the first to file in the real estate records wins. See 9-334(c) and 9-334(e)(1). Unsurprisingly, though, a number of special situations arise. The first is the now-familiar purchase money security interest. Suppose the real estate mortgage is of record. The seller of the fence will sell for credit only if it holds a superior interest after installation. In a world without purchase money rights, a subordination agreement would be negotiated, but again a judgment has been made that simply permitting the creation of a superior interest without negotiation is the better approach. This idea is implemented in 9-334(d).

This covers the highlights of 9-334. There are some miscellaneous rules that overlay these familiar basics. Two of these—9-334(e)(2) and 9-334(e)(3)—create priorities in the chattel secured creditor without jumping through the special fixture filing hoops. Subsection (e)(2) deals with certain readily removable chattels, which are, notwithstanding that quality, deemed to be fixtures under state real estate law. Subsection (e)(2) can almost be understood as a cutback on the breadth of the fixture definition in 9-102(a)(41). Subsection (e)(3), in turn, addresses cases where the real estate lien arises after the Article 9 interest in fixtures has been perfected and the real estate lien is obtained by legal or equitable proceedings. You should note the special priority of construction mortgages in 9-334(h). So far we've said that a purchase money secured chattel financier can trump a preexisting real estate mortgage. That rule is cutback by 9-334(h), which has the effect of providing that the earlier filed construction mortgage retains priority.

All of this is important if somewhat mechanical. What we have said almost nothing about so far is what actually counts as a fixture, and this is far from mechanical. 9-102(a)(41) provides that fixtures are goods "that have become so related to particular real property that an interest in them arises under real property law." This tells us only that we need look outside of Article 9.

Yeadon Fabric Domes, Inc. v. Maine Sports Complex, LLC

Supreme Judicial Court of Maine, 2006.
901 A.2d 200.

■ Calkins, J.

Yeadon Fabric Domes, Inc. appeals from a judgment entered in the District Court in favor of Yeadon, Harriman Brothers, Inc., and Kiser & Kiser Company, against Maine Sports Complex, LLC (MSC). The judgment set the order of priority among MSC's creditors. Yeadon contends that the court erred when it held that Harriman's and Kiser's mechanic's liens had priority over its perfected security interest in a fixture attached to MSC's land. In resolving this matter, we are called upon to determine whether two apparently conflicting statutes can be harmonized: 10 MRS 4012, which gives [Article 9] perfected security interests priority over title 10 liens, and 9-334(c), which subordinates security interests in fixtures to conflicting interests of encumbrancers. We interpret 10 MRS 4012 to refer only to personal property and not to fixtures. With that interpretation,

10 MRS 4012 is inapplicable to this case, and, pursuant to 9-334(c), Yeadon's security interest is subordinate to the mechanic's liens of Harriman and Kiser. Thus, we affirm the judgment.

In 2001, MSC entered into a series of business transactions for the purpose of building a sports complex in Hampden. It purchased real estate and gave a mortgage to the seller, H.O. Bouchard, Inc. It engaged Kiser to provide engineering services for the construction of the complex. MSC entered into a contract to purchase an inflatable, fabric dome from Yeadon, along with the materials and equipment required to erect and operate the dome. MSC contracted with Harriman to provide groundwork for the sports complex. MSC also obtained a loan from Bangor Savings Bank, giving the bank a mortgage, which was later assigned to Steven Hoksch. MSC defaulted on its obligations to these various entities * * * .

Yeadon had filed a financing statement for the dome and equipment with the Secretary of State on July 22, 2002. It brought a forcible entry and detainer action for personalty pursuant to 14 MRS 6012 against MSC, seeking to recover the dome. The court dismissed the action after concluding that the dome was a fixture and not personal property. Subsequently, on February 27, 2004, Yeadon recorded a financing statement in the Penobscot County Registry of Deeds.

Yeadon filed a collection action against MSC, which was consolidated with other collection actions that had been filed by Harriman and Kiser. Both Harriman and Kiser had filed mechanic's lien claims, pursuant to 10 MRS 3253, and brought court actions to enforce their lien claims, pursuant to 10 MRS 3255. After motions for summary judgment, motions for default, and hearings, the court issued a final judgment detailing the order of priority of MSC's creditors and the amounts owed by MSC. The court found that Kiser began its work for MSC on December 3, 2001, and that Harriman began its work on December 7, 2001. The court put Yeadon last in the order of priority. * * *

The issue in this case is whether the court erred in determining the order of priority afforded to Harriman's and Kiser's mechanic's liens and to Yeadon's security interest in the dome. There are several statutes that bear on the question of priority. There are the statutes in Maine's version of the Uniform Commercial Code dealing with secured transactions, and there is also a statute in title 10.

Maine's version of the UCC sets out requirements concerning security interests and how to perfect them. Generally speaking, a financing statement must be filed to perfect a security interest. 9-310(a). A security interest is perfected by filing unless certain exceptions apply, none of which are applicable here. 9-310(a). A security interest in fixtures may be perfected by filing the financing statement in either of two places: in the registry of deeds for the county where the related real property is located, or in the Secretary of State's office. 9-501(a). * * * Thus, for goods that are, or are to become, fixtures, the secured party who wishes to perfect a security interest should file the financing statement in the county registry of deeds if the filing is to be a fixture filing, or with the Secretary of State.

A fixture filing is defined as "the filing of a financing statement covering goods that are or are to become fixtures and satisfying 9-502, subsections (a) and (b)." 9-102(a)(40). 9-502 lists the information that a financing statement must contain to qualify as a fixture filing. 9-502(a), (b).

The provision in Maine's version of the UCC dealing with the priority of security interests in fixtures is 9-334. The general rule is that "a security interest in fixtures is subordinate to a conflicting interest of an encumbrancer or owner of the related real property other than the debtor." 9-334(c). An encumbrance is defined as "a right, other than an ownership interest, in real property." 9-102(a)(32). The term "includes mortgages and other liens on real property." 9-102(a)(32).

There are exceptions to the general rule and several alternatives by which a security interest in fixtures has priority over conflicting interests. The alternatives that are most likely to fit the factual situation of this case are found in 9-334(d) and (e). The first of these alternatives is in 9-334(d), which gives a perfected security interest in fixtures priority when the debtor has an interest of record in, or is in possession of, the real property; the security interest in fixtures is a purchase-money security interest; the encumbrancer's interest arose before the goods became fixtures; and the security interest was perfected by a fixture filing before or within twenty days of the time the goods became fixtures. Another alternative is 9-334(e)(1), which states that a perfected security interest in fixtures has priority if:

> (a) The debtor has an interest of record in the real property or is in possession of the real property and the security interest:
>
> (i) Is perfected by a fixture filing before the interest of the encumbrancer or owner is of record; and
>
> (ii) Has priority over any conflicting interest of a predecessor in title of the encumbrancer or owner ....

There is also the alternative in 9-334(e)(3), which states that a perfected security interest in fixtures has priority if "[t]he conflicting interest is a lien on the real property obtained by legal or equitable proceedings after the security interest was perfected by any method permitted by this Article."

The final statute that bears on this case is in title 10, which contains the statute authorizing the mechanic's liens filed by Harriman and Kiser. See 10 MRS 3251. Specifically, 10 MRS 4012 states: "A security interest perfected in accordance with Title 11 has priority over any lien created or referred to by this Title unless the person claiming the lien has possession of the goods subject to the lien."

Yeadon filed a financing statement covering the dome and equipment with the Secretary of State on July 22, 2002, and with the registry of deeds on February 27, 2004. The court determined that the dome with its equipment is a fixture. The claims of Kiser and Harriman are pursuant to the mechanic's lien statute. 10 MRS 3251. Kiser began work on December 3, 2001, filed its lien on November 18, 2002, and filed its enforcement action on February 10, 2003. Harriman began work on December 7, 2001, filed its lien on August 27, 2002, and filed the enforcement action on October 17, 2002.

The issue is whether the District Court correctly placed Yeadon's priority after Harriman and Kiser. *** Yeadon perfected its security interest when it filed a financing statement with the Secretary of State on July 22, 2002. This filing did not qualify as a fixture filing, but 9-501(a)(2) provides that a security interest in goods that are, or are to become, fixtures can be perfected by filing with the Secretary of State. There is no requirement that a fixture filing be made in order to perfect a security interest in fixtures. Yeadon's later filing with the registry of deeds on February 27, 2004, qualified as a fixture filing.

The significance of a fixture filing, as compared to a filing with the Secretary of State, is shown in 9-334. A fixture filing is necessary for a security interest in fixtures to obtain priority pursuant to sections 9-334(d) and (e)(1). In order for Yeadon to obtain priority over Harriman and Kiser pursuant to 9-334(d), which is one of the exceptions to the general rule that security interests in fixtures are subordinate, Yeadon's security interest had to be perfected by a fixture filing before the dome became a fixture or within twenty days thereafter. The record is not clear as to when the dome became a fixture, but it had obviously become a fixture before July 21, 2003, the date of the forcible entry and detainer hearing. As Yeadon's fixture filing was not made until February 2004, it was not made within twenty days of the time the dome became a fixture. Thus, 9-334(d) is of no help to Yeadon.

To obtain priority over Harriman and Kiser pursuant to 9-334(e)(1), Yeadon's security interest had to be perfected by a fixture filing before the Harriman or Kiser interests became of record. Because Yeadon's fixture filing was not made until 2004 and both Harriman's and Kiser's title 10 liens were of record in 2002, Yeadon does not have priority over Harriman and Kiser pursuant to 9-334(e)(1).

The final provision in 9-334 worth discussion is 9-334(e)(3), which gives priority to a security interest in fixtures over a conflicting interest that is a lien on the real property obtained by legal or equitable proceedings after the perfection of the security interest, regardless of whether the security interest was perfected by a fixture filing or a filing with the Secretary of State. This alternative does not assist Yeadon because the mechanic's liens held by Harriman and Kiser are not liens obtained by legal or equitable proceedings. Mechanic's liens are *enforced* by legal proceedings, but they are *obtained* by operation of statute and the filing of the liens pursuant to the statute. See 10 MRS 3251, 3253, 3255.

Yeadon does not come within the alternatives in 9-334 that give priority to security interests in fixtures over conflicting interests. Thus, the general rule in 9-334(c) subordinating a security interest in fixtures to a conflicting interest of an encumbrancer applies, and Yeadon's security interest is subordinate to Harriman's and Kiser's mechanic's liens unless 10 MRS 4012 gives Yeadon priority.

Section 4012 plainly states that a security interest perfected in accordance with title 11 has priority over any non-possessory lien created by title 10. If the plain meaning of section 4012 controls, Yeadon's security interest takes priority over Harriman's and Kiser's mechanic's liens. On its face, section 4012 is in direct conflict with the rule in 9-334(c) that security interests in fixtures are subordinate to conflicting interests of an encumbrancer. No cases interpreting section 4012 have been called to our attention, and our independent research has not uncovered any.

When two statutes appear to be inconsistent, we should harmonize them if at all possible. It is tempting to try to harmonize the statutes by interpreting the term "encumbrancer" in 9-334(c) as not applying to the holder of a mechanic's lien. * * * However, the term "encumbrance" is defined in 9-102(a)(32) as "a right, other than an ownership interest, in real property" and "includes mortgages and other liens on real property." Thus, an interpretation of 9-334(c) that excludes holders of mechanic's liens from being encumbrancers appears disingenuous.

Another possibility for harmonizing the two statutes is to interpret section 4012 as giving a security interest in fixtures priority over any title 10 non-possessory lien only when the title 10 lien is created after the date the security interest is perfected. In other words, we could interpret section 4012 as giving priority to the creditor who is first in time. A first in time interpretation, however, requires additional language concerning when the security interest is "perfected" and when the title 10 lien is "created." This interpretation is not a reasonable one because it requires reading into section 4012 far more language than appears in it. Furthermore, because a detailed first in time priority for security interests in fixtures is contained in 9-334(e)(1), the goal of harmonizing the statutes would be defeated unless the additional requirements of 9-334(e)(1) were also read into section 4012.

The most reasonable interpretation of section 4012 is that it does not apply to fixtures. There are several reasons why this interpretation is desirable. First, the chapter in which section 4012 is located appears to deal only with liens on personal property. Second, it is highly doubtful that the Legislature intended to enact a statute that is directly contrary to another statute. If section 4012 applies to fixtures, then section 4012 is directly contrary to 9-334(c), a result we doubt the Legislature intended. Third, 9-334 contains considerably more detail regarding the situations in which conflicting interests in a fixture can arise than does section 4012, and it therefore makes sense to construe the more general section 4012 to fit with the more specific 9-334. Fourth, because section 4012 was included in the errors and inconsistencies legislation following the enactment of the Maine UCC, the Legislature itself saw section 4012 as consistent with the priorities established in title 11.

For these reasons, we conclude that interpreting section 4012 as not applying to fixtures is a reasonable interpretation that comports with the Legislature's intention and harmonizes section 4012 with 9-334(c). Under this interpretation of section 4012, the statute is not applicable to Yeadon's security interest in the fixture. The liens of Harriman and Kiser have priority over Yeadon's security interest because 9-334(c) subordinates Yeadon's security interest in the fixture to the mechanic's liens. * * *

CHAPTER TEN

THE SECURED CREDITOR IN BANKRUPTCY

This is the final chapter of the book, and we will spend it focusing on different chapters, in particular Chapters 7, 11 and 13 of the Bankruptcy Code. Many security interests are ultimately resolved in a bankruptcy proceeding, and that possibility is part of the background against which all security interests must be considered. Section I of this chapter sets forth a brief overview of the Bankruptcy Code as applied to a secured creditor in personal property. Section II addresses the avoiding powers of the trustee in bankruptcy. Section III sets forth the framework for establishing the value of the position of the secured creditor in a bankruptcy case.

SECTION I. OVERVIEW OF KEY BANKRUPTCY CODE PROVISIONS

Section 8 of Article I of the U.S. Constitution empowers Congress "[t]o establish an uniform Rule of Naturalization, and uniform Laws on the subject of Bankruptcies throughout the United States." Congress exercised this power repeatedly during the 19th Century, as federal bankruptcy laws came into force and then expired of their own accord. The adoption of the Bankruptcy Act of 1898 changed this. Since that time to the present date, we have had a federal bankruptcy statute in place. The statute has changed substantially during that period. The reorganization provisions were created in the 1930's in response to the Great Depression and were put firmly in place in the Chandler Act of 1938. So they remained, on the whole, until 1978, when the present Bankruptcy Code was put in place. Since then, substantial amendments were passed in 1984, 1994 and 2005.

As noted above, the Bankruptcy Code is divided into chapters. Chapters 1, 3 and 5 contain general provisions that apply in the other chapters.

Chapter 7 addresses liquidations; Chapter 9, municipal debtors; Chapter 11, reorganizations; Chapter 12, family farmers; and Chapter 13, wage earners. A bankruptcy proceeding is initiated by the filing of a bankruptcy petition, which designates the applicable chapter of the Bankruptcy Code. The debtor—the entity that will be in bankruptcy—may file the petition on its own behalf—this is a voluntary filing, see BC 301—or a group of three creditors owed more than roughly $10,000—the amount is adjusted periodically—in unsecured claims may force the debtor into bankruptcy in an involuntary filing. See BC 303. As the titles themselves suggest, each chapter has certain eligibility requirements and the substance of the chapters varies considerably. Chapter 7 contemplates that the assets of the debtor will be sold and the resulting cash will be distributed to creditors pursuant to state-law priorities, in-bankruptcy priorities, and the basic pro-rata distribution rule applicable in bankruptcy. See BC 507 and BC 726. The debtor gives up control of the assets to a trustee, who may operate the business pending sale. In turn, an individual filing under Chapter 7 receives a discharge of its debts. See BC 727.

The idea of a discharge—a fresh start—has long been part of this nation's bankruptcy policy. As the Supreme Court emphasized in Wetmore v. Markoe, 196 U.S. 68 (1904):

> Systems of bankruptcy are designed to relieve the honest debtor from the weight of indebtedness which has become oppressive, and to permit him to have a fresh start in business or commercial life, freed from the obligation and responsibilities which may have resulted from business misfortunes.

The vision behind this is that we want debtors to be productive members of society. An oppressive debt burden—regardless of the manner in which the debts were created—saps the energy of the debtor. There is little reason to try to be productive if your best efforts offer no hope of full repayment of debt or if every dollar earned must be paid over immediately to creditors. The consequence of the discharge is that creditors are no longer entitled to collect their debts from the debtor. See BC 524. The personal liability—the in-personam liability—faced by the debtor is ended and the debtor can move forward free of the burdens imposed by that liability. The discharge is not absolute: the debtor will forfeit it for various bad acts, see BC 727(a), and an ever-increasing list of debts are excluded from the discharge. See BC 523. The list of nondischargeable debts includes those arising out of willful and malicious injuries, fraud and false pretenses, and student loans, absent undue hardship. Chapters 9, 11, 12 and 13 all contemplate a reorganization of the debtor.

Turn more directly to the position of the secured creditor in bankruptcy. Four ideas are of particular importance. First, the filing itself immediately alters the opportunities available to the secured creditor. The filing creates an automatic stay of actions against the debtor and its property. See BC 362. For example, the secured creditor is barred from repossessing collateral under 9-609 or selling it under 9-610. Instead, the secured creditor must seek relief from the automatic stay under BC 362(d):

> (d) On request of a party in interest and after notice and a hearing, the court shall grant relief from the stay provided under subsection (a) of this section, such as by terminating, annulling, modifying, or conditioning such stay -
>
> (1) for cause, including the lack of adequate protection of an interest in property of such party in interest;
>
> (2) with respect to a stay of an act against property under subsection (a) of this section, if -
>
> (A) the debtor does not have an equity in such property; and
>
> (B) such property is not necessary to an effective reorganization ...

(This omits BC 362(d)(3), which has a special provision covering security interests in real estate.) Thus, a bankruptcy petition prevents the secured creditor from invoking the defining property rights of the secured creditor. At a minimum, these rights are delayed, and only if the secured creditor can navigate BC 362(d) successfully will these rights again be meaningful.

Second, the petition filing means that transactions that took place before bankruptcy will be reexamined. For secured creditors, this means that the trustee (or the debtor if the debtor has remained in control and is acting as a debtor-in-possession) will scrutinize the position of the secured creditor to bring to bear the trustee's avoiding powers. The avoiding powers permit the trustee to invalidate particular prepetition transactions. The trustee will start by examining whether the secured creditor perfected its security interest appropriately under applicable law. As explained below, BC 544(a) empowers the trustee to avoid—that is, to strip away and preserve for the benefit of the estate—unperfected security interests. Much of the litigation in bankruptcy over the secured creditor's position thus turns on whether the secured creditor has complied with Article 9's rules. The trustee will turn to the time that the secured creditor perfected its interest. Even if the secured creditor filed a financing statement perfect in form, a late financing statement, as explained below, will create a preference under BC 547, and the trustee once again will be able to avoid the security interest. Finally, even if the financing statement was filed at the right time, the secured creditor still is at risk. Payments received by the secured creditor will also be examined as preferences under BC 547, as will grants of security interests.

Third, assuming the security interest survives the avoiding powers, we will have to assess how we will value and treat the position of the secured creditor. BC 506(a) calls for the judge to value the collateral securing the obligation owed to the secured creditor. If the collateral is worth more than the amount owed to the secured creditor, the creditor is said to be oversecured. Under BC 506(b), an oversecured creditor is entitled to interest during the bankruptcy proceeding up to the amount of the oversecurity. More often than not, the secured creditor is undersecured, meaning that the value of the collateral is less than the amount of the debt. In that case, BC 506(a) splits the debt into two pieces—bifurcates it, as the phrase goes—into a secured claim equal to the value of the collateral and an unsecured claim for the rest. So, for example, take a secured creditor with a security interest on equipment found by the bankruptcy judge under BC 506(a) to be worth $1,000. The secured creditor is owed $3,000 as of the bankruptcy petition. Under BC 506(a), the creditor will hold a secured claim of $1,000 and an unsecured claim of $2,000. With these claims in hand, we will be able to assess the secured creditor's rights in the case.

Fourth and finally, in a reorganization under Chapter 11, the secured creditor's claim must be dealt with. That is complicated, but Chapter 11 contemplates a consensual process subject to rules that kick in when the parties can't agree (the so-called cramdown rules). Chapter 11 embraces "absolute priority" meaning that superior claimants are entitled to be paid in full before any claimants below them claim any value. Secured creditors are to collect in front of unsecured creditors, who take before preferred shareholders, who take before common stockholders. But parties can agree to deviate from that and do so with some frequency. Of course, any agreement reached undoubtedly reflects the alternative that the debtor can impose without agreement. That alternative is set forth in BC 1129(b)(2)(A). That is a lengthy provision but it provides for the secured creditor to retain its security interest and to be paid, often over time, the full amount of its claim, at least in cases in which anyone below the secured creditor in priority takes value under the plan. Do recognize that the actual terms of the secured loan—key terms such as the maturity date and the interest rate—can be changed dramatically from those in the original loan.

SECTION II. TRUSTEE AVOIDING POWERS

The "avoiding powers" of the trustee in bankruptcy facilitate the marshaling of the estate. The estate's right to property is, in the first instance, derived from the debtor itself. BC 541. But the trustee (for purposes of augmenting the estate) also acquires powers that the debtor itself does not enjoy. These powers are designed to give the trustee, and hence the estate, greater rights in property than the debtor would have outside of bankruptcy. Although state law (such as Article 9) provides a baseline for determining the force or extent of the trustee's powers, inevitably, the trustee is using federal (bankruptcy) law to displace state-created rights and interests. These powers that are given to the trustee but that are not derived from the debtor are of two sorts. First of all, the trustee inherits the rights of the *existing unsecured creditors* of the debtor, so that if any one of them would have the power to set aside a transaction, the trustee "inherits" that power, and may use it for the benefit of the unsecured creditors generally.

Under the rule of Moore v. Bay, 284 U.S. 4 (1931), the trustee's power is greater than that of the actual creditors. An actual creditor can set aside a transfer only up to the amount it is owed. When the trustee steps into the shoes of an actual unsecured creditor, however, he can set aside the entire transfer, regardless of the amount of the claim held by the actual creditor whose rights the trustee assumes. BC 544(b), however, does not loom large for secured creditors under Article 9 because actual unsecured creditors do not have interests superior to that of even unperfected secured creditors. Recall 9-317. In addition to inheriting the rights that existing creditors possess, the trustee is given rights that no one—neither the debtor nor existing creditors—actually enjoys outside of bankruptcy. These form the remainder of the avoiding powers we shall be examining.

A. THE TRUSTEE AS IDEAL LIEN CREDITOR

BC 544(a) gives the trustee the rights of a fictional (or hypothetical) contract creditor with a judicial lien or execution lien on any personal property the debtor may claim an interest in. This gives us a measuring rod, so to speak, for determining who prevails in a contest between the trustee and adverse claimants: If an imaginary creditor with the characteristics of a BC 544(a)(1) creditor would prevail as against the adverse interest, the trustee wins. Not only does the trustee win, but BC 544(a) goes on to say that he may "avoid" the interest, making the unlucky claimant an unsecured creditor for purposes of bankruptcy. See also BC 551 (stating that the avoided transfer is preserved "for the benefit of the estate").

It is necessary to become accustomed to two things here: the trustee's rights are being measured by those of a third party, and this particular third party is a hypothetical one. To understand the importance of BC 544(a) in relation to Article 9 security interests, you should examine, with care, not only BC 544(a), but also 9-317.

10-1: THE HYPOTHETICAL LIEN CREDITOR POWER

- Debtor borrows $5,000 from Finco and gives Finco a security interest in its machine. This machine is worth $10,000 and is Debtor's only asset.
- Finco fails to make a proper Article 9 filing. Debtor had long before borrowed $10,000 from Bank on an unsecured basis. Debtor also owes its suppliers $5,000.
- Debtor files a petition in bankruptcy. The trustee convinces the bankruptcy judge to set aside Finco's security interest and he sells the machine for $10,000.
- ¤ How should the proceeds be divided?

B. PREFERENCES IN BANKRUPTCY

In their most basic form, preferences are simply transfers that favor one existing creditor over another. Debtor prefers Creditor A to Creditor B if it pays A before B. Favoring A over B is not usually not a fraudulent conveyance—assuming Debtor is not motivated by an actual desire to delay, hinder, or defraud B—because the antecedent debt to A is fair consideration for the transfer (of cash presumably) that Debtor makes to A. Debtor plans to pay B eventually, but would simply prefer to pay A first. See Shelley v. Boothe, 73 Mo. 74 (1880) ("While the effect of such preference must, to the extent that it is made, necessarily be to defer or hinder or delay other creditors, the mere knowledge of the preferred creditor that such will be its effect, and the debtor intended it should have that effect, will not be sufficient to avoid the transaction ....").

Outside of bankruptcy (or other collective proceedings), preferences do not seem inherently objectionable. Indeed, it is a corollary of the idea that every creditor is left to its own devices to ensure that it is repaid that one creditor could be repaid (or secured) before another. Any system that prevented preferences would necessarily be a collective system in which creditors could not recover from their debtor without accounting for the interests of the other creditors. Our basic rule is that outside of bankruptcy, satisfaction of existing debts is the responsibility of the individual creditors. Each creditor must use its own powers of persuasion (as well as the powers of the courts) to seek repayment. Its efforts are not compromised if someone else is less vigorous in seeking repayment; on the other hand, it cannot complain if another is more vigorous and has satisfied its claim against the debtor first.

Inside of bankruptcy, preferences generally do not take place, at least with respect to prepetition debts. Creditors share in the property of the debtor not according to the wishes of the debtor or the trustee nor according to their speed or diligence, but according to the priorities they agreed to when they initially entered into the transaction with the debtor. If they bargained to be secured creditors, they get paid first (up to the value of their secured claim); if they did not, they share equally in the remainder (subject to a few exceptions—workers' claims for back wages, for example, are given priority over other unsecured claims up to a specified statutory amount). See BC 507, BC 725, BC 726, BC 507.

We cannot, however, expect the two sets of rules to live harmoniously side-by-side. Bankruptcy law is founded on the principle that, when the debtor is insolvent, the interests of the creditors are best served if the creditors work together, even though a creditor might profit if it pursued individual remedies. Creditors, however, do not wake up suddenly and discover that the debtor is insolvent. Some of the creditors may know that the collective proceeding is imminent and take advantage of this knowledge to have their own claims satisfied (to the extent possible) and opt out of the collective proceeding altogether. Sometimes debtors, knowing that bankruptcy is imminent, pay first the creditors that they like or that they think they will need in the future. By the time the bankruptcy petition is actually filed, those creditors that remained would discover that they had the worst of both worlds: they have to share equally in a small pool of assets.

Preference law is essentially a transitional rule that prevents individual creditors from opting out of the collective proceeding once that event becomes imminent. Like many other legal rules, the preference provision of the Bankruptcy Code leans towards per se rules rather than loose standards in deciding what is a preference. The idea of these rules is to pick up most of the transfers that are objectionable (creditors or debtors taking special action in anticipation of the collective proceeding) and to leave untouched transactions that are unobjectionable (for example, payment of gas and electricity bills in the ordinary course). In evaluating the Bankruptcy Code's preference rule, which is in BC 547, you should ask how well the drafters succeeded.

In section 60 of the Bankruptcy Act of 1898, much of the sorting between objectionable and unobjectionable transactions was done by two prerequisites to finding a voidable preference: (a) that the debtor was insolvent when the event under question took place; and (b) that the recipient of the preference "knew or had reason to know" of that insolvency. The subjective "knew or had reason to know" test—probably the most litigated question under the preference provisions of the Bankruptcy Act of 1898—has been dropped in the Bankruptcy Code as a requirement of receiving a preference. The insolvency requirement, however, remains, although there is a presumption that the debtor is insolvent during the 90 days before the filing of a petition. See BC 547(b)(3); BC 547(f); BC 101(32).

Read BC 547 closely. The general provisions are contained in BC 547(b). The section gives the trustee the power to avoid some "transfers" of "interests of the debtor in property" made for or on account of "antecedent debts." There is a voidable preference only if the requirements of BC 547(b) are met. Even if they are met, BC 547(c) may nonetheless release the transaction from the clutches of the trustee. If the trustee avoids the transfer, it is again preserved for the benefit of the estate, BC 551. To get a feel for the basic issues raised by BC 547(b) for secured creditors, consider the following hypotheticals:

10-2: NO ANTECEDENT DEBT, NO PREFERENCE

- On February 1st, Debtor borrows $10,000 from Finco and gives Finco a security interest in its machine. This machine is worth $10,000 and is Debtor's only asset. Finco perfects the interest appropriately on that date.
- Two months later, Debtor files for bankruptcy.

    ¤ Has Finco received a preference under BC 547(b)?

10-3: ANTECEDENT DEBT, PREFERENCE

- On February 1st, Debtor borrows $10,000 from Finco.
- On March 1st, Debtor gives Finco a security interest in its machine. This machine is worth $10,000 and is Debtor's only asset. Finco perfects the interest appropriately on that date.
- Two months later, Debtor files for bankruptcy.
- ¤ Has Finco received a preference under BC 547(b)?

What transfers may the trustee avoid? "Transfer" is defined broadly; it means "every mode, direct or indirect, absolute or conditional, voluntary or involuntary, of disposing of or parting with property or with an interest in property, including retention of title as a security interest and foreclosure of the debtor's equity of redemption." BC 101(54). A transfer is a voidable preference under BC 547(b) only if five conditions are met. First, the transfer must be "to or for the benefit of a creditor." If a debtor gives a creditor a security interest or cash, the transfer is made directly to the creditor. Second, the transfer must also be "for or on account of an antecedent debt owed by the debtor before the transfer was made." In any transaction in which a voidable preference is a possibility, you must always ask two questions: (1) When was the debt incurred? (2) When was the transfer made? As long as the transfer was made at the same time as the debt was incurred or before the debt was incurred, there can be, by definition, no voidable preference.

Third, the transfer must also have been made while the debtor was insolvent. "Insolvent" is a defined term, BC 101(32). A debtor is insolvent within that definition when its debts, at fair valuation, exceed the fair value of its property. Proving insolvency may be very difficult, for it requires you to find "fair values" of assets and liabilities, instead of accounting or book values, and also will require you to value contingent liabilities (e.g., tort suits by asbestosis victims) and contingent assets (e.g., the value of a lawsuit against insurance carriers). BC 547(f) is designed to avoid that inquiry, at least sometimes, by providing that the debtor is presumed to have been insolvent on and during the 90 days immediately preceding the date of the filing of the petition.

Fourth, the transfer must have been made on or within 90 days of the filing of the petition or within one year of the filing of the petition if the creditor is an insider. This provision is a change from the 1898 Act. Under the 1898 Act, the general preference period was longer (four months instead of 90 days) and there was no special provision for insiders. In addition, there was a requirement that the creditor knew or had reason to know of the debtor's insolvency.

The final requirement of a voidable preference is that it makes the creditor better off than if no transfer had been made and the creditor had only enjoyed what rights it had in the collective proceeding. The idea is that the creditor cannot be trying to opt out of the collective proceeding if the transfer brings it no special advantages. This can be of particular importance to a secured creditor, for if it is fully secured, a payment made to it—a "transfer" of cash—may be saved from being a voidable preference principally because of this requirement.

10-4: PAYMENTS TO FULLY SECURED CREDITORS
- On February 1st, Debtor borrows $10,000 from Finco and gives Finco a security interest in its machine. This machine is worth $10,000. Finco perfects the interest appropriately on that date.
- On February 2nd, Debtor borrows $10,000 from Bank on an unsecured basis.
- Two months later, Finco pressures Debtor to sell the machine and turn over its proceeds to Finco. Debtor sells the machine for $10,000, its fair market value, and gives the money to Finco.
- One day later, Debtor files for bankruptcy, having assets of $5,000.
- ¤ Has Finco received a preference under BC 547(b)?

10-5: SYNERGIES AND FULLY SECURED CREDITORS
- Debtor has two machines. The first machine, alone, is worth $10,000, the second machine, alone, is worth $5,000, but together they are worth $17,000. On February 1st, Debtor borrows $10,000 from Finco and gives Finco a security interest in the first machine.
- On February 2nd, Debtor borrows $10,000 from Bank on an unsecured basis.
- Two months later, Finco pressures Debtor to sell the first machine and turn over its proceeds to Finco. Debtor sells that machine for $10,000, its fair market value standing alone, and gives the money to Finco.
- One day later, Debtor files for bankruptcy, having only the second machine, which is worth $5,000.
- ¤ Has Finco received a preference under BC 547(b)?

Antecedence is the core idea in BC 547(b). Given that, an enormous amount turns on the timing of the creation of the debt and the allegedly preferential transfer. This poses special problems for secured creditors. When does a debtor "transfer" an interest in property in a secured transaction? Is it when the secured party files? When the security interest attaches? When the security interest becomes perfected? BC 547(e) provides the answers to at least some of these questions; we will look at it shortly. Consider it as you examine the following fact pattern:

10-6: LATE FILINGS AND SECURED CREDITORS

- On February 1st, Debtor borrows $10,000 from Finco and gives Finco a security interest in its machine. This machine is worth $10,000. Finco does not perfect.
- On February 2nd, Debtor borrows $10,000 from Bank on an unsecured basis.
- On March 1st, Finco files an appropriate financing statement to perfect its security interest.
- One month later, Finco pressures Debtor to sell the machine and turn over its proceeds to Finco. Debtor sells the machine for $10,000, its fair market value, and gives the money to Finco.
- One day later, Debtor files for bankruptcy, having assets of $5,000.
- ¤ Has Finco received a preference under BC 547(b)?

Section 547(e) tells us that a transfer of a security interest is "deemed" to take place at the time the interest takes effect as between the parties (or, to use the language of Article 9, at the time of attachment), provided that the interest is perfected within thirty days of the time it takes effect, BC 547(e)(2)(A). If perfection takes place at a later time, the transfer is "deemed" to take effect at that time, BC 547(e)(2)(B), and the transfer is "deemed" to take effect just before the filing of the petition, if the security interest is not perfected by the time the petition is filed or within thirty days of the time the transfer takes effect between the parties, BC 547(e)(2)(C). "Perfection," as used in BC 547(e)(2), is defined in BC 547(e)(1). For personal property and fixtures, the time of perfection is "when a creditor on a simple contract cannot acquire a judicial lien that is superior." BC 547(e)(3), finally, states that a transfer is not made for purposes of BC 547(e) until the debtor has acquired rights in the collateral.

In looking at the purposes of preference law, note that preferences can be conceived of in two distinct ways. On the one hand are "last minute grabs." On the other hand are "tardy perfections." Both types of actions involve eve-of-bankruptcy opt-outs from the oncoming collective proceeding. A preference section, however, that reached only transfers of property by or from a debtor, would not successfully reach cases of tardy perfections. For, in those cases, the problem is one of priority, not property. A security interest is granted when it attaches—the "transfer" of "property" occurs then. But bankruptcy is concerned with rights among claimants. A secured creditor who does not take the additional steps for perfection will lose its security interest and be treated as an unsecured creditor for purposes of bankruptcy, BC 544(a). Perfecting the security interest after it is granted, and on the eve of bankruptcy, therefore, avoids the trustee's use of BC 544(a) and involves opt-out just as if the creditor had been paid. A preference section presumably needs to reach such actions. BC 547 does so by manipulating the date of transfer, and BC 547(e) exists to provide that manipulation. Although BC 547(e) appears complex when first approached, much of its mystery can be avoided by remembering that it exists to treat tardy perfections equivalently with transfers of property. If the issue is not one of a tardy perfection of an interest previously transferred, BC 547(e) is not involved.

Bear in mind the consequences that follow from finding that the transfer, for purposes of BC 547, did not take place at the time that the security interest became effective between the parties: once a party has given "value" to the debtor, it becomes a creditor and the debtor will have incurred a "debt" within the meaning of BC 101(5) and BC 101(12). If the transfer is found to take place at some later time, there is a potential voidable preference, because the transfer, taking place *after* the debt has been incurred, will be made on account of an *antecedent* debt, thus meeting the requirement of BC 547(b)(2). In this way, tardy perfections are treated the same as last-minute grabs.

C. THE ARTICLE 9 FLOATING LIEN IN BANKRUPTCY

One of the major innovations of Article 9 was to make it easy for asset-based lenders to take a security interest in collateral of the debtor that was constantly changing. Article 9 largely rejects both the 19th-century doctrine that "a man cannot give what he hath not" and the doctrine that required a creditor to maintain control over disposition of the collateral in order to have a security interest that was enforceable against third parties. See 9-204. If Finco wants to acquire a security interest in all of Debtor's inventory, it need only make an Article 9 filing and ensure that Debtor sign a single security agreement that gives it an interest in all of Debtor's inventory, then existing or thereafter acquired.

Outside of a bankruptcy proceeding, Finco, assuming it is the first to file or perfect, will prevail over all other creditors of Debtor, unless one of them enables Debtor to acquire specific inventory and obtains a super-priority under 9-324(b) by, among other things, providing Finco with notice of its interest before Debtor acquires the collateral. Will Finco also prevail in a bankruptcy proceeding? We know that, as a general matter, it will because the trustee, as the representative of the general creditors who have hypothetically reduced all their claims to judgment as of the date of the filing of the petition, loses to a perfected secured creditor under BC 544(a). But is Finco's interest in recently-acquired inventory a voidable preference? Has there been a transfer to Finco on the eve of Debtor's demise that violates the "anti-tardy-perfection" or "anti-last minute grab" policies? Has there been a manipulation by Finco to improve its position in the expectation of an imminent bankruptcy proceeding?

The following problems address the consequences to a secured creditor of changes in its collateral during the preference period.

10-7: NEW PROPERTY AND SECURED CREDITORS

- On February 1st, Bank lends Debtor $10,000. Debtor signs a security agreement granting Bank a security interest in all of its property, then existing or thereafter acquired. On that date, Bank makes a proper Article 9 filing.
- On February 12th, Debtor acquires a machine.
- On March 1st, Debtor files for bankruptcy.
- ¤ Has Bank received a preference under BC 547(b)? See BC 547(e)(3).

10-8: FLOATING COLLATERAL AND SECURED CREDITORS

- On February 1st, Bank lends Debtor $10,000. Debtor signs a security agreement granting Bank a security interest in all of its inventory, then existing or thereafter acquired. On that date, Bank makes a proper Article 9 filing. Debtor has $10,000 in inventory.

- On March 1st, Debtor files for bankruptcy. Debtor again has $10,000 in inventory, but all of this inventory has been acquired since February 1st.

- ¤ Has Bank received a preference under BC 547(b)? See BC 547(e)(3); BC 547(c)(5). Suppose that Debtor had only $8,000 in inventory on February 1st. Does that change your answer?

COMMENTS AND QUESTIONS: THE EVOLUTION OF BC 547(c)(5)

When it passed the 1978 Bankruptcy Reform Act, Congress thought that secured creditors who had a "floating lien"—that is, a lien over a certain class of a debtor's property such as inventory or accounts—could persuade the debtor to increase the value of those assets (and hence decrease the value of others). An increase in the total value of the inventory might result from pressure that a finance company exercised upon the debtor during the 90-day preference period. You should consider how likely such manipulations are and whether or in what respects the rules Congress enacted in BC 547 (particularly in (c)(5)) are under- or over-inclusive.

This particular controversy was the subject of intense attention before the passage of the 1978 Act. See Anthony T. Kronman, The Treatment of Security Interests in After-Acquired Property Clauses Under the Proposed Bankruptcy Act, 124 U. Pa. L. Rev. 110 (1975). BC 547(e)(3) tries to kill the technical arguments that underlay that controversy by *postponing* the moment of transfer until the debtor acquires rights in the collateral. If a creditor has a security interest in inventory and the debtor acquires new inventory in the 90-day period, the security interests that are thereby created (that "attach" to use the language of Article 9) are voidable preferences within the meaning of BC 547(b) (provided its other requirements (such as the debtor's insolvency) are met). The question we face in examining a floating lien, therefore, is whether any of the exceptions in BC 547(c) apply. BC 547(c)(5) provides that a perfected security interest in inventory or accounts is not a voidable preference unless (a) the new security interest improves the position of the secured creditor and (b) that improvement of position is "to the prejudice of other creditors holding unsecured claims." The transfers are not voidable if, when totaled together, they do not reduce the amount that the debtor owed the secured creditor that was unsecured at the time the preference period began to run or the time the secured creditor first extended value under the security agreement, whichever was later.

SECTION III. VALUATION AND ITS CONSEQUENCES

In a typical reorganization case involving a secured creditor, the debtor will hope to retain the collateral and pay the secured creditor some amount over time. We will need to assess the value of the secured creditor's position. The first sentence of BC 506(a)(1) addresses this issue:

> An allowed claim of a creditor secured by a lien on property in which the estate has an interest, or that is subject to setoff under section 553 of this title, is a secured claim to the extent of the value of such creditor's interest in the estate's interest in such property, or to the extent of the amount subject to setoff, as the case may be, and is an unsecured claim to the extent that the value of such creditor's interest or the amount so subject to setoff is less than the amount of such allowed claim.

This is not crystal clear: What exactly is the "value of such creditor's interest in the estate's interest in such property"? Is this just the value of the collateral or is it something else? Could we argue that by focusing on the creditor's interest that this points us to state law and what the secured creditor could have done with the collateral?

Once that argument was up for grabs, but the Supreme Court's decision in United Savings Ass'n v. Timbers of Inwood Forest Assocs., 484 U.S. 365 (1988) resolved this. Prior to *Timbers*, secured creditors argued that adequate protection of their security interest under BC 361 required that the time value of money be recognized. After all, reasoned the secured creditors, had the secured creditor foreclosed on the property, it could have immediately reinvested the proceeds. The "creditor's interest" in BC 506(a)(1) therefore should look to the outcome under state law, and adequate protection of that interest required compensation for the loss of interest on the foreclosure proceeds. See, e.g., Crocker National Bank v. American Mariner Industries, Inc. (In re American Mariner Industries, Inc.), 734 F.2d 426 (9th Cir. 1984). See also Douglas G. Baird & Thomas H. Jackson, Corporate Reorganizations and the Treatment of Diverse Ownership Interests: A Comment on Adequate Protection of Secured Creditors in Bankruptcy, 51 U. Chi. L. Rev. 97 (1984).

The Court rejected this out of hand: "[t]he phrase 'value of such creditor's interest' in BC 506(a) means 'the value of the collateral.'" *Timbers*, 484 U.S. at 372. The Court noted that the lead-in phrase was intended to encompass cases in which the secured creditor took an interest in only part of the debtor's property. Otherwise, we were not to look to outcomes under state law, but were instead to use the value of the collateral to determine the amount of the creditor's secured claim.

Post-*Timbers*, we should understand the first sentence of BC 506(a)(1) to provide that the creditor has a secured claim equal to the value of the collateral and that the balance of its allowed claim is unsecured. But, this sentence says nothing about *how* to value the collateral—whether to use a standard of retail, wholesale or something else—but only specifies that it is the collateral that must be valued. It is the second sentence of BC 506(a)(1) that tells us how to value the collateral:

> Such value shall be determined in light of the purpose of the
> valuation and of the proposed disposition or use of such proper-
> ty, and in conjunction with any hearing on such disposition or
> use or on a plan affecting such creditor's interest.

What standard should be used to value this property? Wholesale? Retail? Foreclosure value? Some combination of these? This is very open-ended, but it does suggest strongly that we cannot have a single standard applicable in all situations. At the same time, to take the language of the statute seriously, we must take disposition and use into account.

At one point, this was an open question, but with the Supreme Court's decision in *Rash*, set forth below, we got something of an answer (or do we; judge for yourself, and pay special attention to footnote 6). And Congress jumped in in 2005 and created a new special valuation rule for individual debtors in Chapter 7 and Chapter 13 cases (see BC 506(a)(2)). Note also that BC 506 was reorganized in making those changes but you will have no trouble matching the current numbering with the numbering in place when the case that follows was decided.

Associates Commercial Corp. v. Rash

United States Supreme Court, 1997.

520 U.S. 953.

■ JUSTICE GINSBURG delivered the opinion of the Court

We resolve in this case a dispute concerning the proper application of BC 506(a) when a bankrupt debtor has exercised the "cram down" option for which BC 1325(a)(5)(B) provides. Specifically, when a debtor, over a secured creditor's objection, seeks to retain and use the creditor's collateral in a Chapter 13 plan, is the value of the collateral to be determined by (1) what the secured creditor could obtain through foreclosure sale of the property (the "foreclosure-value" standard); (2) what the debtor would have to pay for comparable property (the "replacement-value" standard); or (3) the midpoint between these two measurements? We hold that BC 506(a) directs application of the replacement-value standard.

I

In 1989, respondent Elray Rash purchased for $73,700 a Kenworth tractor truck for use in his freight-hauling business. Rash made a downpayment on the truck, agreed to pay the seller the remainder in 60 monthly installments, and pledged the truck as collateral on the unpaid balance. The seller assigned the loan, and its lien on the truck, to petitioner Associates Commercial Corporation (ACC).

In March 1992, Elray and Jean Rash filed a joint petition and a repayment plan under Chapter 13 of the Bankruptcy Code (Code), BC 1301-BC 1330. At the time of the bankruptcy filing, the balance owed to ACC on the truck loan was $41,171. Because it held a valid lien on the truck, ACC was listed in the bankruptcy petition as a creditor holding a secured claim. Under the Code, ACC's claim for the balance owed on the truck was secured only to the extent of the value of the collateral; its claim over and above the value of the truck was unsecured. See BC 506(a).

To qualify for confirmation under Chapter 13, the Rashes' plan had to satisfy the requirements set forth in BC 1325(a). The Rashes' treatment of ACC's secured claim, in particular, is governed by subsection (a)(5). Under this provision, a plan's proposed treatment of secured claims can be confirmed if one of three conditions is satisfied: the secured creditor accepts the plan, see BC 1325(a)(5)(A); the debtor surrenders the property securing the claim to the creditor, see BC 1325(a)(5)(C); or the debtor invokes the so-called "cram down" power, see BC 1325(a)(5)(B). Under the cram down option, the debtor is permitted to keep the property over the objection of the creditor; the creditor retains the lien securing the claim, see BC 1325(a)(5)(B)(i), and the debtor is required to provide the creditor with payments, over the life of the plan, that will total the present value of the allowed secured claim, i.e., the present value of the collateral, see BC 1325(a)(5)(B)(ii). The value of the allowed secured claim is governed by BC 506(a).

The Rashes' Chapter 13 plan invoked the cram down power. It proposed that the Rashes retain the truck for use in the freight-hauling business and pay ACC, over 58 months, an amount equal to the present value of the truck. That value, the Rashes' petition alleged, was $28,500. ACC objected to the plan and asked the Bankruptcy Court to lift the automatic stay so ACC could repossess the truck. ACC also filed a proof of claim alleging that its claim was fully secured in the amount of $41,171. The Rashes filed an objection to ACC's claim.

The Bankruptcy Court held an evidentiary hearing to resolve the dispute over the truck's value. At the hearing, ACC and the Rashes urged different valuation benchmarks. ACC maintained that the proper valuation was the price the Rashes would have to pay to purchase a like vehicle, an amount ACC's expert estimated to be $41,000. The Rashes, however, maintained that the proper valuation was the net amount ACC would realize upon foreclosure and sale of the collateral, an amount their expert estimated to be $31,875. The Bankruptcy Court agreed with the Rashes and fixed the amount of ACC's secured claim at $31,875; that sum, the court found, was the net amount ACC would realize if it exercised its right to repossess and sell the truck. The Bankruptcy Court thereafter approved the plan, and the United States District Court for the Eastern District of Texas affirmed.

A panel of the Court of Appeals for the Fifth Circuit reversed. On rehearing en banc, however, the Fifth Circuit affirmed the District Court, holding that ACC's allowed secured claim was limited to $31,875, the net foreclosure value of the truck. In re Rash, 90 F.3d 1036 (1996).

In reaching its decision, the Fifth Circuit highlighted, first, a conflict it perceived between the method of valuation ACC advanced, and the law of Texas defining the rights of secured creditors. In the Fifth Circuit's view, valuing collateral in a federal bankruptcy proceeding under a replacement-value standard—thereby setting an amount generally higher than what a secured creditor could realize pursuing its state-law foreclosure remedy—would "chang[e] the extent to which ACC is secured from what obtained under state law prior to the bankruptcy filing." 90 F.3d, at 1041. Such a departure from state law, the Fifth Circuit said, should be resisted by the federal forum unless "clearly compel[led]" by the Code. Id., at 1042.

The Fifth Circuit then determined that the Code provision governing valuation of security interests, BC 506(a), does not compel a replacement-value approach. Instead, the court reasoned, the first sentence of BC 506(a) requires that collateral be valued from the creditor's perspective. And because "the creditor's interest is in the nature of a security interest, giving the creditor the right to repossess and sell the collateral and nothing more[,] .... the valuation should start with what the creditor could realize by exercising that right." Ibid. This foreclosure-value standard, the Fifth Circuit found, was consistent with the other relevant provisions of the Code, economic analysis, and the legislative history of the pertinent provisions. Judge Smith, joined by five other judges, dissented, urging that the Code dictates a replacement-value standard.

Courts of Appeals have adopted three different standards for valuing a security interest in a bankruptcy proceeding when the debtor invokes the cram down power to retain the collateral over the creditor's objection. In contrast to the Fifth Circuit's foreclosure-value standard, a number of Circuits have followed a replacement-value approach. See, e.g., In re Taffi, 96 F.3d 1190, 1191-1192 (C.A.9 1996) (en banc), cert. pending sub nom. Taffi v. United States, No. 96-881. Other courts have settled on the midpoint between foreclosure value and replacement value. See In re Hoskins, 102 F.3d 311, 316 (C.A.7 1996). We granted certiorari to resolve this conflict among the Courts of Appeals, and we now reverse the Fifth Circuit's judgment.

II

The Bankruptcy Code provision central to the resolution of this case is BC 506(a), which states:

> An allowed claim of a creditor secured by a lien on property in which the estate has an interest ... is a secured claim to the extent of the value of such creditor's interest in the estate's interest in such property, ... and is an unsecured claim to the extent that the value of such creditor's interest ... is less than the amount of such allowed claim. Such value shall be determined in light of

the purpose of the valuation and of the proposed disposition or use of such property .... BC 506(a).

Over ACC's objection, the Rashes' repayment plan proposed, pursuant to BC 1325(a)(5)(B), continued use of the property in question, i.e., the truck, in the debtor's trade or business. In such a "cram down" case, we hold, the value of the property (and thus the amount of the secured claim under BC 506(a)) is the price a willing buyer in the debtor's trade, business, or situation would pay to obtain like property from a willing seller.

Rejecting this replacement-value standard, and selecting instead the typically lower foreclosure-value standard, the Fifth Circuit trained its attention on the first sentence of BC 506(a). In particular, the Fifth Circuit relied on these first sentence words: a claim is secured "to the extent of the value of such *creditor's interest* in the estate's interest in such property." See 90 F.3d, at 1044 (citing BC 506(a)) (emphasis added). The Fifth Circuit read this phrase to instruct that the "starting point for the valuation [is] what the creditor could realize if it sold the estate's interest in the property according to the security agreement," namely, through "repossess[ing] and sell [ing] the collateral." 90 F.3d, at 1044.

We do not find in the BC 506(a) first sentence words—"the creditor's interest in the estate's interest in such property"—the foreclosure-value meaning advanced by the Fifth Circuit. Even read in isolation, the phrase imparts no valuation standard: A direction simply to consider the "value of such creditor's interest" does not expressly reveal how that interest is to be valued.

Reading the first sentence of BC 506(a) as a whole, we are satisfied that the phrase the Fifth Circuit considered key is not an instruction to equate a "creditor's interest" with the net value a creditor could realize through a foreclosure sale. The first sentence, in its entirety, tells us that a secured creditor's claim is to be divided into secured and unsecured portions, with the secured portion of the claim limited to the value of the collateral. To separate the secured from the unsecured portion of a claim, a court must compare the creditor's claim to the value of "such property," i.e., the collateral. That comparison is sometimes complicated. A debtor may own only a part interest in the property pledged as collateral, in which case the court will be required to ascertain the "estate's interest" in the collateral. Or, a creditor may hold a junior or subordinate lien, which would require the court to ascertain the creditor's interest in the collateral. The BC 506(a) phrase referring to the "creditor's interest in the estate's interest in such property" thus recognizes that a court may encounter, and in such instances must evaluate, limited or partial interests in collateral. The first full sentence of BC 506(a), in short, tells a court what it must evaluate, but it does not say more; it is not enlightening on how to value collateral.

The second sentence of BC 506(a) does speak to the how question. "Such value," that sentence provides, "shall be determined in light of the purpose of the valuation and of the proposed disposition or use of such property." BC 506(a). By deriving a foreclosure-value standard from BC 506(a)'s first sentence, the Fifth Circuit rendered inconsequential the sentence that expressly addresses how "value shall be determined."

As we comprehend BC 506(a), the "proposed disposition or use" of the collateral is of paramount importance to the valuation question. If a secured creditor does not accept a debtor's Chapter 13 plan, the debtor has two options for handling allowed secured claims: surrender the collateral to the creditor, see BC 1325(a)(5)(C); or, under the cram down option, keep the collateral over the creditor's objection and provide the creditor, over the life of the plan, with the equivalent of the present value of the collateral, see BC 1325(a)(5)(B). The "disposition or use" of the collateral thus turns on the alternative the debtor chooses—in one case the collateral will be surrendered to the creditor, and in the other, the collateral will be retained and used by the debtor. Applying a foreclosure-value standard when the cram down option is invoked attributes no significance to the different consequences of the debtor's choice to surrender the property or retain it. A replacement-value standard, on the other hand, distinguishes retention from surrender and renders meaningful the key words "disposition or use."

Tying valuation to the actual "disposition or use" of the property points away from a foreclosure-value standard when a Chapter 13 debtor, invoking cram down power, retains and uses the property. Under that option, foreclosure is averted by the debtor's choice and over the creditor's objection. From the creditor's perspective as well as the debtor's, surrender and retention are not equivalent acts.

When a debtor surrenders the property, a creditor obtains it immediately, and is free to sell it and reinvest the proceeds. We recall here that ACC sought that very advantage. If a debtor keeps the property and continues to use it, the creditor obtains at once neither the property nor its value and is exposed to double risks: The debtor may again default and the property may deteriorate from extended use. Adjustments in the interest rate and secured creditor demands for more "adequate protection," BC 361, do not fully offset these risks. See 90 F.3d, at 1066 (Smith, J., dissenting) ("vast majority of reorganizations fail ... leaving creditors with only a fraction of the compensation due them"; where, as here, "collateral depreciates rapidly, the secured creditor may receive far less in a failed reorganization than in a prompt foreclosure").

Of prime significance, the replacement-value standard accurately gauges the debtor's "use" of the property. It values "the creditor's interest in the collateral in light of the proposed [repayment plan] reality: no foreclosure sale and economic benefit for the debtor derived from the collateral equal to ... its [replacement] value." In re Winthrop Old Farm Nurseries, 50 F.3d, at 75. The debtor in this case elected to use the collateral to generate an income stream. That actual use, rather than a foreclosure sale that will not take place, is the proper guide under a prescription hinged to the property's "disposition or use."

The Fifth Circuit considered the replacement-value standard disrespectful of state law, which permits the secured creditor to sell the collateral, thereby obtaining its net foreclosure value "and nothing more." In allowing Chapter 13 debtors to retain and use collateral over the objection of secured creditors, however, the Bankruptcy Code has reshaped debtor and creditor rights in marked departure from state law. See, e.g., [9-609, 9-610]. The Code's cram down option displaces a secured creditor's state-law right to obtain immediate foreclosure upon a debtor's default. That change, ordered by federal law, is attended by a direction that courts look to the "proposed disposition or use" of the collateral in determining its value. It no more disrupts state law to make "disposition or use" the guide for valuation than to authorize the rearrangement of rights the cram down power entails.

Nor are we persuaded that the split-the-difference approach adopted by the Seventh Circuit provides the appropriate solution. See In re Hoskins, 102 F.3d, at 316. Whatever the attractiveness of a standard that picks the midpoint between foreclosure and replacement values, there is no warrant for it in the Code.[5] BC 506(a) calls for the value the property possesses in light of the "disposition or use" in fact "proposed," not the various disposi-

---

[5] As our reading of BC 506(a) makes plain, we also reject a ruleless approach allowing use of different valuation standards based on the facts and circumstances of individual cases. Cf. In re Valenti, 105 F.3d 55, 62-63 (C.A.2 1997) (permissible for bankruptcy courts to determine valuation standard case-by-case).

tions or uses that might have been proposed. The Seventh Circuit rested on the "economics of the situation," In re Hoskins, 102 F.3d, at 316, only after concluding that the statute suggests no particular valuation method. We agree with the Seventh Circuit that "a simple rule of valuation is needed" to serve the interests of predictability and uniformity. Id., at 314. We conclude, however, that BC 506(a) supplies a governing instruction less complex than the Seventh Circuit's "make two valuations, then split the difference" formulation.

In sum, under BC 506(a), the value of property retained because the debtor has exercised the BC 1325(a)(5)(B) "cram down" option is the cost the debtor would incur to obtain a like asset for the same "proposed ... use."[6]

For the foregoing reasons, the judgment of the Court of Appeals is reversed, and the case is remanded for further proceedings consistent with this opinion.

It is so ordered.

■ JUSTICE STEVENS, dissenting.

Although the meaning of BC 506(a) is not entirely clear, I think its text points to foreclosure as the proper method of valuation in this case. The first sentence in BC 506(a) tells courts to determine the value of the "*creditor's* interest in the estate's interest" in the property. BC 506(a) (emphasis added). This language suggests that the value should be determined from the creditor's perspective, i.e., what the collateral is worth, on the open market, in the creditor's hands, rather than in the hands of another party.

---

[6] Our recognition that the replacement-value standard, not the foreclosure-value standard, governs in cram down cases leaves to bankruptcy courts, as triers of fact, identification of the best way of ascertaining replacement value on the basis of the evidence presented. Whether replacement value is the equivalent of retail value, wholesale value, or some other value will depend on the type of debtor and the nature of the property. We note, however, that replacement value, in this context, should not include certain items. For example, where the proper measure of the replacement value of a vehicle is its retail value, an adjustment to that value may be necessary: A creditor should not receive portions of the retail price, if any, that reflect the value of items the debtor does not receive when he retains his vehicle, items such as warranties, inventory storage, and reconditioning. Nor should the creditor gain from modifications to the property—e.g., the addition of accessories to a vehicle—to which a creditor's lien would not extend under state law.

The second sentence explains that "[s]uch value shall be determined in light of the purpose of the valuation and of the proposed disposition or use of such property." Ibid. In this context, the "purpose of the valuation" is determined by BC 1325(a)(5)(B). Commonly known as the Code's "cram down" provision, this section authorizes the debtor to keep secured property over the creditor's objections in a Chapter 13 reorganization, but, if he elects to do so, directs the debtor to pay the creditor the "value" of the secured claim. The "purpose" of this provision, and hence of the valuation under BC 506(a), is to put the creditor in the same shoes as if he were able to exercise his lien and foreclose.*

It is crucial to keep in mind that BC 506(a) is a provision that applies throughout the various chapters of the bankruptcy code; it is, in other words, a "utility" provision that operates in many different contexts. Even if the words "proposed disposition or use" did not gain special meaning in the cram down context, this would not render them surplusage because they have operational significance in their many other Code applications. In this context, I also think the foreclosure standard best comports with economic reality. Allowing any more than the foreclosure value simply grants a general windfall to undersecured creditors at the expense of unsecured creditors. Cf. In re Hoskins, 102 F.3d 311, 320 (C.A.7 1996) (Easterbrook, concurring in judgment). As Judge Easterbrook explained in rejecting the split-the-difference approach as a general rule, see id., at 318-320, a foreclosure-value standard is also consistent with the larger statutory scheme by keeping the respective recoveries of secured and unsecured creditors the same throughout the various bankruptcy chapters.

---

* The Court states that "surrender and retention are not equivalent acts" from the creditor's perspective because he does not receive the property and is exposed to the risk of default and deterioration. I disagree. That the creditor does not receive the property is irrelevant because, as BC 1325(a)(5)(B)(ii) directs, he receives the present value of his security interest. Present value includes both the underlying value and the time-value of that interest. The time value component similarly vitiates the risk concern. Higher risk uses of money must pay a higher premium to offset the same opportunity cost. In this case, for instance, the creditor was receiving nine percent interest, see In re Rash, 90 F.3d 1036, 1039 (C.A.5 1996) (en banc), well over the prevailing rate for an essentially risk-free loan, such as a United States Treasury Bond. Finally, the concern with deterioration is addressed by another provision of the Code, BC 361, which authorizes the creditor to demand "adequate protection," including increased payments, to offset any derogation of his security interest during a cram down.

Accordingly, I respectfully dissent.

10-9: GOING CONCERN VALUE AFTER *RASH*

- Suppose that the debtor is a printing firm with two assets, a printing press and the plates that go with it. Suppose that, together, the assets are worth $220 if sold together, while the press is worth $110 if liquidated separately and the plates are worth $40. Replacement costs of the assets are estimated to be, respectively, $135 and $45.
- Bank is owed $110 and has a security interest on the press. Finco is also owed $110 and has a security interest on the plates. General unsecured creditors are owed $100.
- ¤ How should going concern value be divided after *Rash*? What values should apply to each of the secured creditors?

COMMENTS AND QUESTIONS

1. For more on *Rash*, see Chris Lenhart, Toward a Midpoint Valuation Standard in Cram Down: Ointment for the *Rash* Decision, 83 Cornell L. Rev. 1821 (1998); see also Edie Walters, An Ambiguous Answer: The Effect of Associates Commercial Corp. v. Rash on Chapter 11 and Chapter 13 Collateral Valuation, 35 Hous. L. Rev. 953 (1998).

2. As noted in the introduction to *Rash*, the 2005 amendments to the Bankruptcy Code made a number of important changes that relate to the result in *Rash*. The Code now contains a separate valuation rule for individuals set out in BC 506(a)(2). Be sure to examine that carefully to see how much of *Rash* continues to apply, though do note that *Rash* interprets BC 506 and that applies generally throughout the Code to all cases. The 2005 amendments also added a new hanging paragraph at the bottom of BC 1325(a). That limits the extent to which BC 506 applies at all in Chapter 13 cramdowns. Consider whether that amendment would apply in *Rash* itself.

INDEX

References are to pages.